VIZ GRAPHIC NOVEL

MERMAID'S SCAR™

STORY AND ART BY
RUMIKO TAKAHASHI

CONTENTS

This volume contains the series MERMAID'S DREAM, MERMAID'S PROMISE, and MERMAID'S SCAR in their entirety.

STORY AND ART BY
RUMIKO TAKAHASHI

English Adaptation/Matt Thorn
Touch-Up art & Lettering/Wayne Truman
Cover Design/Viz Graphics
Editors/Trish Ledoux & Annette Roman
Director of Sales & Marketing/Dallas Middaugh
Marketing Manager/Renee Solberg
Sales Representative/Mike Roberson
Assistant Editor/Toshifumi Yoshida

Publisher/Seiji Horibuchi
Editor-in-Chief/Hyoe Narita

Printed in Canada

Vizit us at **www.viz.com** and our online magazines at **www.j-pop.com** and **www.animerica-mag.com** and **www.pulp-mag.com!**

Get your free Viz Shop-By-Mail catalog!
(800) 394-3042 or fax (415) 546-7086

Published by Viz Communications, Inc.
P.O. Box 77010 • San Francisco, CA 94107
10 9 8 7 6 5 4 3
First printing, October 1995
Third Printing, July 2201

MERMAID SAGA GRAPHIC NOVELS

MERMAID FOREST
MERMAID'S SCAR
MERMAID'S GAZE

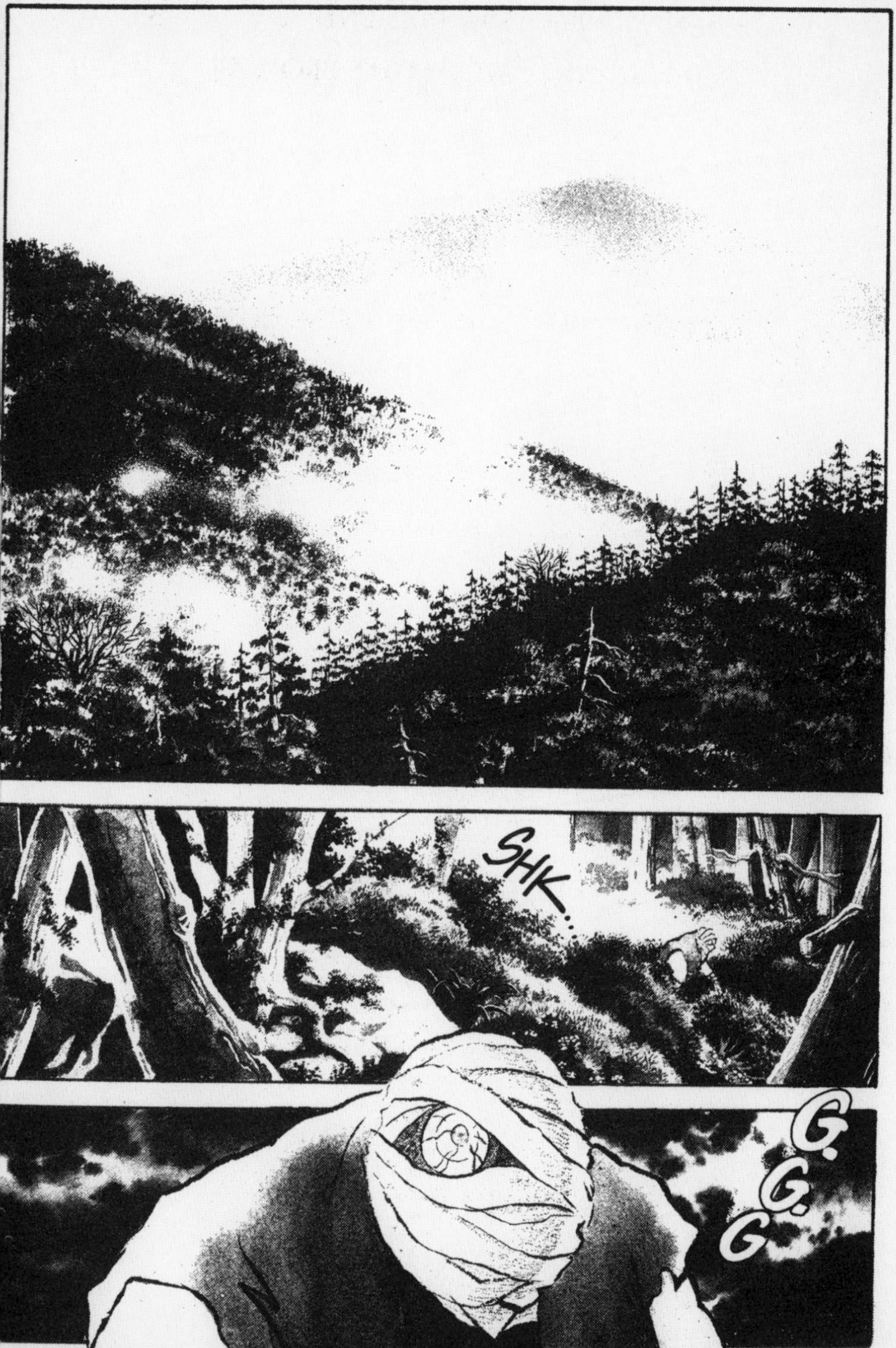
SHK...
G. G. G

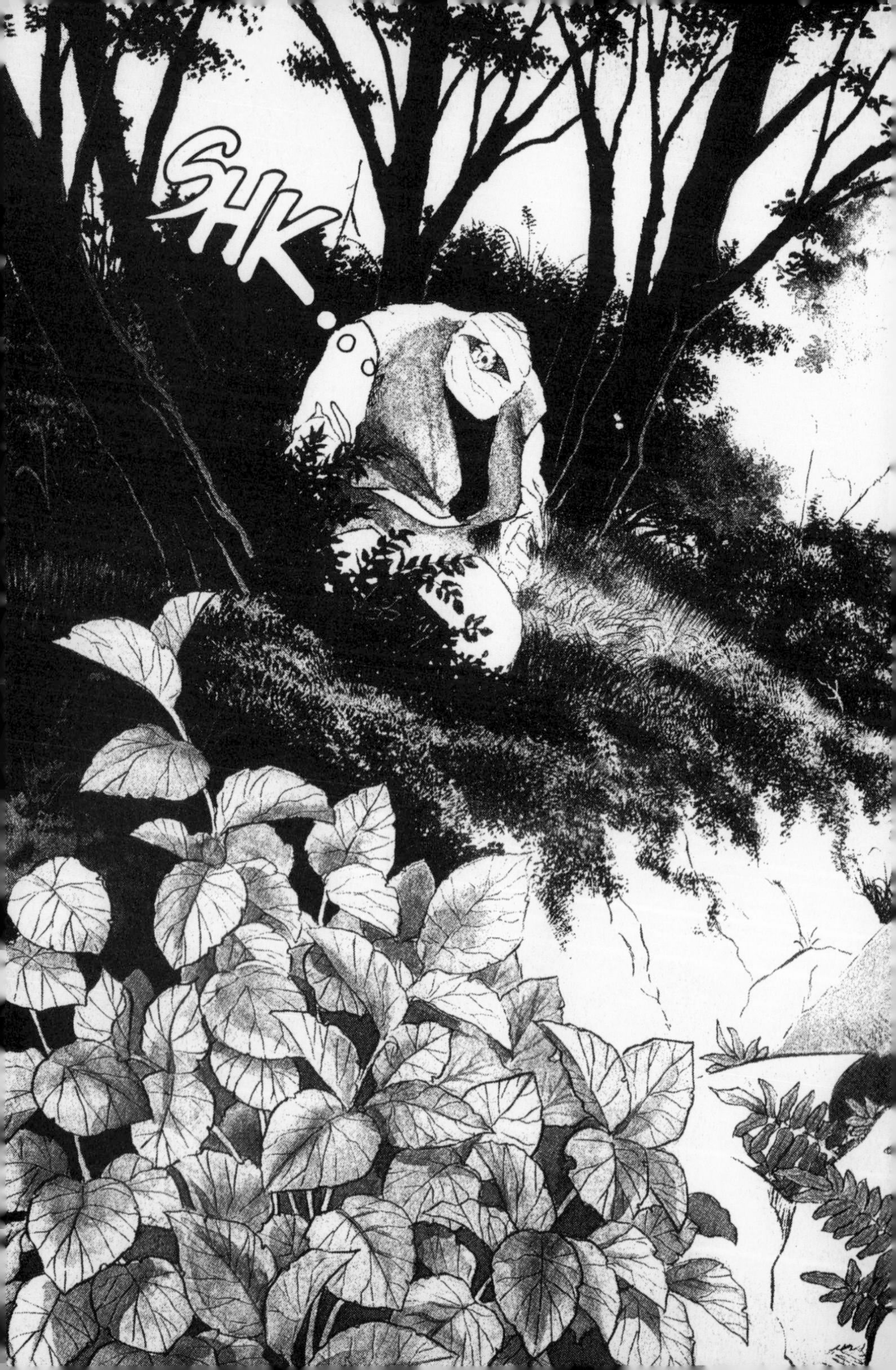
SHK

CHAPTER ONE
DREAM'S END

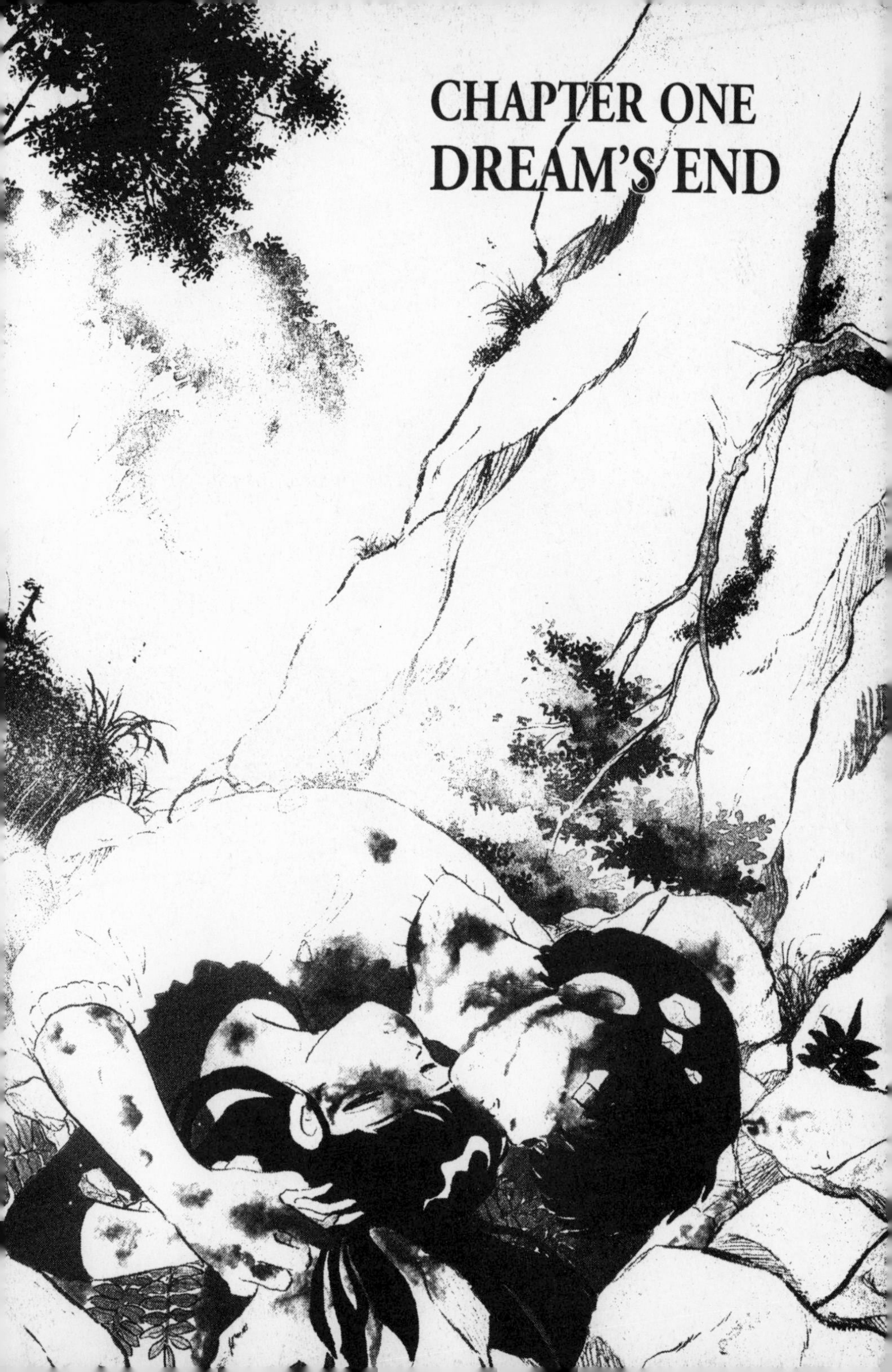

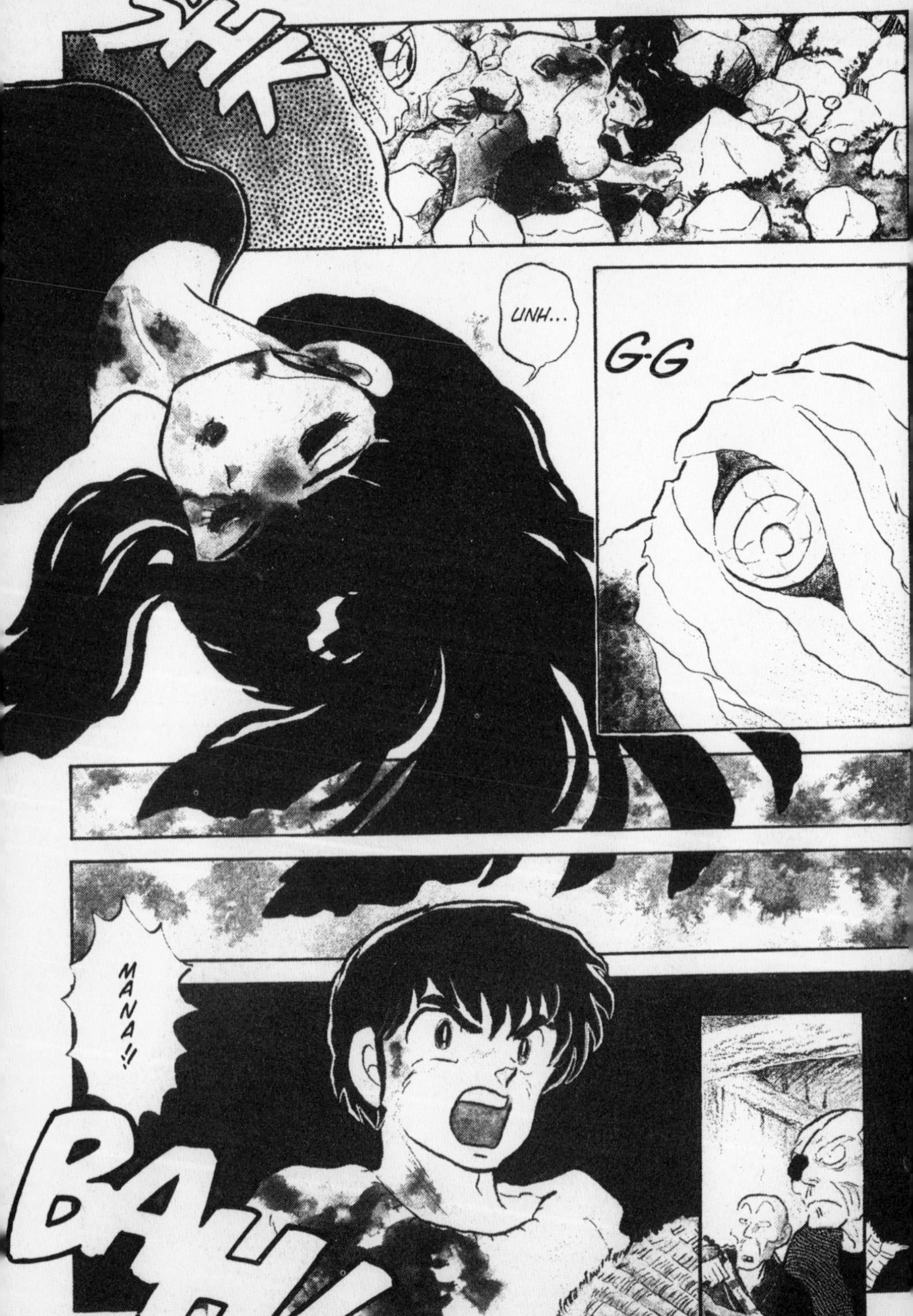
SHK
UNH...
G-G
MANA!!
BAH!

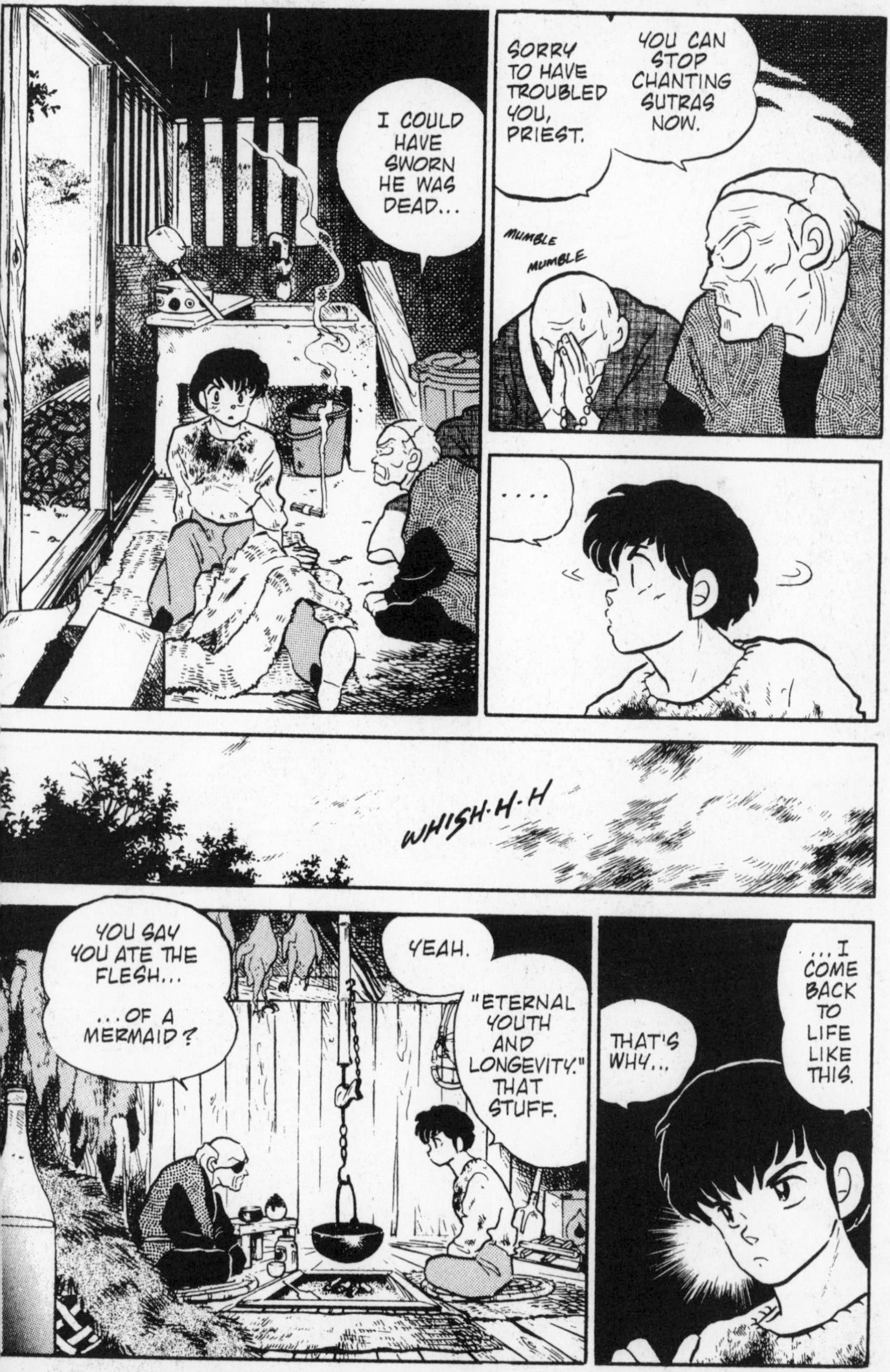
I COULD HAVE SWORN HE WAS DEAD...
SORRY TO HAVE TROUBLED YOU, PRIEST.
YOU CAN STOP CHANTING SUTRAS NOW.
MUMBLE
MUMBLE
....
WHISH-H-H
YOU SAY YOU ATE THE FLESH...
...OF A MERMAID?
YEAH.
"ETERNAL YOUTH AND LONGEVITY." THAT STUFF.
THAT'S WHY...
...I COME BACK TO LIFE LIKE THIS.

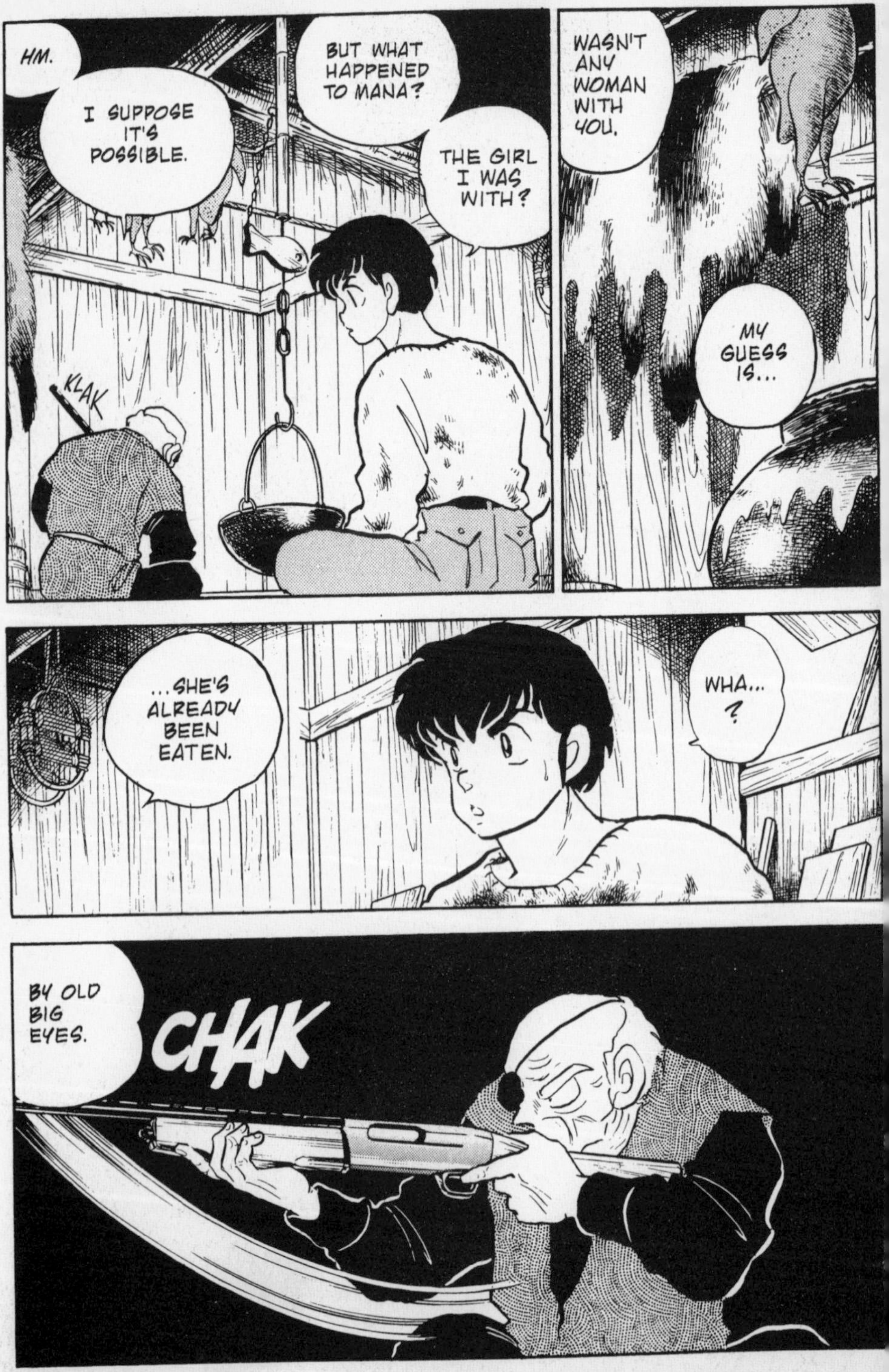
HM.
I SUPPOSE IT'S POSSIBLE.
BUT WHAT HAPPENED TO MANA?
THE GIRL I WAS WITH?
KLAK
WASN'T ANY WOMAN WITH YOU.
MY GUESS IS...
...SHE'S ALREADY BEEN EATEN.
WHA...?
BY OLD BIG EYES.
CHAK

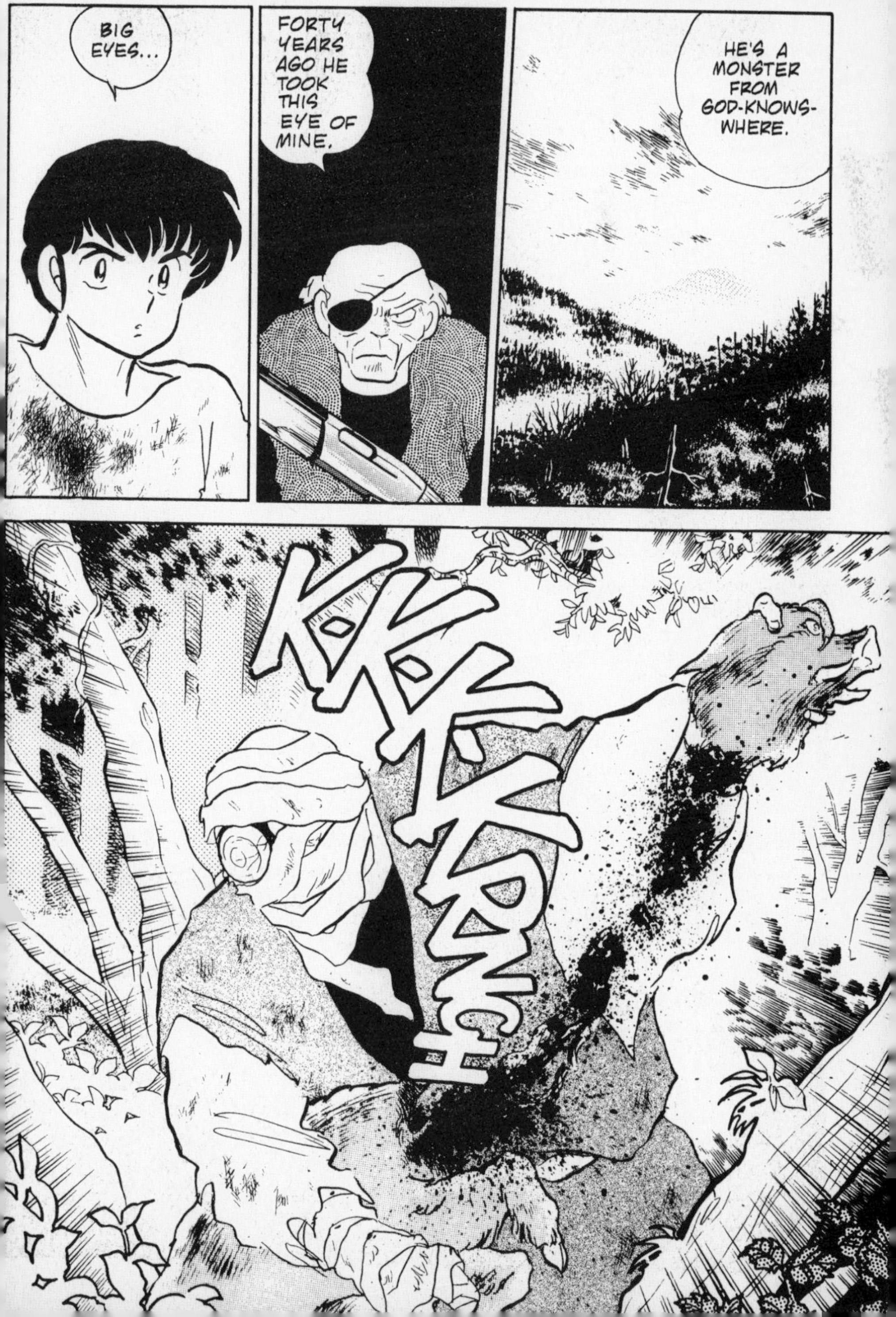
BIG EYES...
FORTY YEARS AGO HE TOOK THIS EYE OF MINE.
HE'S A MONSTER FROM GOD-KNOWS-WHERE.
KRKRKRUNCH

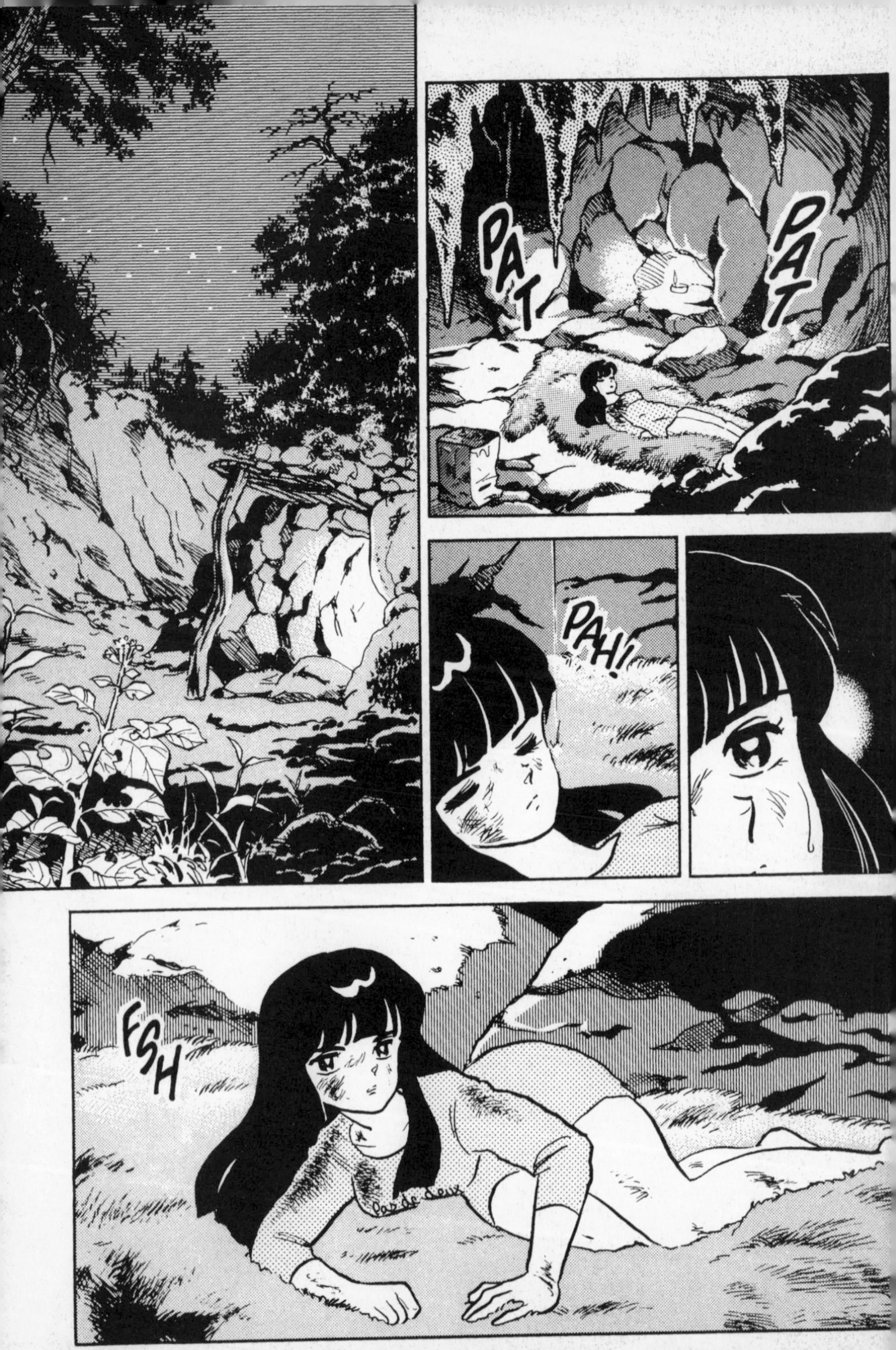
PAT
PAT
PAH!
FSH
pas de deux

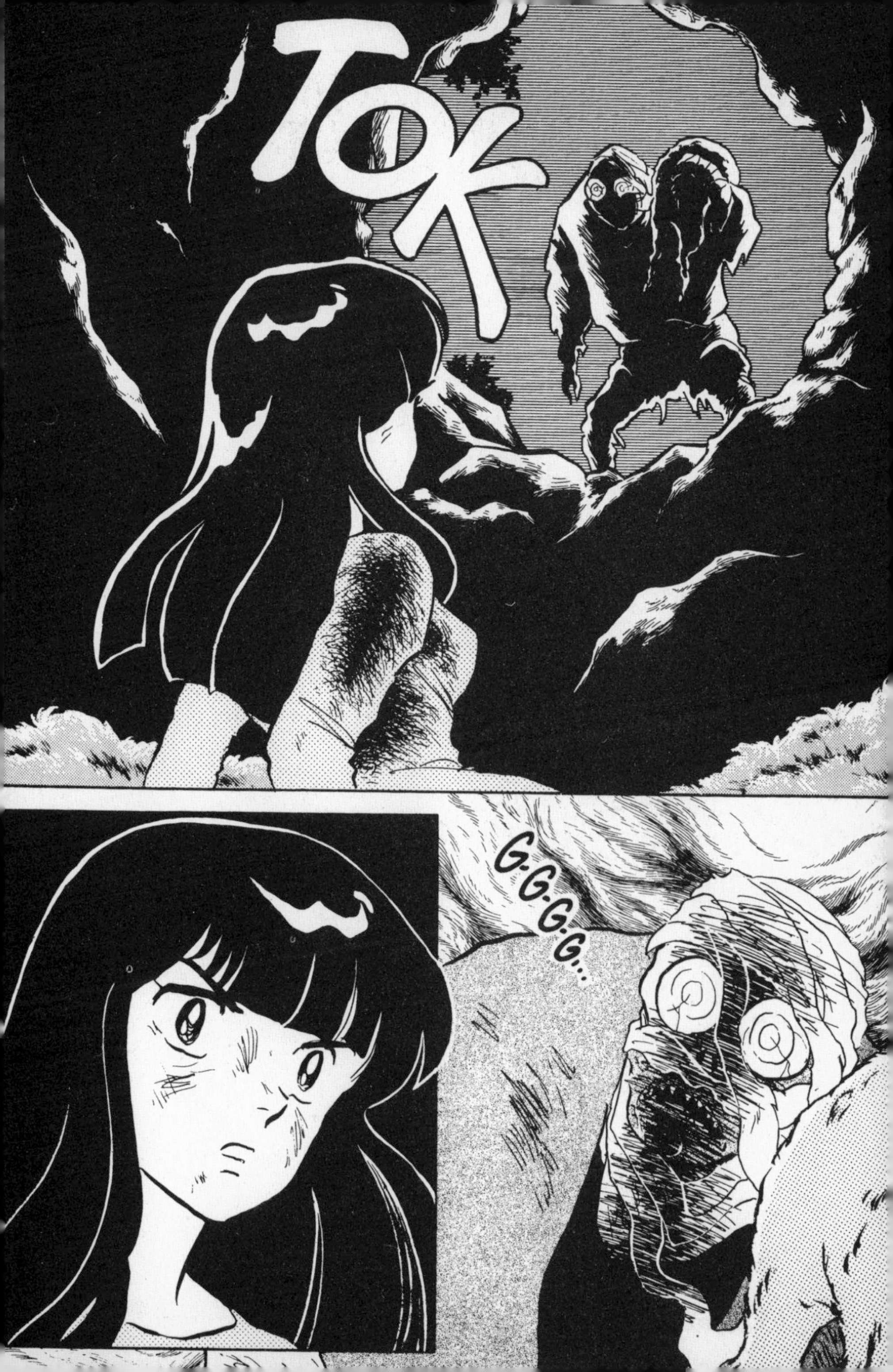
TOK
G-G-G-G...

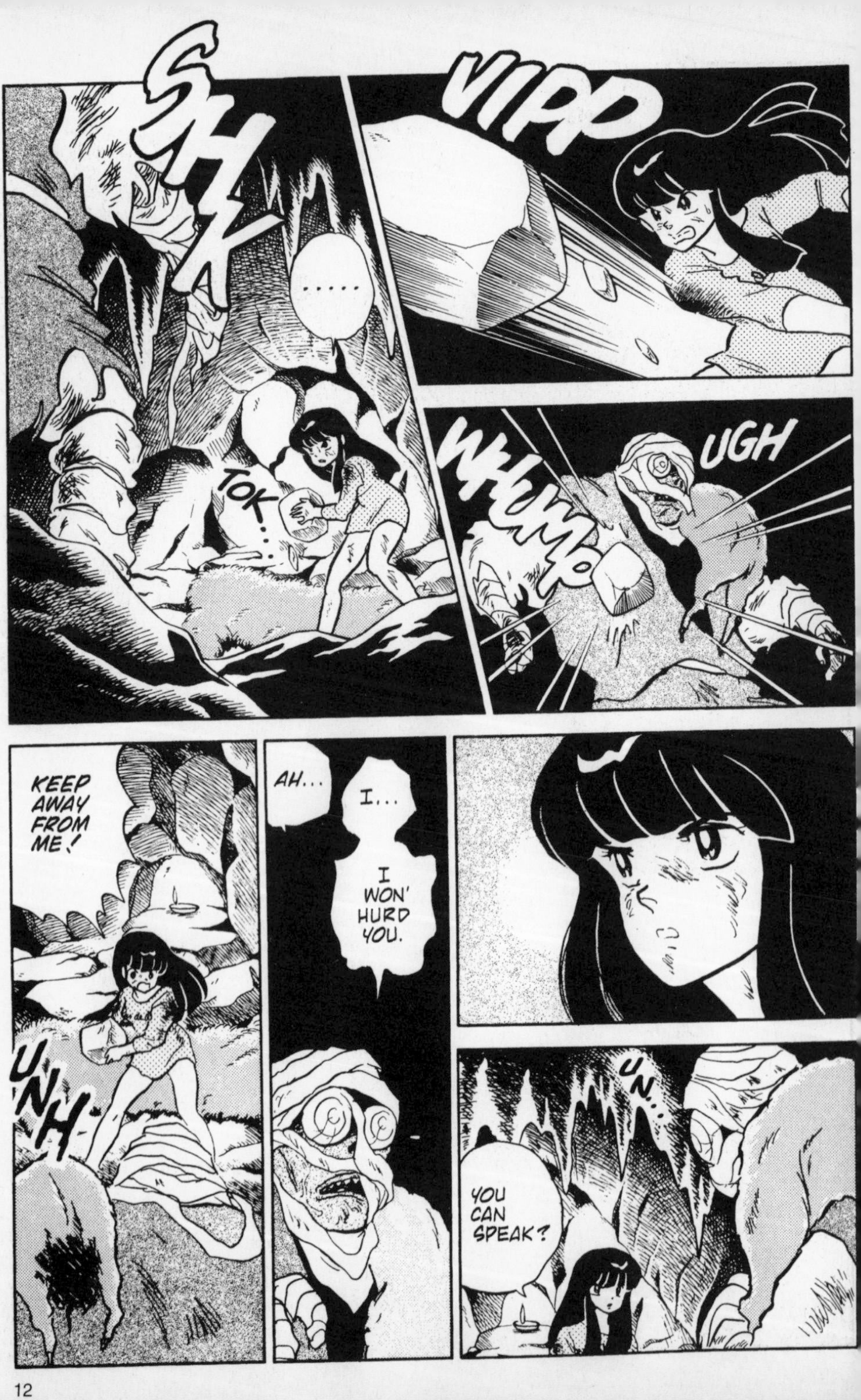
SHAK
.....
TOK...
VIPP
WHUMP
UGH
KEEP AWAY FROM ME!
UNH
AH...
I...
I WON' HURD YOU.
UN...
YOU CAN SPEAK?

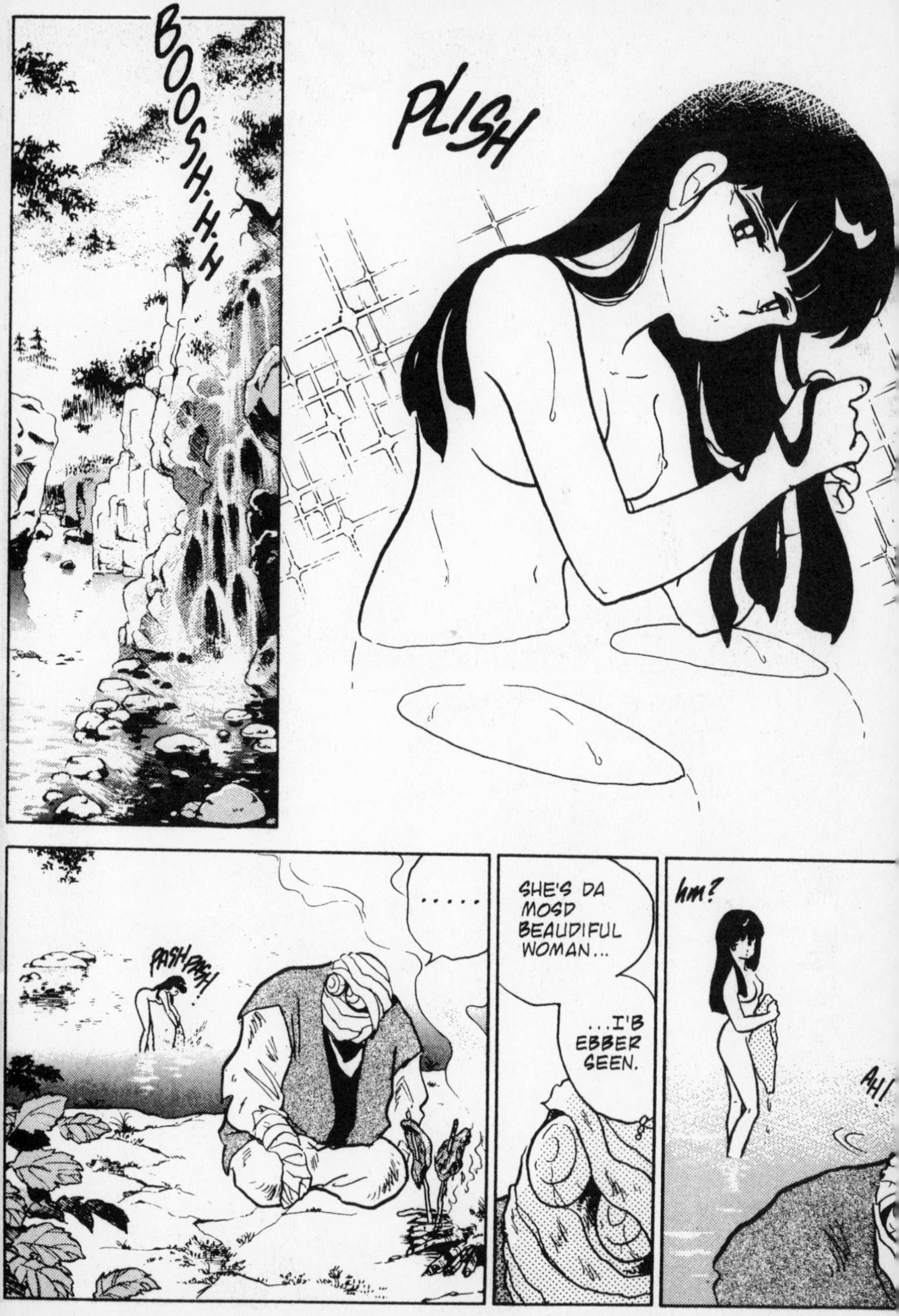
BOOSH-H-H
PLISH
PASH PASH
.....
SHE'S DA MOSD BEAUDIFUL WOMAN...
...I'B EBBER SEEN.
hm?
AH!

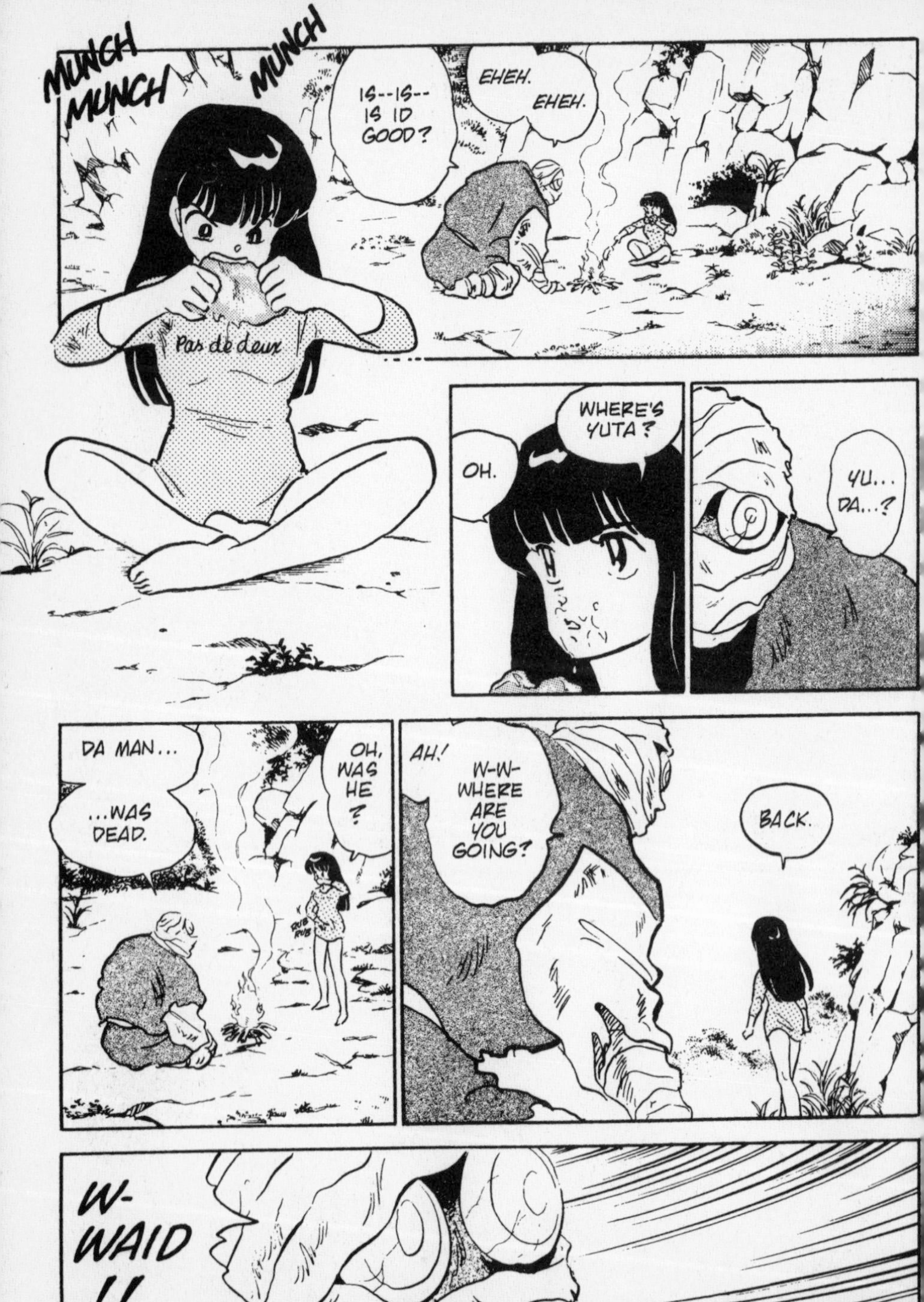
MUNCH
MUNCH
MUNCH
IS--IS-- IS ID GOOD?
EHEH. EHEH.
WHERE'S YUTA?
OH.
YU... DA...?
DA MAN...
...WAS DEAD.
OH, WAS HE?
RUB RUB
AH!
W-W-WHERE ARE YOU GOING?
BACK.
W-WAID!!

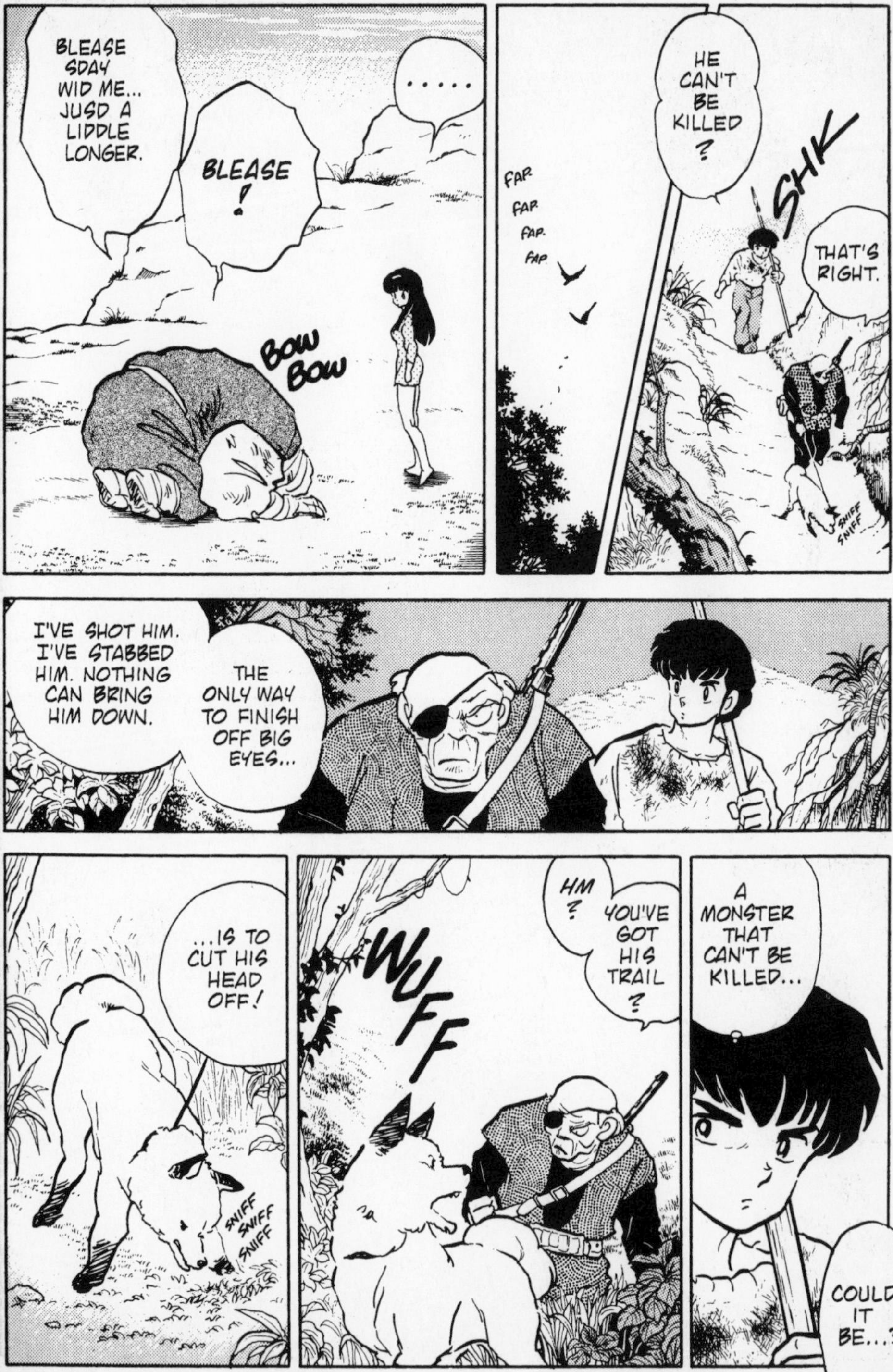
BLEASE SDAY WID ME... JUSD A LIDDLE LONGER.
BLEASE!
......
BOW BOW
FAP FAP FAP FAP
HE CAN'T BE KILLED?
SHK
THAT'S RIGHT.
SNIFF SNIFF
I'VE SHOT HIM. I'VE STABBED HIM. NOTHING CAN BRING HIM DOWN.
THE ONLY WAY TO FINISH OFF BIG EYES...
...IS TO CUT HIS HEAD OFF!
SNIFF SNIFF SNIFF
WUFF
HM?
YOU'VE GOT HIS TRAIL?
A MONSTER THAT CAN'T BE KILLED...
COULD IT BE...?

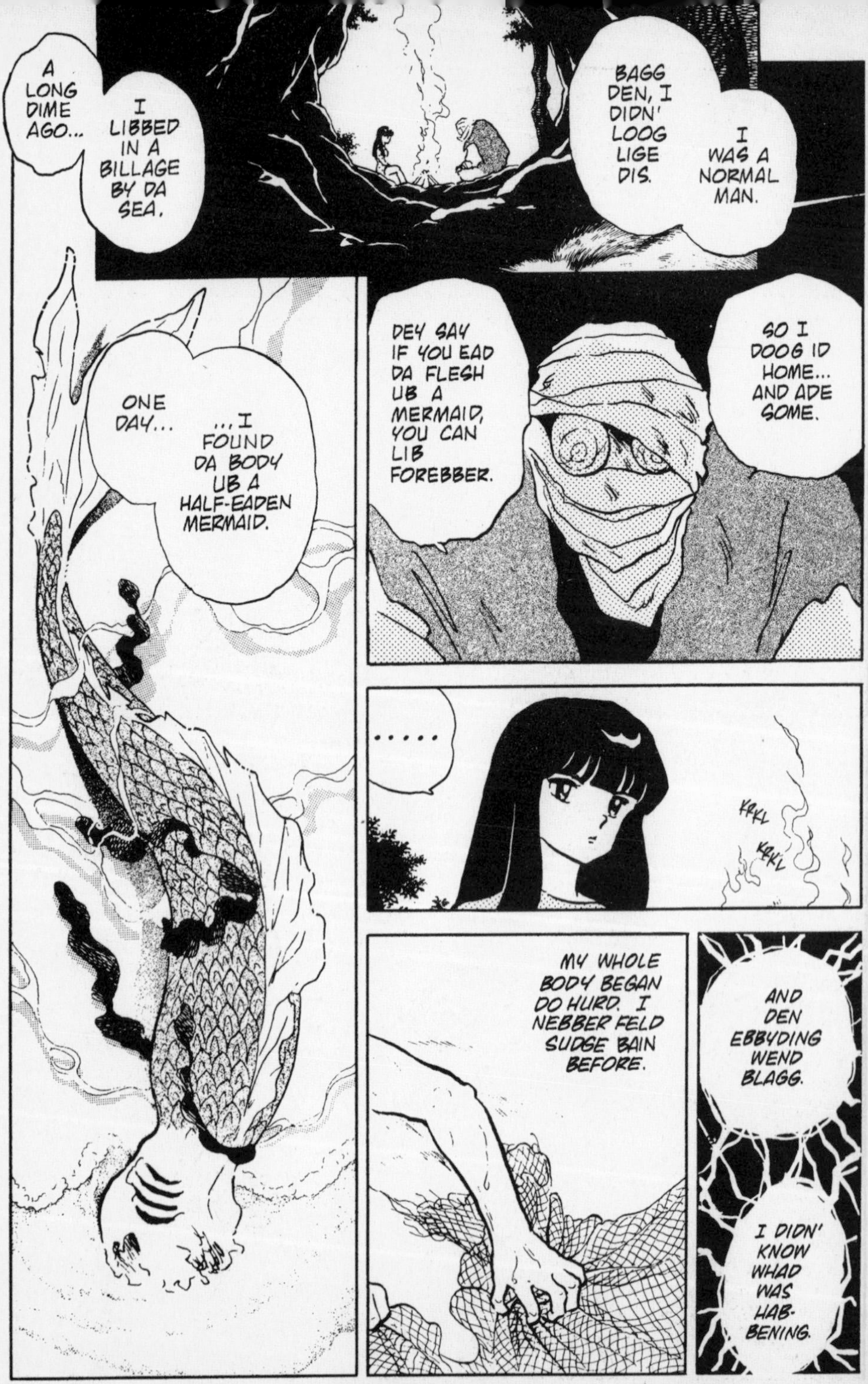
A LONG DIME AGO...
I LIBBED IN A BILLAGE BY DA SEA.
BAGG DEN, I DIDN' LOOG LIGE DIS.
I WAS A NORMAL MAN.
ONE DAY...
...I FOUND DA BODY UB A HALF-EADEN MERMAID.
DEY SAY IF YOU EAD DA FLESH UB A MERMAID, YOU CAN LIB FOREBBER.
SO I DOOG ID HOME... AND ADE SOME.
.....
KRKL
KRKL
MY WHOLE BODY BEGAN DO HURD. I NEBBER FELD SUDGE BAIN BEFORE.
AND DEN EBBYDING WEND BLAGG.
I DIDN' KNOW WHAD WAS HAB-BENING.

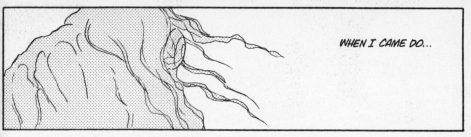

WHEN I CAME DO...

...MY FADDER
...AND MY MUDDER...

...EBBYONE
IN DA WHOLE
BILLAGE...
WAS...

GU-GU

M-
MONSTER
!!

MONSTER!!

A BILLAGE
WOMAN
WAS
SCREAMING
AND
SCREAMING.

I WAS AFRAID.

I RAN.

I RAN...

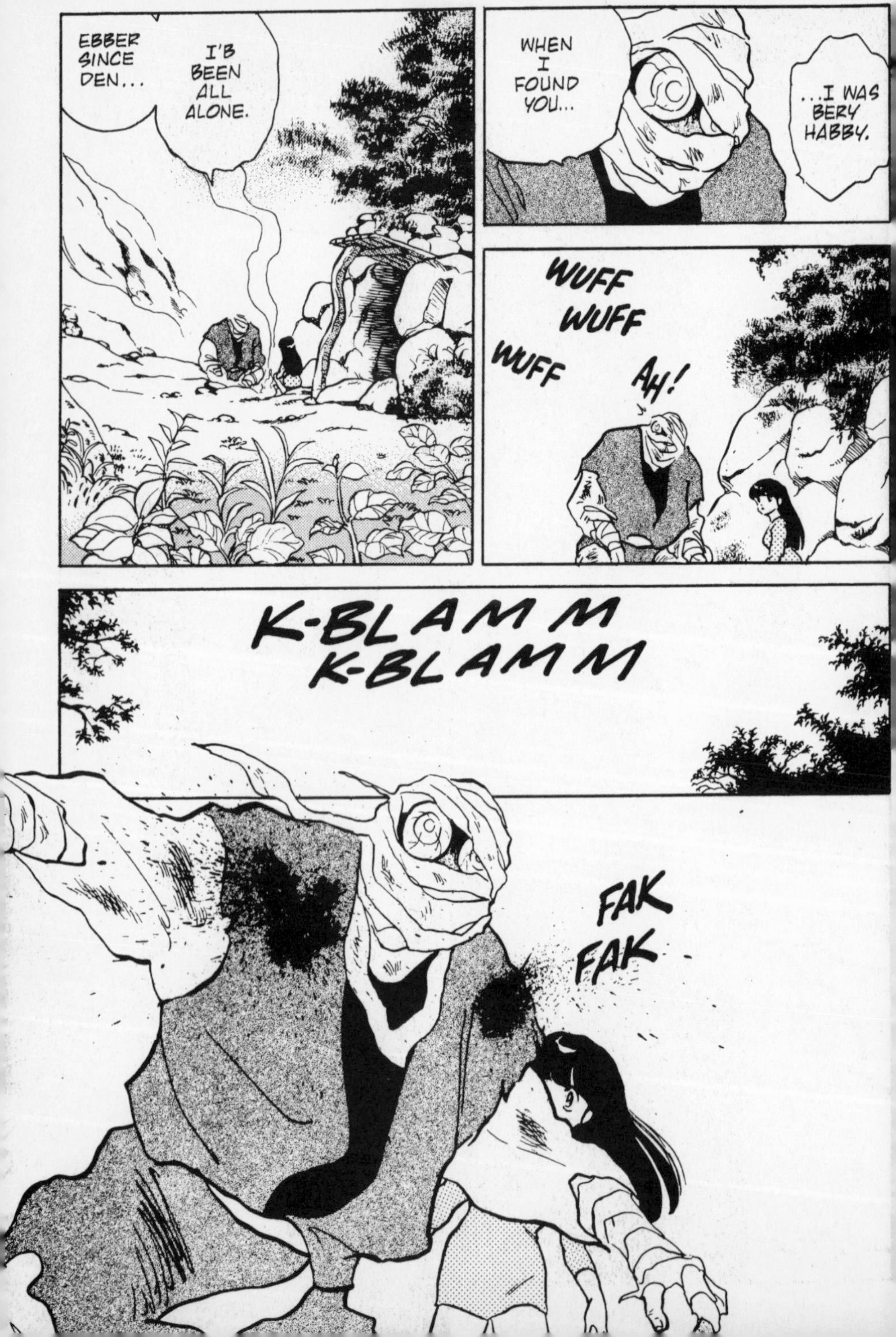
EBBER SINCE DEN...
I'B BEEN ALL ALONE.
WHEN I FOUND YOU...
...I WAS BERY HABBY.
WUFF
WUFF
WUFF
AH!
K-BLAMM
K-BLAMM
FAK
FAK

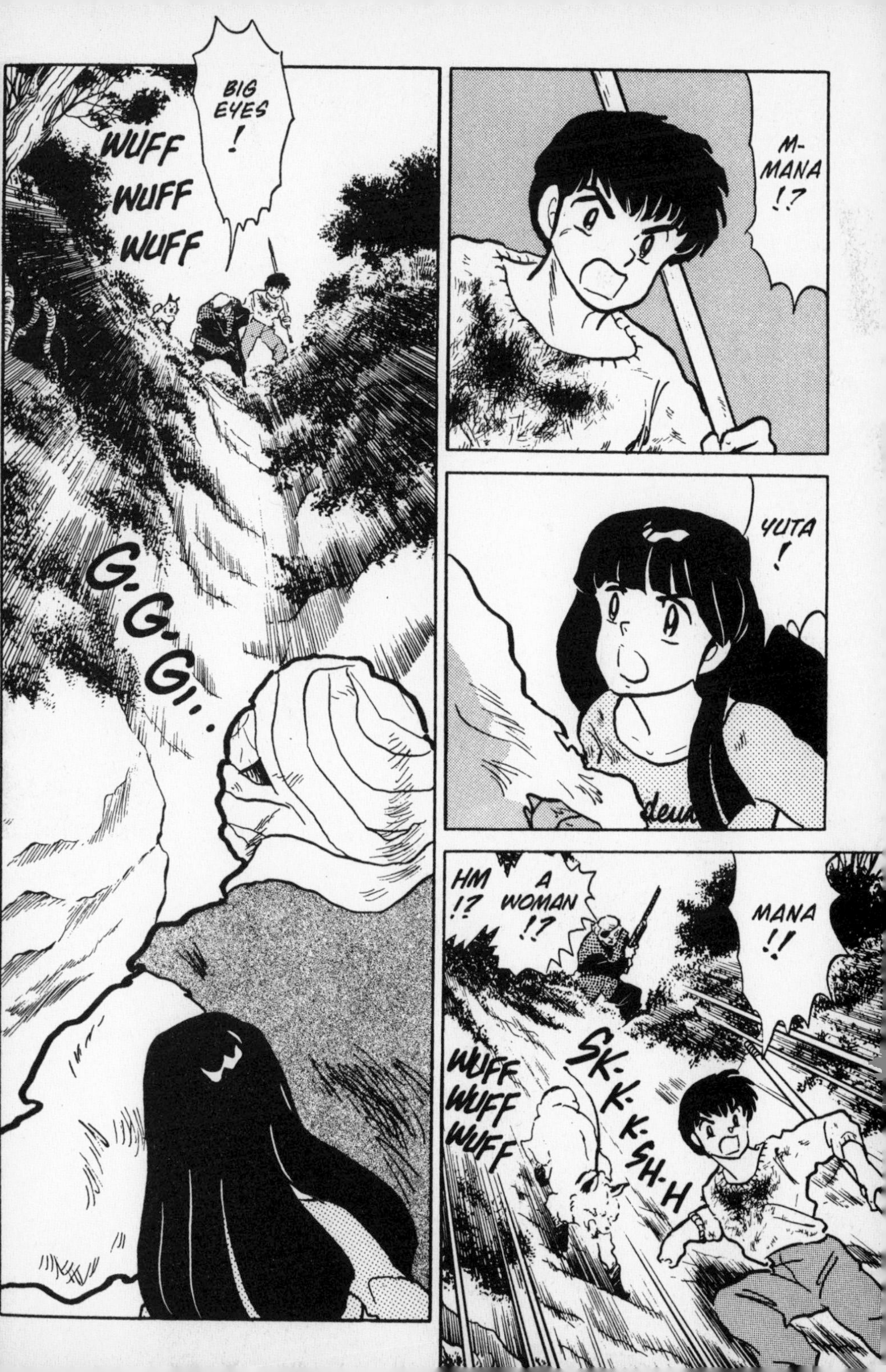
BIG EYES !
WUFF WUFF WUFF
G-G-G!..
M-MANA !?
YUTA !
HM !?
A WOMAN !?
MANA !!
WUFF WUFF WUFF
SK-K-K-SH-H

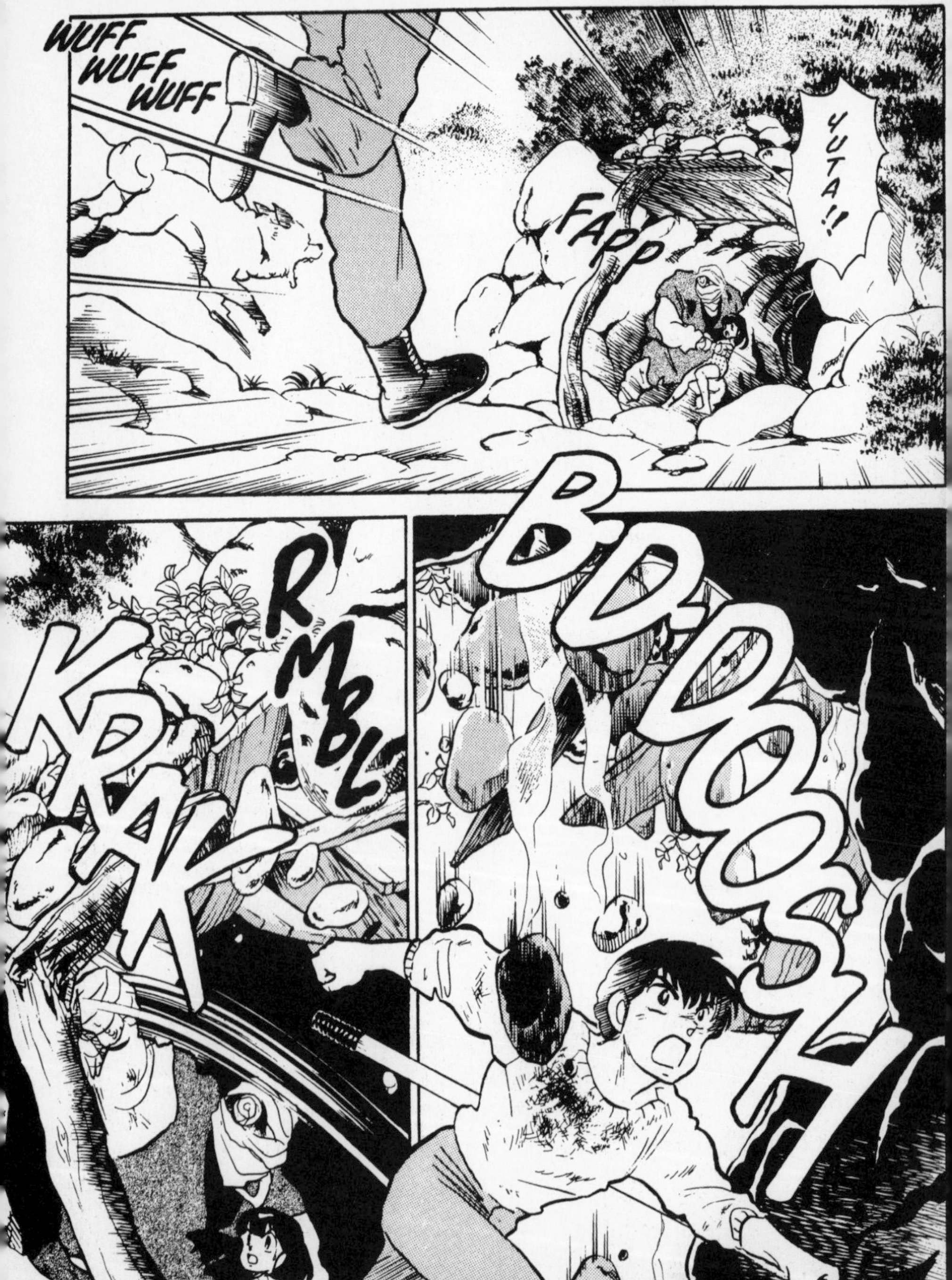
WUFF WUFF WUFF
FAPP
YUTA!!
KRAK
RMBL
BDOOOMH

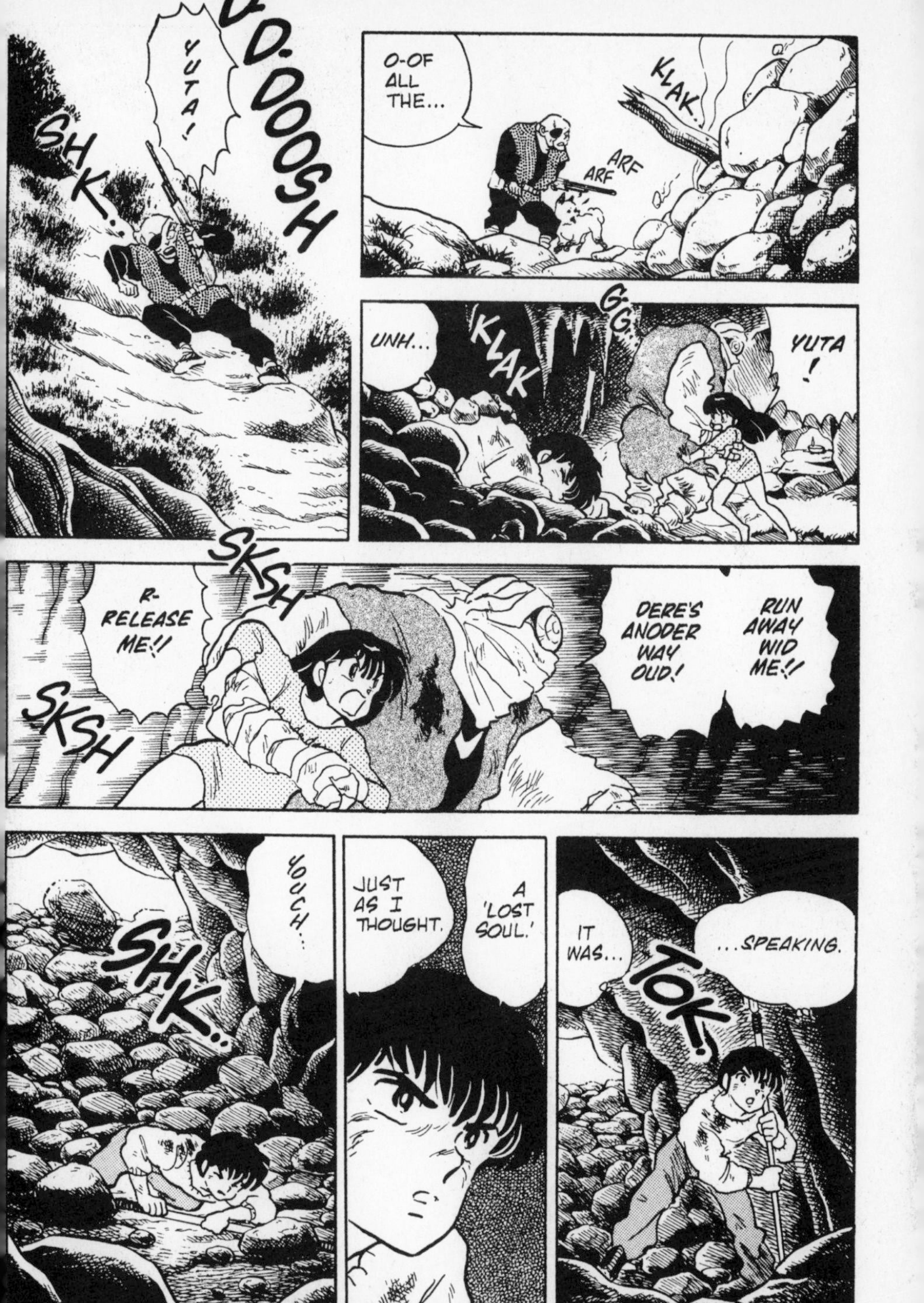
YUTA!
DO-DOOOSH
SHK...
O-OF ALL THE...
KLAK...
ARF ARF
UNH...
KLAK
GG...
YUTA!
R-RELEASE ME!!
SKSH
SKSH
DERE'S ANODER WAY OUD!
RUN AWAY WID ME!!
SHK...
YOUCH...
JUST AS I THOUGHT.
A 'LOST SOUL.'
IT WAS...
TOK!
...SPEAKING.

YUTA! YUTA·A!!

MANA...

WHY....?

RELEASE ME!!

IS ID BECAUSE I'M UGLY ?

FAPP

I MAY LOOG LIGE DIS... BUD MY HARD...

...MY HEART--!!

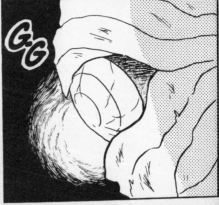

GG

FLUMP

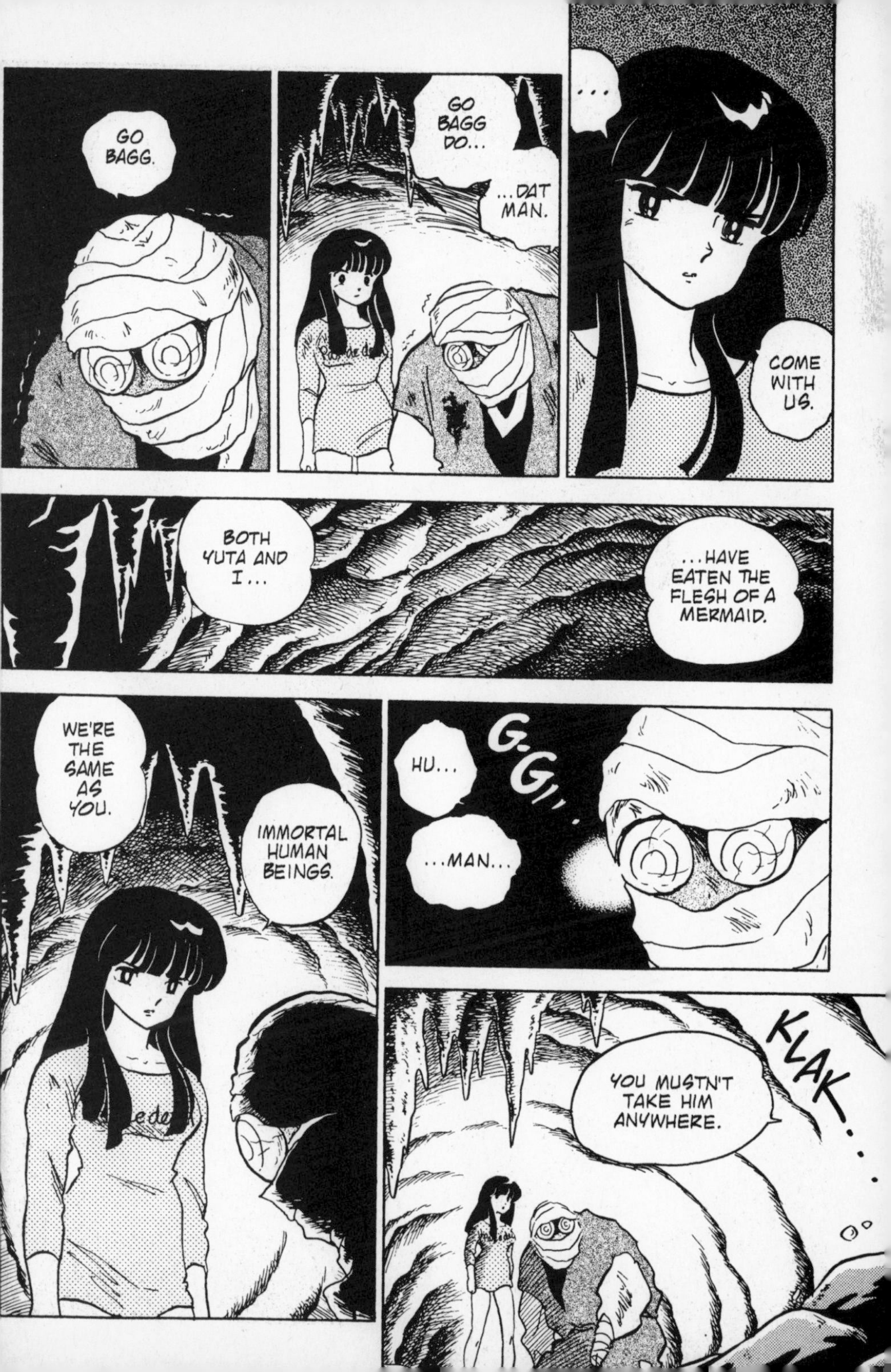
GO BAGG.
GO BAGG DO...
...DAT MAN.
...
COME WITH US.
BOTH YUTA AND I...
...HAVE EATEN THE FLESH OF A MERMAID.
WE'RE THE SAME AS YOU.
IMMORTAL HUMAN BEINGS.
HU...
G-G!!
...MAN...
KLAK...
YOU MUSTN'T TAKE HIM ANYWHERE.

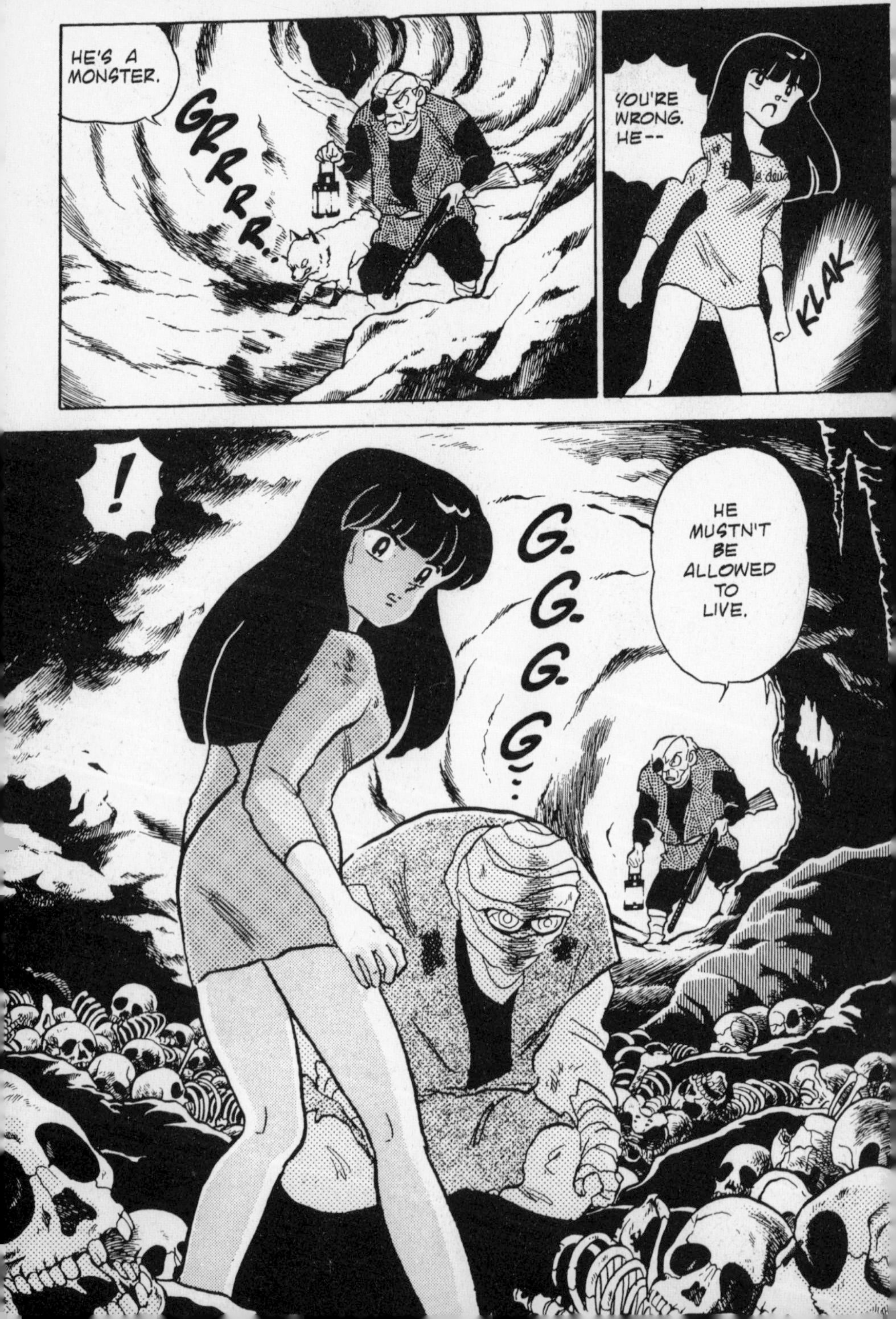
HE'S A MONSTER.
GRRRR...
YOU'RE WRONG. HE--
KLAK
!
G. G. G. G...
HE MUSTN'T BE ALLOWED TO LIVE.

MANA!!

G.G.G...

TOK

BLAMM
BLAMM
BLAMM

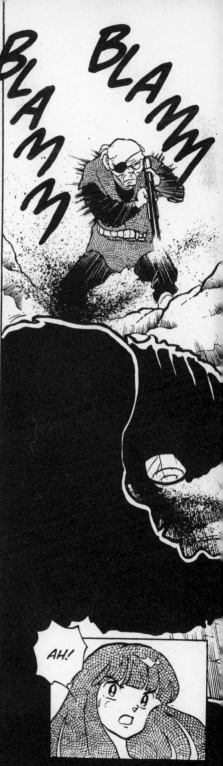

SOMEDIMES... I BEGOME DIZZY...

...I DON' KNOW WHAD I'M DOING...

AH!

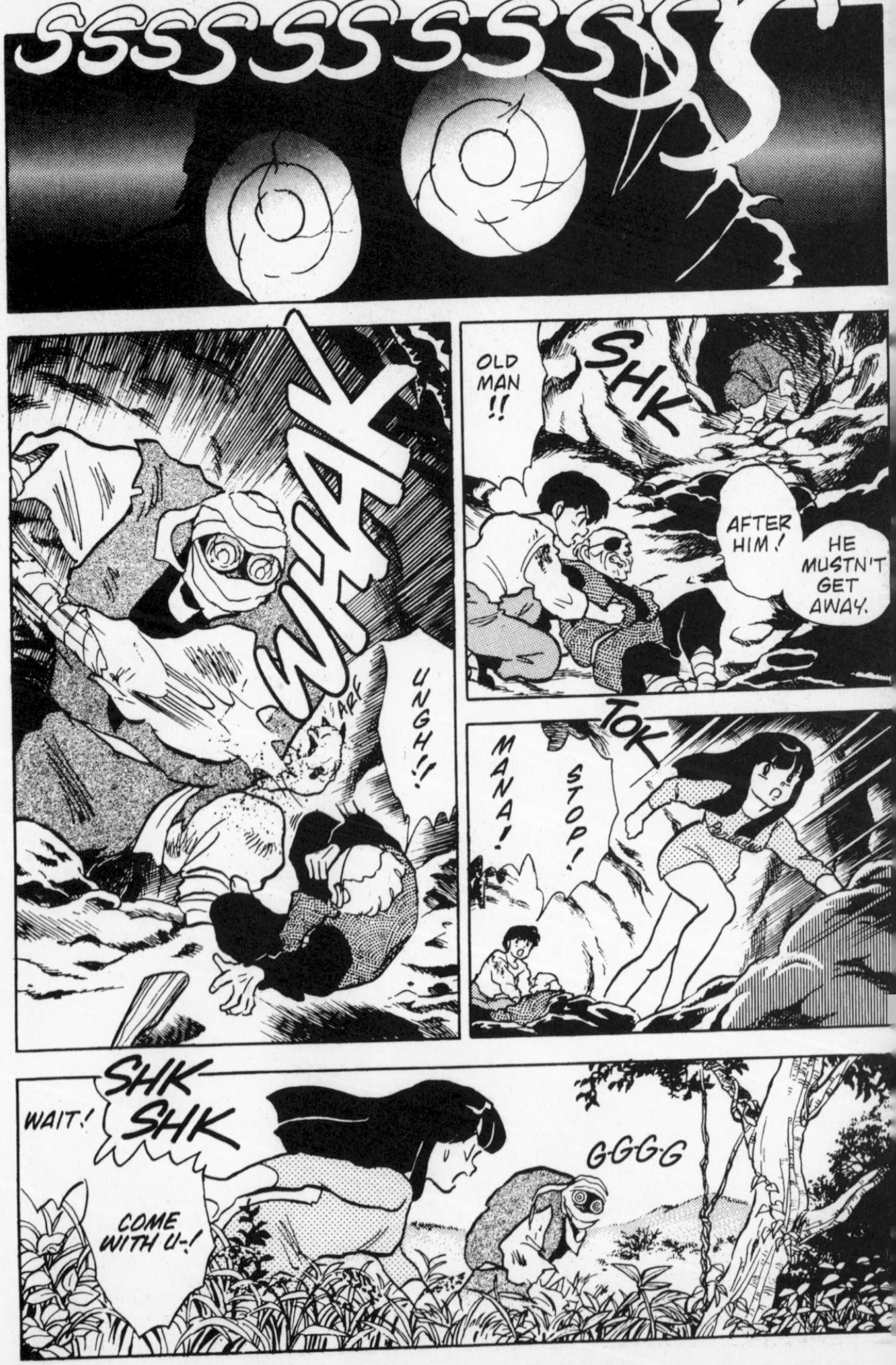
SSSSSSSSSSS
WHAK
ARF
UNGH!!
OLD MAN !!
SHK
AFTER HIM!
HE MUSTN'T GET AWAY.
TOK
MANA!
STOP!
SHK SHK
WAIT!
COME WITH U-!
G-G-G-G

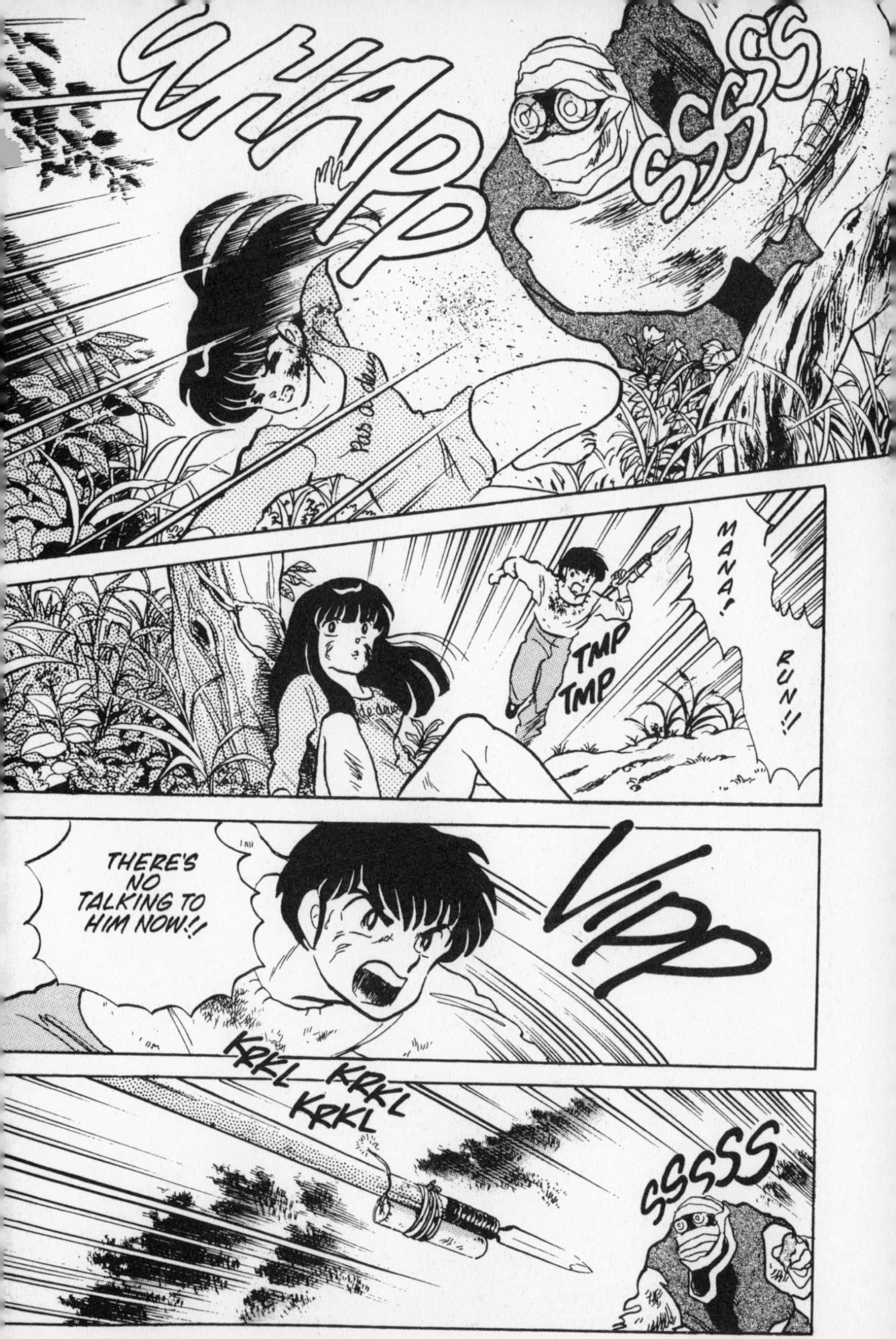
WHAP
SSSSS
TMP TMP
MANA!
RUN!!
THERE'S NO TALKING TO HIM NOW!!
VIP
KRKL KRKL KRKL
SSSSS

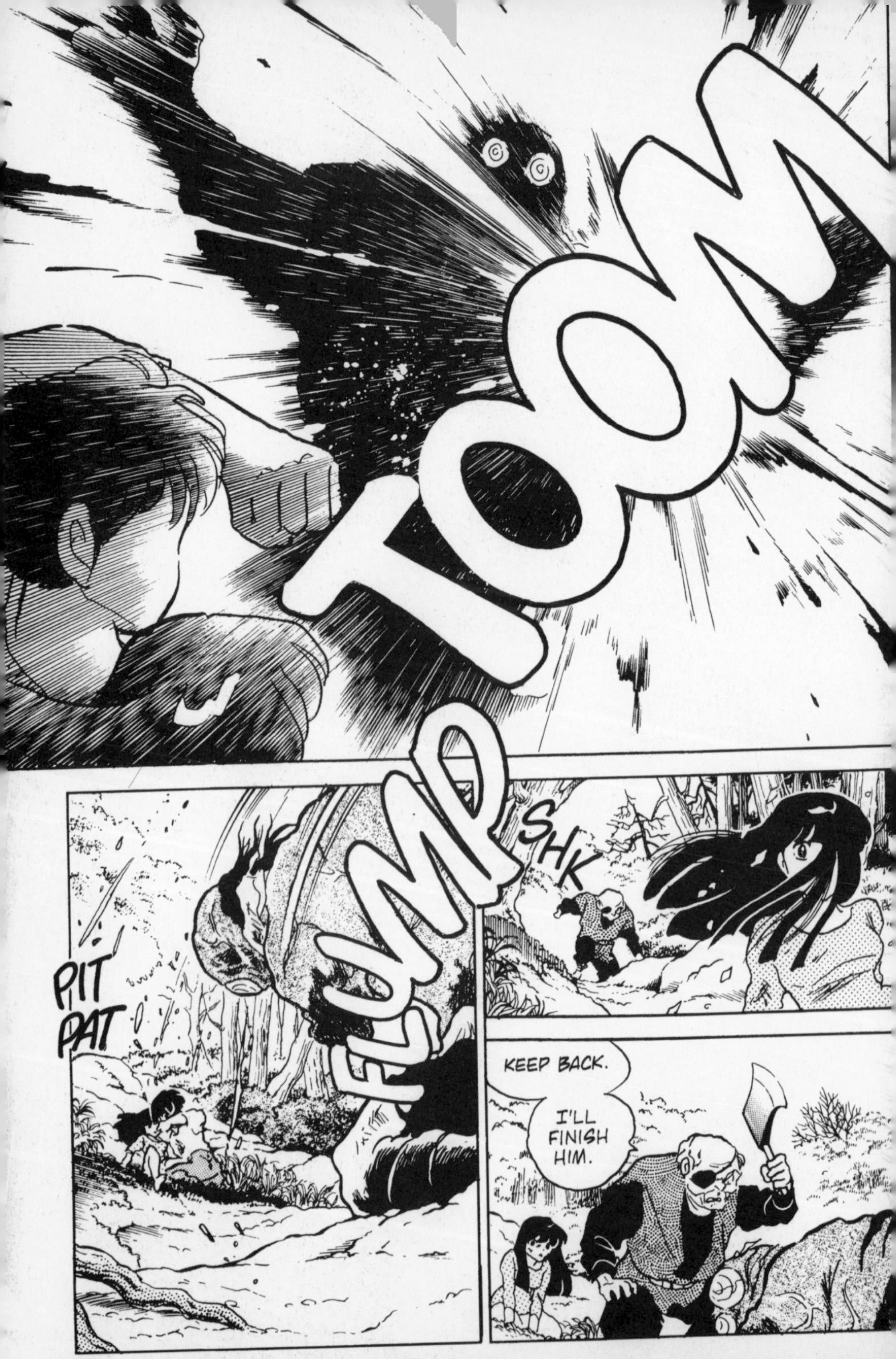

TOOM
FUMP
SHK
PIT
PAT
KEEP BACK.
I'LL FINISH HIM.

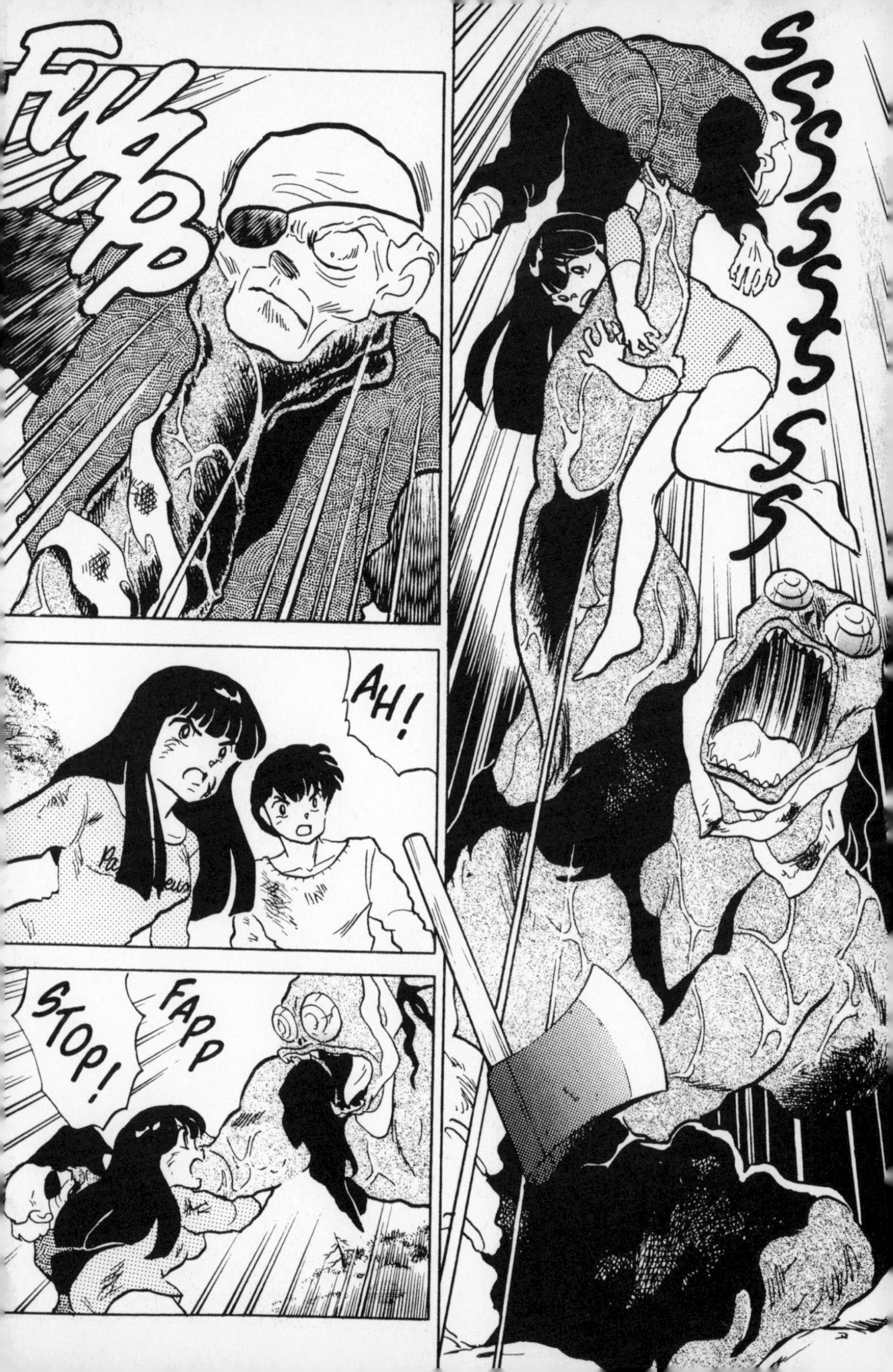
FWAP
AH!
STOP!
FAPP
SSSSSSSS

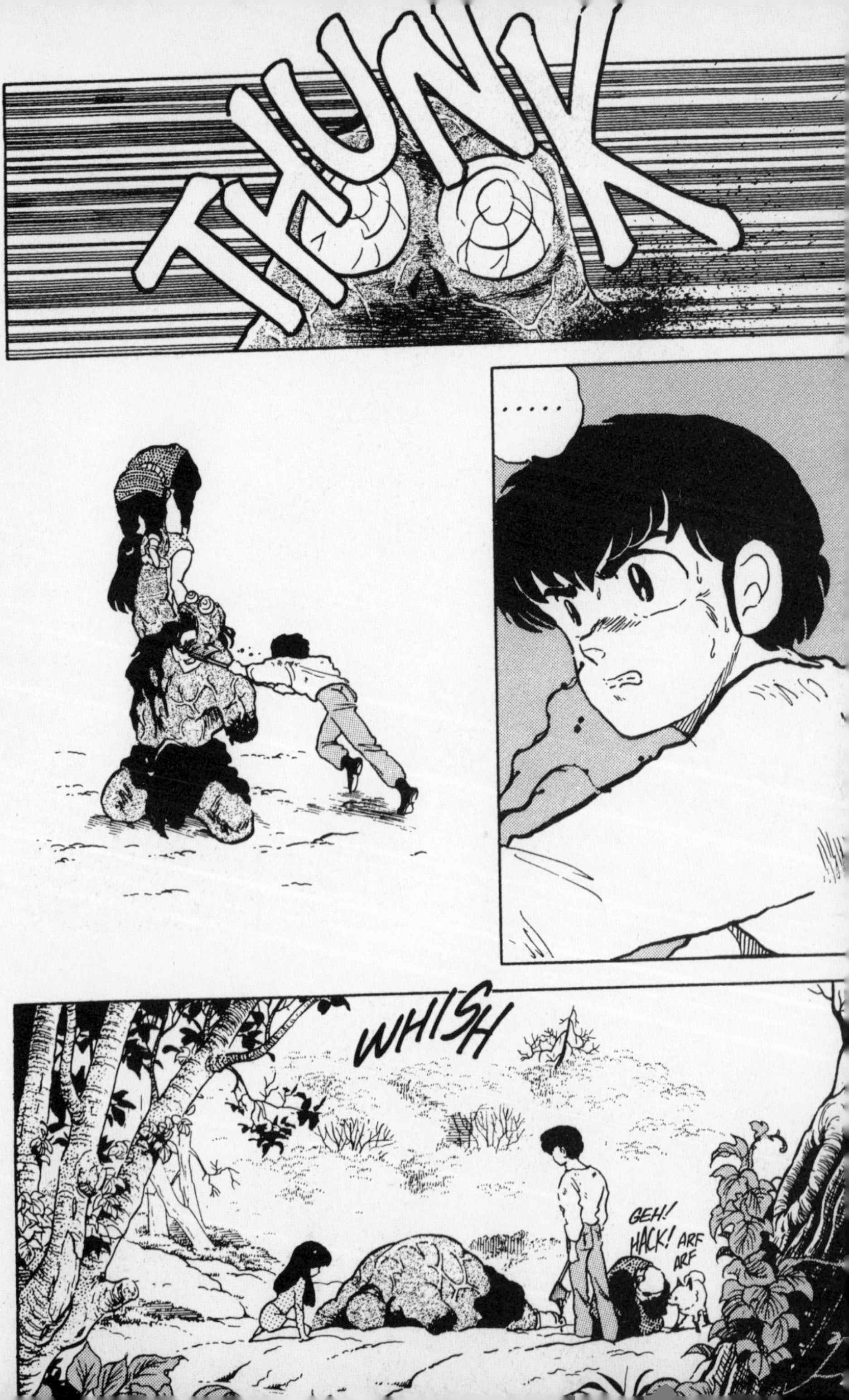
THUNK
......
WHISH
GEH! HACK!
ARF ARF

...NA...

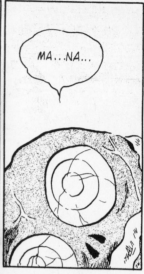

MA...NA...

YOU... YOU RECOGNIZE ME?

MANA...

I'M RIGHT HERE.

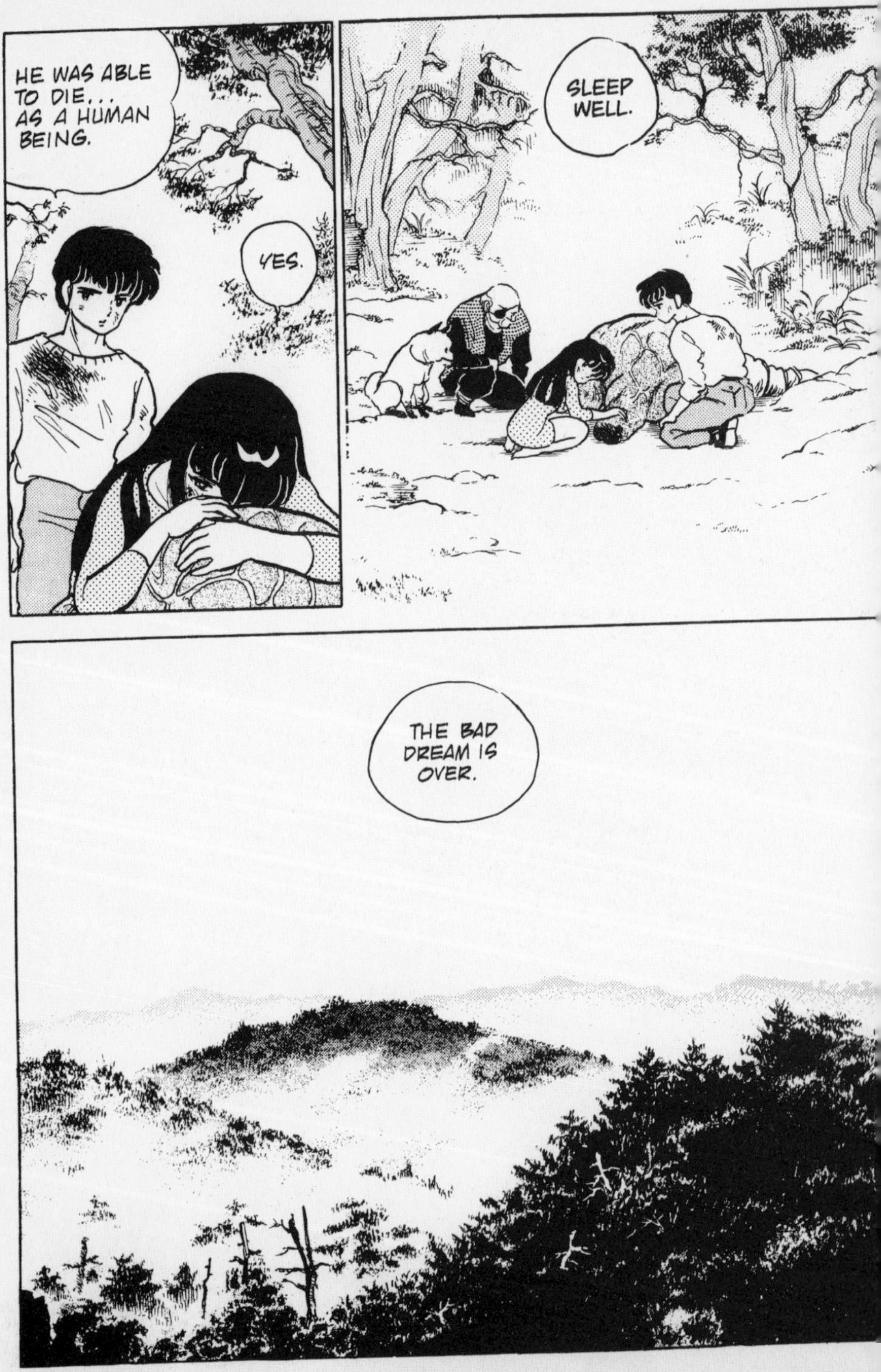
HE WAS ABLE TO DIE... AS A HUMAN BEING.
YES.
SLEEP WELL.
THE BAD DREAM IS OVER.

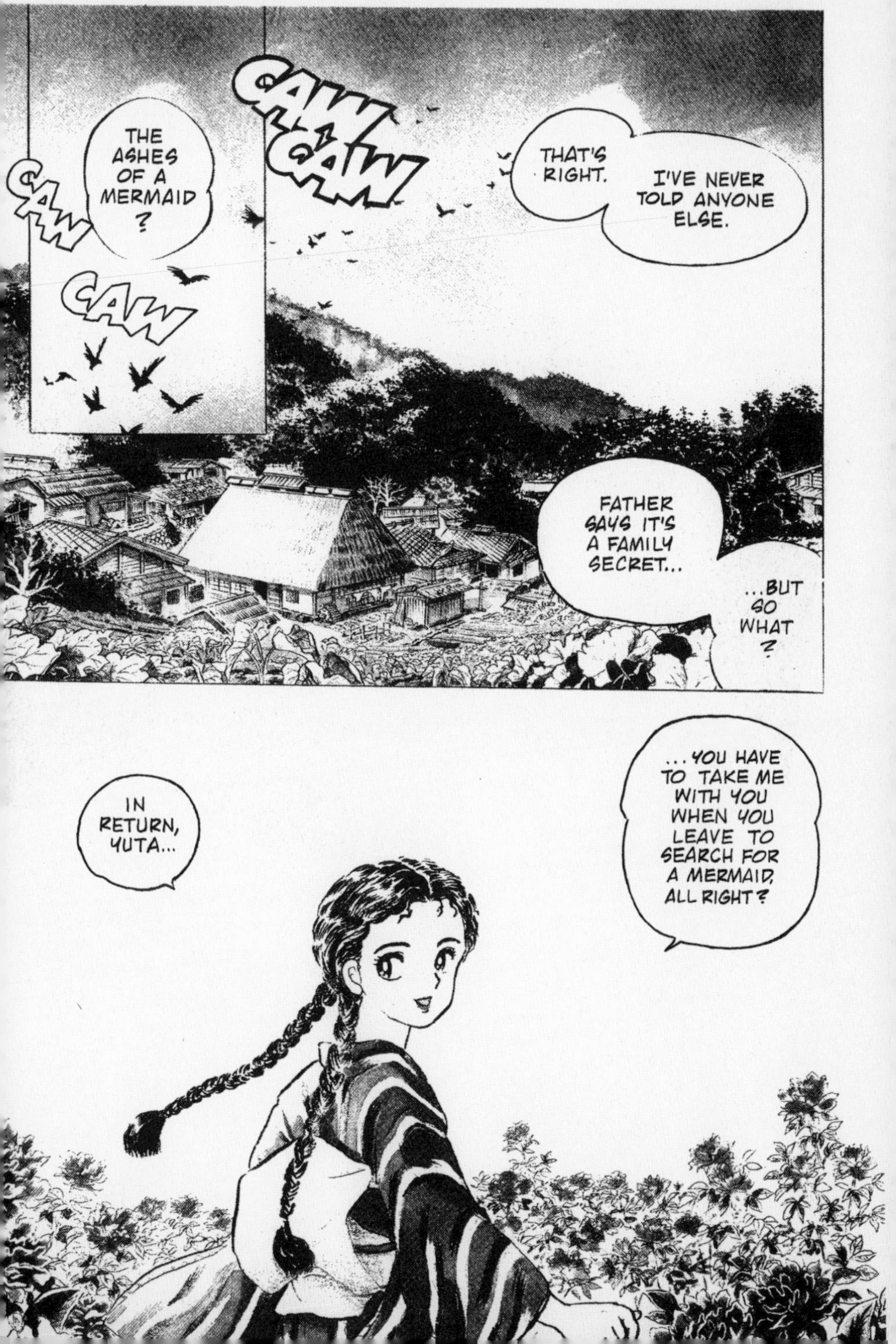
CAW
THE ASHES OF A MERMAID?
CAW
CAW CAW
THAT'S RIGHT.
I'VE NEVER TOLD ANYONE ELSE.
FATHER SAYS IT'S A FAMILY SECRET...
...BUT SO WHAT?
IN RETURN, YUTA...
...YOU HAVE TO TAKE ME WITH YOU WHEN YOU LEAVE TO SEARCH FOR A MERMAID, ALL RIGHT?

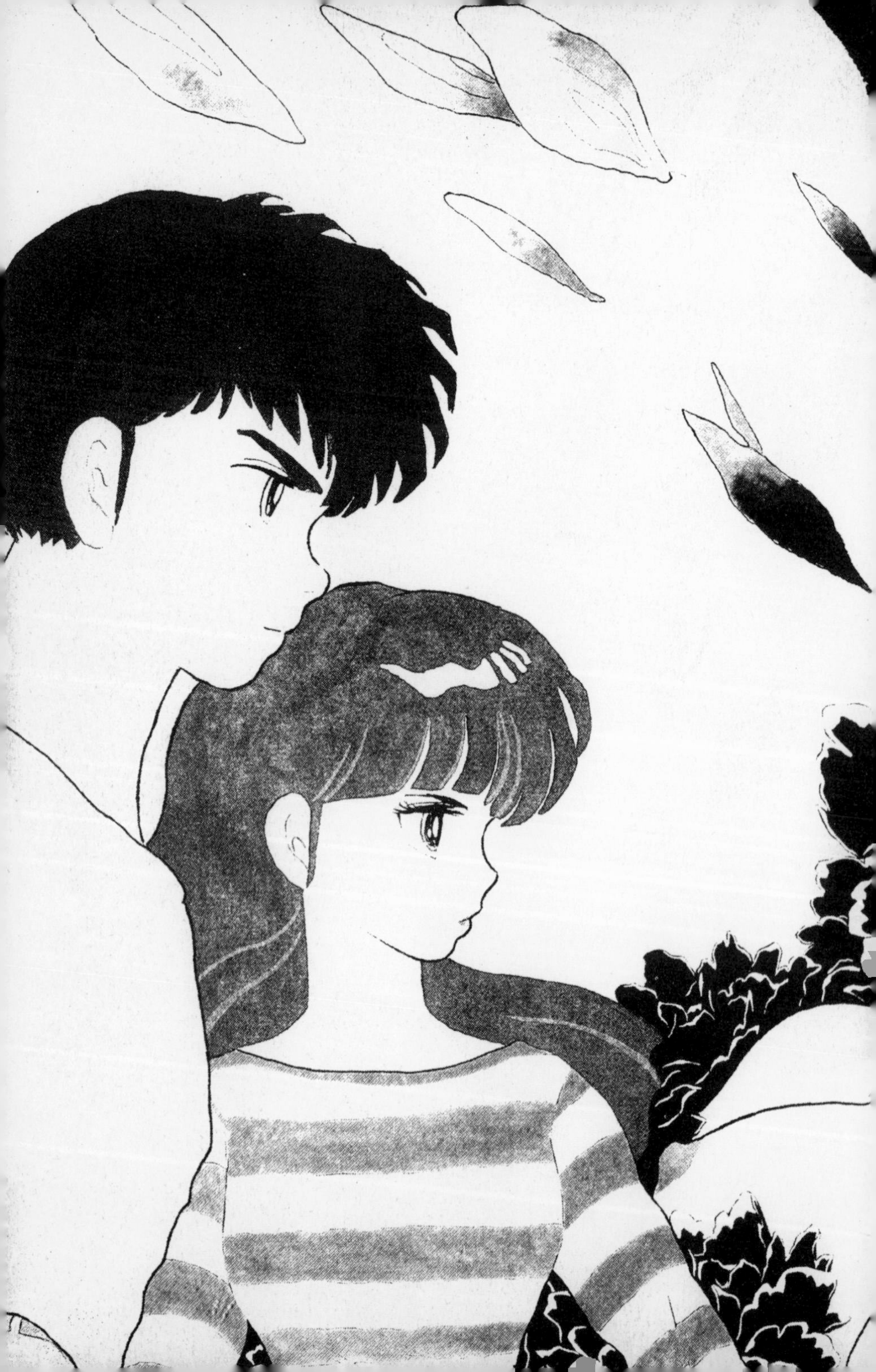

CHAPTER TWO
MERMAID'S PROMISE
PART ONE

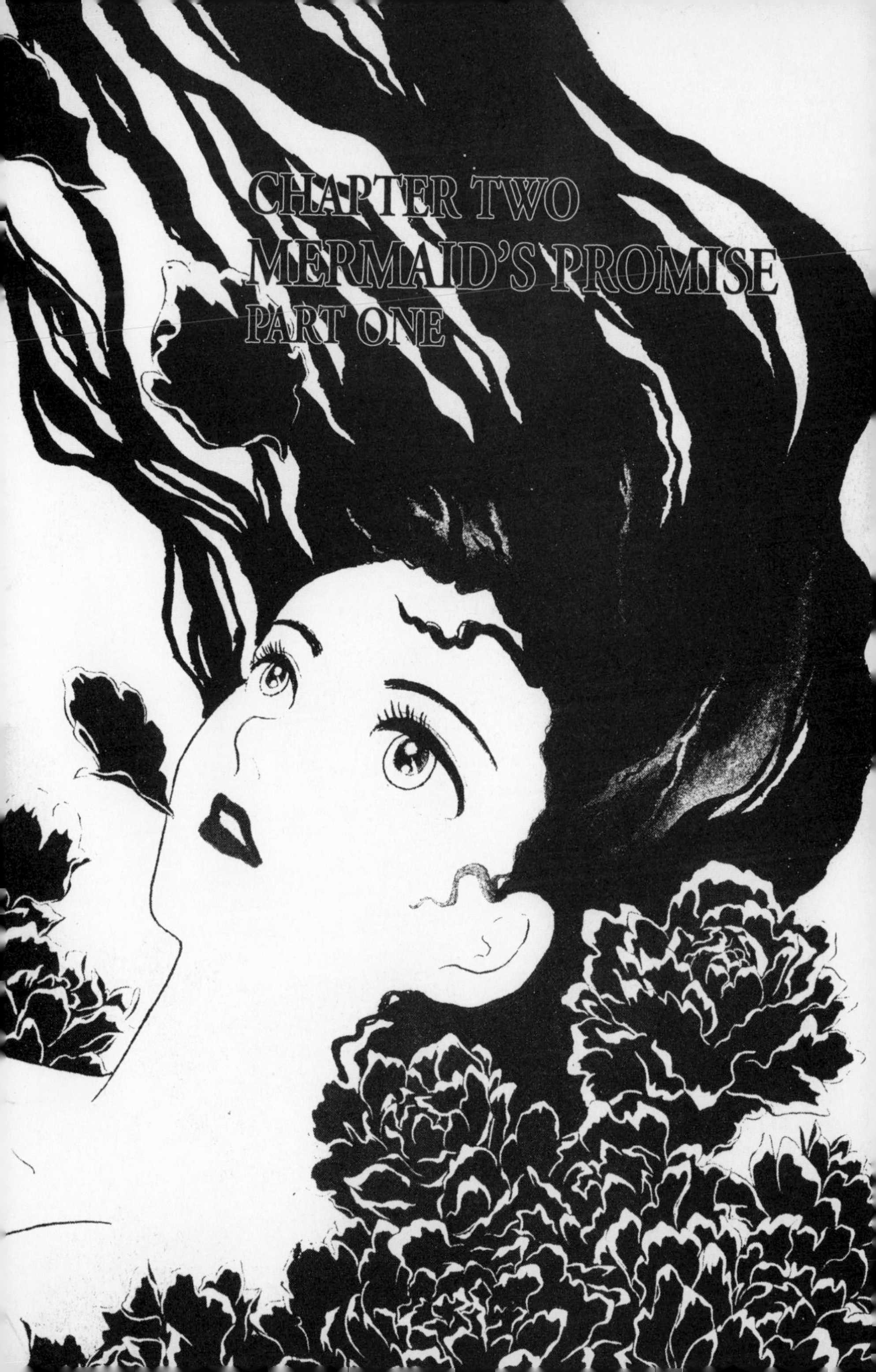

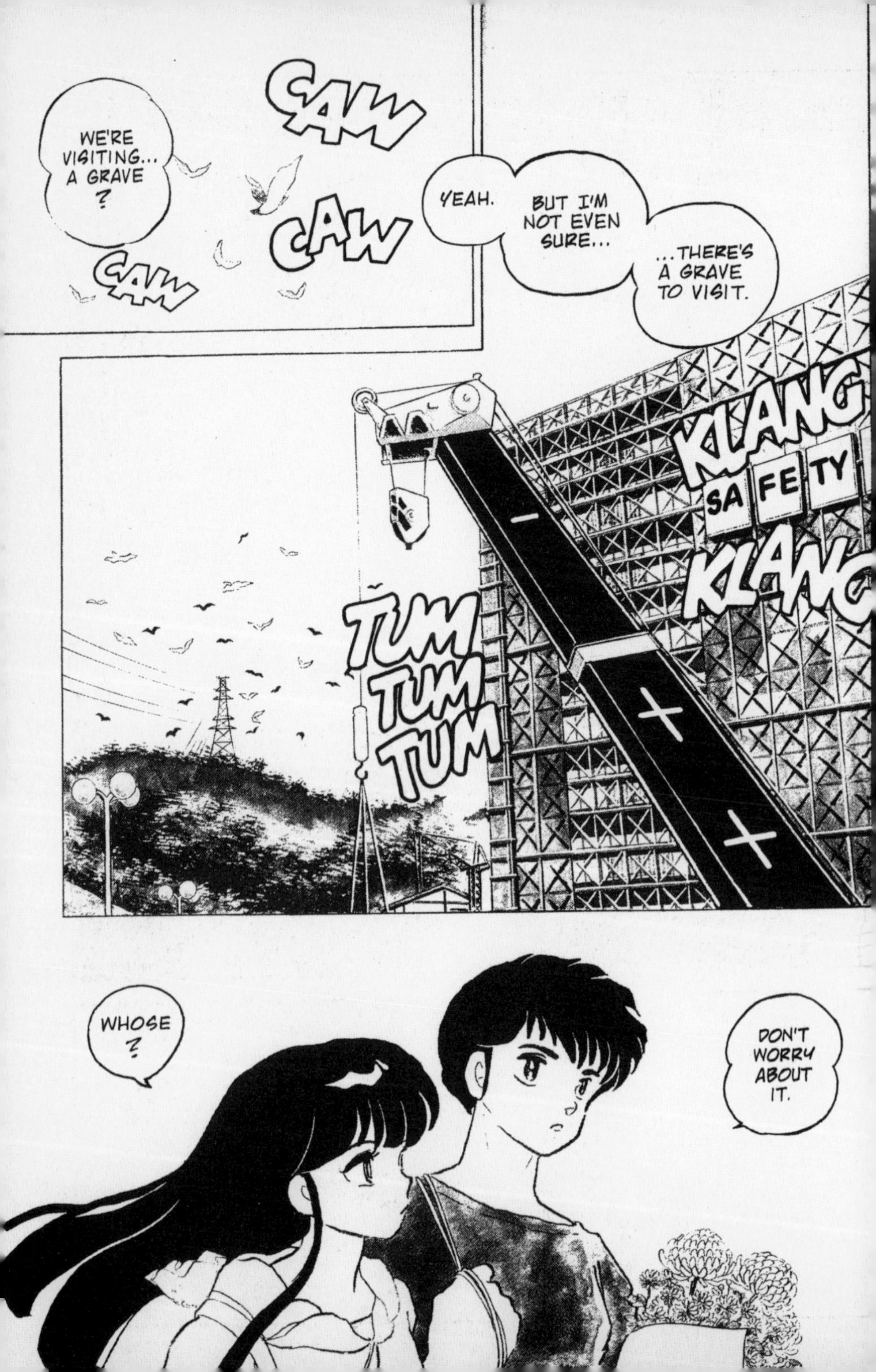

WE'RE VISITING... A GRAVE ?
CAW
CAW
CAW
YEAH.
BUT I'M NOT EVEN SURE...
...THERE'S A GRAVE TO VISIT.
KLANG
SAFETY
KLANG
TUM TUM TUM
WHOSE ?
DON'T WORRY ABOUT IT.

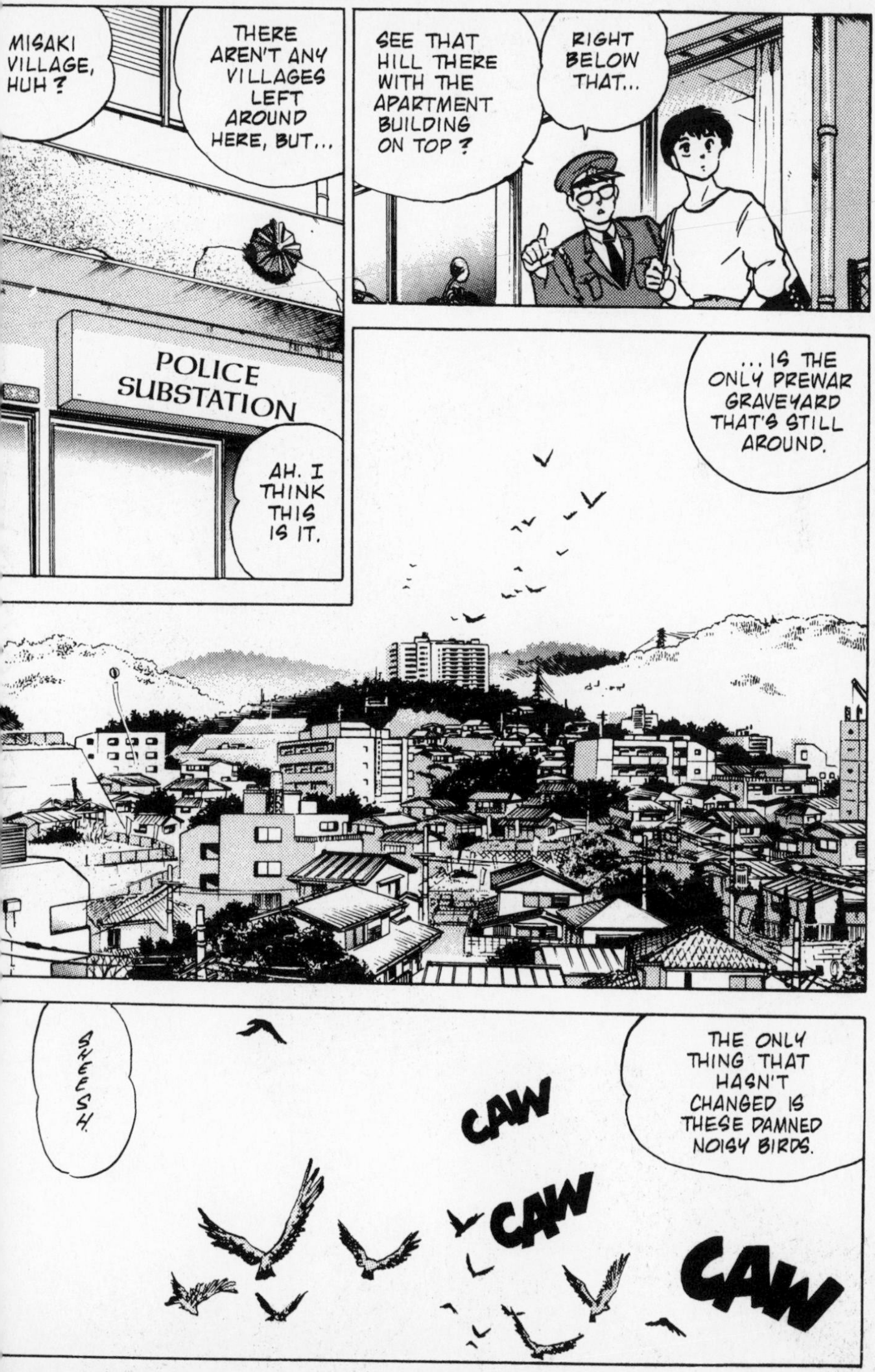
MISAKI VILLAGE, HUH ?
THERE AREN'T ANY VILLAGES LEFT AROUND HERE, BUT...
POLICE SUBSTATION
AH. I THINK THIS IS IT.
SEE THAT HILL THERE WITH THE APARTMENT BUILDING ON TOP ?
RIGHT BELOW THAT...
...IS THE ONLY PREWAR GRAVEYARD THAT'S STILL AROUND.
SHEESH.
THE ONLY THING THAT HASN'T CHANGED IS THESE DAMNED NOISY BIRDS.
CAW
CAW
CAW

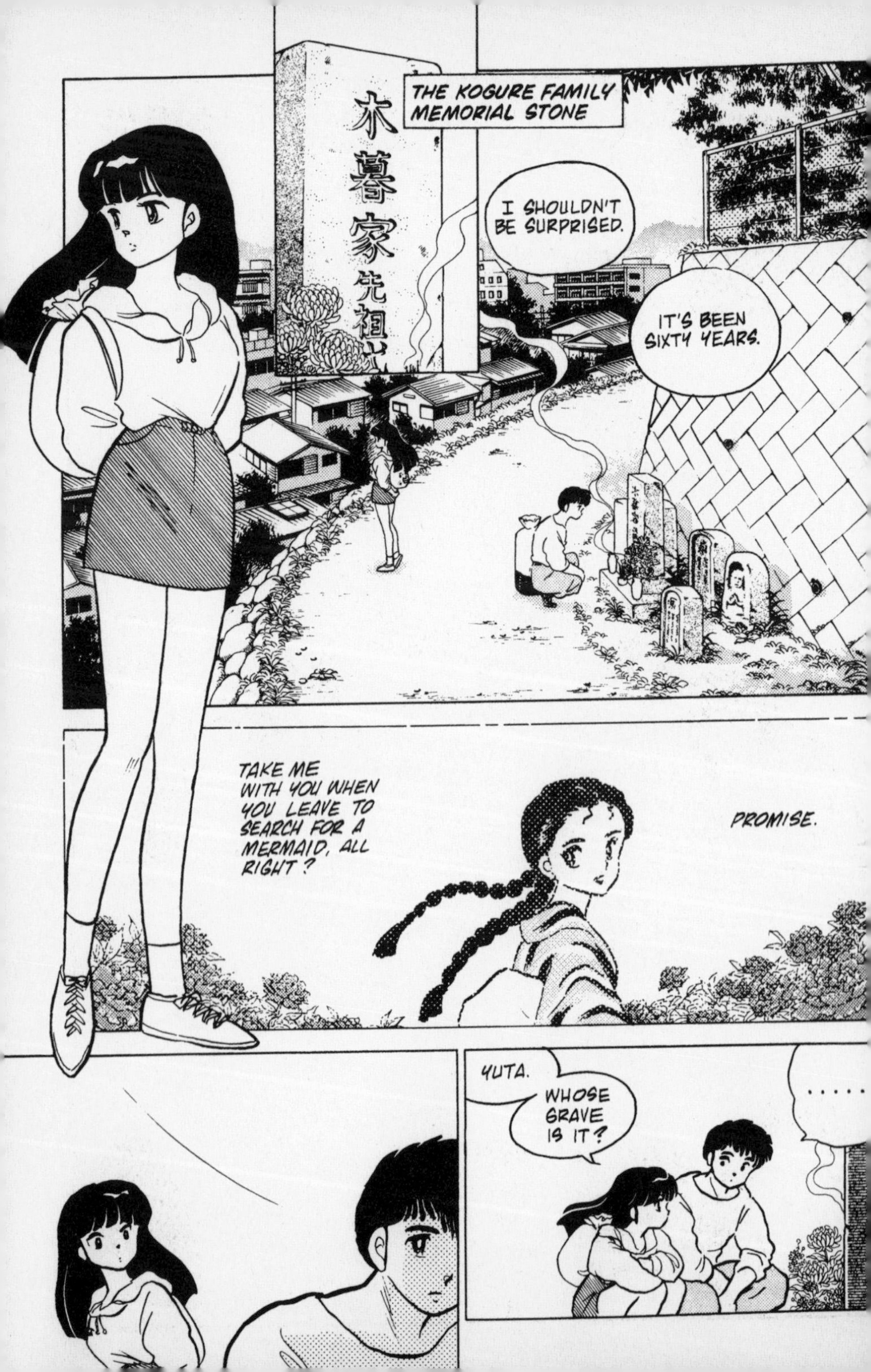
THE KOGURE FAMILY MEMORIAL STONE
木暮家先祖
I SHOULDN'T BE SURPRISED.
IT'S BEEN SIXTY YEARS.
TAKE ME WITH YOU WHEN YOU LEAVE TO SEARCH FOR A MERMAID, ALL RIGHT?
PROMISE.
YUTA.
WHOSE GRAVE IS IT?
.....

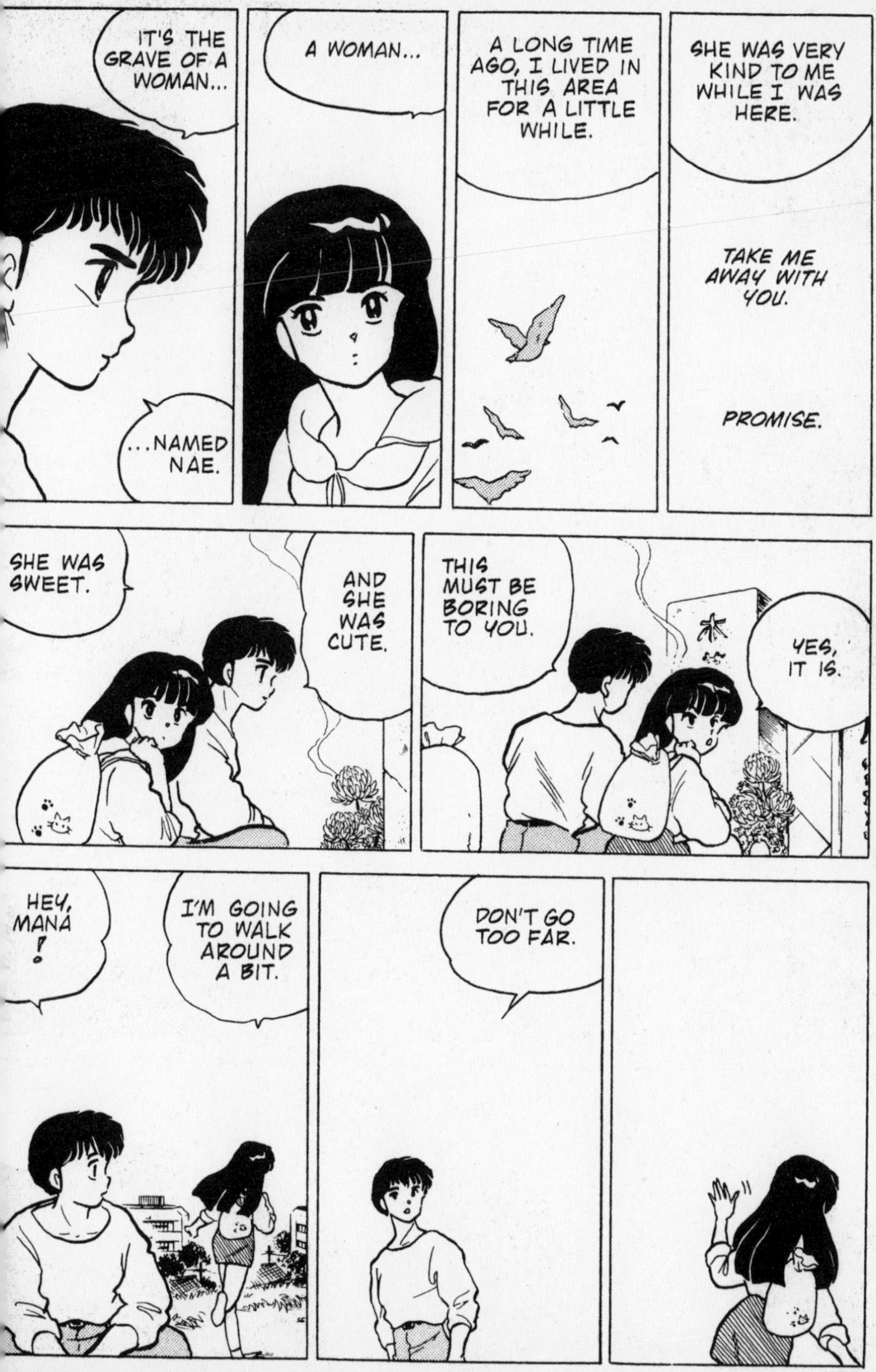
IT'S THE GRAVE OF A WOMAN...
...NAMED NAE.
A WOMAN...
A LONG TIME AGO, I LIVED IN THIS AREA FOR A LITTLE WHILE.
SHE WAS VERY KIND TO ME WHILE I WAS HERE.
TAKE ME AWAY WITH YOU.
PROMISE.
SHE WAS SWEET.
AND SHE WAS CUTE.
THIS MUST BE BORING TO YOU.
YES, IT IS.
HEY, MANA!
I'M GOING TO WALK AROUND A BIT.
DON'T GO TOO FAR.

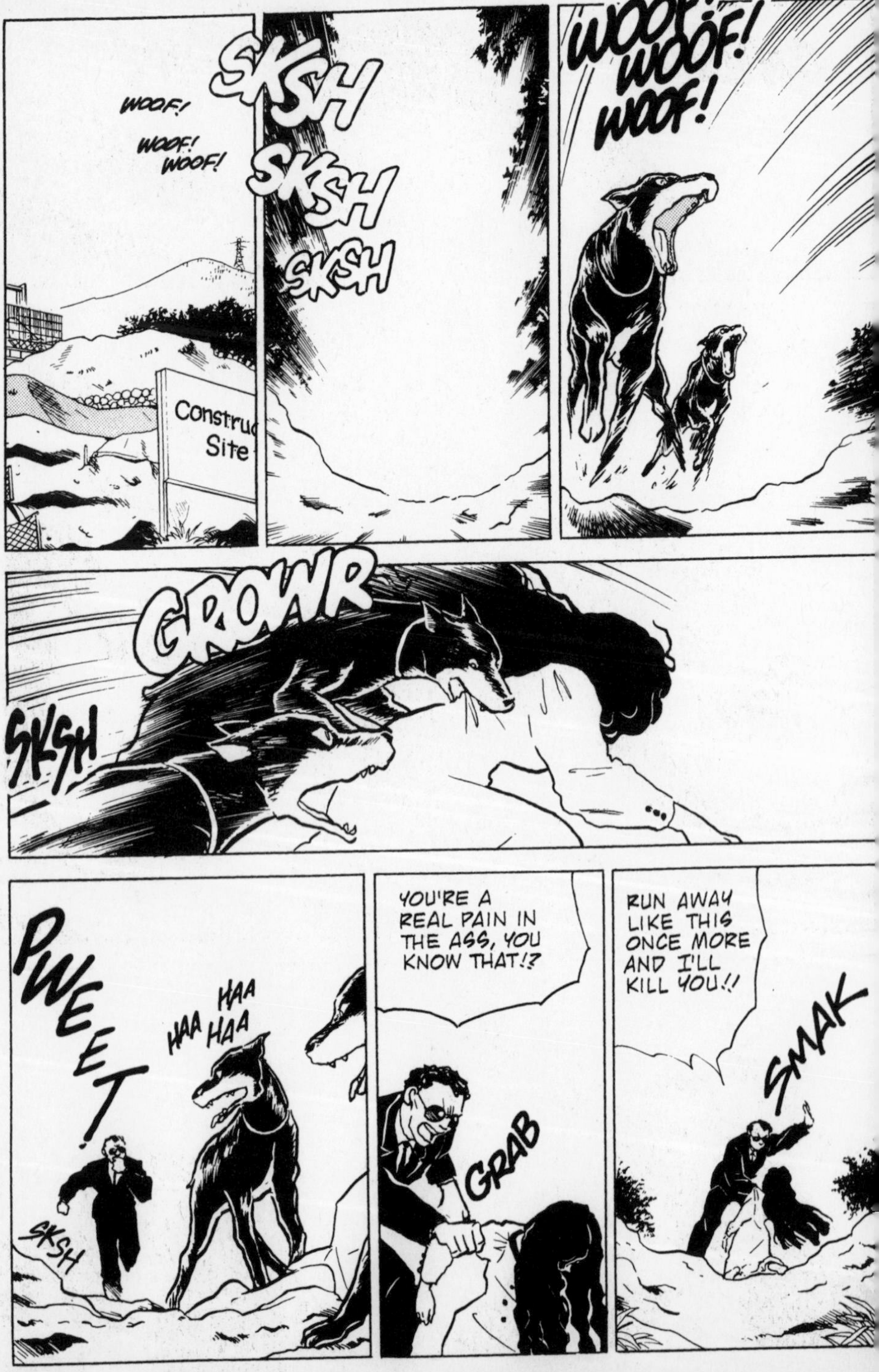
WOOF!
WOOF!
WOOF!
Construc
Site
SKSH
SKSH
SKSH
WOOF!
WOOF!
WOOF!
GROWR
SKSH
PWEET!
SKSH
HAA HAA
HAA HAA
YOU'RE A REAL PAIN IN THE ASS, YOU KNOW THAT!?
GRAB
RUN AWAY LIKE THIS ONCE MORE AND I'LL KILL YOU!!
SMAK

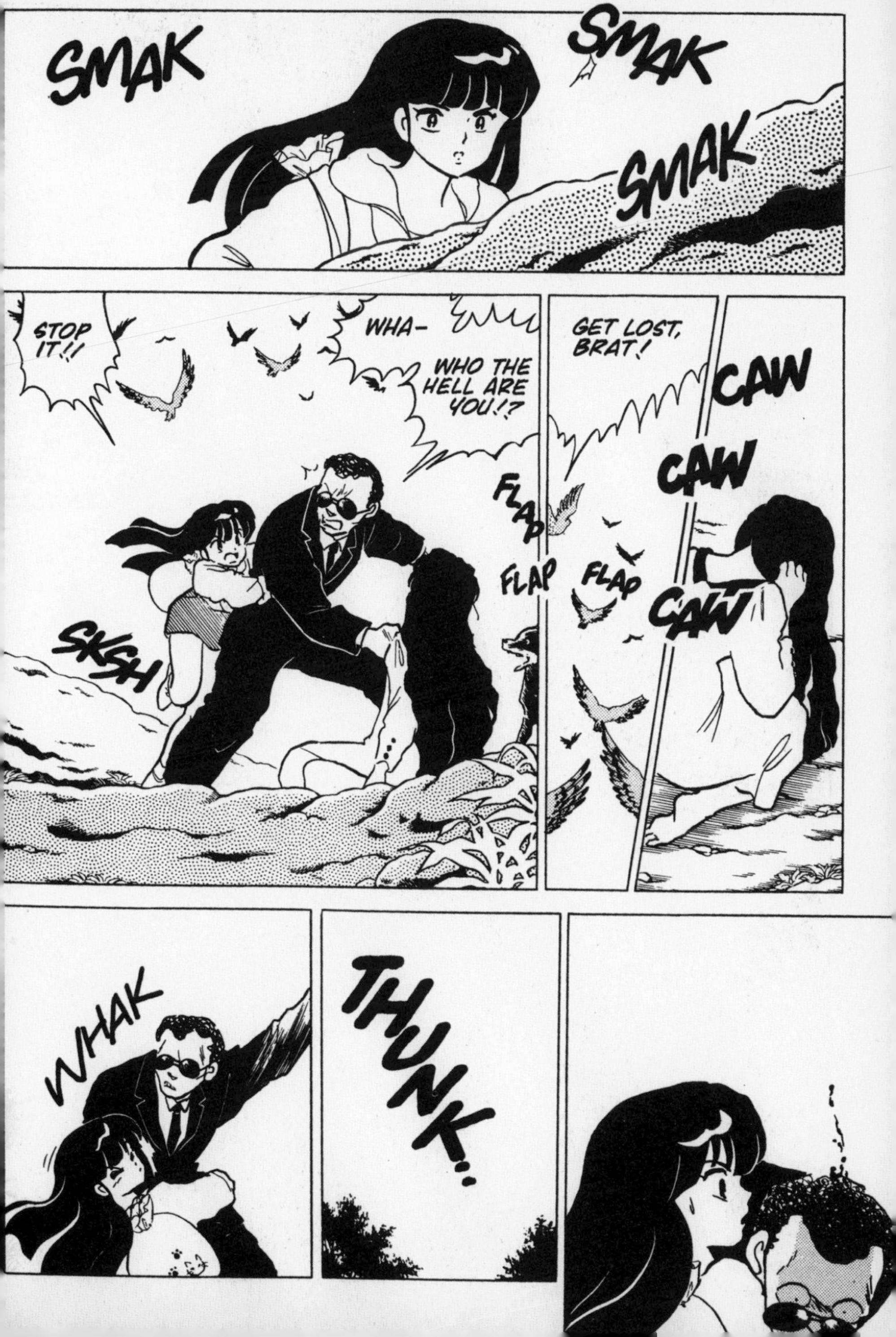
SMAK
SMAK
SMAK
STOP IT!!
WHA-
WHO THE HELL ARE YOU!?
SKSH
FLAP
FLAP
GET LOST, BRAT!
FLAP
CAW
CAW
CAW
WHAK
THUNK!!

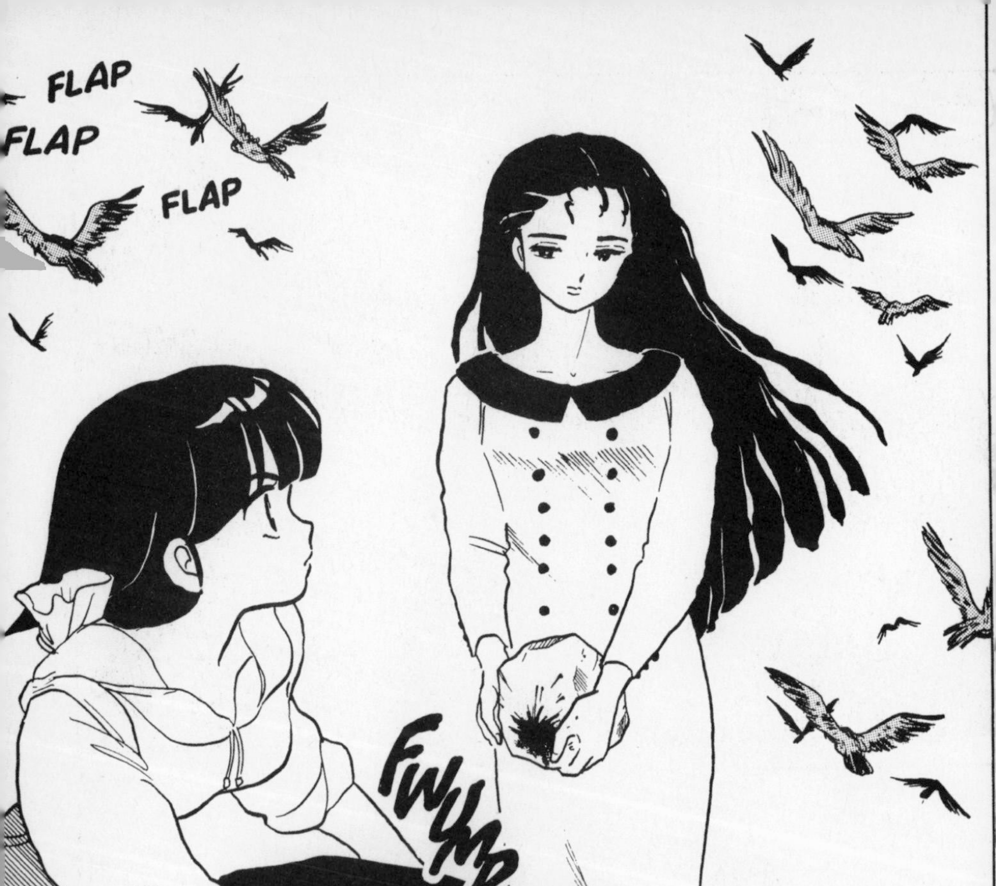
FLAP
FLAP
FLAP
FWUMP
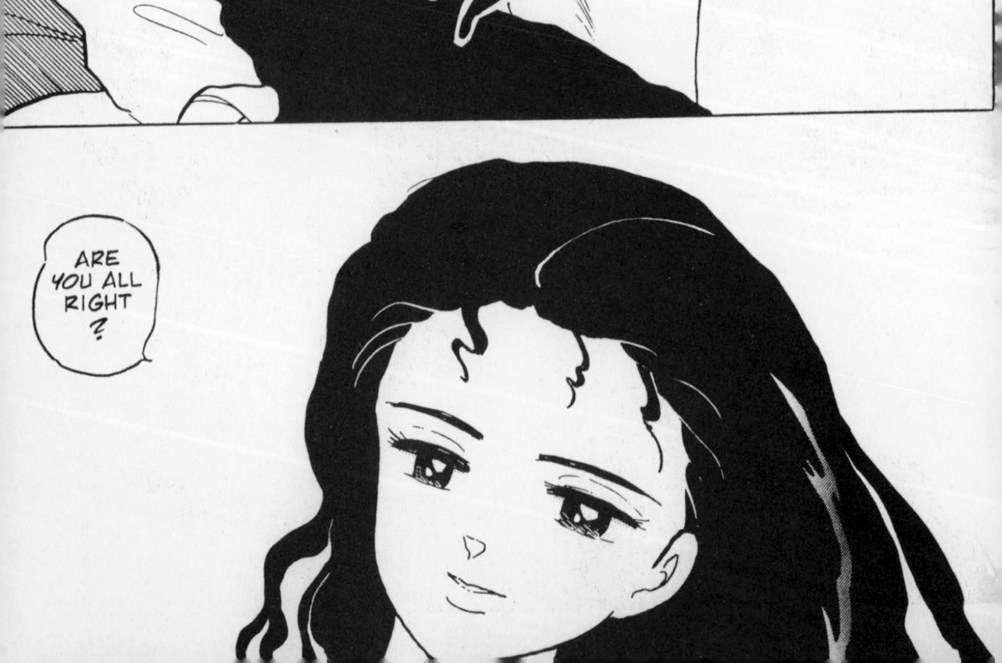
ARE YOU ALL RIGHT ?

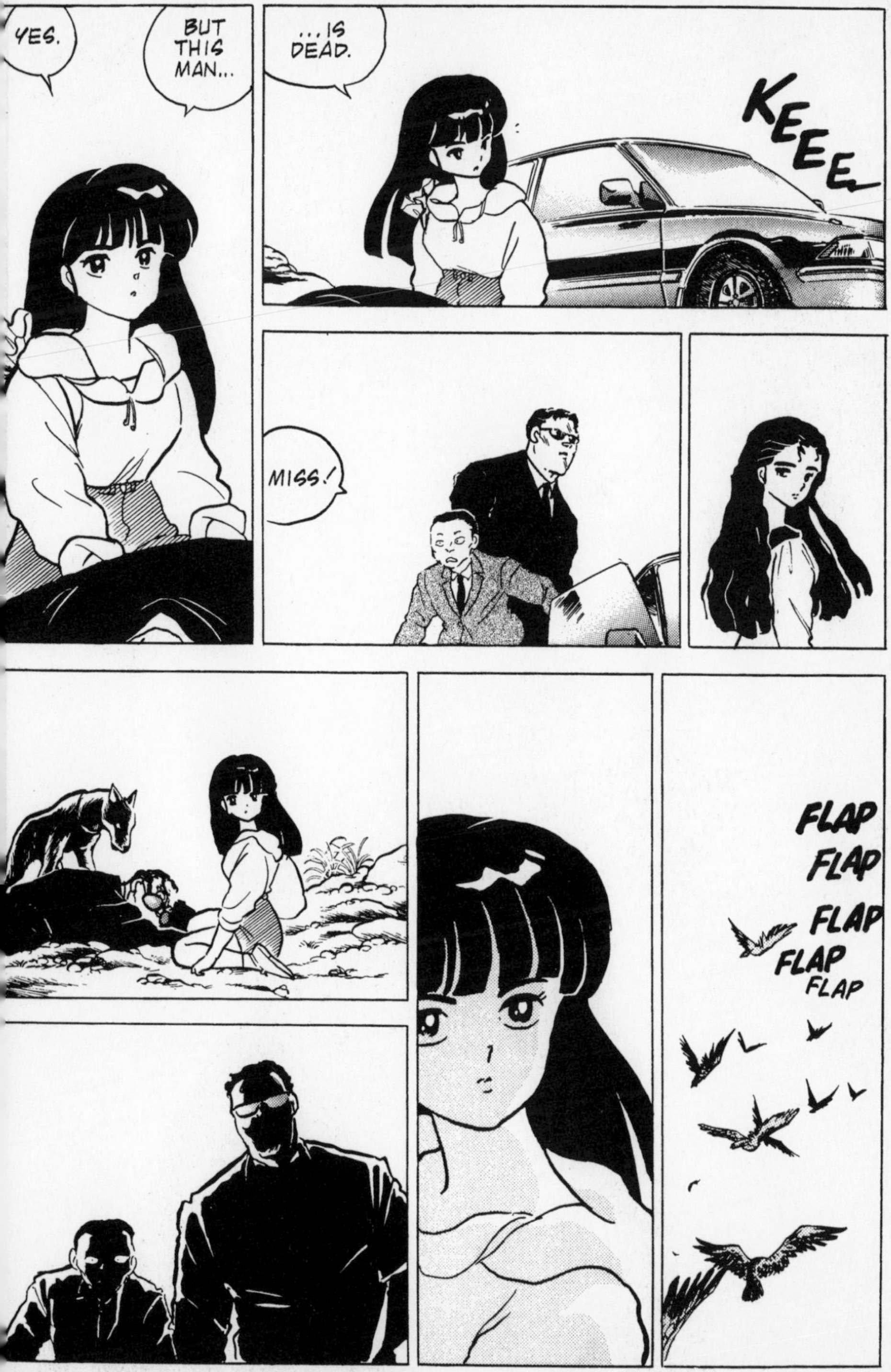
YES.
BUT THIS MAN...
...IS DEAD.
KEEE
MISS!
FLAP
FLAP
FLAP
FLAP
FLAP

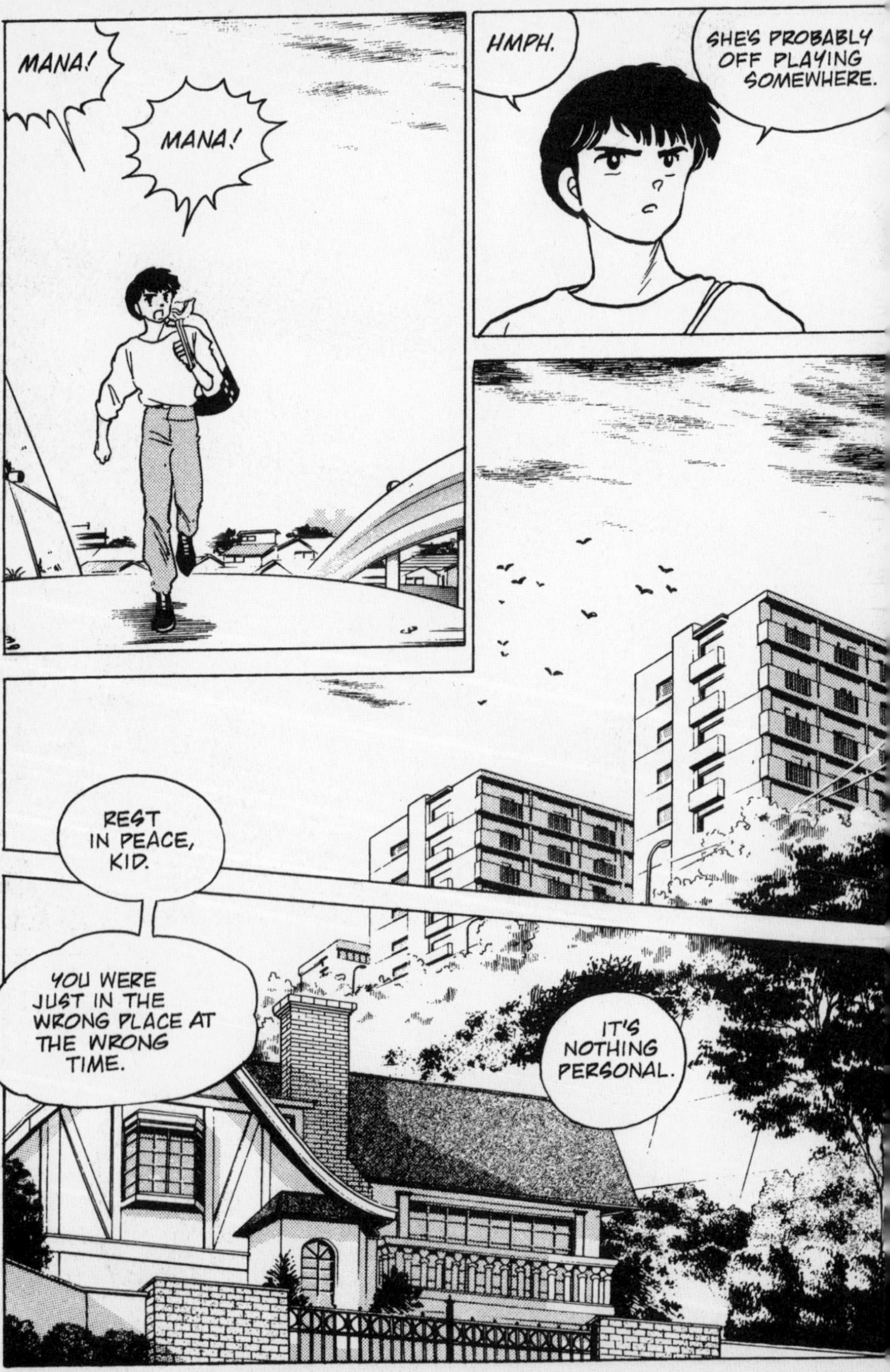
MANA!
MANA!
HMPH.
SHE'S PROBABLY OFF PLAYING SOMEWHERE.
REST IN PEACE, KID.
YOU WERE JUST IN THE WRONG PLACE AT THE WRONG TIME.
IT'S NOTHING PERSONAL.

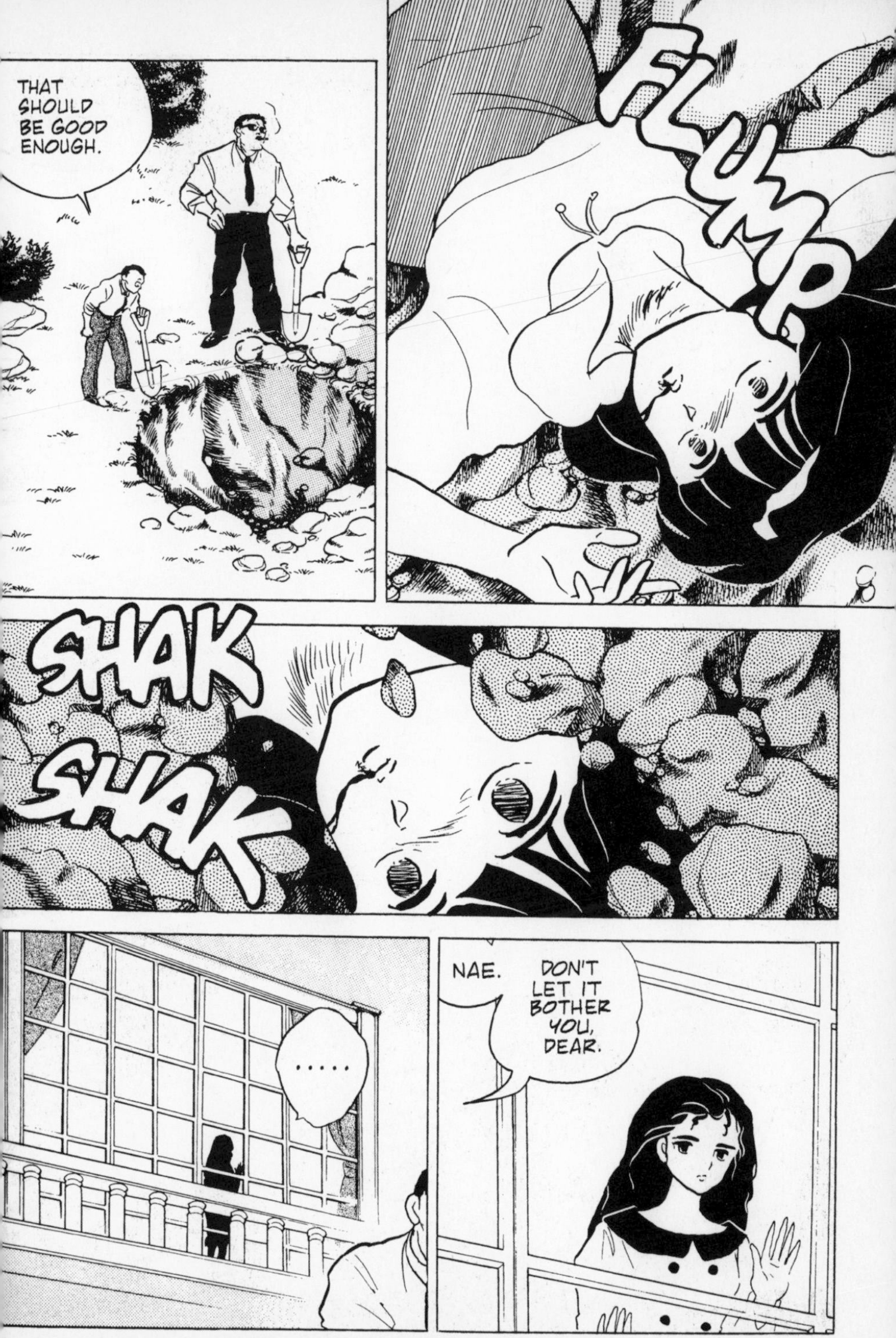

THAT SHOULD BE GOOD ENOUGH.
FLUMP
SHAK SHAK
.....
NAE. DON'T LET IT BOTHER YOU, DEAR.

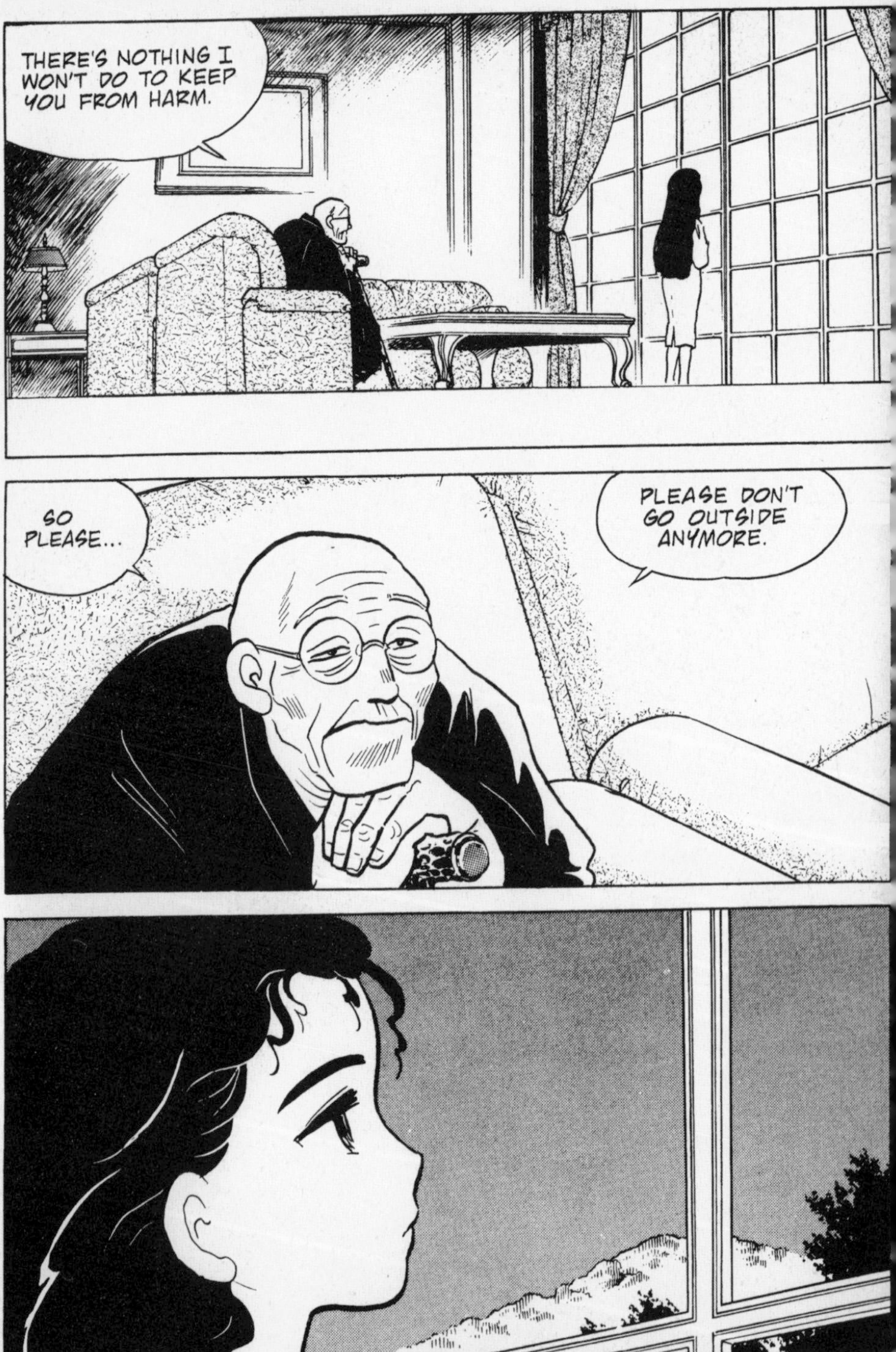
THERE'S NOTHING I WON'T DO TO KEEP YOU FROM HARM.
SO PLEASE...
PLEASE DON'T GO OUTSIDE ANYMORE.

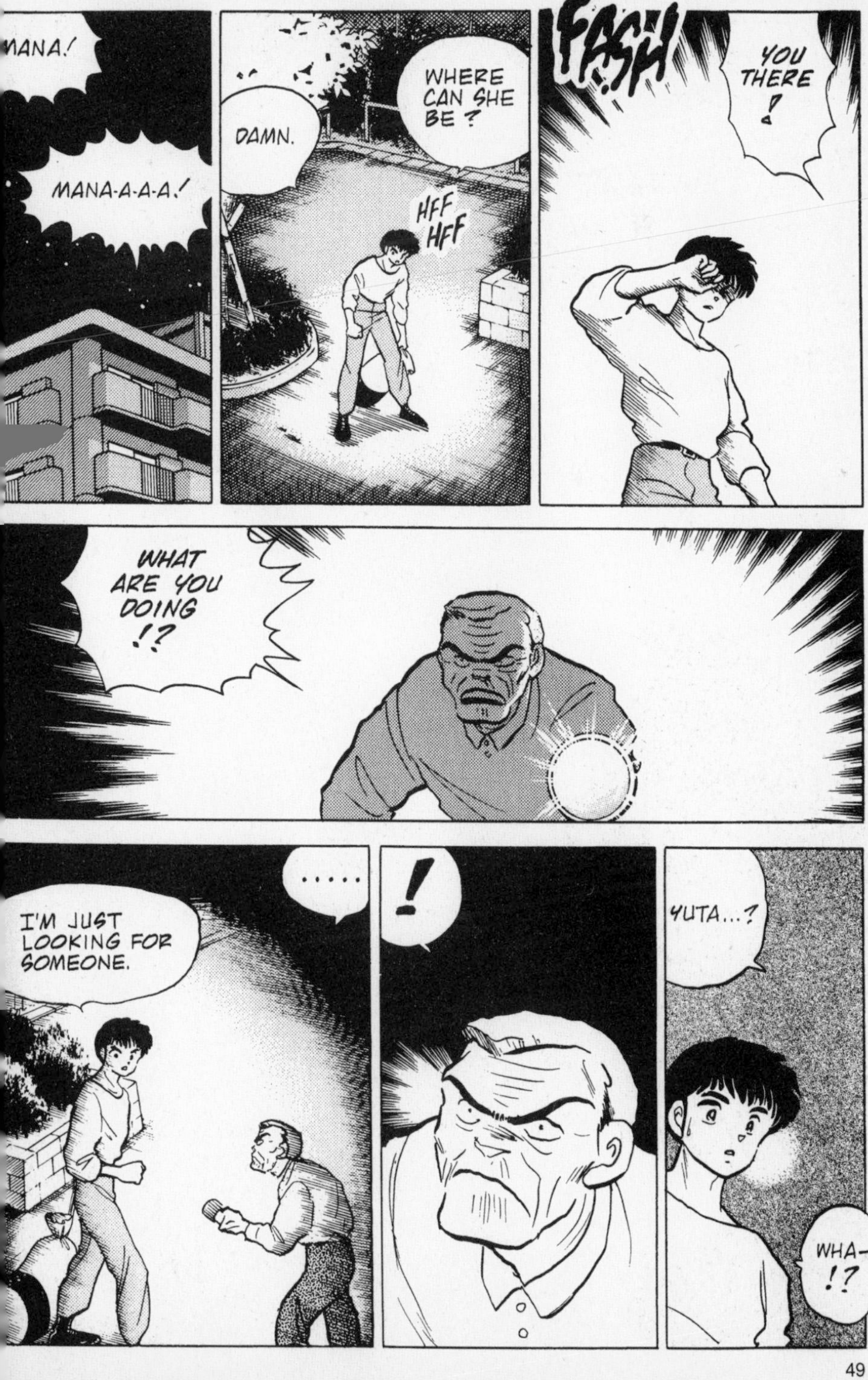
MANA!
MANA-A-A-A!
DAMN.
WHERE CAN SHE BE?
HFF HFF
FASH
YOU THERE!
WHAT ARE YOU DOING!?
I'M JUST LOOKING FOR SOMEONE.
......
!
YUTA...?
WHA-!?

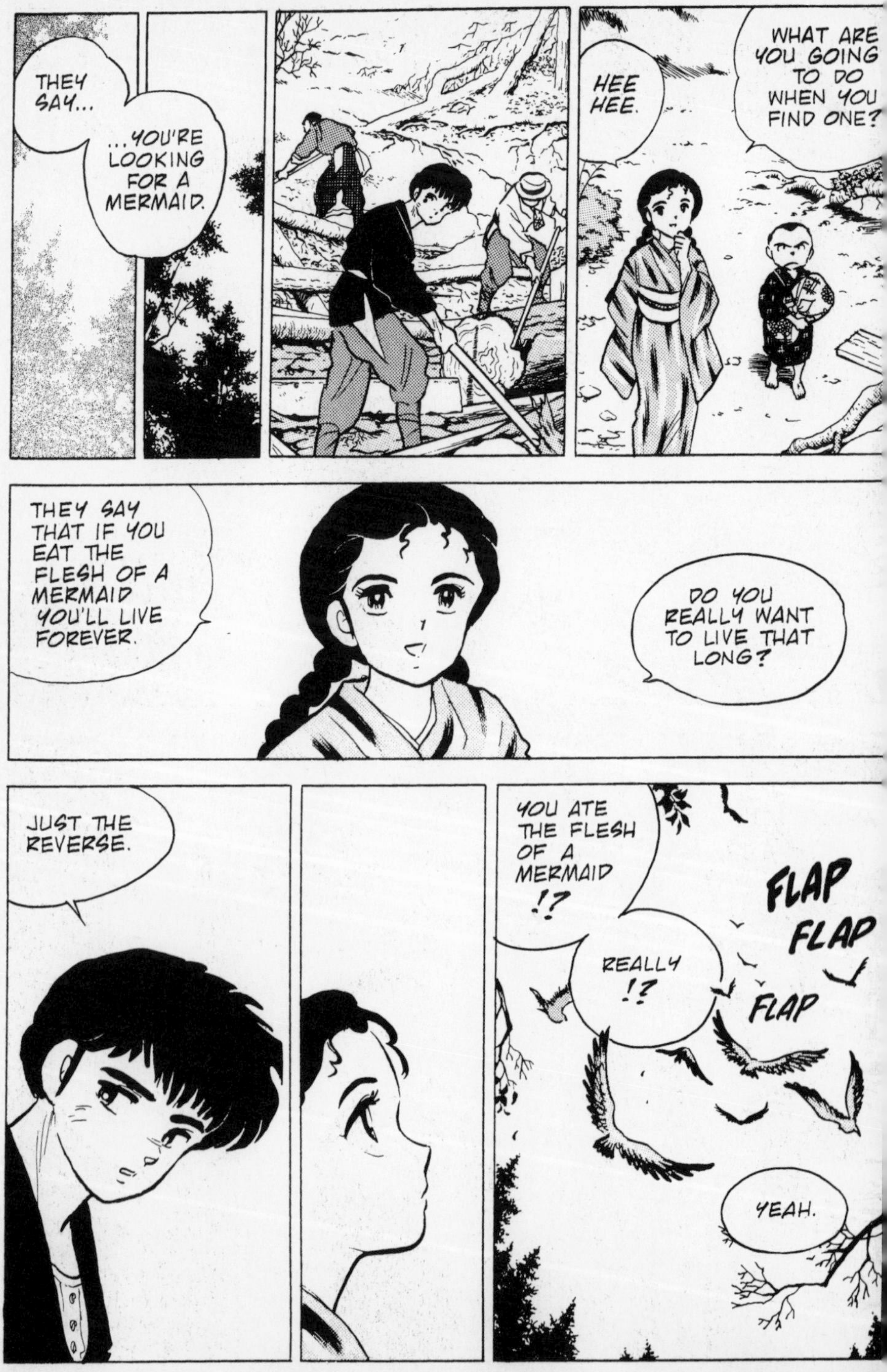
THEY SAY...
...YOU'RE LOOKING FOR A MERMAID.
HEE HEE.
WHAT ARE YOU GOING TO DO WHEN YOU FIND ONE?
THEY SAY THAT IF YOU EAT THE FLESH OF A MERMAID YOU'LL LIVE FOREVER.
DO YOU REALLY WANT TO LIVE THAT LONG?
JUST THE REVERSE.
YOU ATE THE FLESH OF A MERMAID !?
REALLY !?
FLAP
FLAP
FLAP
YEAH.

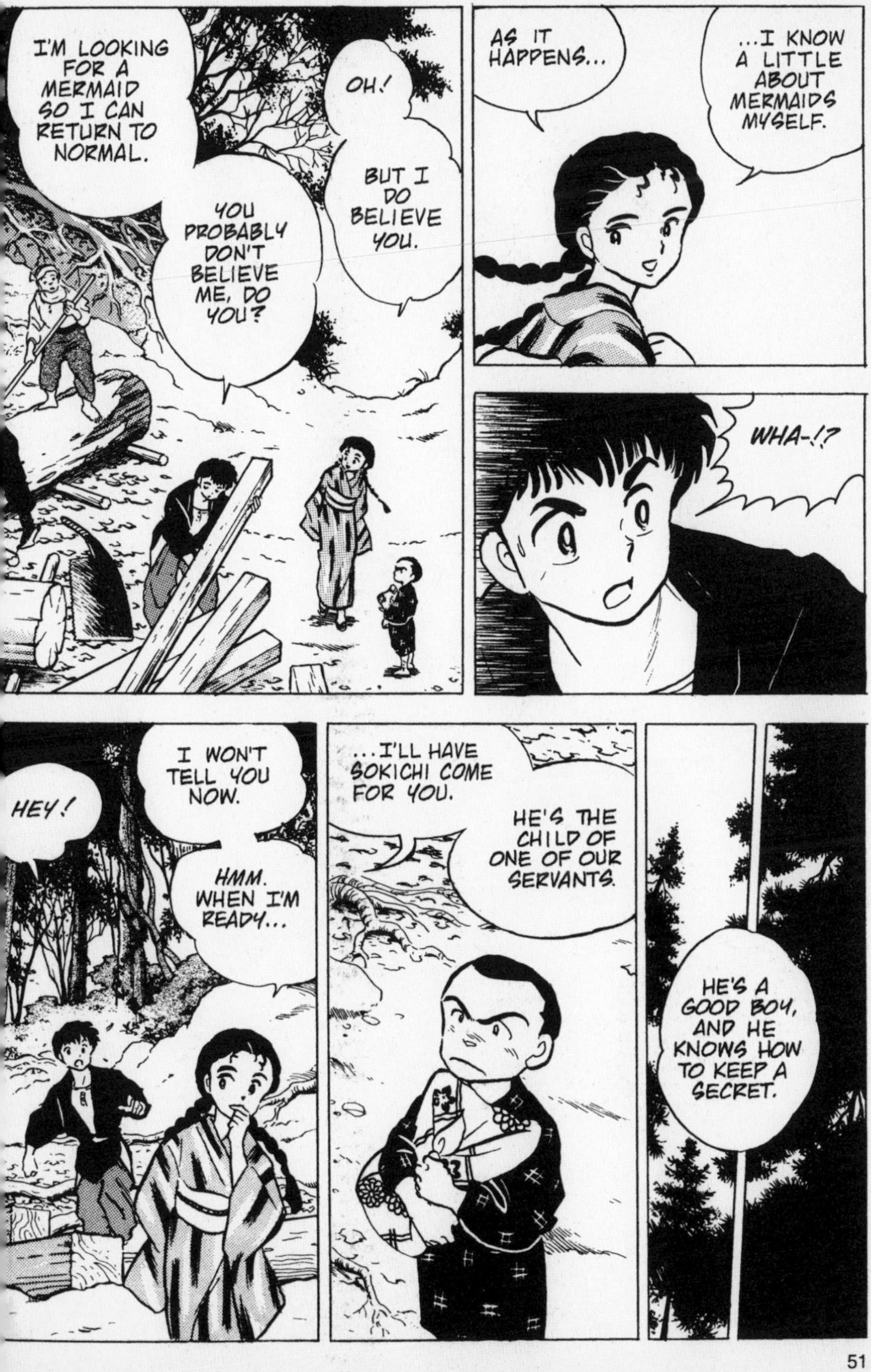
I'M LOOKING FOR A MERMAID SO I CAN RETURN TO NORMAL.
YOU PROBABLY DON'T BELIEVE ME, DO YOU?
OH!
BUT I DO BELIEVE YOU.
AS IT HAPPENS...
...I KNOW A LITTLE ABOUT MERMAIDS MYSELF.
WHA-!?
HEY!
I WON'T TELL YOU NOW.
HMM. WHEN I'M READY...
...I'LL HAVE SOKICHI COME FOR YOU.
HE'S THE CHILD OF ONE OF OUR SERVANTS.
HE'S A GOOD BOY, AND HE KNOWS HOW TO KEEP A SECRET.

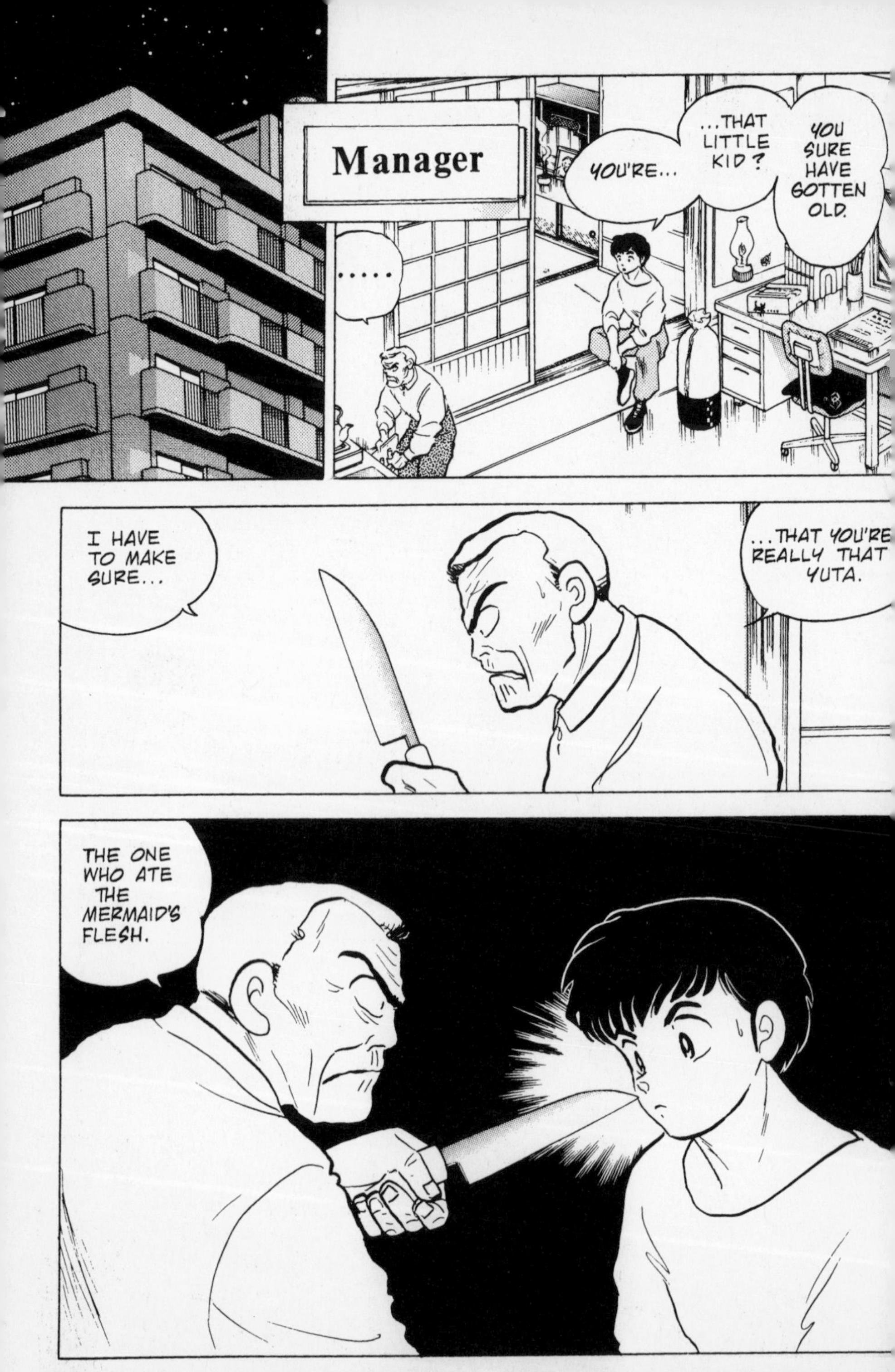
Manager
......
YOU'RE...
...THAT LITTLE KID?
YOU SURE HAVE GOTTEN OLD.
I HAVE TO MAKE SURE...
...THAT YOU'RE REALLY THAT YUTA.
THE ONE WHO ATE THE MERMAID'S FLESH.

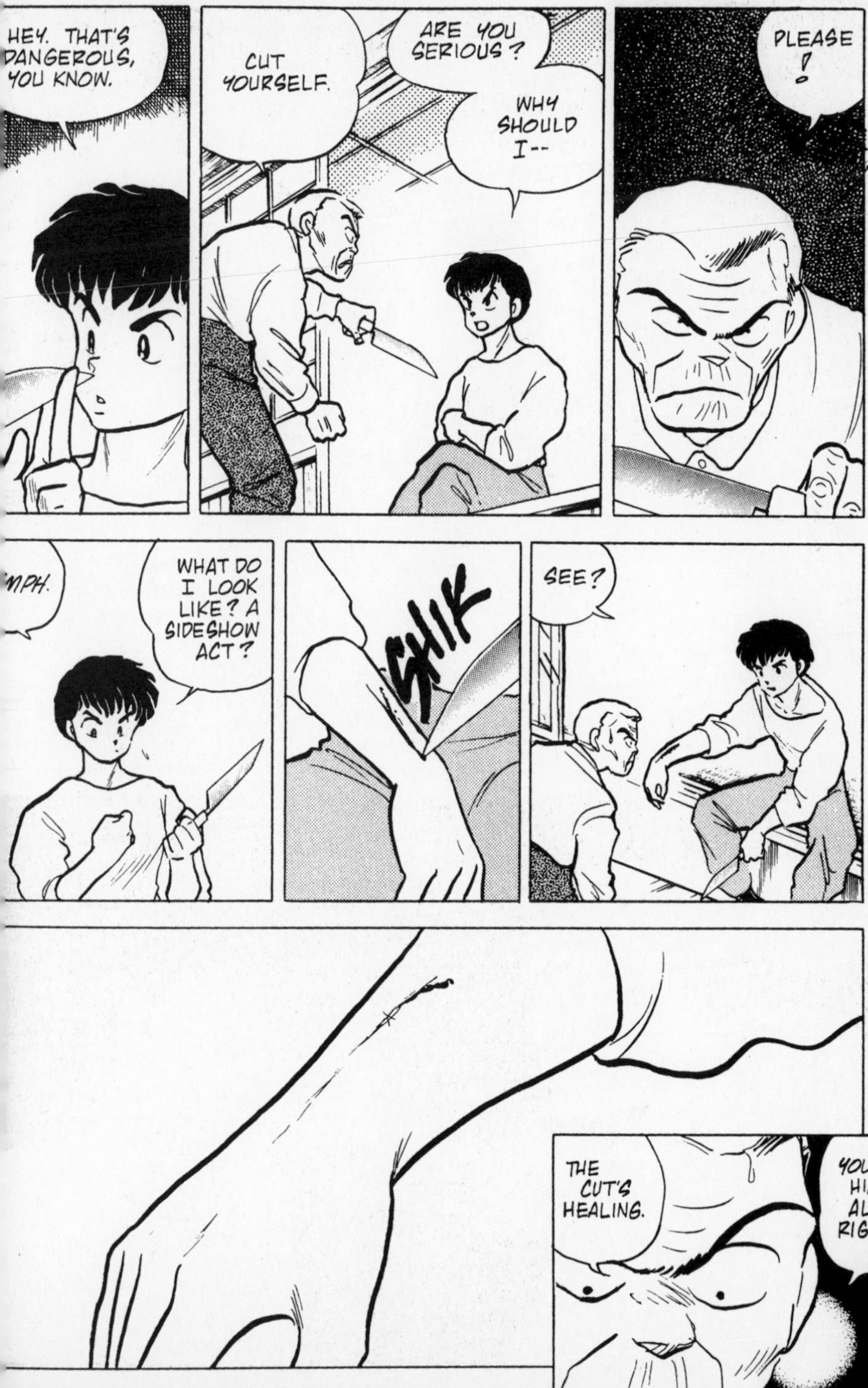
HEY. THAT'S DANGEROUS, YOU KNOW.
CUT YOURSELF.
ARE YOU SERIOUS?
WHY SHOULD I--
PLEASE!
MPH.
WHAT DO I LOOK LIKE? A SIDESHOW ACT?
SHIK
SEE?
THE CUT'S HEALING.
YOU'RE HIM ALL RIGHT.

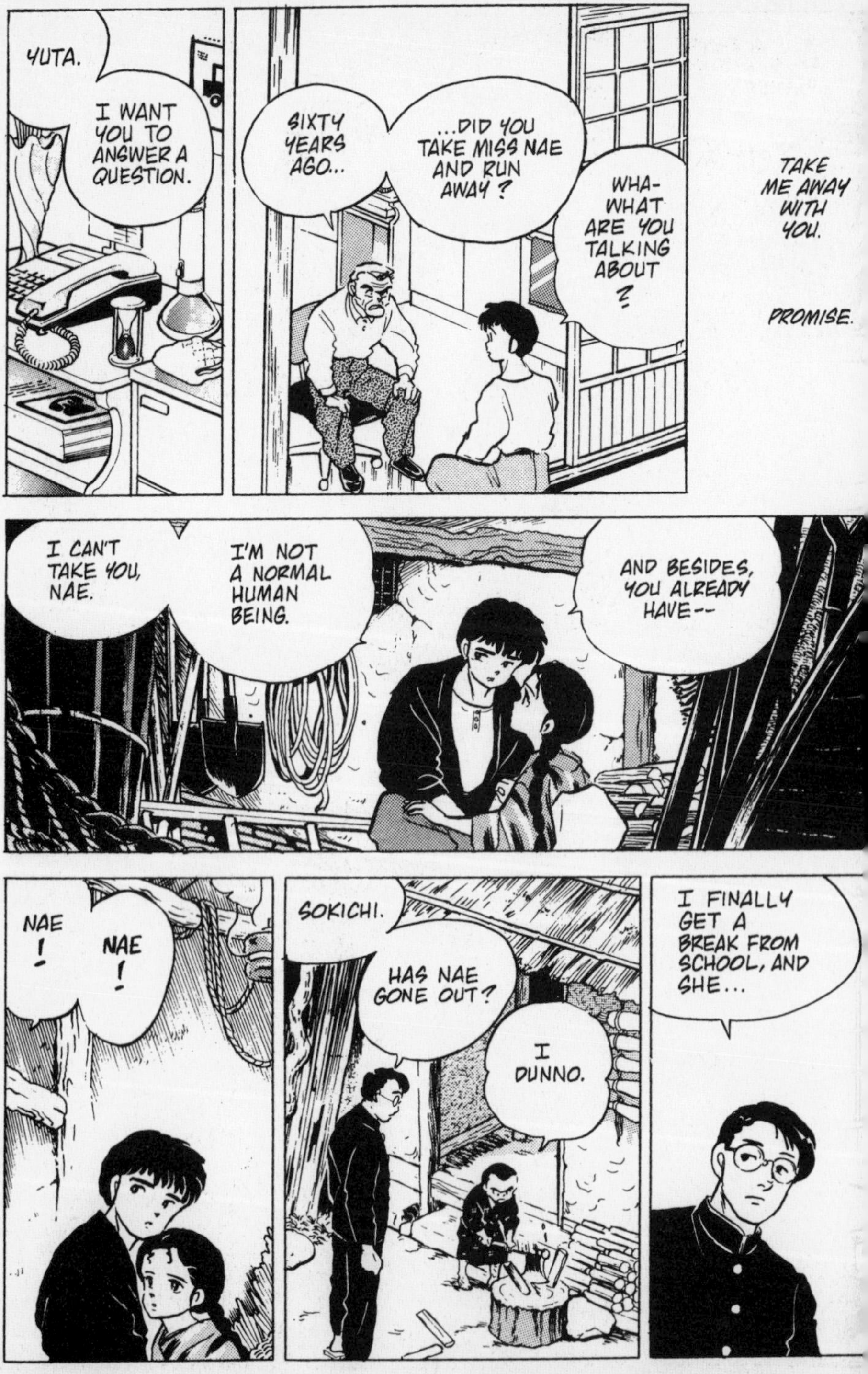
YUTA.
I WANT YOU TO ANSWER A QUESTION.
SIXTY YEARS AGO...
...DID YOU TAKE MISS NAE AND RUN AWAY?
WHA-WHAT ARE YOU TALKING ABOUT??
TAKE ME AWAY WITH YOU.
PROMISE.
I CAN'T TAKE YOU, NAE.
I'M NOT A NORMAL HUMAN BEING.
AND BESIDES, YOU ALREADY HAVE--
NAE!
NAE!
SOKICHI.
HAS NAE GONE OUT?
I DUNNO.
I FINALLY GET A BREAK FROM SCHOOL, AND SHE...

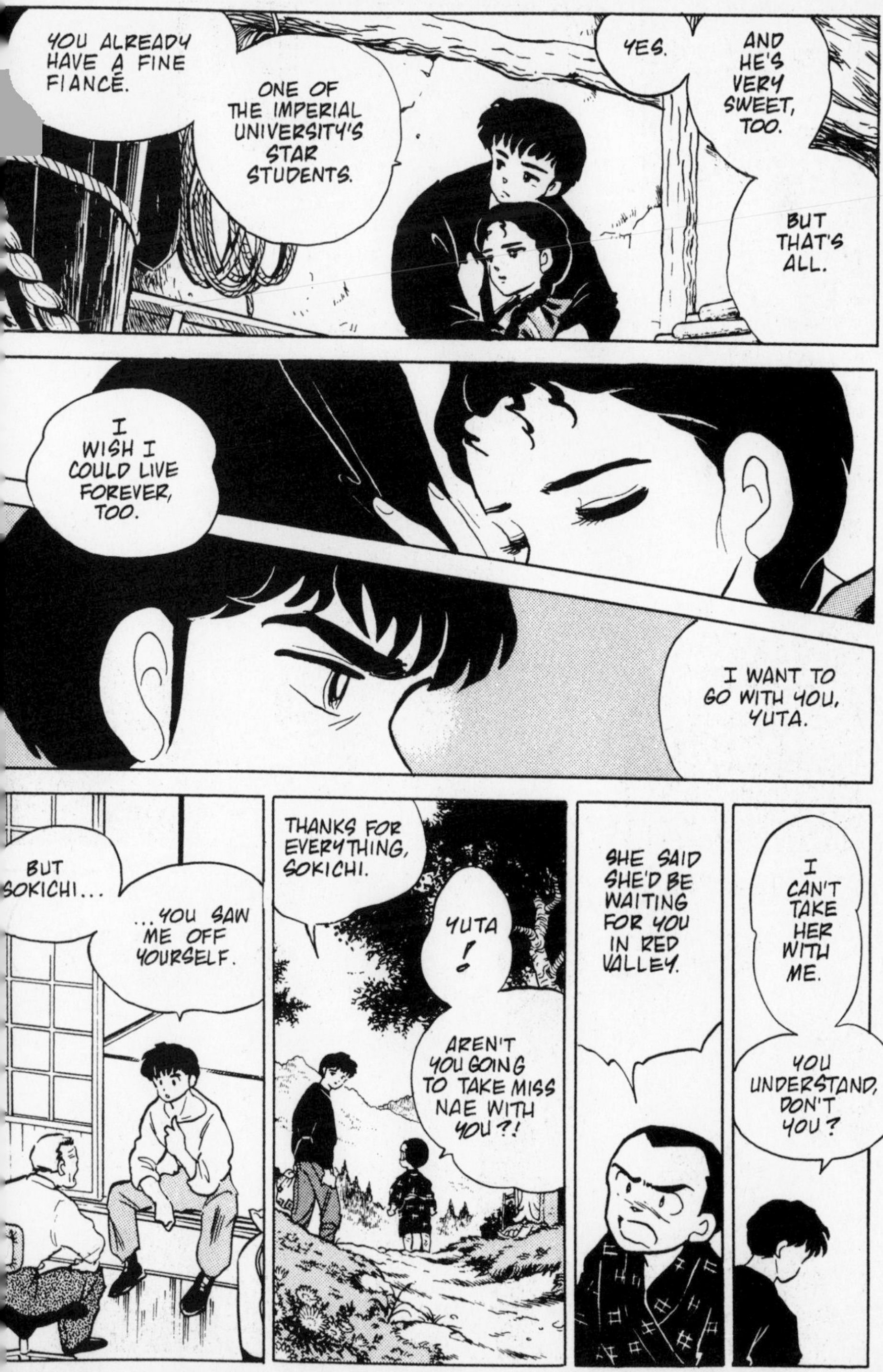
YOU ALREADY HAVE A FINE FIANCÉ.
ONE OF THE IMPERIAL UNIVERSITY'S STAR STUDENTS.
YES.
AND HE'S VERY SWEET, TOO.
BUT THAT'S ALL.
I WISH I COULD LIVE FOREVER, TOO.
I WANT TO GO WITH YOU, YUTA.
BUT SOKICHI...
...YOU SAW ME OFF YOURSELF.
THANKS FOR EVERYTHING, SOKICHI.
YUTA!
AREN'T YOU GOING TO TAKE MISS NAE WITH YOU?!
SHE SAID SHE'D BE WAITING FOR YOU IN RED VALLEY.
I CAN'T TAKE HER WITH ME.
YOU UNDERSTAND, DON'T YOU?

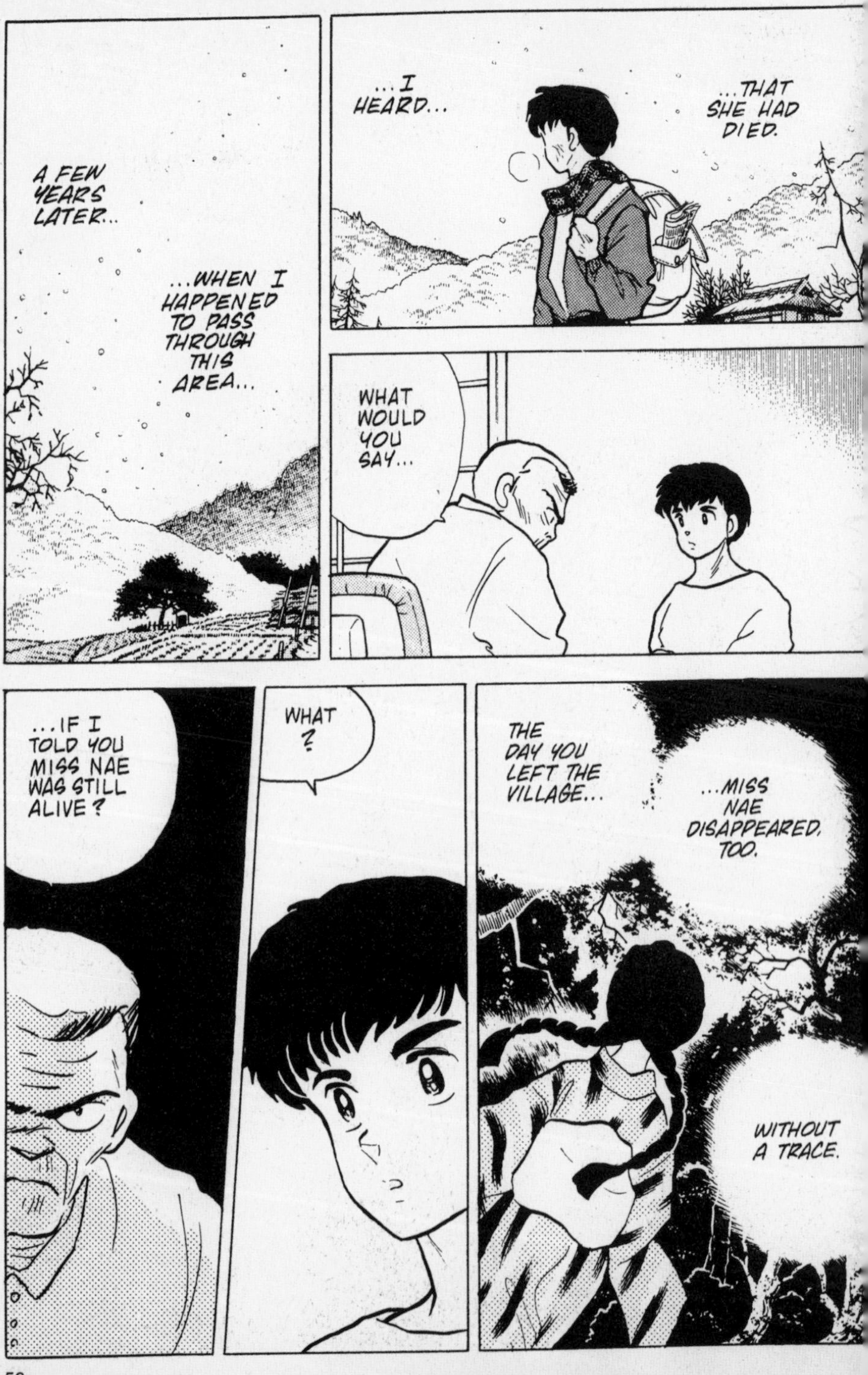
A FEW YEARS LATER...
...WHEN I HAPPENED TO PASS THROUGH THIS AREA...
...I HEARD...
...THAT SHE HAD DIED.
WHAT WOULD YOU SAY...
...IF I TOLD YOU MISS NAE WAS STILL ALIVE?
WHAT?
THE DAY YOU LEFT THE VILLAGE...
...MISS NAE DISAPPEARED, TOO.
WITHOUT A TRACE.

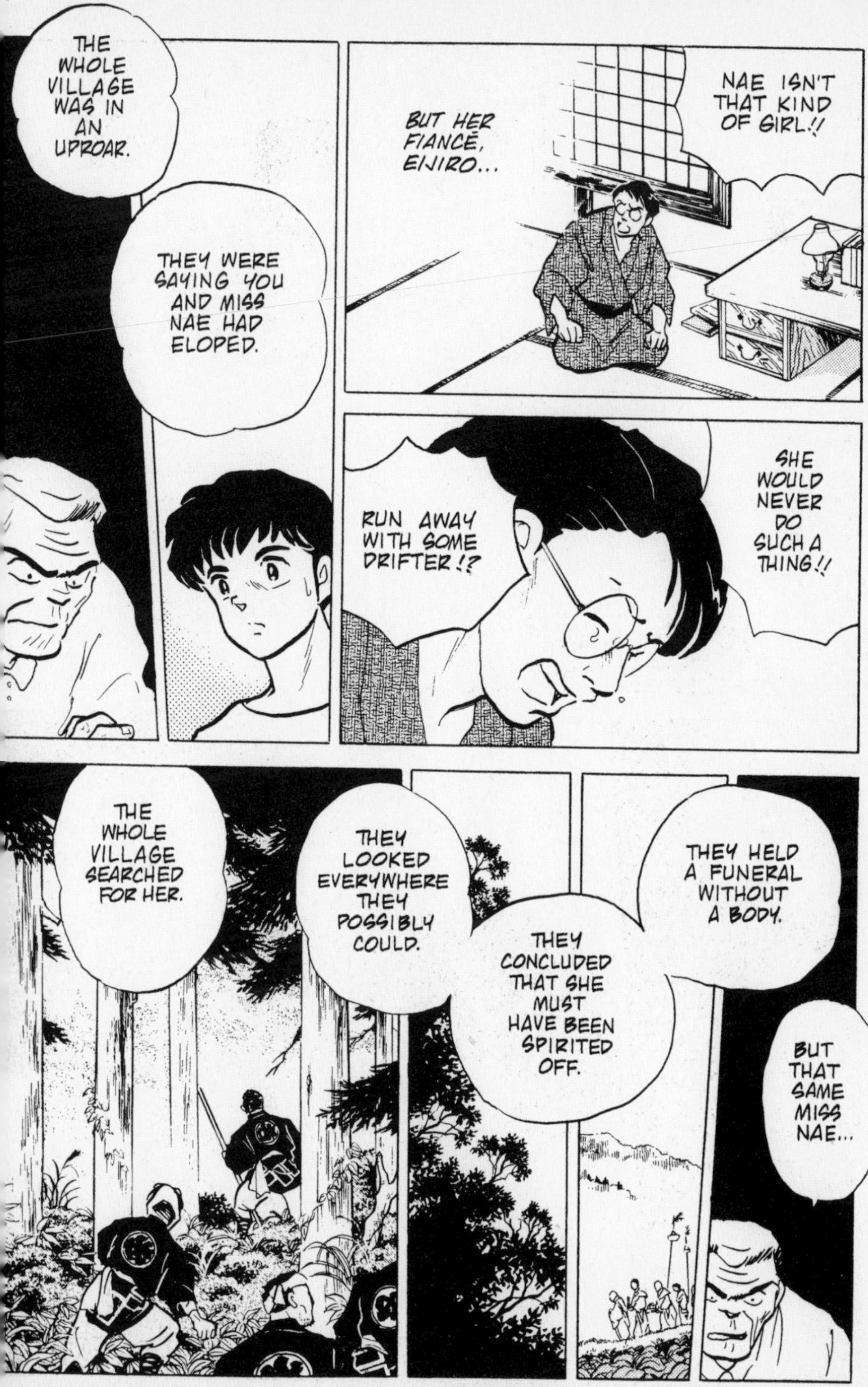
THE WHOLE VILLAGE WAS IN AN UPROAR.
THEY WERE SAYING YOU AND MISS NAE HAD ELOPED.
BUT HER FIANCÉ, EIJIRO...
NAE ISN'T THAT KIND OF GIRL!!
RUN AWAY WITH SOME DRIFTER!?
SHE WOULD NEVER DO SUCH A THING!!
THE WHOLE VILLAGE SEARCHED FOR HER.
THEY LOOKED EVERYWHERE THEY POSSIBLY COULD.
THEY CONCLUDED THAT SHE MUST HAVE BEEN SPIRITED OFF.
THEY HELD A FUNERAL WITHOUT A BODY.
BUT THAT SAME MISS NAE...

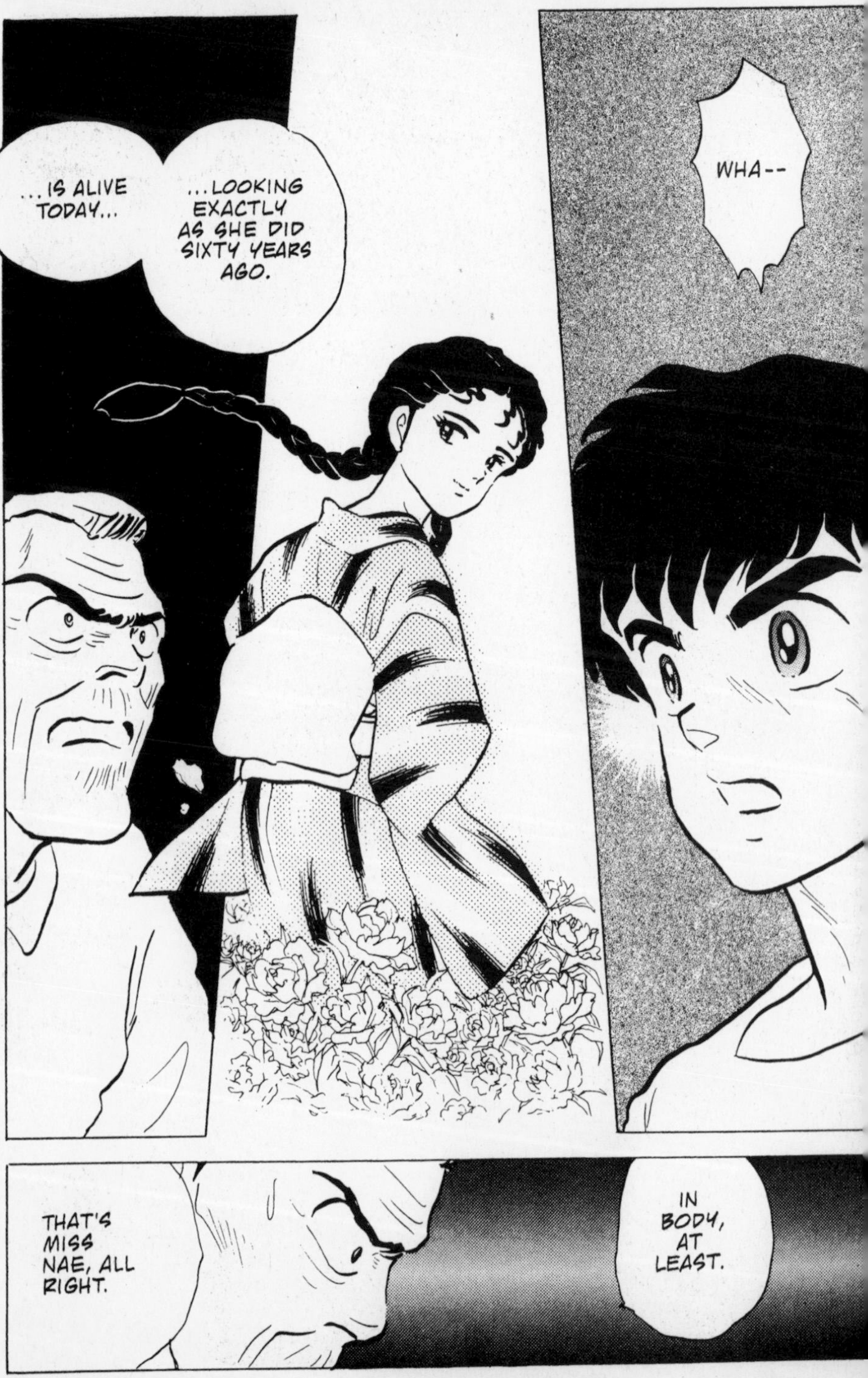

...IS ALIVE TODAY...
...LOOKING EXACTLY AS SHE DID SIXTY YEARS AGO.
WHA--
THAT'S MISS NAE, ALL RIGHT.
IN BODY, AT LEAST.

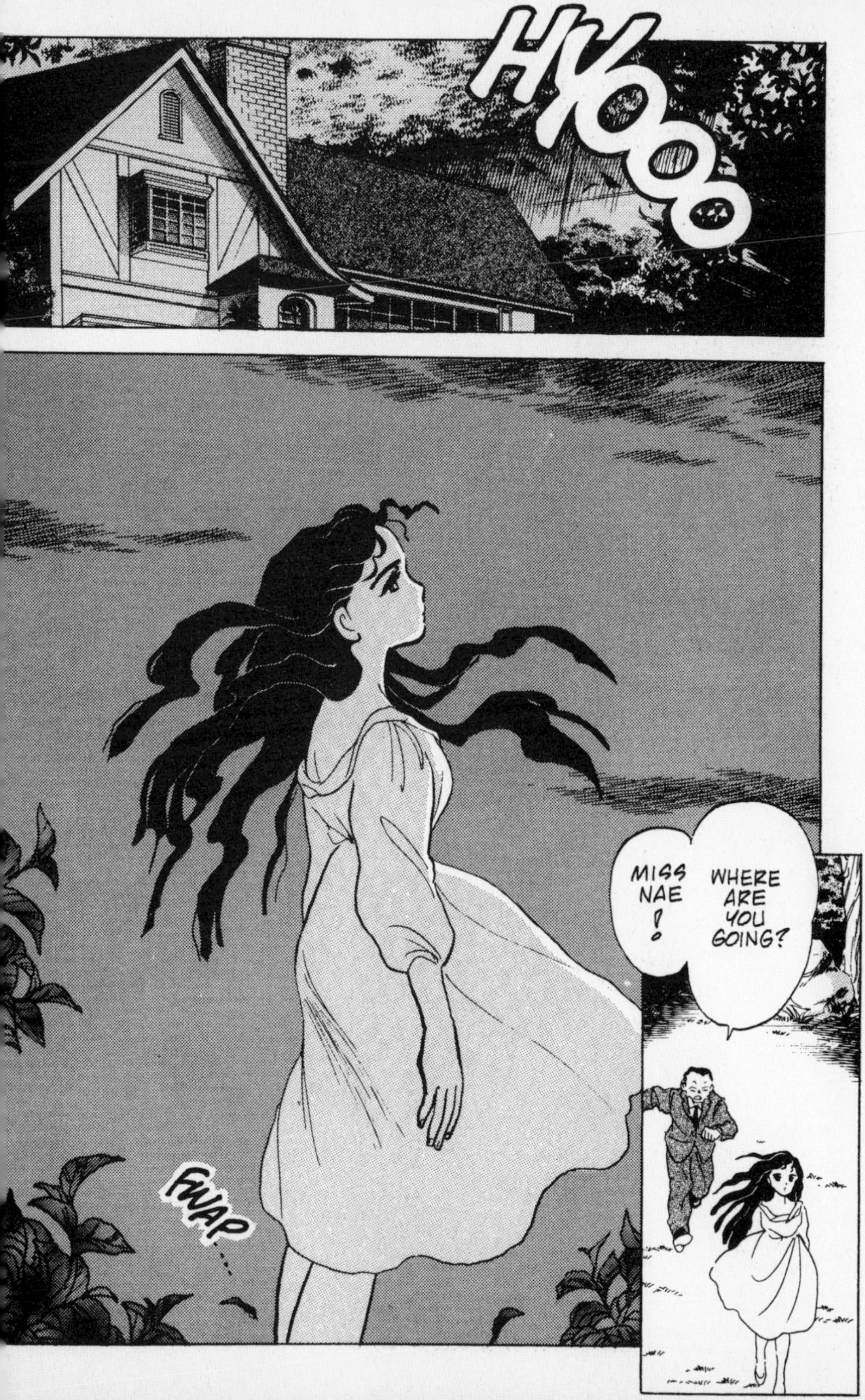HYOOO
MISS NAE!
WHERE ARE YOU GOING?
FWAP...

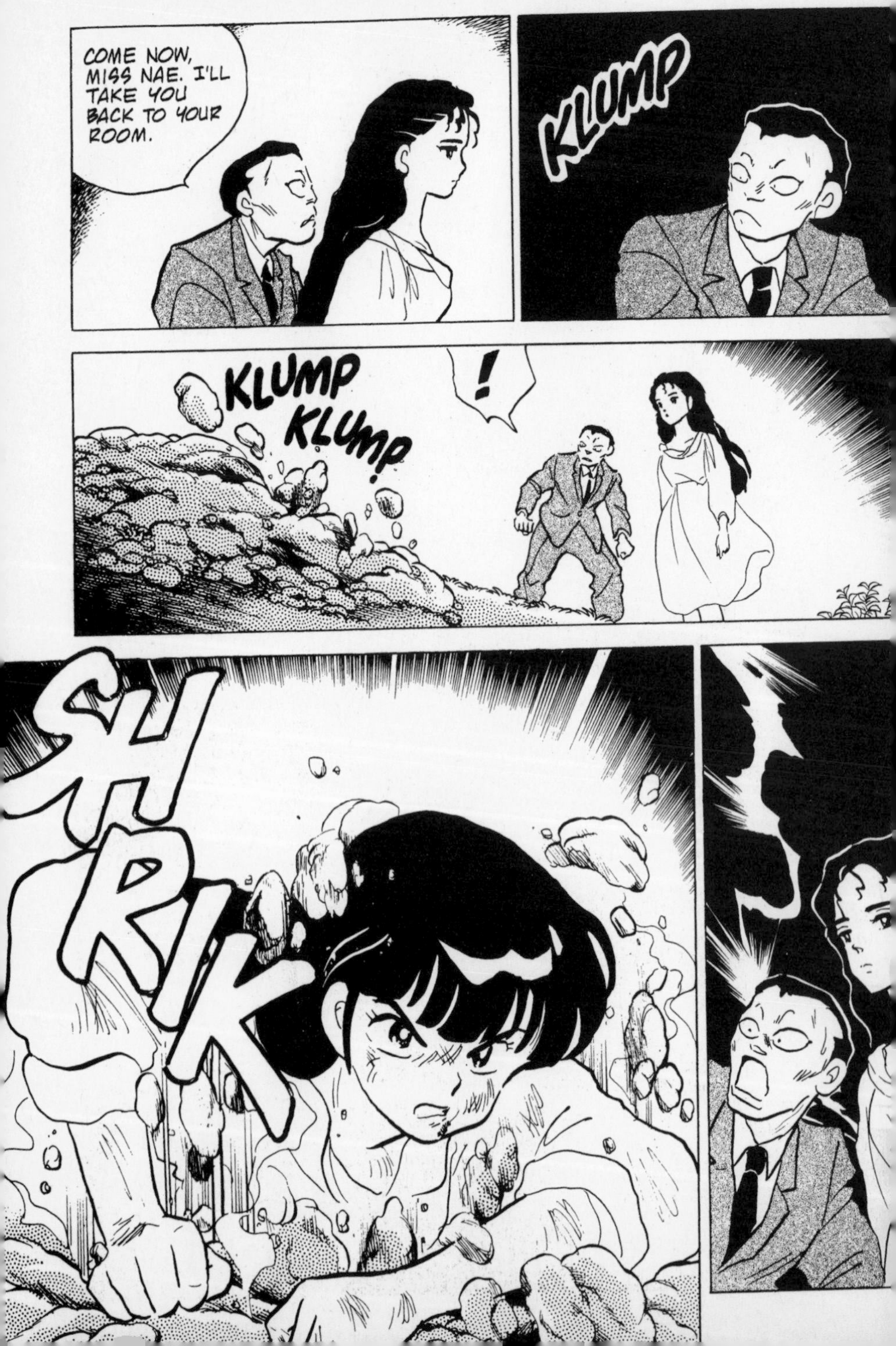
COME NOW, MISS NAE. I'LL TAKE YOU BACK TO YOUR ROOM.
KLUMP
KLUMP KLUMP
!
SHRIK

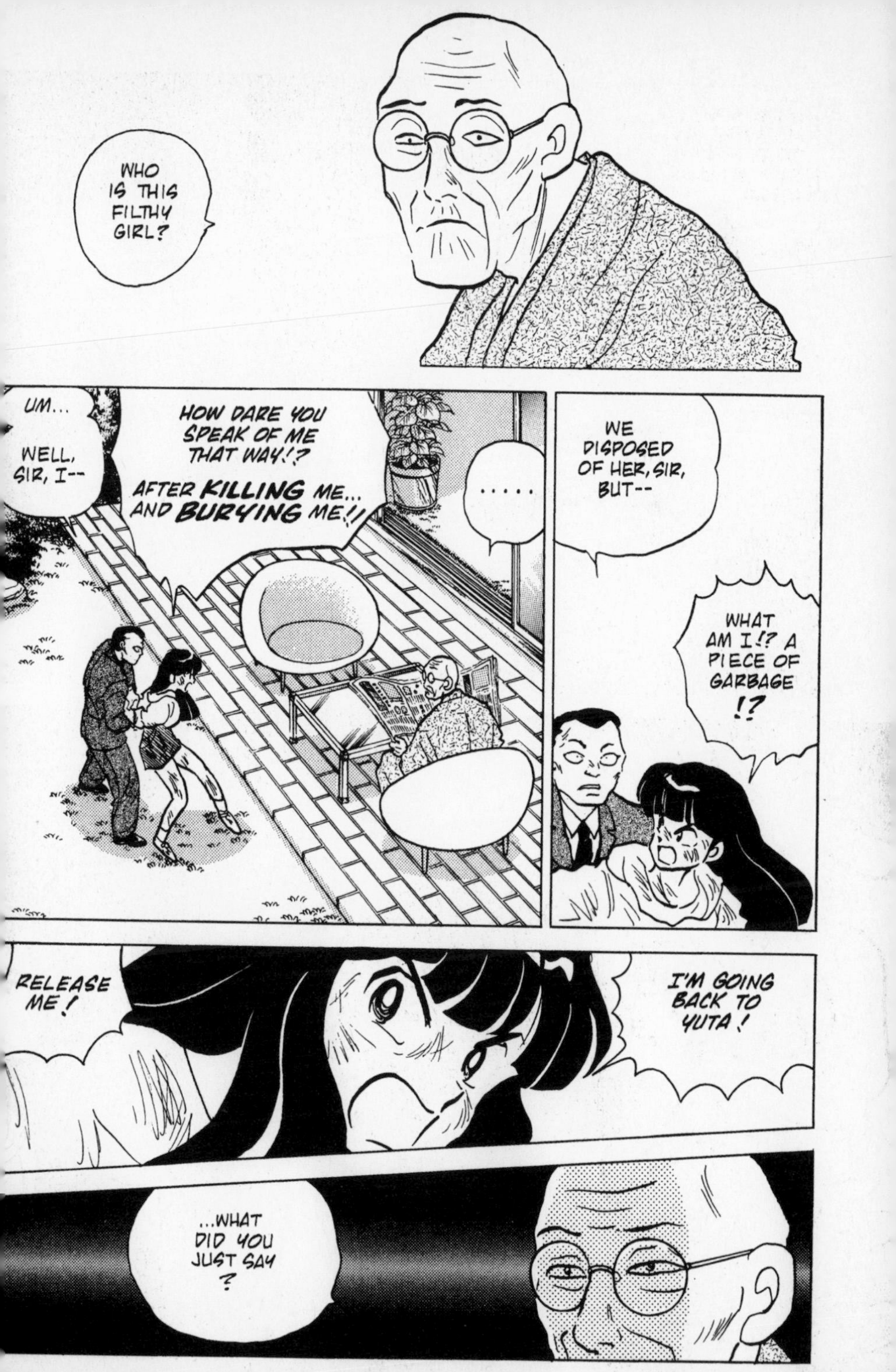

WHO IS THIS FILTHY GIRL?
UM... WELL, SIR, I--
HOW DARE YOU SPEAK OF ME THAT WAY!?
AFTER KILLING ME... AND BURYING ME!!
.....
WE DISPOSED OF HER, SIR, BUT--
WHAT AM I!? A PIECE OF GARBAGE !?
RELEASE ME!
I'M GOING BACK TO YUTA!
...WHAT DID YOU JUST SAY ?

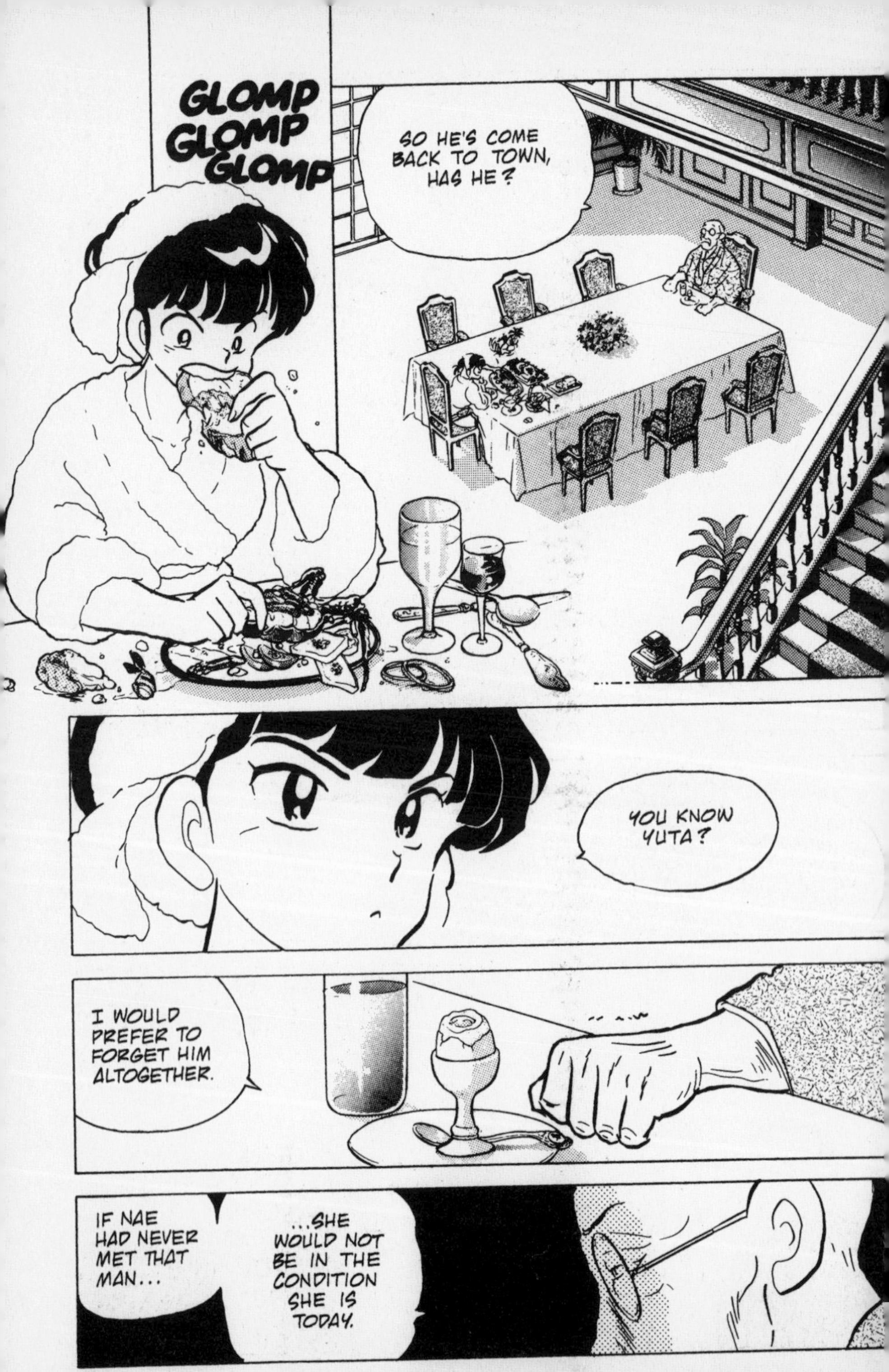
GLOMP GLOMP GLOMP
SO HE'S COME BACK TO TOWN, HAS HE?
YOU KNOW YUTA?
I WOULD PREFER TO FORGET HIM ALTOGETHER.
IF NAE HAD NEVER MET THAT MAN...
...SHE WOULD NOT BE IN THE CONDITION SHE IS TODAY.

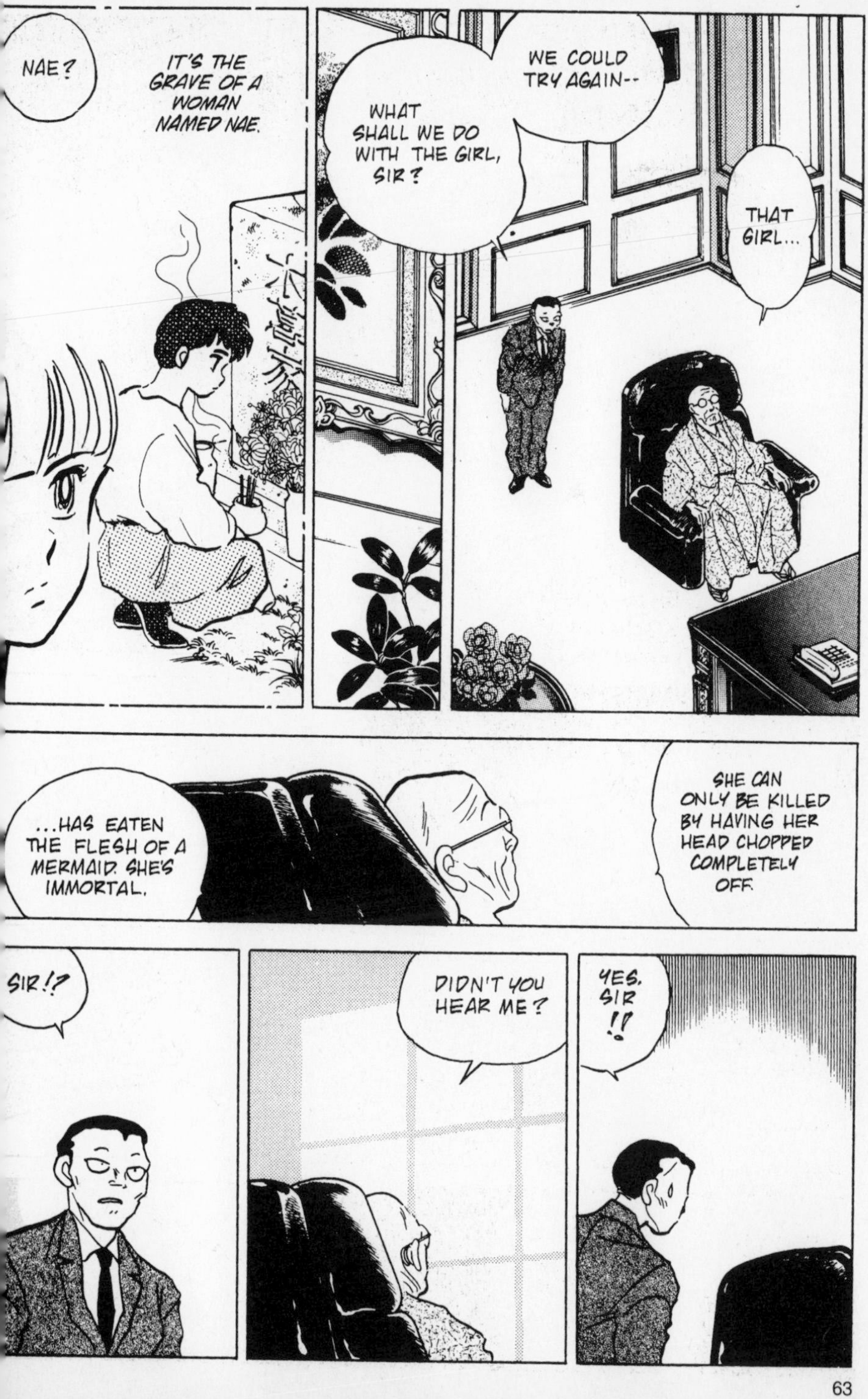
NAE?
IT'S THE GRAVE OF A WOMAN NAMED NAE.
WHAT SHALL WE DO WITH THE GIRL, SIR?
WE COULD TRY AGAIN--
THAT GIRL...
...HAS EATEN THE FLESH OF A MERMAID. SHE'S IMMORTAL.
SHE CAN ONLY BE KILLED BY HAVING HER HEAD CHOPPED COMPLETELY OFF.
SIR!?
DIDN'T YOU HEAR ME?
YES. SIR!!

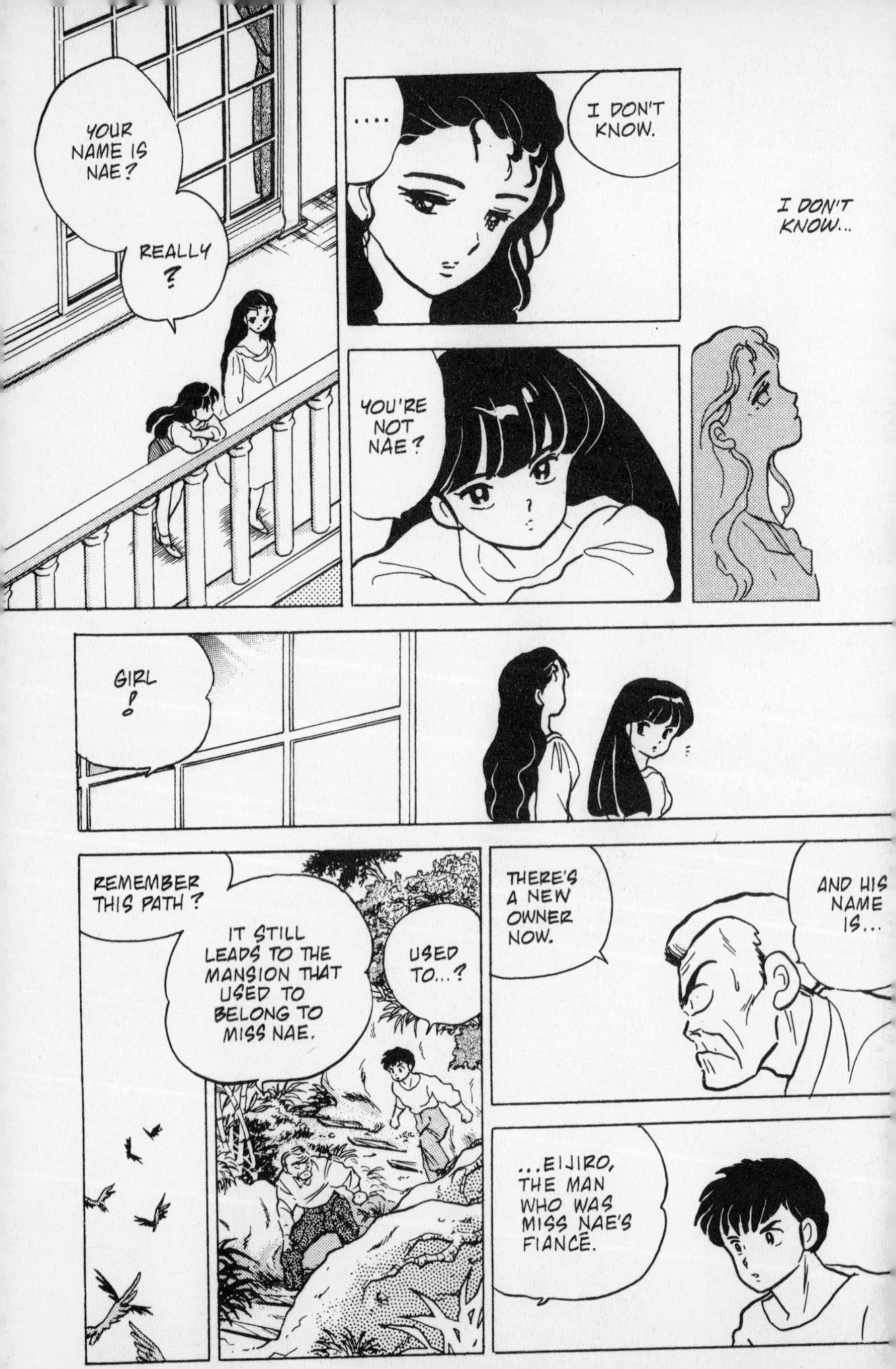
YOUR NAME IS NAE?
REALLY ?
....
I DON'T KNOW.
I DON'T KNOW...
YOU'RE NOT NAE?
GIRL !
REMEMBER THIS PATH?
IT STILL LEADS TO THE MANSION THAT USED TO BELONG TO MISS NAE.
USED TO...?
THERE'S A NEW OWNER NOW.
AND HIS NAME IS...
...EIJIRO, THE MAN WHO WAS MISS NAE'S FIANCÉ.

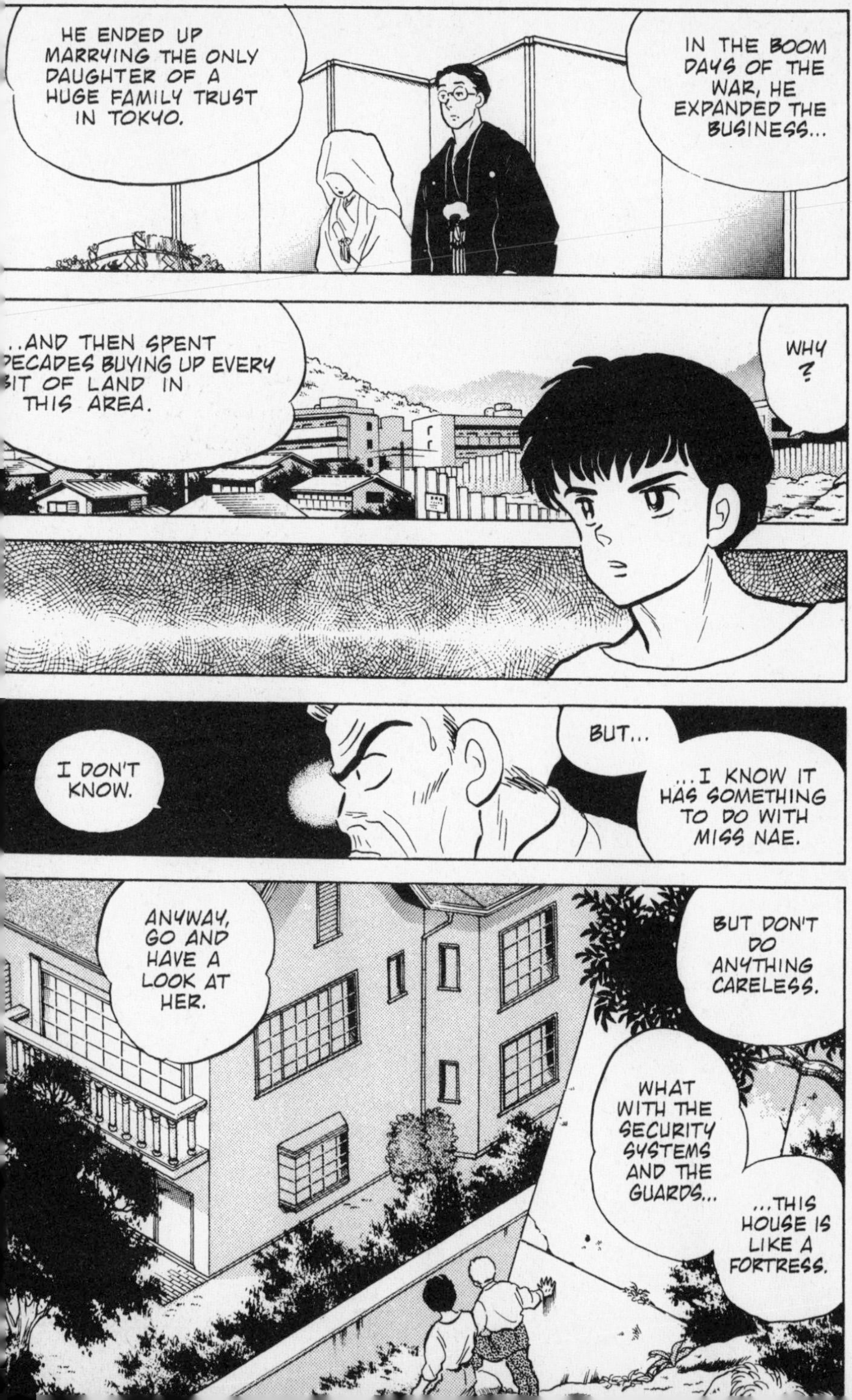
HE ENDED UP MARRYING THE ONLY DAUGHTER OF A HUGE FAMILY TRUST IN TOKYO.
IN THE BOOM DAYS OF THE WAR, HE EXPANDED THE BUSINESS...
...AND THEN SPENT DECADES BUYING UP EVERY BIT OF LAND IN THIS AREA.
WHY?
I DON'T KNOW.
BUT...
...I KNOW IT HAS SOMETHING TO DO WITH MISS NAE.
ANYWAY, GO AND HAVE A LOOK AT HER.
BUT DON'T DO ANYTHING CARELESS.
WHAT WITH THE SECURITY SYSTEMS AND THE GUARDS...
...THIS HOUSE IS LIKE A FORTRESS.

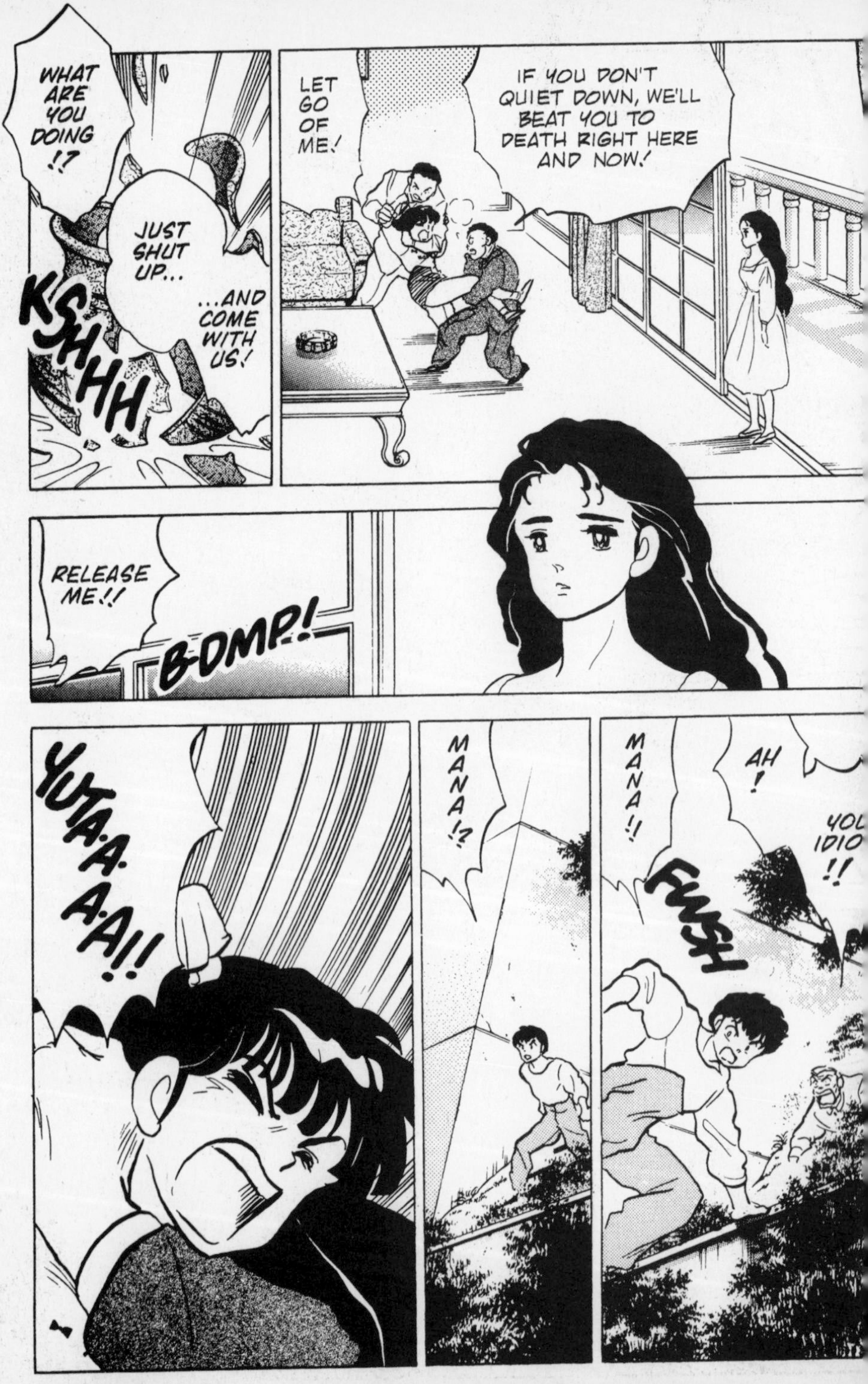
WHAT ARE YOU DOING !?
JUST SHUT UP...
...AND COME WITH US!
KSHHHH
LET GO OF ME!
IF YOU DON'T QUIET DOWN, WE'LL BEAT YOU TO DEATH RIGHT HERE AND NOW!
RELEASE ME!!
B-DMP!
YUTA-A-A-A!!
MANA!?
MANA!!
AH!
FWISH
YOU IDIO !!

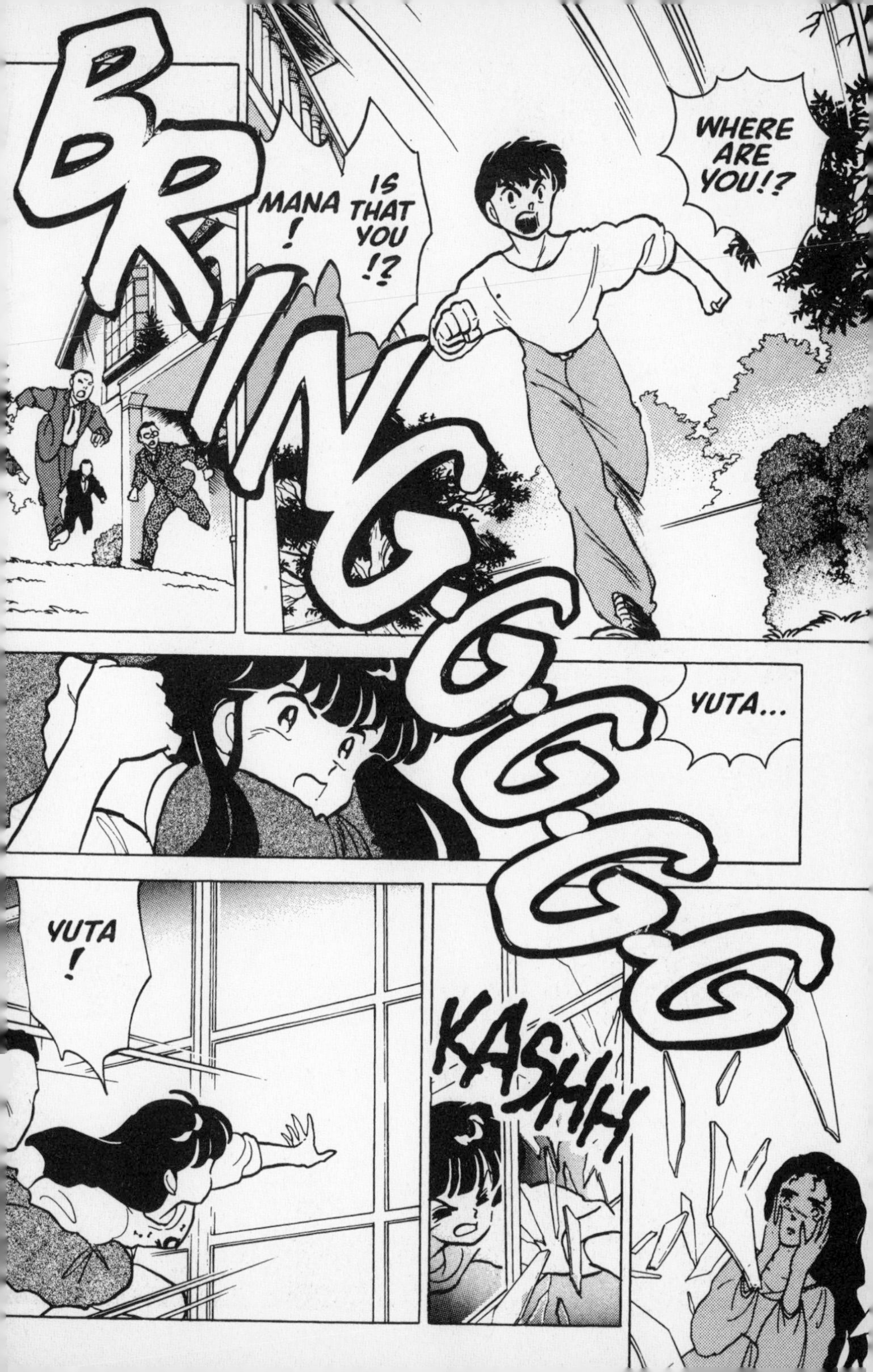

BRINGGGGGG
MANA!
IS THAT YOU!?
WHERE ARE YOU!?
YUTA...
YUTA!
KASHH

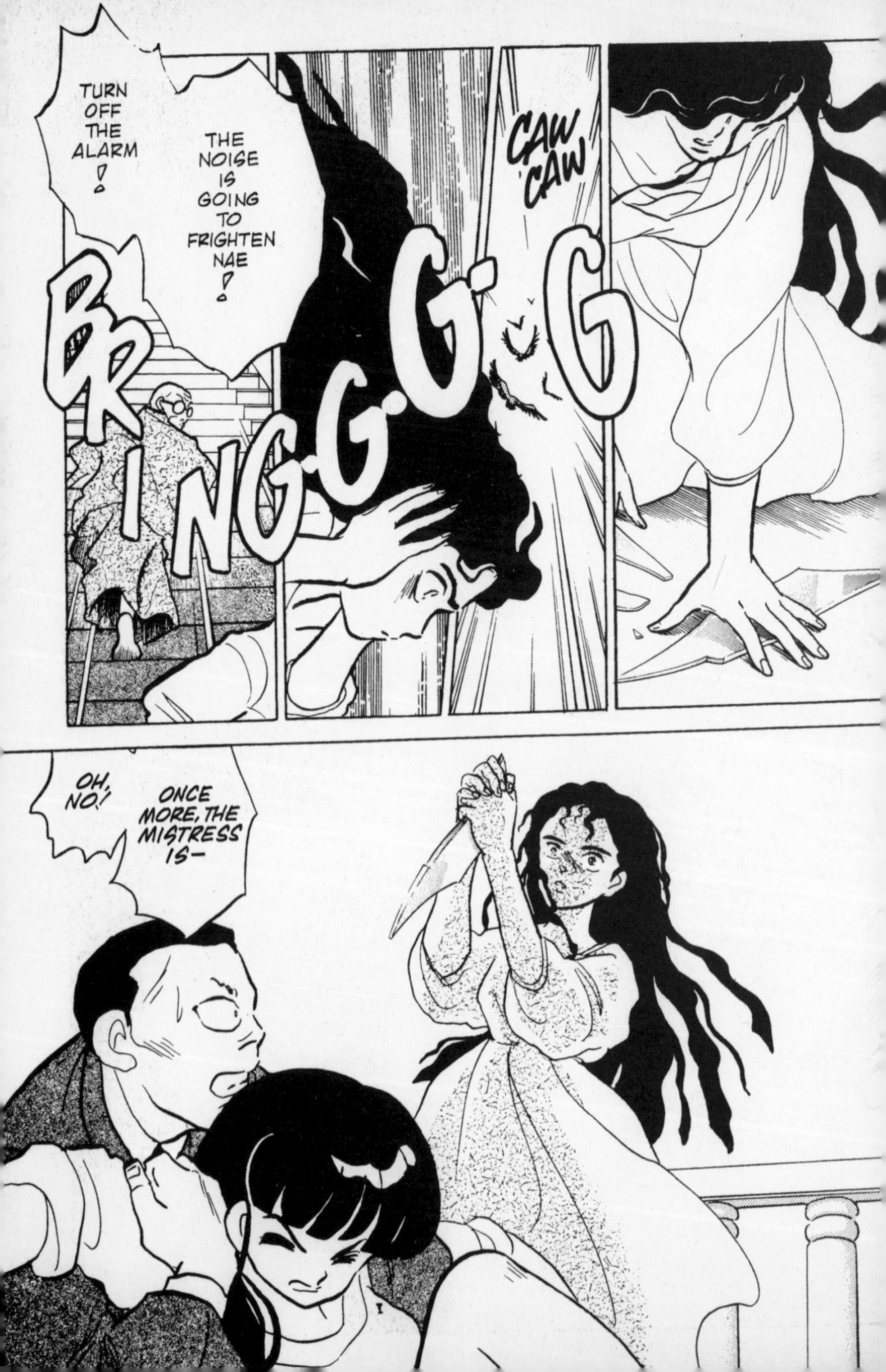
TURN OFF THE ALARM!
THE NOISE IS GOING TO FRIGHTEN NAE!
BRINGGGG
CAW CAW
OH, NO!
ONCE MORE, THE MISTRESS IS—

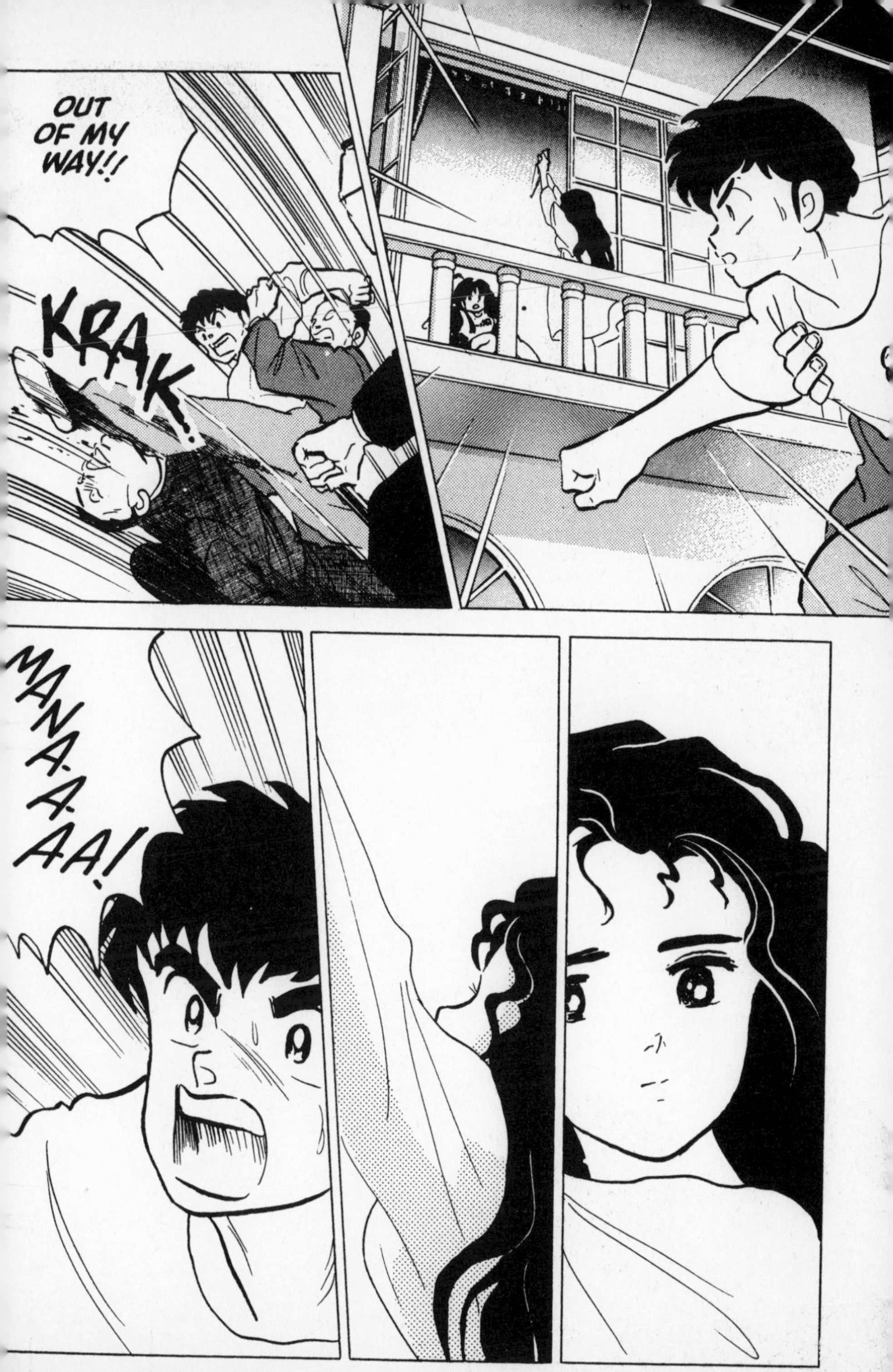
OUT OF MY WAY!!
KRAK!
MANA-A-A-AA!

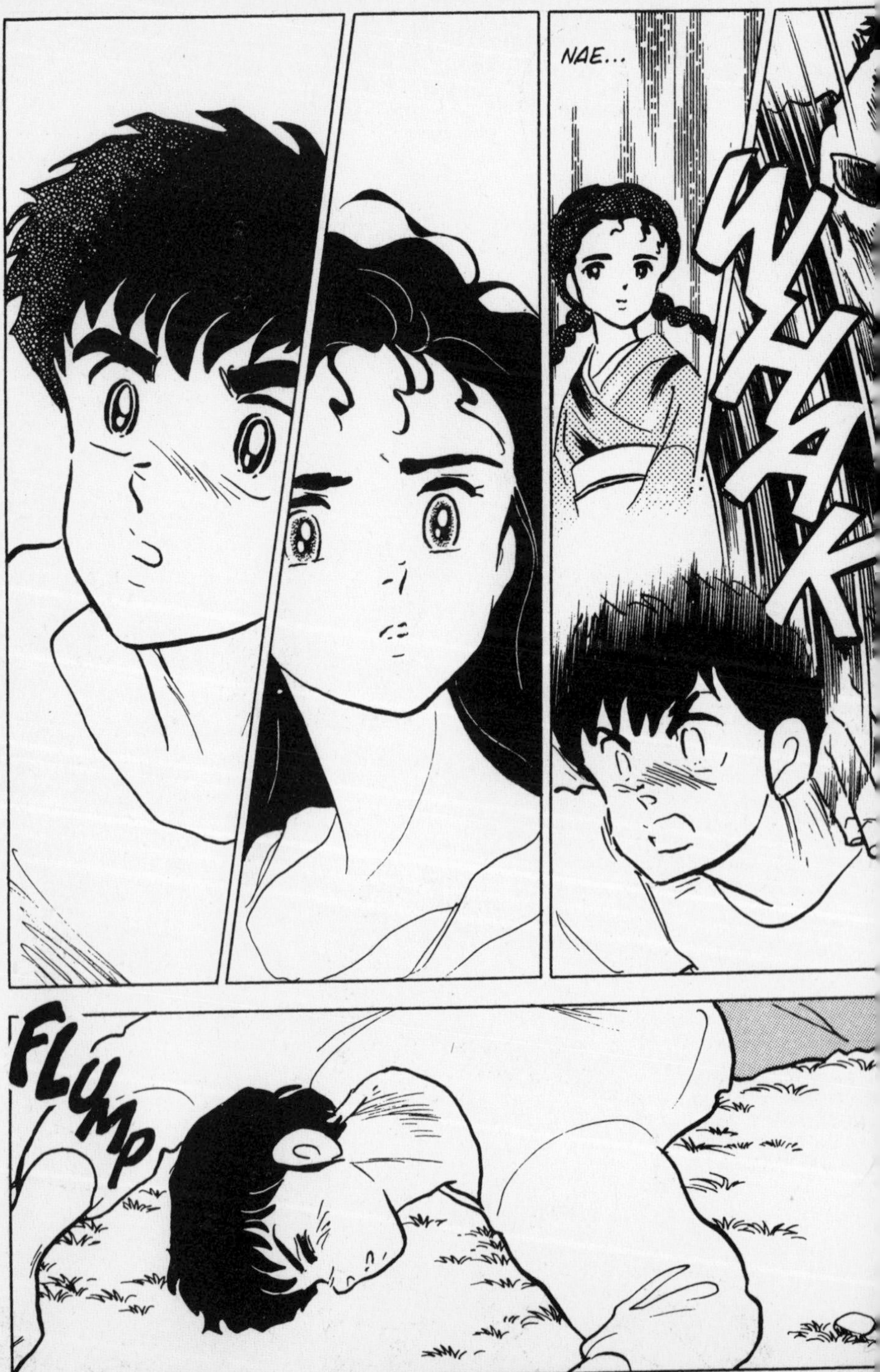
NAE...
WHAK
FLUMP

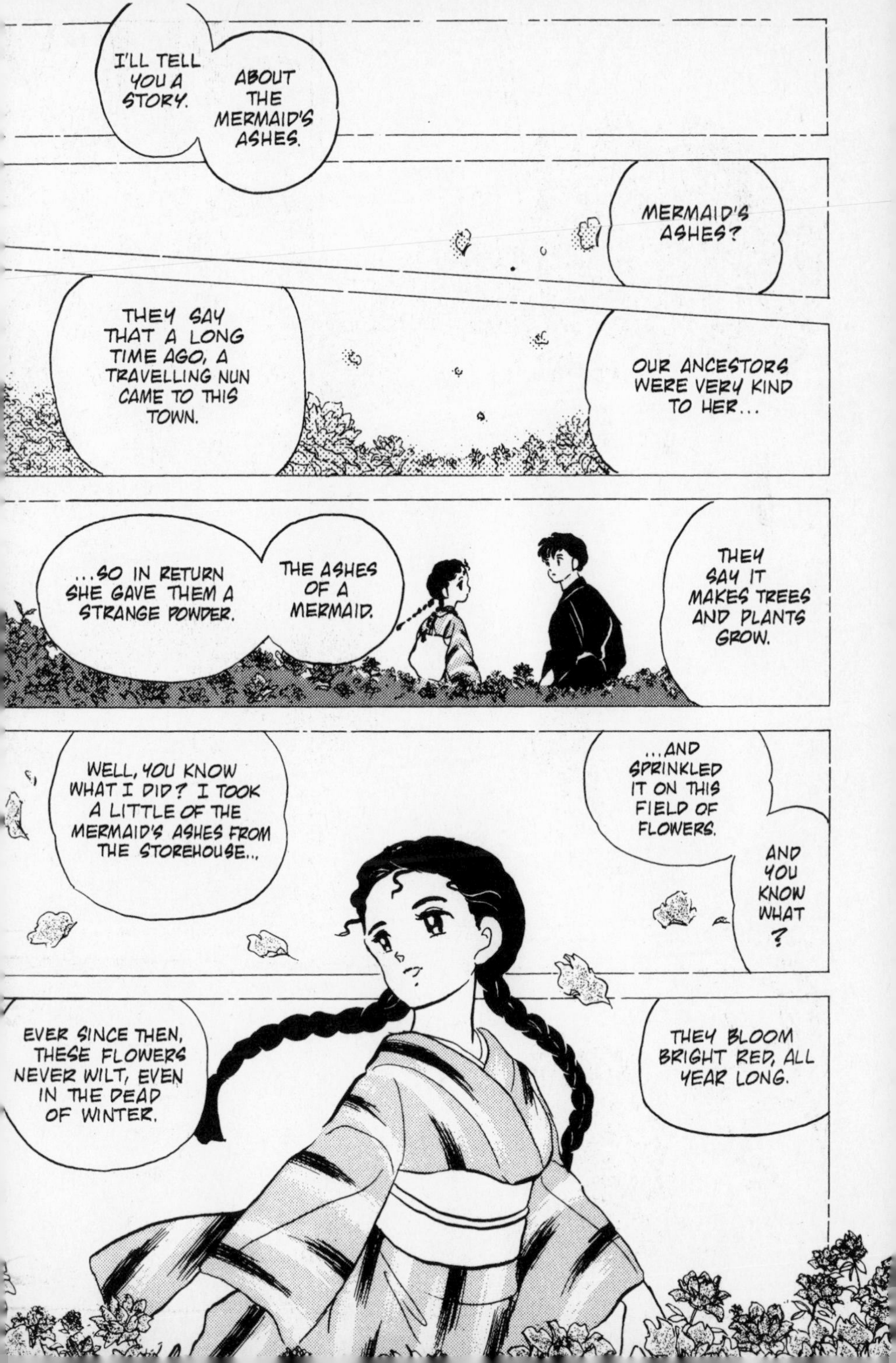
I'LL TELL YOU A STORY.
ABOUT THE MERMAID'S ASHES.
MERMAID'S ASHES?
THEY SAY THAT A LONG TIME AGO, A TRAVELLING NUN CAME TO THIS TOWN.
OUR ANCESTORS WERE VERY KIND TO HER...
...SO IN RETURN SHE GAVE THEM A STRANGE POWDER.
THE ASHES OF A MERMAID.
THEY SAY IT MAKES TREES AND PLANTS GROW.
WELL, YOU KNOW WHAT I DID? I TOOK A LITTLE OF THE MERMAID'S ASHES FROM THE STOREHOUSE...
...AND SPRINKLED IT ON THIS FIELD OF FLOWERS.
AND YOU KNOW WHAT?
EVER SINCE THEN, THESE FLOWERS NEVER WILT, EVEN IN THE DEAD OF WINTER.
THEY BLOOM BRIGHT RED, ALL YEAR LONG.

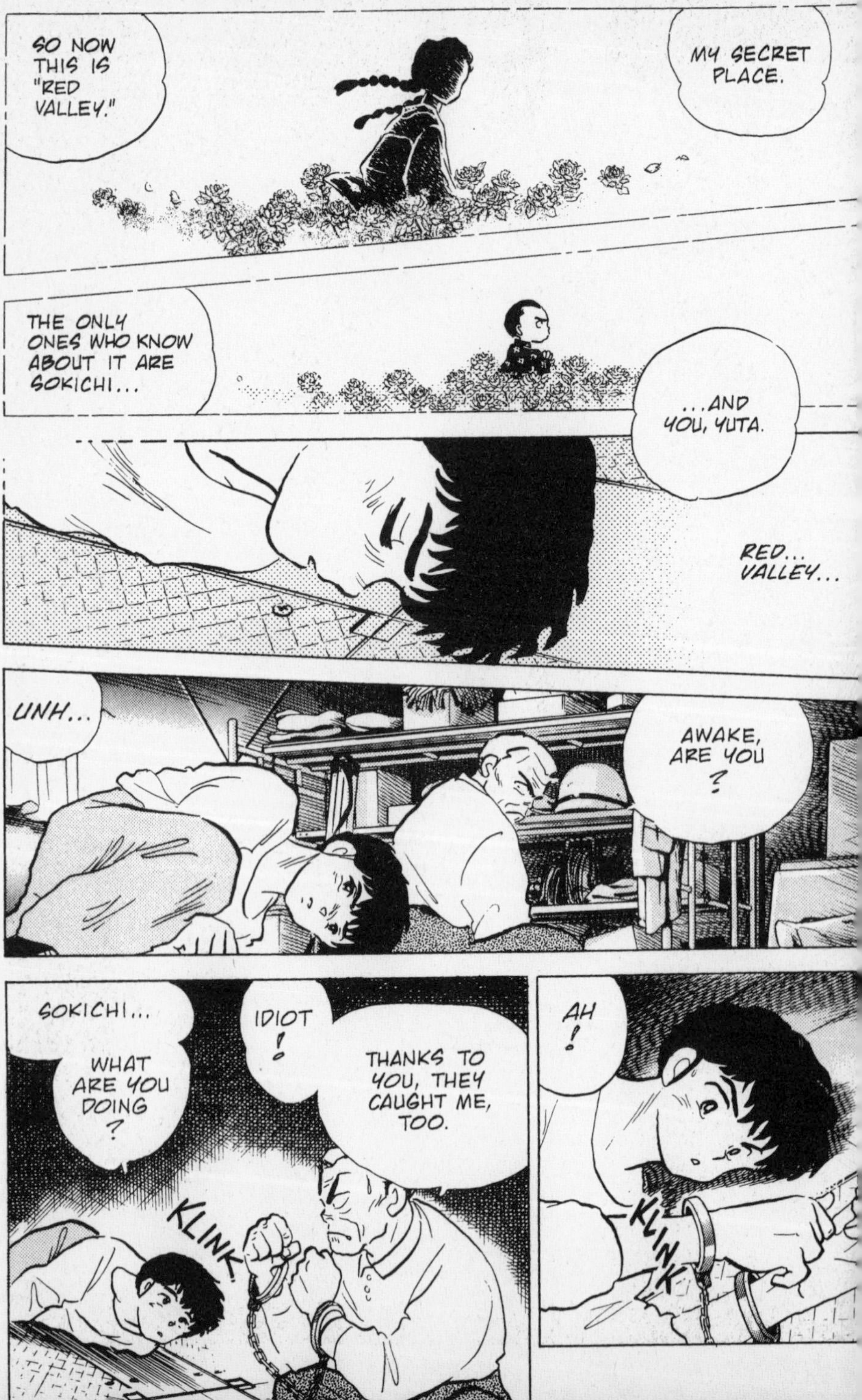
SO NOW THIS IS "RED VALLEY."
MY SECRET PLACE.
THE ONLY ONES WHO KNOW ABOUT IT ARE SOKICHI...
...AND YOU, YUTA.
RED... VALLEY...
UNH...
AWAKE, ARE YOU?
SOKICHI...
WHAT ARE YOU DOING?
IDIOT!
THANKS TO YOU, THEY CAUGHT ME, TOO.
KLINK
AH!
KLINK

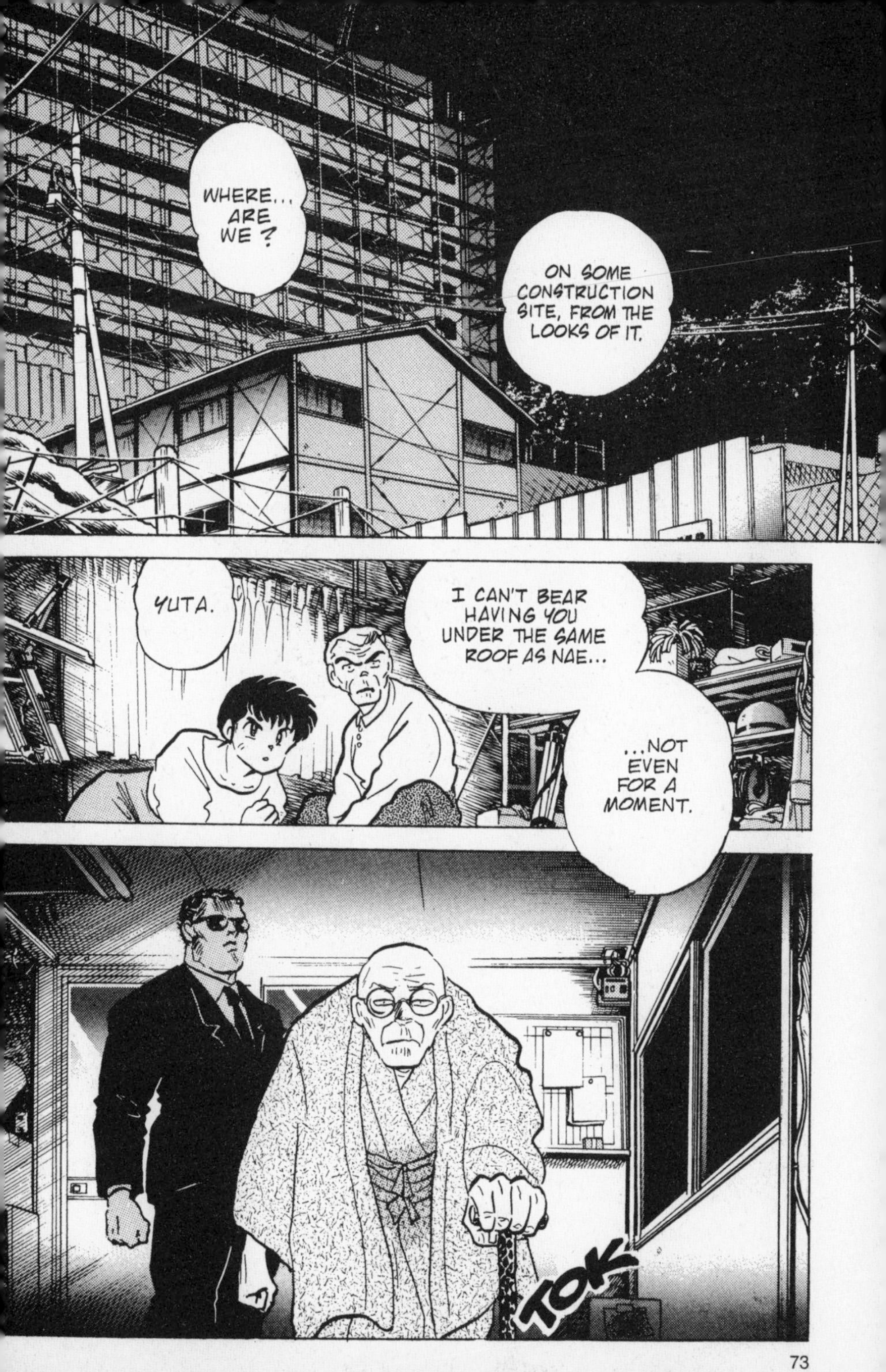
WHERE... ARE WE ?
ON SOME CONSTRUCTION SITE, FROM THE LOOKS OF IT.
YUTA.
I CAN'T BEAR HAVING YOU UNDER THE SAME ROOF AS NAE...
...NOT EVEN FOR A MOMENT.
TOK

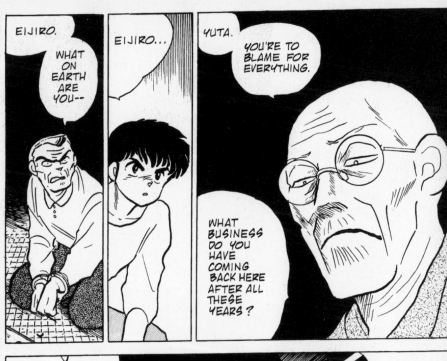

EIJIRO. WHAT ON EARTH ARE YOU--

EIJIRO...

YUTA. YOU'RE TO BLAME FOR EVERYTHING.

WHAT BUSINESS DO YOU HAVE COMING BACK HERE AFTER ALL THESE YEARS?

WH-WHY, YOU-! WHAT HAVE YOU DONE WITH MANA!?

WHAT DID YOU DO TO NAE!?

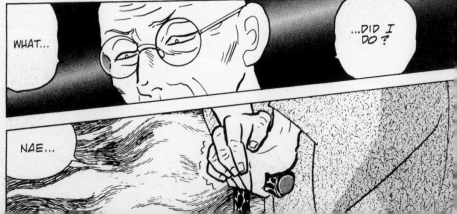

WHAT...

...DID I DO?

NAE...

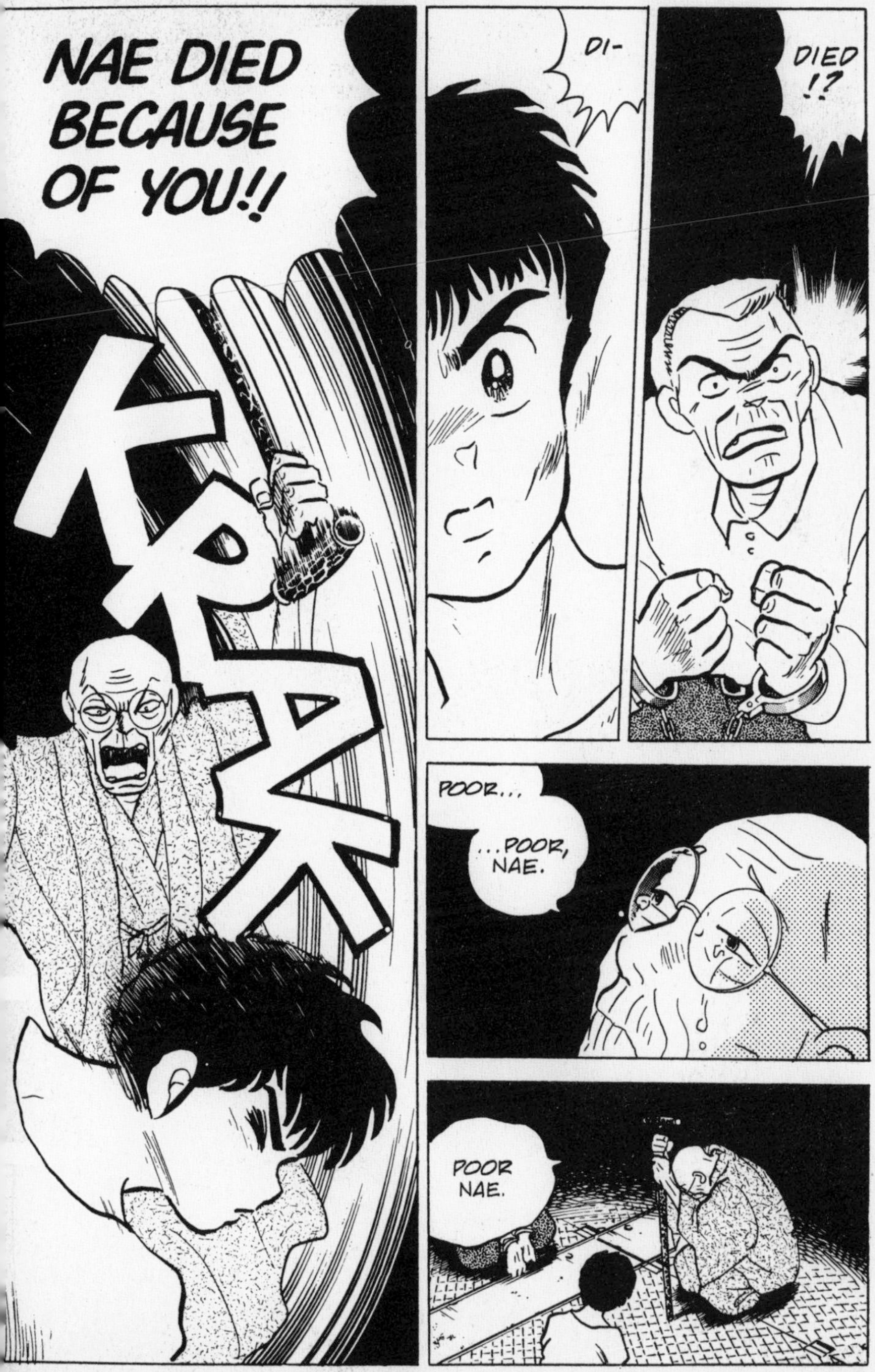
NAE DIED BECAUSE OF YOU!!
KRAK
DI-
DIED !?
POOR...
...POOR, NAE.
POOR NAE.

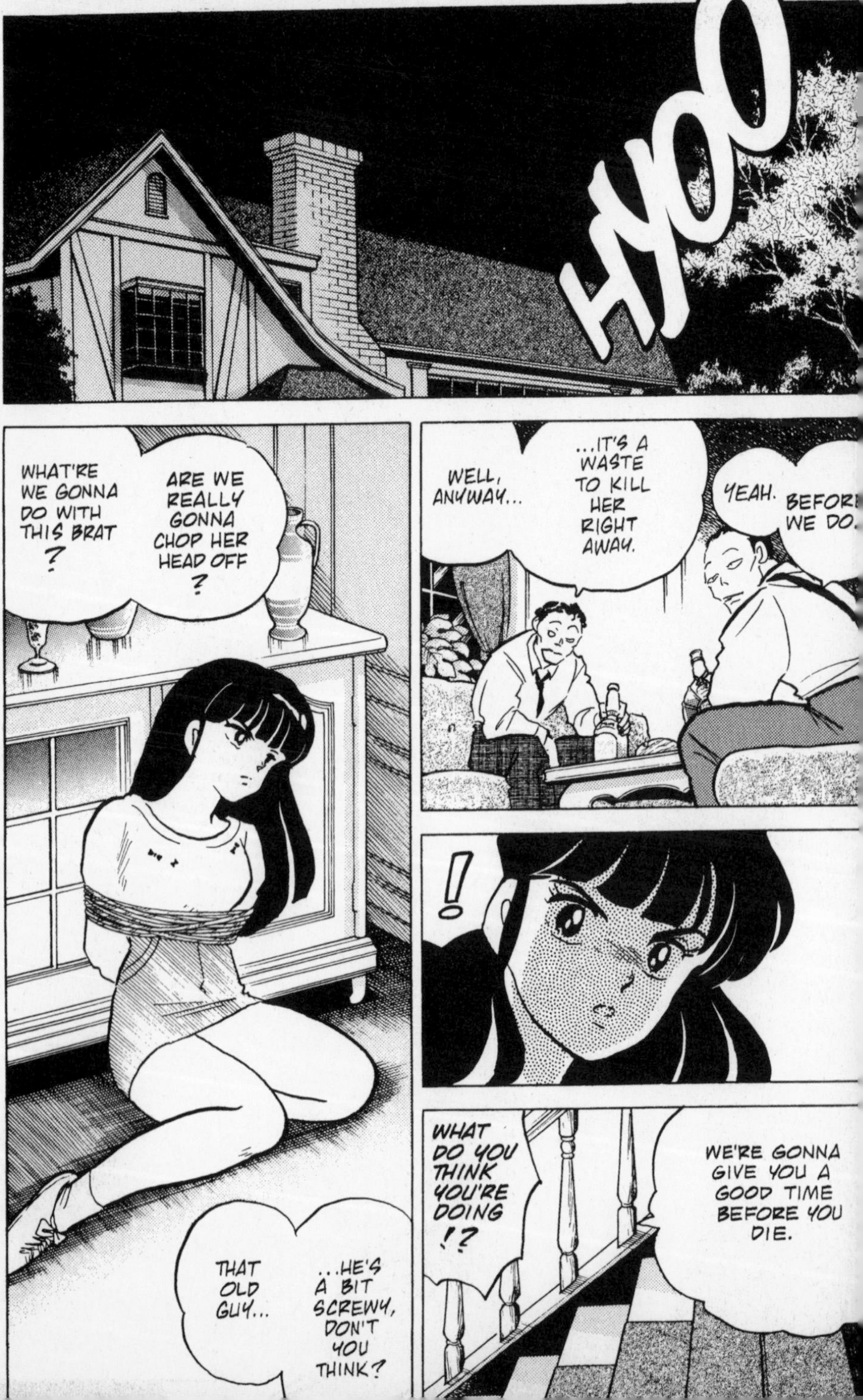
HYOO
WHAT'RE WE GONNA DO WITH THIS BRAT?
ARE WE REALLY GONNA CHOP HER HEAD OFF?
WELL, ANYWAY...
...IT'S A WASTE TO KILL HER RIGHT AWAY.
YEAH.
BEFORE WE DO...
!
THAT OLD GUY...
...HE'S A BIT SCREWY, DON'T YOU THINK?
WHAT DO YOU THINK YOU'RE DOING!?
WE'RE GONNA GIVE YOU A GOOD TIME BEFORE YOU DIE.

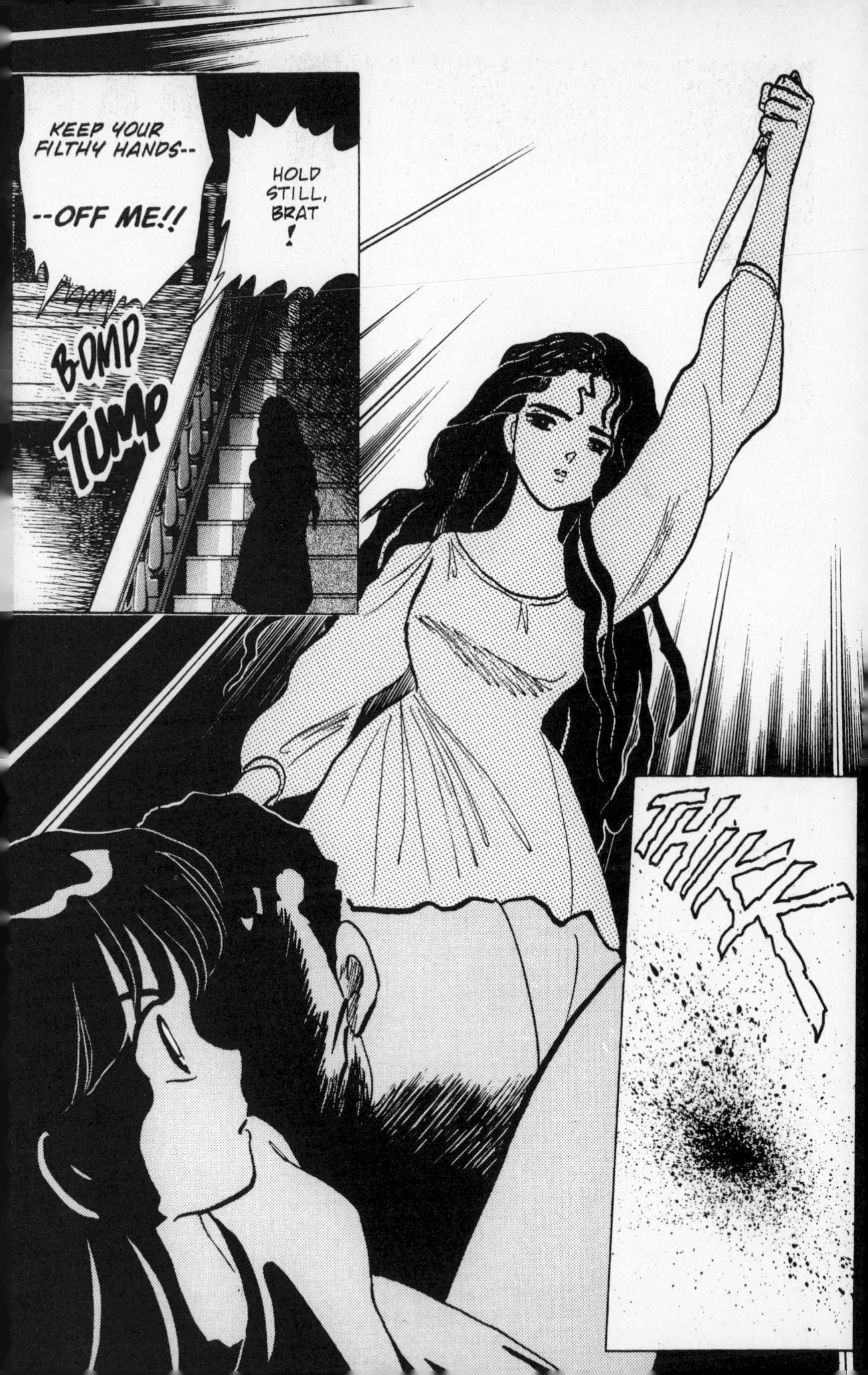
KEEP YOUR FILTHY HANDS--
--OFF ME!!
HOLD STILL, BRAT!
BOMP
TUMP
THKK

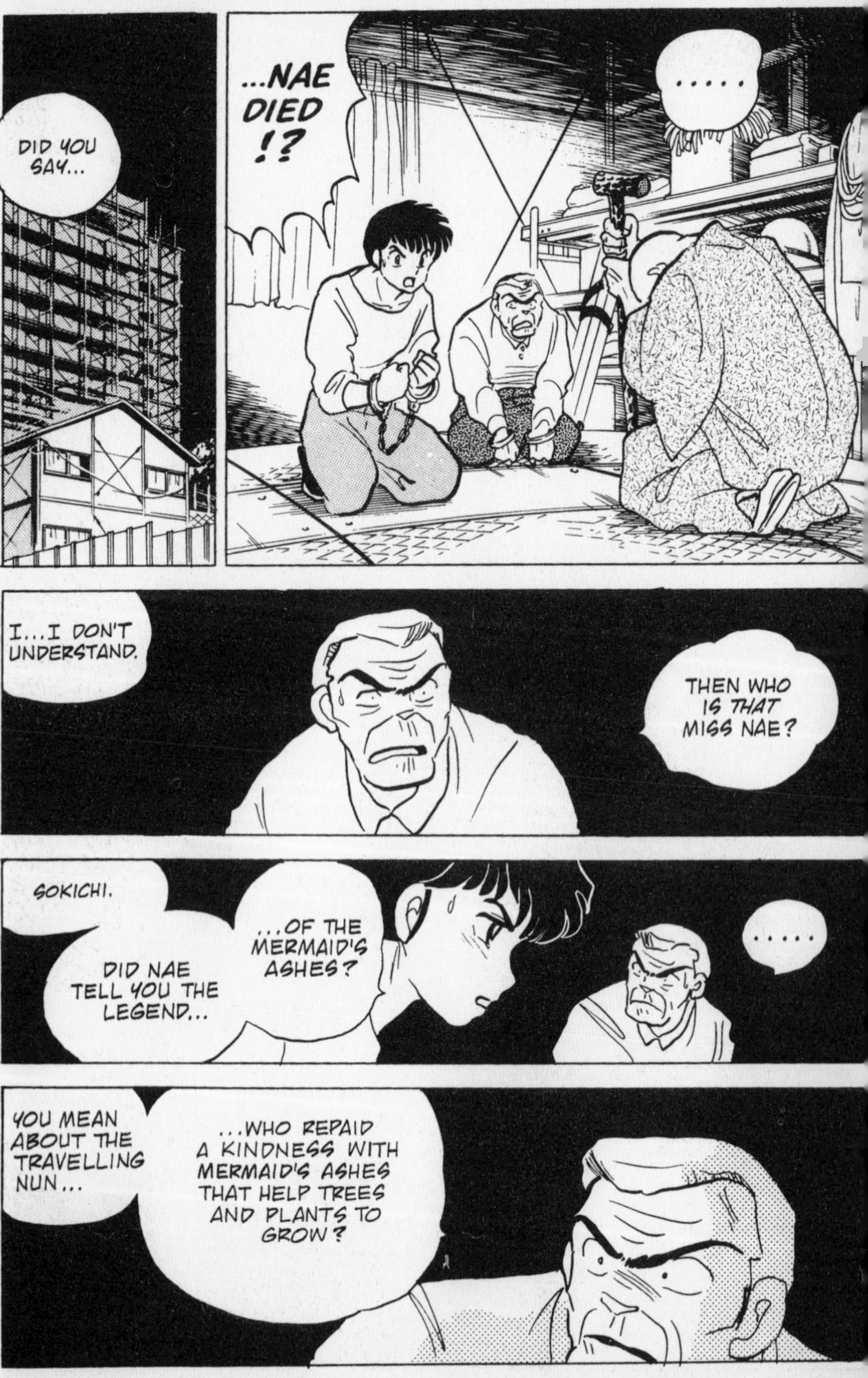
DID YOU SAY...
...NAE DIED !?
.....
I...I DON'T UNDERSTAND.
THEN WHO IS THAT MISS NAE?
SOKICHI.
DID NAE TELL YOU THE LEGEND...
...OF THE MERMAID'S ASHES?
.....
YOU MEAN ABOUT THE TRAVELLING NUN...
...WHO REPAID A KINDNESS WITH MERMAID'S ASHES THAT HELP TREES AND PLANTS TO GROW?

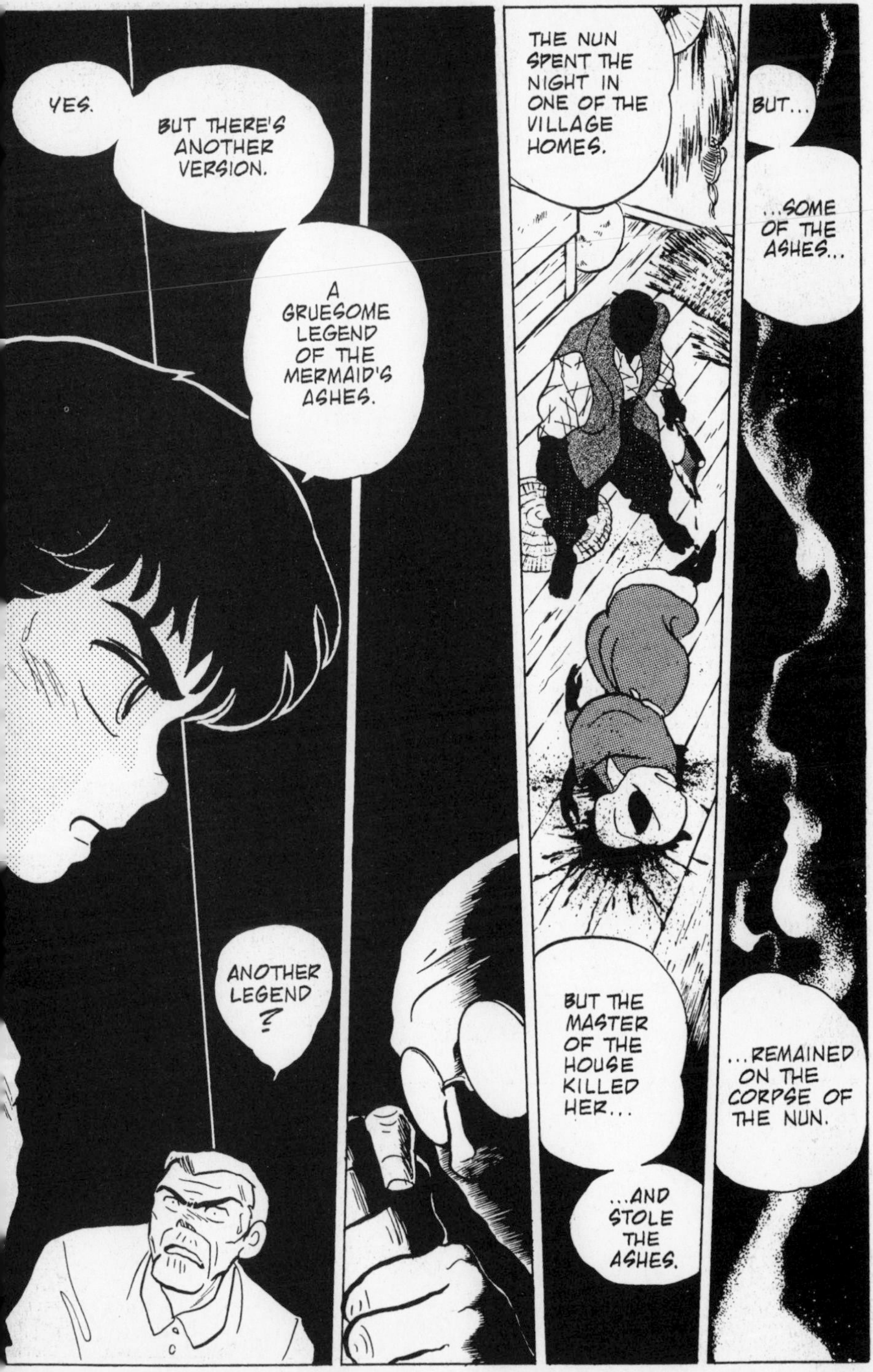
YES.
BUT THERE'S ANOTHER VERSION.
A GRUESOME LEGEND OF THE MERMAID'S ASHES.
ANOTHER LEGEND?
THE NUN SPENT THE NIGHT IN ONE OF THE VILLAGE HOMES.
BUT THE MASTER OF THE HOUSE KILLED HER...
...AND STOLE THE ASHES.
BUT...
...SOME OF THE ASHES...
...REMAINED ON THE CORPSE OF THE NUN.

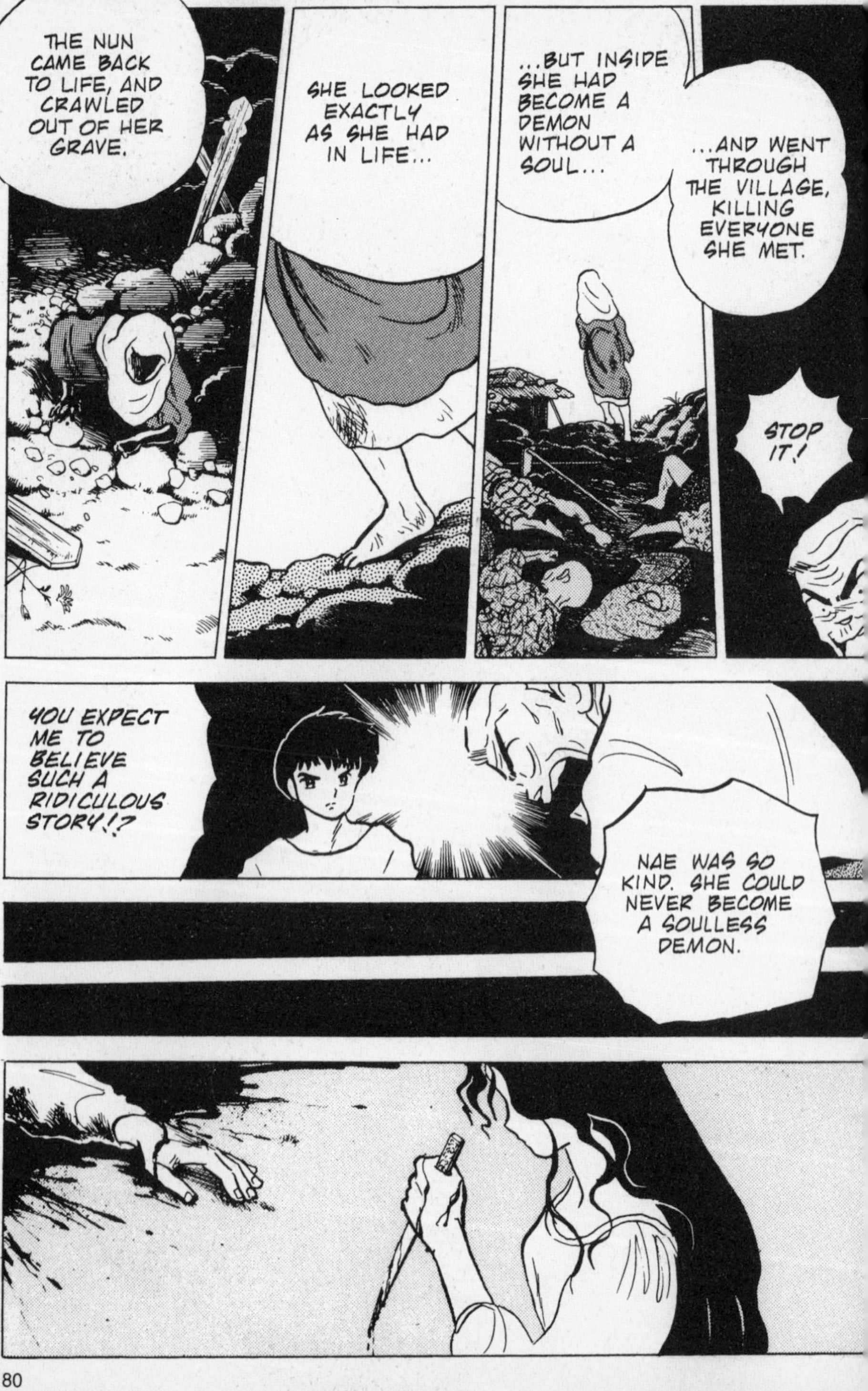
THE NUN CAME BACK TO LIFE, AND CRAWLED OUT OF HER GRAVE.
SHE LOOKED EXACTLY AS SHE HAD IN LIFE...
...BUT INSIDE SHE HAD BECOME A DEMON WITHOUT A SOUL...
...AND WENT THROUGH THE VILLAGE, KILLING EVERYONE SHE MET.
STOP IT!
YOU EXPECT ME TO BELIEVE SUCH A RIDICULOUS STORY!?
NAE WAS SO KIND. SHE COULD NEVER BECOME A SOULLESS DEMON.

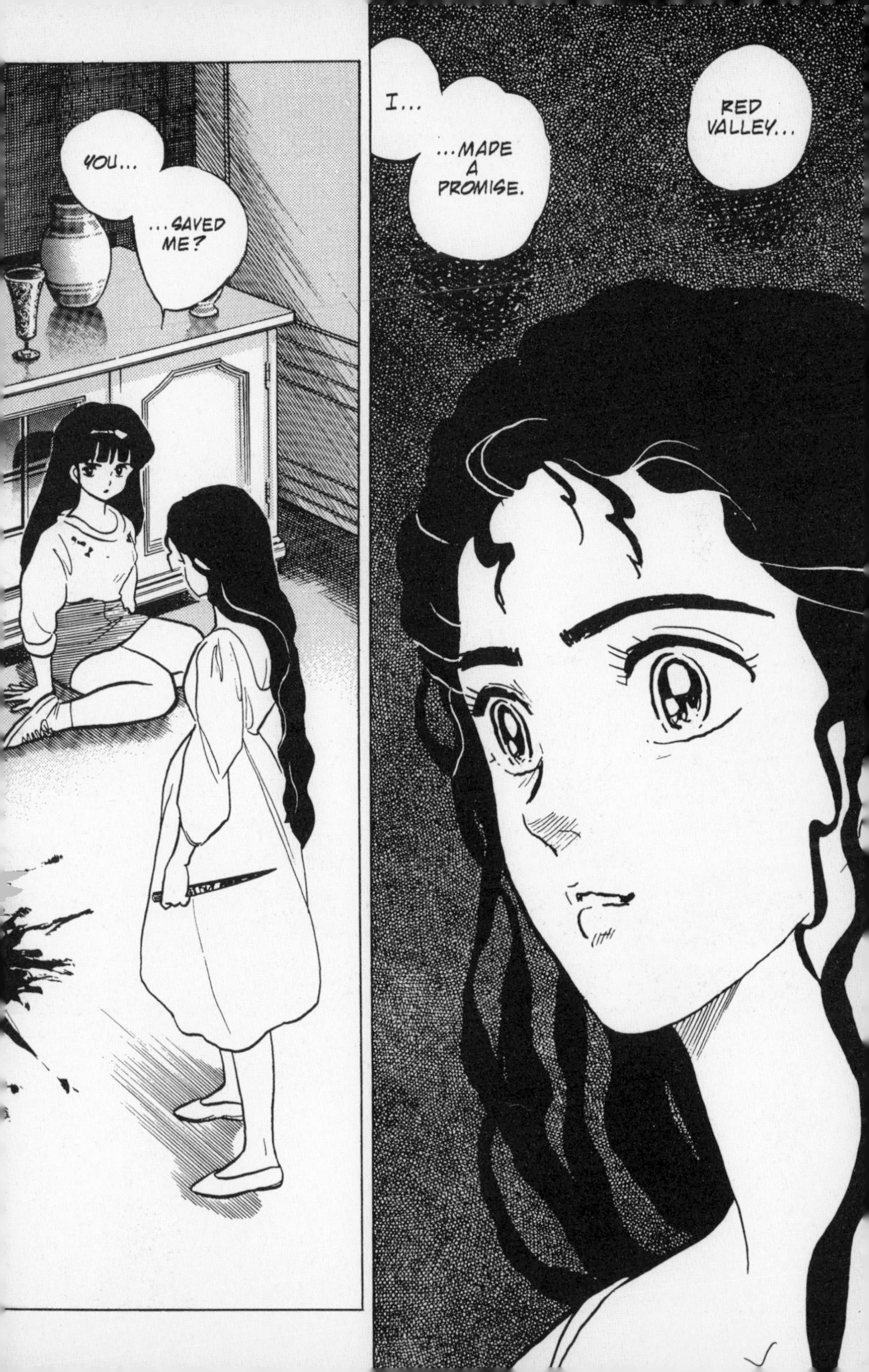
YOU...
...SAVED ME?
I...
...MADE A PROMISE.
RED VALLEY...

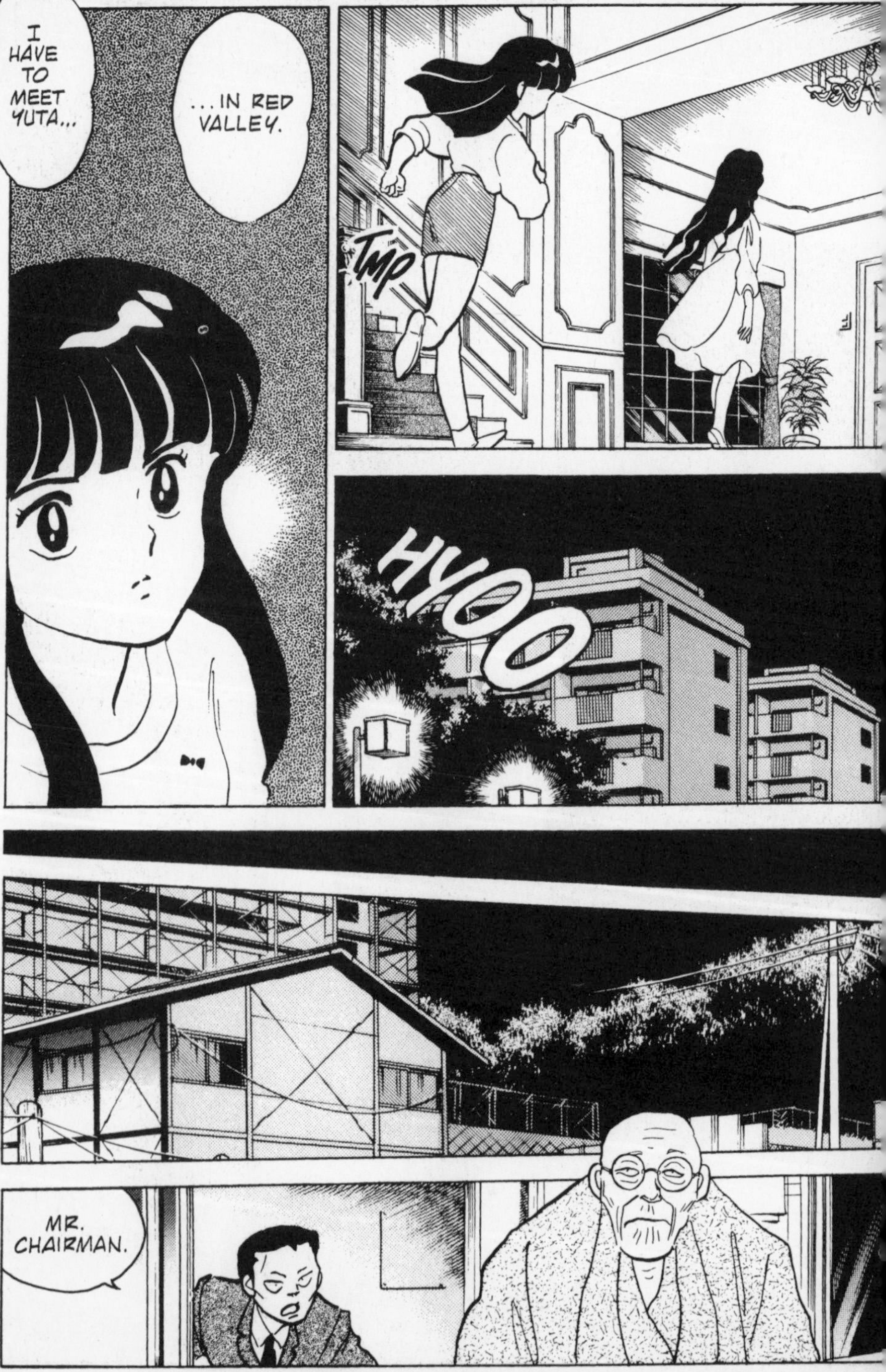
I HAVE TO MEET YUTA...
...IN RED VALLEY.
TMP
HYOO
MR. CHAIRMAN.

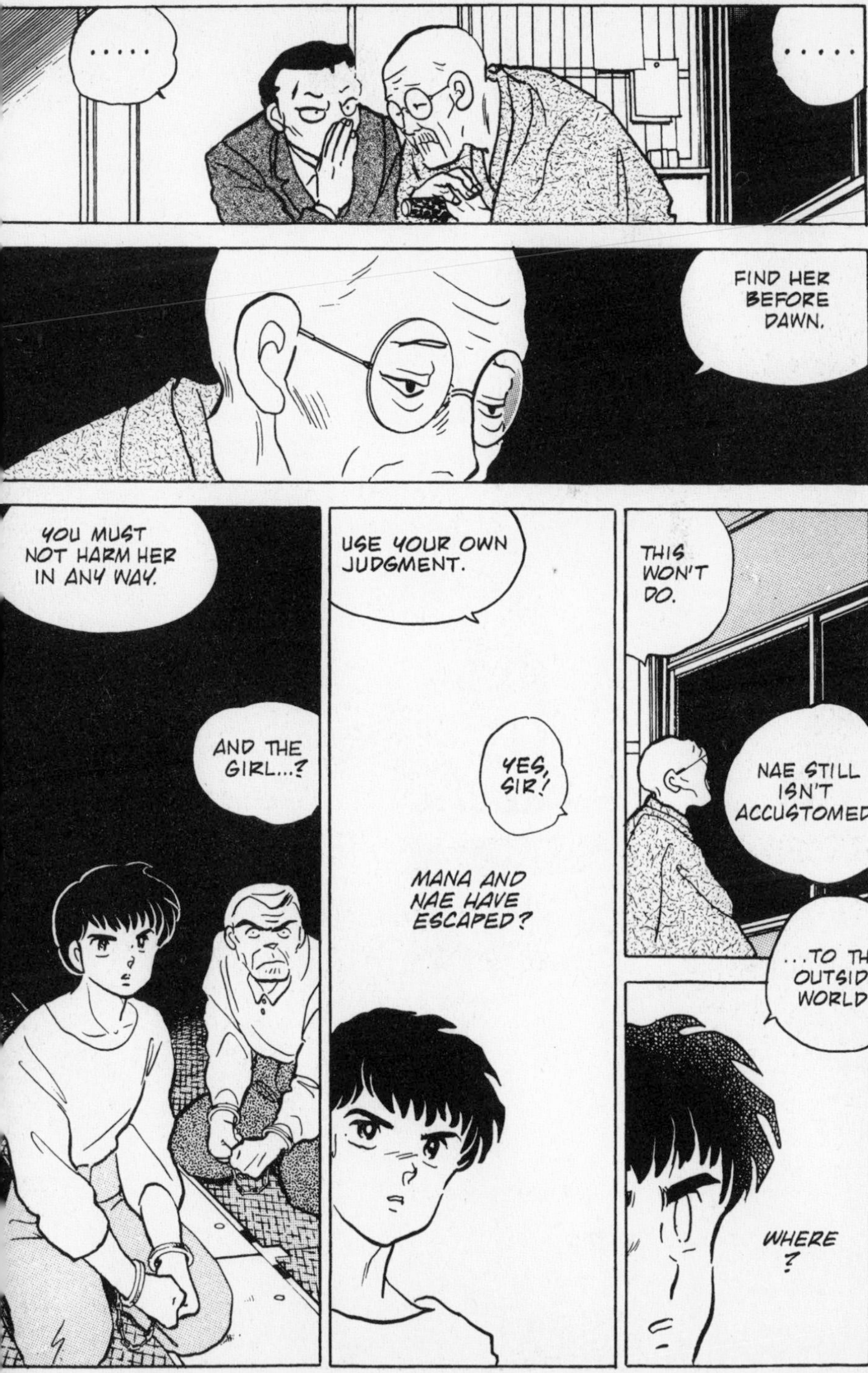
.....
.....
FIND HER BEFORE DAWN.
YOU MUST NOT HARM HER IN ANY WAY.
AND THE GIRL...?
USE YOUR OWN JUDGMENT.
YES, SIR!
MANA AND NAE HAVE ESCAPED?
THIS WON'T DO.
NAE STILL ISN'T ACCUSTOMED...
...TO THE OUTSIDE WORLD.
WHERE?

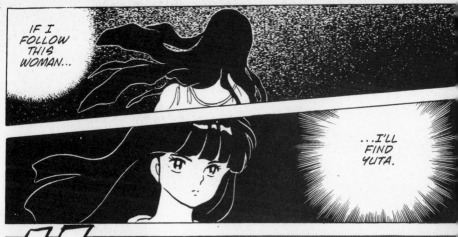

IF I FOLLOW THIS WOMAN...

...I'LL FIND YUTA.

IN RED VALLEY...

CHAPTER TWO
MERMAID'S PROMISE
PART TWO

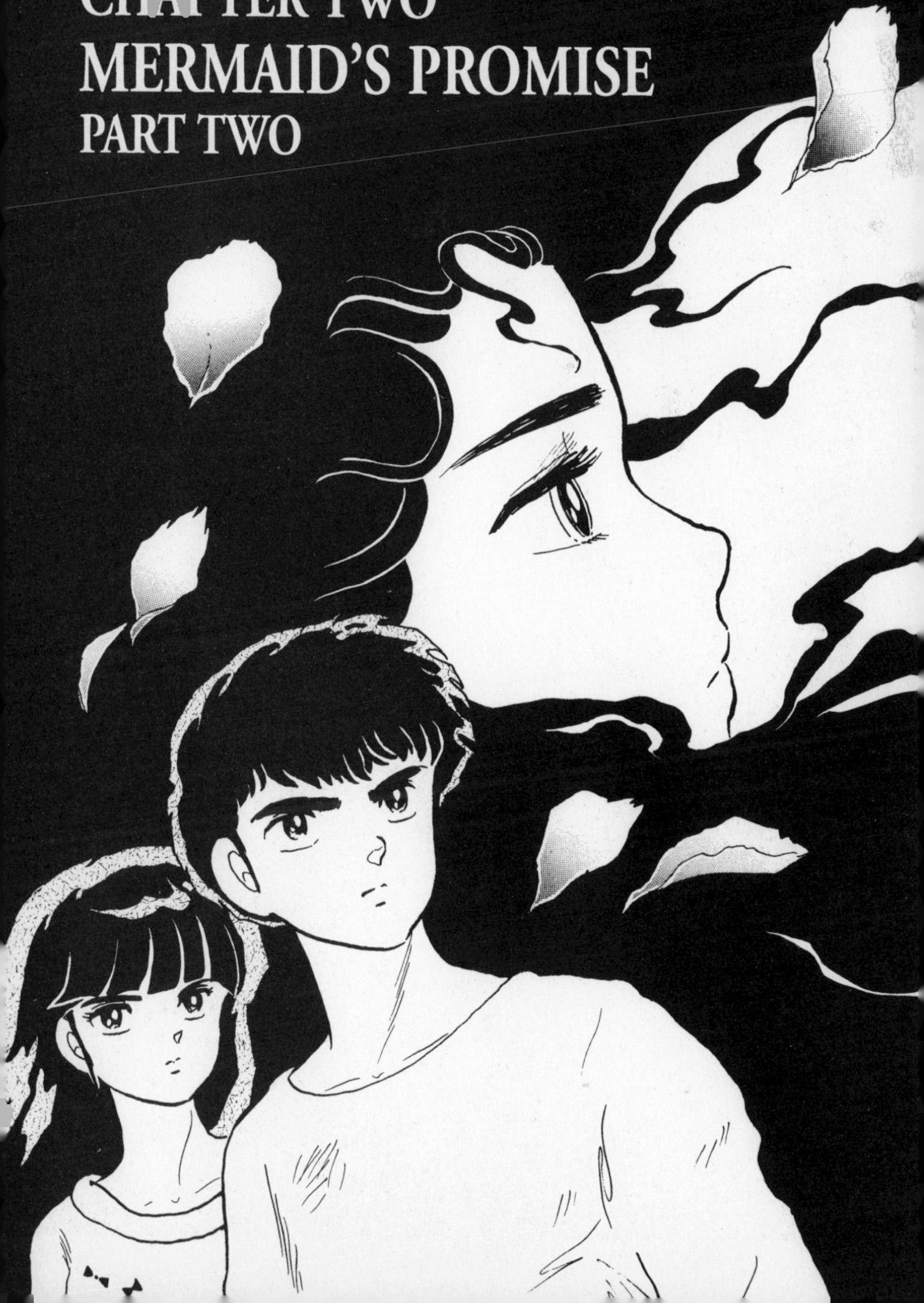

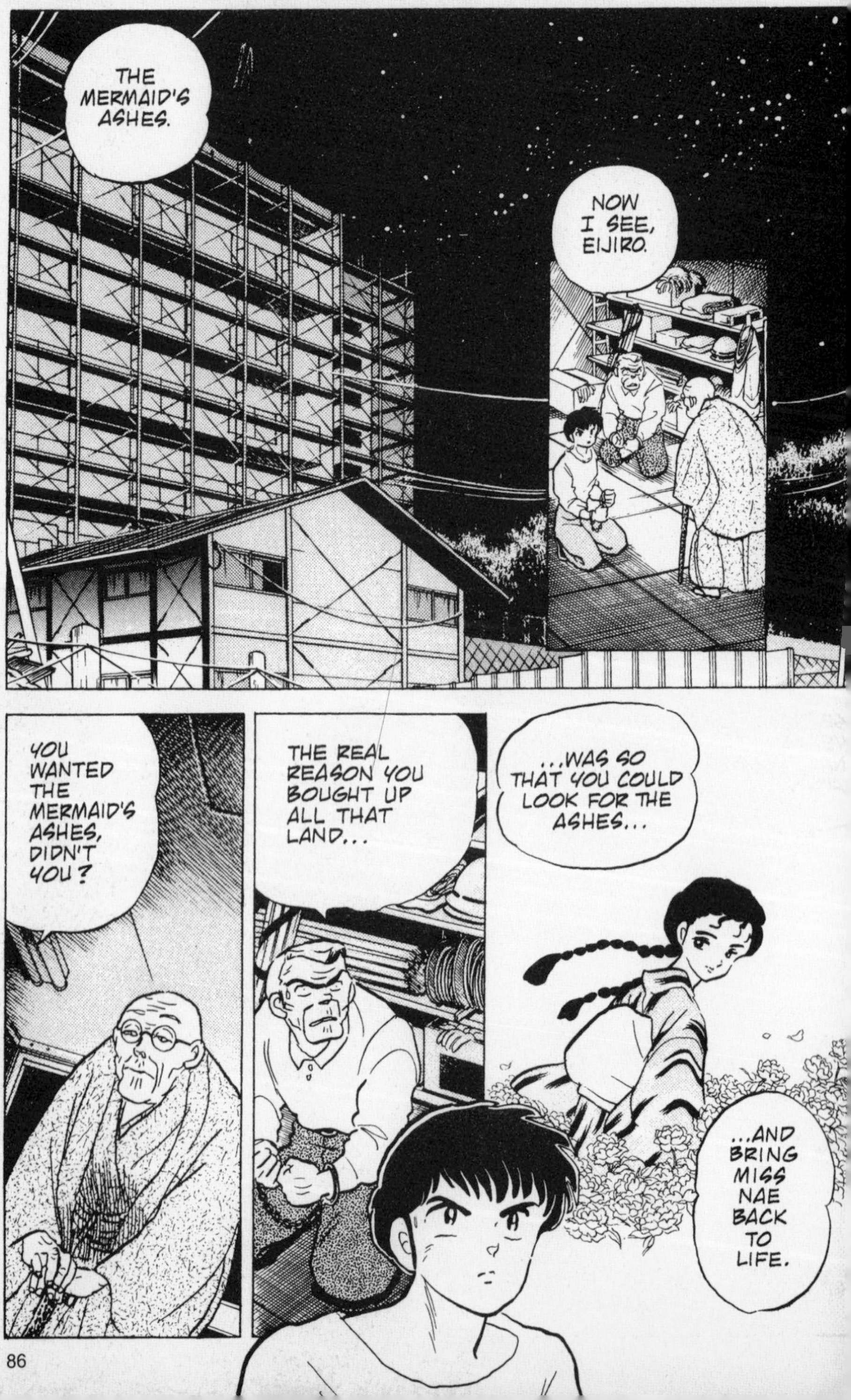
THE MERMAID'S ASHES.
NOW I SEE, EIJIRO.
YOU WANTED THE MERMAID'S ASHES, DIDN'T YOU?
THE REAL REASON YOU BOUGHT UP ALL THAT LAND...
...WAS SO THAT YOU COULD LOOK FOR THE ASHES...
...AND BRING MISS NAE BACK TO LIFE.

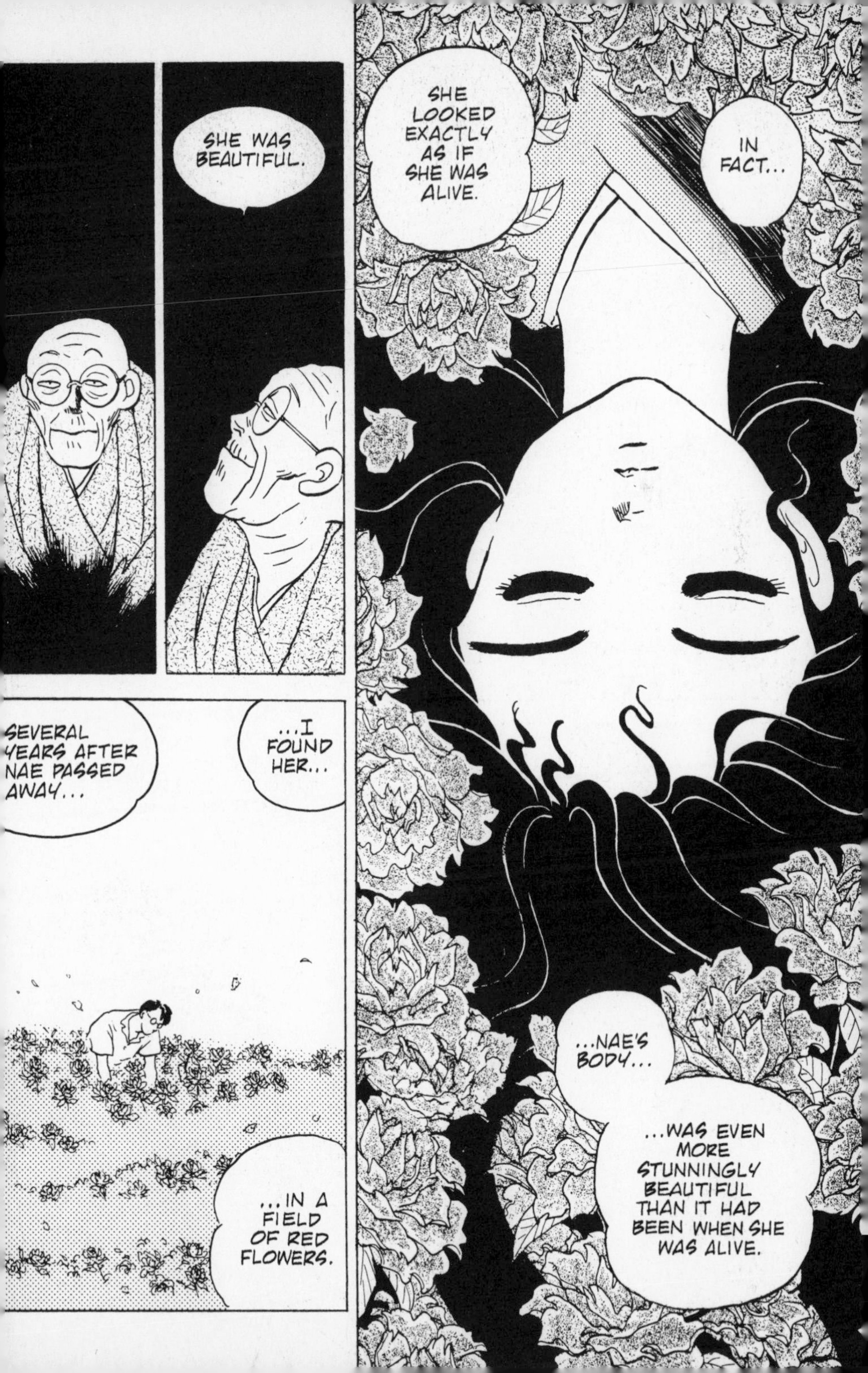
SHE WAS BEAUTIFUL.
SEVERAL YEARS AFTER NAE PASSED AWAY...
...I FOUND HER...
...IN A FIELD OF RED FLOWERS.
SHE LOOKED EXACTLY AS IF SHE WAS ALIVE.
IN FACT...
...NAE'S BODY...
...WAS EVEN MORE STUNNINGLY BEAUTIFUL THAN IT HAD BEEN WHEN SHE WAS ALIVE.

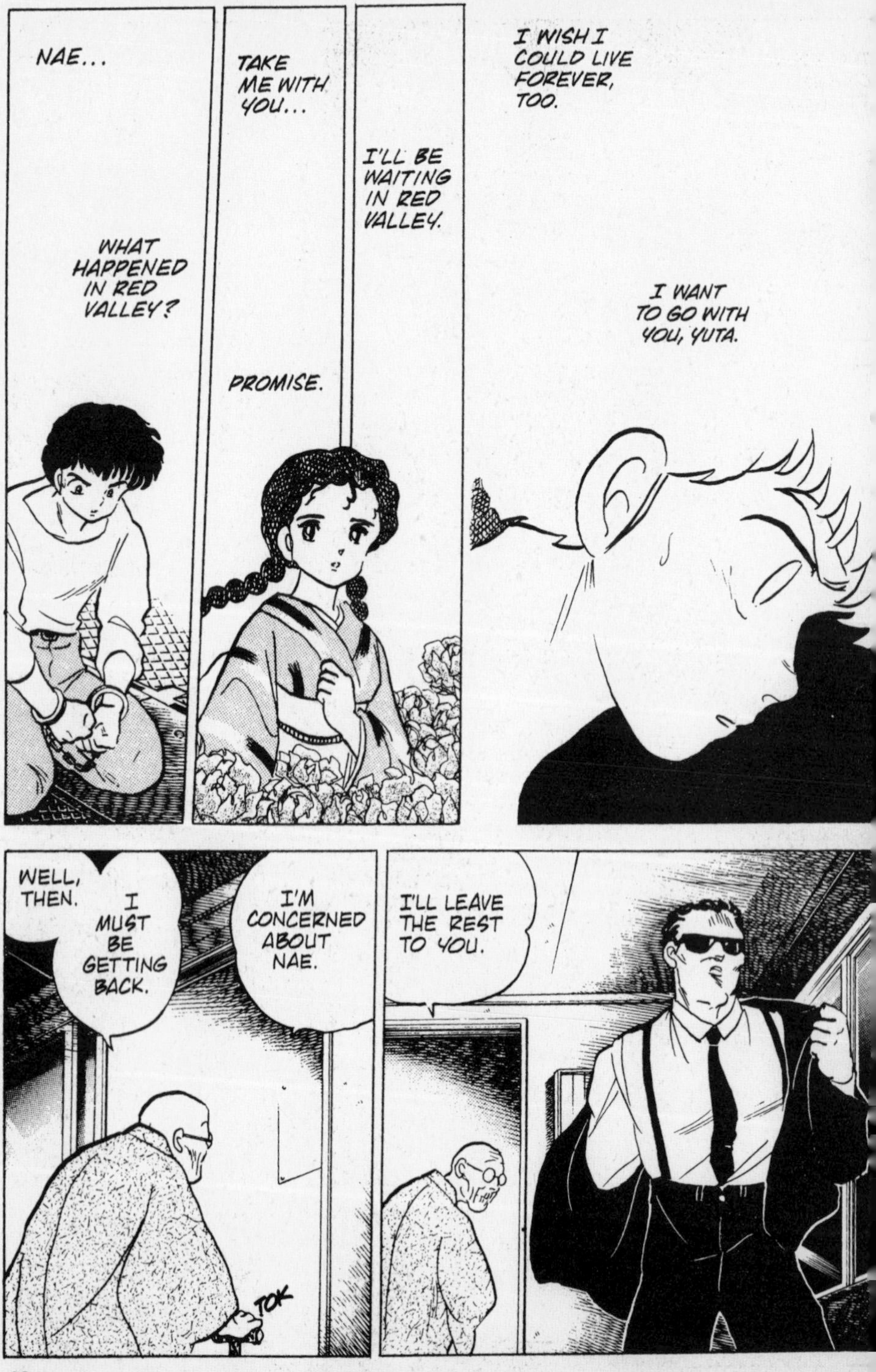
NAE...
WHAT HAPPENED IN RED VALLEY?
TAKE ME WITH YOU...
PROMISE.
I'LL BE WAITING IN RED VALLEY.
I WISH I COULD LIVE FOREVER, TOO.
I WANT TO GO WITH YOU, YUTA.
WELL, THEN.
I MUST BE GETTING BACK.
TOK
I'M CONCERNED ABOUT NAE.
I'LL LEAVE THE REST TO YOU.

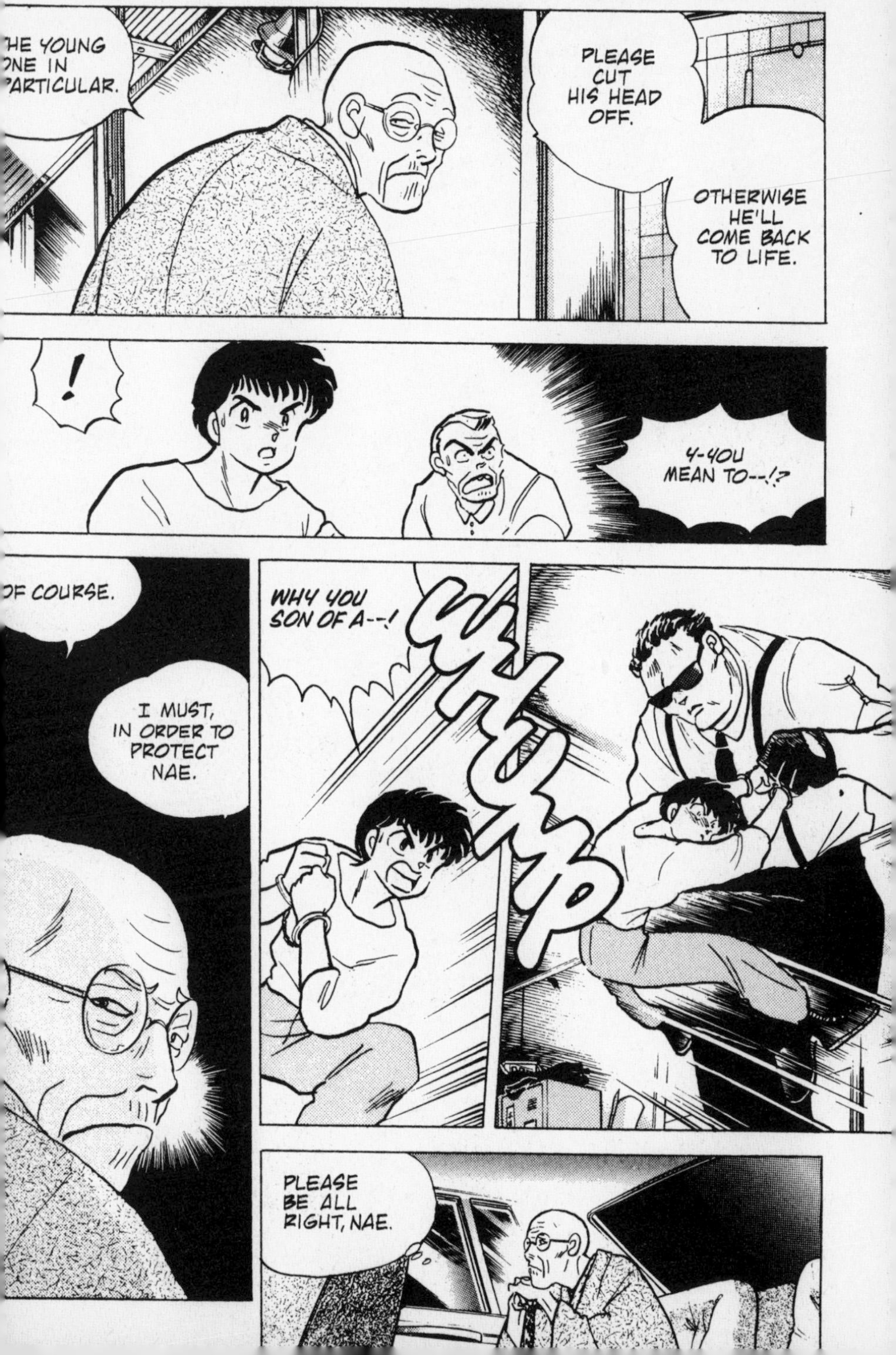

THE YOUNG ONE IN PARTICULAR.
PLEASE CUT HIS HEAD OFF.
OTHERWISE HE'LL COME BACK TO LIFE.
!
Y-YOU MEAN TO--!?
OF COURSE.
I MUST, IN ORDER TO PROTECT NAE.
WHY YOU SON OF A--!
WHUMP
PLEASE BE ALL RIGHT, NAE.

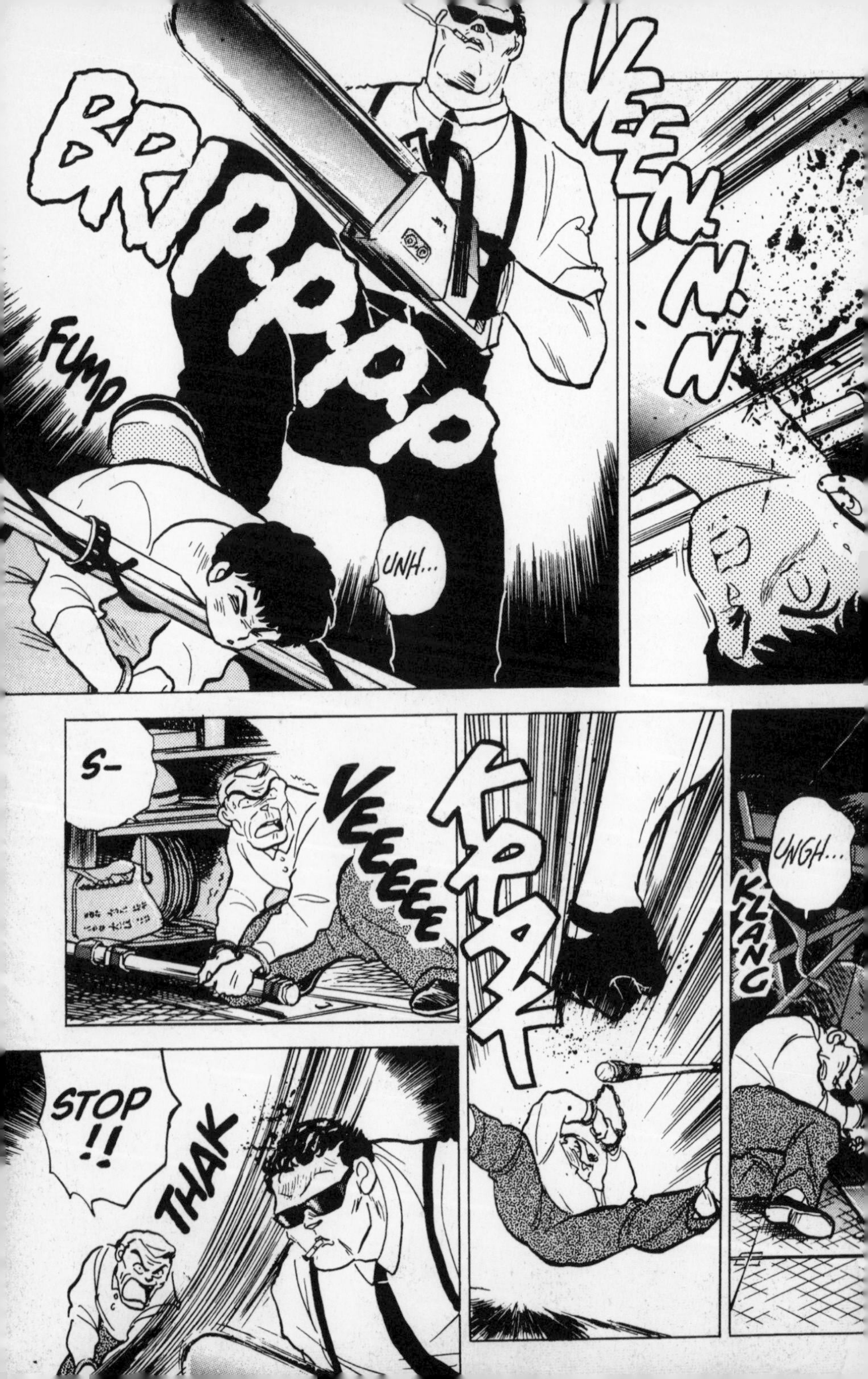
BRRRRP
FUMP
UNH...
VEEN.N.N
S-
VEEEEEE
STOP!!
THAK
KRAK
UNGH...
KLANG

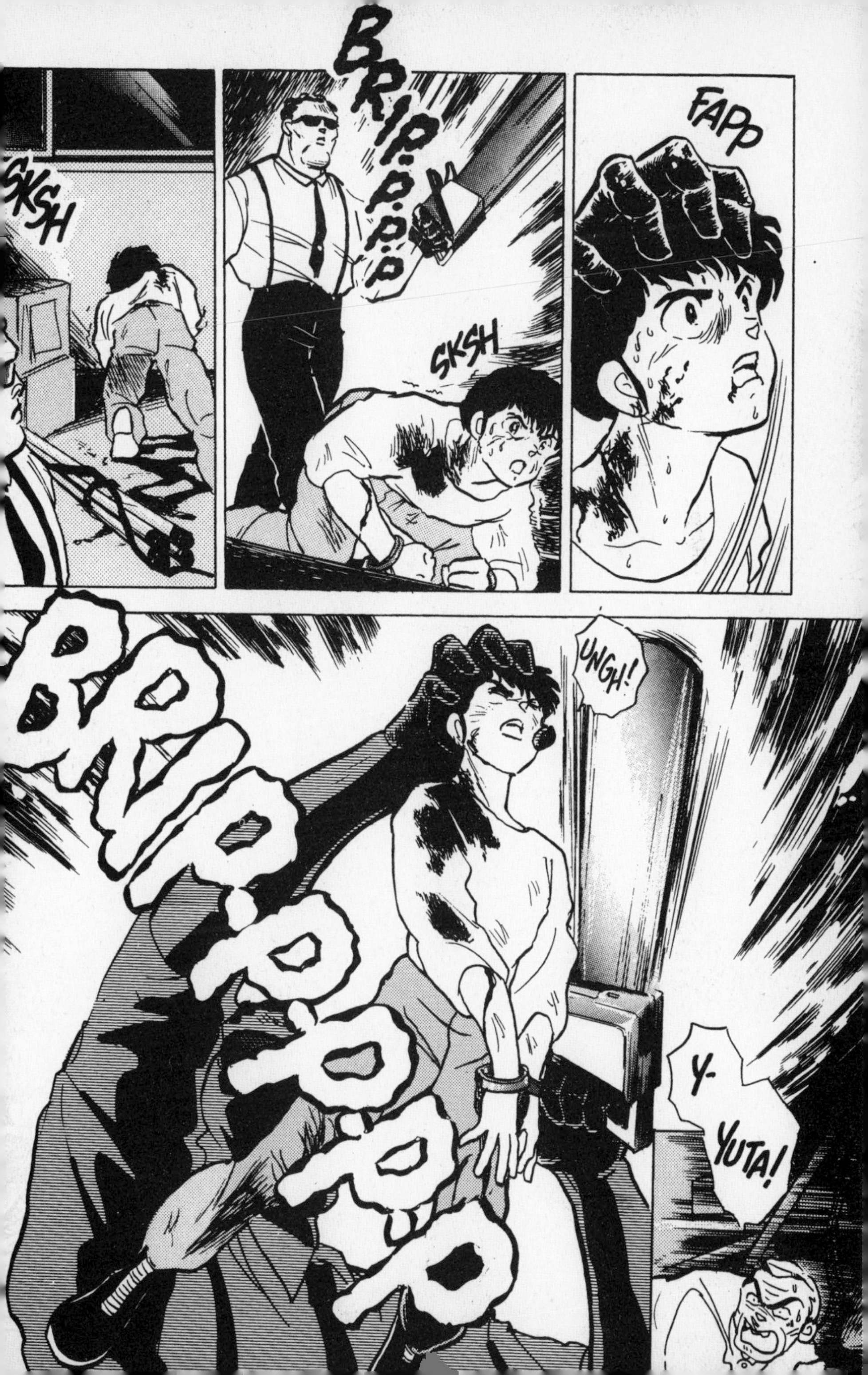
SKSH
BRIP-P-P-P
SKSH
FAPP
BRIPPPPP
UNGH!
Y- YUTA!

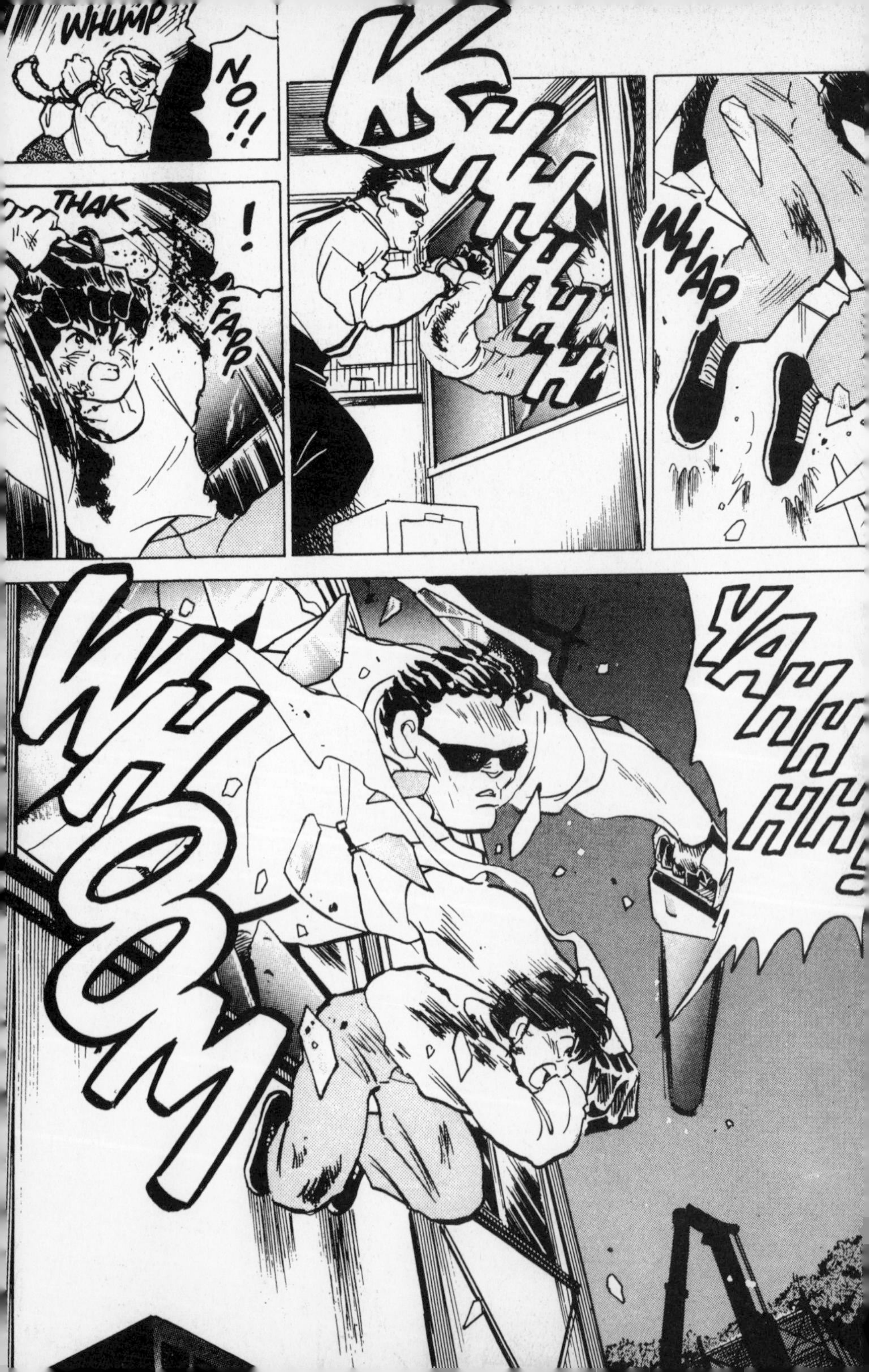
WHUMP
NO!!
THAK
!
FAPP
KAHHHHHH
WHAP
WHOOM
YAHHHHH

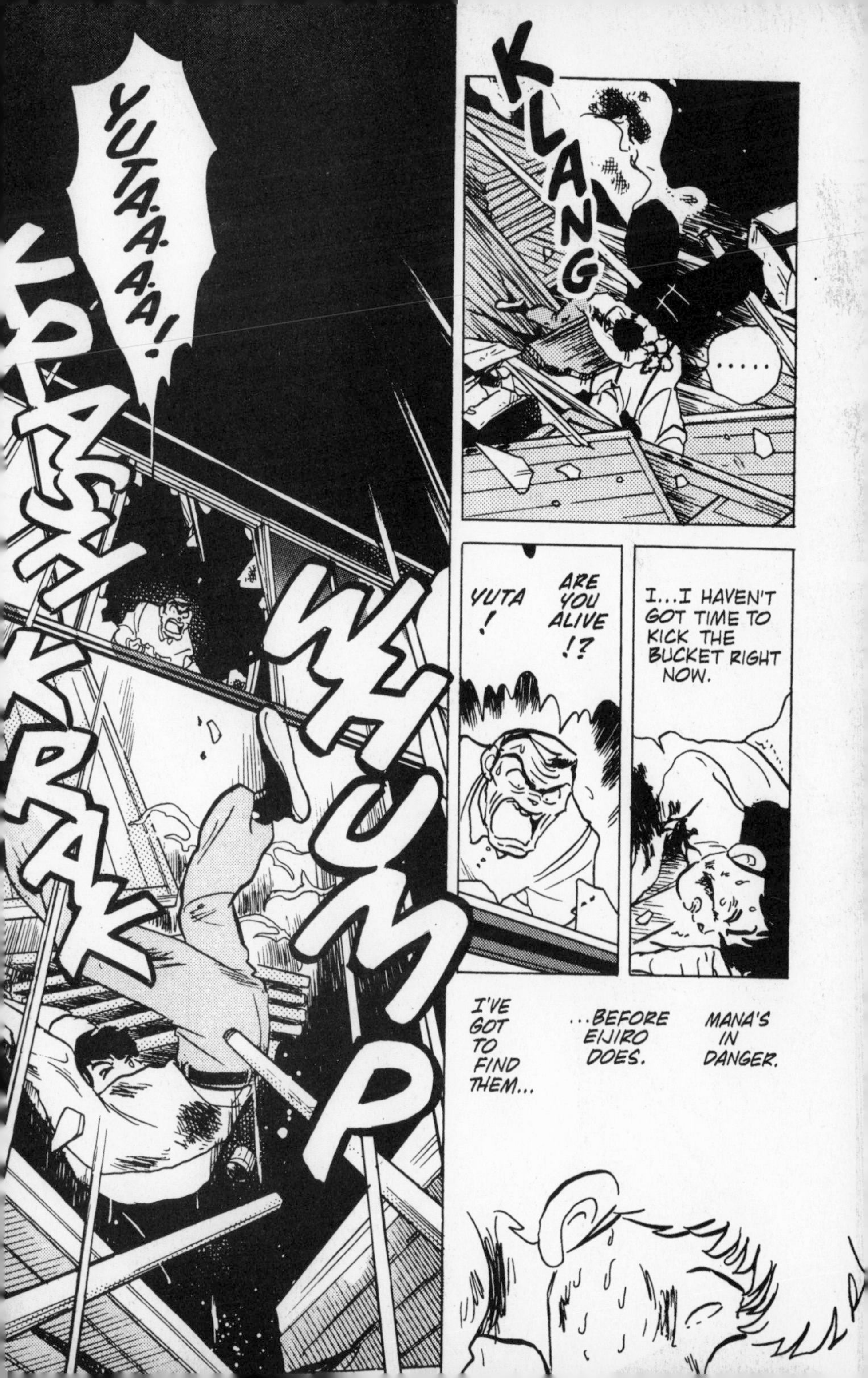
YUTA-A-A-A-A!
ASH
RAK
WHUMP
KLANG
......
YUTA!
ARE YOU ALIVE!?
I...I HAVEN'T GOT TIME TO KICK THE BUCKET RIGHT NOW.
I'VE GOT TO FIND THEM...
...BEFORE EIJIRO DOES.
MANA'S IN DANGER.

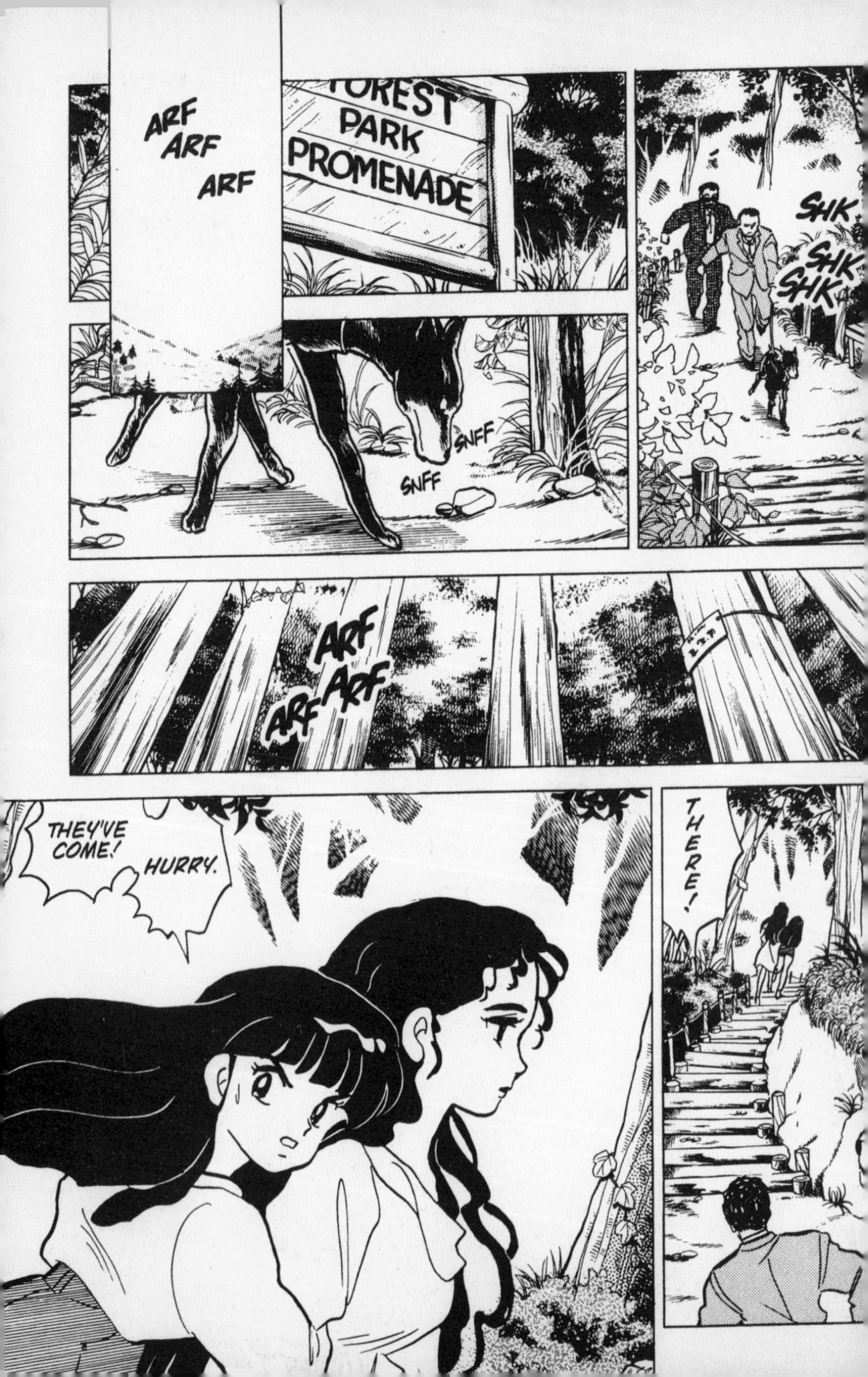
SHK
SHK
SHK
ARF
ARF
ARF
FOREST
PARK
PROMENADE
SNFF
SNFF
ARF
ARF
ARF
THERE!
THEY'VE COME!
HURRY.

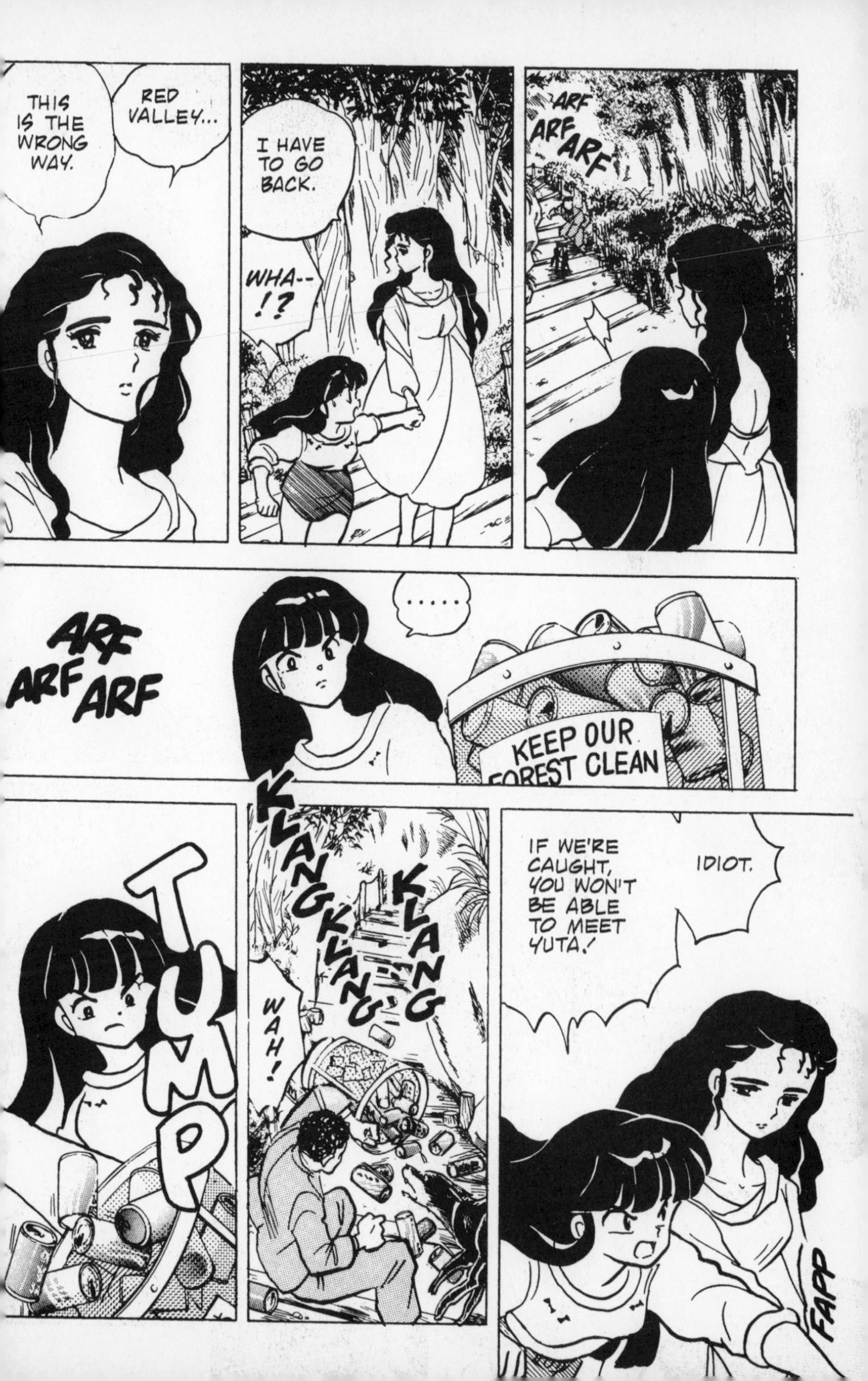

THIS IS THE WRONG WAY.
RED VALLEY...
I HAVE TO GO BACK.
WHA-- !?
ARF ARF ARF
ARF ARF ARF
......
KEEP OUR FOREST CLEAN
TUMP
KLANG KLANG KLANG
WAH!
IF WE'RE CAUGHT, YOU WON'T BE ABLE TO MEET YUTA!
IDIOT.
FAPP

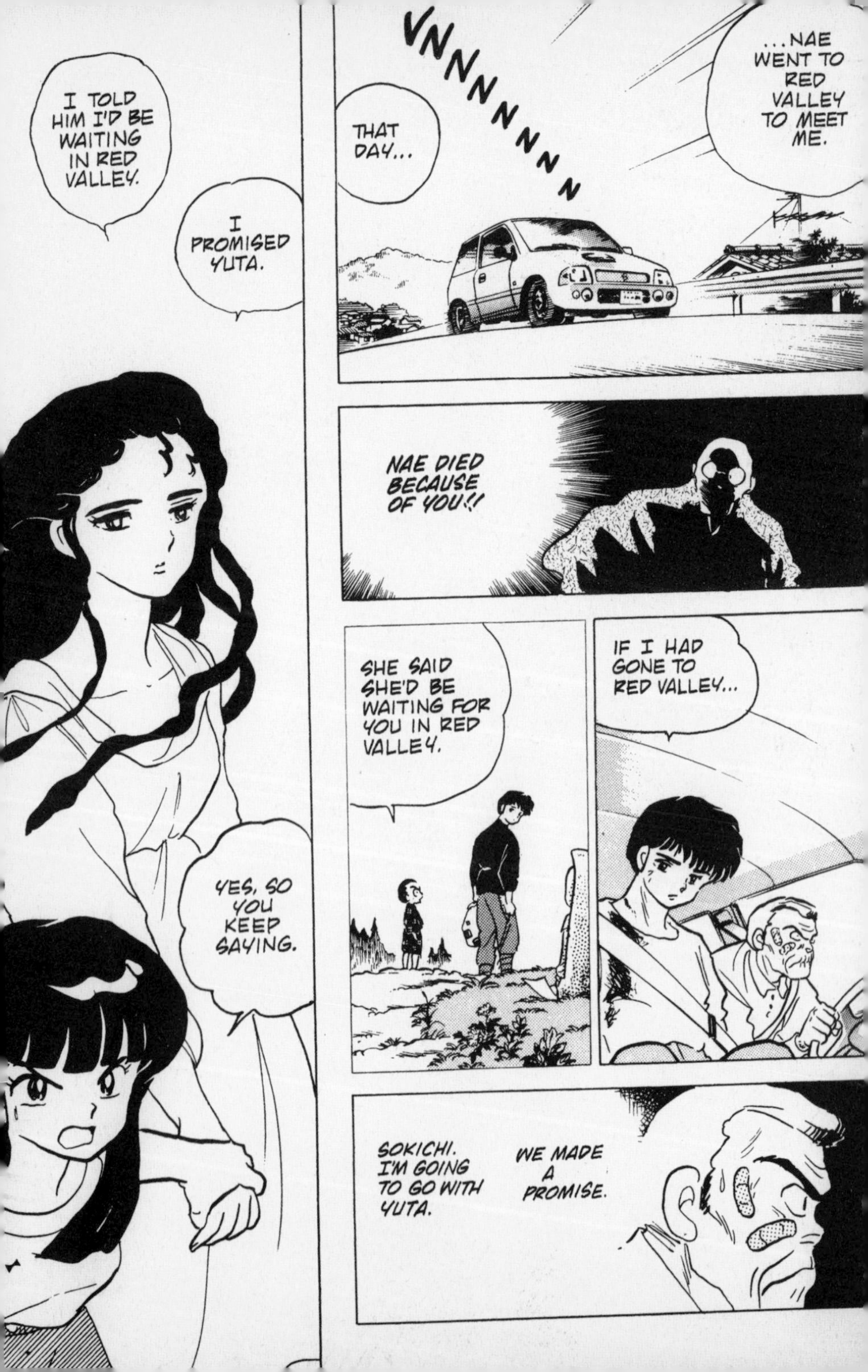
I TOLD HIM I'D BE WAITING IN RED VALLEY.
I PROMISED YUTA.
YES, SO YOU KEEP SAYING.
VNNNNNNNNN
THAT DAY...
...NAE WENT TO RED VALLEY TO MEET ME.
NAE DIED BECAUSE OF YOU!!
SHE SAID SHE'D BE WAITING FOR YOU IN RED VALLEY.
IF I HAD GONE TO RED VALLEY...
SOKICHI. I'M GOING TO GO WITH YUTA.
WE MADE A PROMISE.

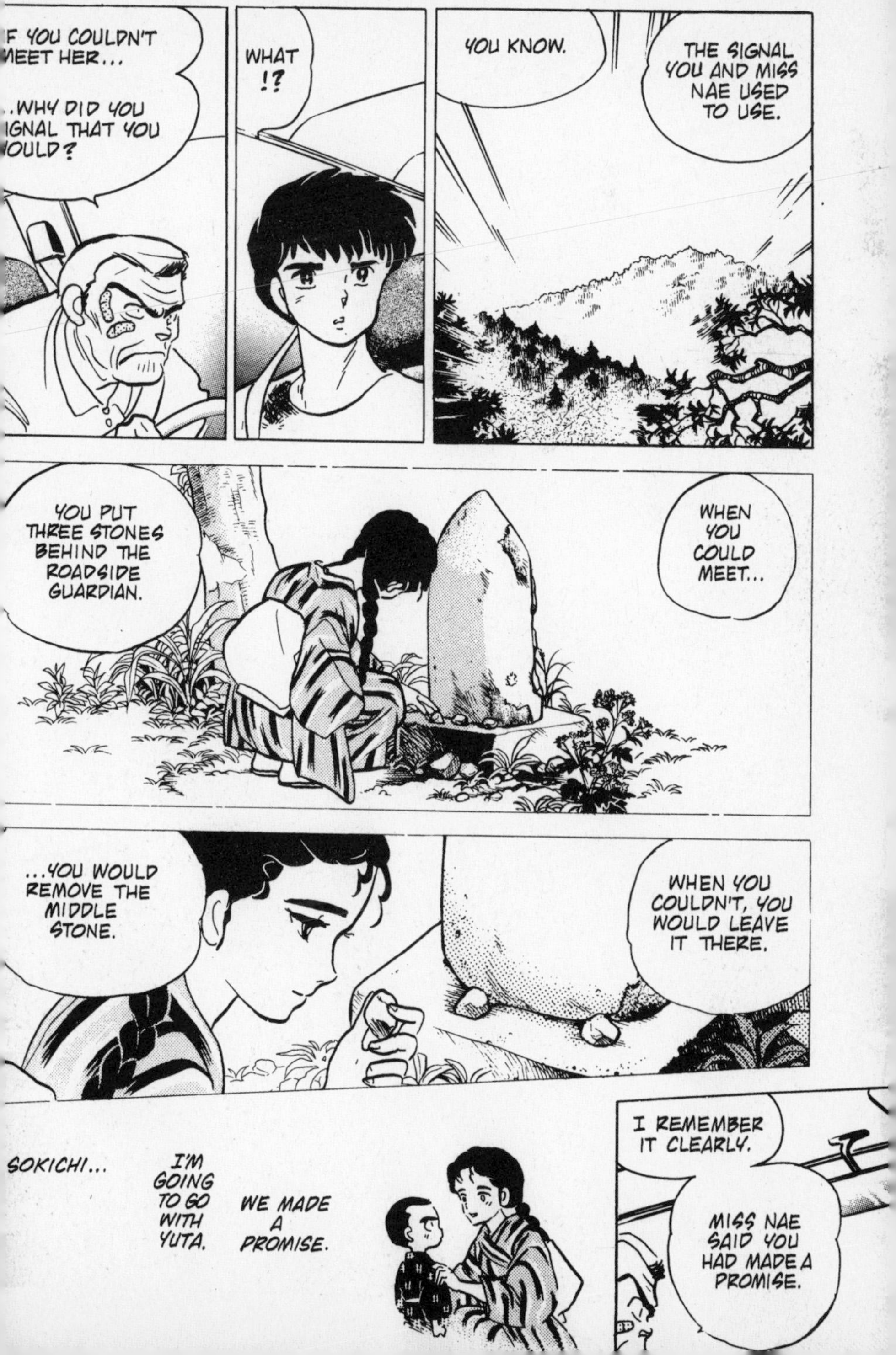

F YOU COULDN'T
MEET HER...
..WHY DID YOU
IGNAL THAT YOU
OULD?
WHAT !?
YOU KNOW.
THE SIGNAL YOU AND MISS NAE USED TO USE.
YOU PUT THREE STONES BEHIND THE ROADSIDE GUARDIAN.
WHEN YOU COULD MEET...
...YOU WOULD REMOVE THE MIDDLE STONE.
WHEN YOU COULDN'T, YOU WOULD LEAVE IT THERE.
SOKICHI...
I'M GOING TO GO WITH YUTA.
WE MADE A PROMISE.
I REMEMBER IT CLEARLY.
MISS NAE SAID YOU HAD MADE A PROMISE.

I... I DIDN'T MOVE THE STONE.

WHICH MEANS SOMEONE ELSE...

..... IT WAS A SMALL VILLAGE.

IT'S POSSIB SOMEONE ELSE KNE ABOUT YO SIGNAL.

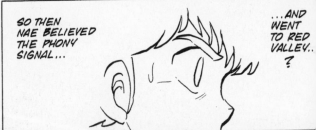

SO THEN NAE BELIEVED THE PHONY SIGNAL...

...AND WENT TO RED VALLEY...?

CASHIER

ANY SIGN?

KITCHEN WARE

DAMN. EVEN IF WE FIND THEM, WE CAN'T DO ANYTHING HERE.

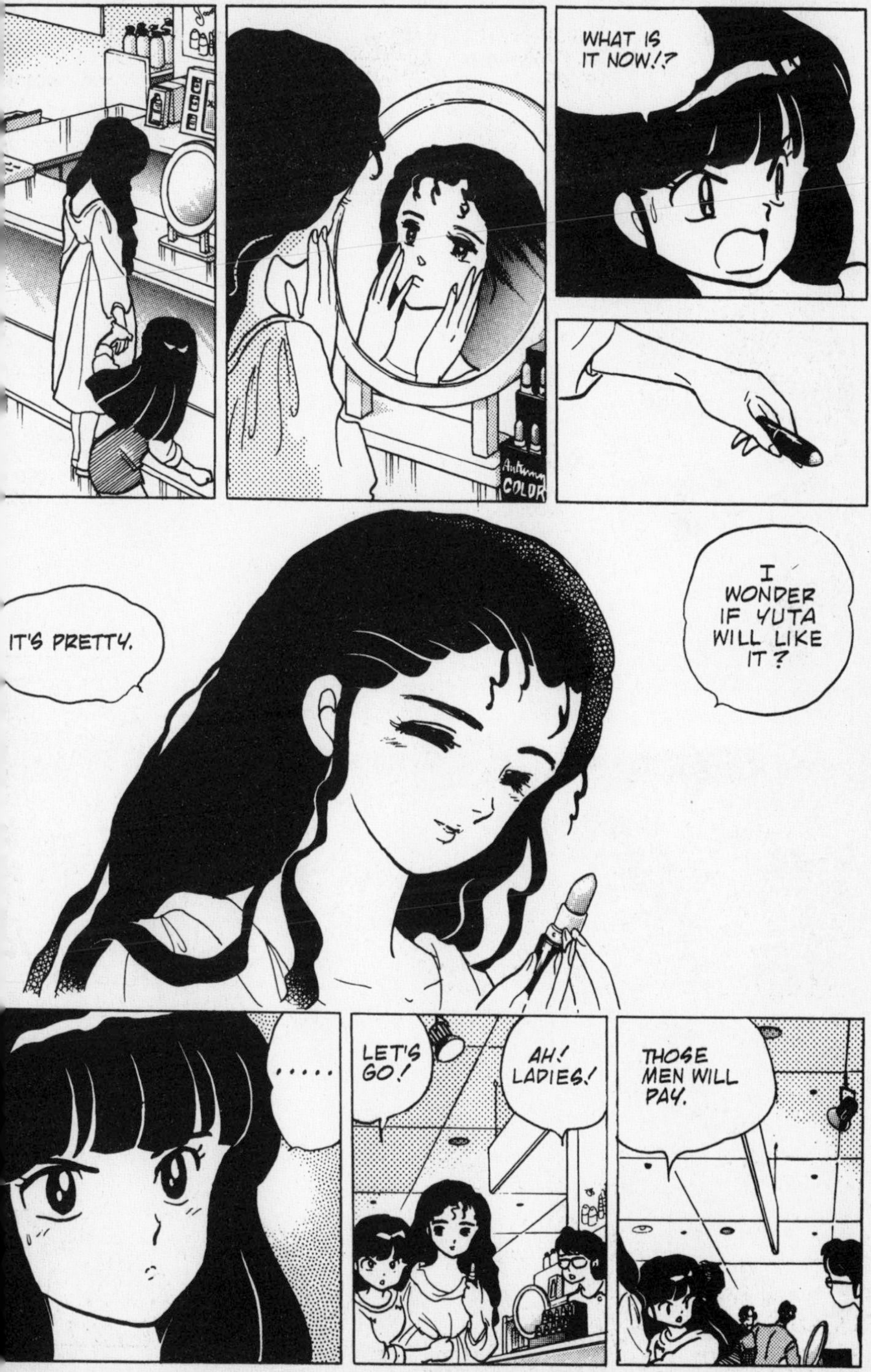
Autumn
COLOR
WHAT IS IT NOW!?
IT'S PRETTY.
I WONDER IF YUTA WILL LIKE IT?
.....
LET'S GO!
AH! LADIES!
THOSE MEN WILL PAY.

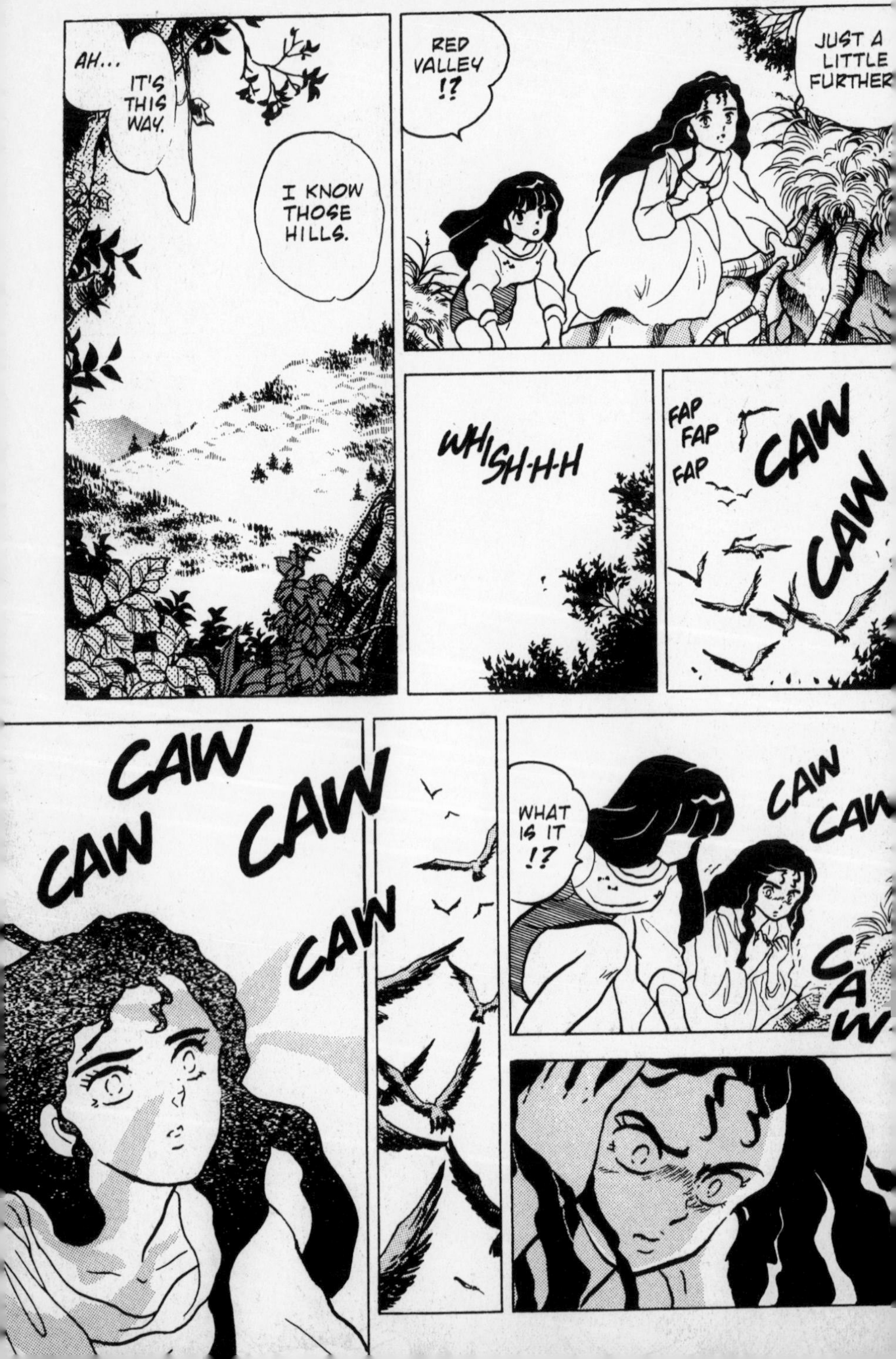
AH...
IT'S THIS WAY.
I KNOW THOSE HILLS.
RED VALLEY !?
JUST A LITTLE FURTHER
WHISH-H-H
FAP FAP FAP
CAW CAW
CAW CAW CAW CAW
WHAT IS IT !?
CAW CAW
CAW

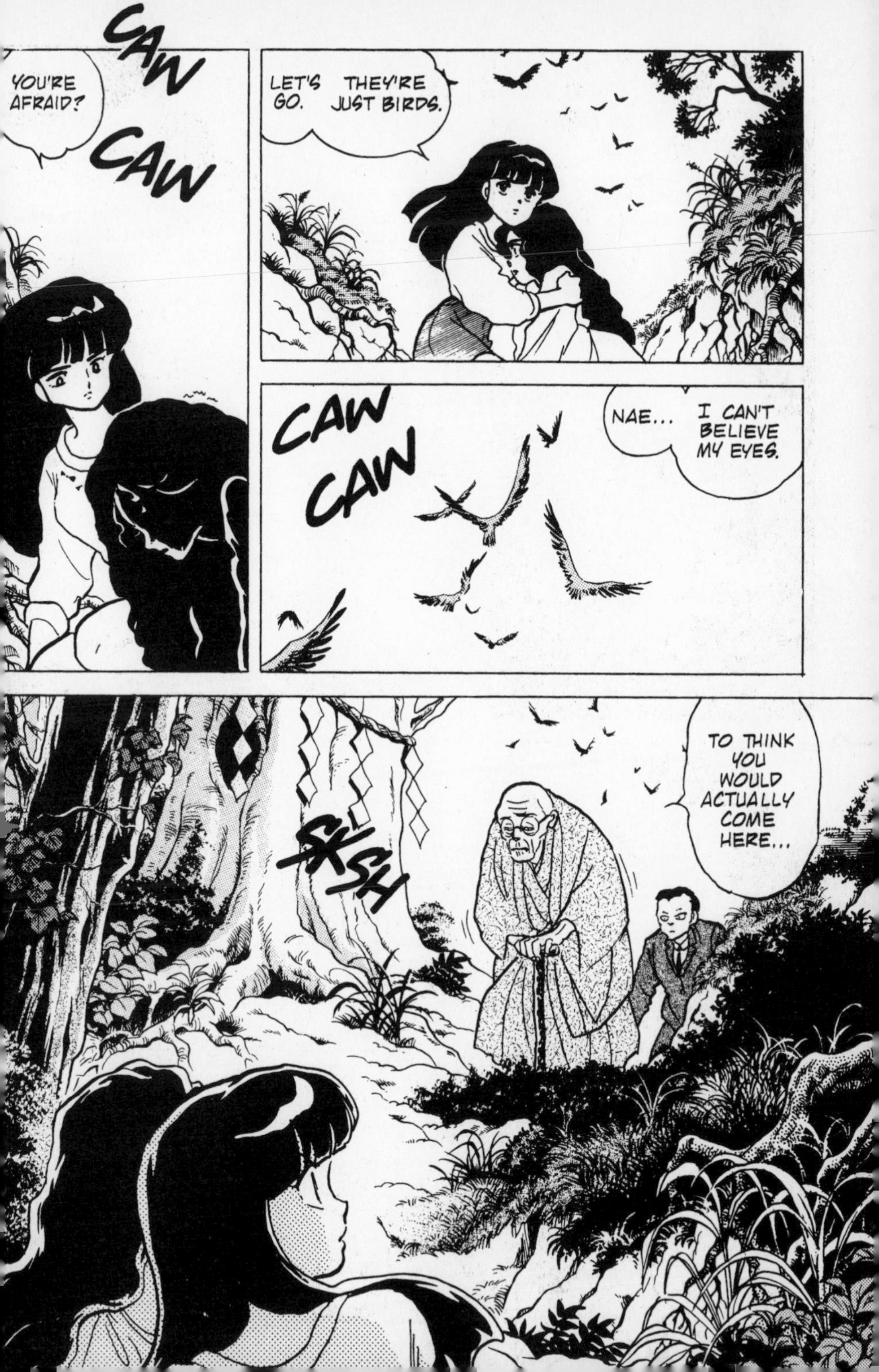
CAW
CAW
YOU'RE AFRAID?
LET'S GO.
THEY'RE JUST BIRDS.
CAW
CAW
NAE...
I CAN'T BELIEVE MY EYES.
SKSH
TO THINK YOU WOULD ACTUALLY COME HERE...

THE OLD MAN!

CAW CAW

LET'S GO HOME, NAE.

YOU CAN'T SURVIVE IN THE OUTSIDE WORLD.

YOU MUSTN'T!

THE YOUNG MISTRESS LOSES CONTROL OF HERSELF WHEN SHE HEARS THE BIRDS CRYING.

SHE WOULD NEVER HARM ME.

CAW CAW CAW

M-MR. CHAIRMAN!

NOW THEN, NAE.

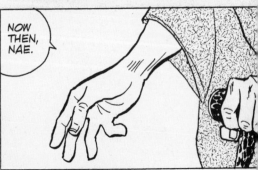

CAW CAW

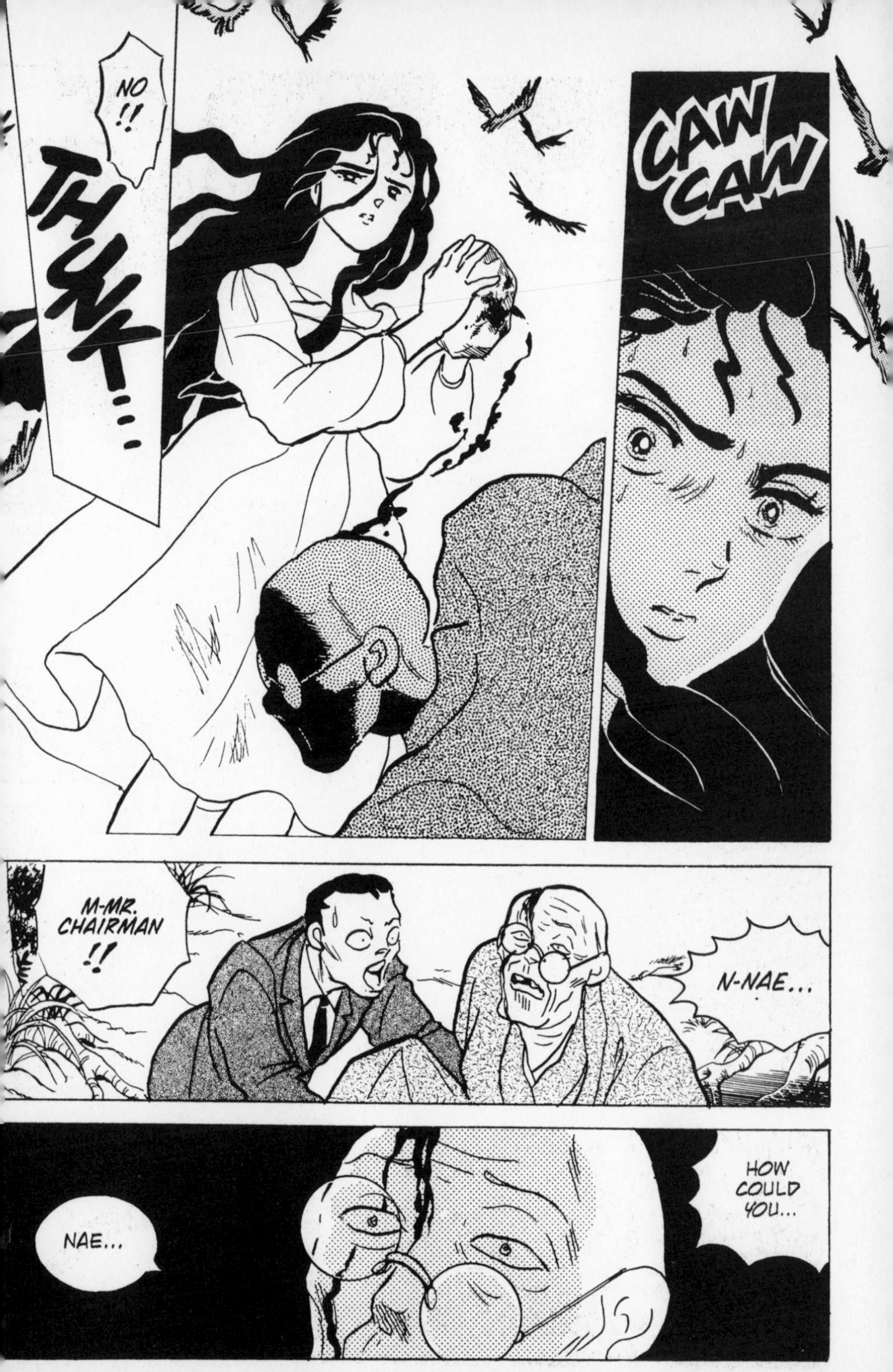
NO !!
THUNK...
CAW CAW
M-MR. CHAIRMAN !!
N-NAE...
NAE...
HOW COULD YOU...

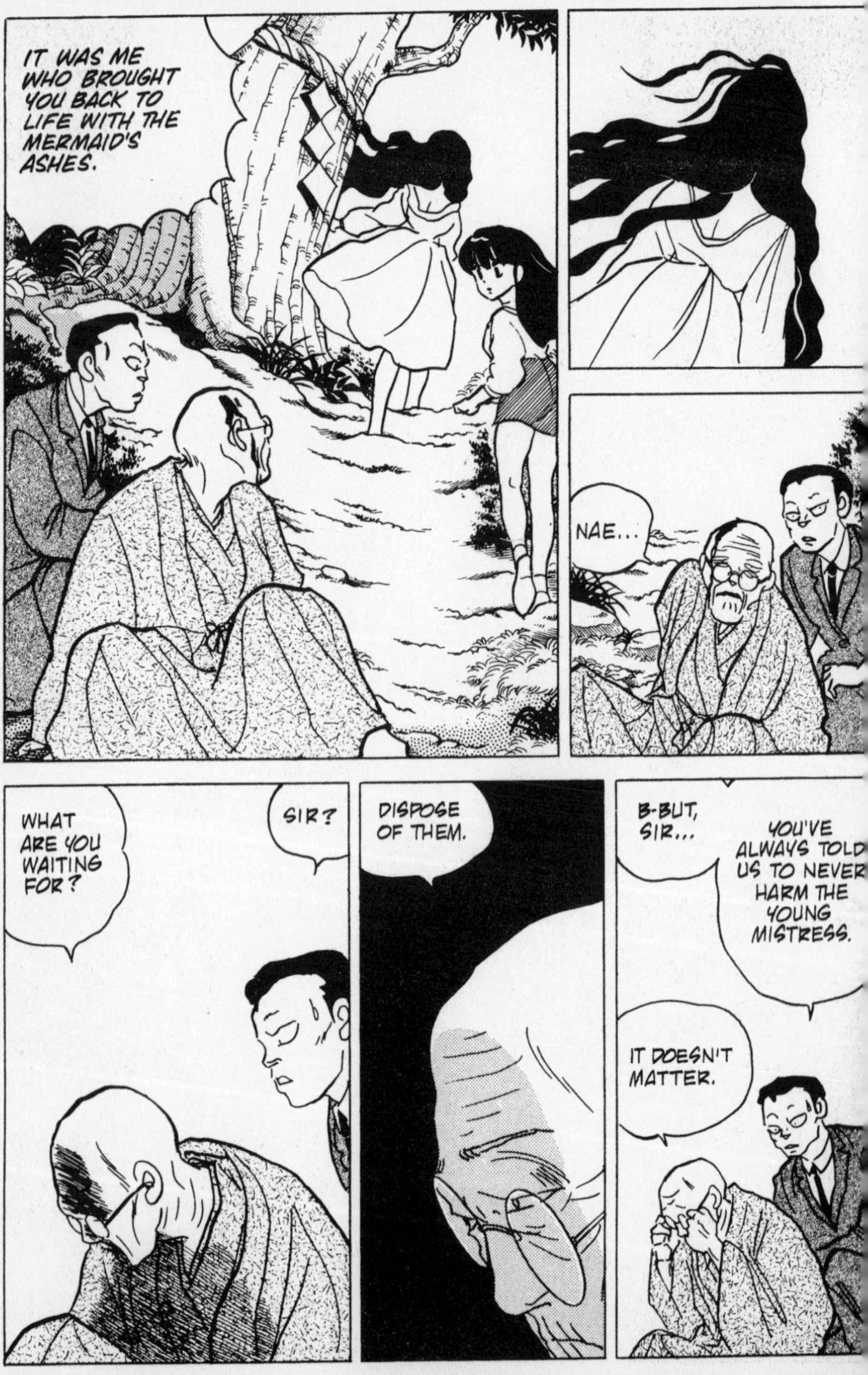
IT WAS ME WHO BROUGHT YOU BACK TO LIFE WITH THE MERMAID'S ASHES.
NAE...
WHAT ARE YOU WAITING FOR?
SIR?
DISPOSE OF THEM.
B-BUT, SIR...
YOU'VE ALWAYS TOLD US TO NEVER HARM THE YOUNG MISTRESS.
IT DOESN'T MATTER.

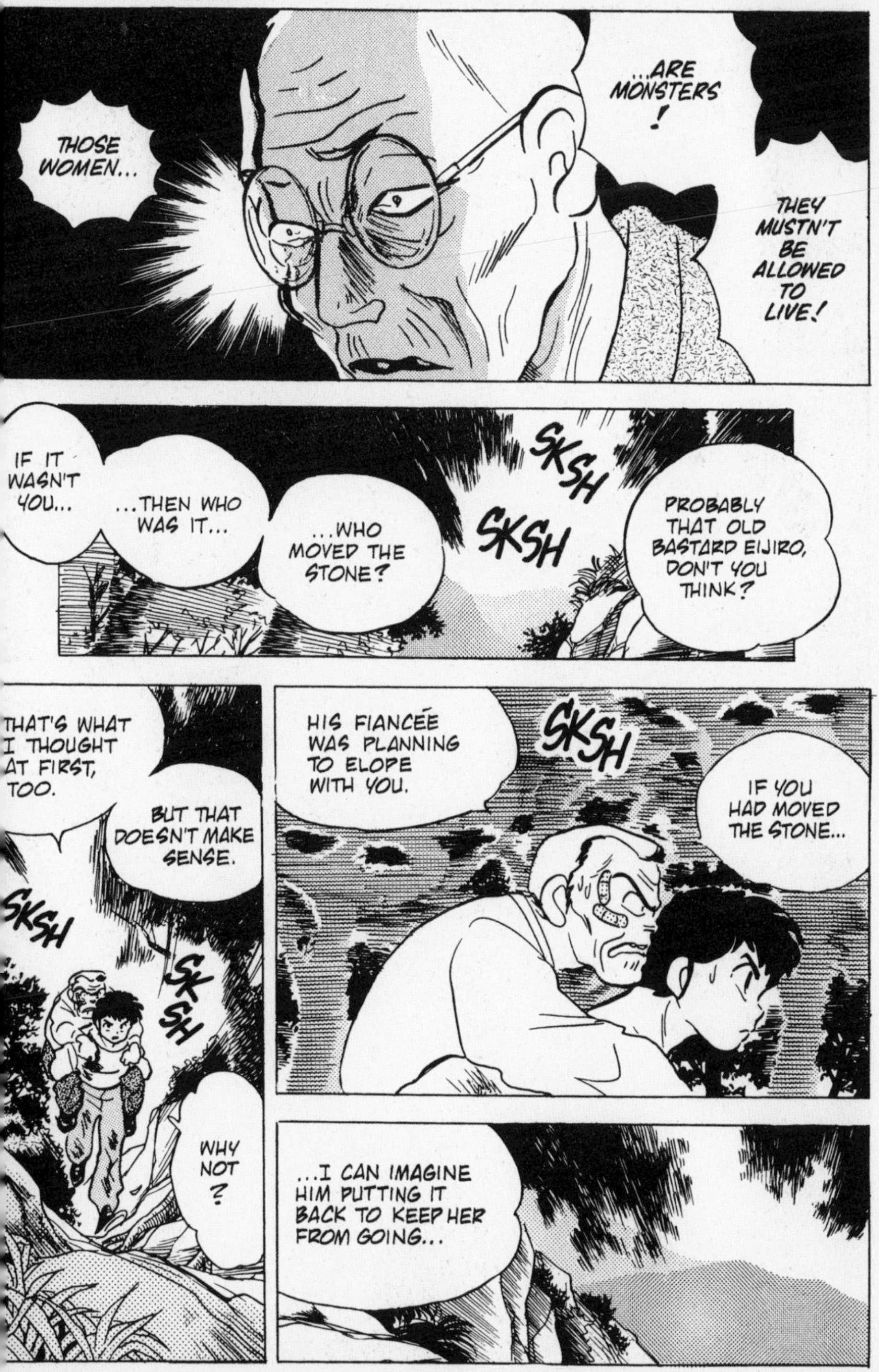
THOSE WOMEN...
...ARE MONSTERS!
THEY MUSTN'T BE ALLOWED TO LIVE!
IF IT WASN'T YOU...
...THEN WHO WAS IT...
...WHO MOVED THE STONE?
SKSH
SKSH
PROBABLY THAT OLD BASTARD EIJIRO, DON'T YOU THINK?
THAT'S WHAT I THOUGHT AT FIRST, TOO.
BUT THAT DOESN'T MAKE SENSE.
SKSH
SKSH
WHY NOT?
HIS FIANCÉE WAS PLANNING TO ELOPE WITH YOU.
SKSH
IF YOU HAD MOVED THE STONE...
...I CAN IMAGINE HIM PUTTING IT BACK TO KEEP HER FROM GOING...

...BUT WHY WOULD HE GO TO THE TROUBLE OF CALLING HER OUT?

YOU WERE GOING TO LEAVE THE VILLAGE ALONE ANYWAY. HE COULD HAVE JUST LEFT IT THERE.

.....

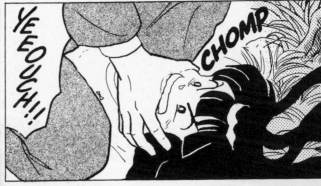

RELEASE ME!!

YEEOUCH!!

CHOMP

YOU LITTLE-!

KRAK

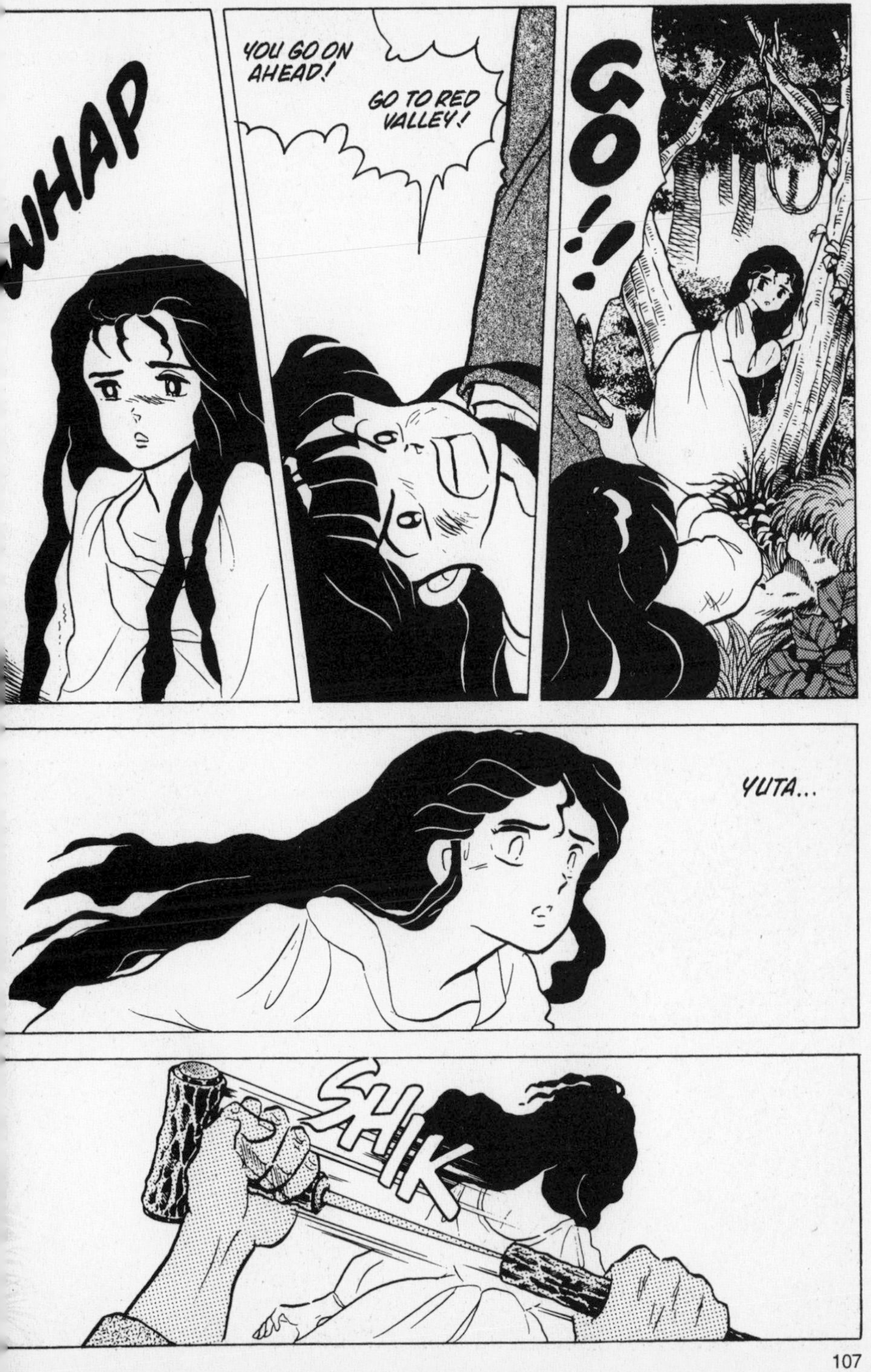
WHAP
YOU GO ON AHEAD!
GO TO RED VALLEY!
GO!!
YUTA...
SHIK

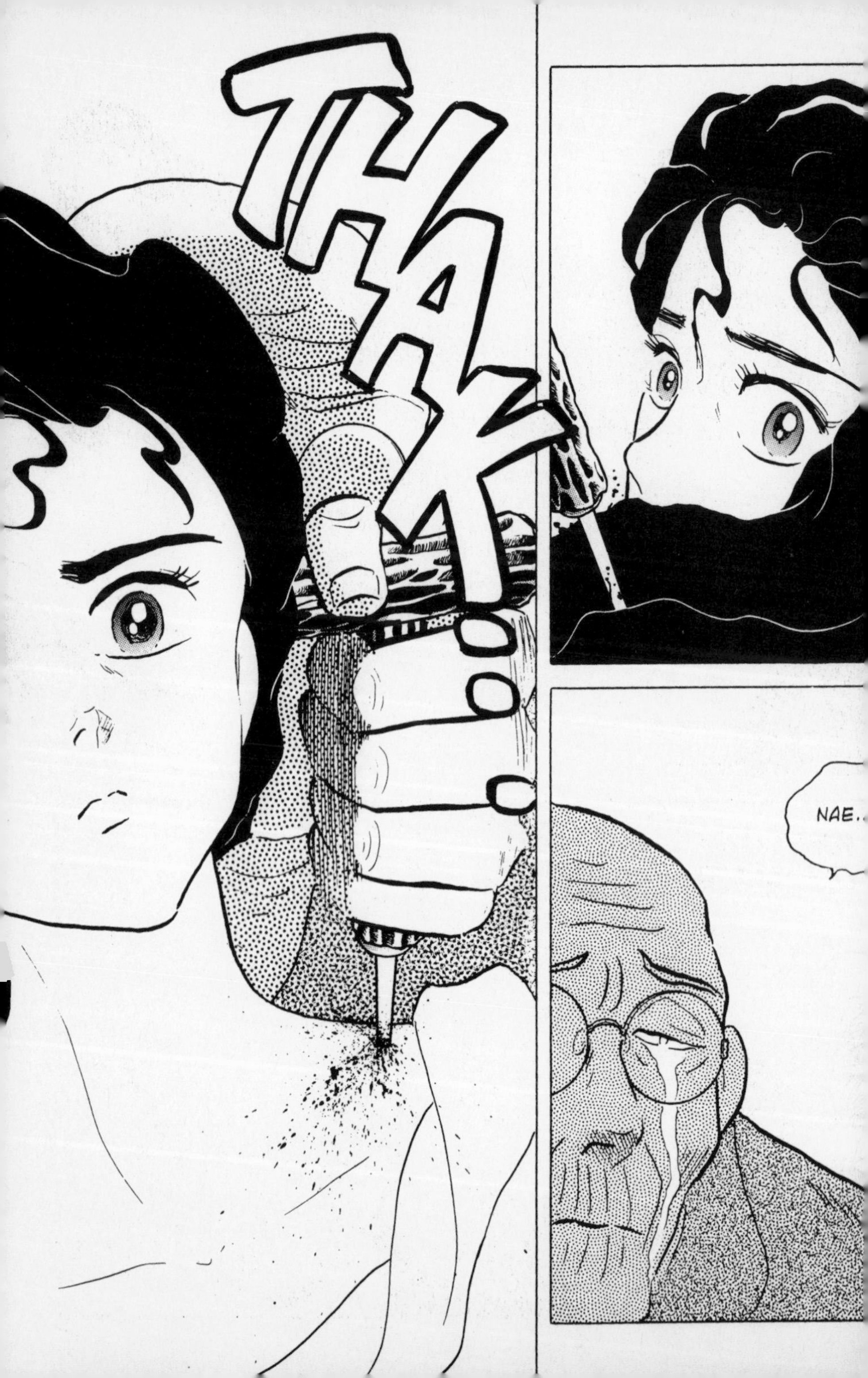
THAK
NAE...

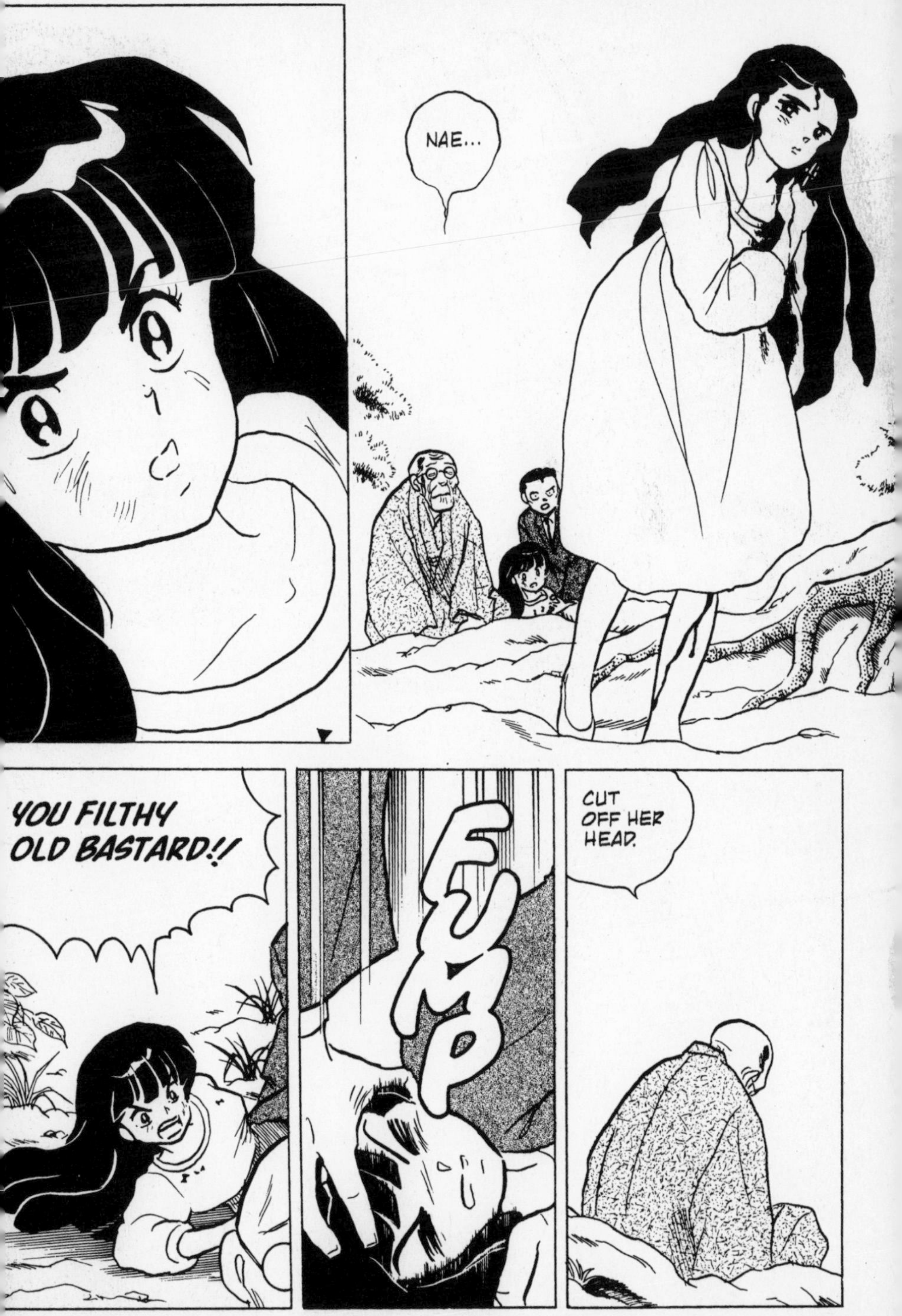
NAE...
YOU FILTHY OLD BASTARD!!
FUMP
CUT OFF HER HEAD.

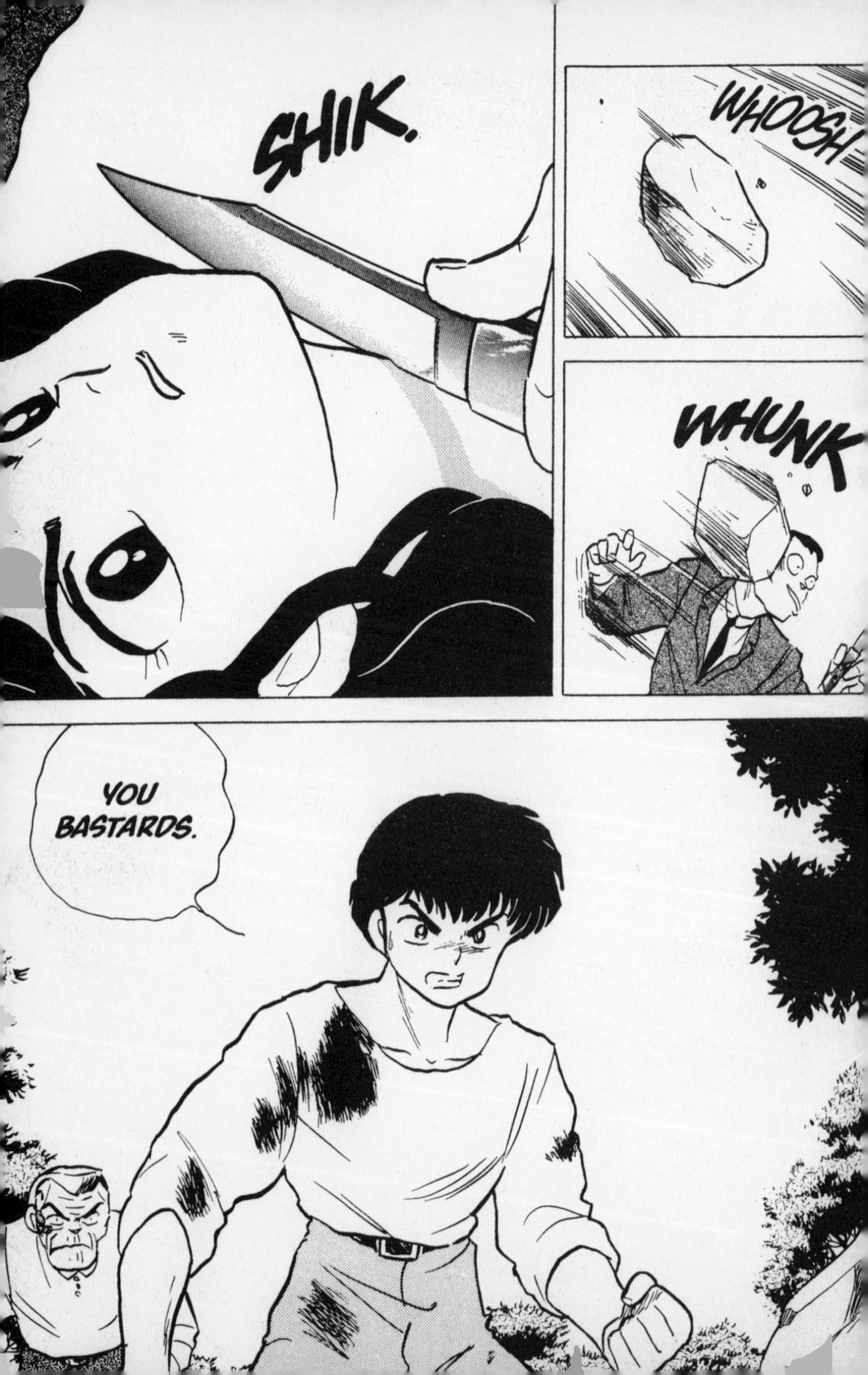
SHIK.
WHOOSH
WHUNK
YOU BASTARDS.

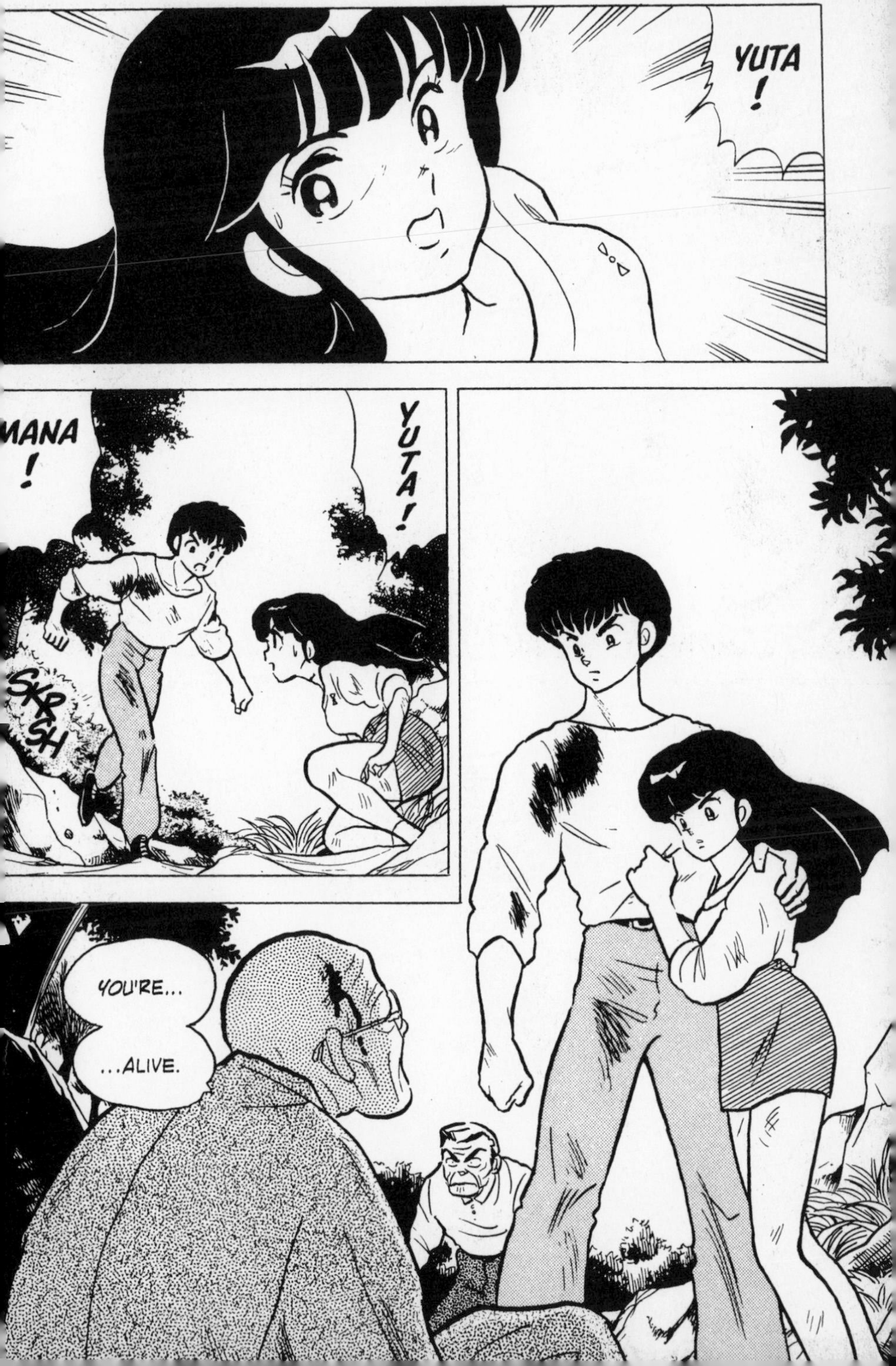
YUTA !
MANA !
YUTA !
SKRSH
YOU'RE...
...ALIVE.

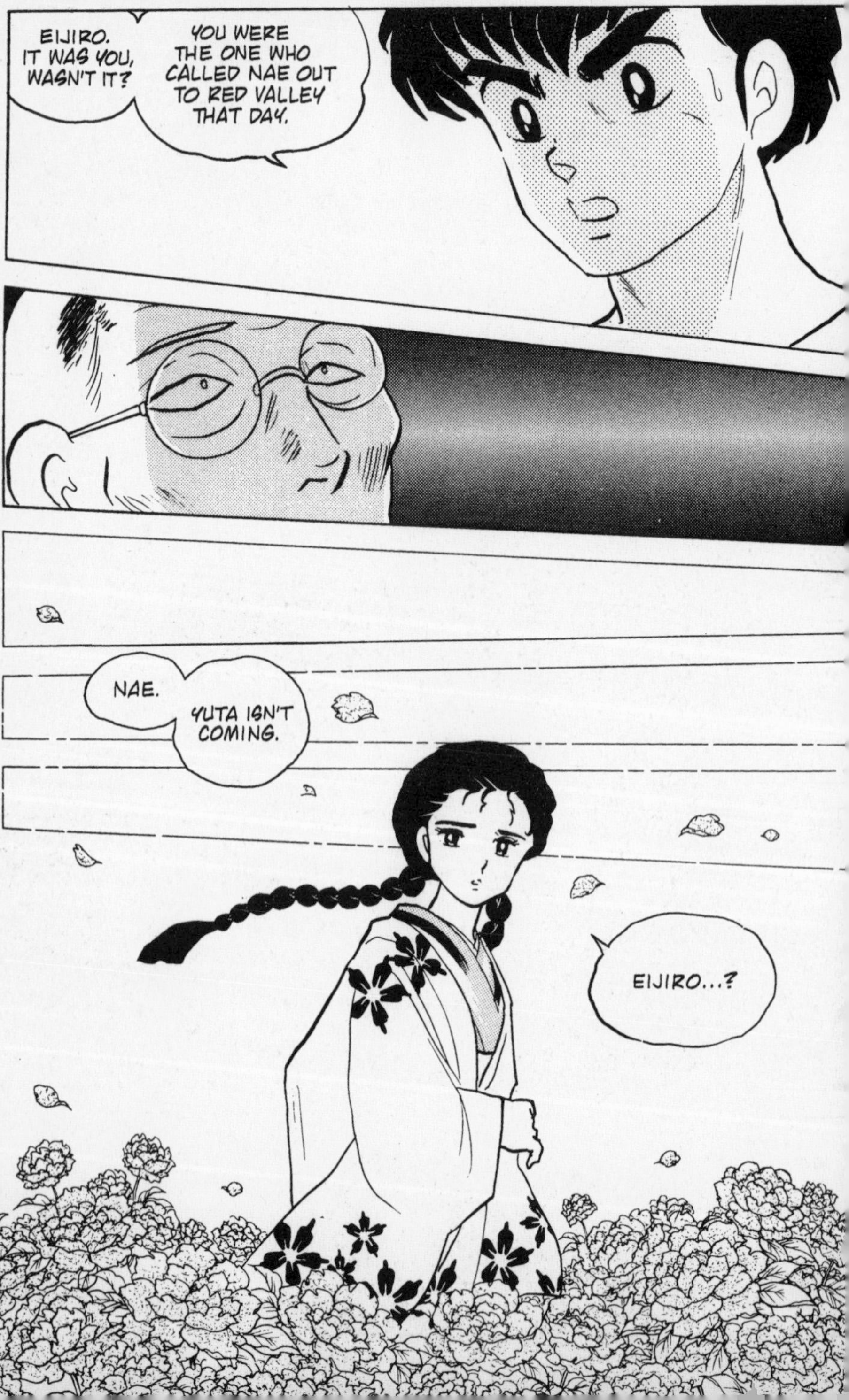
EIJIRO. IT WAS YOU, WASN'T IT?
YOU WERE THE ONE WHO CALLED NAE OUT TO RED VALLEY THAT DAY.
NAE.
YUTA ISN'T COMING.
EIJIRO...?

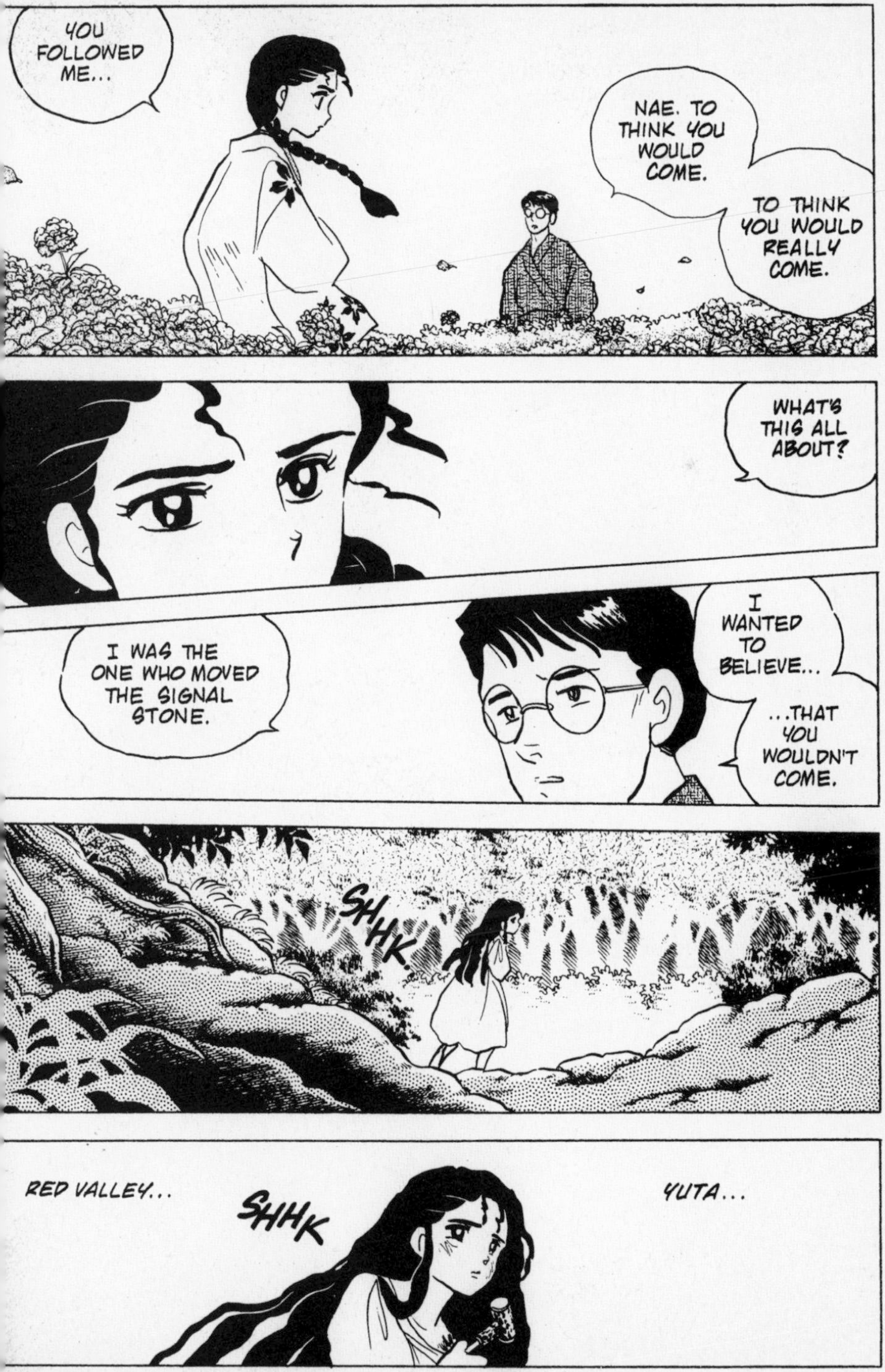
YOU FOLLOWED ME...
NAE. TO THINK YOU WOULD COME.
TO THINK YOU WOULD REALLY COME.
WHAT'S THIS ALL ABOUT?
I WAS THE ONE WHO MOVED THE SIGNAL STONE.
I WANTED TO BELIEVE...
...THAT YOU WOULDN'T COME.
SHHK
RED VALLEY...
SHHK
YUTA...

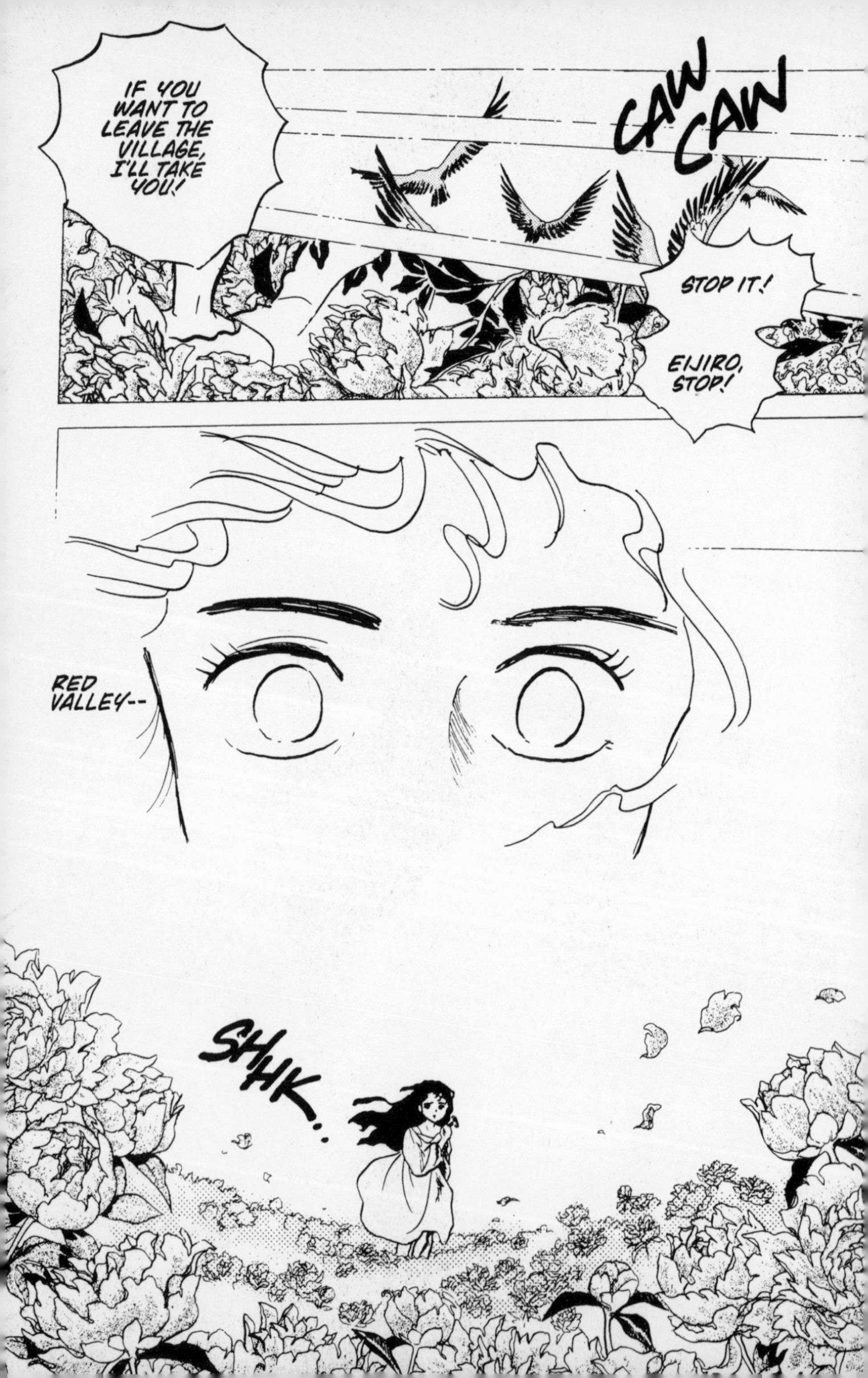

IF YOU WANT TO LEAVE THE VILLAGE, I'LL TAKE YOU!
CAW CAW
STOP IT!
EIJIRO, STOP!
RED VALLEY--
SHHK...

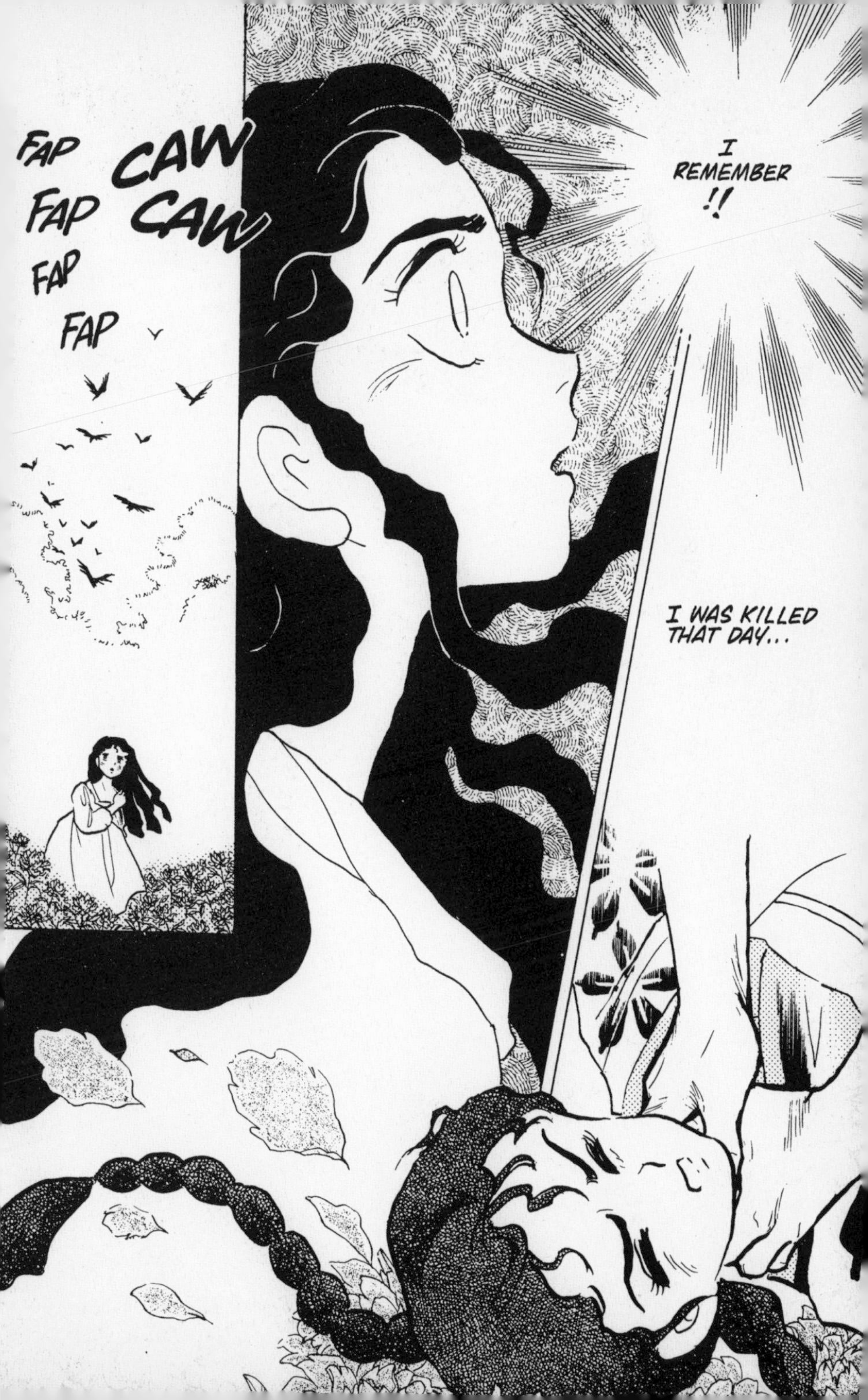
FAP
FAP
FAP
FAP
CAW
CAW
I REMEMBER !!
I WAS KILLED THAT DAY...

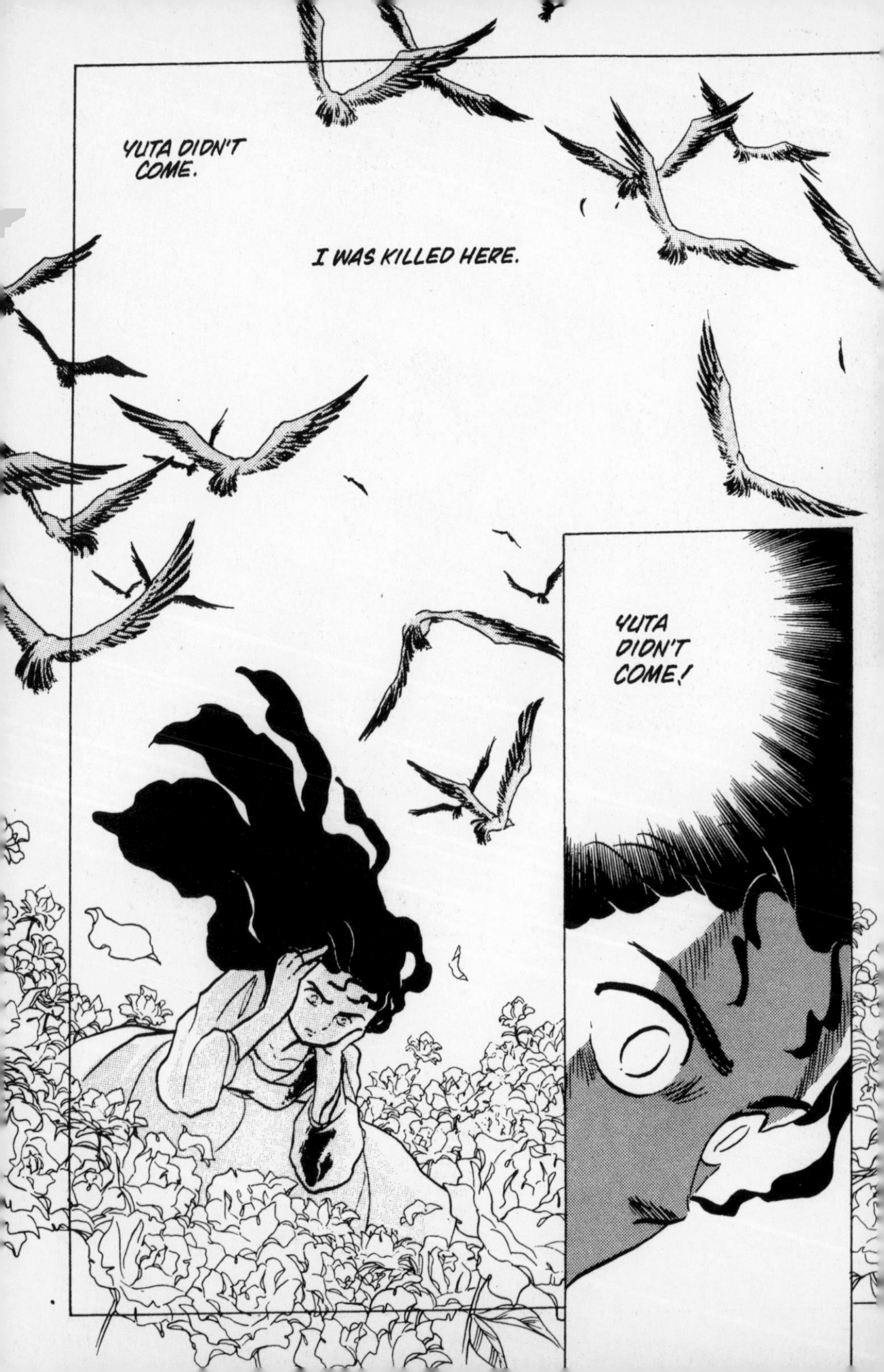
YUTA DIDN'T COME.
I WAS KILLED HERE.
YUTA DIDN'T COME!

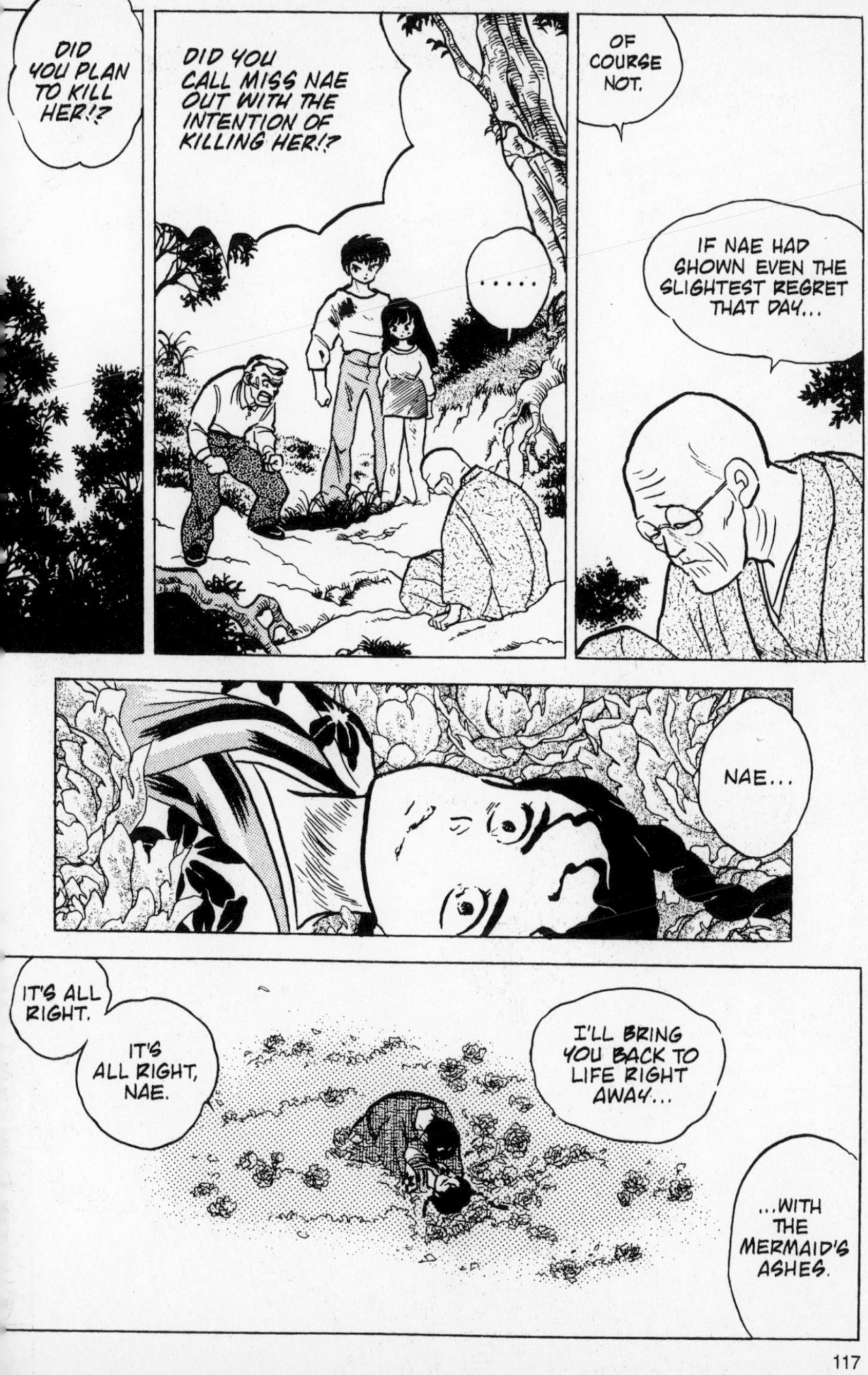
DID YOU PLAN TO KILL HER!?
DID YOU CALL MISS NAE OUT WITH THE INTENTION OF KILLING HER!?
.....
OF COURSE NOT.
IF NAE HAD SHOWN EVEN THE SLIGHTEST REGRET THAT DAY...
NAE...
IT'S ALL RIGHT.
IT'S ALL RIGHT, NAE.
I'LL BRING YOU BACK TO LIFE RIGHT AWAY...
...WITH THE MERMAID'S ASHES.

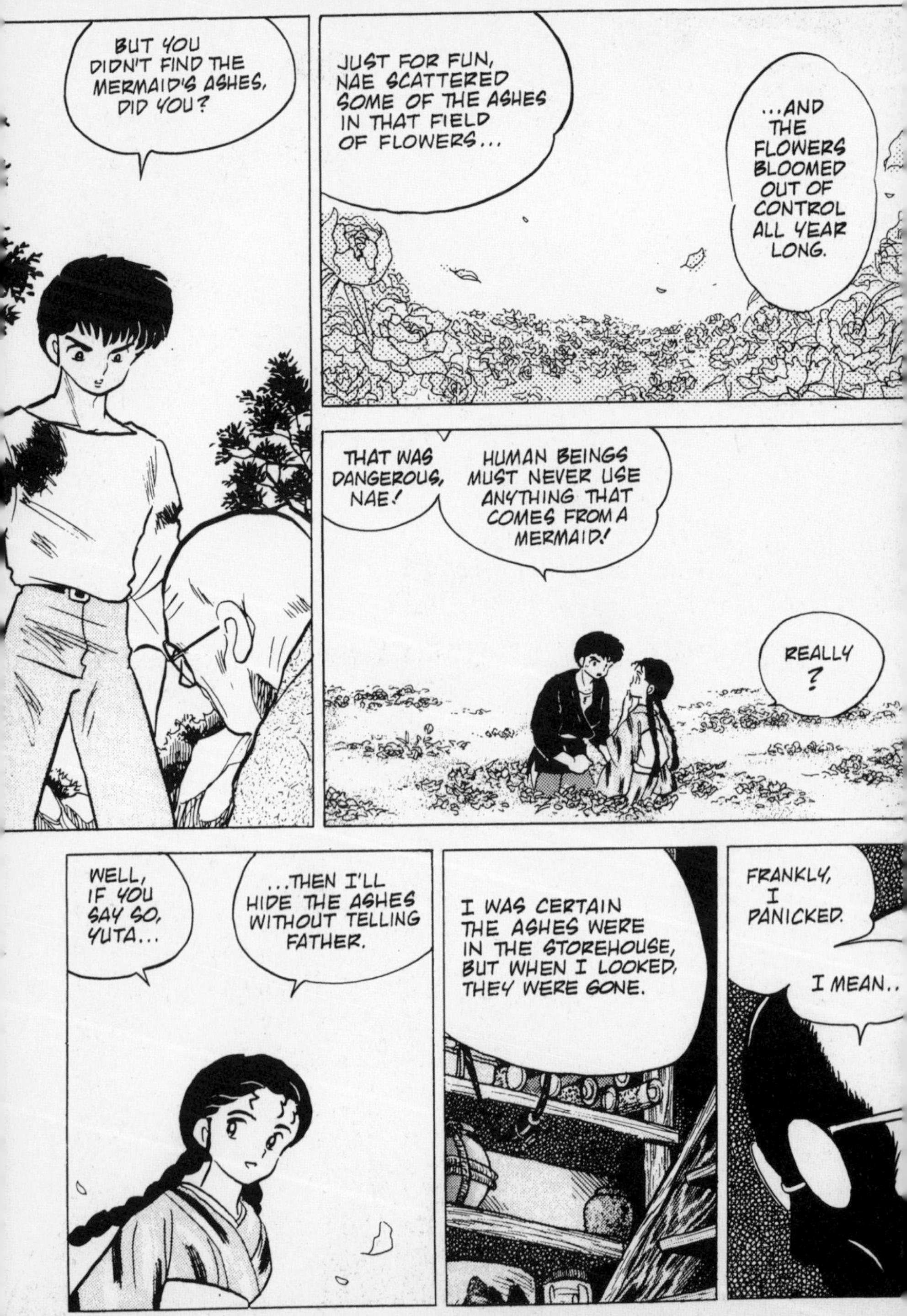
BUT YOU DIDN'T FIND THE MERMAID'S ASHES, DID YOU?
JUST FOR FUN, NAE SCATTERED SOME OF THE ASHES IN THAT FIELD OF FLOWERS...
...AND THE FLOWERS BLOOMED OUT OF CONTROL ALL YEAR LONG.
THAT WAS DANGEROUS, NAE!
HUMAN BEINGS MUST NEVER USE ANYTHING THAT COMES FROM A MERMAID!
REALLY?
WELL, IF YOU SAY SO, YUTA...
...THEN I'LL HIDE THE ASHES WITHOUT TELLING FATHER.
I WAS CERTAIN THE ASHES WERE IN THE STOREHOUSE, BUT WHEN I LOOKED, THEY WERE GONE.
FRANKLY, I PANICKED.
I MEAN...

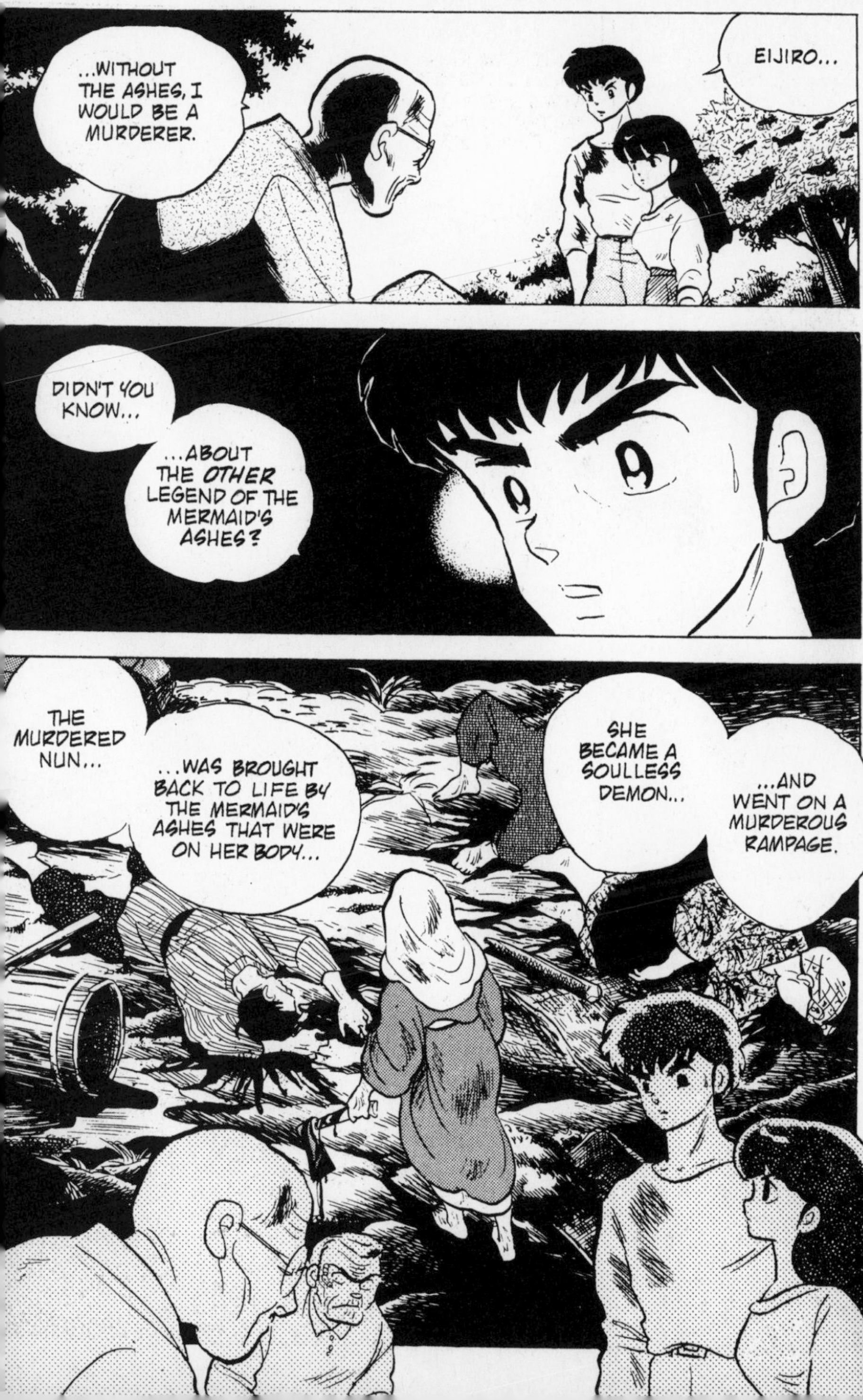
...WITHOUT THE ASHES, I WOULD BE A MURDERER.
EIJIRO...
DIDN'T YOU KNOW...
...ABOUT THE *OTHER* LEGEND OF THE MERMAID'S ASHES?
THE MURDERED NUN...
...WAS BROUGHT BACK TO LIFE BY THE MERMAID'S ASHES THAT WERE ON HER BODY...
SHE BECAME A SOULLESS DEMON...
...AND WENT ON A MURDEROUS RAMPAGE.

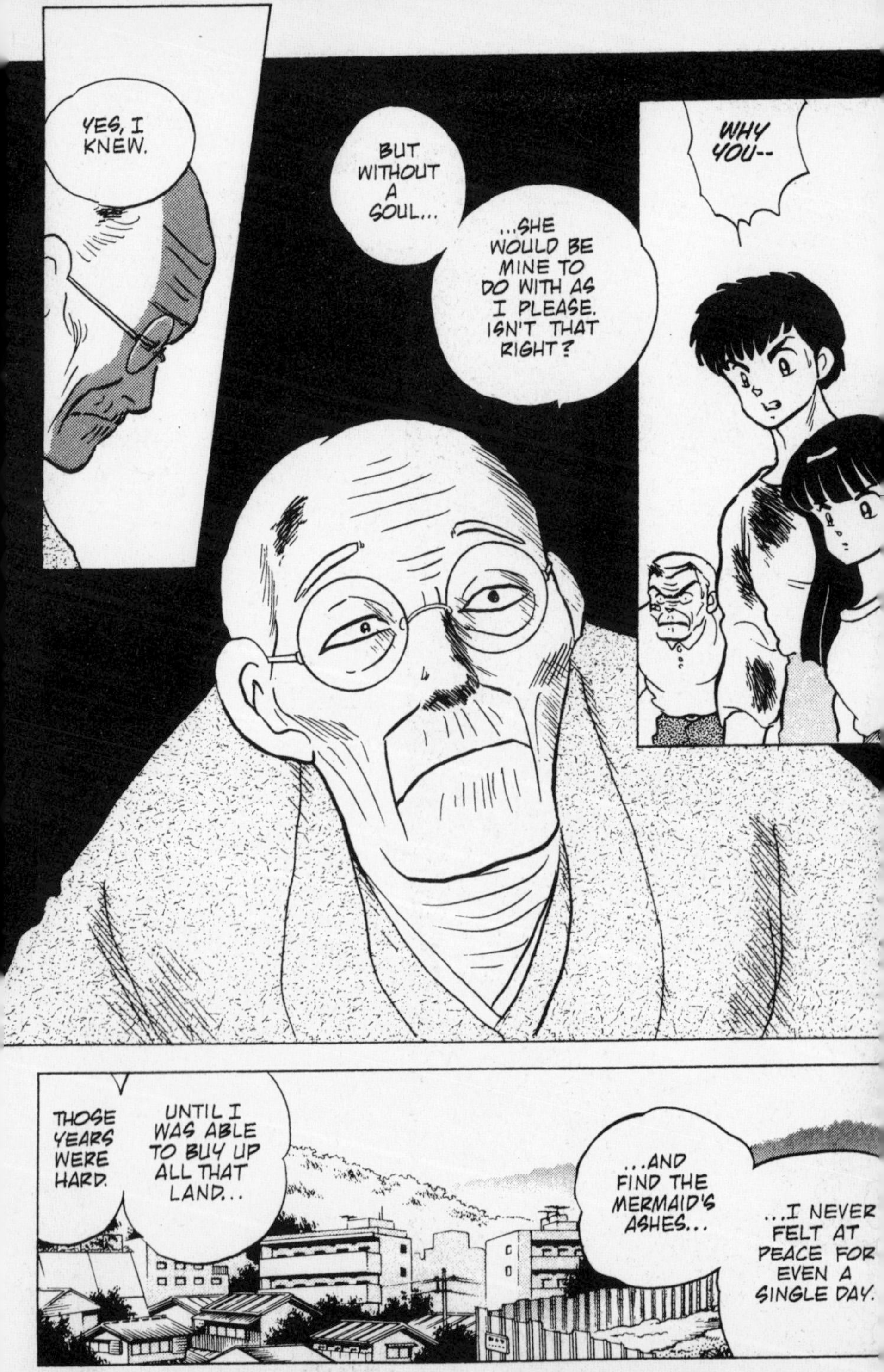
YES, I KNEW.
BUT WITHOUT A SOUL...
...SHE WOULD BE MINE TO DO WITH AS I PLEASE. ISN'T THAT RIGHT?
WHY YOU--
THOSE YEARS WERE HARD.
UNTIL I WAS ABLE TO BUY UP ALL THAT LAND...
...AND FIND THE MERMAID'S ASHES...
...I NEVER FELT AT PEACE FOR EVEN A SINGLE DAY.

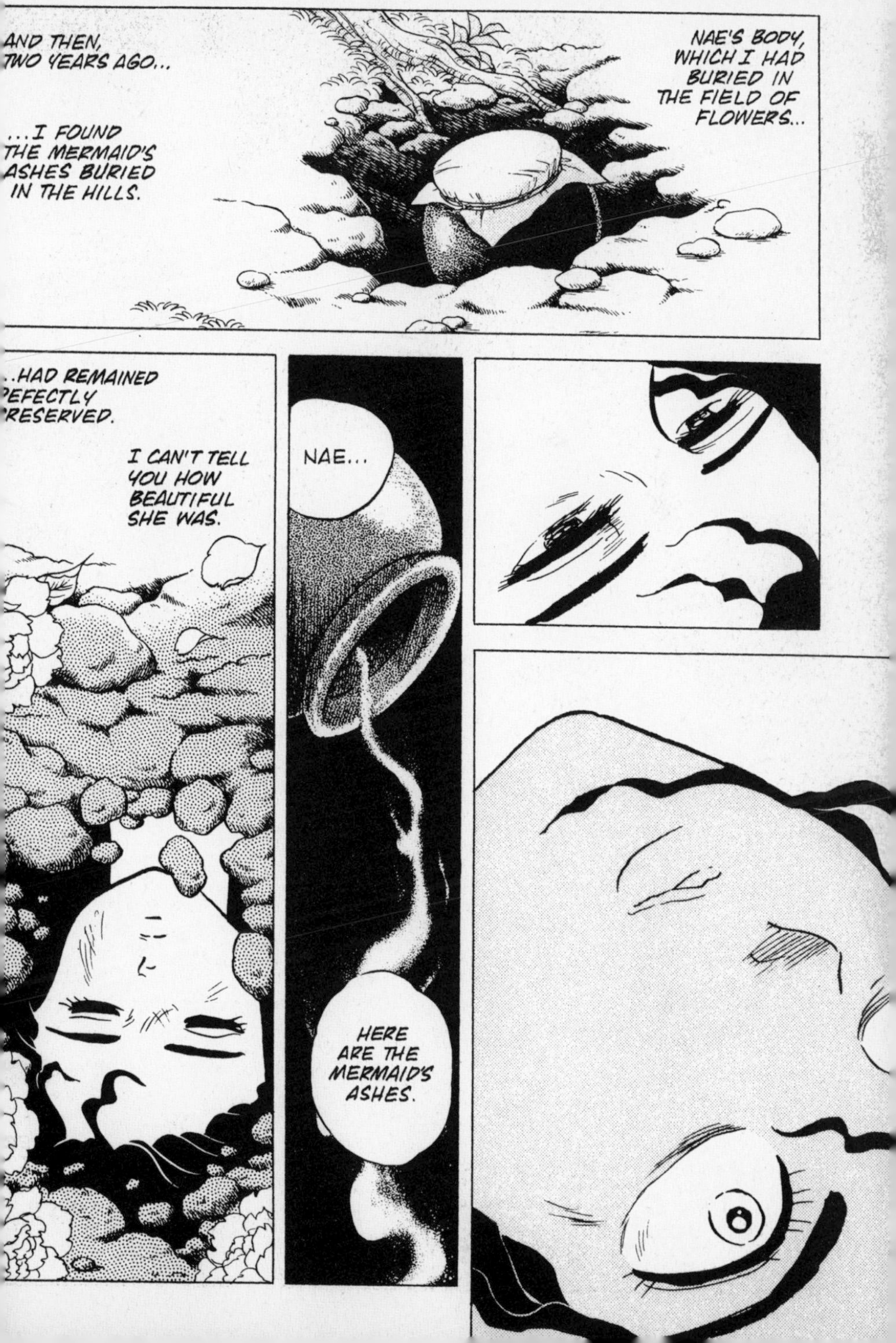
AND THEN, TWO YEARS AGO...
...I FOUND THE MERMAID'S ASHES BURIED IN THE HILLS.
NAE'S BODY, WHICH I HAD BURIED IN THE FIELD OF FLOWERS...
..HAD REMAINED PEFECTLY RESERVED.
I CAN'T TELL YOU HOW BEAUTIFUL SHE WAS.
NAE...
HERE ARE THE MERMAID'S ASHES.

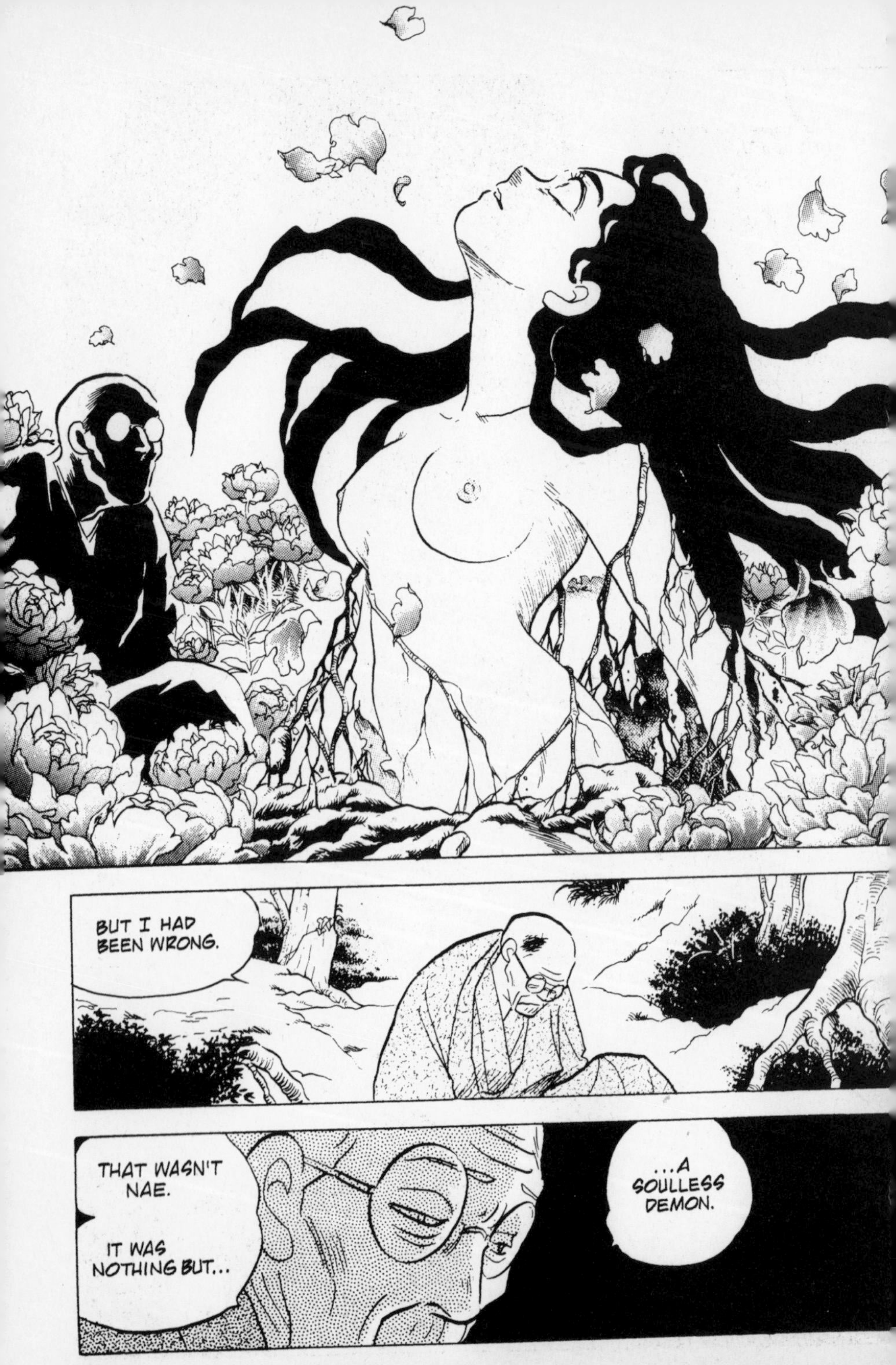
BUT I HAD BEEN WRONG.
THAT WASN'T NAE.
IT WAS NOTHING BUT...
...A SOULLESS DEMON.

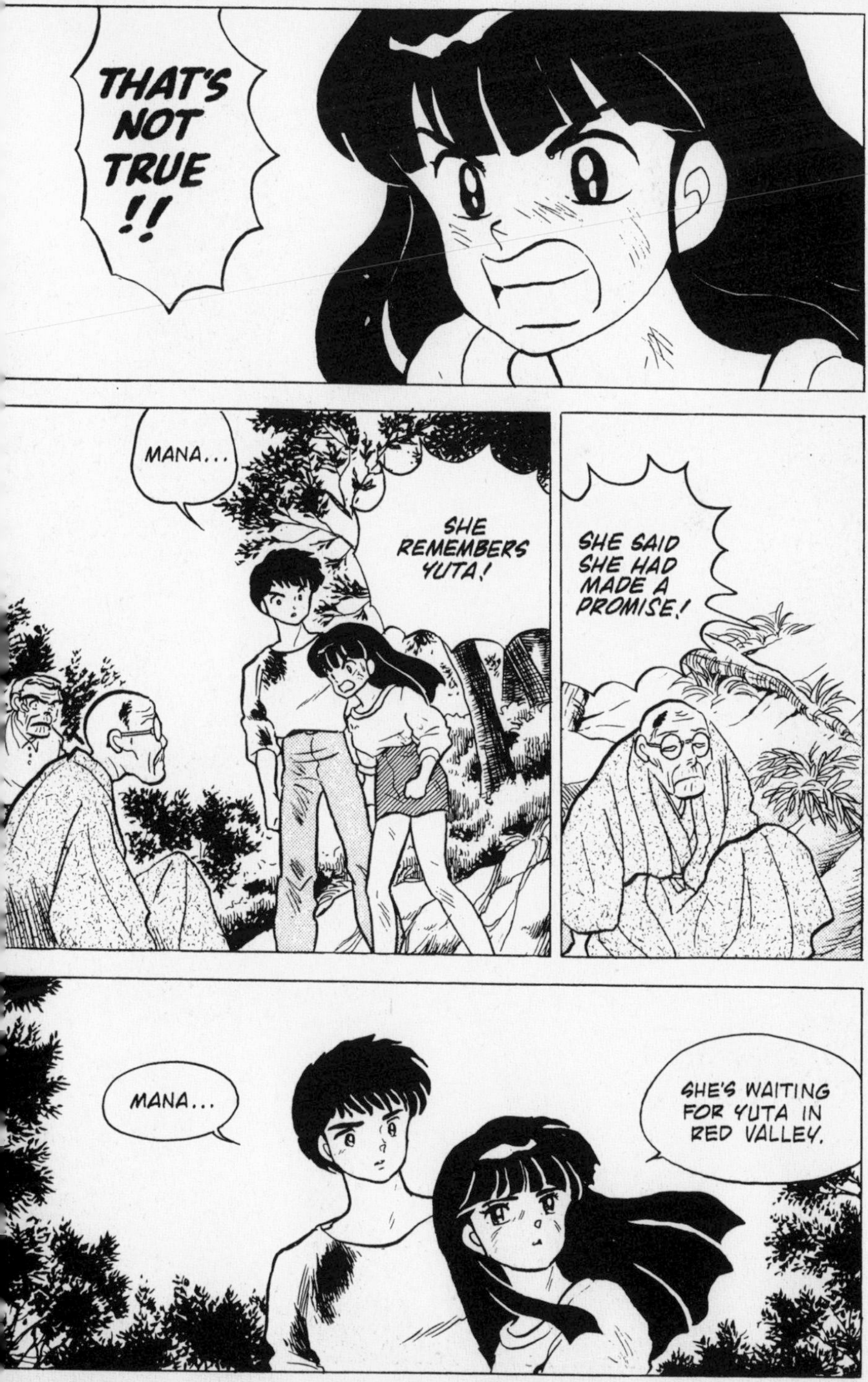
THAT'S NOT TRUE!!
MANA...
SHE REMEMBERS YUTA!
SHE SAID SHE HAD MADE A PROMISE!
MANA...
SHE'S WAITING FOR YUTA IN RED VALLEY.

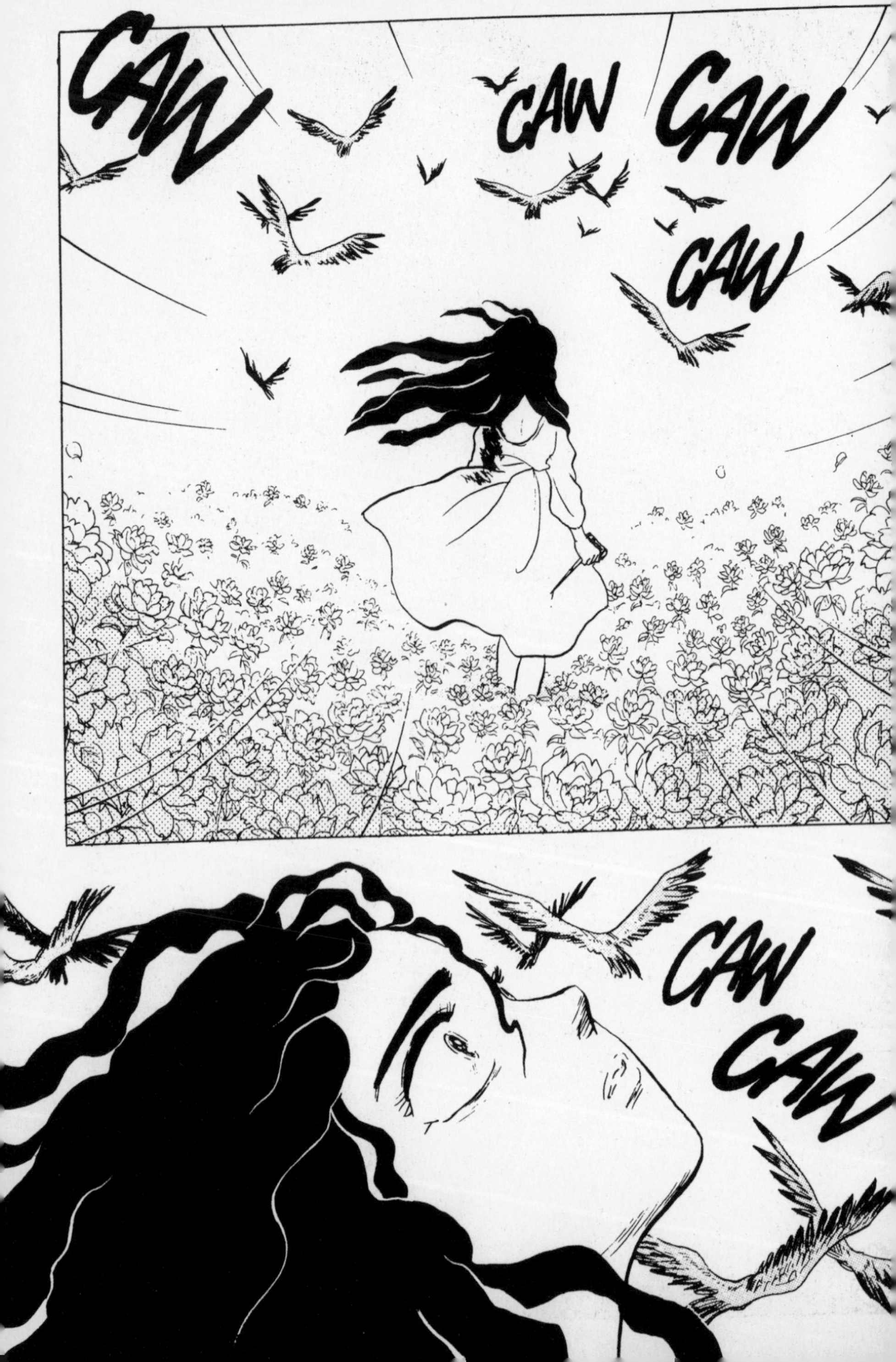
CAW
CAW
CAW
CAW
CAW
CAW

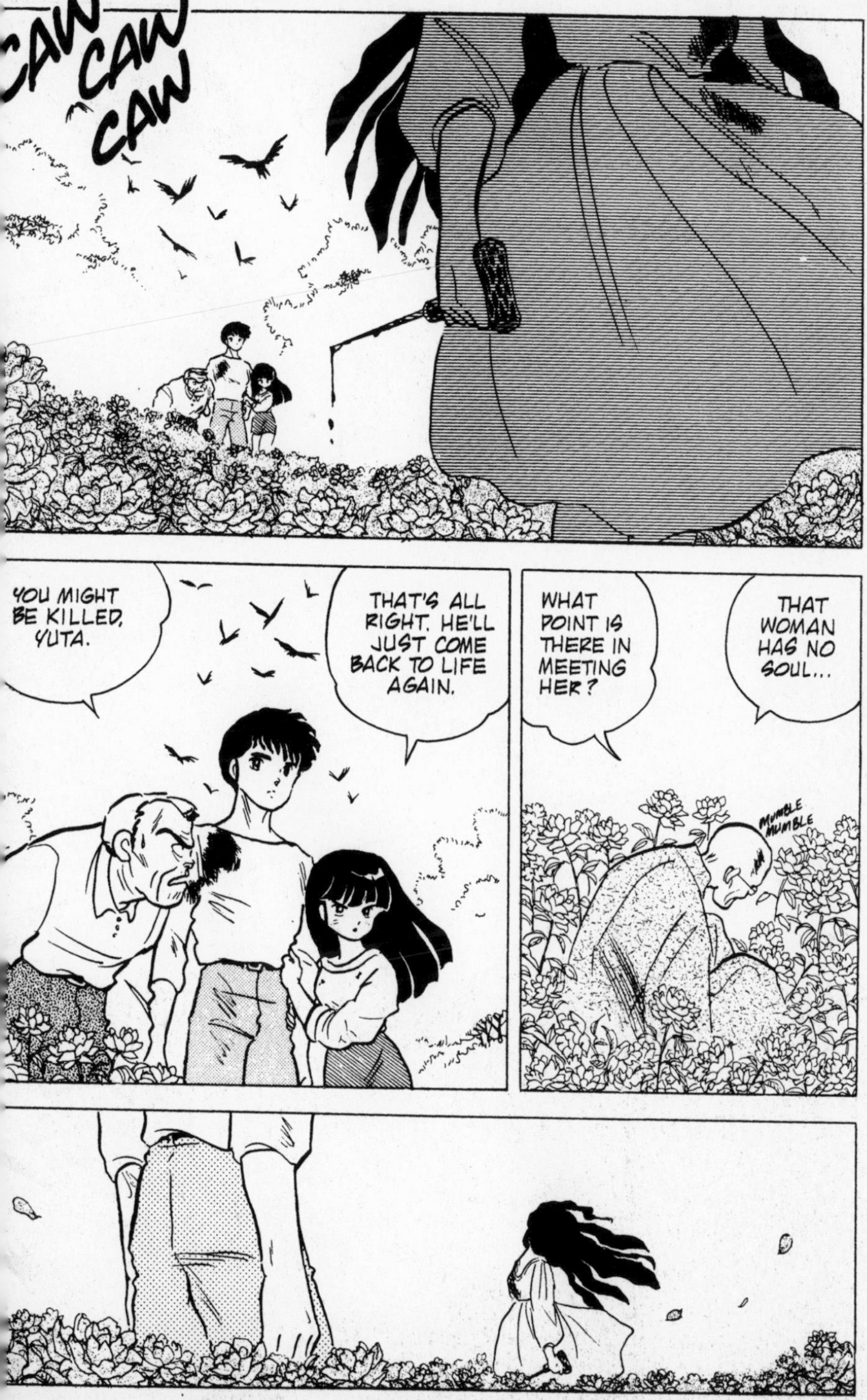
CAW CAW CAW
YOU MIGHT BE KILLED, YUTA.
THAT'S ALL RIGHT. HE'LL JUST COME BACK TO LIFE AGAIN.
WHAT POINT IS THERE IN MEETING HER?
THAT WOMAN HAS NO SOUL...
MUMBLE MUMBLE

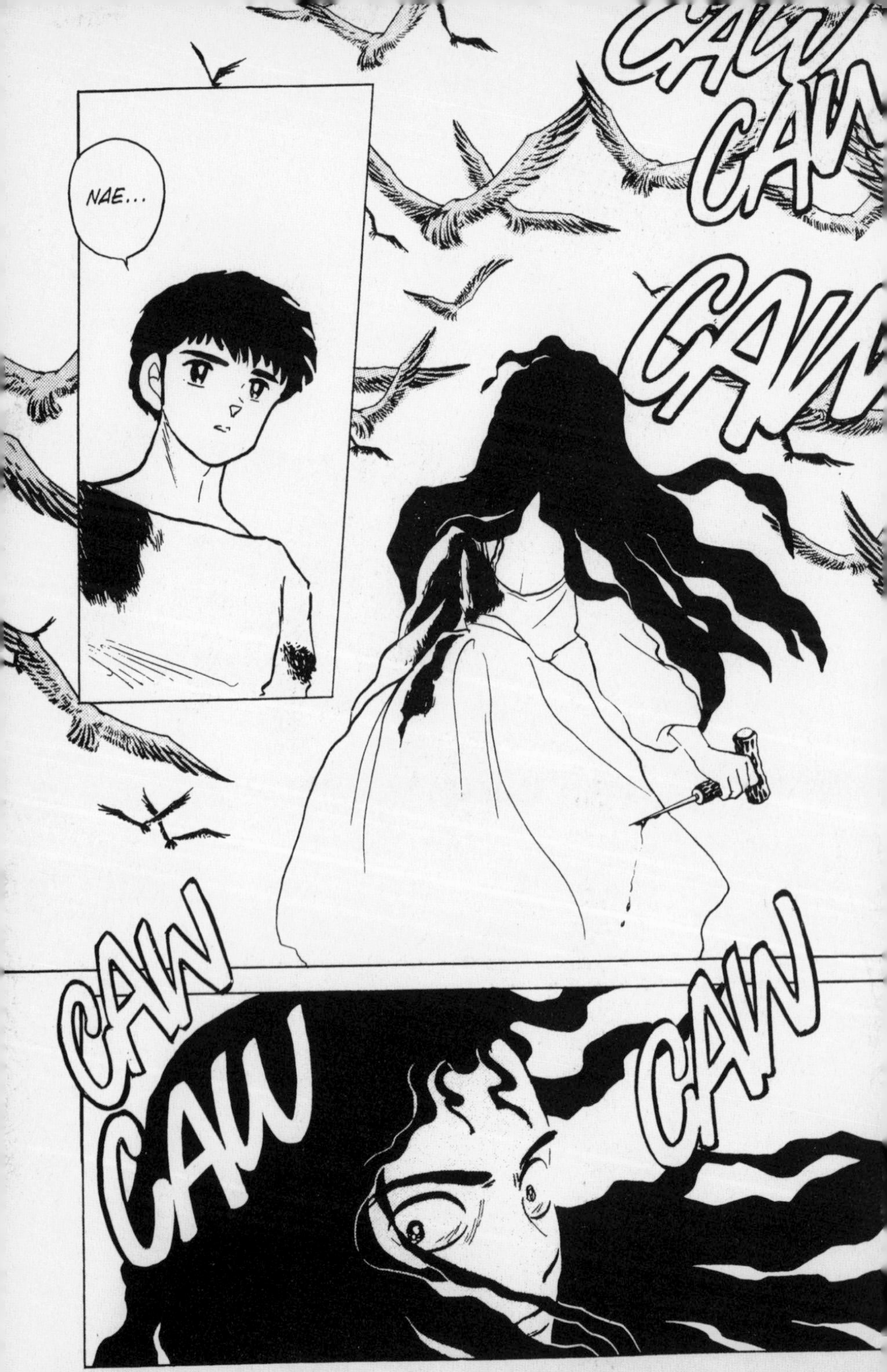
NAE...
CAW
CAW
CAW
CAW
CAW
CAW

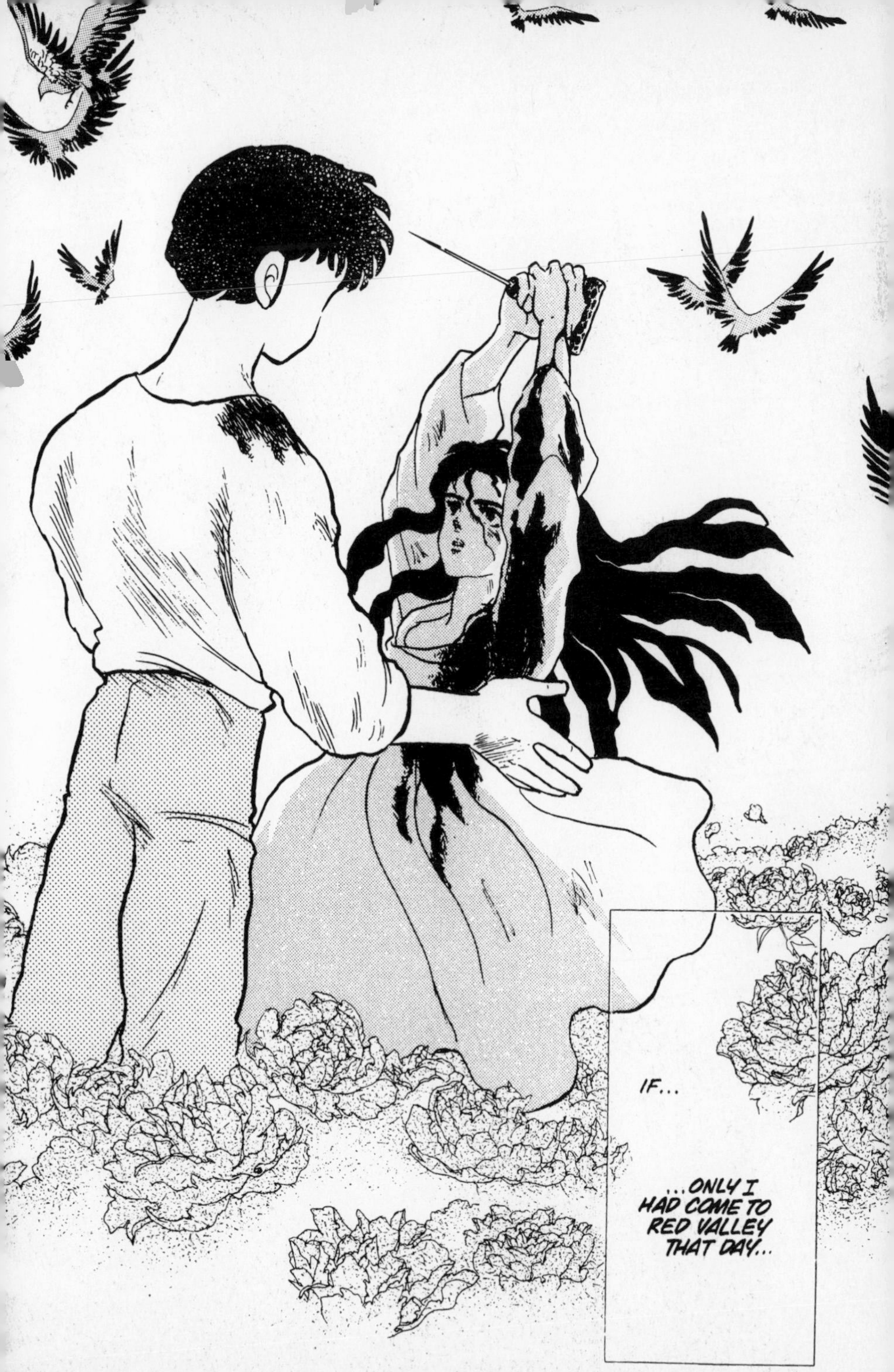
IF...
...ONLY I HAD COME TO RED VALLEY THAT DAY...

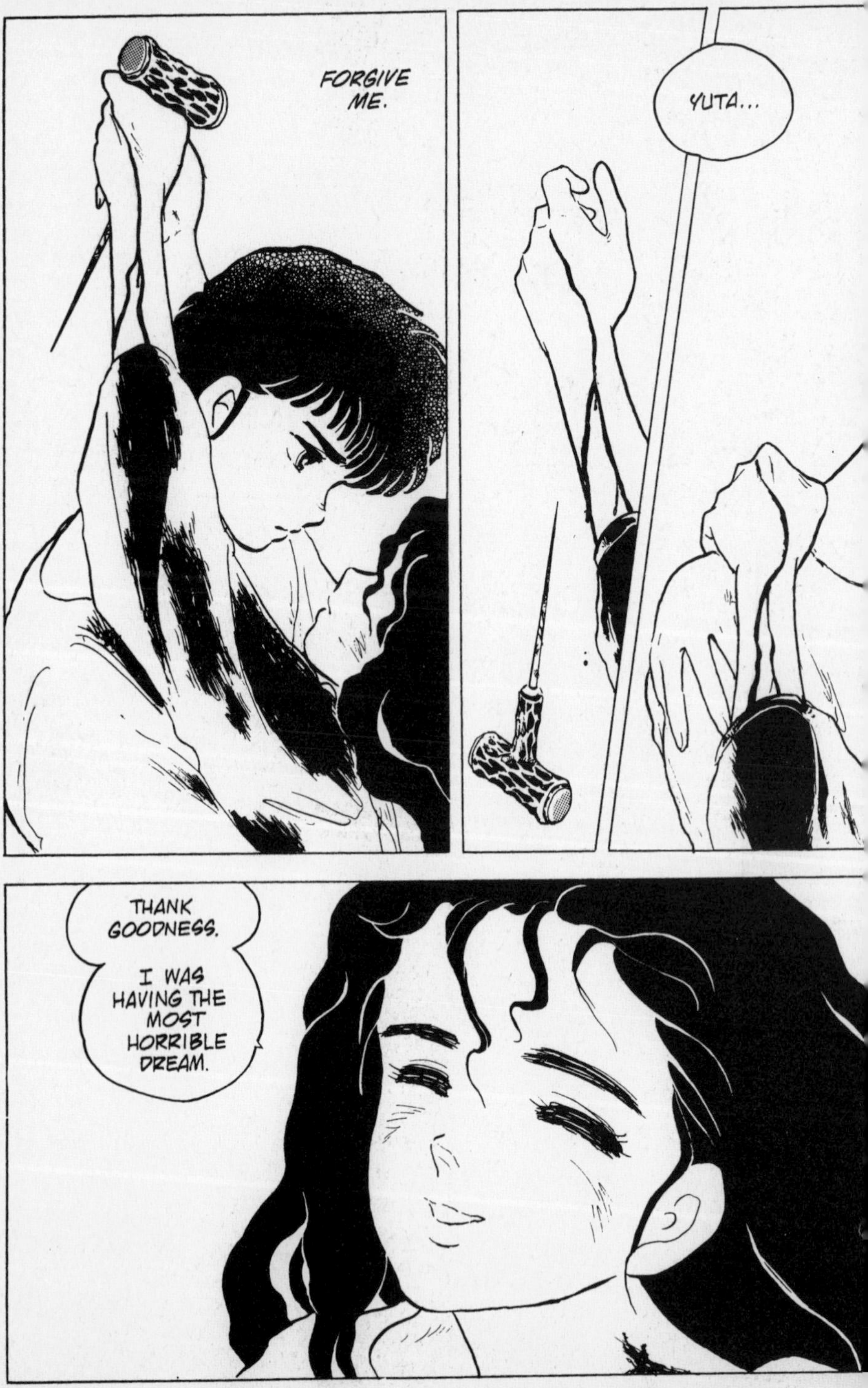
FORGIVE ME.
YUTA...
THANK GOODNESS.
I WAS HAVING THE MOST HORRIBLE DREAM.

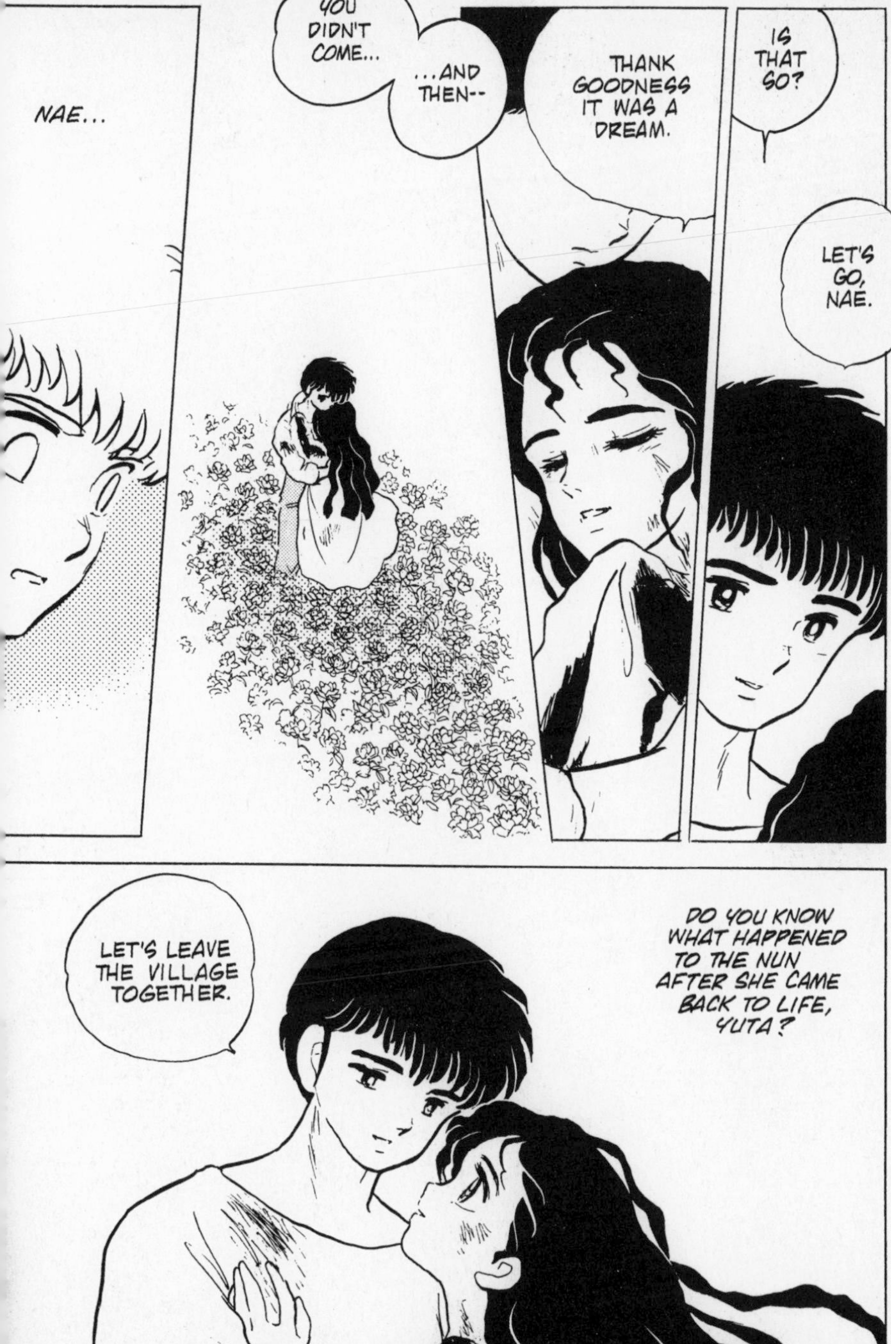
NAE...
YOU DIDN'T COME...
...AND THEN--
THANK GOODNESS IT WAS A DREAM.
IS THAT SO?
LET'S GO, NAE.
LET'S LEAVE THE VILLAGE TOGETHER.
DO YOU KNOW WHAT HAPPENED TO THE NUN AFTER SHE CAME BACK TO LIFE, YUTA?

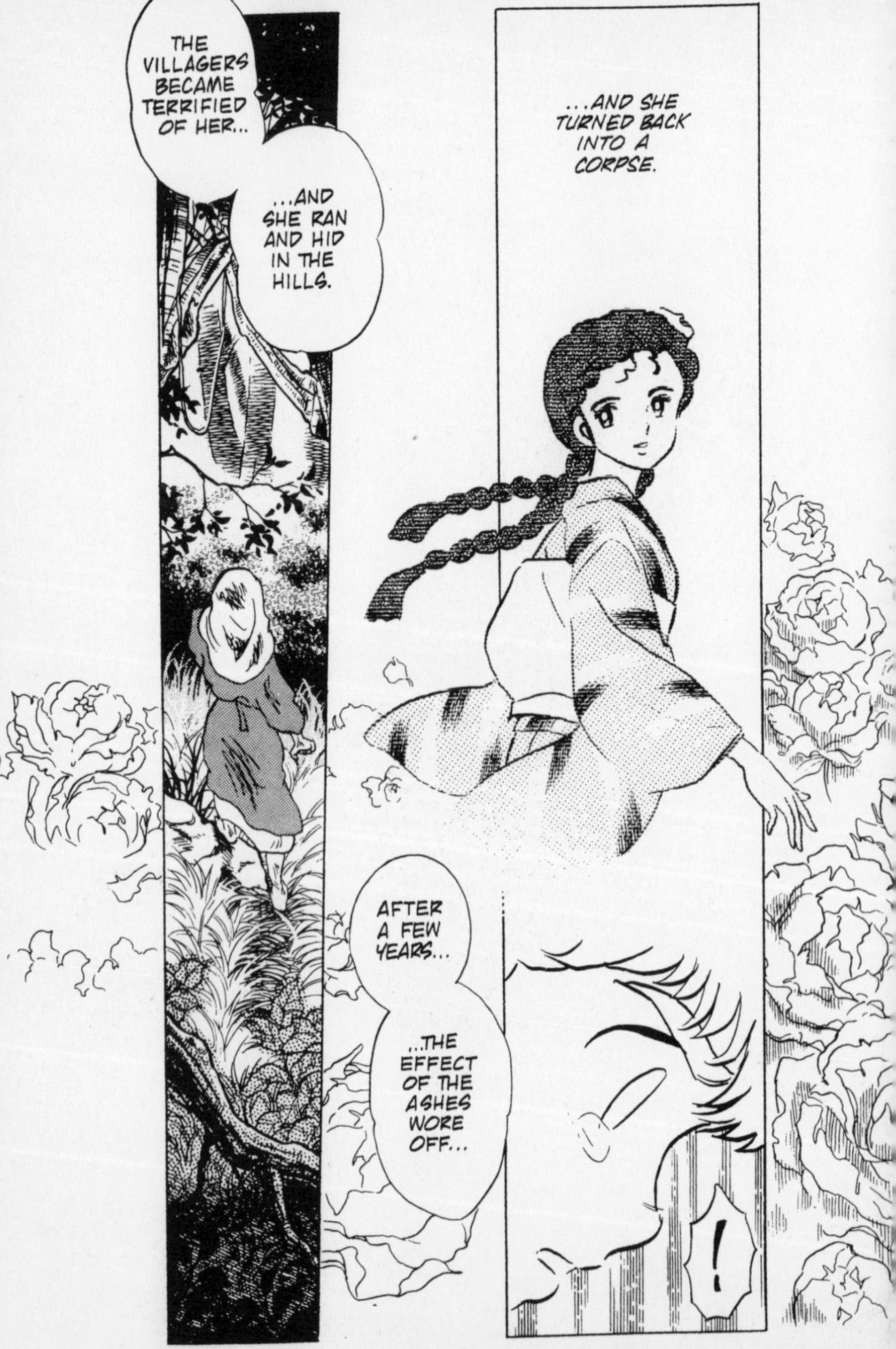
THE VILLAGERS BECAME TERRIFIED OF HER...
...AND SHE RAN AND HID IN THE HILLS.
AFTER A FEW YEARS...
...THE EFFECT OF THE ASHES WORE OFF...
...AND SHE TURNED BACK INTO A CORPSE.
!

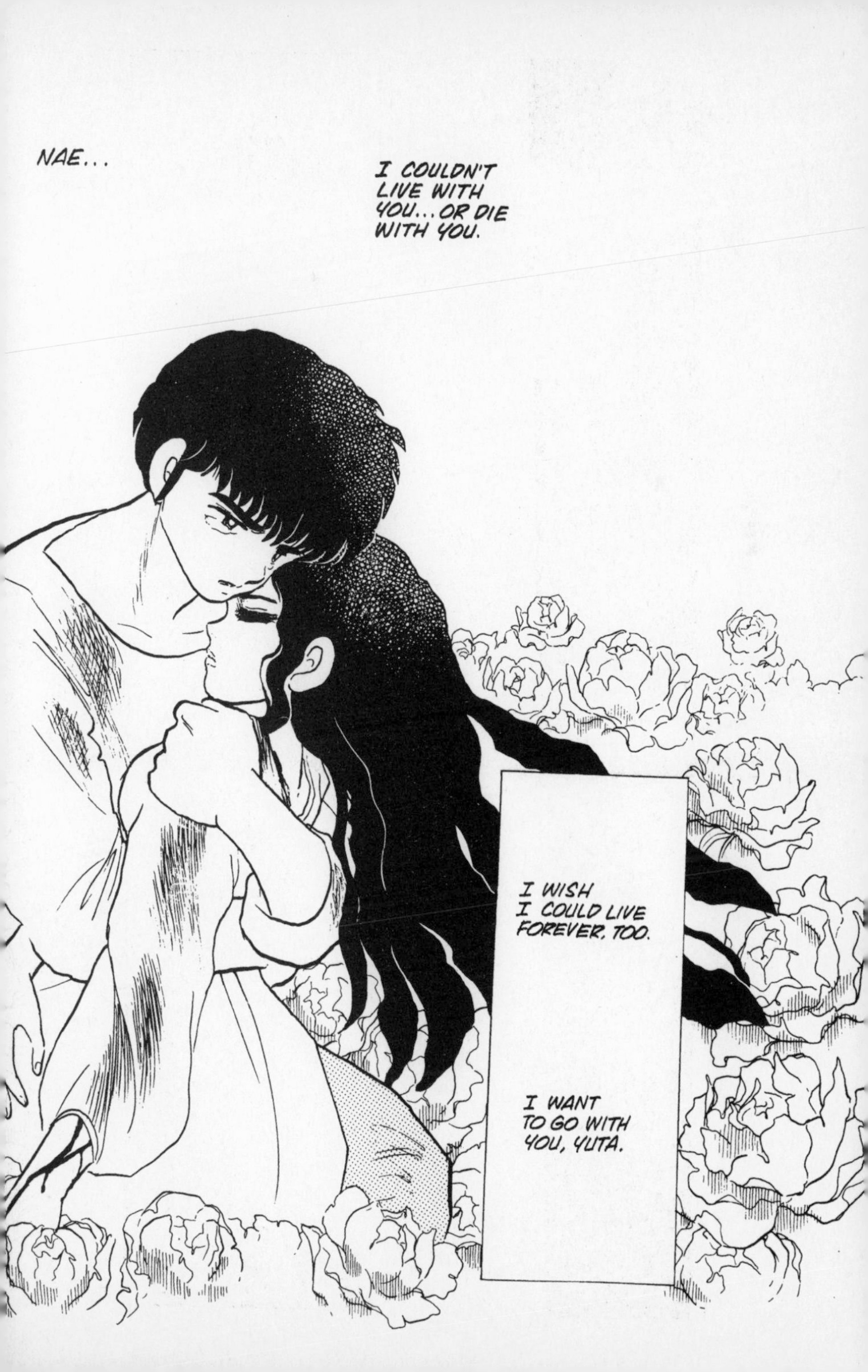
NAE...
I COULDN'T LIVE WITH YOU... OR DIE WITH YOU.
I WISH I COULD LIVE FOREVER, TOO.
I WANT TO GO WITH YOU, YUTA.

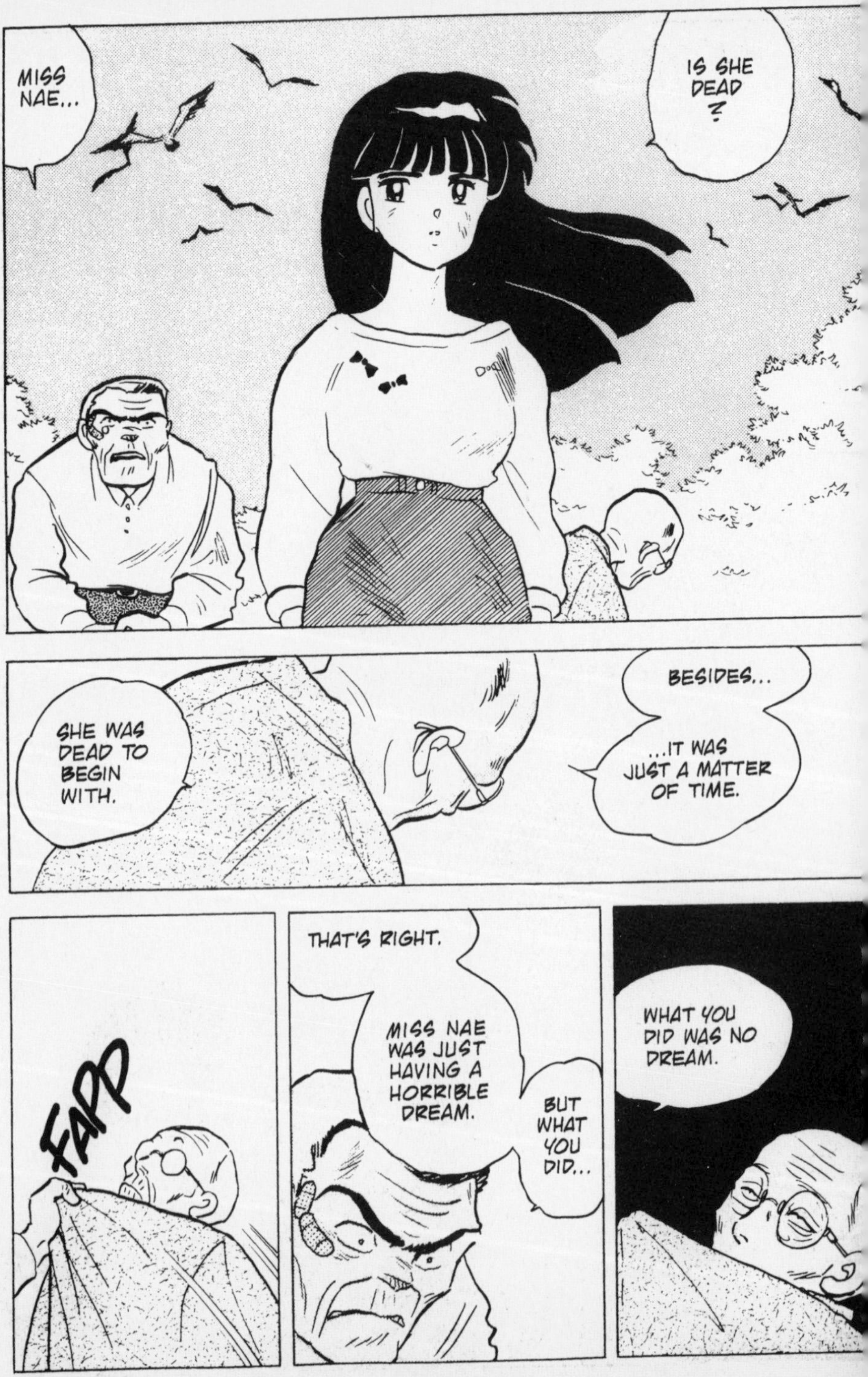
MISS NAE...
IS SHE DEAD?
SHE WAS DEAD TO BEGIN WITH.
BESIDES...
...IT WAS JUST A MATTER OF TIME.
FAPP
THAT'S RIGHT.
MISS NAE WAS JUST HAVING A HORRIBLE DREAM.
BUT WHAT YOU DID...
WHAT YOU DID WAS NO DREAM.

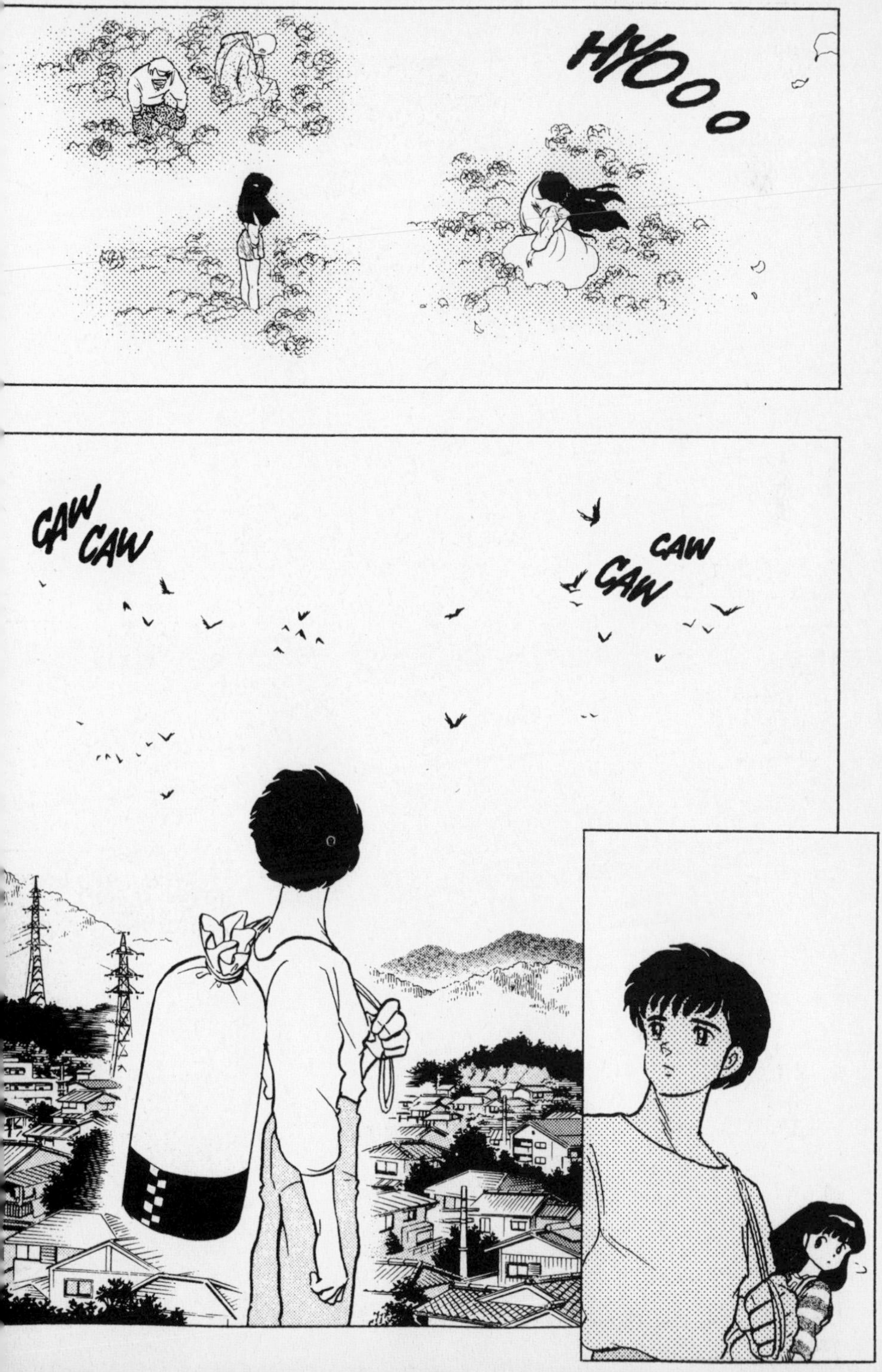
HYOOO
CAW CAW
CAW CAW

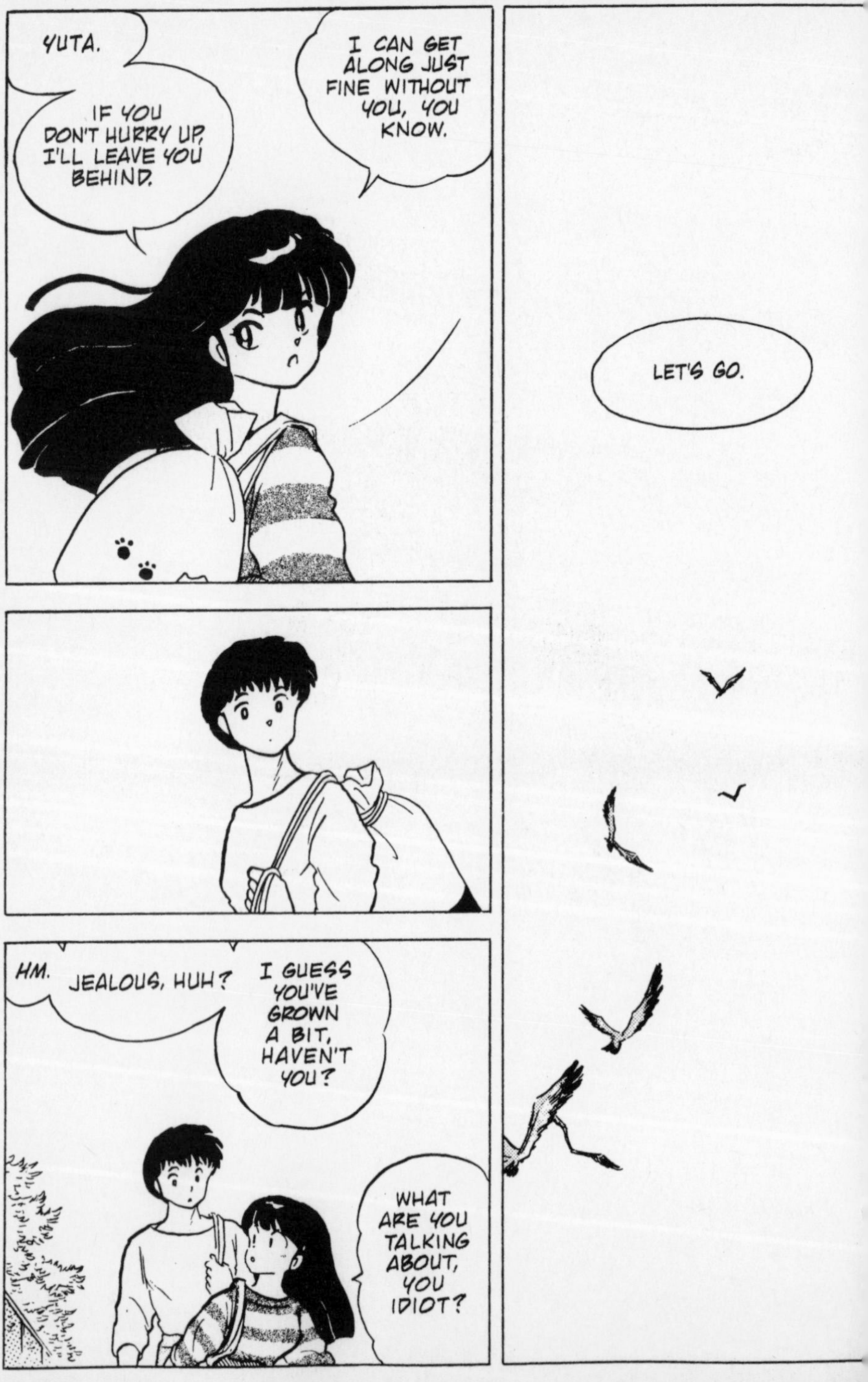
YUTA.
IF YOU DON'T HURRY UP, I'LL LEAVE YOU BEHIND.
I CAN GET ALONG JUST FINE WITHOUT YOU, YOU KNOW.
HM.
JEALOUS, HUH?
I GUESS YOU'VE GROWN A BIT, HAVEN'T YOU?
WHAT ARE YOU TALKING ABOUT, YOU IDIOT?
LET'S GO.

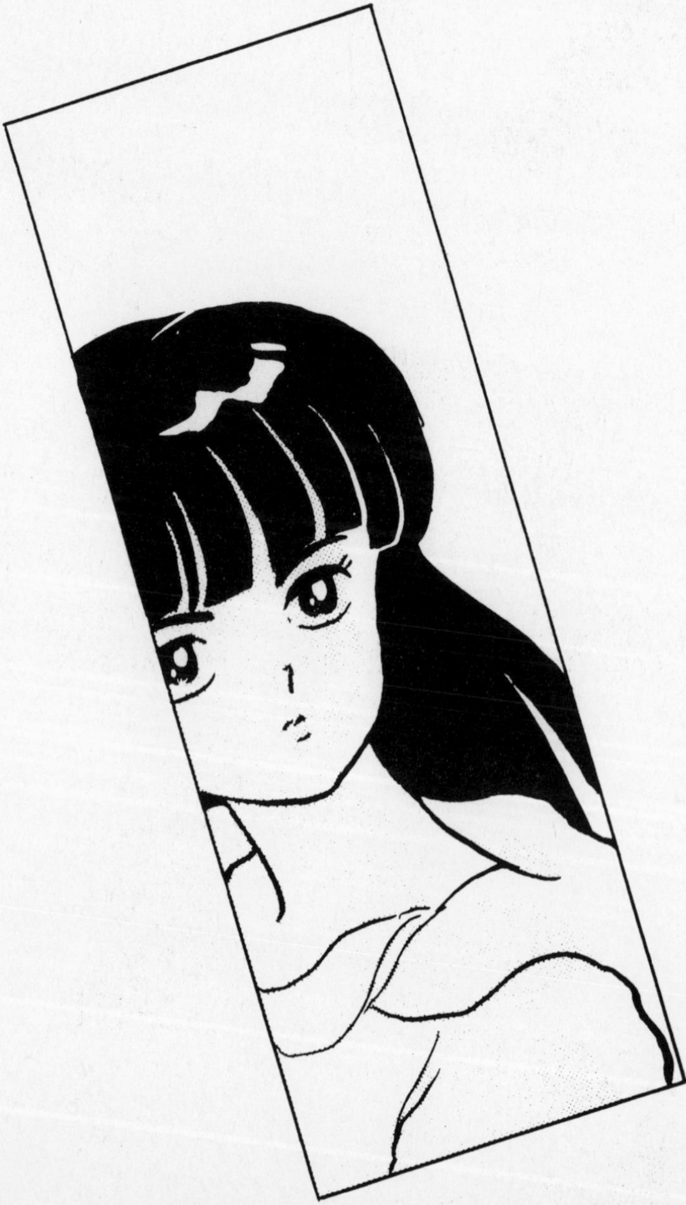

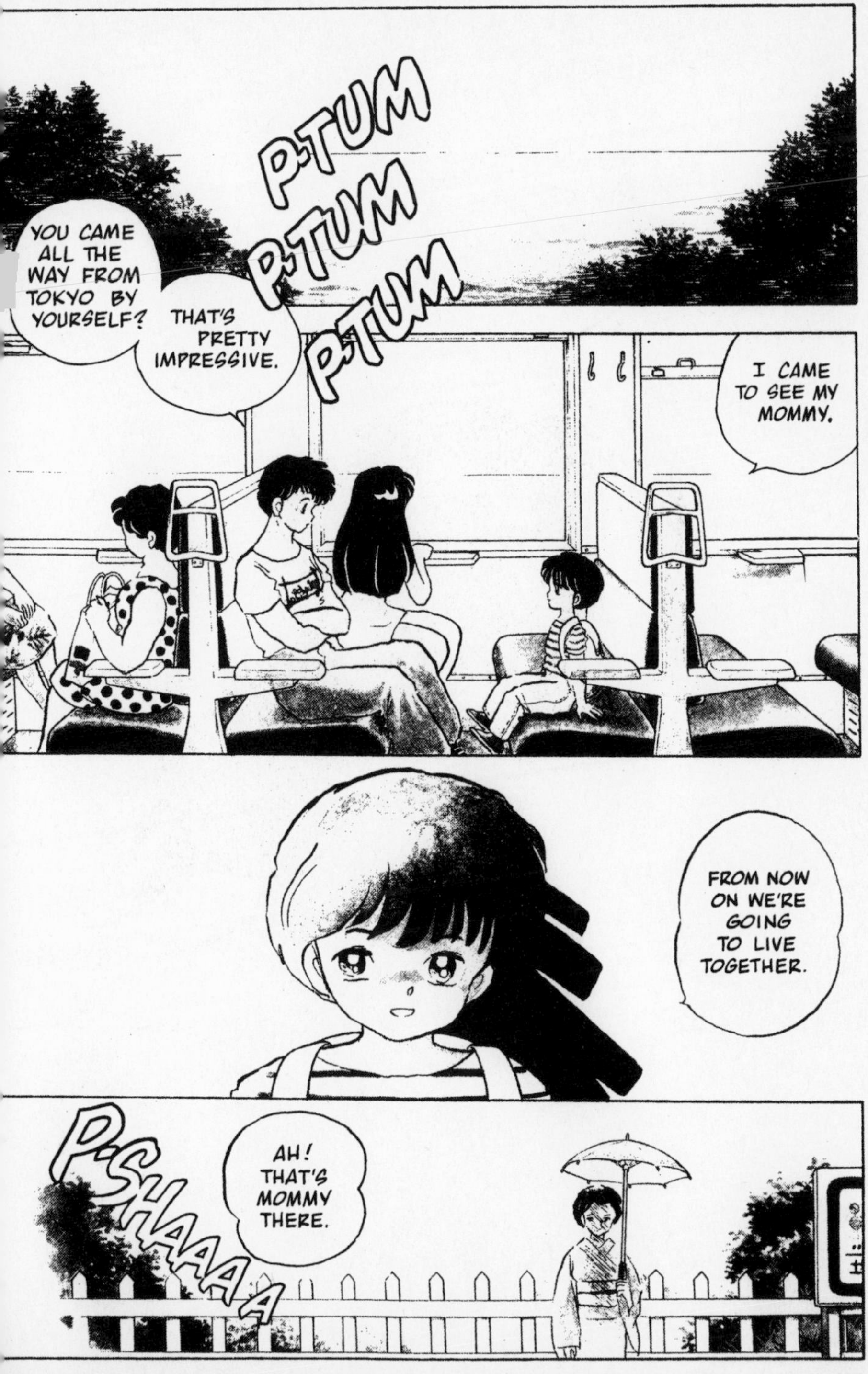
P-TUM P-TUM P-TUM
YOU CAME ALL THE WAY FROM TOKYO BY YOURSELF?
THAT'S PRETTY IMPRESSIVE.
I CAME TO SEE MY MOMMY.
FROM NOW ON WE'RE GOING TO LIVE TOGETHER.
P-SHAAAA
AH! THAT'S MOMMY THERE.

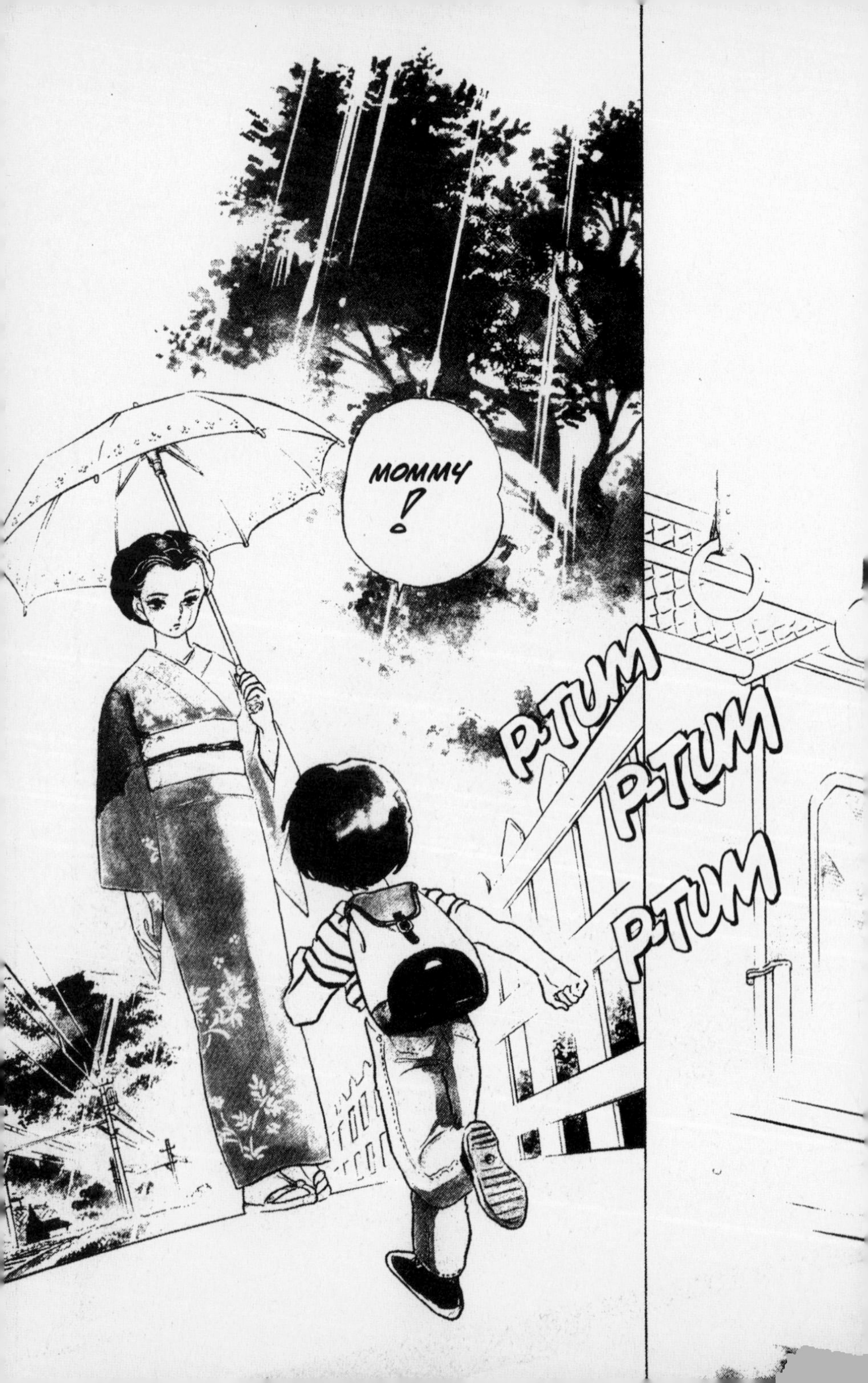
MOMMY!
P-TUM
P-TUM
P-TUM

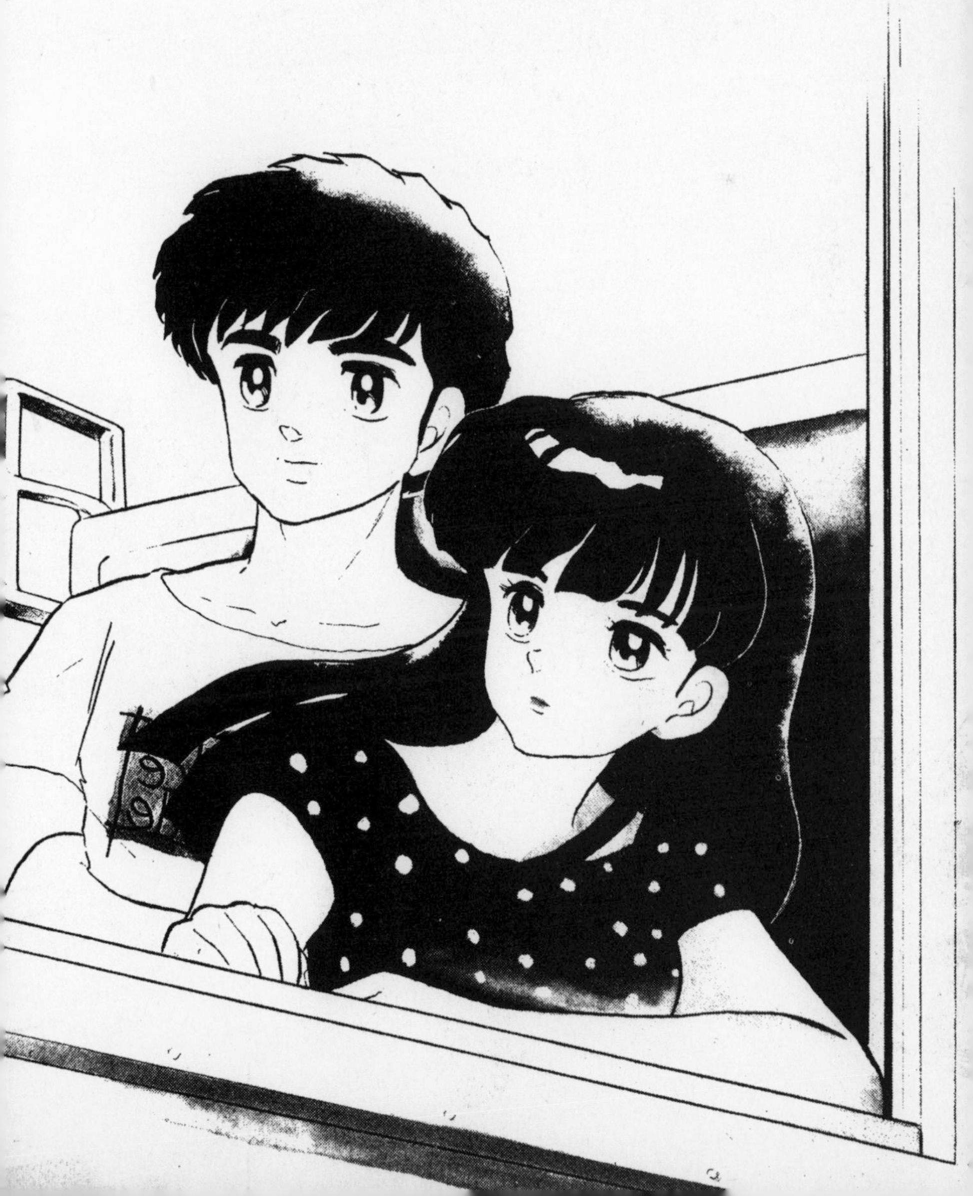

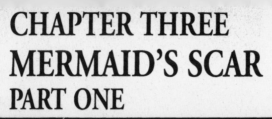

CHAPTER THREE
MERMAID'S SCAR
PART ONE

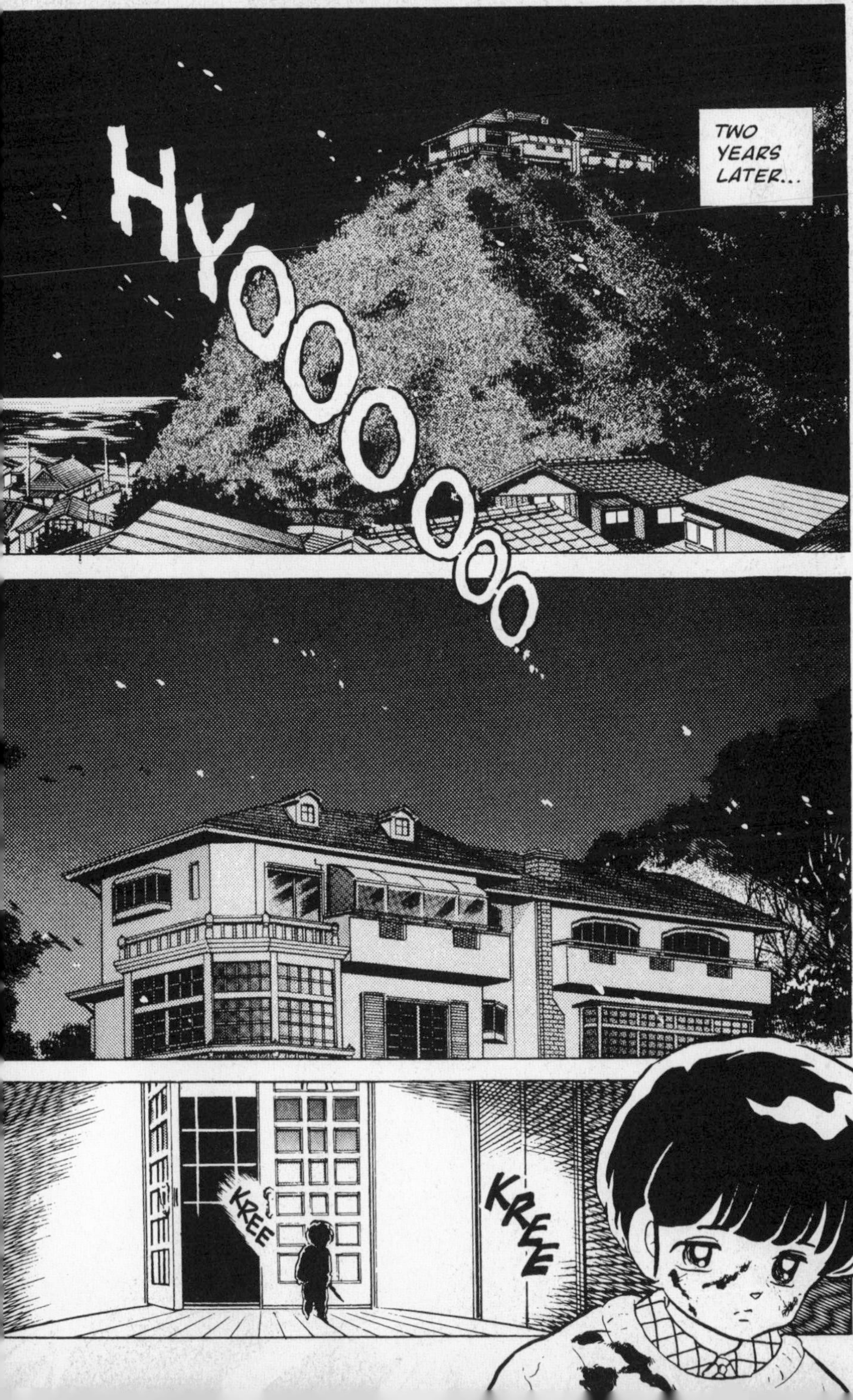
HYOOOOOO
TWO YEARS LATER...
KREE
KREE

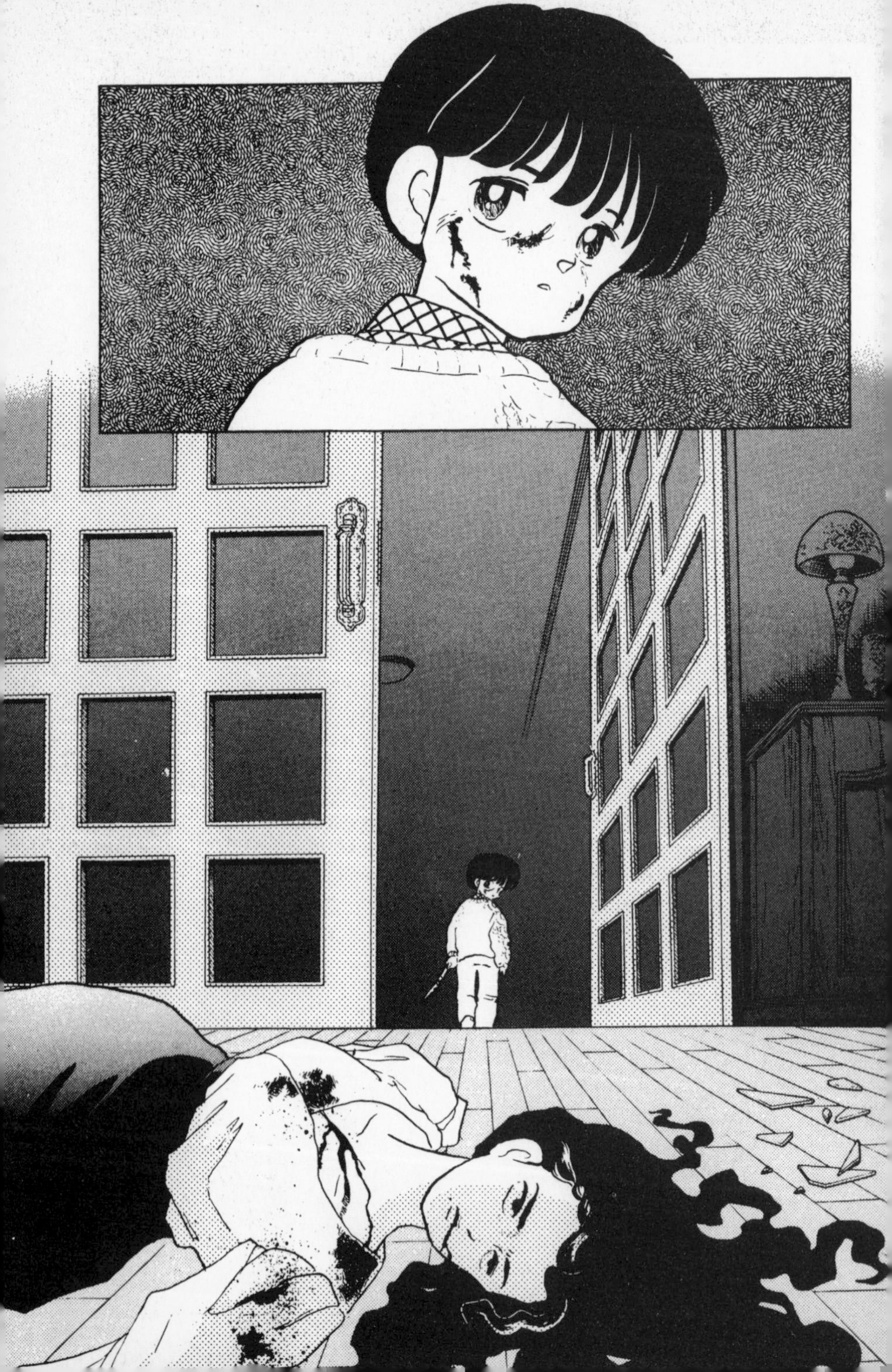

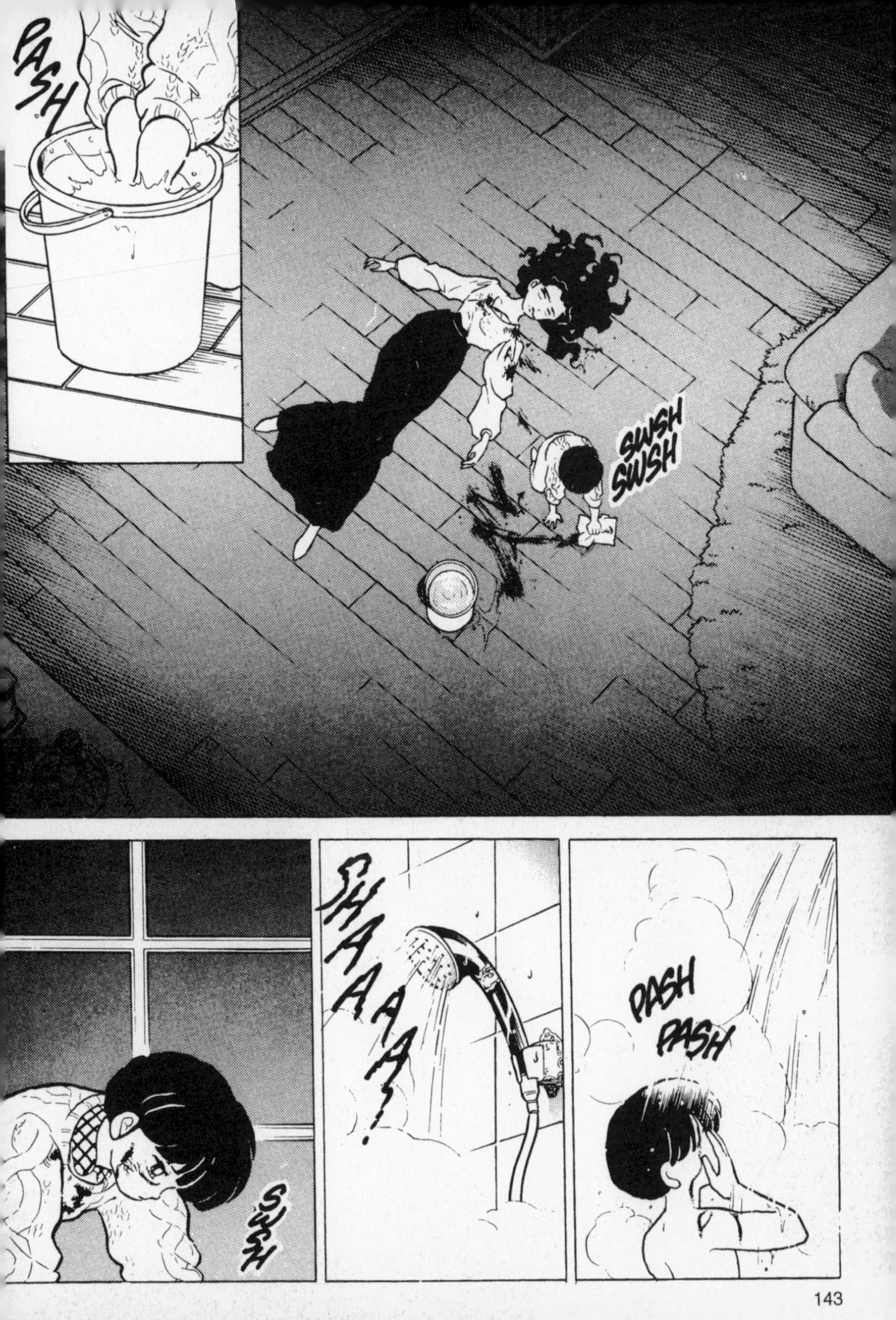
PASH
SWSH SWSH
SWSH
SHAAAAA!
PASH PASH

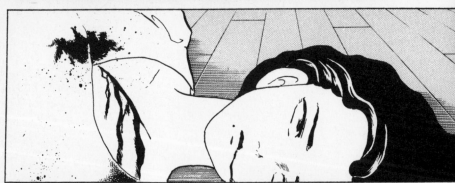

MOMMY...

144

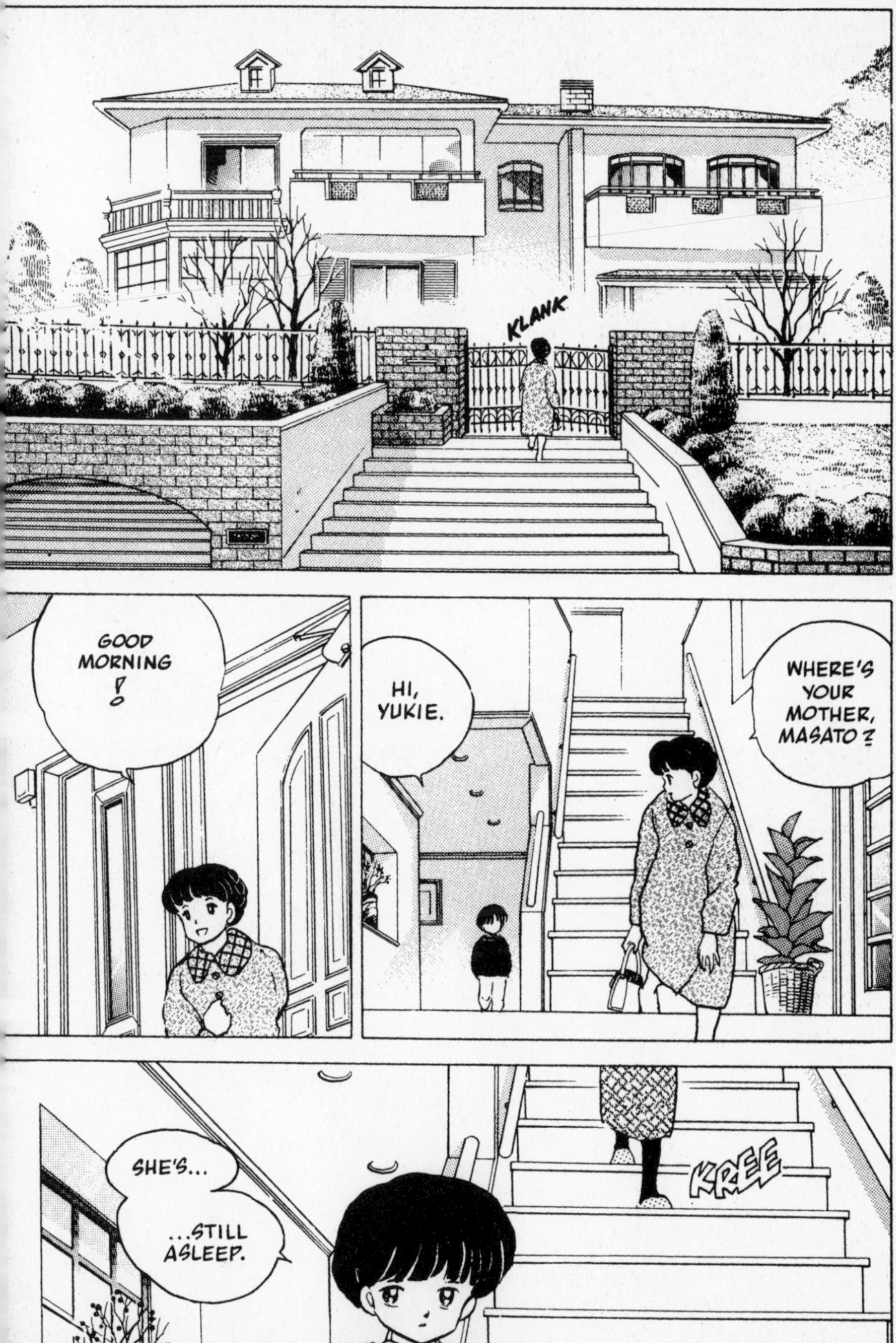
KLANK
GOOD MORNING!
HI, YUKIE.
WHERE'S YOUR MOTHER, MASATO?
SHE'S...
...STILL ASLEEP.
KREE

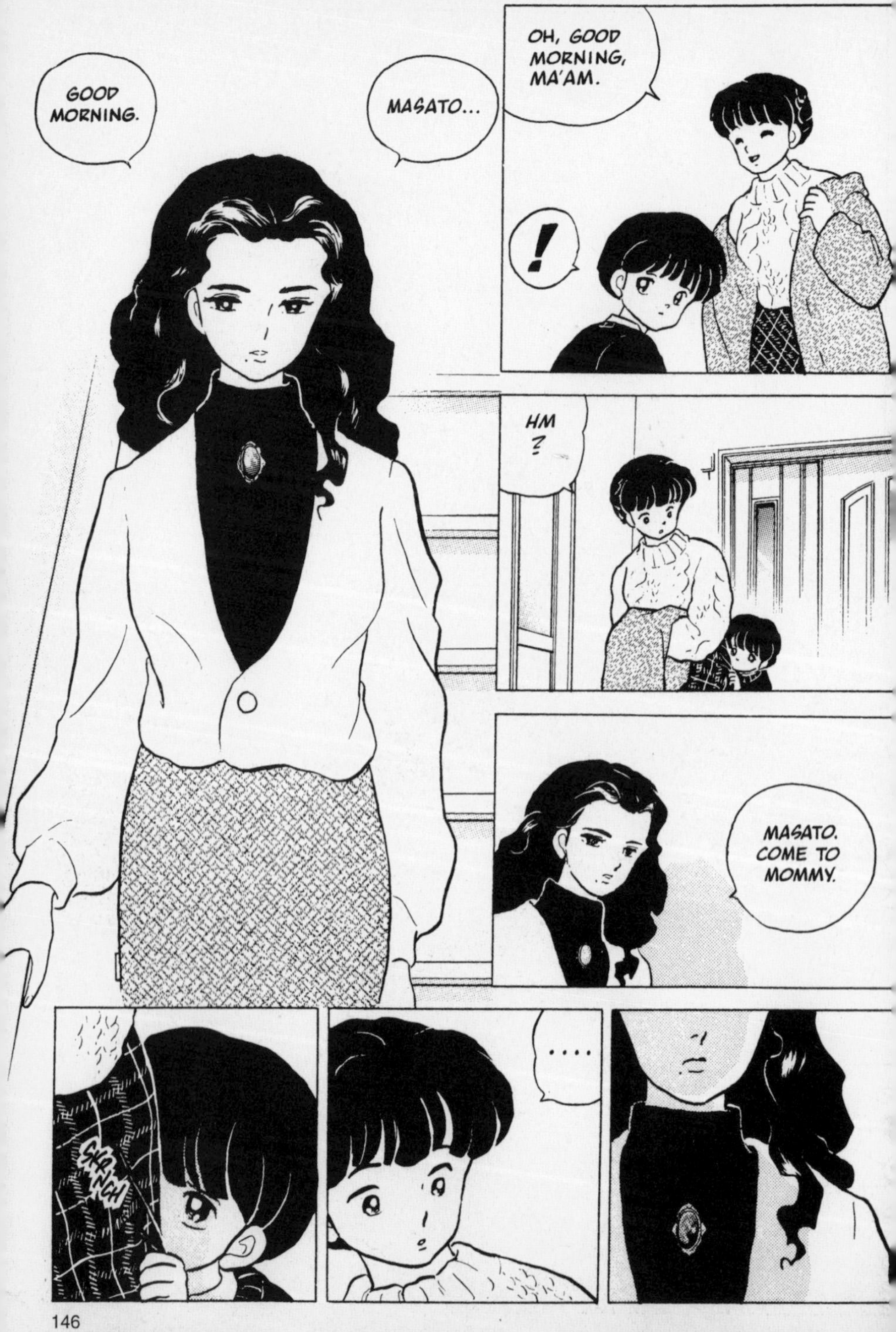
GOOD MORNING.
MASATO...
OH, GOOD MORNING, MA'AM.
!
HM ?
MASATO. COME TO MOMMY.
SKRNCH
....

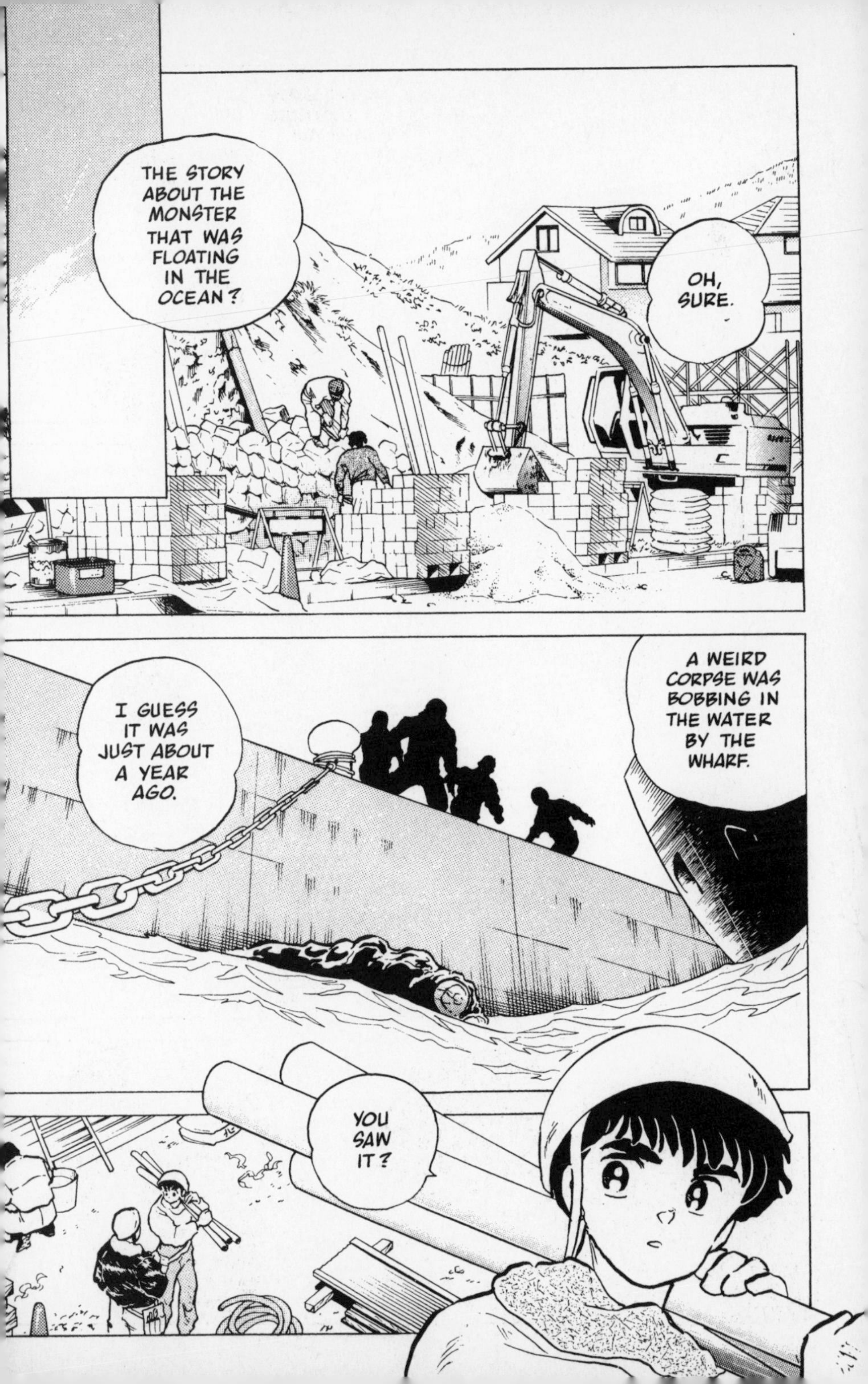
THE STORY ABOUT THE MONSTER THAT WAS FLOATING IN THE OCEAN?
OH, SURE.
I GUESS IT WAS JUST ABOUT A YEAR AGO.
A WEIRD CORPSE WAS BOBBING IN THE WATER BY THE WHARF.
YOU SAW IT?

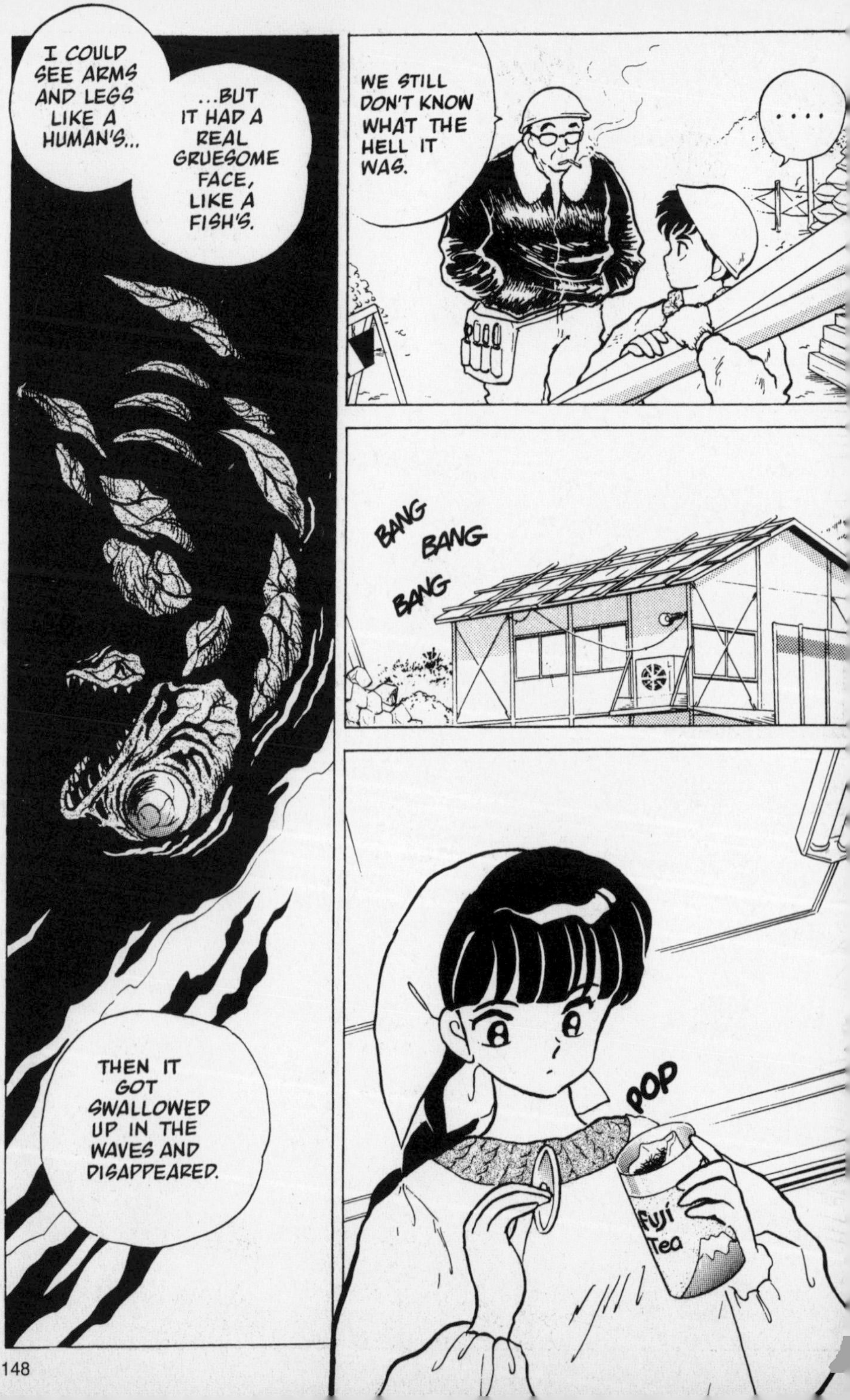
I COULD SEE ARMS AND LEGS LIKE A HUMAN'S...
...BUT IT HAD A REAL GRUESOME FACE, LIKE A FISH'S.
THEN IT GOT SWALLOWED UP IN THE WAVES AND DISAPPEARED.
WE STILL DON'T KNOW WHAT THE HELL IT WAS.
....
BANG
BANG
BANG
POP
Fuji Tea

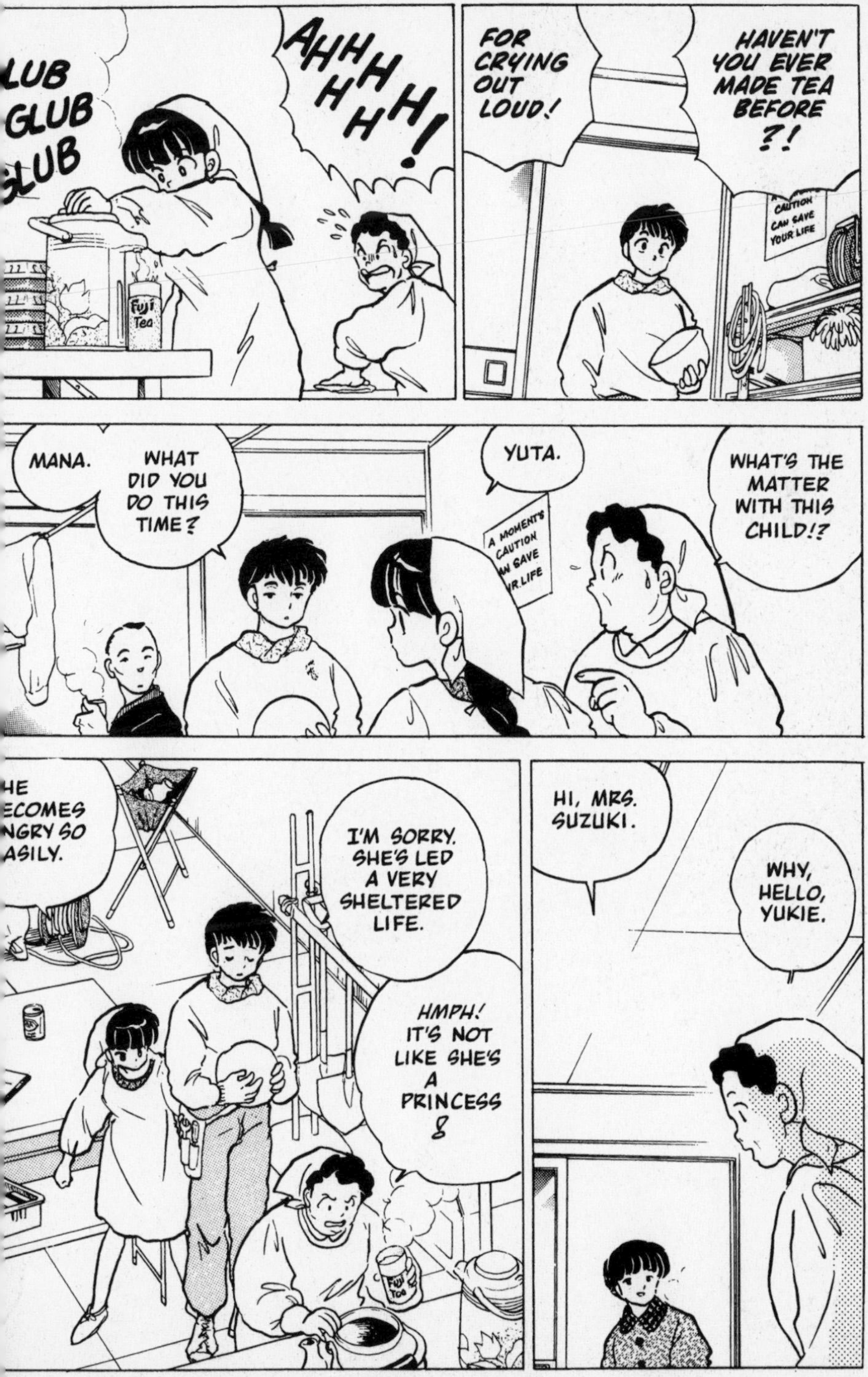
LUB GLUB GLUB
Fuji Tea
AHHHHHH!
FOR CRYING OUT LOUD!
HAVEN'T YOU EVER MADE TEA BEFORE?!
CAUTION CAN SAVE YOUR LIFE
MANA.
WHAT DID YOU DO THIS TIME?
YUTA.
A MOMENT'S CAUTION
WHAT'S THE MATTER WITH THIS CHILD!?
HE ECOMES NGRY SO ASILY.
I'M SORRY. SHE'S LED A VERY SHELTERED LIFE.
HMPH! IT'S NOT LIKE SHE'S A PRINCESS!
HI, MRS. SUZUKI.
WHY, HELLO, YUKIE.

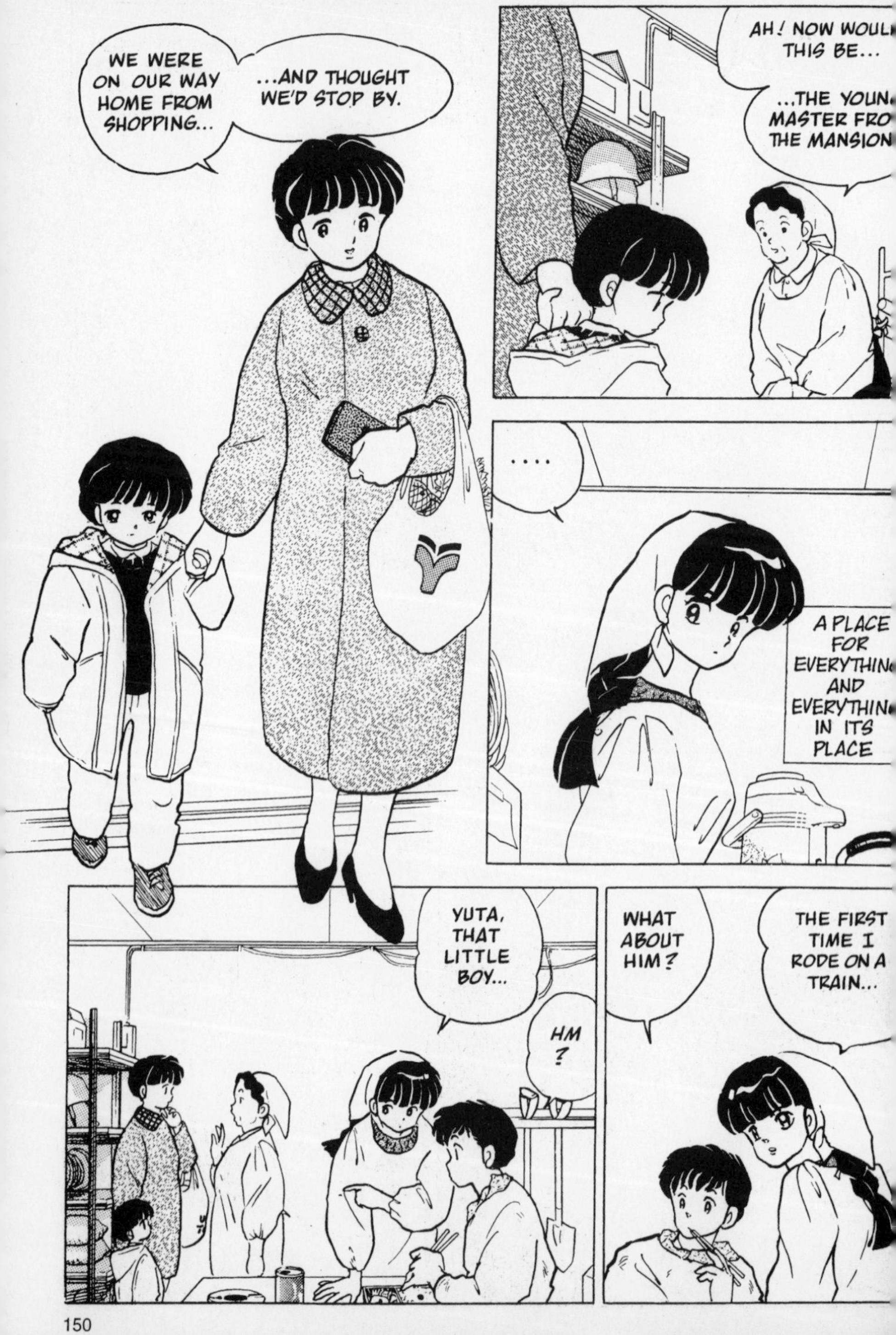

WE WERE ON OUR WAY HOME FROM SHOPPING...
...AND THOUGHT WE'D STOP BY.
AH! NOW WOUL THIS BE...
...THE YOUN MASTER FRO THE MANSION
....
A PLACE FOR EVERYTHIN AND EVERYTHIN IN ITS PLACE
YUTA, THAT LITTLE BOY...
HM?
WHAT ABOUT HIM?
THE FIRST TIME I RODE ON A TRAIN...

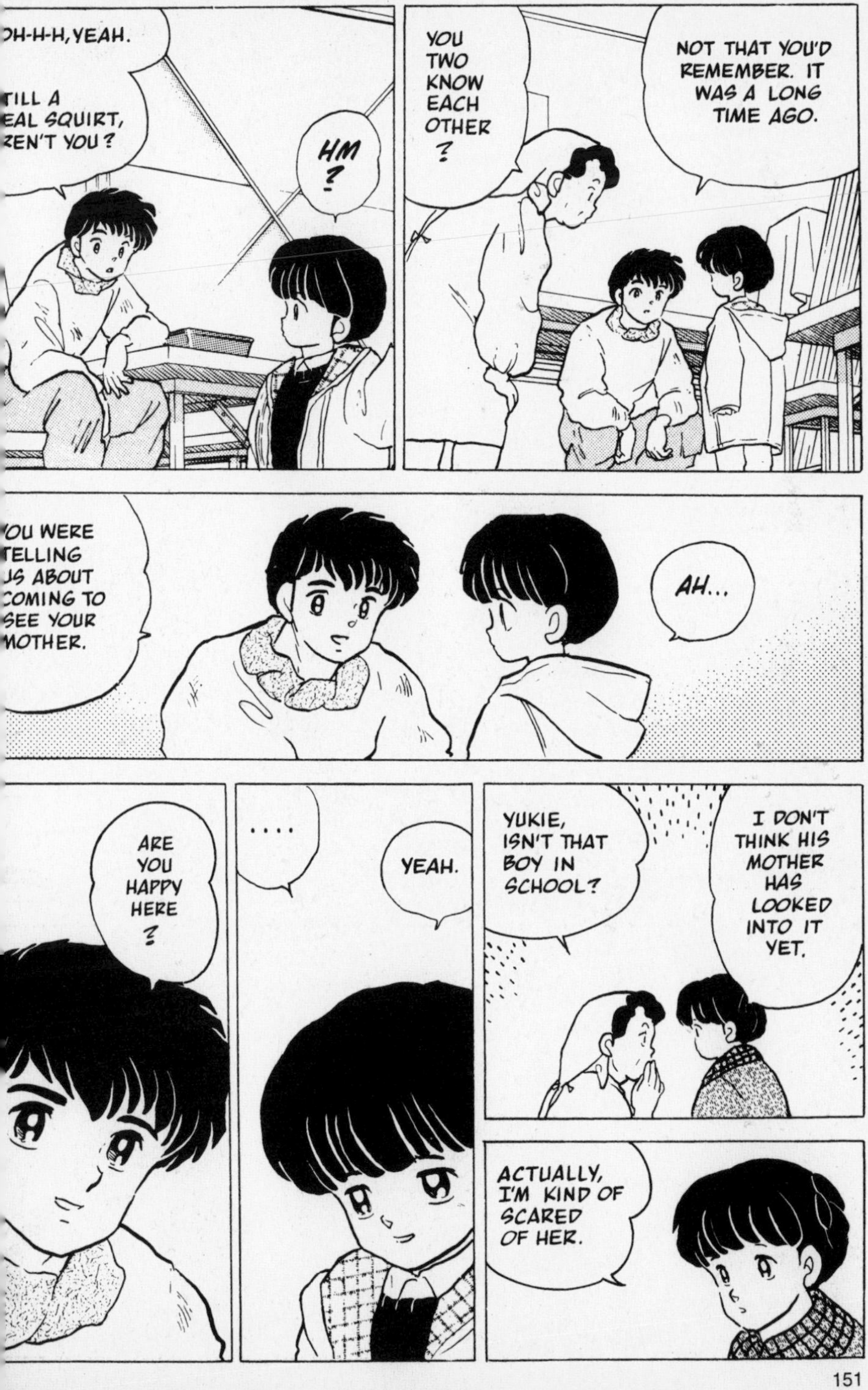

OH-H-H, YEAH.
TILL A EAL SQUIRT, REN'T YOU?
HM?
YOU TWO KNOW EACH OTHER?
NOT THAT YOU'D REMEMBER. IT WAS A LONG TIME AGO.
OU WERE TELLING US ABOUT COMING TO SEE YOUR MOTHER.
AH...
ARE YOU HAPPY HERE?
....
YEAH.
YUKIE, ISN'T THAT BOY IN SCHOOL?
I DON'T THINK HIS MOTHER HAS LOOKED INTO IT YET.
ACTUALLY, I'M KIND OF SCARED OF HER.

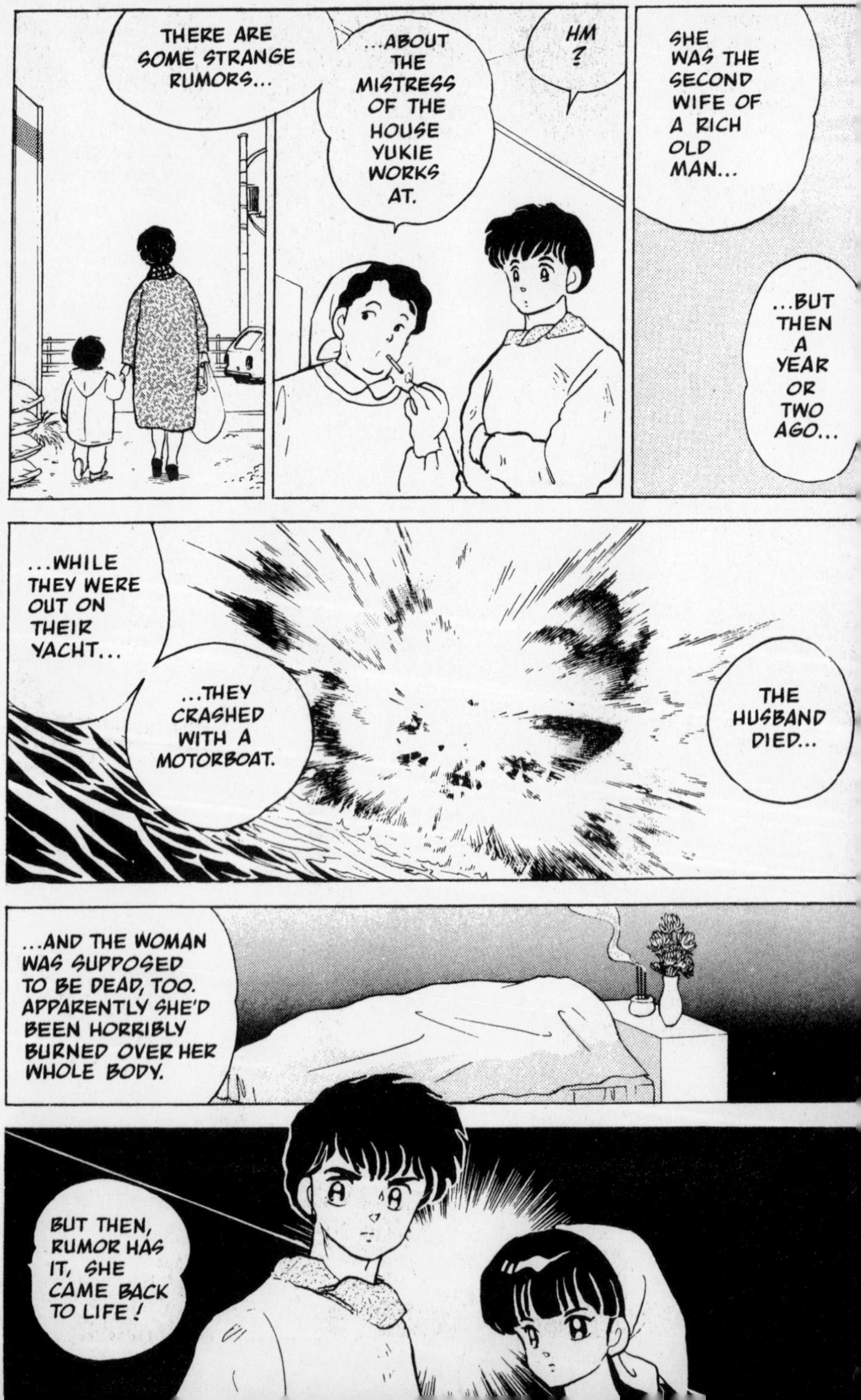
THERE ARE SOME STRANGE RUMORS...
...ABOUT THE MISTRESS OF THE HOUSE YUKIE WORKS AT.
HM?
SHE WAS THE SECOND WIFE OF A RICH OLD MAN...
...BUT THEN A YEAR OR TWO AGO...
...WHILE THEY WERE OUT ON THEIR YACHT...
...THEY CRASHED WITH A MOTORBOAT.
THE HUSBAND DIED...
...AND THE WOMAN WAS SUPPOSED TO BE DEAD, TOO. APPARENTLY SHE'D BEEN HORRIBLY BURNED OVER HER WHOLE BODY.
BUT THEN, RUMOR HAS IT, SHE CAME BACK TO LIFE!

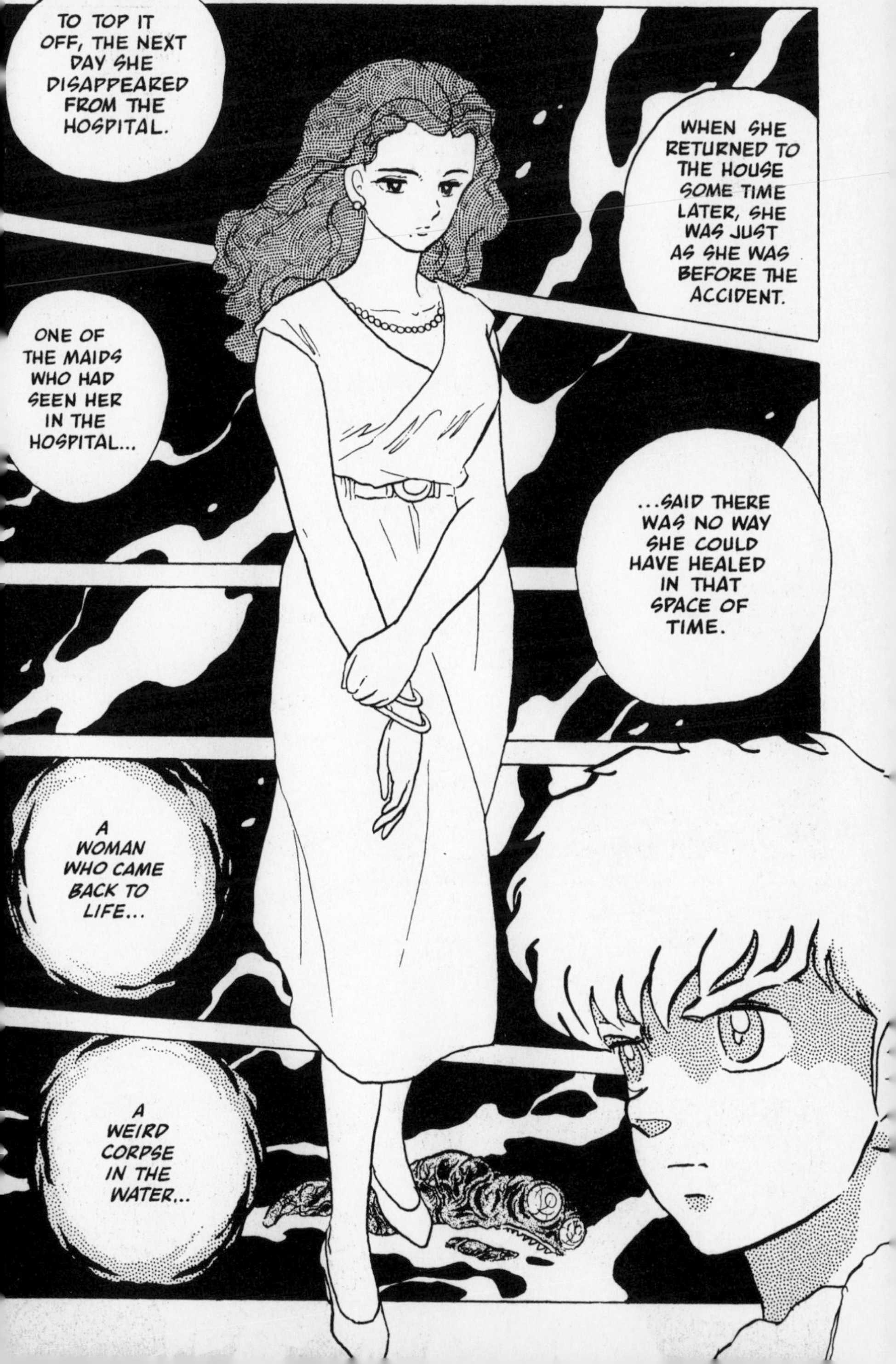
TO TOP IT OFF, THE NEXT DAY SHE DISAPPEARED FROM THE HOSPITAL.
WHEN SHE RETURNED TO THE HOUSE SOME TIME LATER, SHE WAS JUST AS SHE WAS BEFORE THE ACCIDENT.
ONE OF THE MAIDS WHO HAD SEEN HER IN THE HOSPITAL...
...SAID THERE WAS NO WAY SHE COULD HAVE HEALED IN THAT SPACE OF TIME.
A WOMAN WHO CAME BACK TO LIFE...
A WEIRD CORPSE IN THE WATER...

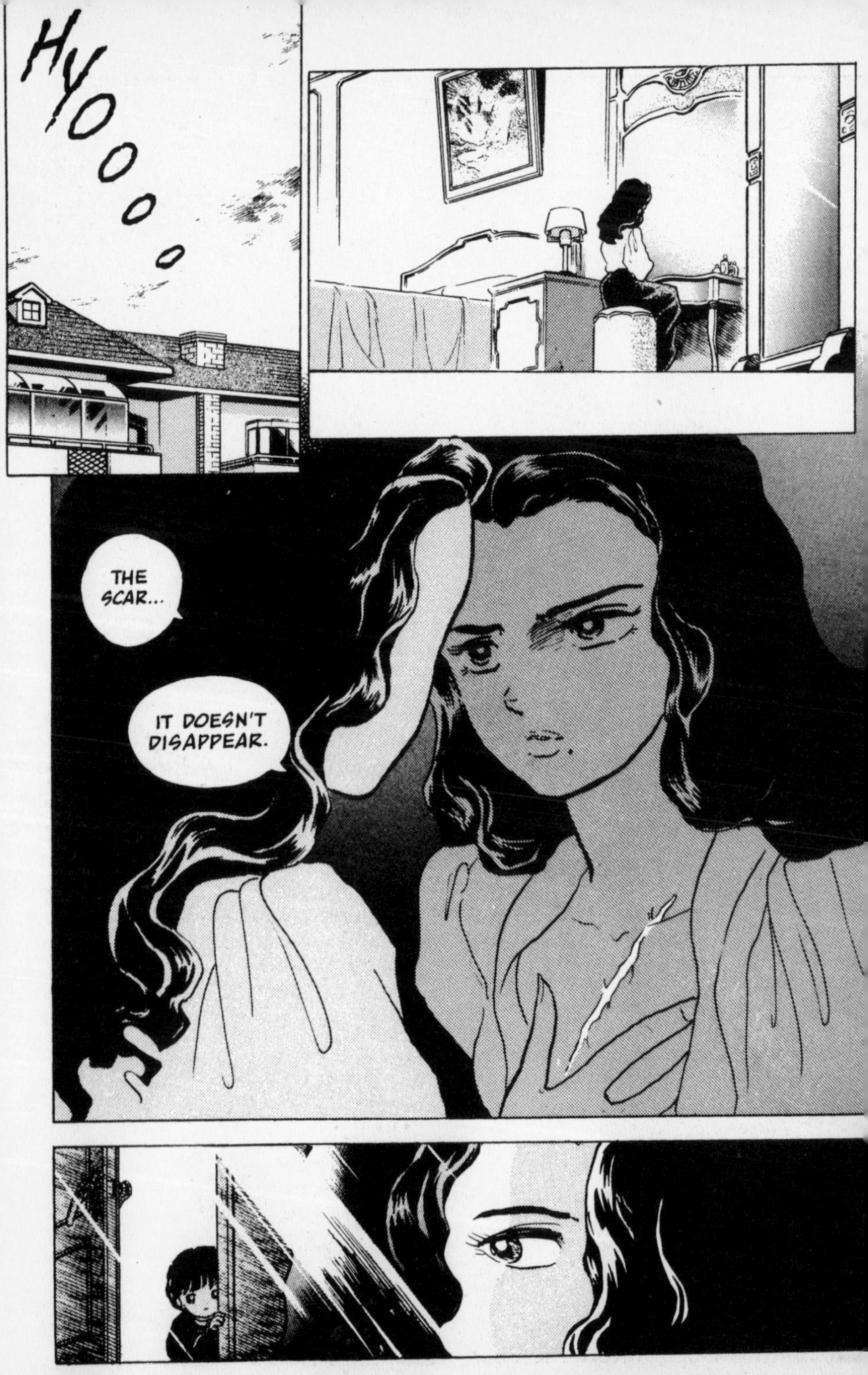
HYOOOO
THE SCAR...
IT DOESN'T DISAPPEAR.

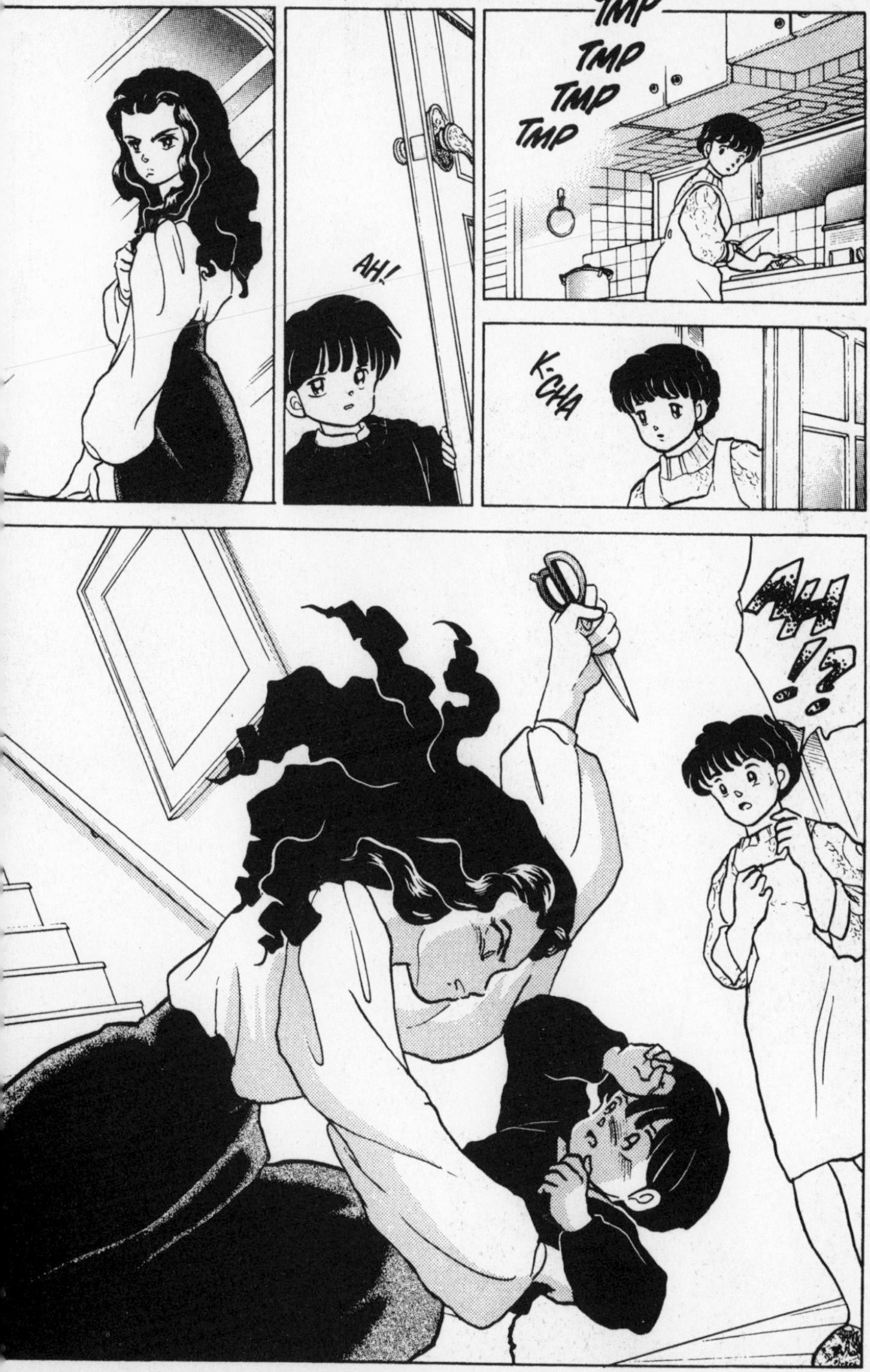
TMP
TMP
TMP
TMP
K-CHA
AH!
AH!?

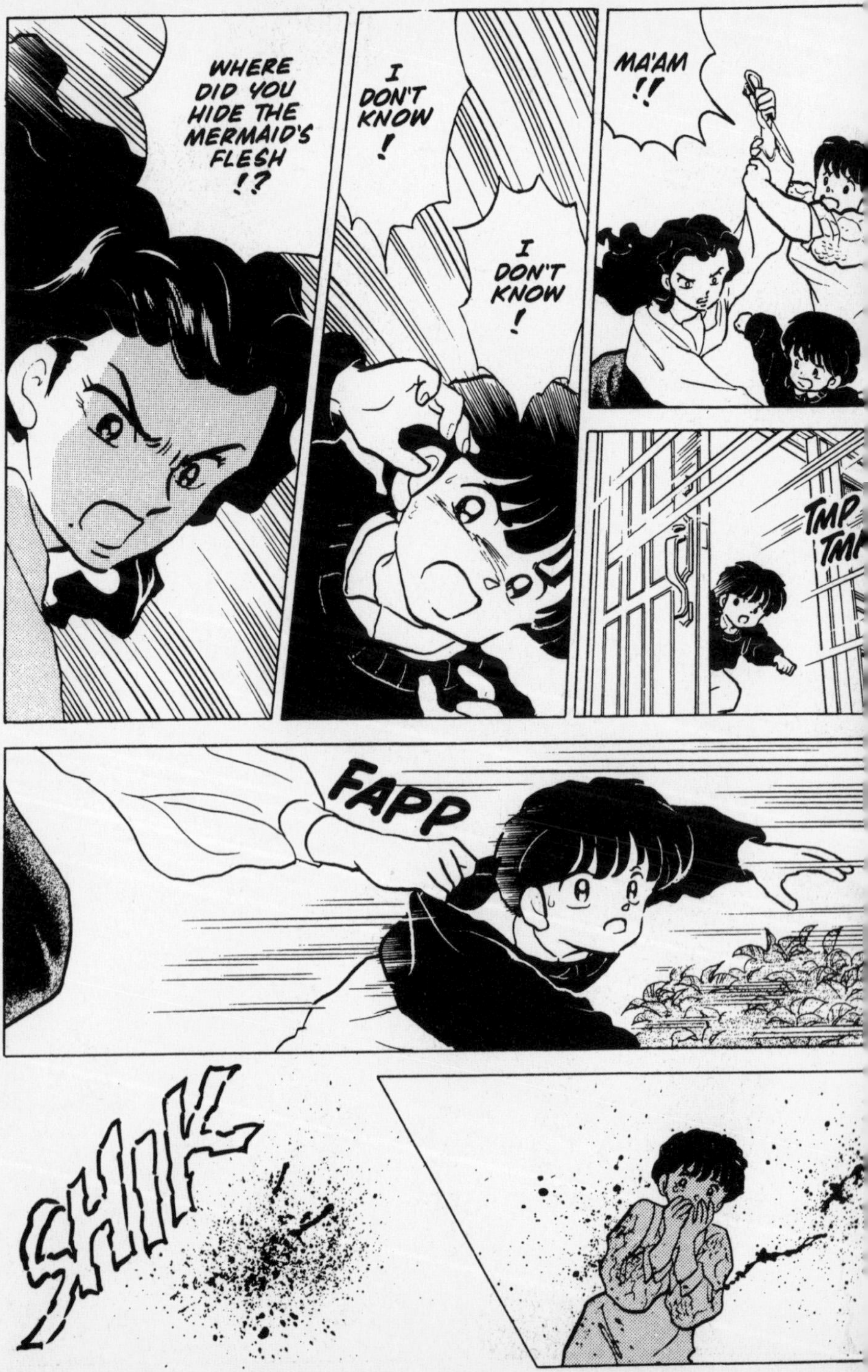
WHERE DID YOU HIDE THE MERMAID'S FLESH !?
I DON'T KNOW !
I DON'T KNOW !
MA'AM !!
TMP TMP
FAPP
SHIK

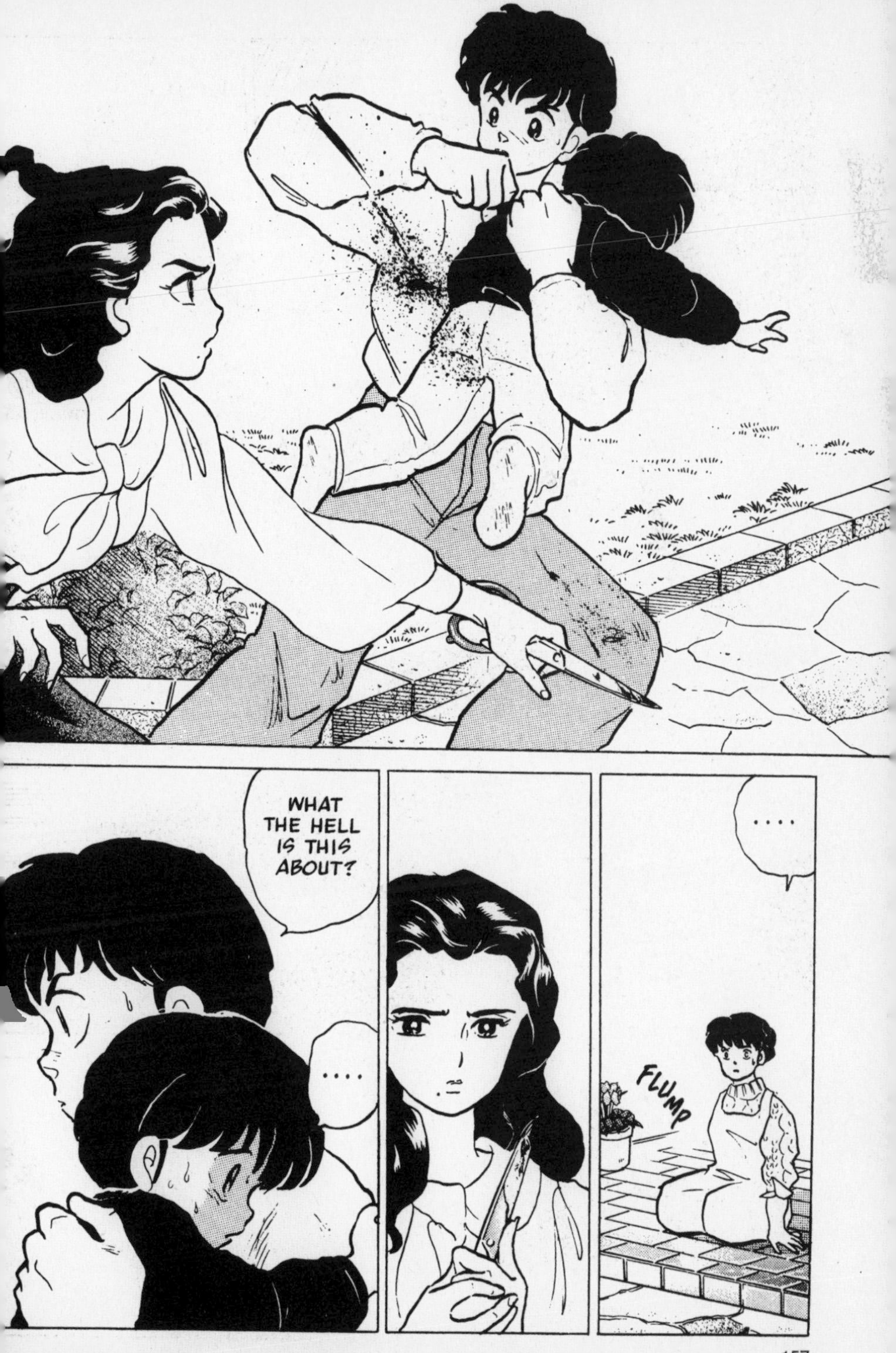
WHAT THE HELL IS THIS ABOUT?
....
....
FLUMP

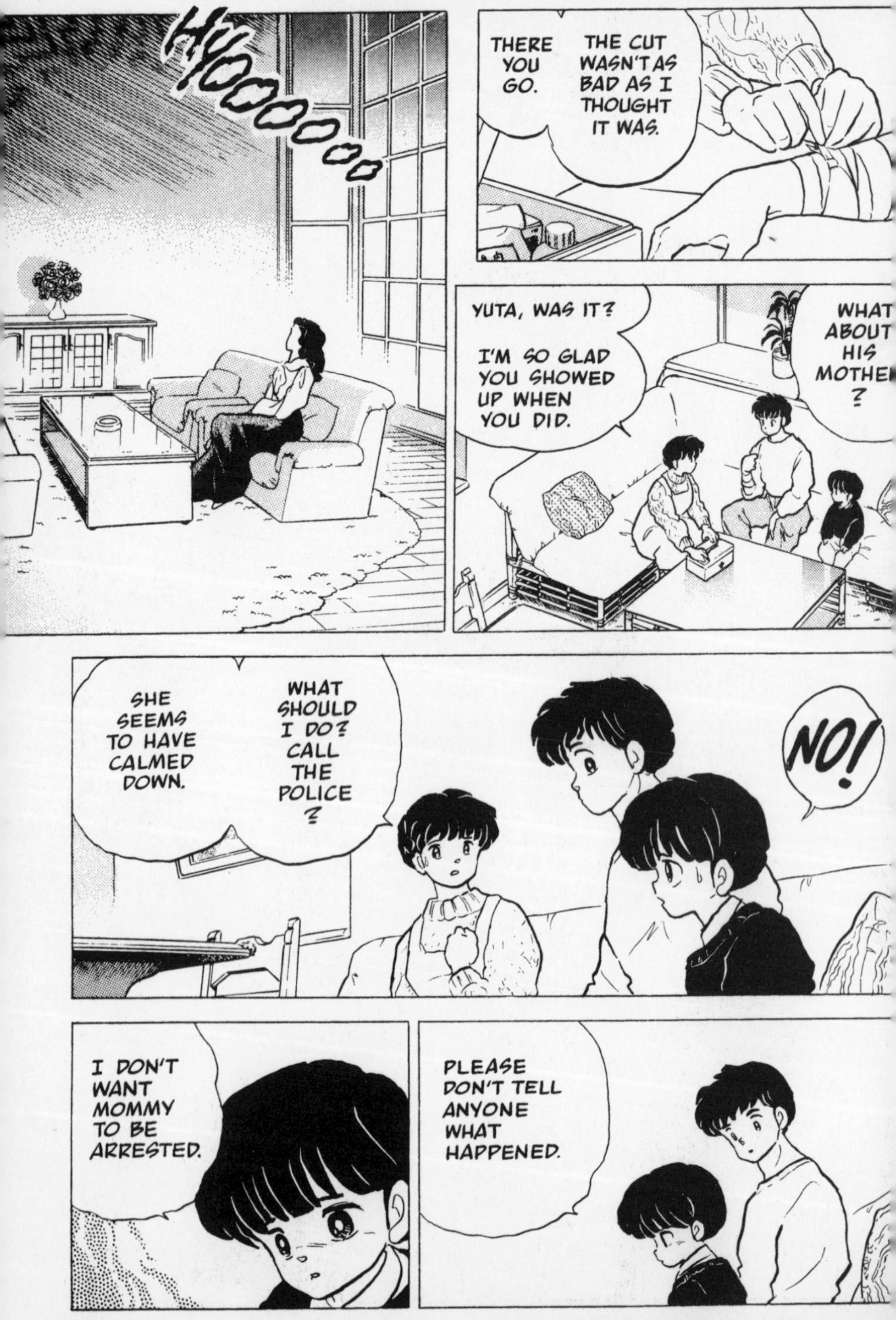
HYOOOOOOO
THERE YOU GO.
THE CUT WASN'T AS BAD AS I THOUGHT IT WAS.
YUTA, WAS IT?
I'M SO GLAD YOU SHOWED UP WHEN YOU DID.
WHAT ABOUT HIS MOTHE ?
SHE SEEMS TO HAVE CALMED DOWN.
WHAT SHOULD I DO? CALL THE POLICE?
NO!
I DON'T WANT MOMMY TO BE ARRESTED.
PLEASE DON'T TELL ANYONE WHAT HAPPENED.

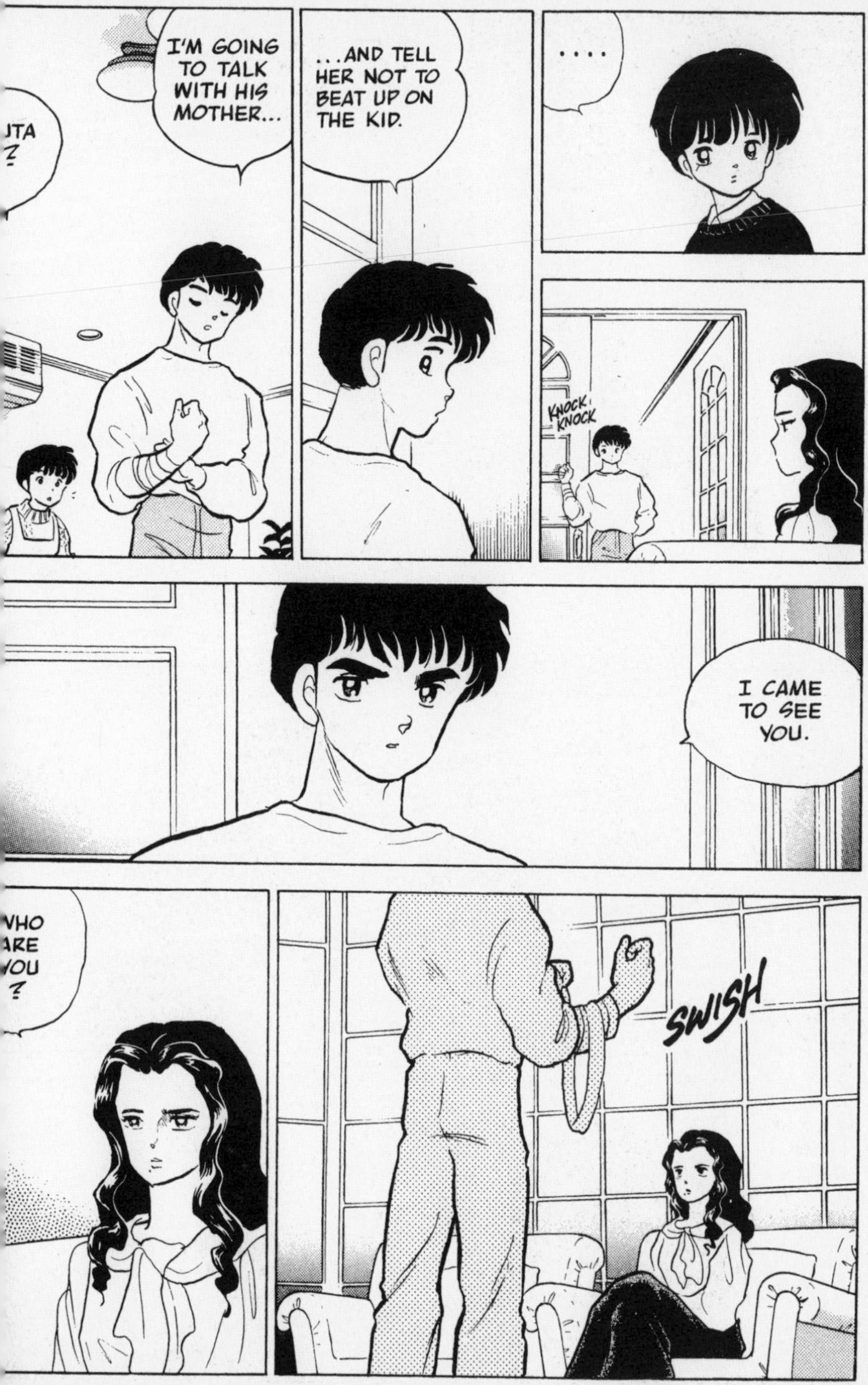
I'M GOING TO TALK WITH HIS MOTHER...
...AND TELL HER NOT TO BEAT UP ON THE KID.
....
KNOCK KNOCK
I CAME TO SEE YOU.
SWISH

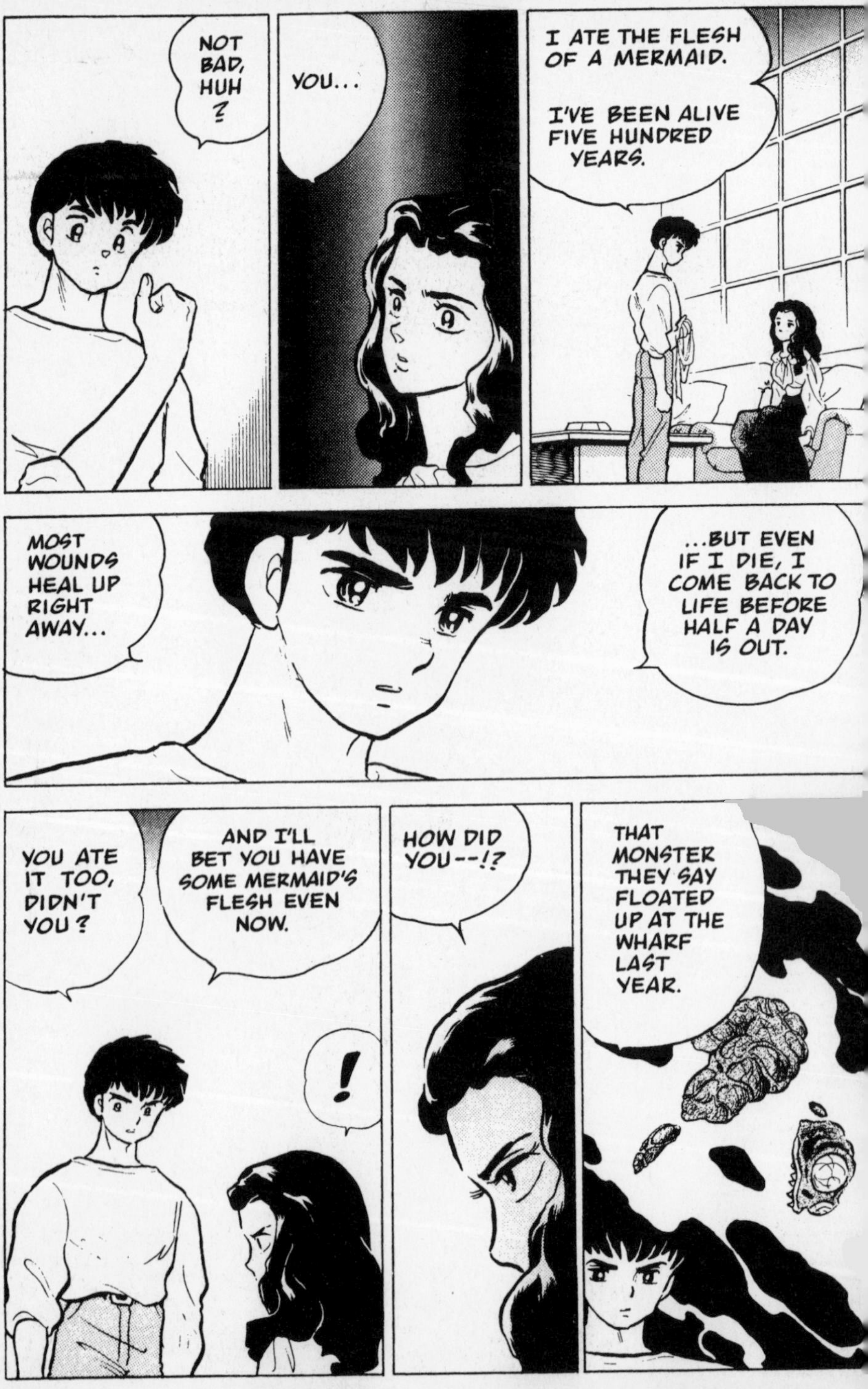
NOT BAD, HUH?
YOU...
I ATE THE FLESH OF A MERMAID.
I'VE BEEN ALIVE FIVE HUNDRED YEARS.
MOST WOUNDS HEAL UP RIGHT AWAY...
...BUT EVEN IF I DIE, I COME BACK TO LIFE BEFORE HALF A DAY IS OUT.
YOU ATE IT TOO, DIDN'T YOU?
AND I'LL BET YOU HAVE SOME MERMAID'S FLESH EVEN NOW.
!
HOW DID YOU--!?
THAT MONSTER THEY SAY FLOATED UP AT THE WHARF LAST YEAR.

I'LL BET THAT WAS A "LOST SOUL"...

...SOMEONE WHO ATE THE FLESH OF A MERMAID BUT DIDN'T BECOME IMMORTAL.

MERMAID'S FLESH IS A VIOLENT POISON.

MOST PEOPLE EITHER DIE...

...OR BECOME MONSTERS.

IF WHAT YOU SAY IS TRUE...

MOMMY...

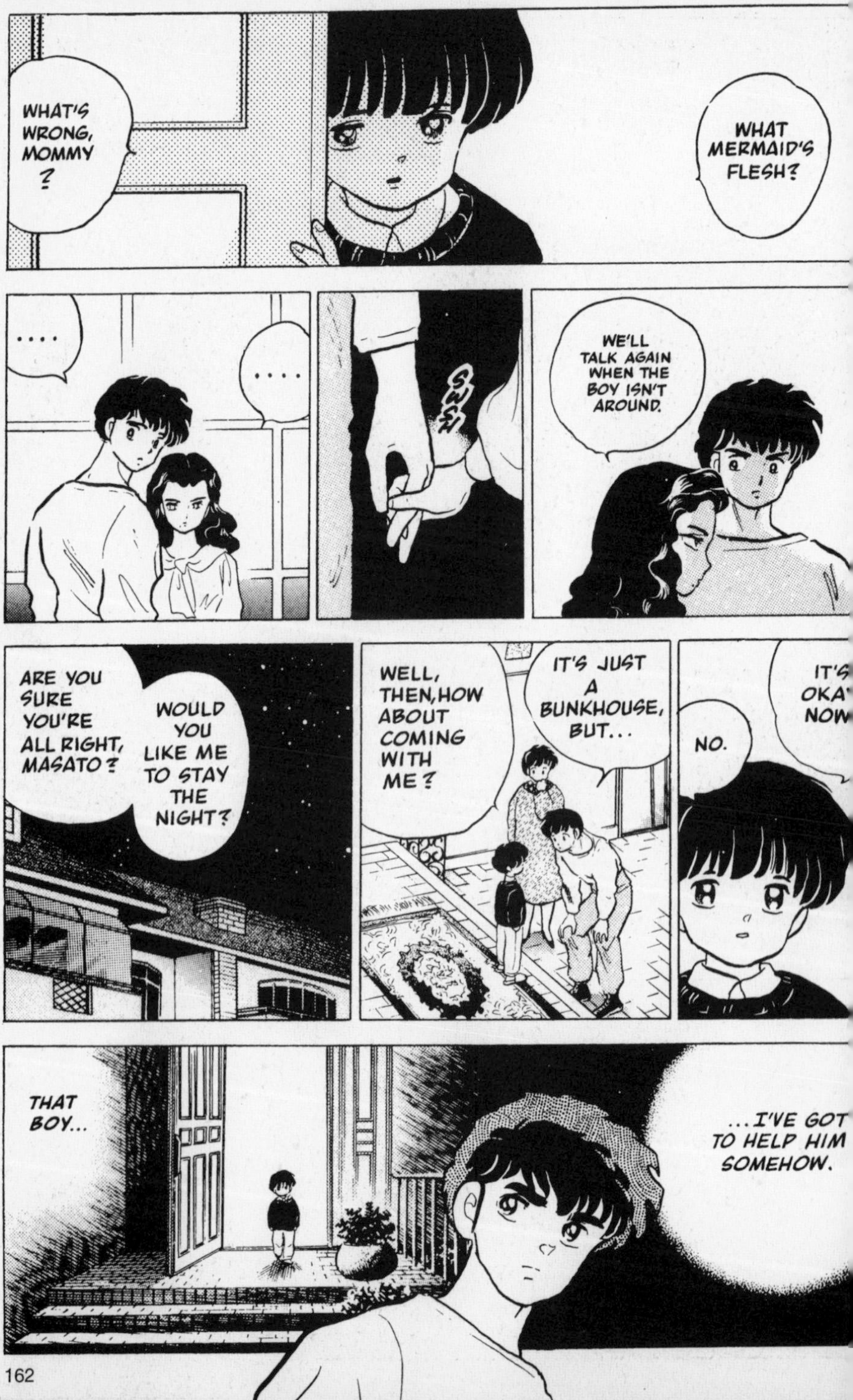
WHAT'S WRONG, MOMMY?
WHAT MERMAID'S FLESH?
....
....
SWISH
WE'LL TALK AGAIN WHEN THE BOY ISN'T AROUND.
ARE YOU SURE YOU'RE ALL RIGHT, MASATO?
WOULD YOU LIKE ME TO STAY THE NIGHT?
WELL, THEN, HOW ABOUT COMING WITH ME?
IT'S JUST A BUNKHOUSE, BUT...
NO.
IT'S OKA NOW
THAT BOY...
...I'VE GOT TO HELP HIM SOMEHOW.

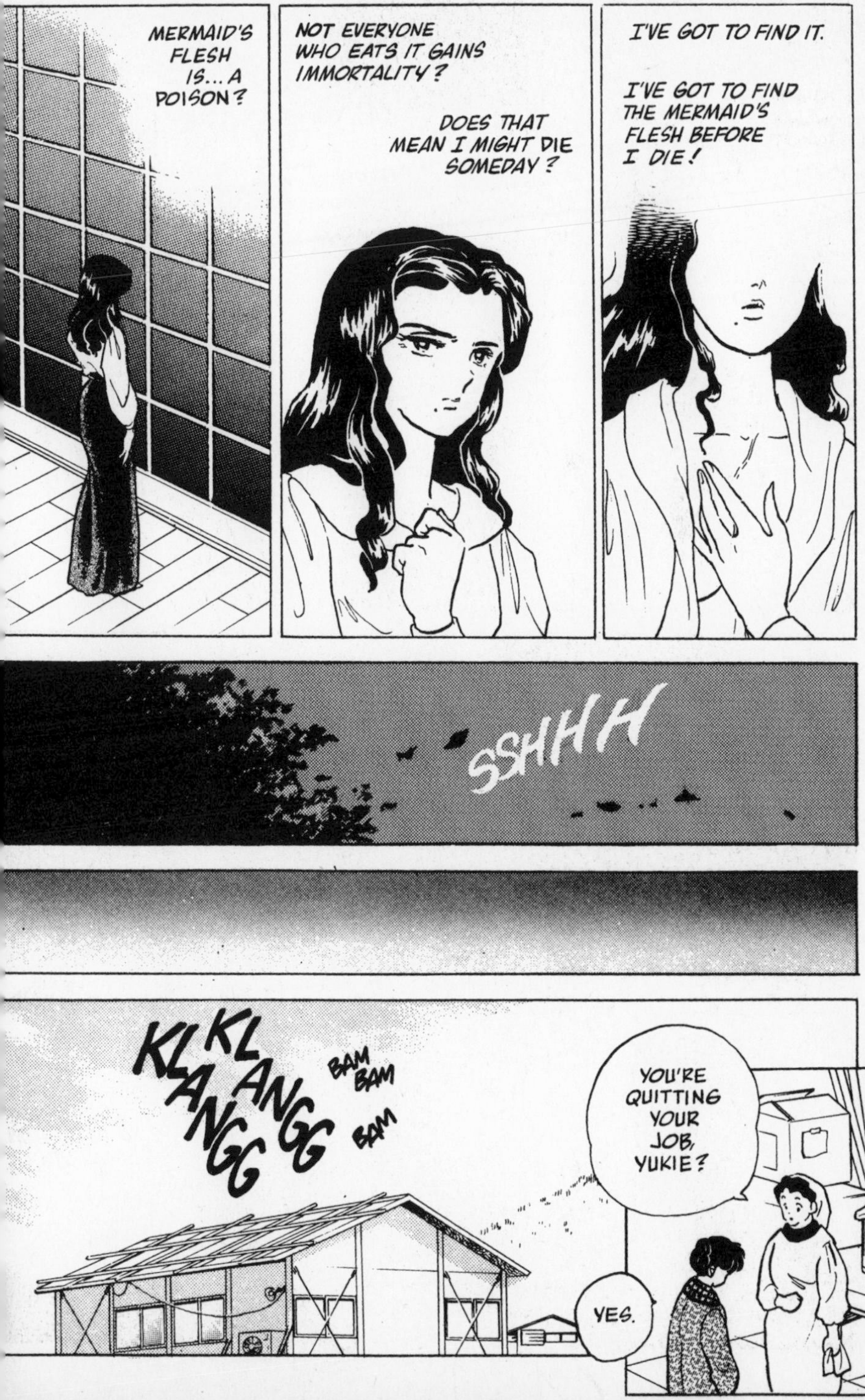
MERMAID'S FLESH IS... A POISON?
NOT EVERYONE WHO EATS IT GAINS IMMORTALITY?
DOES THAT MEAN I MIGHT DIE SOMEDAY?
I'VE GOT TO FIND IT.
I'VE GOT TO FIND THE MERMAID'S FLESH BEFORE I DIE!
SSHHH
KLANGG
KLANGG
BAM BAM
BAM
YOU'RE QUITTING YOUR JOB, YUKIE?
YES.

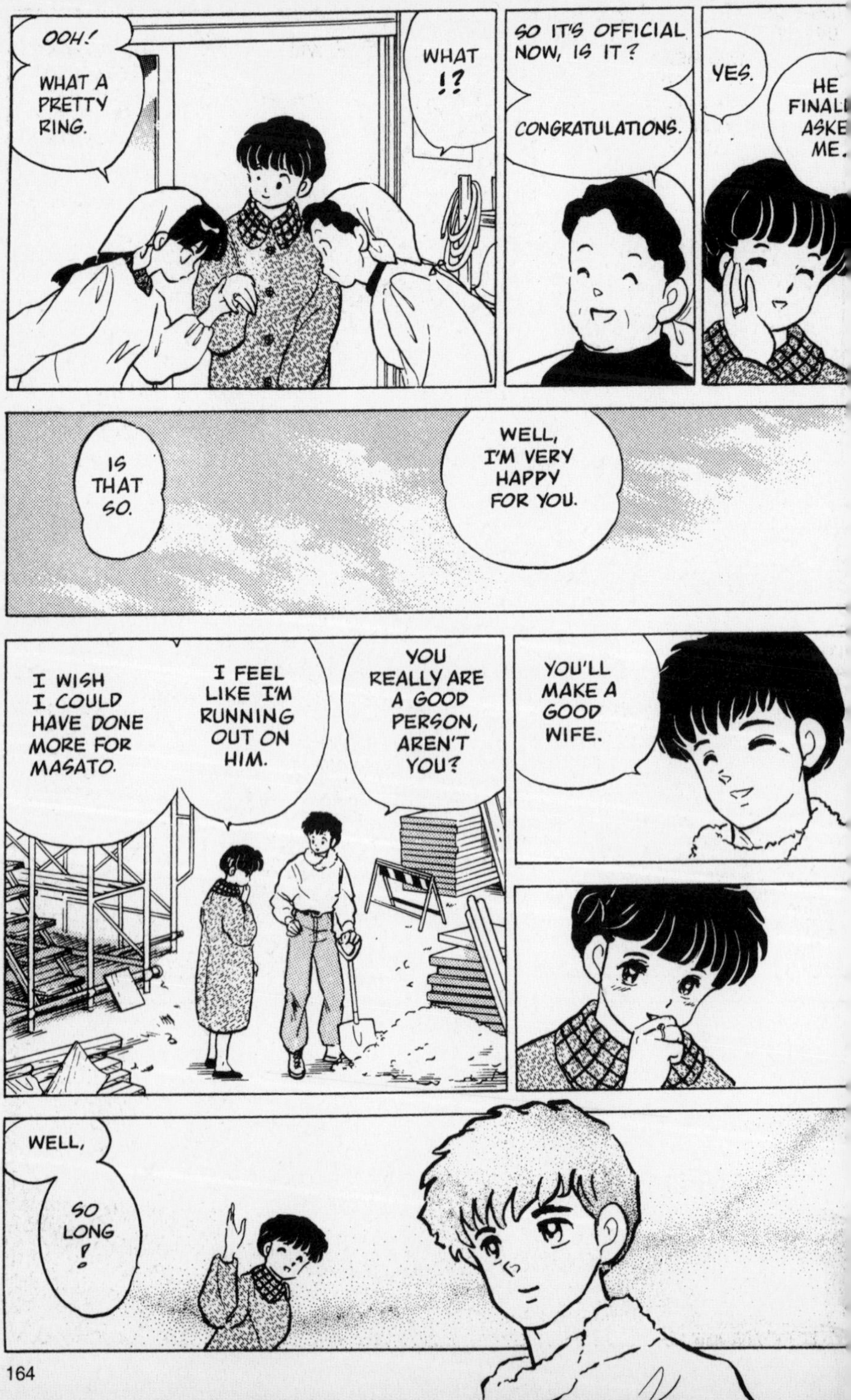
OOH!
WHAT A PRETTY RING.
WHAT !?
SO IT'S OFFICIAL NOW, IS IT?
CONGRATULATIONS.
YES.
HE FINAL ASKE ME.
IS THAT SO.
WELL, I'M VERY HAPPY FOR YOU.
I WISH I COULD HAVE DONE MORE FOR MASATO.
I FEEL LIKE I'M RUNNING OUT ON HIM.
YOU REALLY ARE A GOOD PERSON, AREN'T YOU?
YOU'LL MAKE A GOOD WIFE.
WELL,
SO LONG!

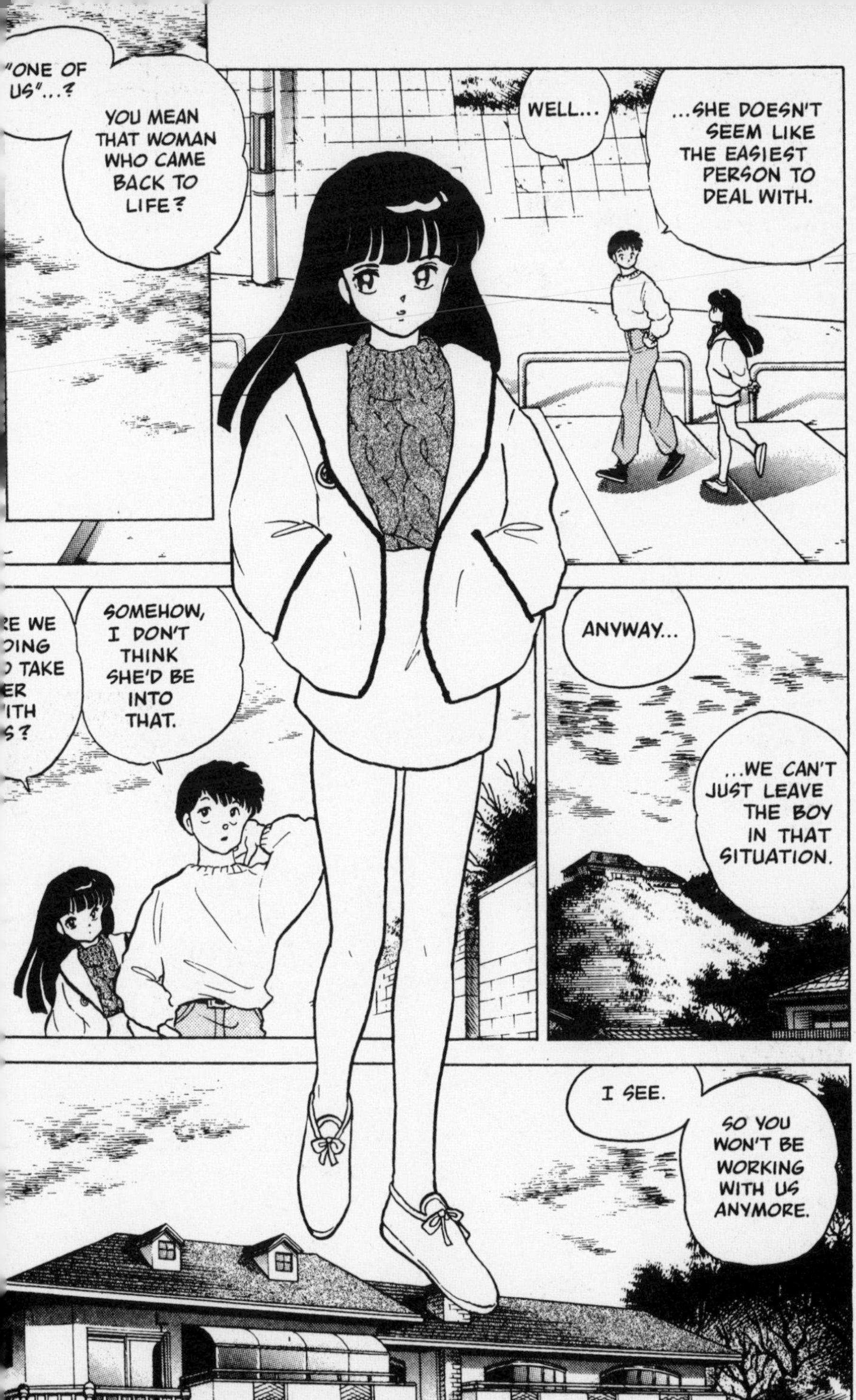
"ONE OF US"...?
YOU MEAN THAT WOMAN WHO CAME BACK TO LIFE?
WELL...
...SHE DOESN'T SEEM LIKE THE EASIEST PERSON TO DEAL WITH.
SOMEHOW, I DON'T THINK SHE'D BE INTO THAT.
ANYWAY...
...WE CAN'T JUST LEAVE THE BOY IN THAT SITUATION.
I SEE.
SO YOU WON'T BE WORKING WITH US ANYMORE.

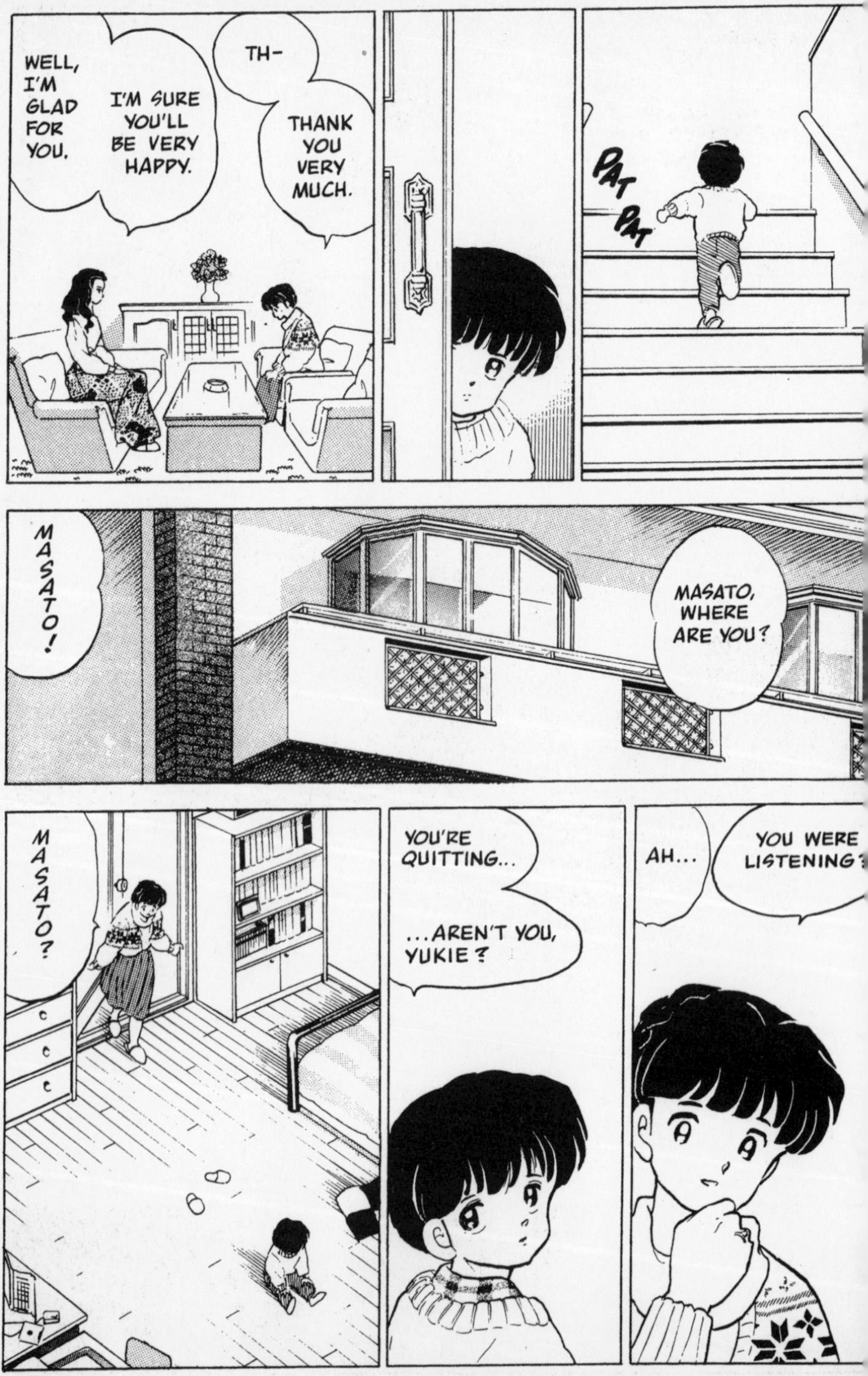
WELL, I'M GLAD FOR YOU.
I'M SURE YOU'LL BE VERY HAPPY.
TH-
THANK YOU VERY MUCH.
PAT PAT
MASATO!
MASATO, WHERE ARE YOU?
MASATO?
YOU'RE QUITTING...
...AREN'T YOU, YUKIE?
AH...
YOU WERE LISTENING?

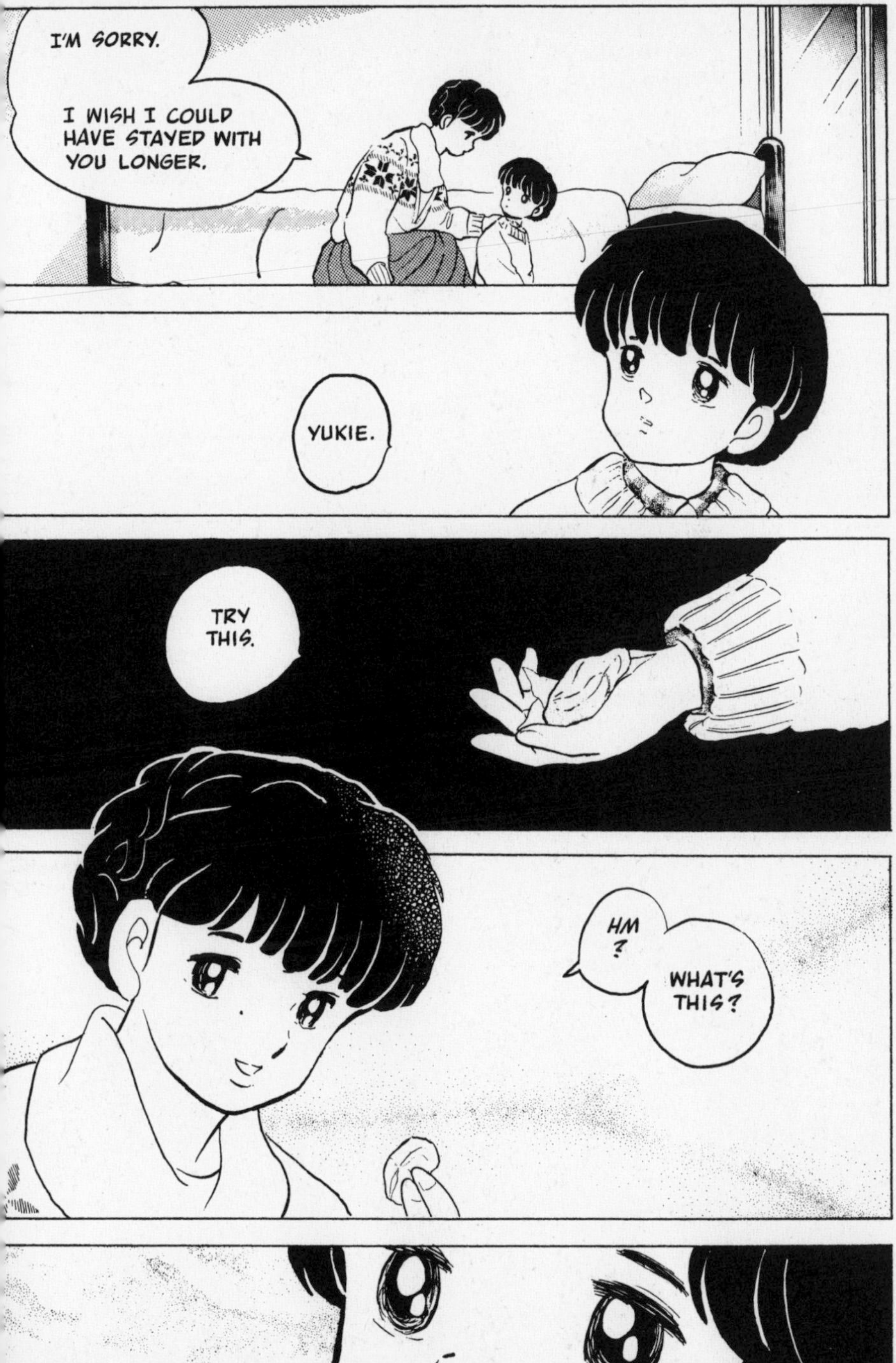
I'M SORRY.
I WISH I COULD HAVE STAYED WITH YOU LONGER.
YUKIE.
TRY THIS.
HM?
WHAT'S THIS?

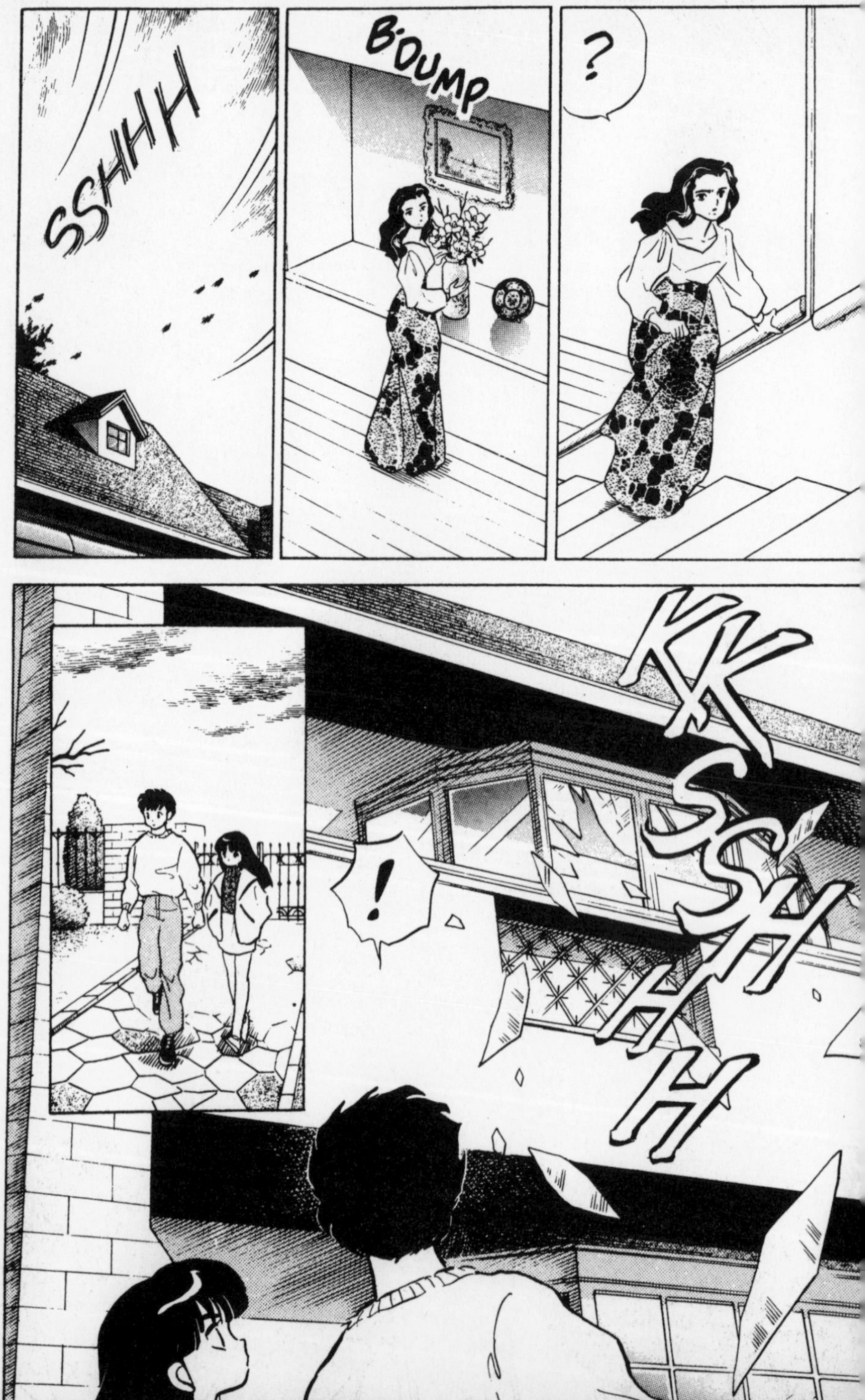
SSHHH
B'OUMP
?
!
KKSSHHHH

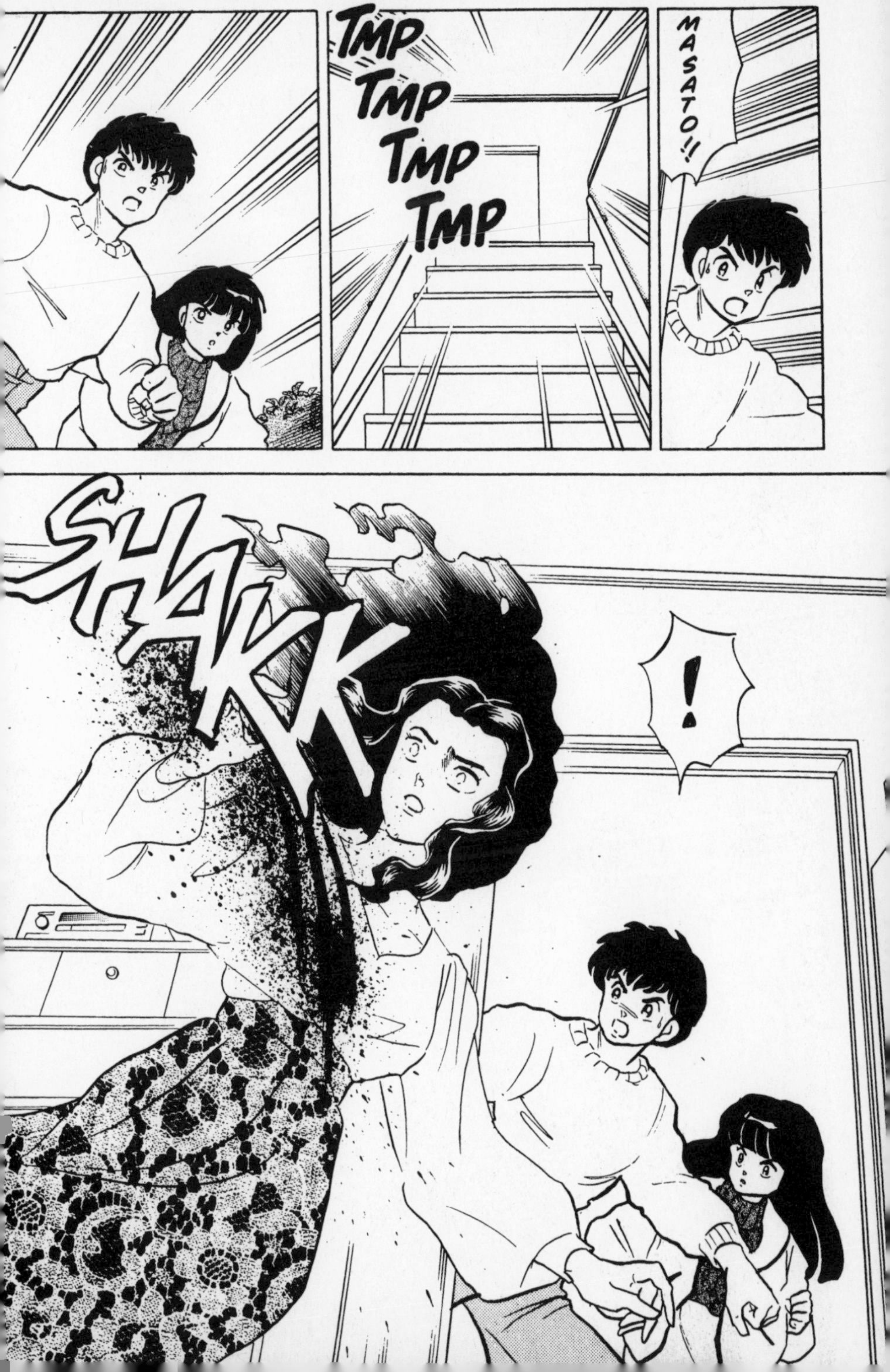

TMP
TMP
TMP
TMP
MASATO!!
SHAKK
!

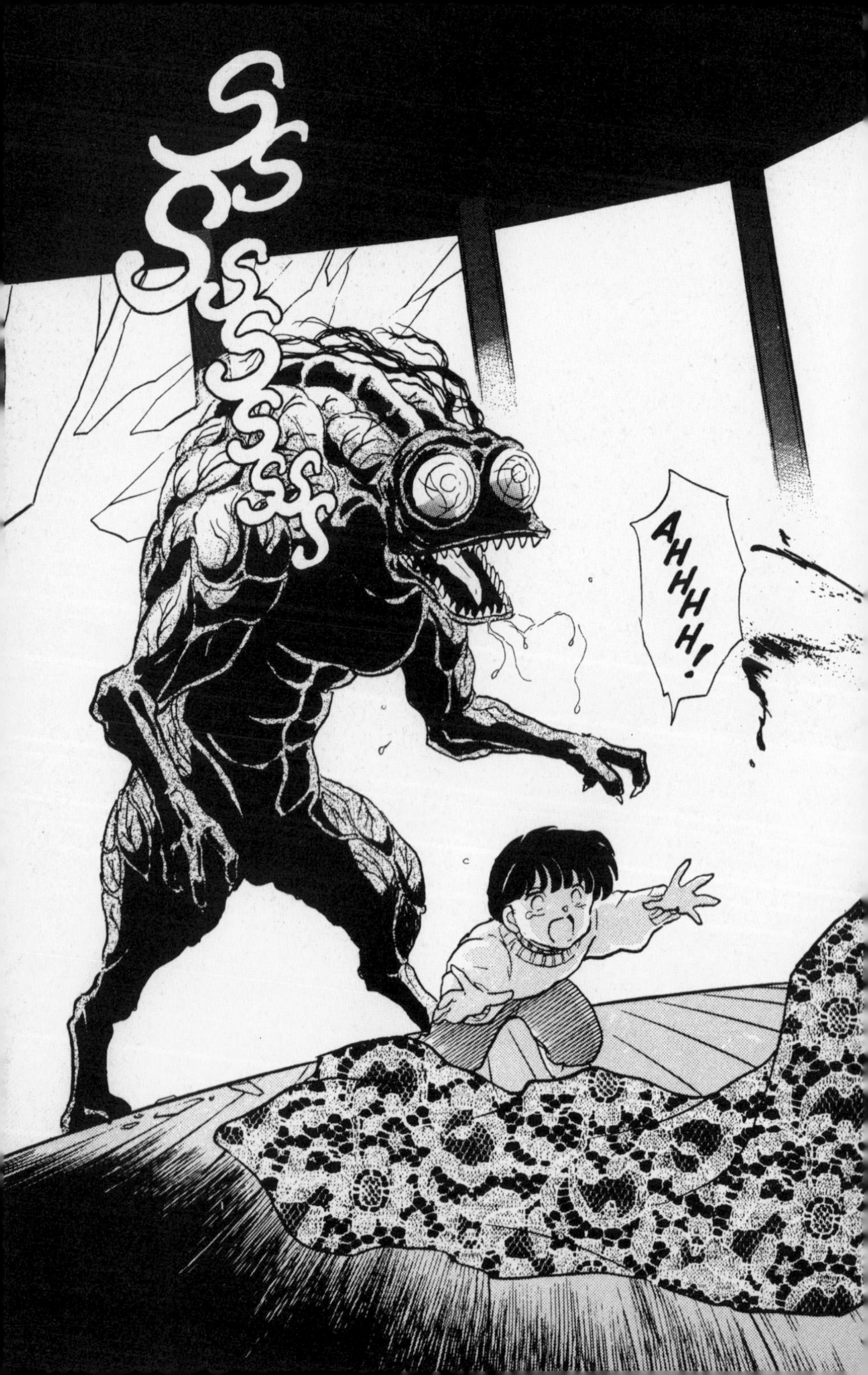
SSSSSSSS
AHHHHH!

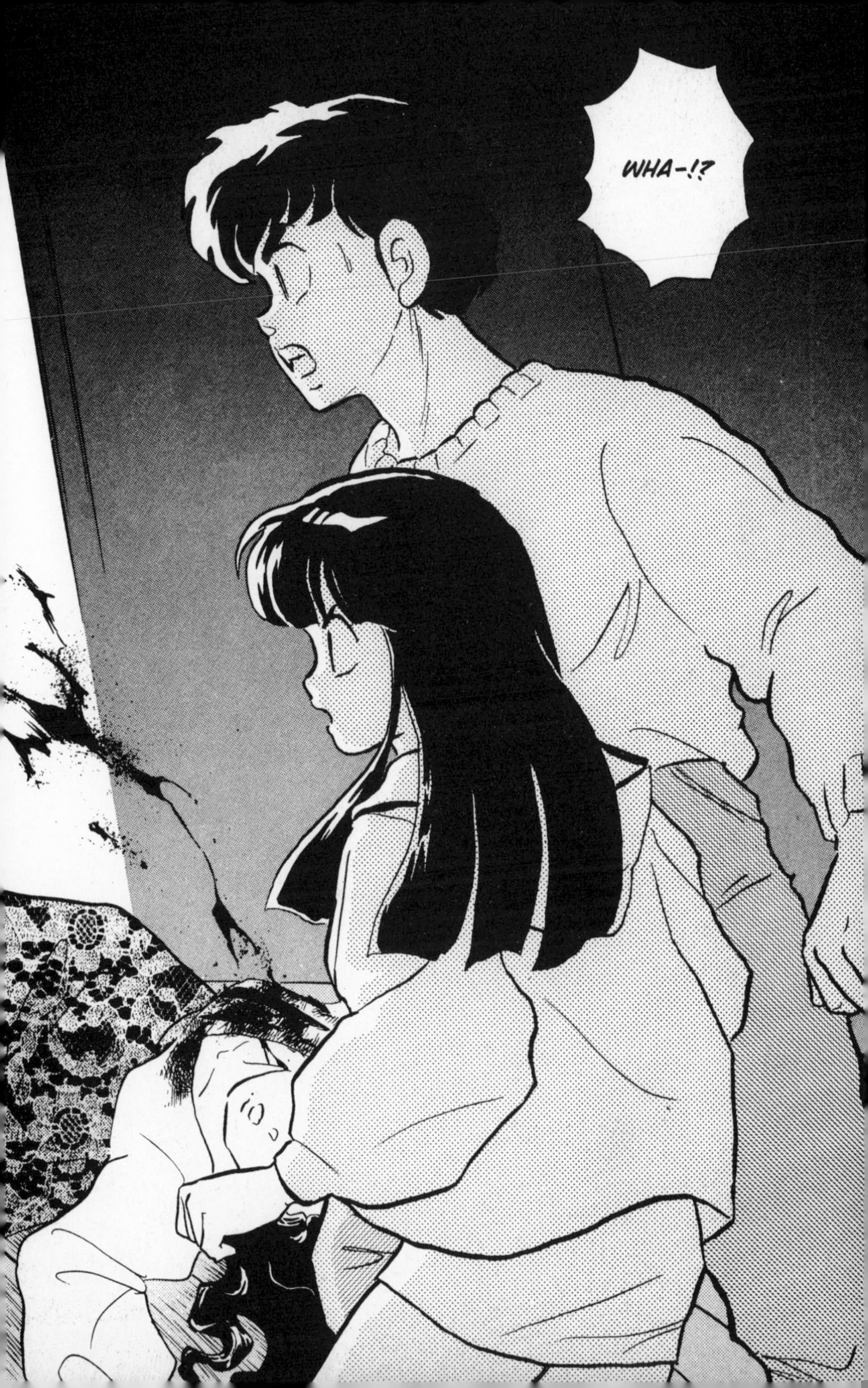
WHA-!?

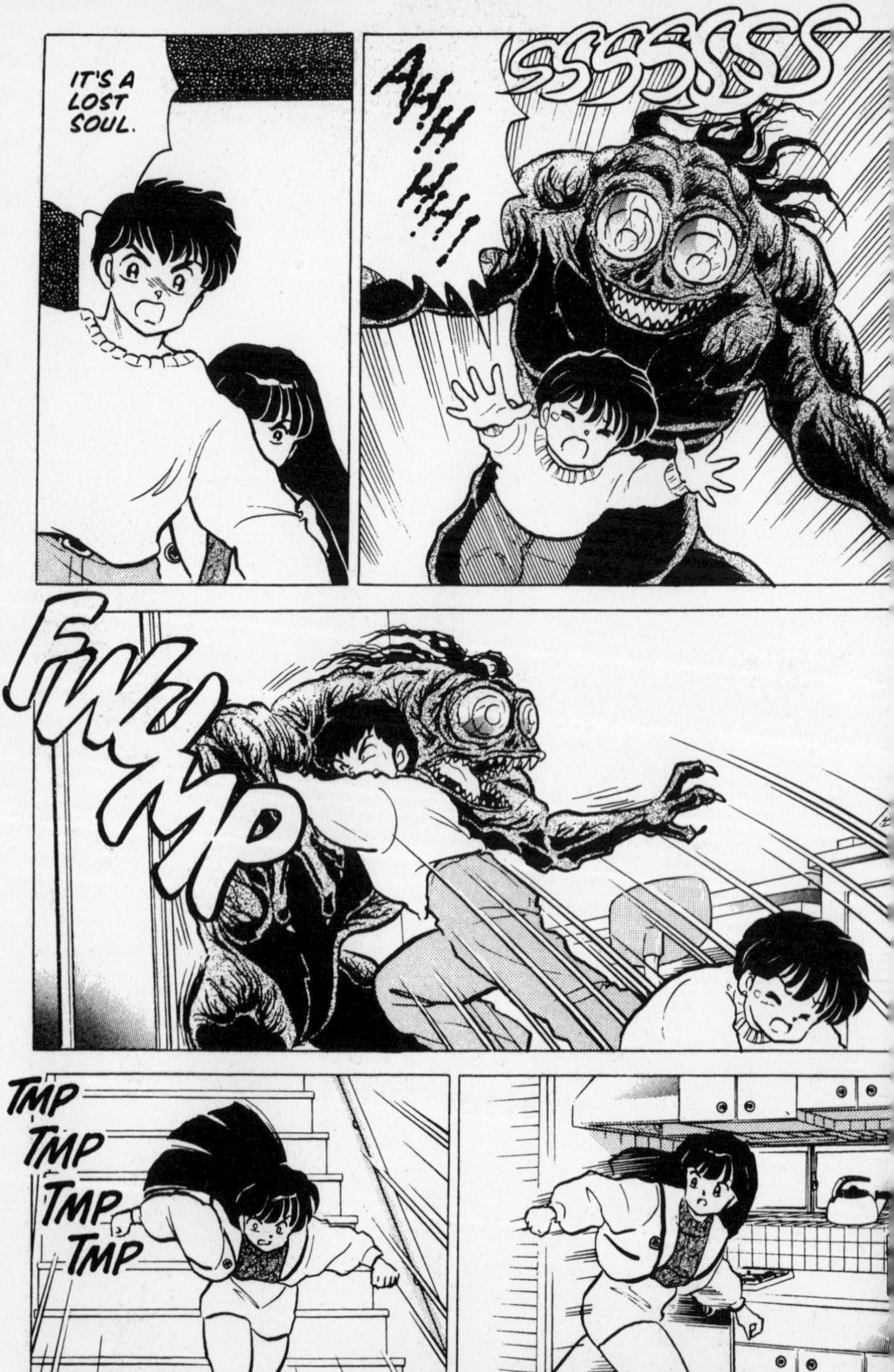
IT'S A LOST SOUL.
AHH HHH!!
SSSSSSS
FWUMP
TMP TMP TMP TMP

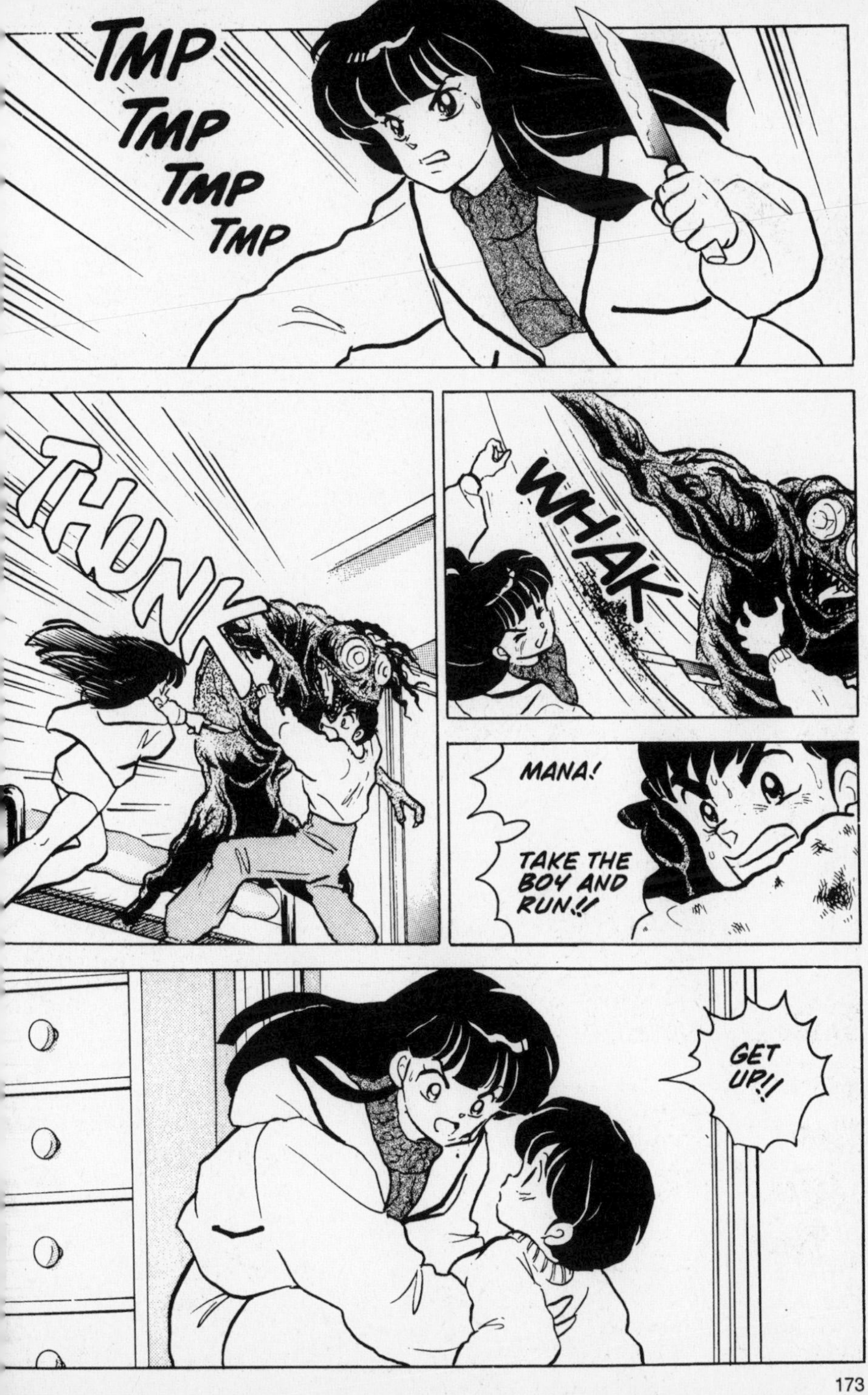
TMP
TMP
TMP
TMP
THUNK
WHAK
MANA!
TAKE THE BOY AND RUN!!
GET UP!!

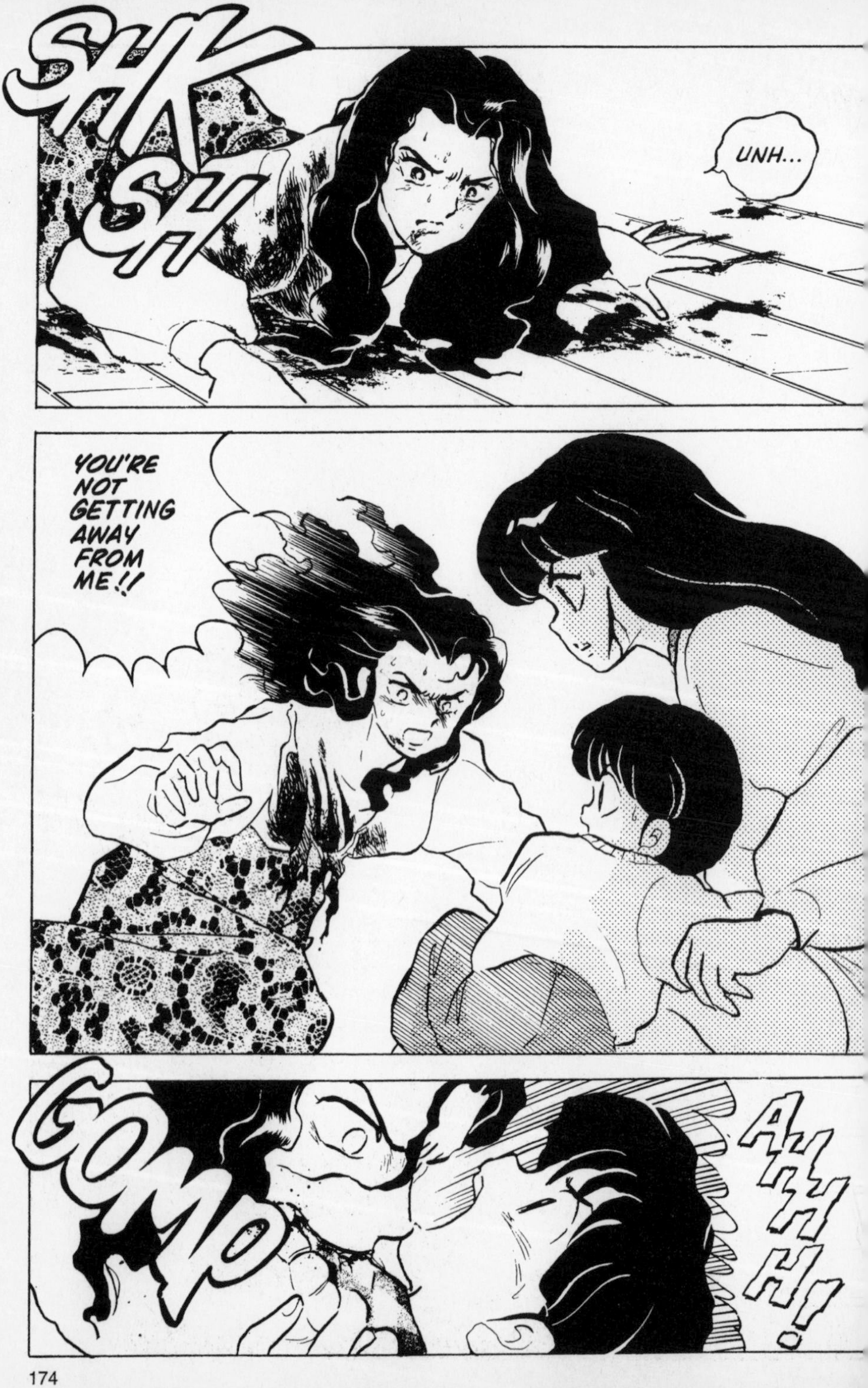
SHK SHK
UNH...
YOU'RE NOT GETTING AWAY FROM ME!!
GOMP
AHHH!

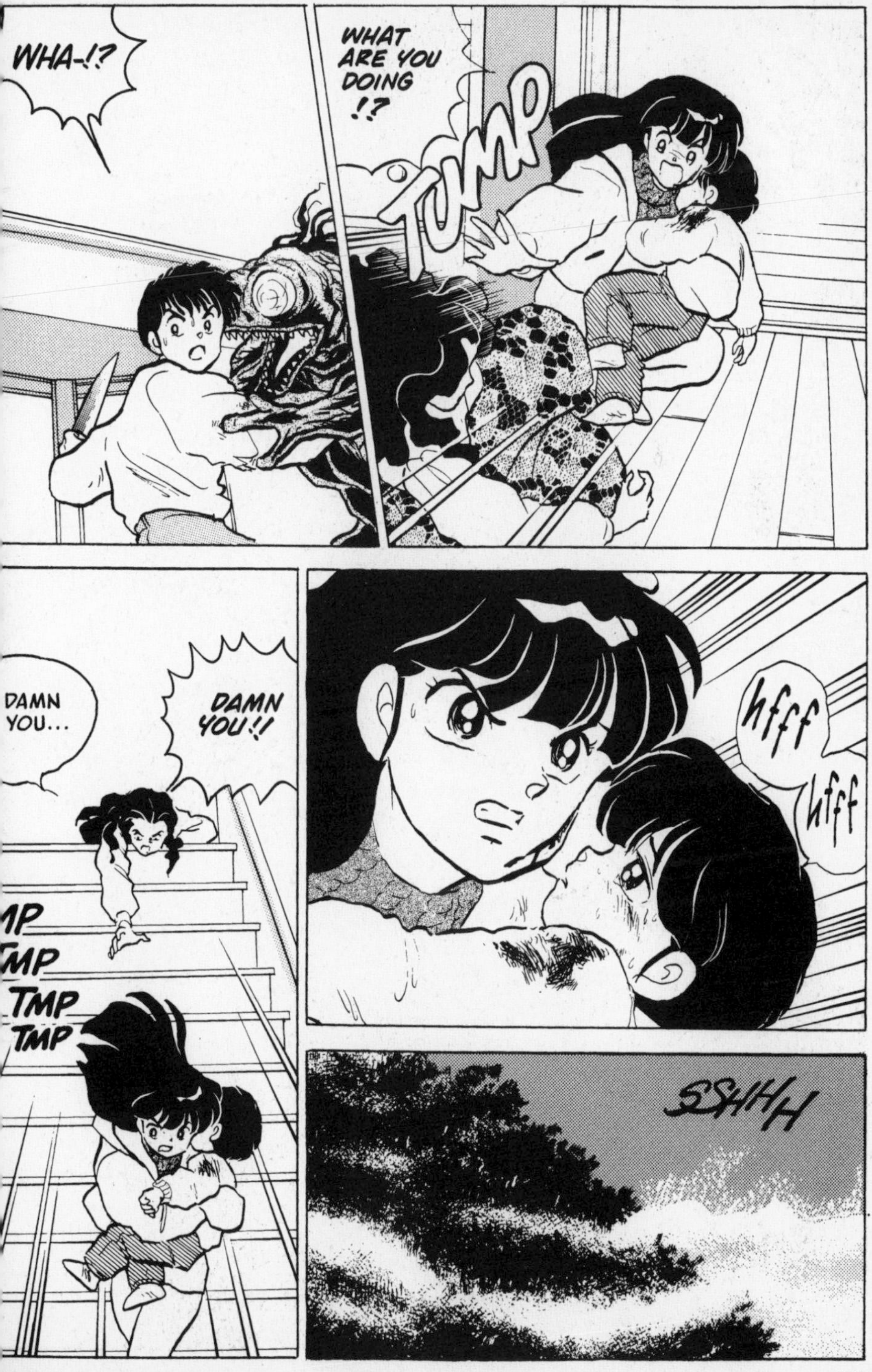
WHA-!?
WHAT ARE YOU DOING !?
TOMP
DAMN YOU...
DAMN YOU!!
TMP
TMP
hfff
hfff

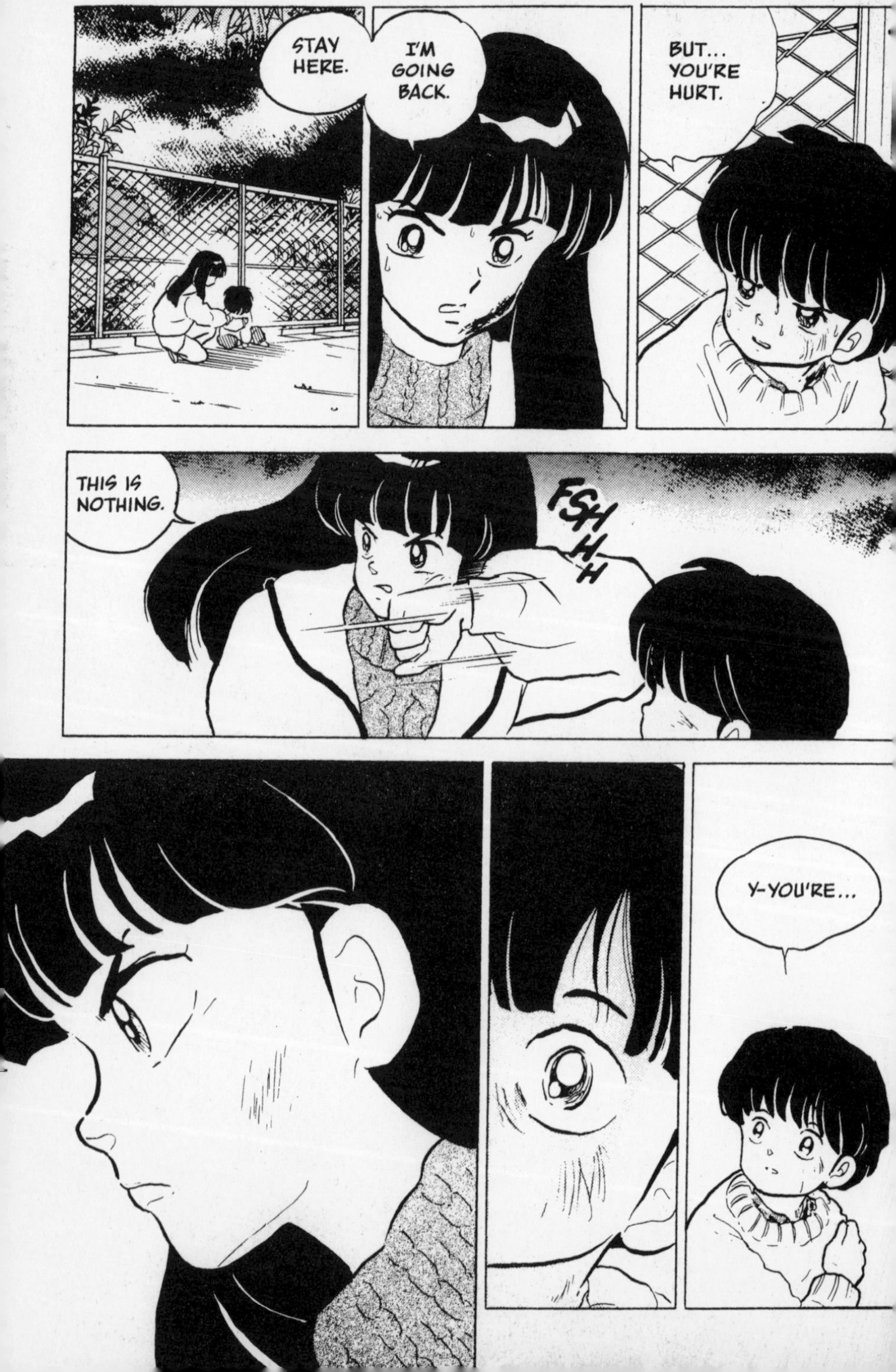

STAY HERE.
I'M GOING BACK.
BUT... YOU'RE HURT.
THIS IS NOTHING.
FSHHH
Y-YOU'RE...

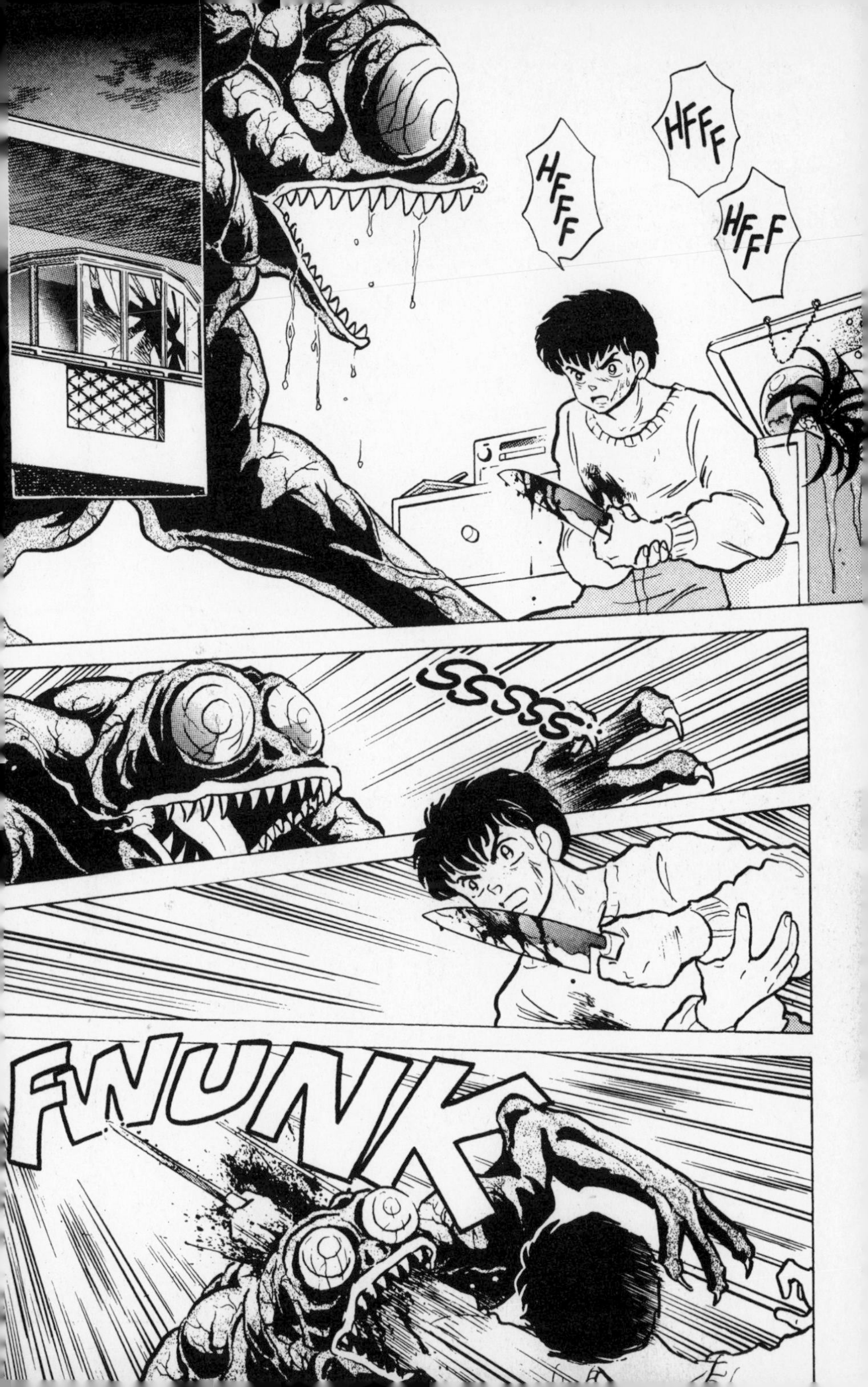
HFFF
HFFFF
HFFF
SSSSS
FWUNK

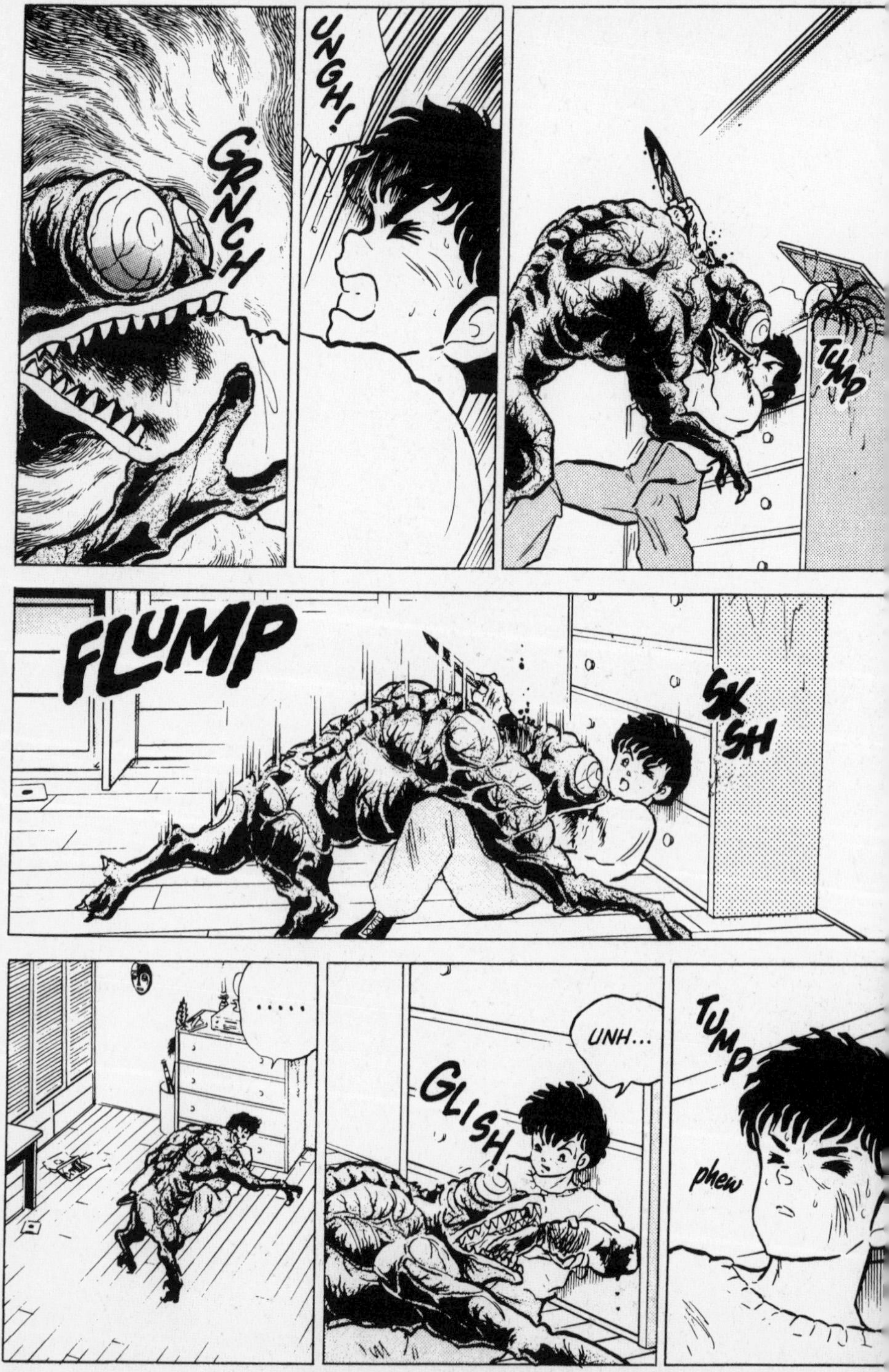
GRNCH
UNGH!
TUMP
FLUMP
SKSH
......
UNH...
GLISH!
TUMP
phew

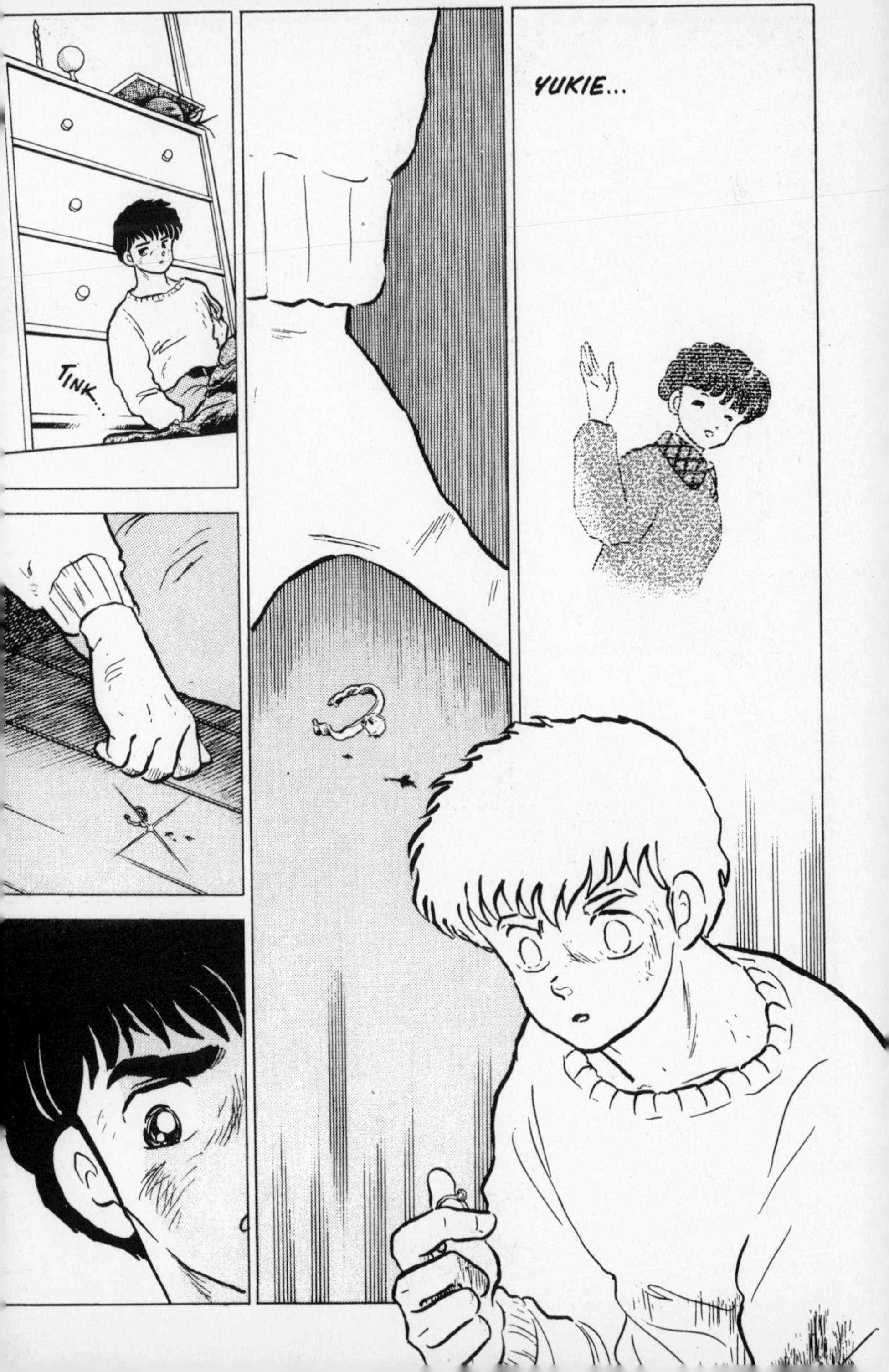
TINK...
YUKIE...

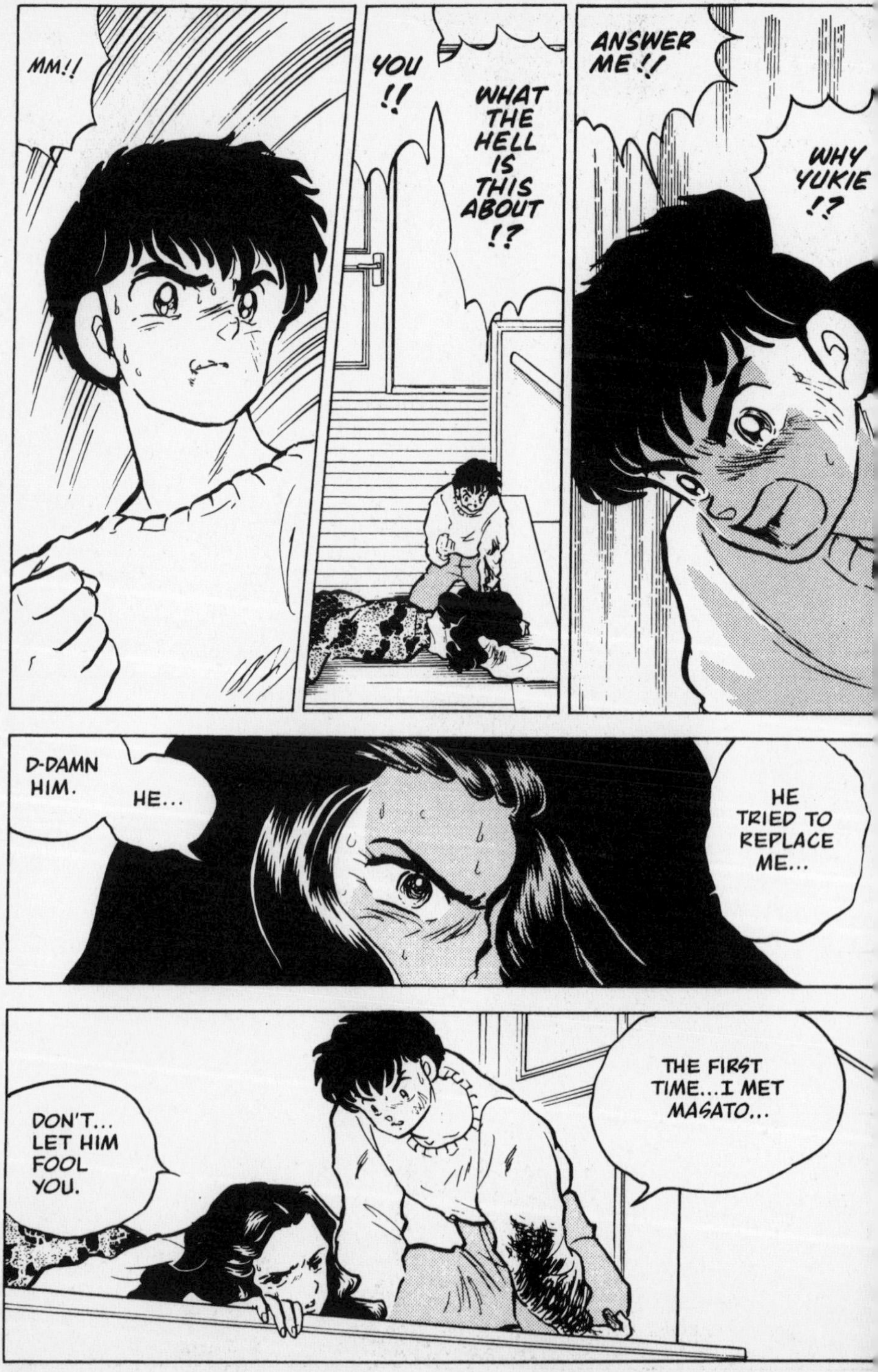
MM!!
YOU !!
WHAT THE HELL IS THIS ABOUT !?
ANSWER ME !!
WHY YUKIE !?
D-DAMN HIM.
HE...
HE TRIED TO REPLACE ME...
DON'T... LET HIM FOOL YOU.
THE FIRST TIME...I MET MASATO...

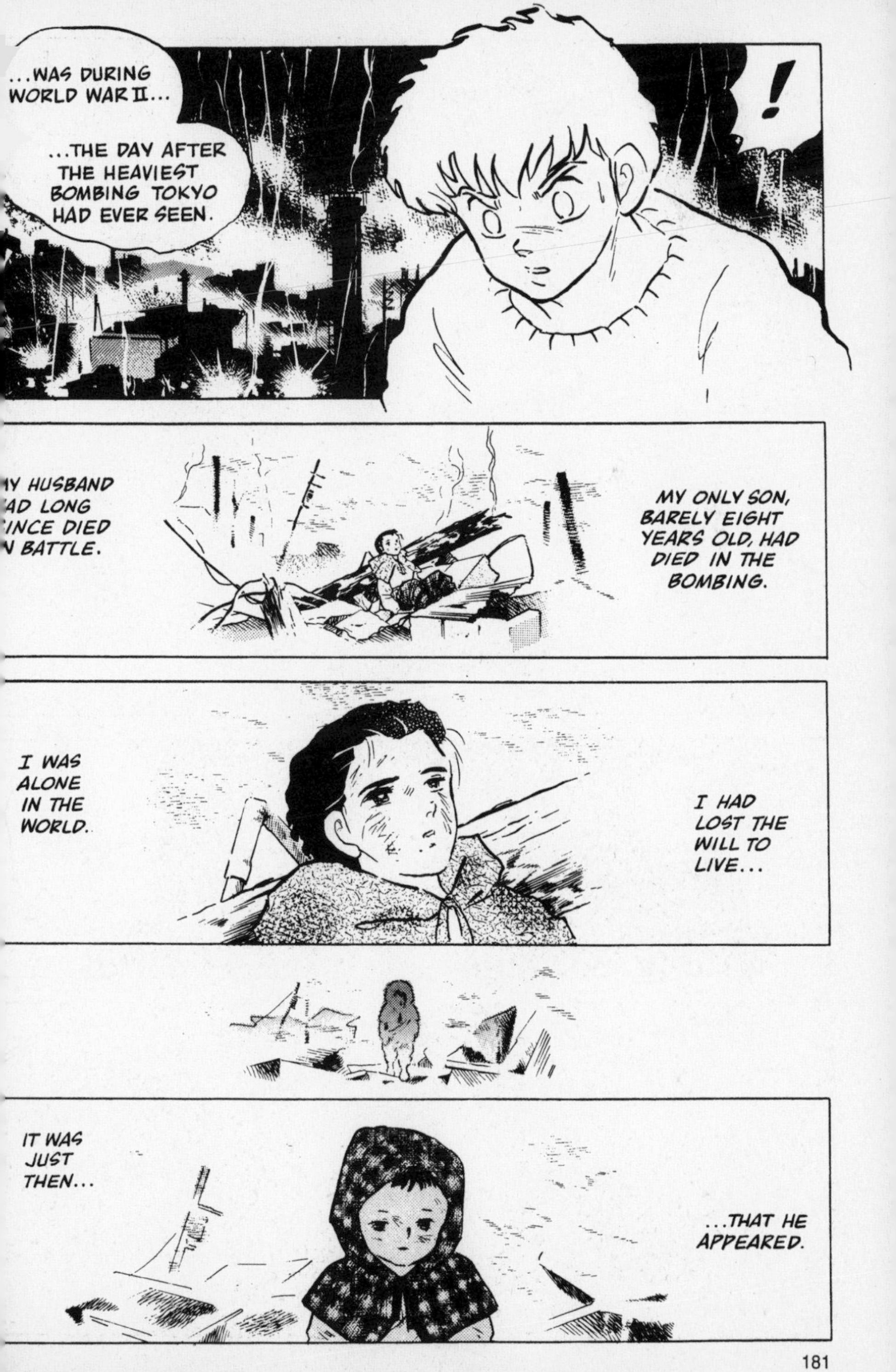

...WAS DURING WORLD WAR II...
...THE DAY AFTER THE HEAVIEST BOMBING TOKYO HAD EVER SEEN.
!
MY HUSBAND HAD LONG SINCE DIED IN BATTLE.
MY ONLY SON, BARELY EIGHT YEARS OLD, HAD DIED IN THE BOMBING.
I WAS ALONE IN THE WORLD.
I HAD LOST THE WILL TO LIVE...
IT WAS JUST THEN...
...THAT HE APPEARED.

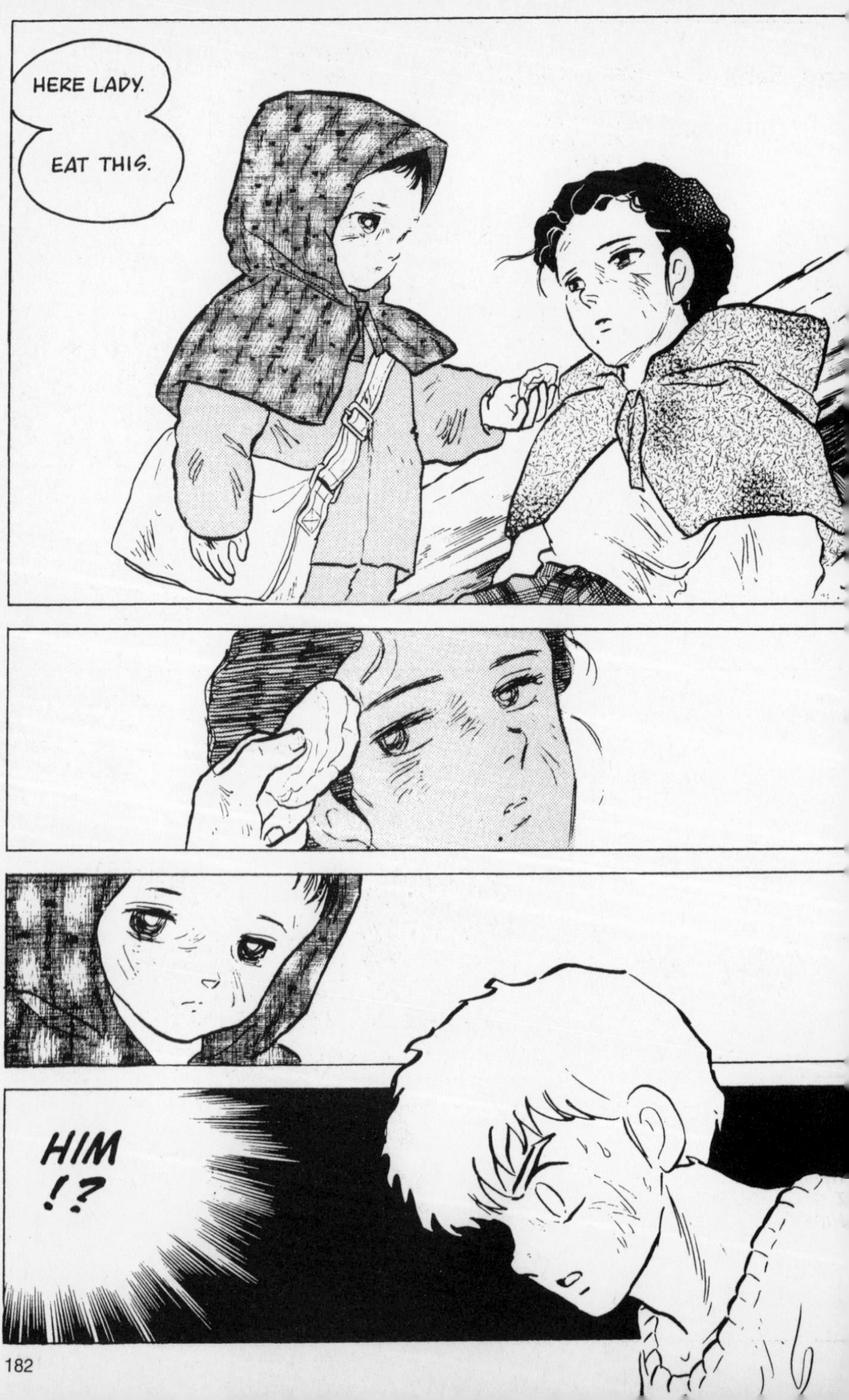
HERE LADY.
EAT THIS.
HIM !?

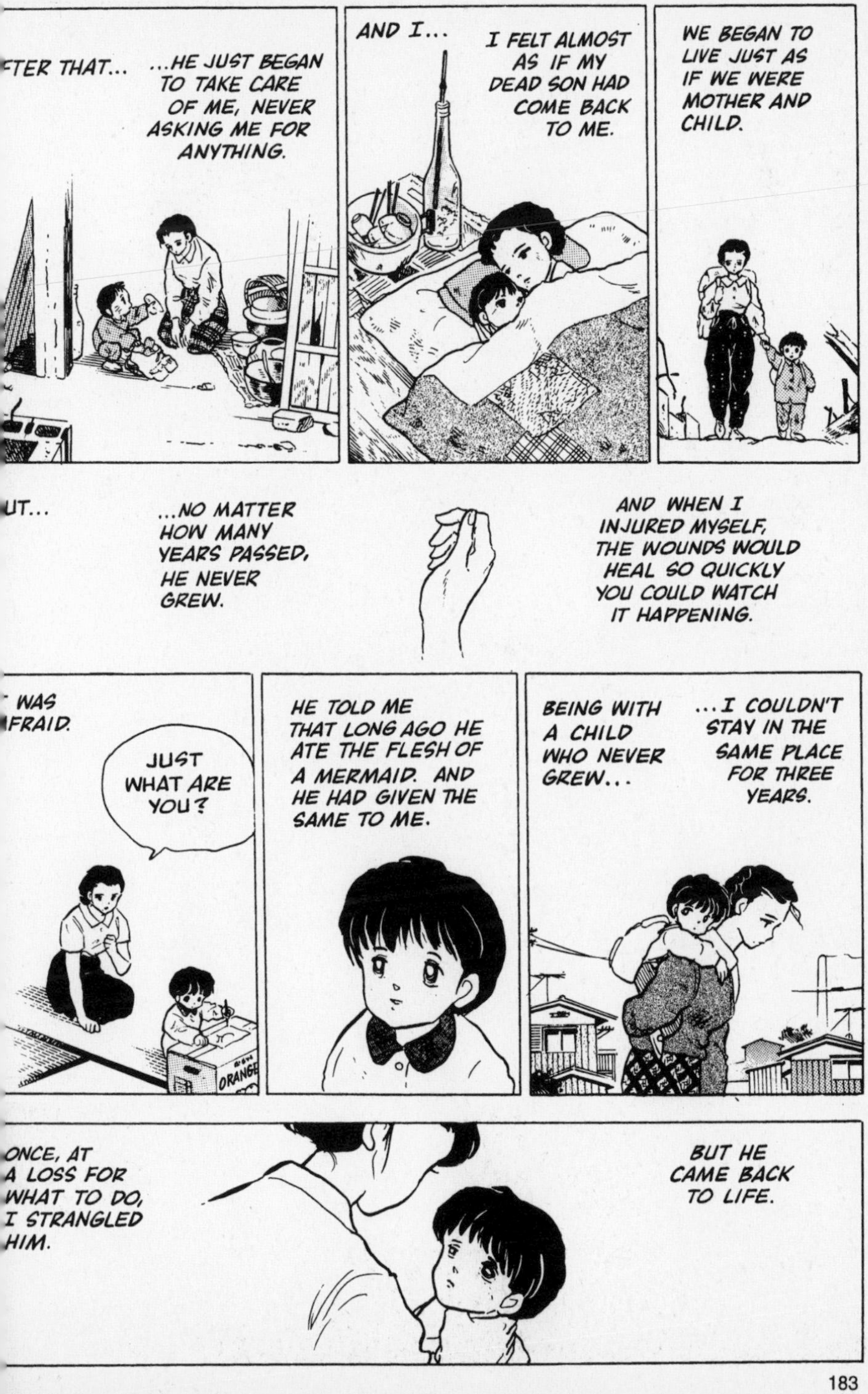
TER THAT...
...HE JUST BEGAN TO TAKE CARE OF ME, NEVER ASKING ME FOR ANYTHING.
AND I...
I FELT ALMOST AS IF MY DEAD SON HAD COME BACK TO ME.
WE BEGAN TO LIVE JUST AS IF WE WERE MOTHER AND CHILD.
UT...
...NO MATTER HOW MANY YEARS PASSED, HE NEVER GREW.
AND WHEN I INJURED MYSELF, THE WOUNDS WOULD HEAL SO QUICKLY YOU COULD WATCH IT HAPPENING.
WAS
FRAID.
JUST WHAT ARE YOU?
ORANGE
HE TOLD ME THAT LONG AGO HE ATE THE FLESH OF A MERMAID. AND HE HAD GIVEN THE SAME TO ME.
BEING WITH A CHILD WHO NEVER GREW...
...I COULDN'T STAY IN THE SAME PLACE FOR THREE YEARS.
ONCE, AT A LOSS FOR WHAT TO DO, I STRANGLED HIM.
BUT HE CAME BACK TO LIFE.

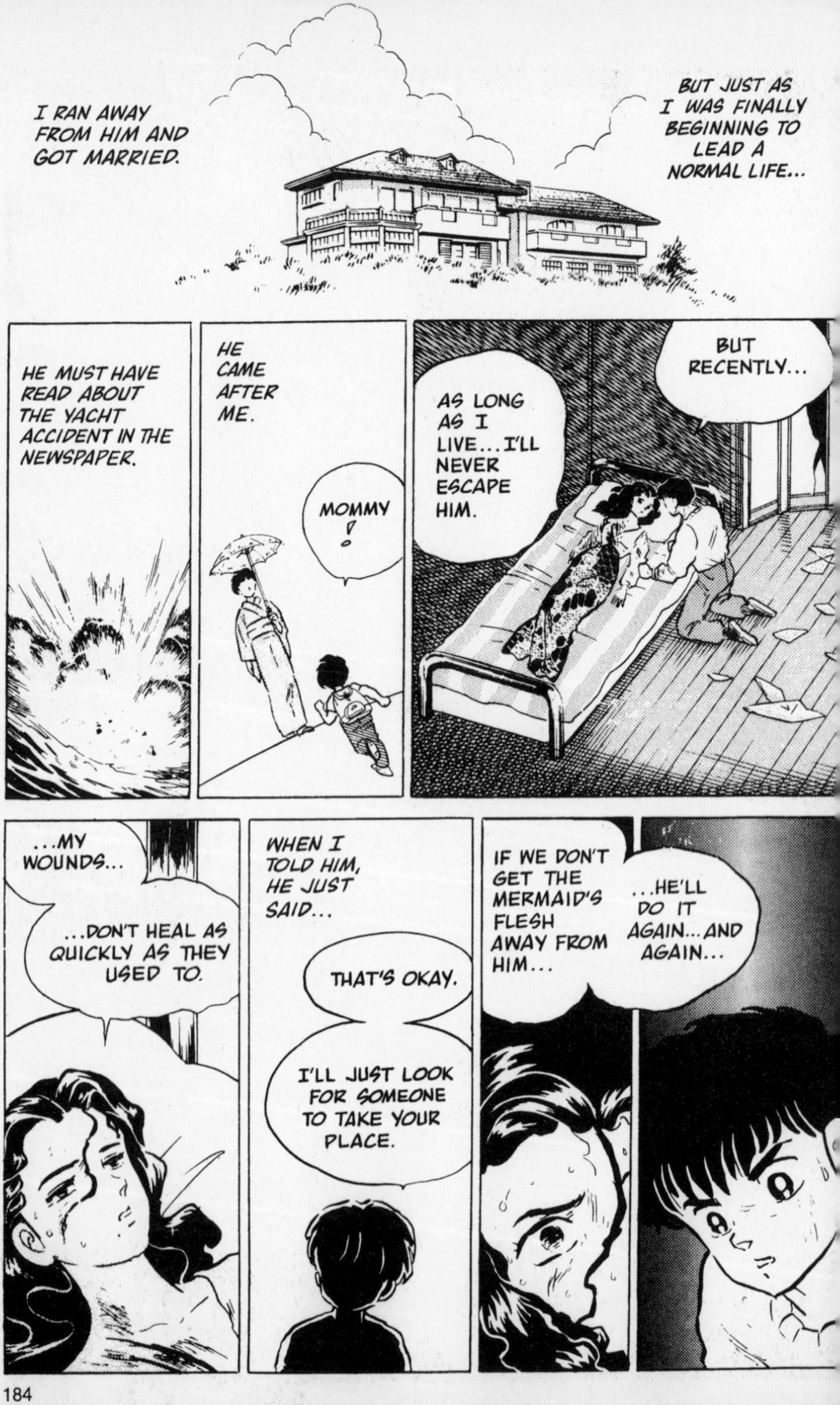
I RAN AWAY FROM HIM AND GOT MARRIED.
BUT JUST AS I WAS FINALLY BEGINNING TO LEAD A NORMAL LIFE...
HE MUST HAVE READ ABOUT THE YACHT ACCIDENT IN THE NEWSPAPER.
HE CAME AFTER ME.
MOMMY!
AS LONG AS I LIVE...I'LL NEVER ESCAPE HIM.
BUT RECENTLY...
...MY WOUNDS...
...DON'T HEAL AS QUICKLY AS THEY USED TO.
WHEN I TOLD HIM, HE JUST SAID...
THAT'S OKAY.
I'LL JUST LOOK FOR SOMEONE TO TAKE YOUR PLACE.
IF WE DON'T GET THE MERMAID'S FLESH AWAY FROM HIM...
...HE'LL DO IT AGAIN...AND AGAIN...

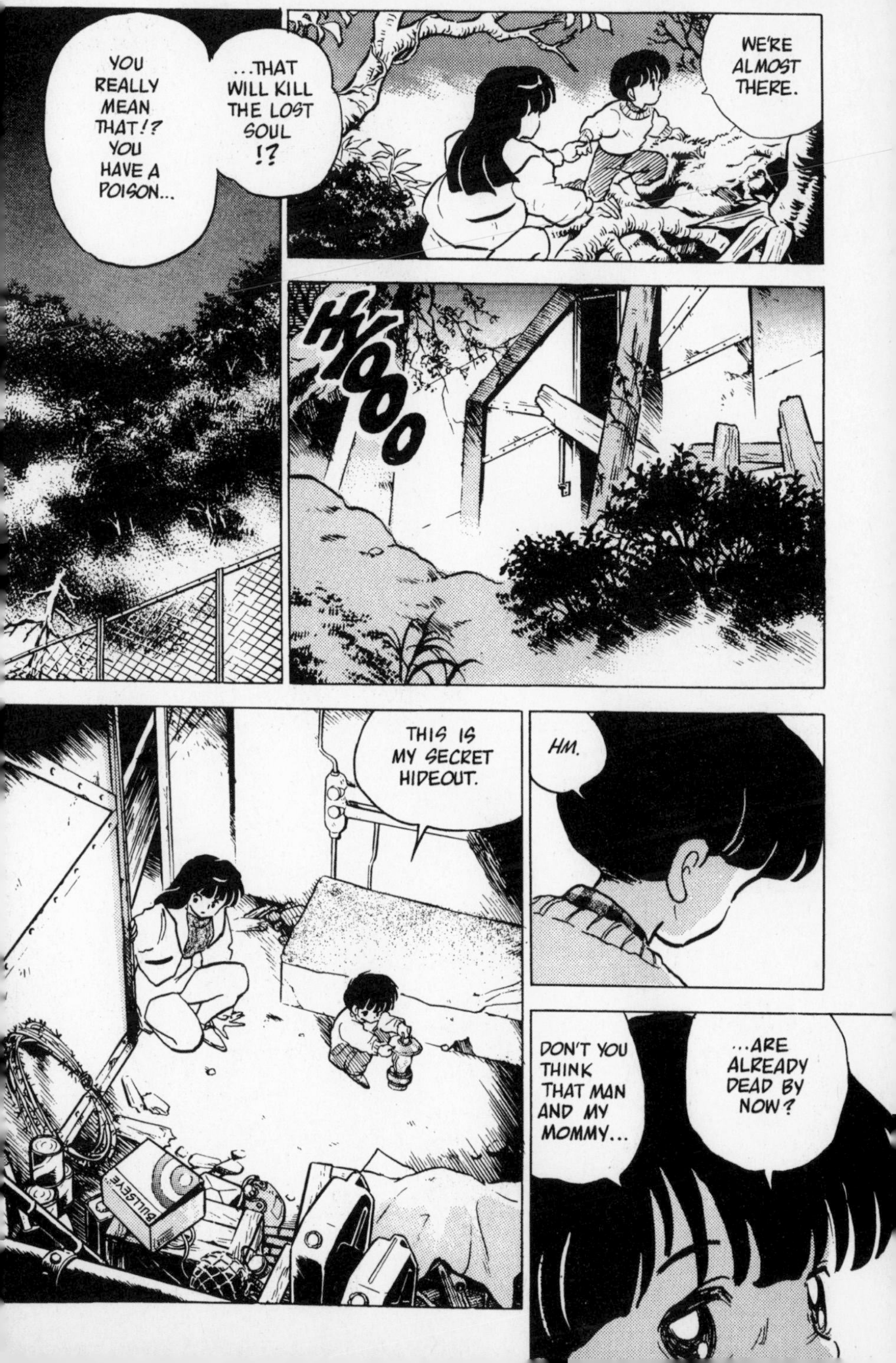
YOU REALLY MEAN THAT!? YOU HAVE A POISON...
...THAT WILL KILL THE LOST SOUL!?
WE'RE ALMOST THERE.
HYOOO
THIS IS MY SECRET HIDEOUT.
BULLSEYE
HM.
DON'T YOU THINK THAT MAN AND MY MOMMY...
...ARE ALREADY DEAD BY NOW?

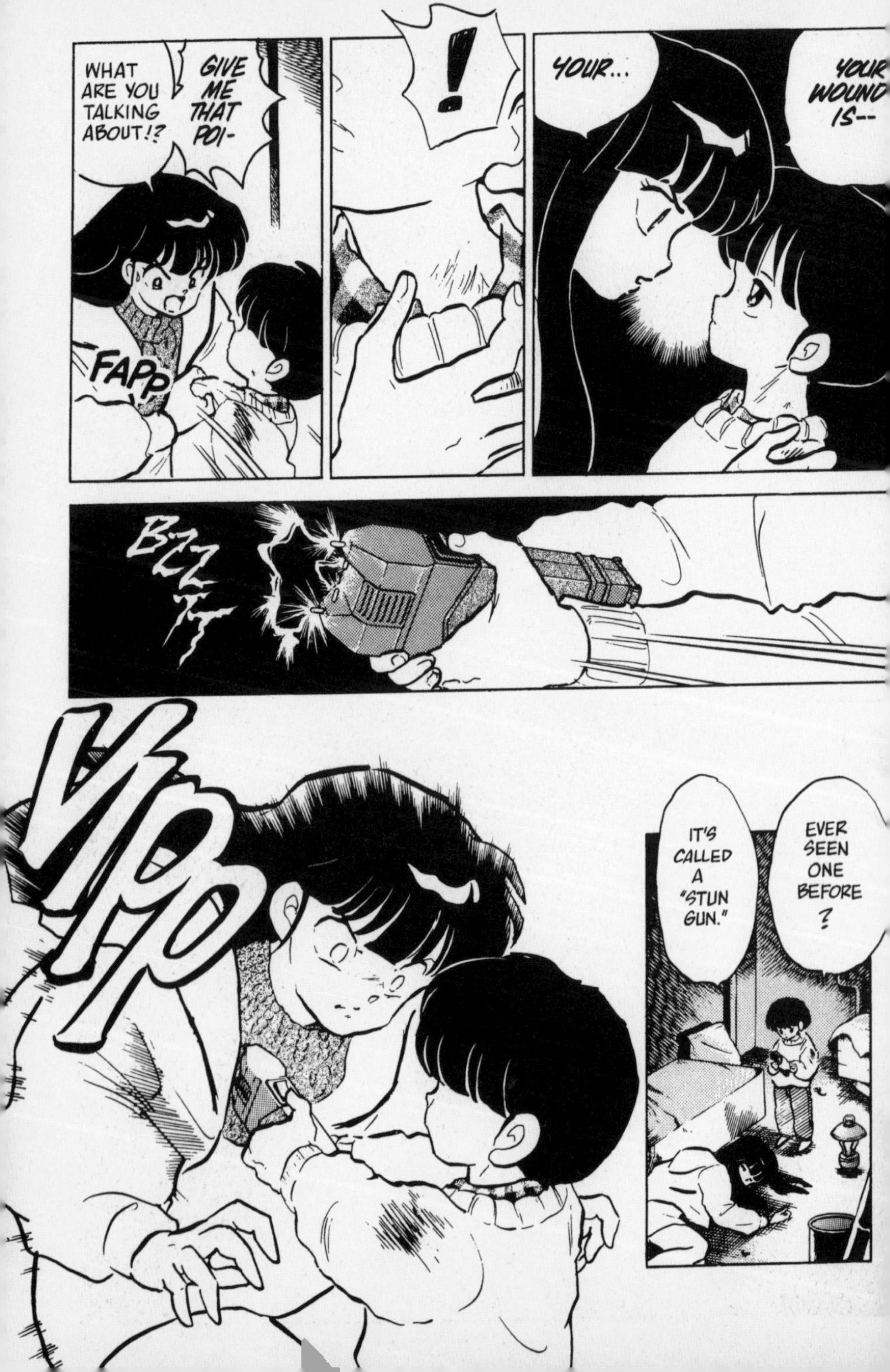
WHAT ARE YOU TALKING ABOUT!?
GIVE ME THAT POI-
FAPP
!
YOUR...
YOUR WOUND IS--
BZZZZT
VIP
IT'S CALLED A "STUN GUN."
EVER SEEN ONE BEFORE?

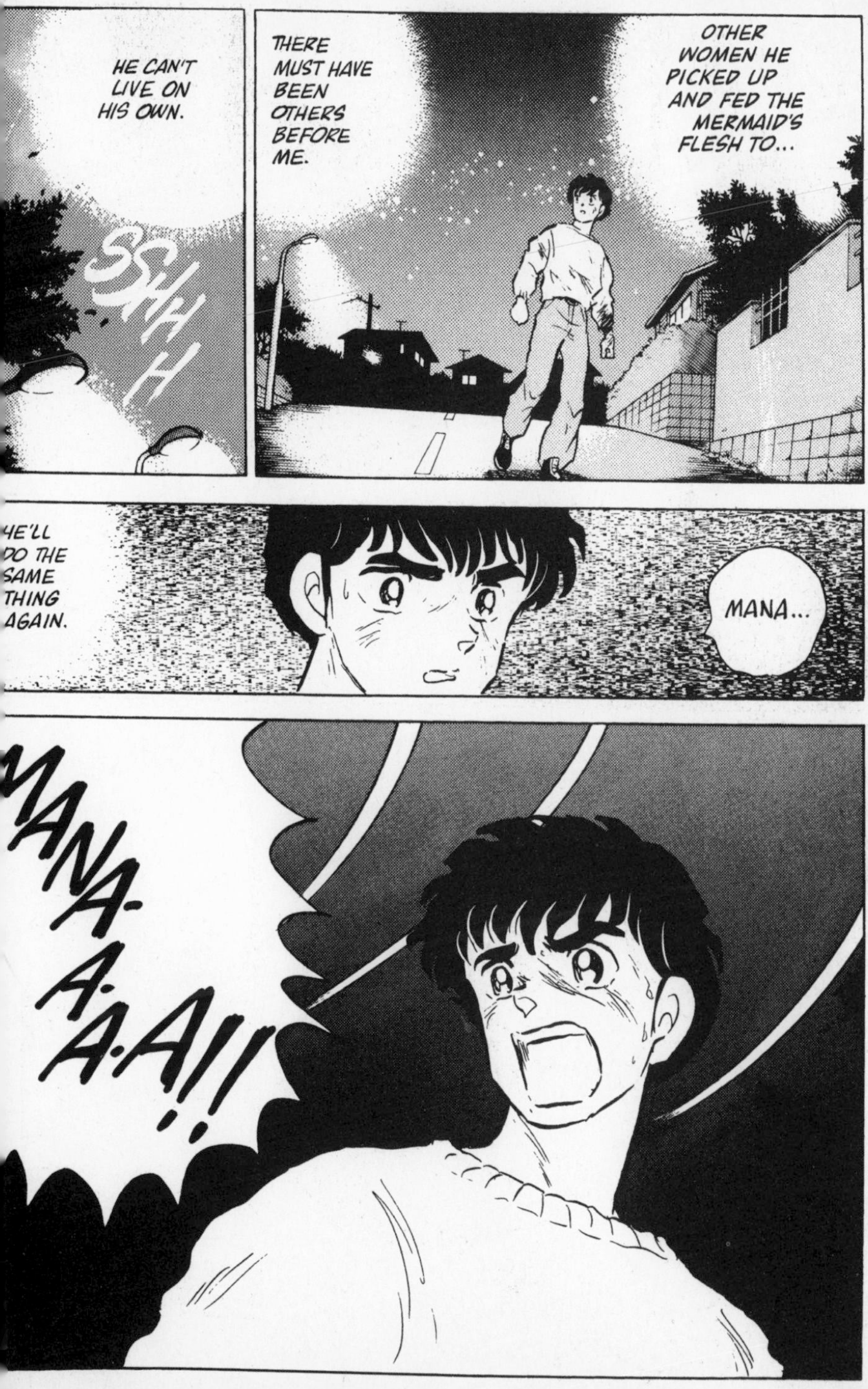
HE CAN'T LIVE ON HIS OWN.
SSHHH
THERE MUST HAVE BEEN OTHERS BEFORE ME.
OTHER WOMEN HE PICKED UP AND FED THE MERMAID'S FLESH TO...
HE'LL DO THE SAME THING AGAIN.
MANA...
MANA-A-A-A!!

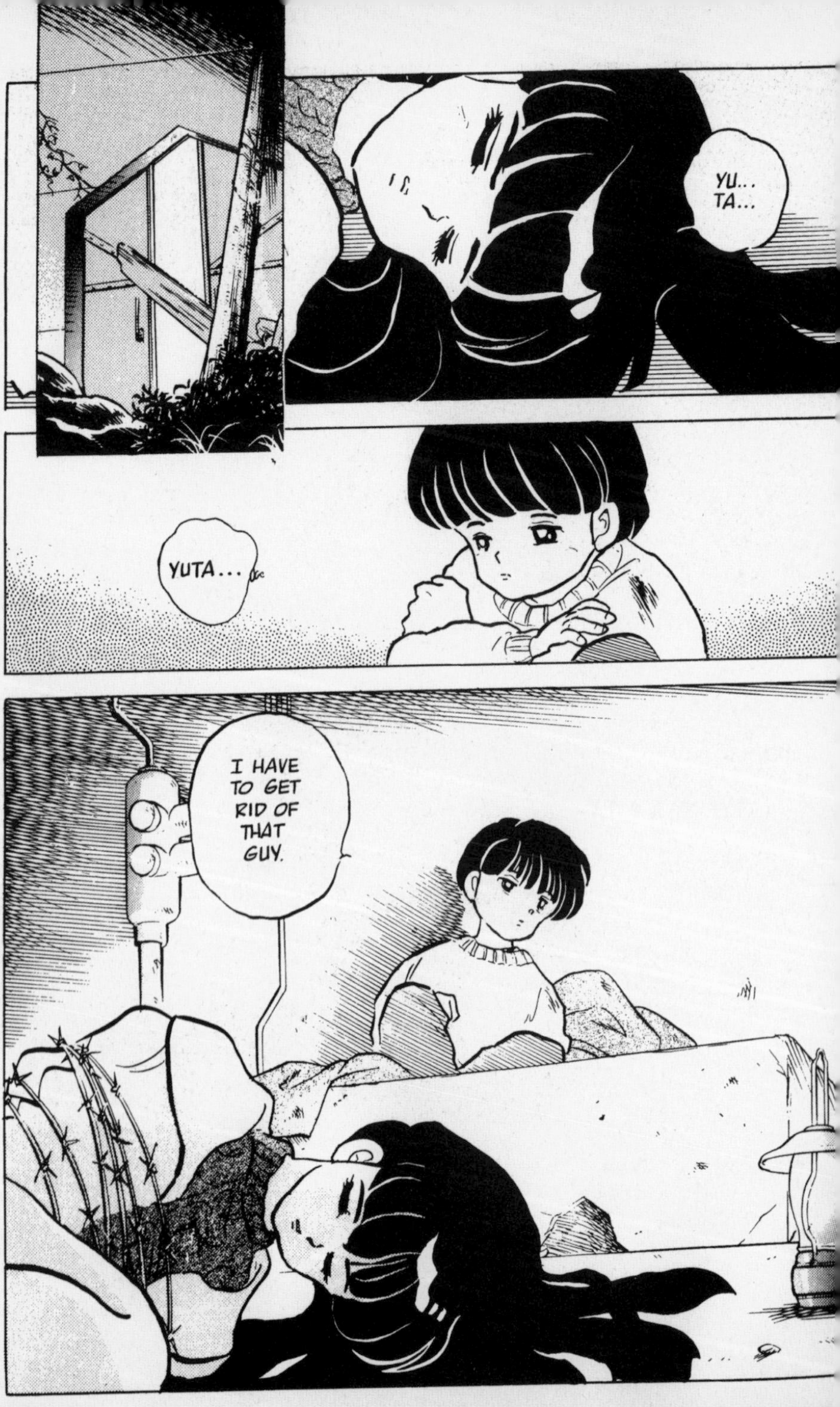
YU... TA...
YUTA...
I HAVE TO GET RID OF THAT GUY.

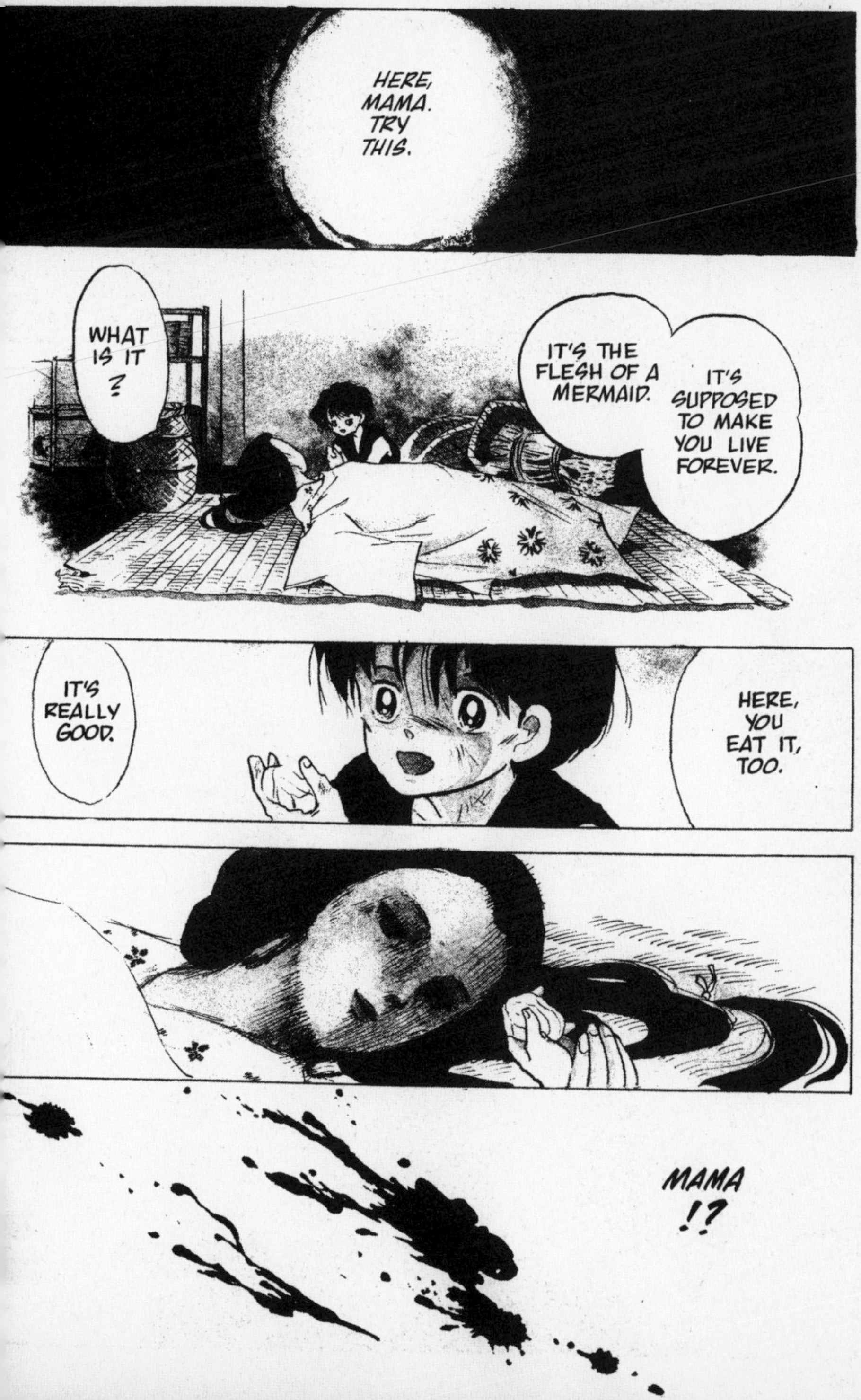
HERE, MAMA. TRY THIS.
WHAT IS IT ?
IT'S THE FLESH OF A MERMAID.
IT'S SUPPOSED TO MAKE YOU LIVE FOREVER.
IT'S REALLY GOOD.
HERE, YOU EAT IT, TOO.
MAMA !?

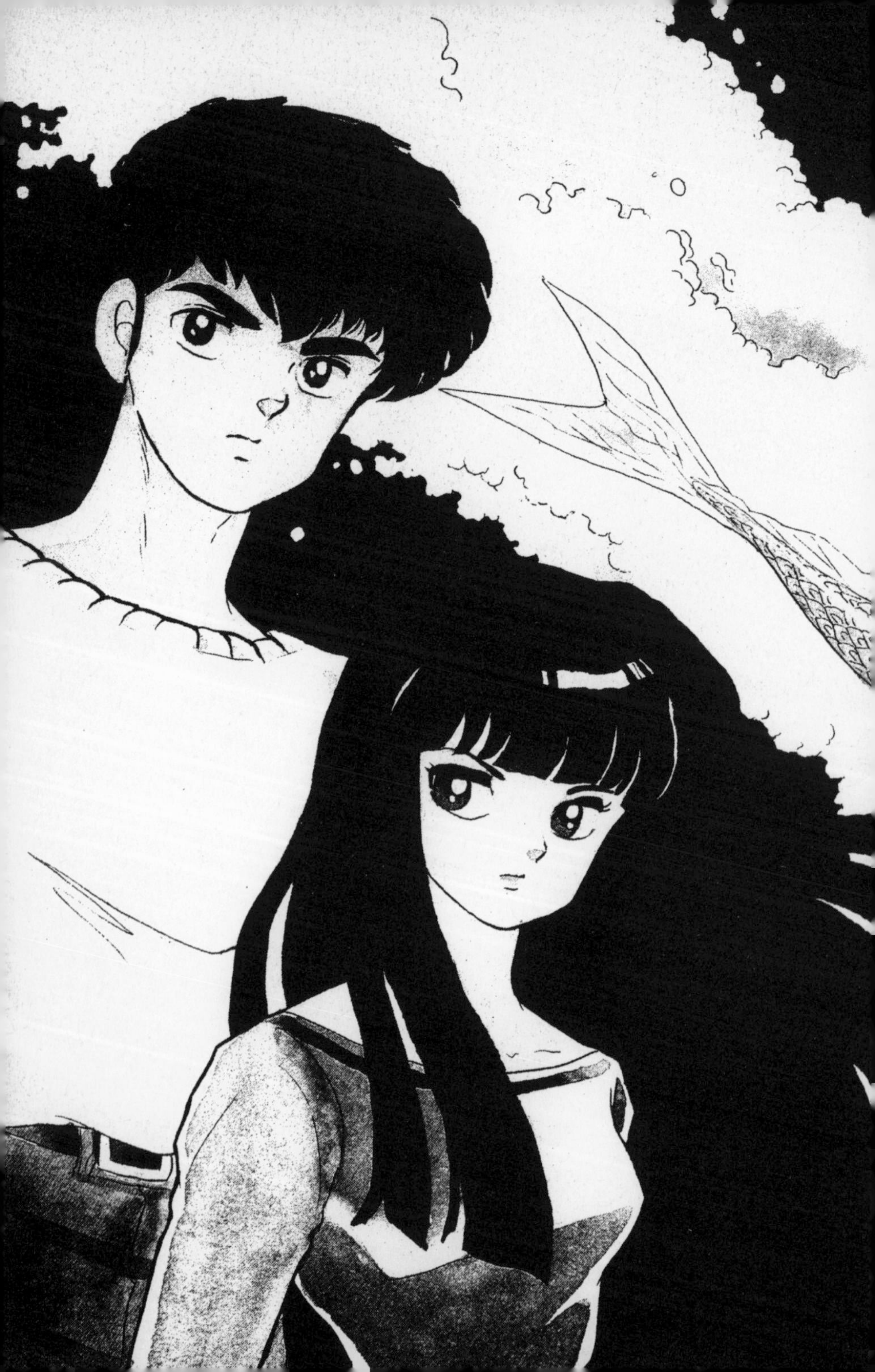

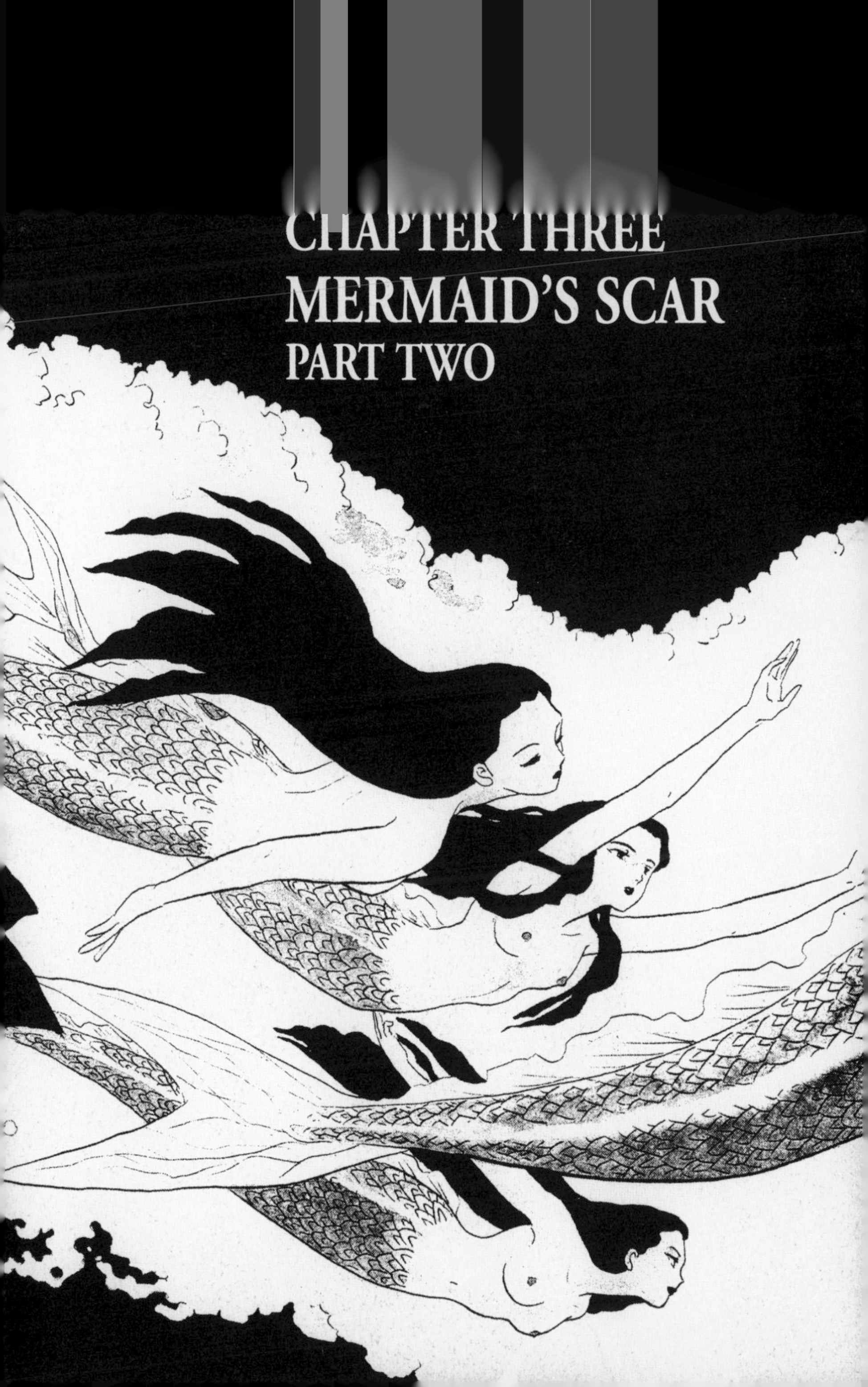
CHAPTER THREE
MERMAID'S SCAR
PART TWO

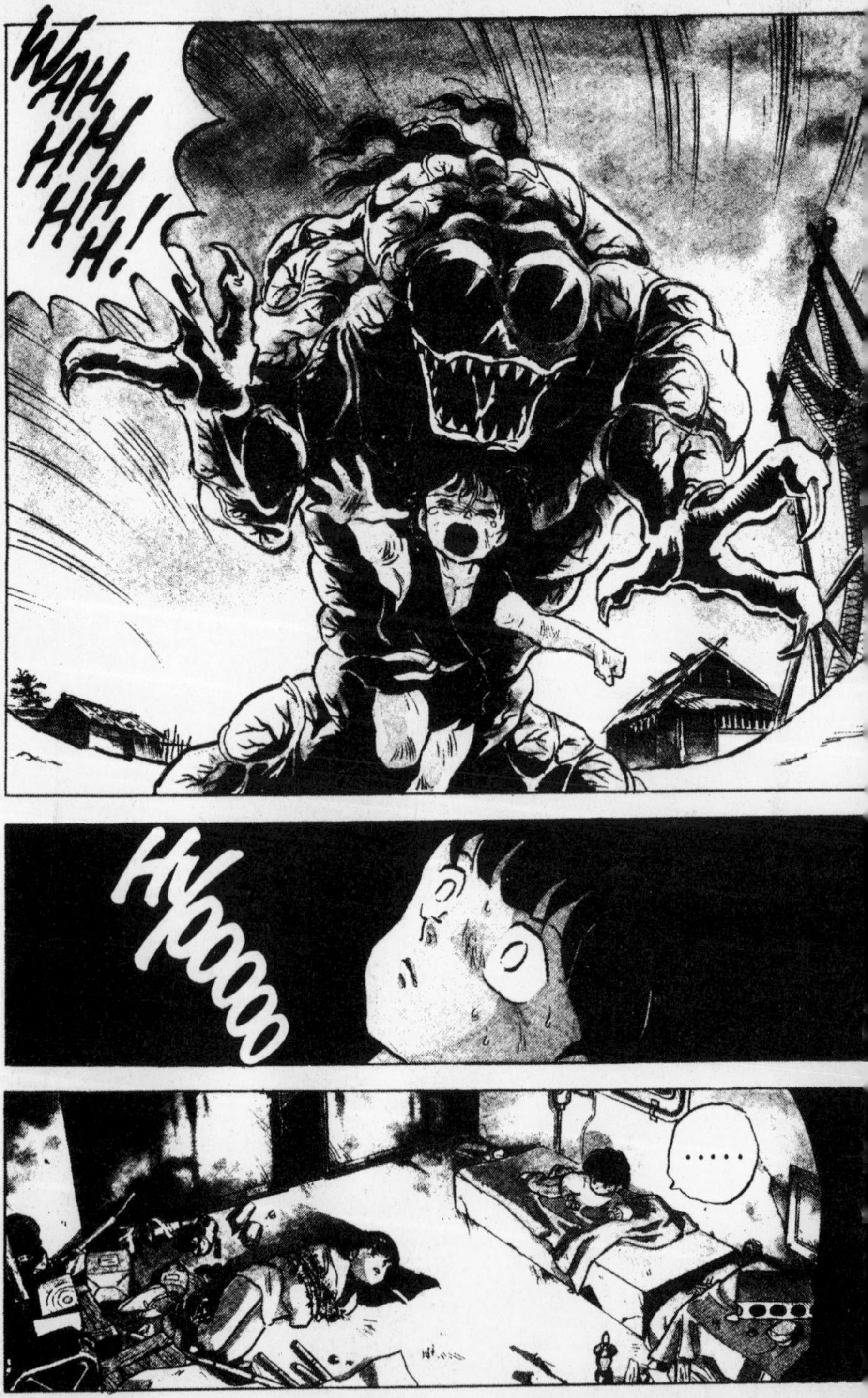
WAHHHHHHHH!
HYooooo
......

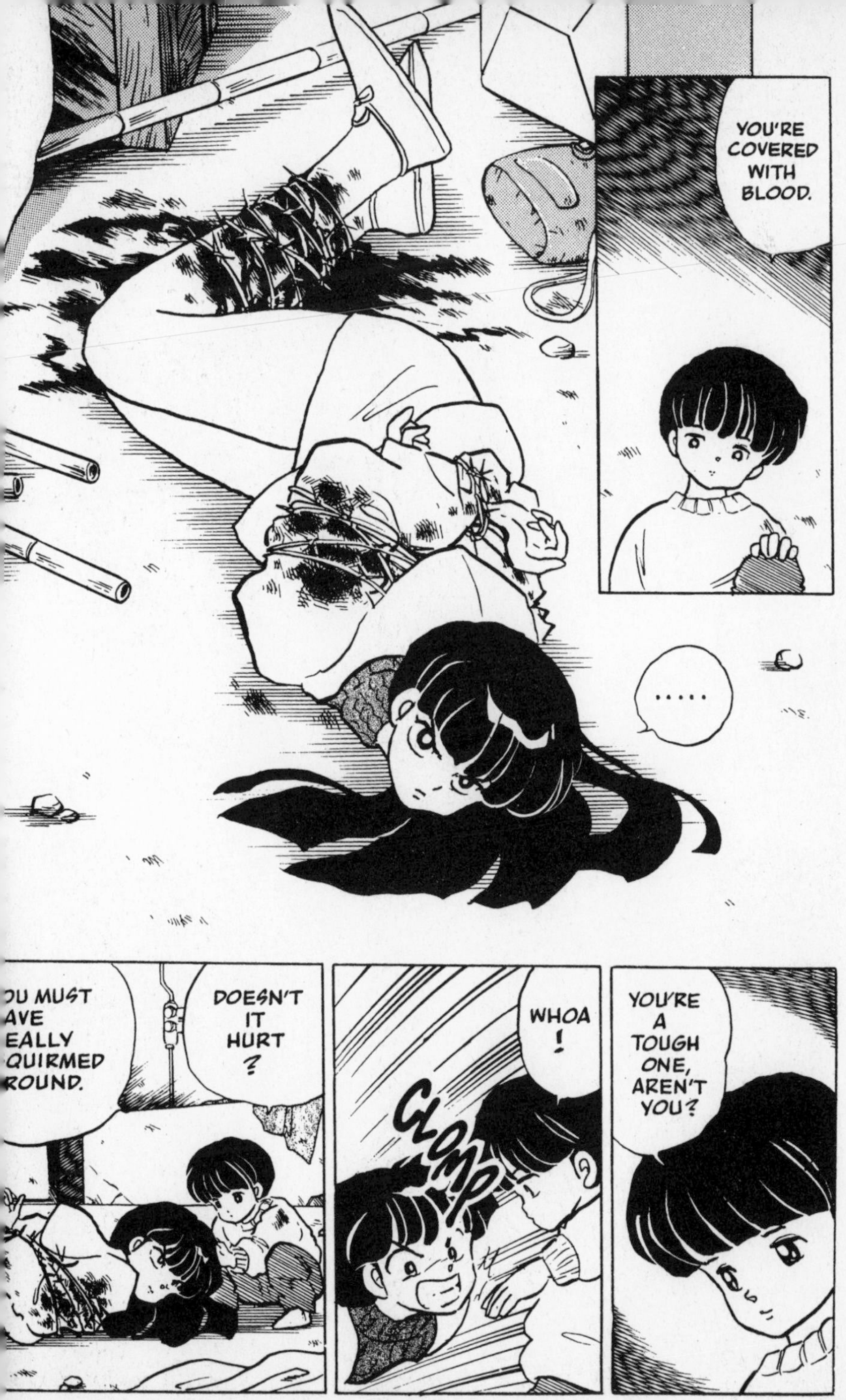

.....
YOU'RE COVERED WITH BLOOD.
OU MUST AVE EALLY QUIRMED ROUND.
DOESN'T IT HURT?
WHOA!
CLOMP
YOU'RE A TOUGH ONE, AREN'T YOU?

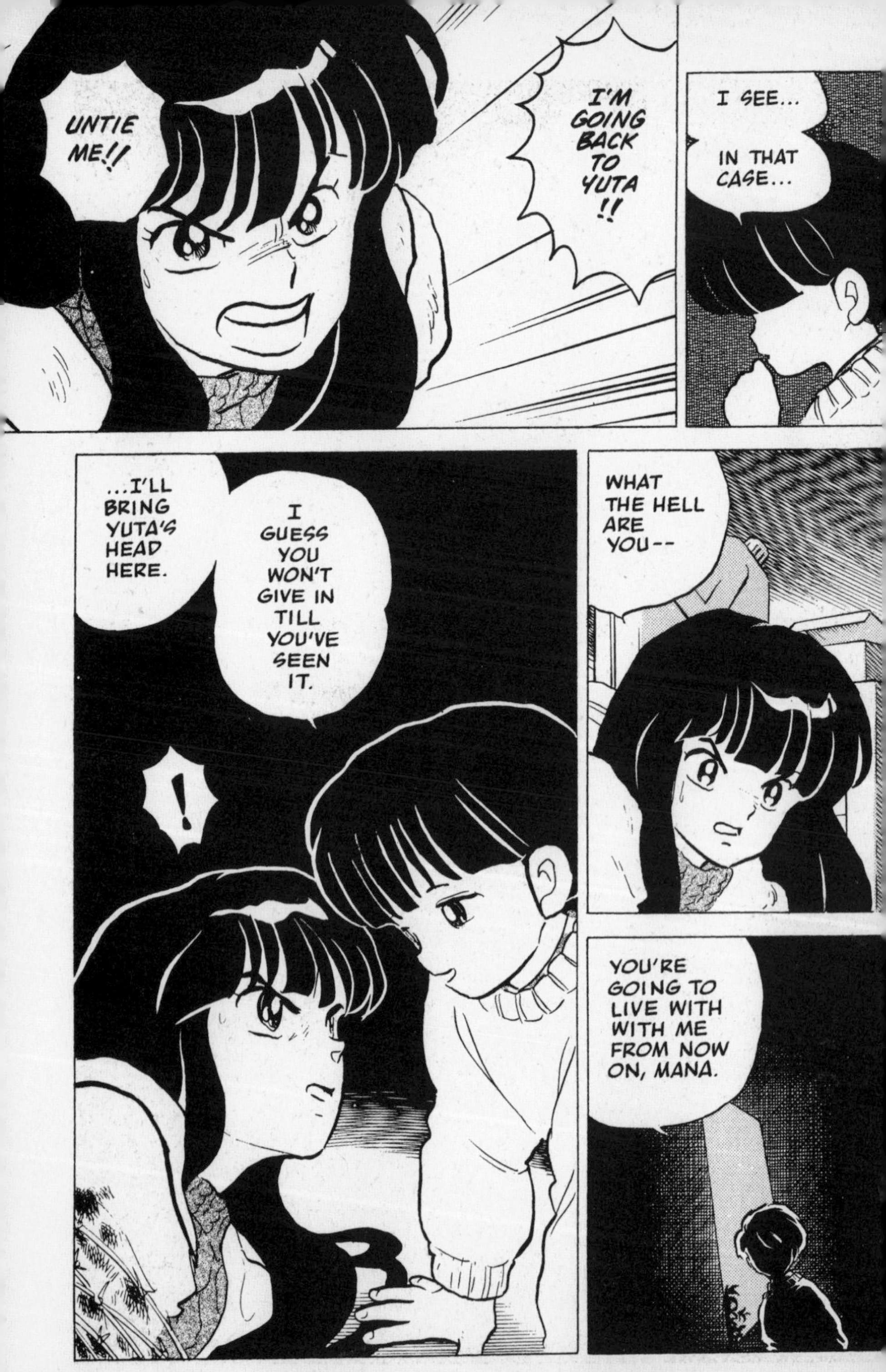
UNTIE ME!!
I'M GOING BACK TO YUTA!!
I SEE...
IN THAT CASE...
...I'LL BRING YUTA'S HEAD HERE.
I GUESS YOU WON'T GIVE IN TILL YOU'VE SEEN IT.
!
WHAT THE HELL ARE YOU--
YOU'RE GOING TO LIVE WITH WITH ME FROM NOW ON, MANA.

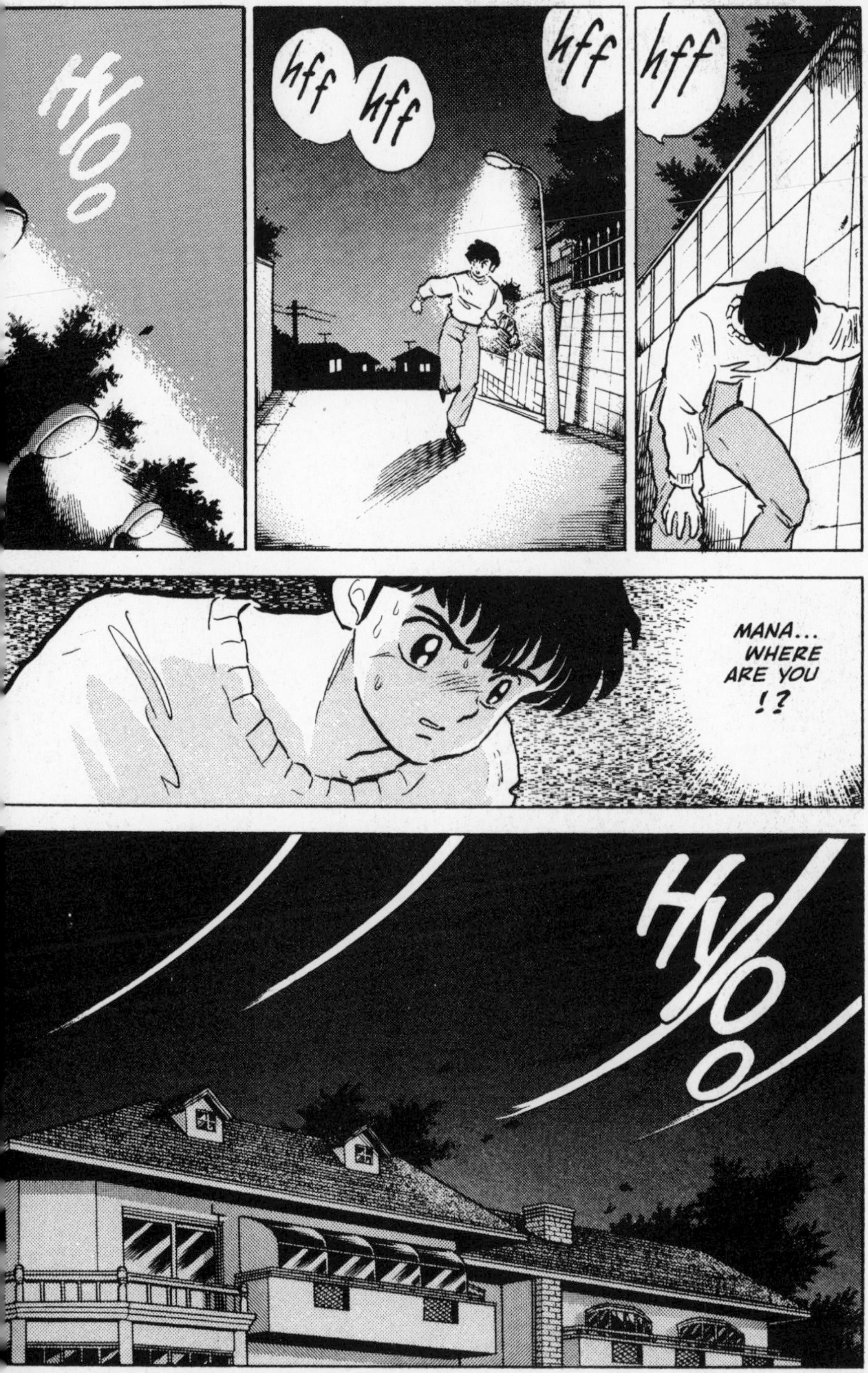
HYOOO
hff
hff
hff
hff
MANA... WHERE ARE YOU !?
HYOOO

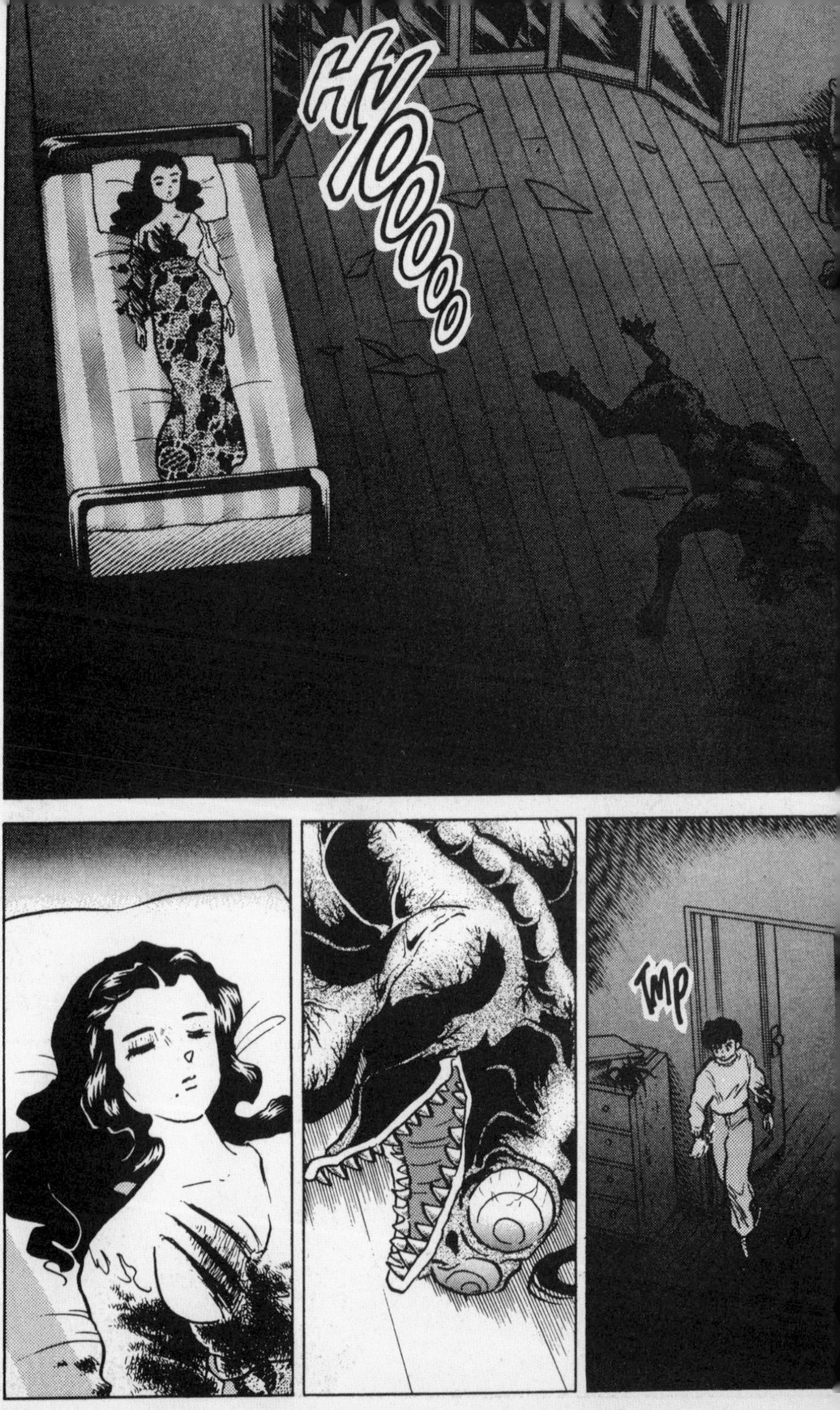
HYOOOOOO
TMP

FLUMP

HEY...

SHE STILL...

...HASN'T COME BACK TO LIFE.

PLEASE.

YOU'VE GOT TO TELL ME WHERE THE KID IS.

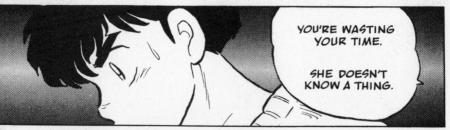

YOU'RE WASTING YOUR TIME.

SHE DOESN'T KNOW A THING.

!

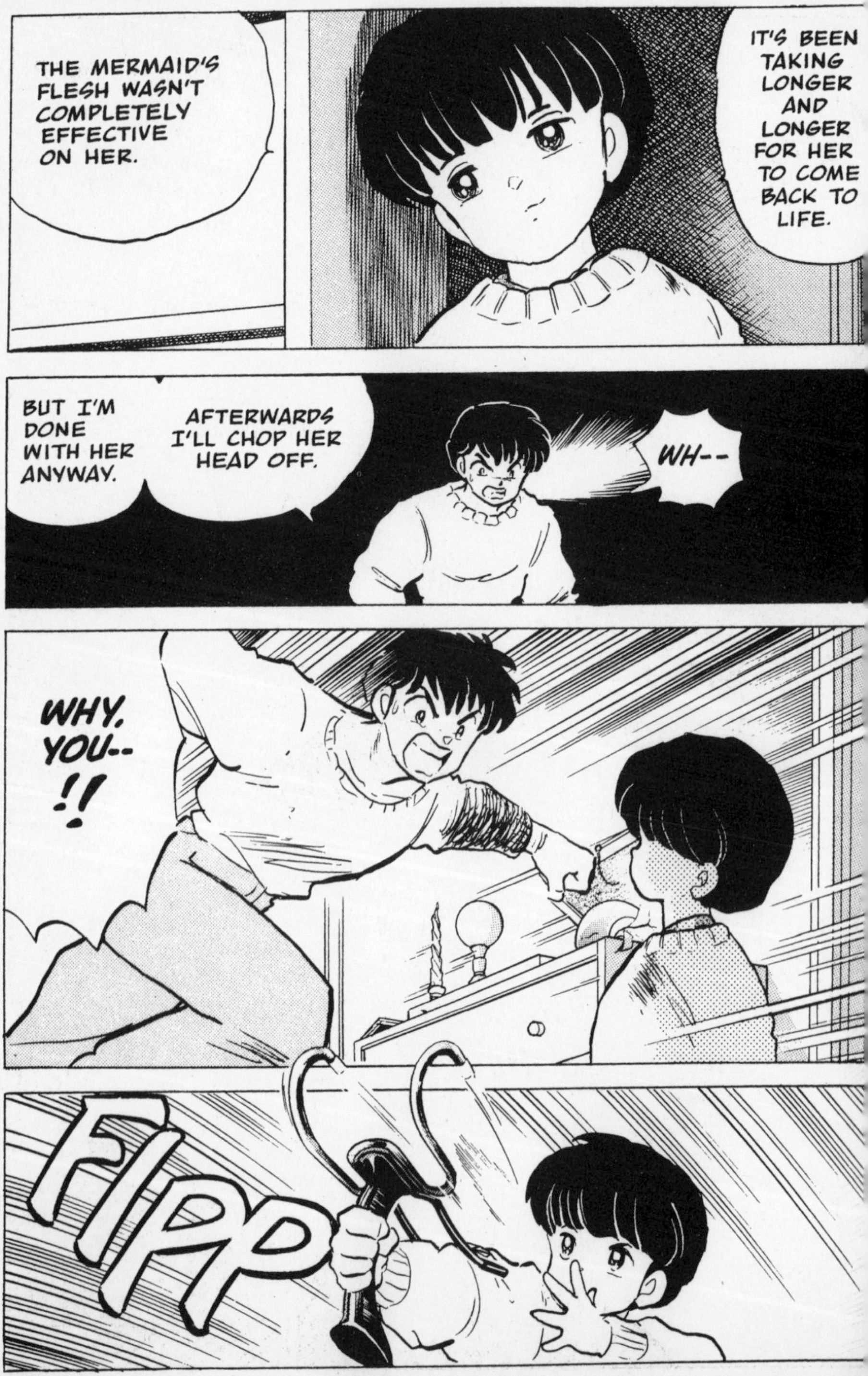
THE MERMAID'S FLESH WASN'T COMPLETELY EFFECTIVE ON HER.
IT'S BEEN TAKING LONGER AND LONGER FOR HER TO COME BACK TO LIFE.
BUT I'M DONE WITH HER ANYWAY.
AFTERWARDS I'LL CHOP HER HEAD OFF.
WH--
WHY, YOU-- !!
FIPP

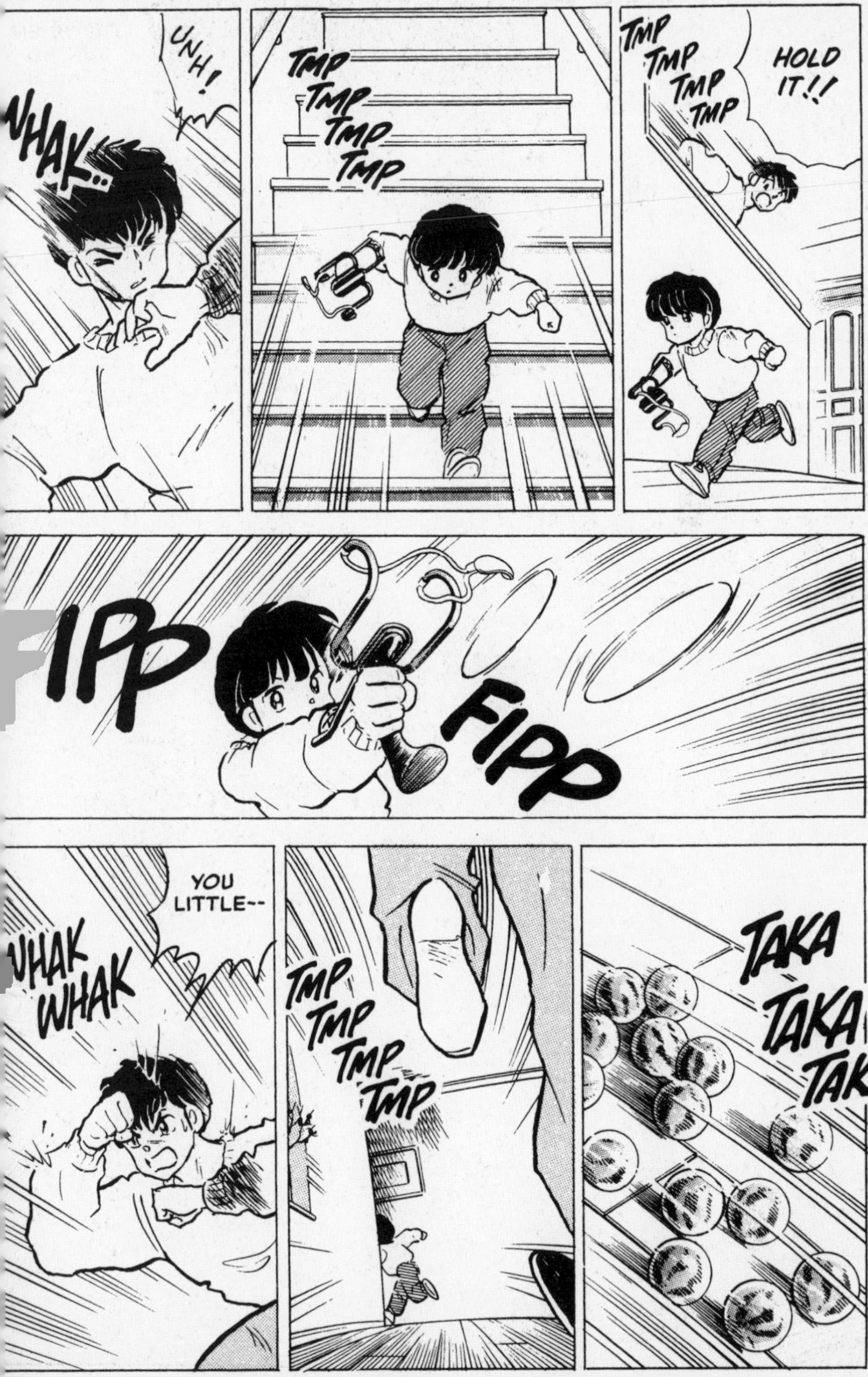
UNH!
WHAK..
TMP TMP TMP TMP
TMP TMP TMP TMP
HOLD IT!!
FIPP
FIPP
YOU LITTLE--
WHAK WHAK
TMP TMP TMP TMP
TAKA TAKA TAKA

WAH!

FWISH

THIK!

!?

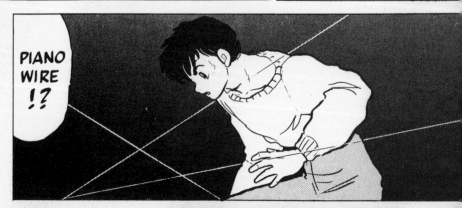

PIANO WIRE !?

HM.

I GUESS I COULDN'T HAVE EXPECTED YOUR HEAD TO COME OFF JUST LIKE THAT.

WH--

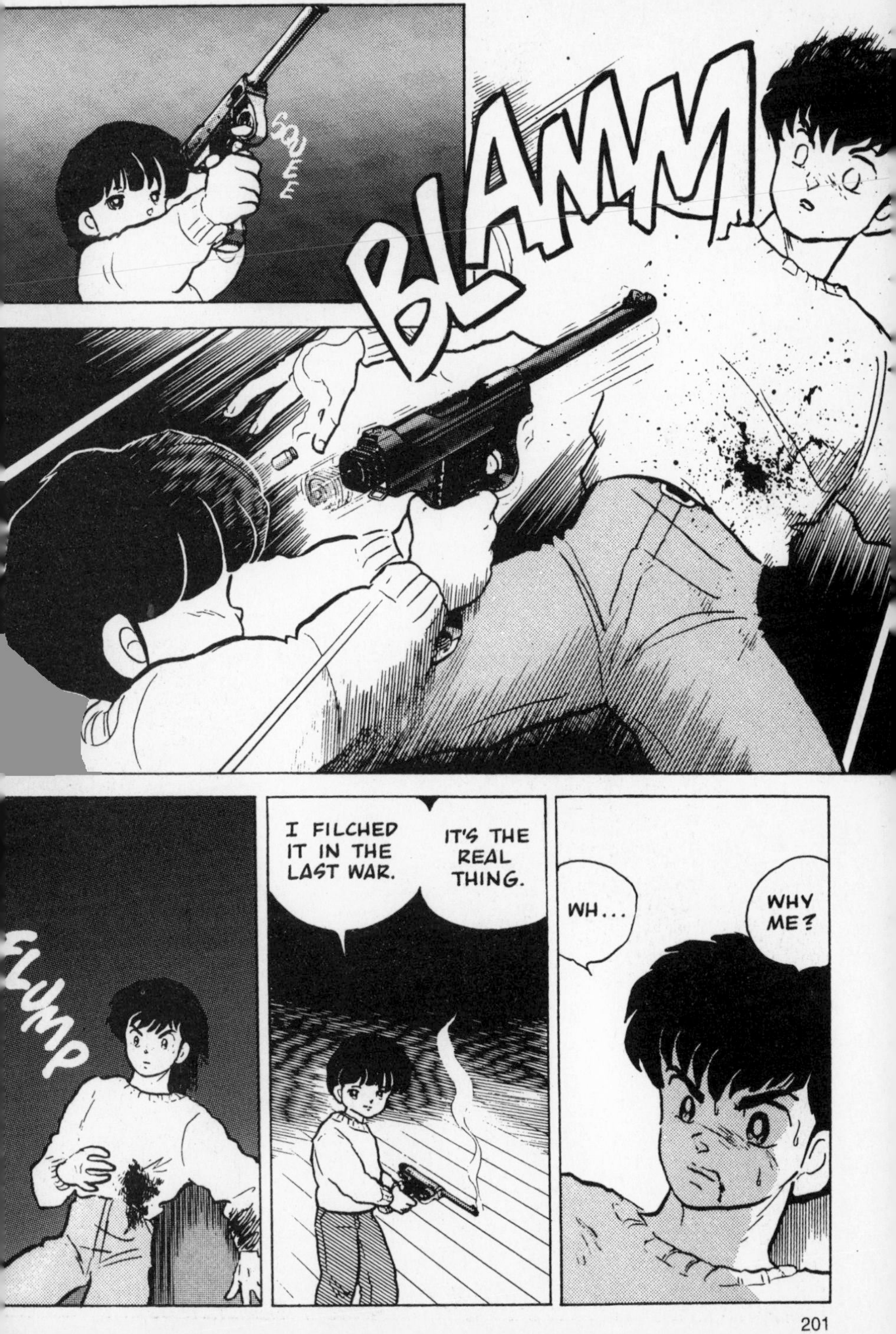
SQUEEE
BLAMM
FLUMP
I FILCHED IT IN THE LAST WAR.
IT'S THE REAL THING.
WH...
WHY ME?

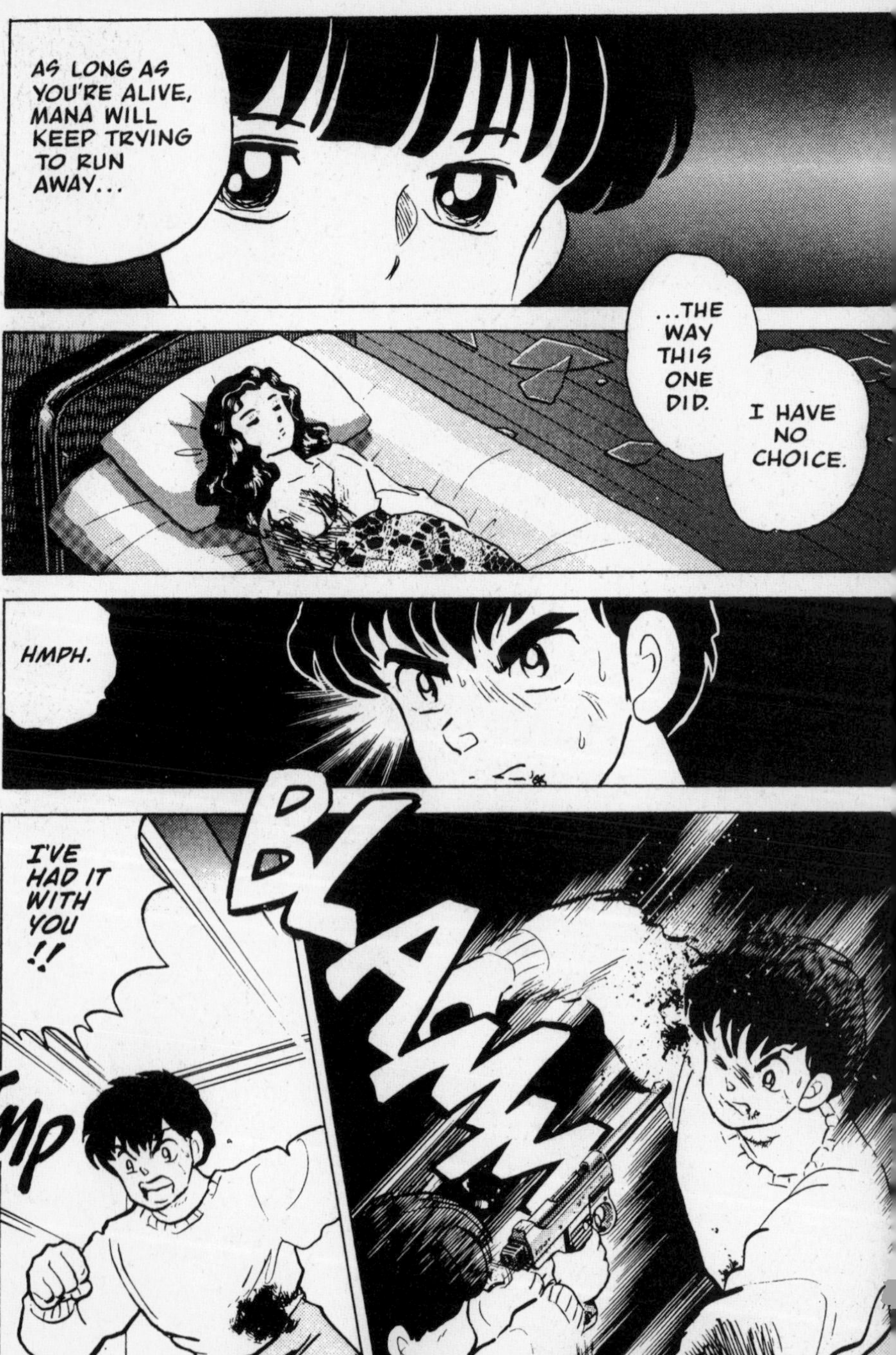
AS LONG AS YOU'RE ALIVE, MANA WILL KEEP TRYING TO RUN AWAY...
...THE WAY THIS ONE DID.
I HAVE NO CHOICE.
HMPH.
I'VE HAD IT WITH YOU !!
TMP
BLAMM

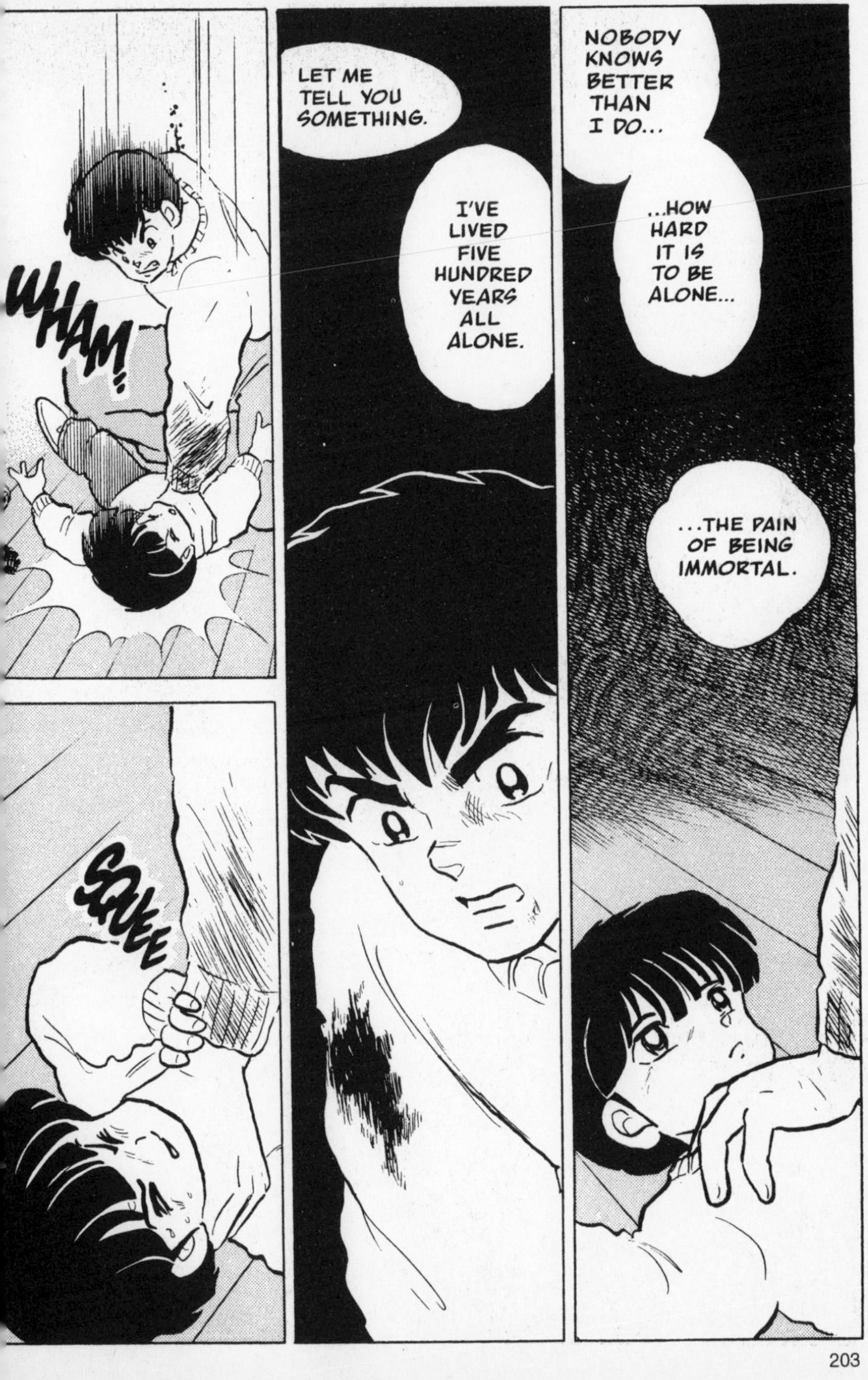
WHAM!
SQUEEE
LET ME TELL YOU SOMETHING.
I'VE LIVED FIVE HUNDRED YEARS ALL ALONE.
NOBODY KNOWS BETTER THAN I DO...
...HOW HARD IT IS TO BE ALONE...
...THE PAIN OF BEING IMMORTAL.

SO I WON'T BUY YOUR EXCUSES!

JUST HOW MANY PEOPLE HAVE YOU FED THE MERMAID'S FLESH!?

SO, THEN...

...JUST KILL ME.

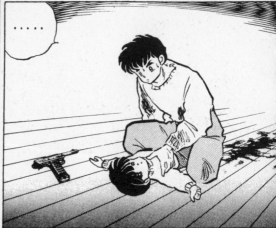

.....

FOOSH!

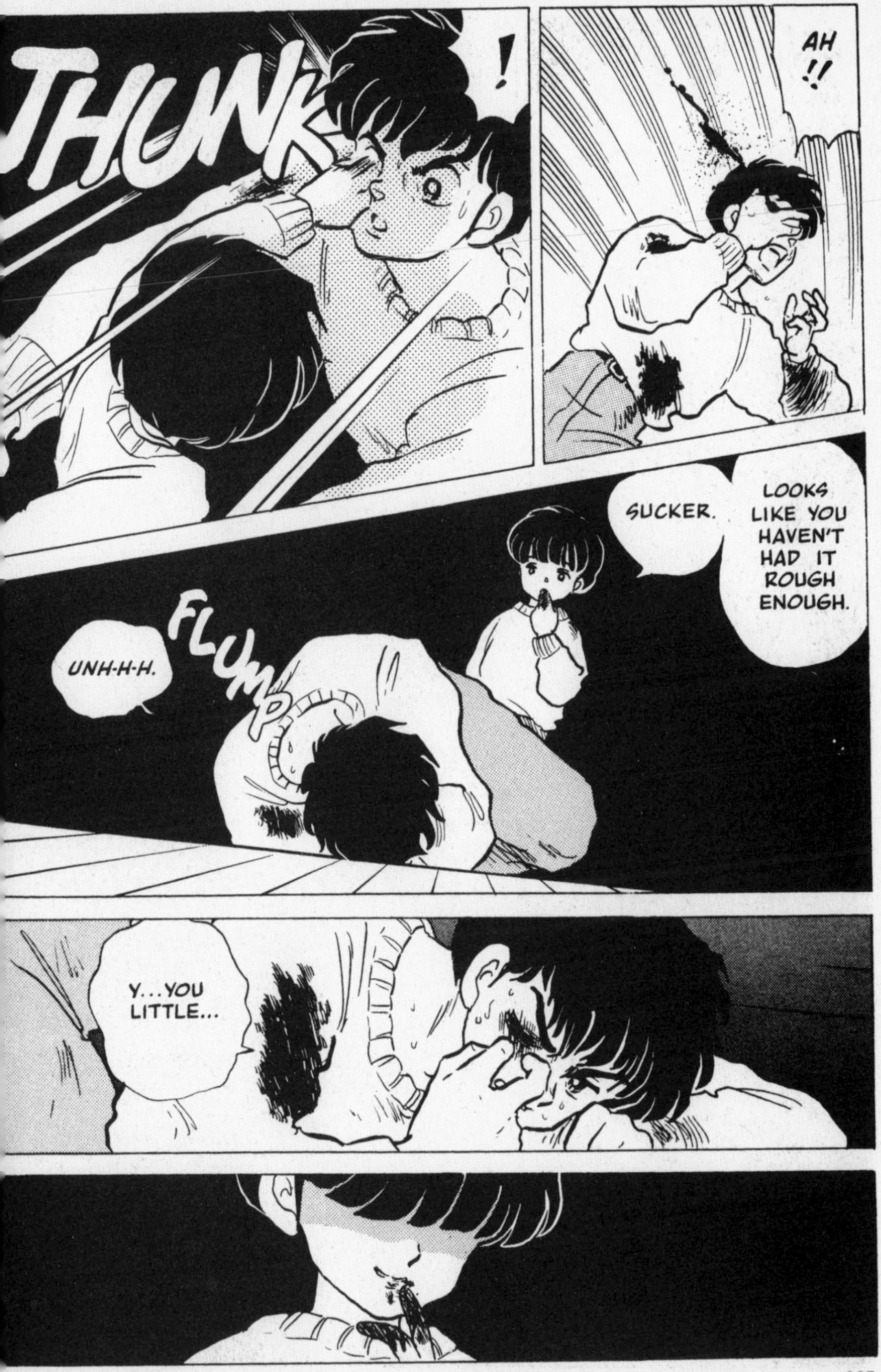
THUNK
!
AH !!
UNH-H-H.
FLUMP
SUCKER.
LOOKS LIKE YOU HAVEN'T HAD IT ROUGH ENOUGH.
Y...YOU LITTLE...

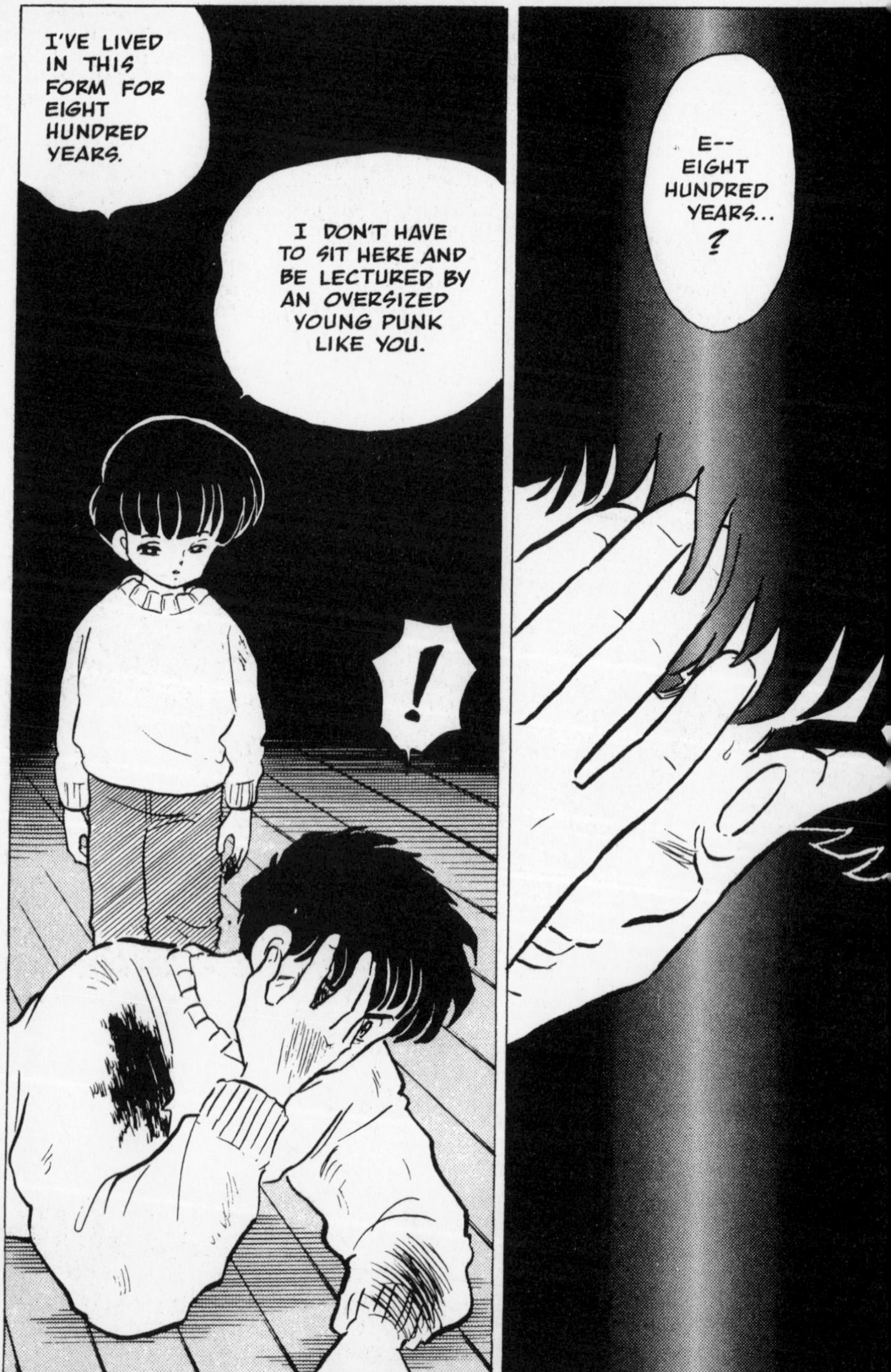
I'VE LIVED IN THIS FORM FOR EIGHT HUNDRED YEARS.
I DON'T HAVE TO SIT HERE AND BE LECTURED BY AN OVERSIZED YOUNG PUNK LIKE YOU.
!
E-- EIGHT HUNDRED YEARS...?

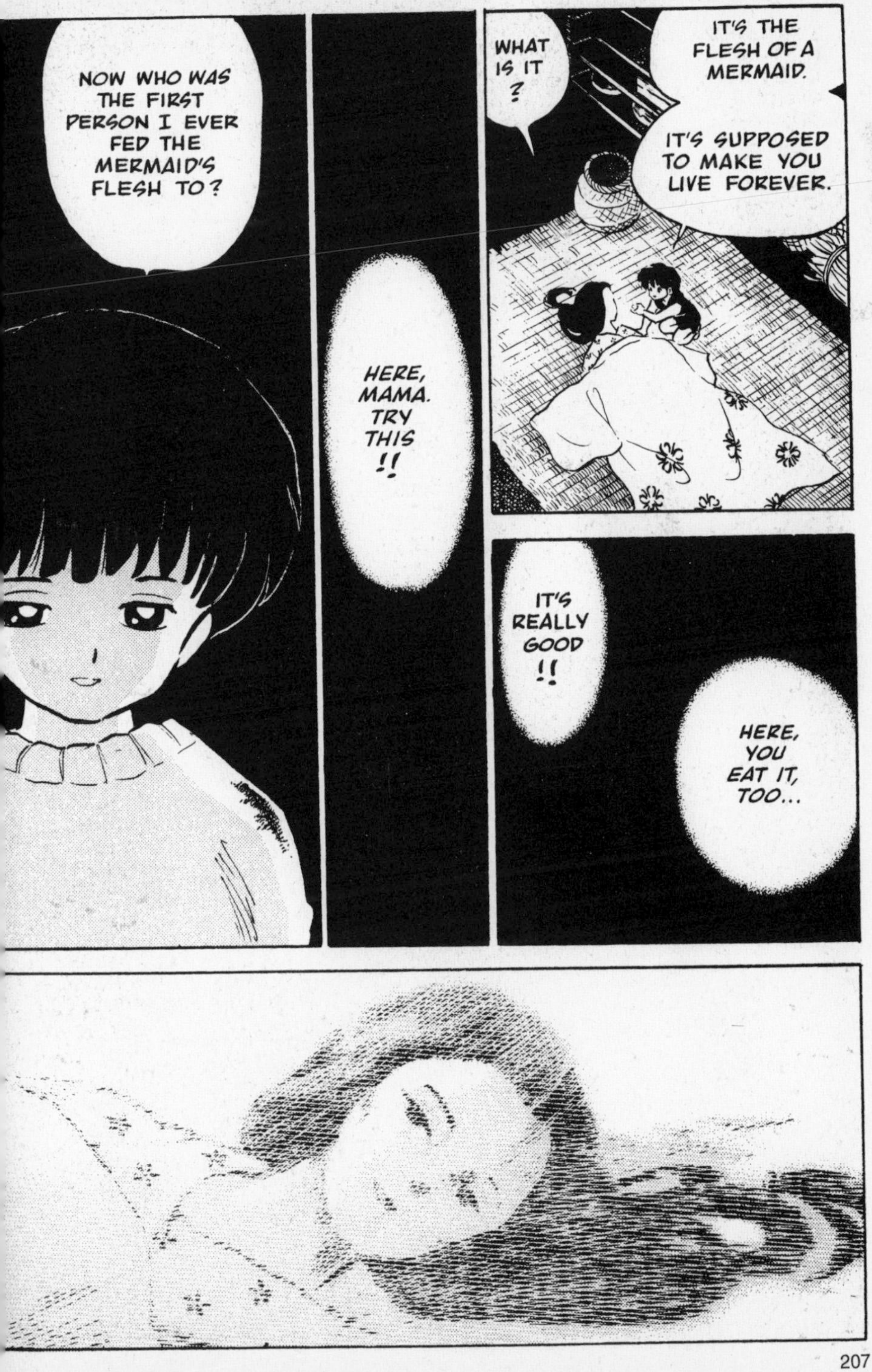
NOW WHO WAS THE FIRST PERSON I EVER FED THE MERMAID'S FLESH TO?
HERE, MAMA. TRY THIS!!
WHAT IS IT?
IT'S THE FLESH OF A MERMAID.
IT'S SUPPOSED TO MAKE YOU LIVE FOREVER.
IT'S REALLY GOOD!!
HERE, YOU EAT IT, TOO...

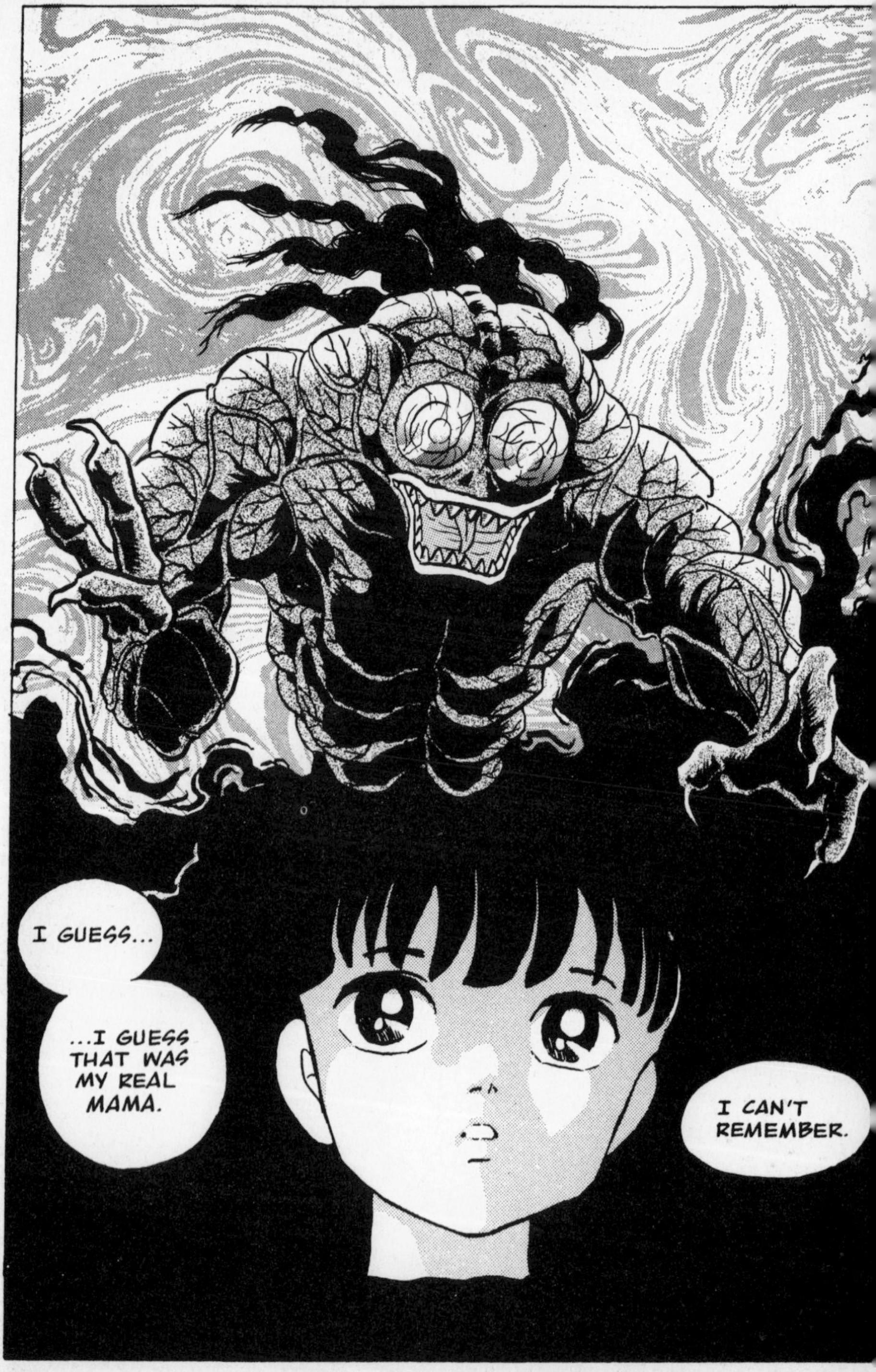
I GUESS...
...I GUESS THAT WAS MY REAL MAMA.
I CAN'T REMEMBER.

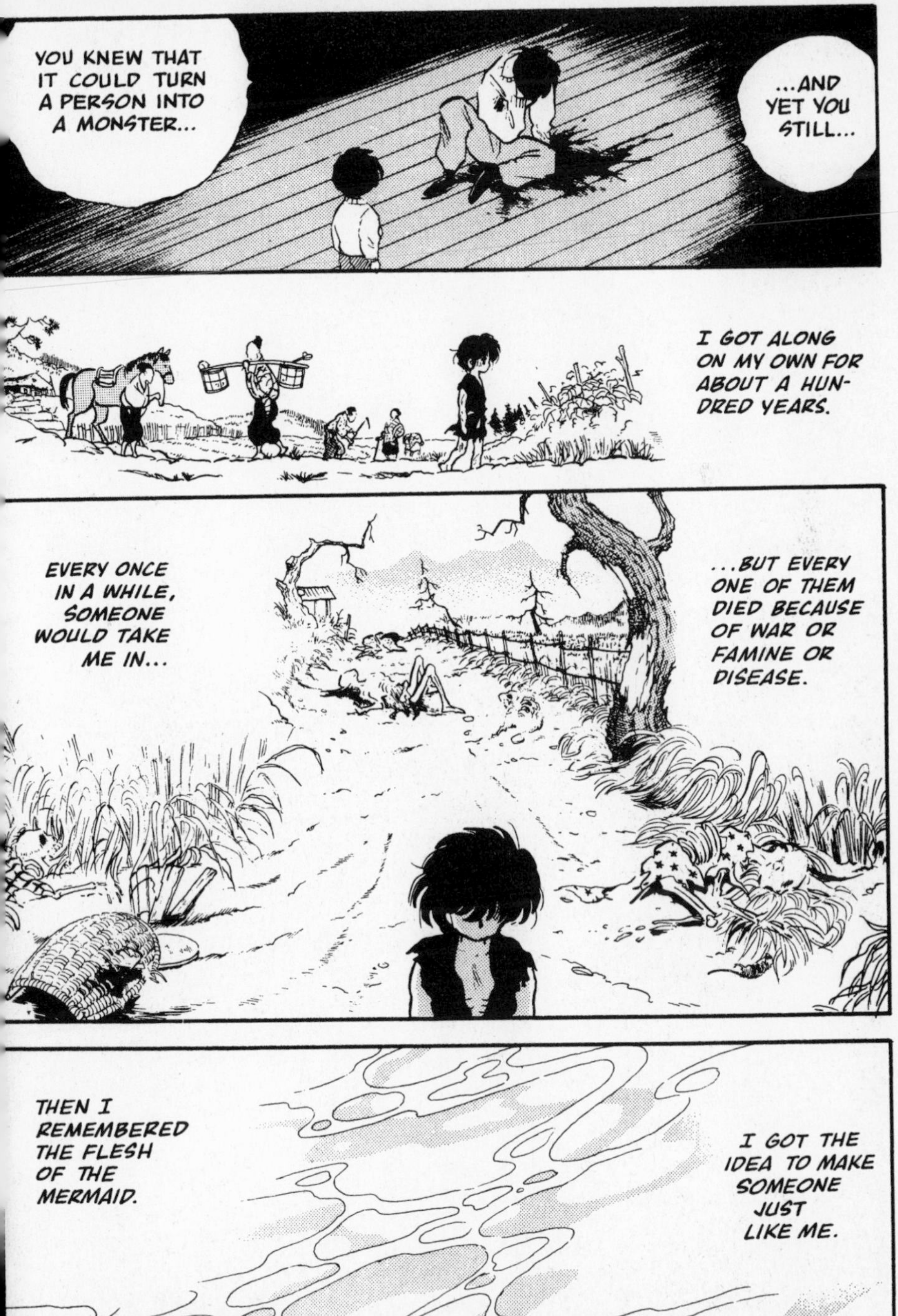
YOU KNEW THAT IT COULD TURN A PERSON INTO A MONSTER...
...AND YET YOU STILL...
I GOT ALONG ON MY OWN FOR ABOUT A HUNDRED YEARS.
EVERY ONCE IN A WHILE, SOMEONE WOULD TAKE ME IN...
...BUT EVERY ONE OF THEM DIED BECAUSE OF WAR OR FAMINE OR DISEASE.
THEN I REMEMBERED THE FLESH OF THE MERMAID.
I GOT THE IDEA TO MAKE SOMEONE JUST LIKE ME.

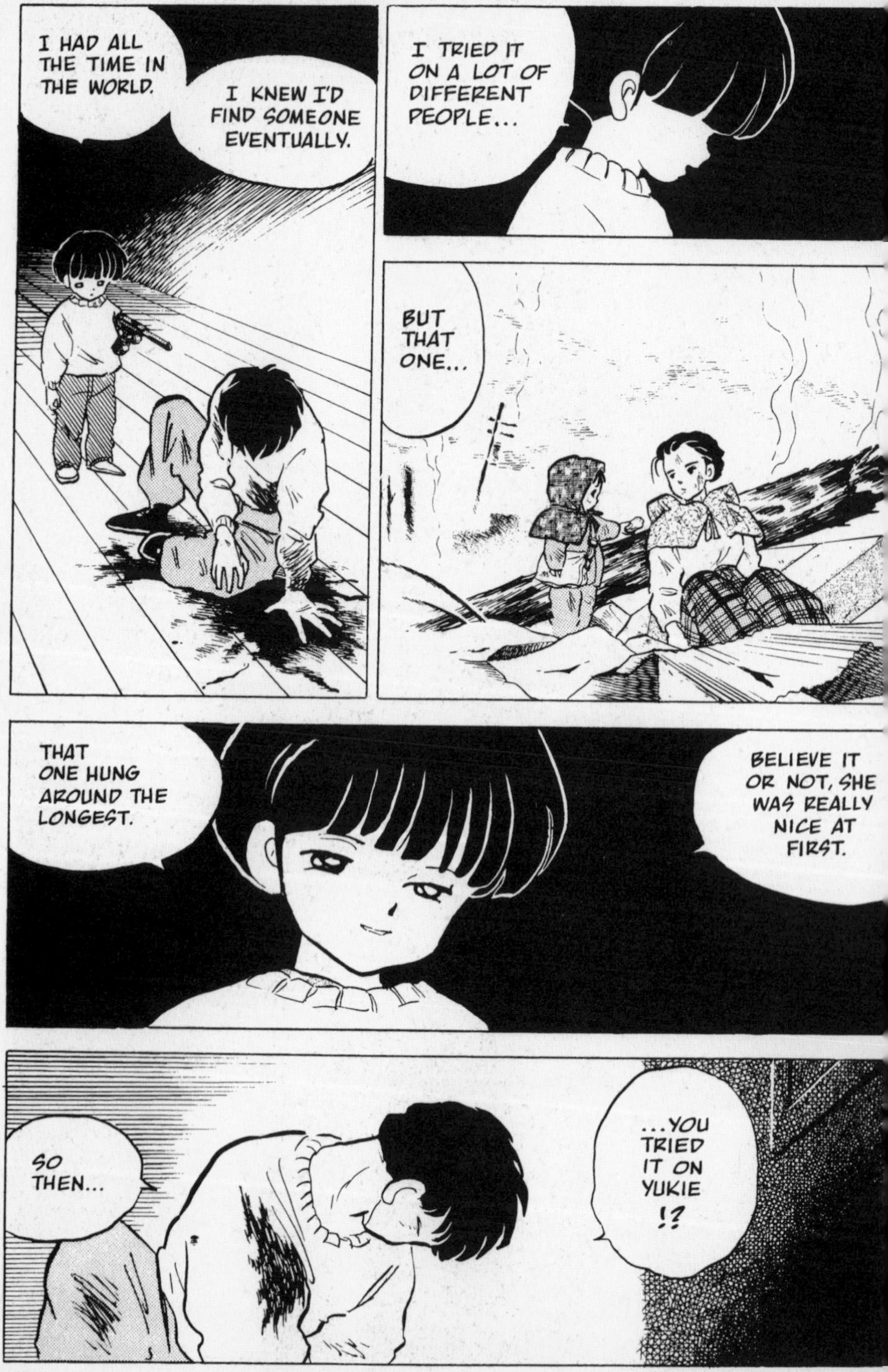
I HAD ALL THE TIME IN THE WORLD.
I KNEW I'D FIND SOMEONE EVENTUALLY.
I TRIED IT ON A LOT OF DIFFERENT PEOPLE...
BUT THAT ONE...
THAT ONE HUNG AROUND THE LONGEST.
BELIEVE IT OR NOT, SHE WAS REALLY NICE AT FIRST.
SO THEN...
...YOU TRIED IT ON YUKIE !?

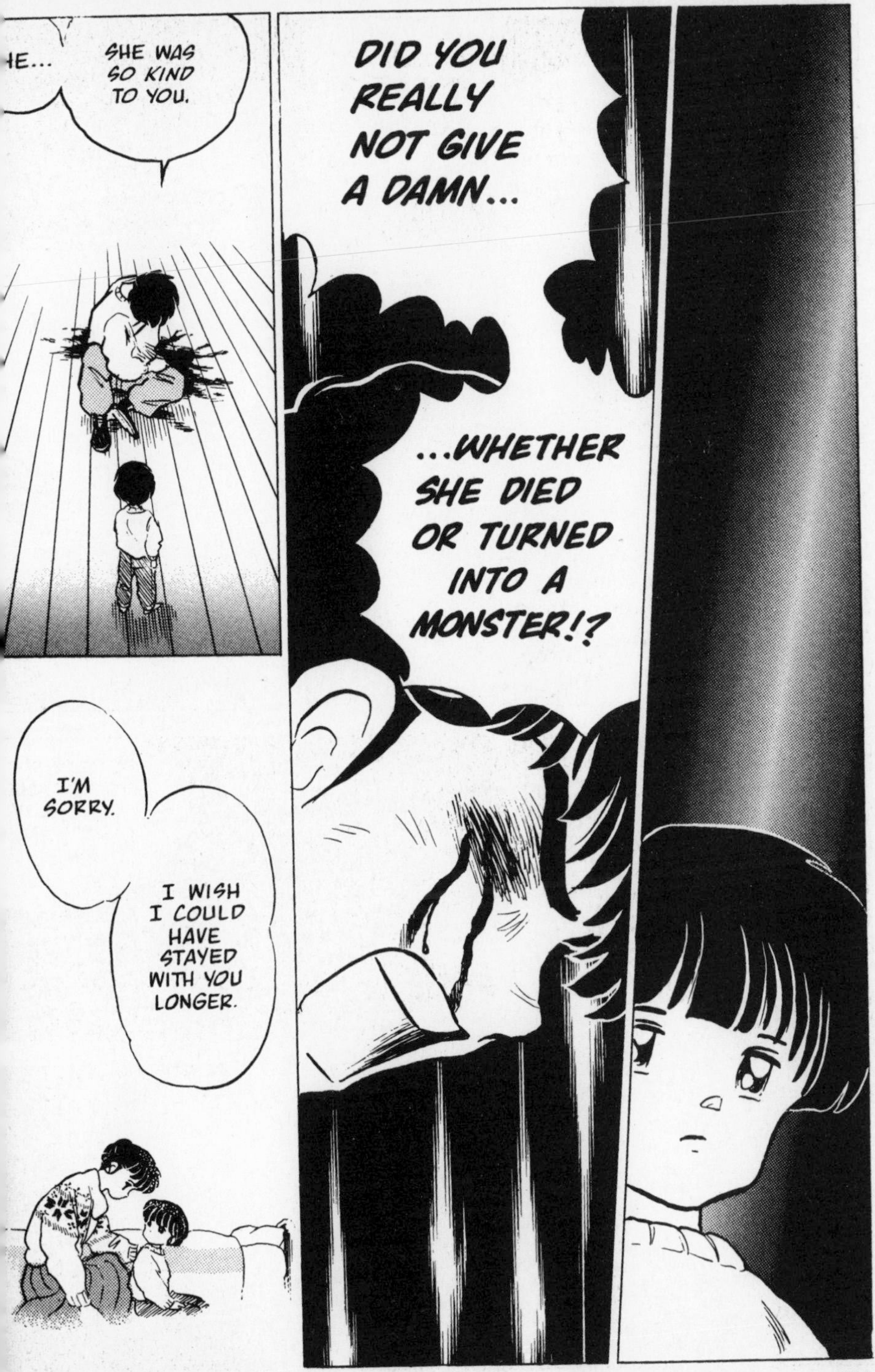
HE...
SHE WAS SO KIND TO YOU.
I'M SORRY.
I WISH I COULD HAVE STAYED WITH YOU LONGER.
DID YOU REALLY NOT GIVE A DAMN...
...WHETHER SHE DIED OR TURNED INTO A MONSTER!?

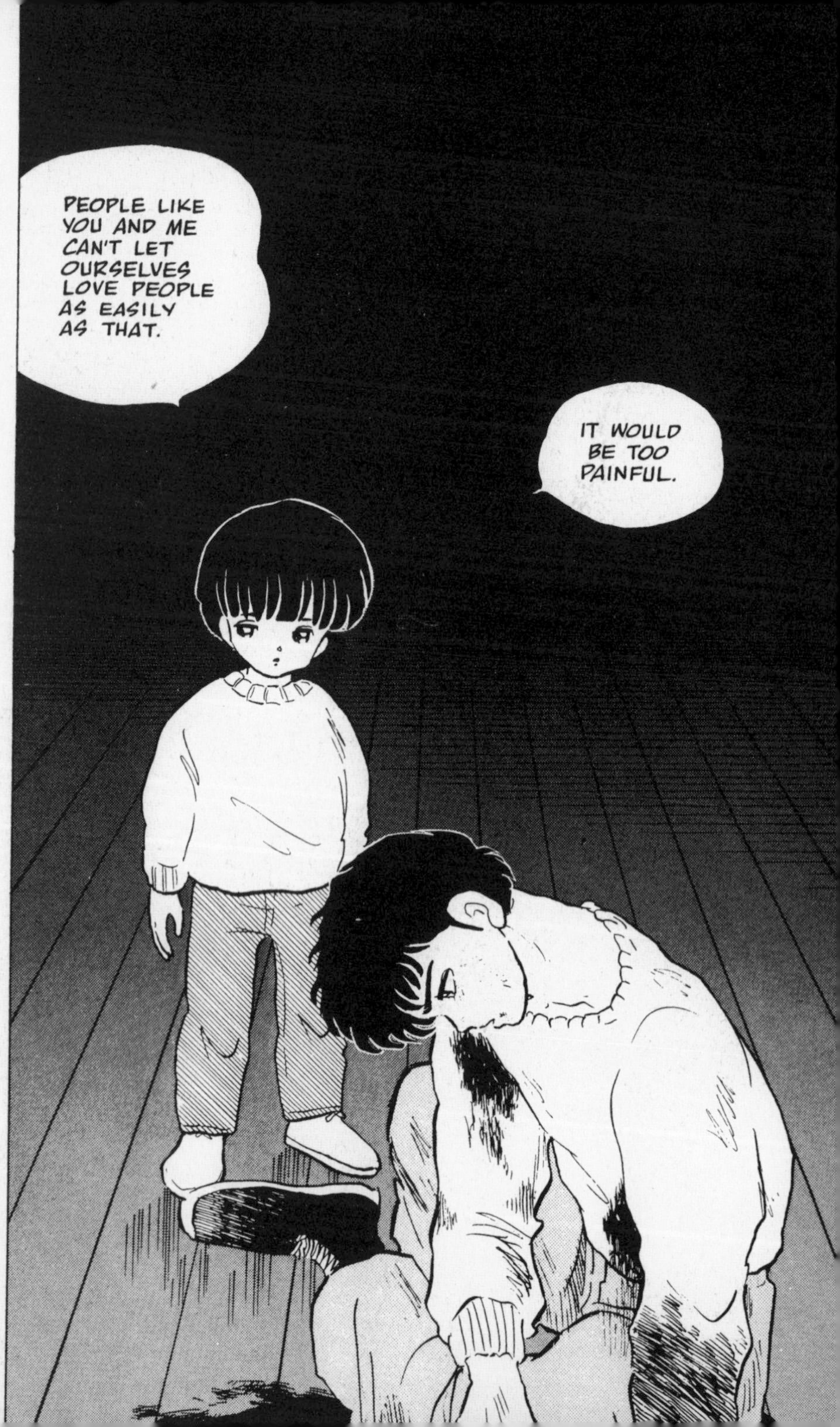
PEOPLE LIKE YOU AND ME CAN'T LET OURSELVES LOVE PEOPLE AS EASILY AS THAT.
IT WOULD BE TOO PAINFUL.

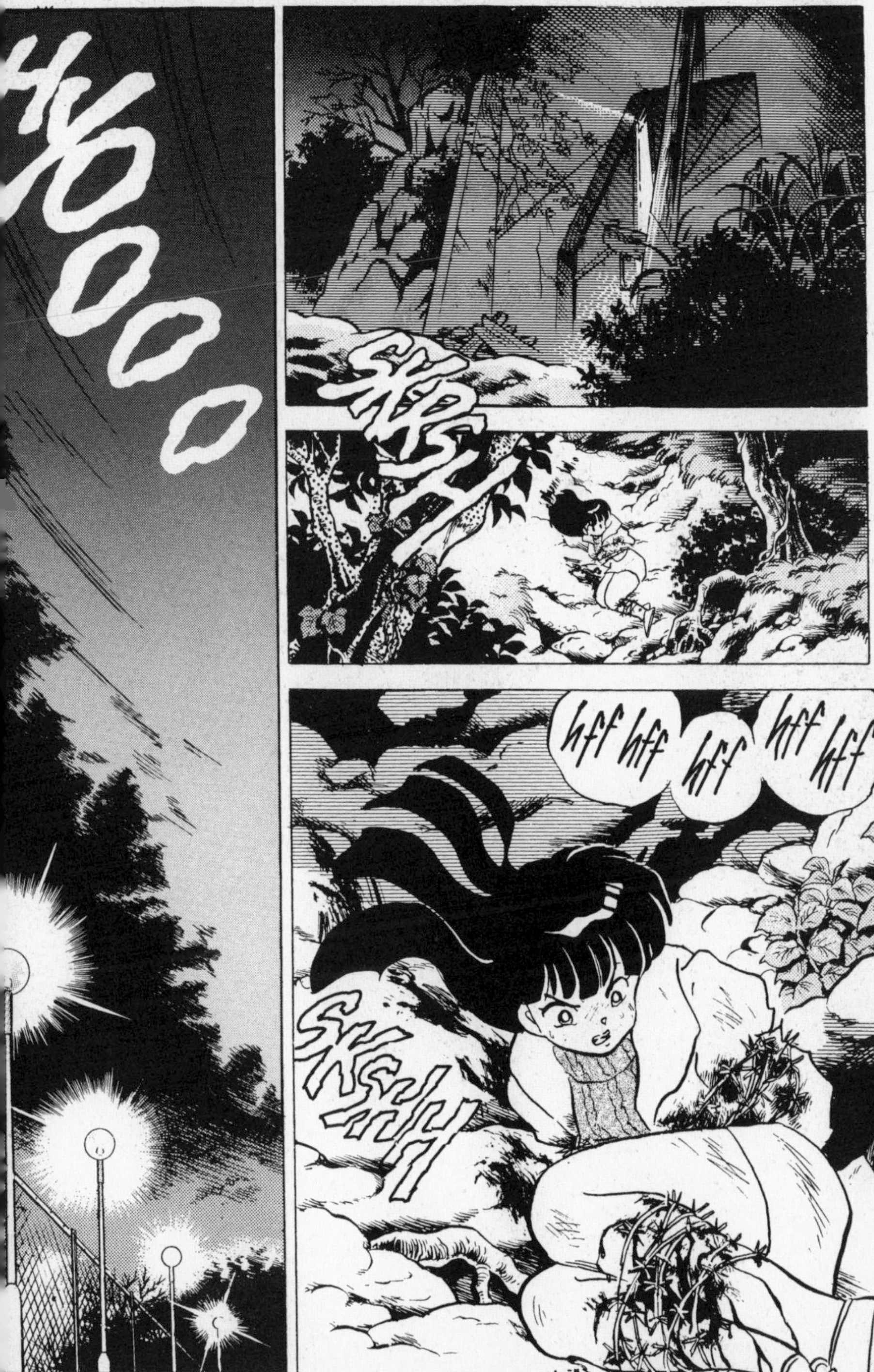
HOOOO
hff hff
hff
hff hff

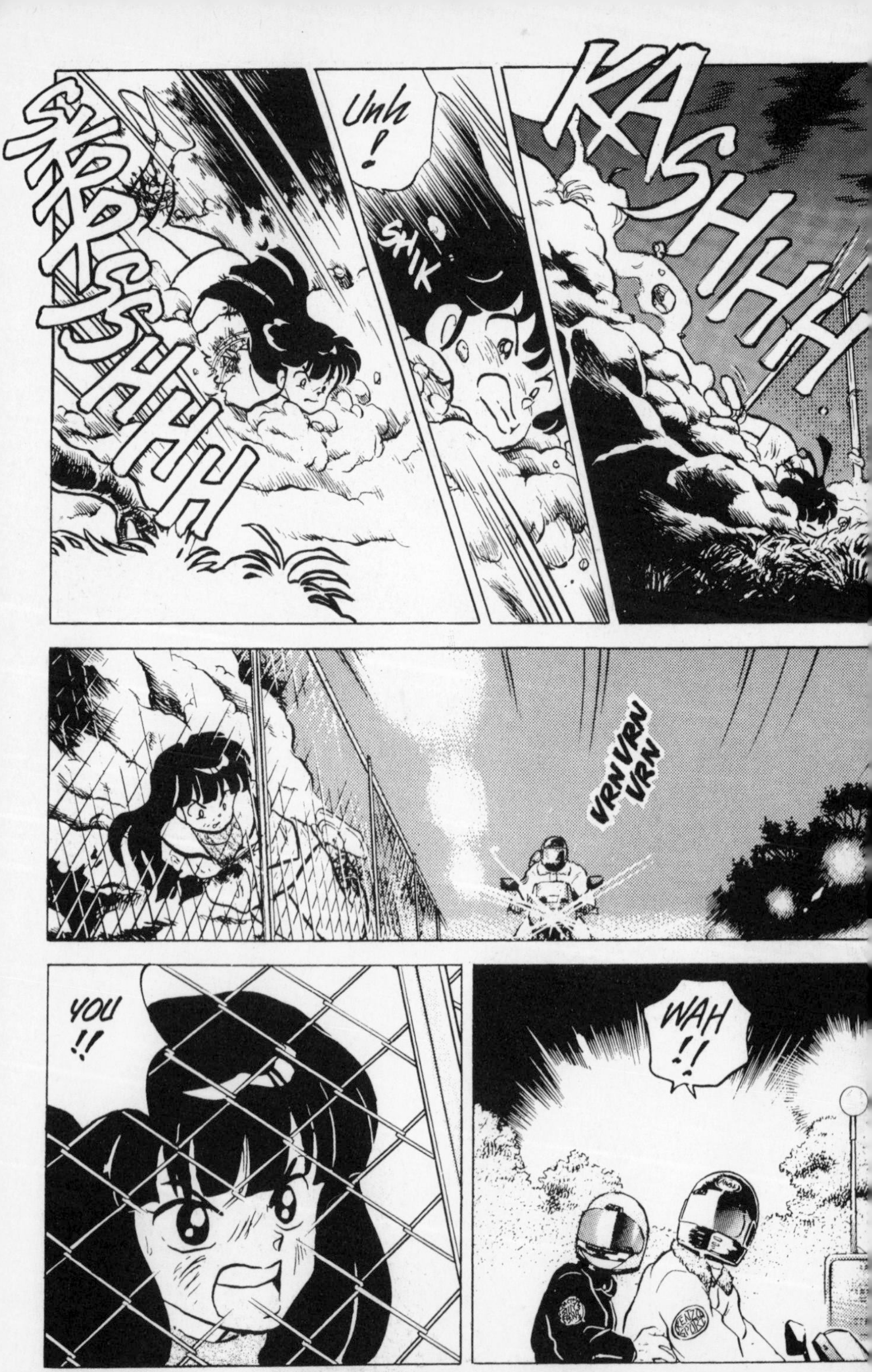
SKRSSHHCH
Unh!
SHIK
KASHHHH
VRN VRN VRN
YOU!!
WAH!!

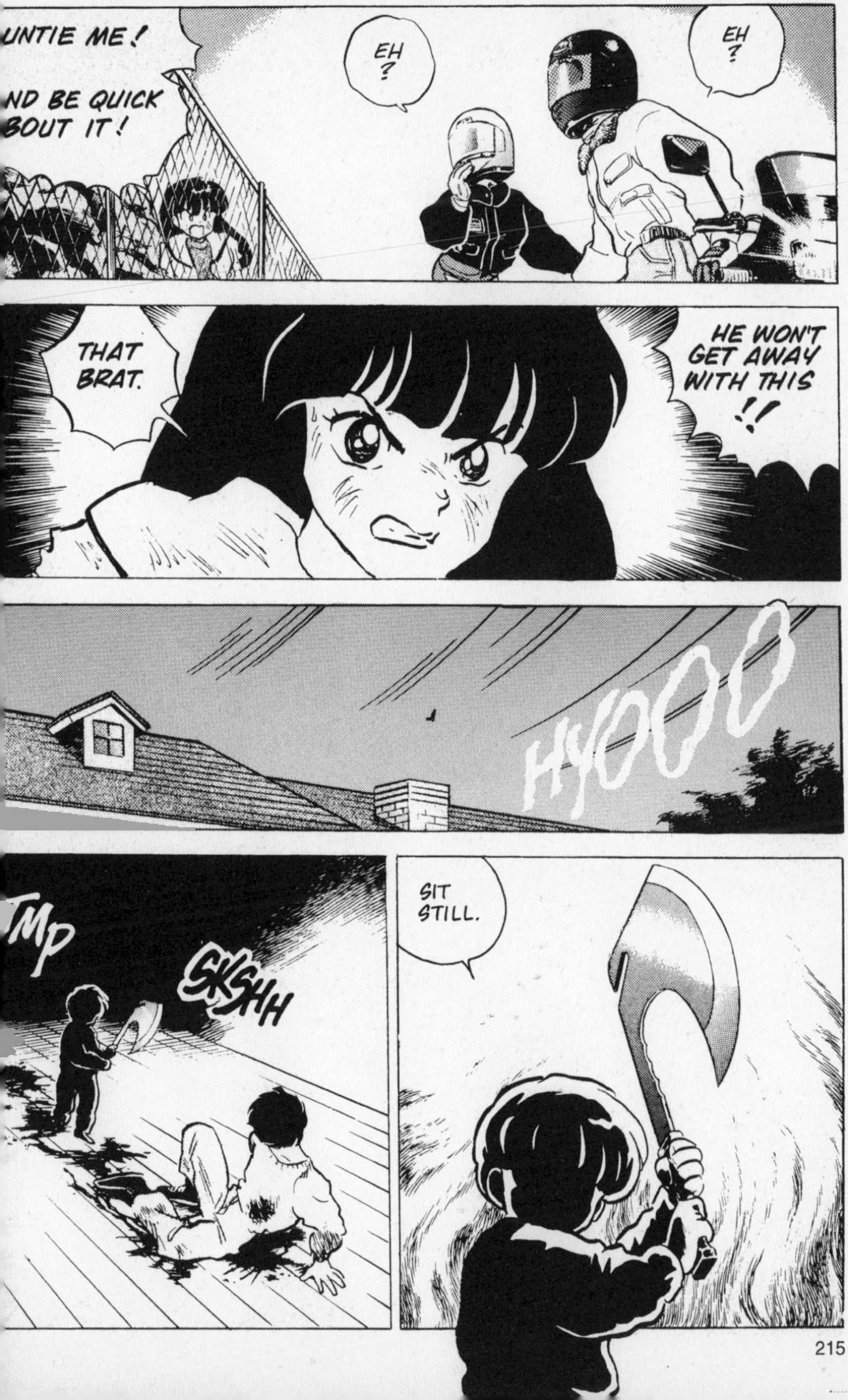

UNTIE ME!
ND BE QUICK
BOUT IT!
EH?
EH?
THAT BRAT.
HE WON'T GET AWAY WITH THIS!!
HYOOO
TMP
SKSHH
SIT STILL.

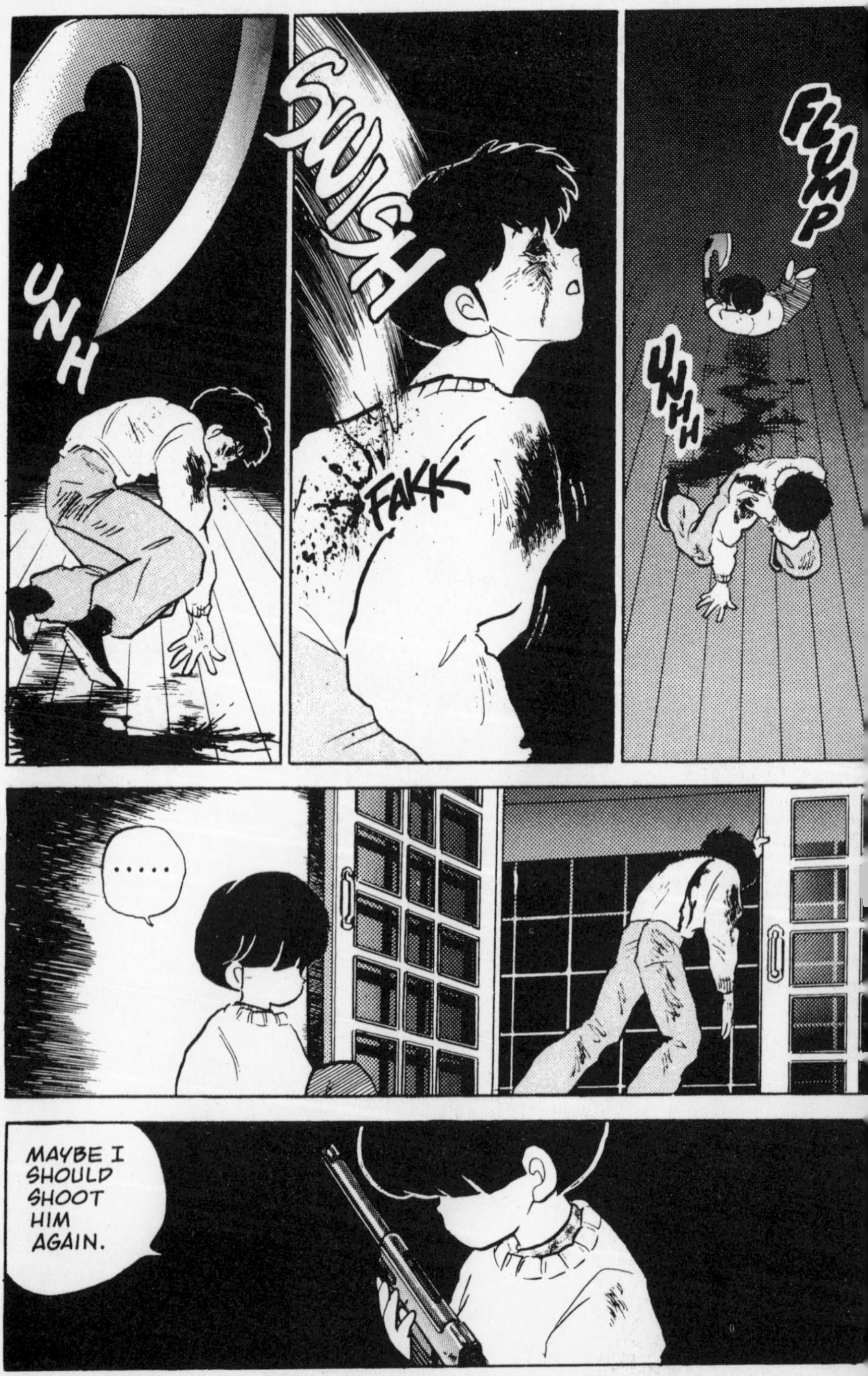
UNH
SWISH
FAKK
FLUMP
UNHH
. . . . .
MAYBE I SHOULD SHOOT HIM AGAIN.

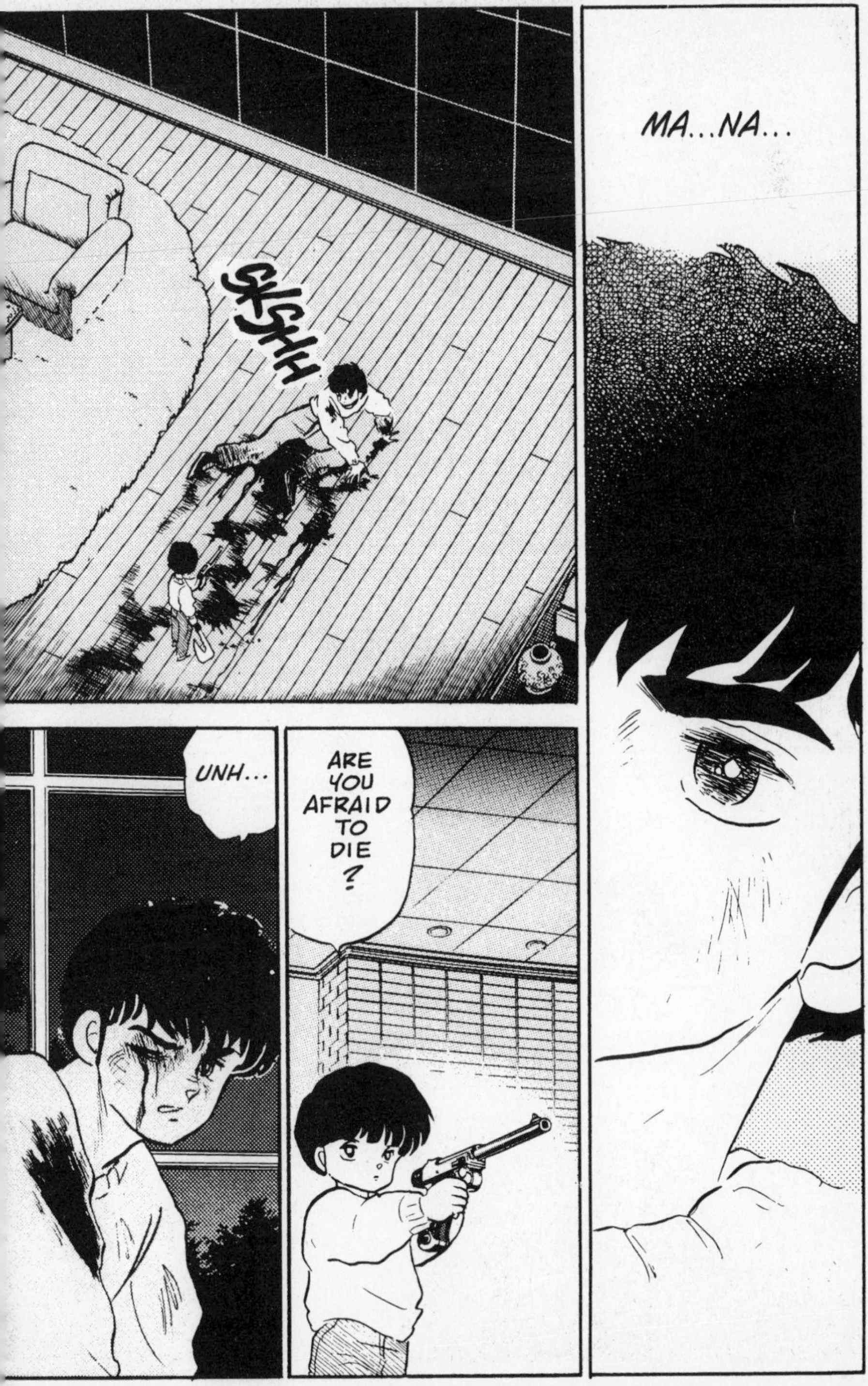
SKSHH
UNH...
ARE YOU AFRAID TO DIE?
MA...NA...

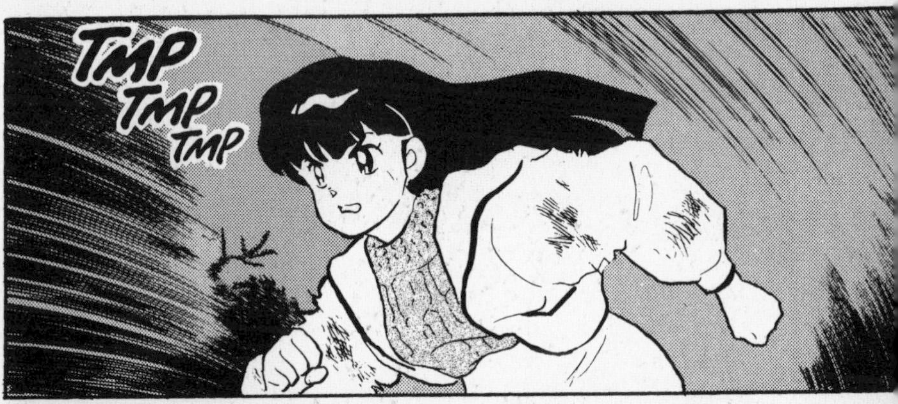
TMP
TMP
TMP

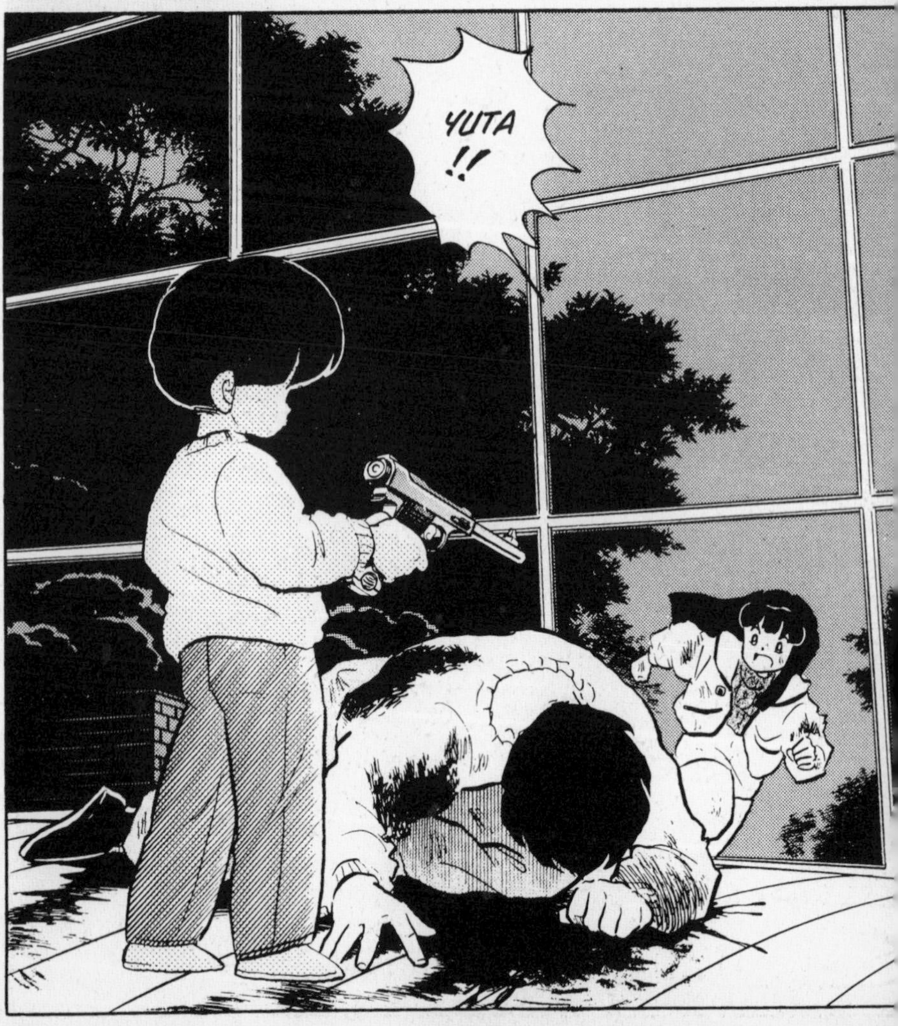
YUTA !!

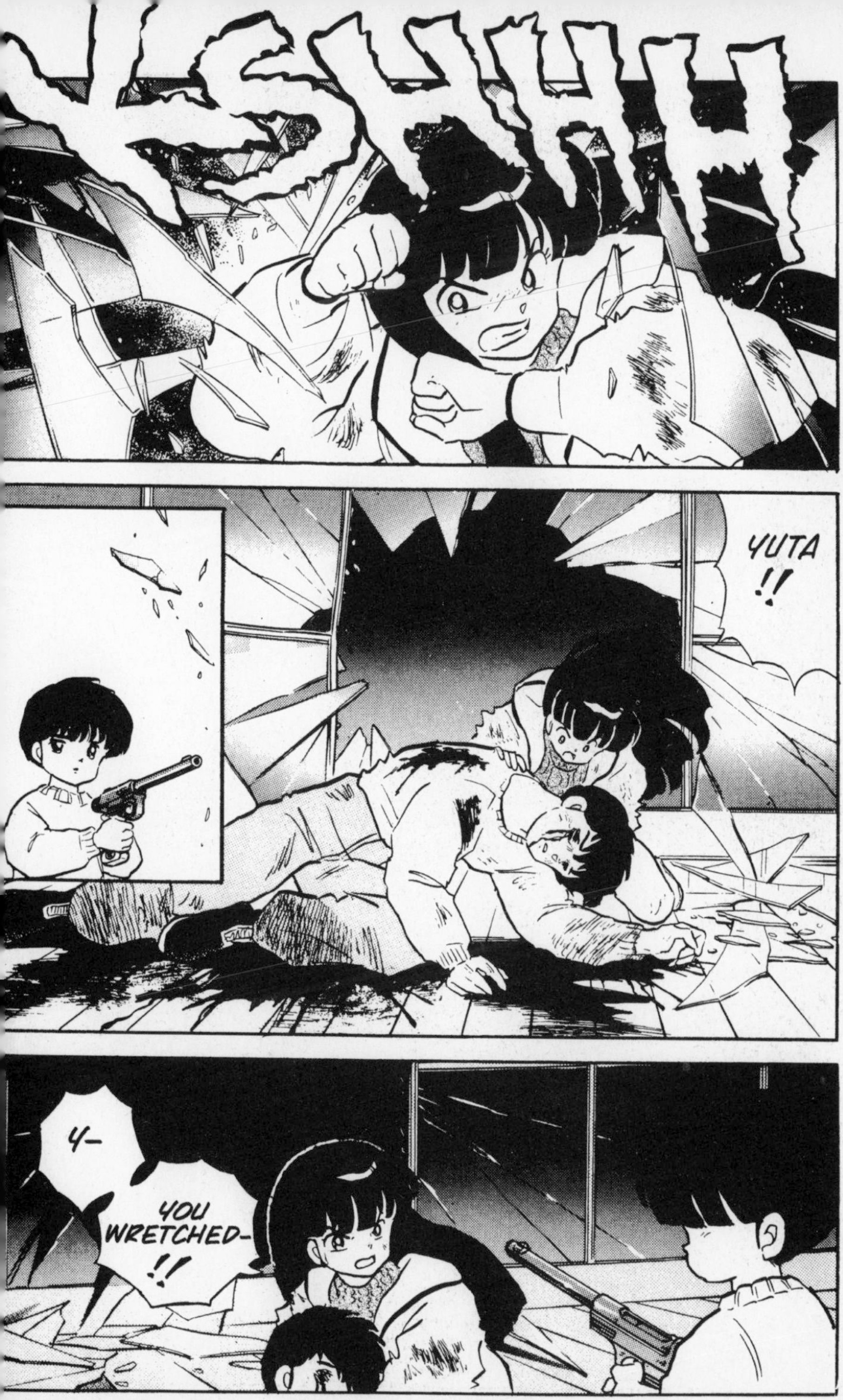

KSSHH
YUTA !!
Y-
YOU WRETCHED- !!

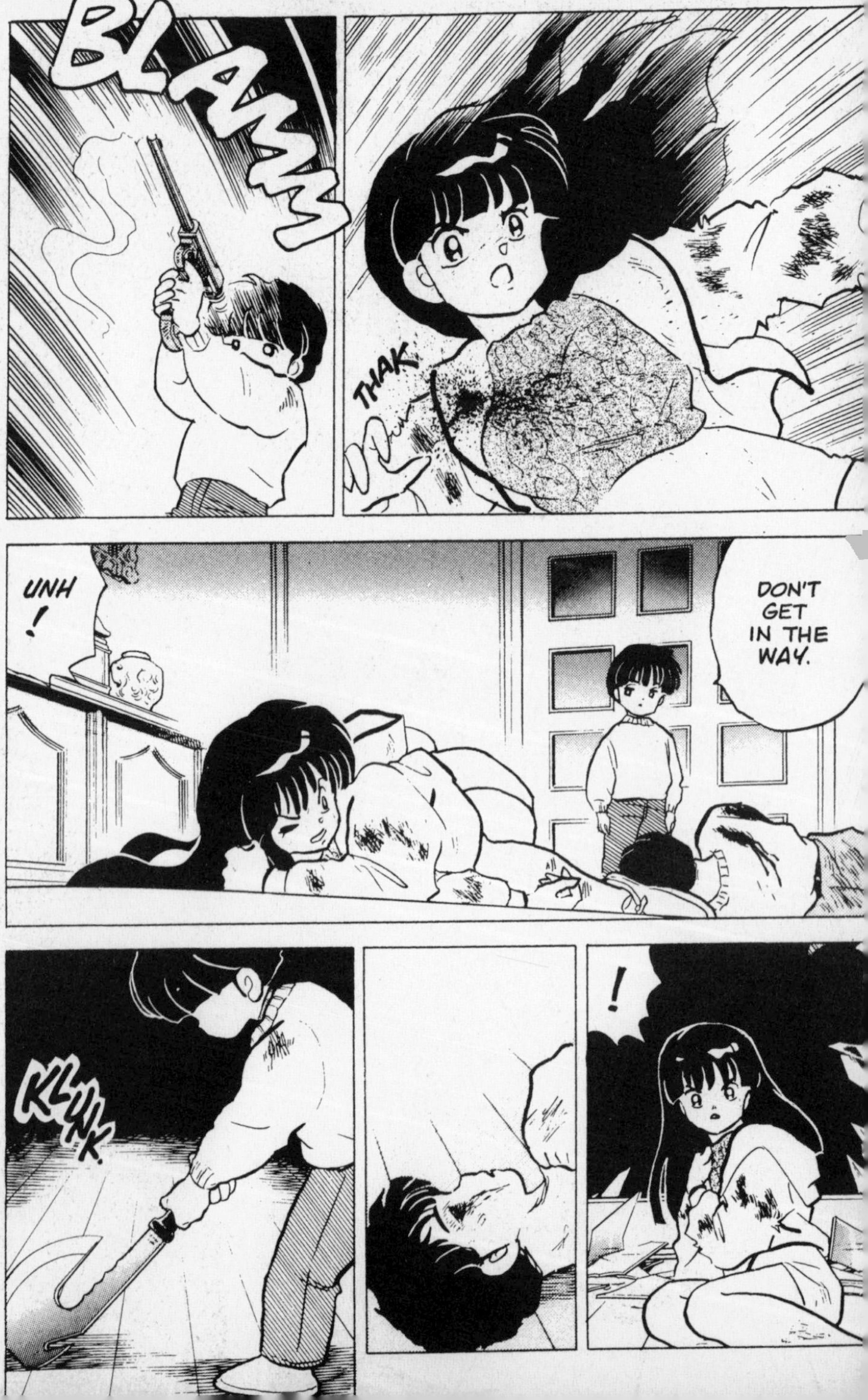
BLAMM
THAK
UNH !
DON'T GET IN THE WAY.
KLUNK.
!

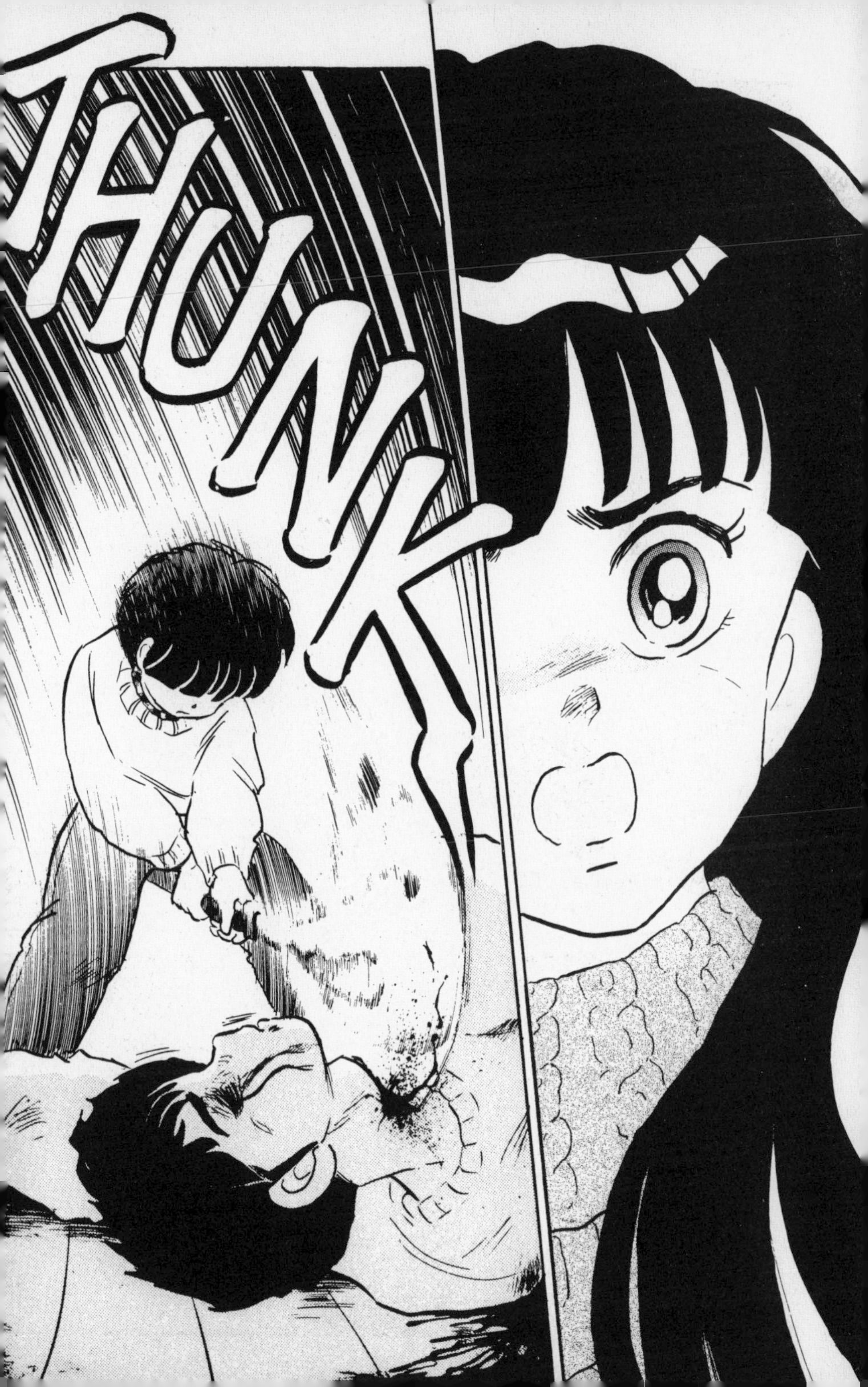
THUNK

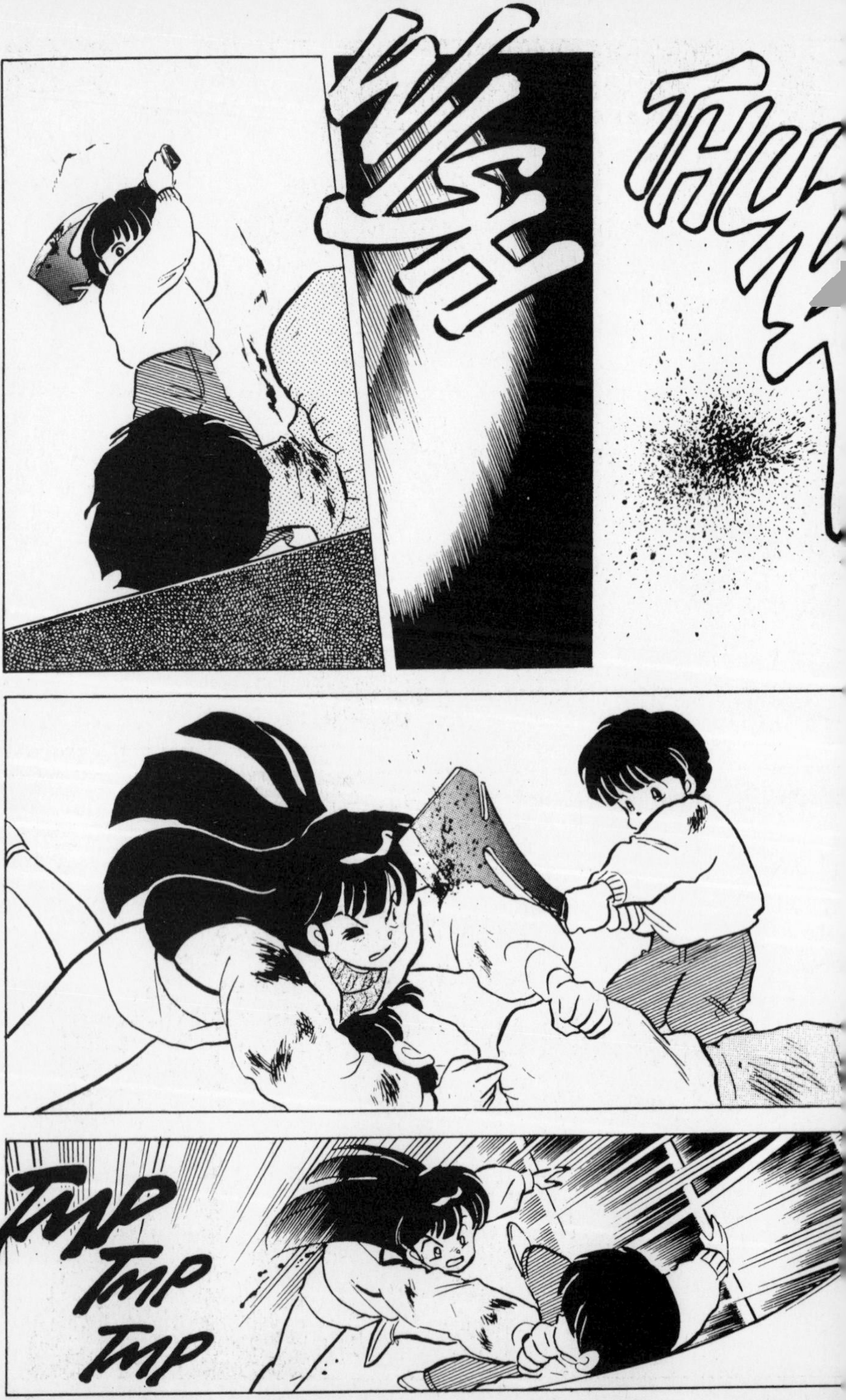
WHISH!
THU
TMP
TMP
TMP

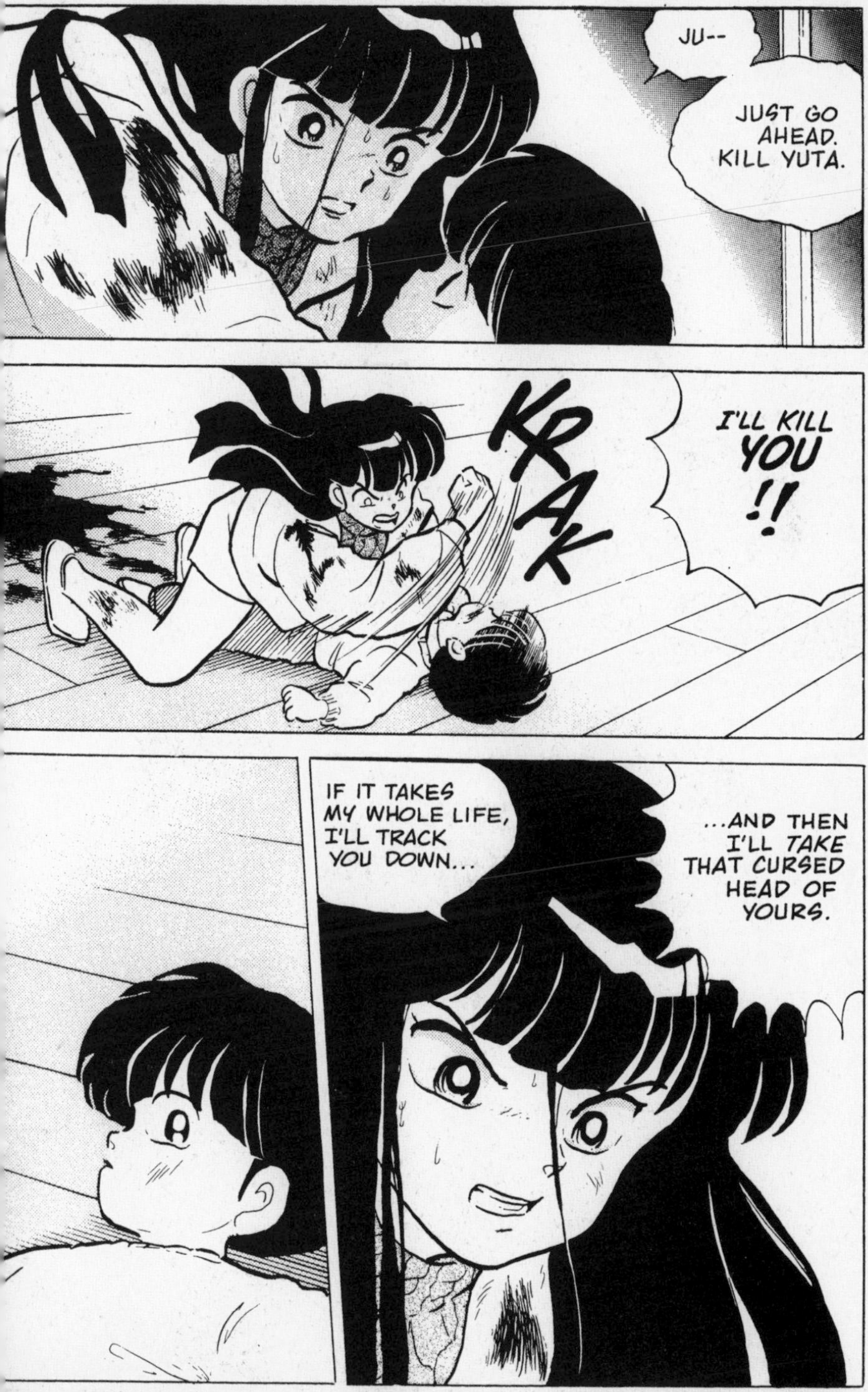
JU--
JUST GO AHEAD. KILL YUTA.
KRAK
I'LL KILL YOU !!
IF IT TAKES MY WHOLE LIFE, I'LL TRACK YOU DOWN...
...AND THEN I'LL TAKE THAT CURSED HEAD OF YOURS.

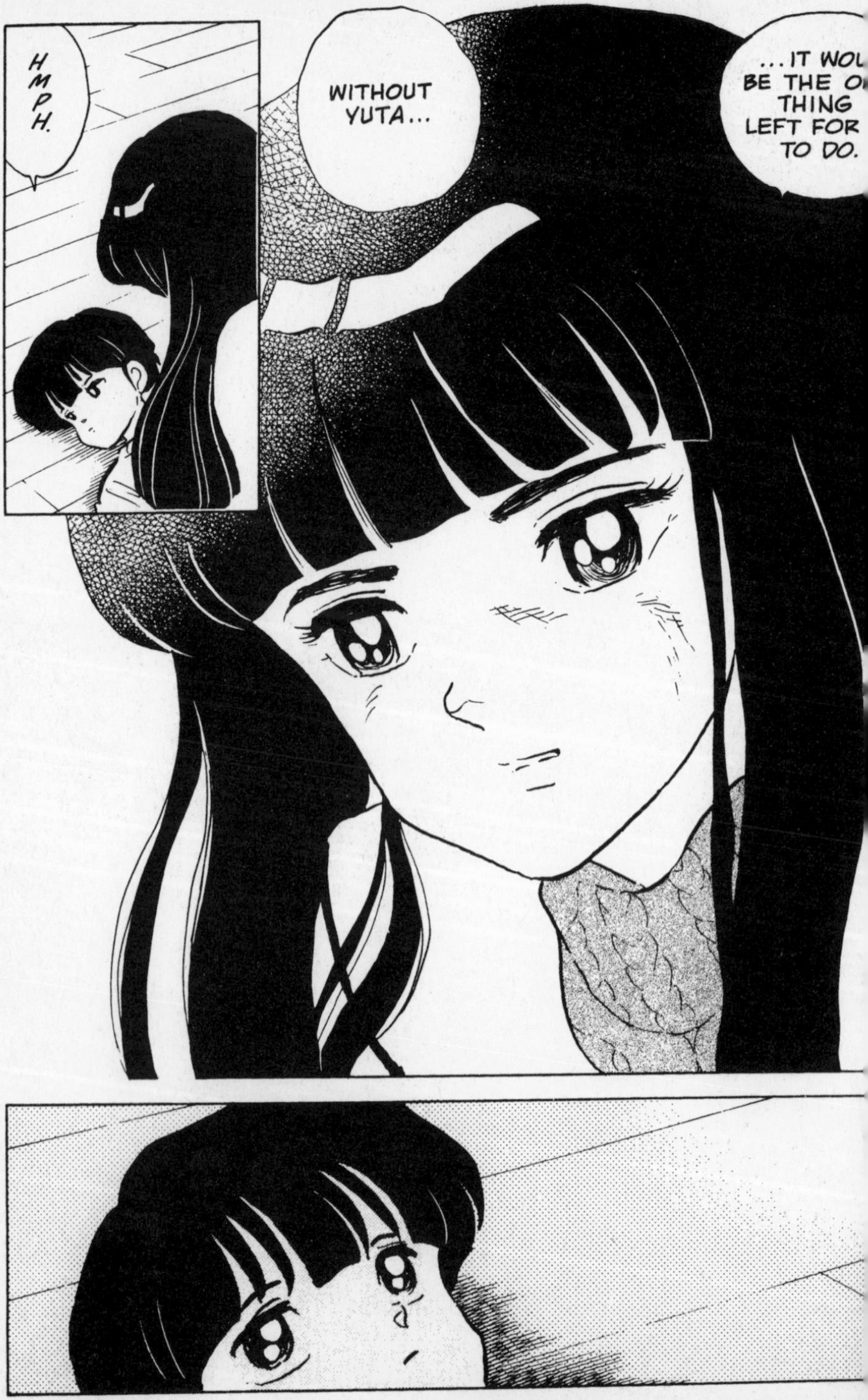
HMPH.
WITHOUT YUTA...
...IT WOU BE THE O THING LEFT FOR TO DO.

FLUMP

WHAT A HORRIBLE GIRL.

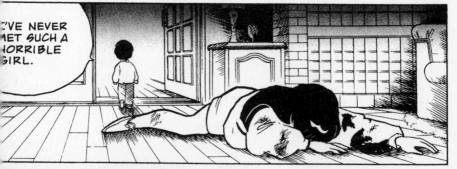

I'VE NEVER MET SUCH A HORRIBLE GIRL.

HEY.

I'VE DECIDED TO LET YOU LIVE A WHILE LONGER.

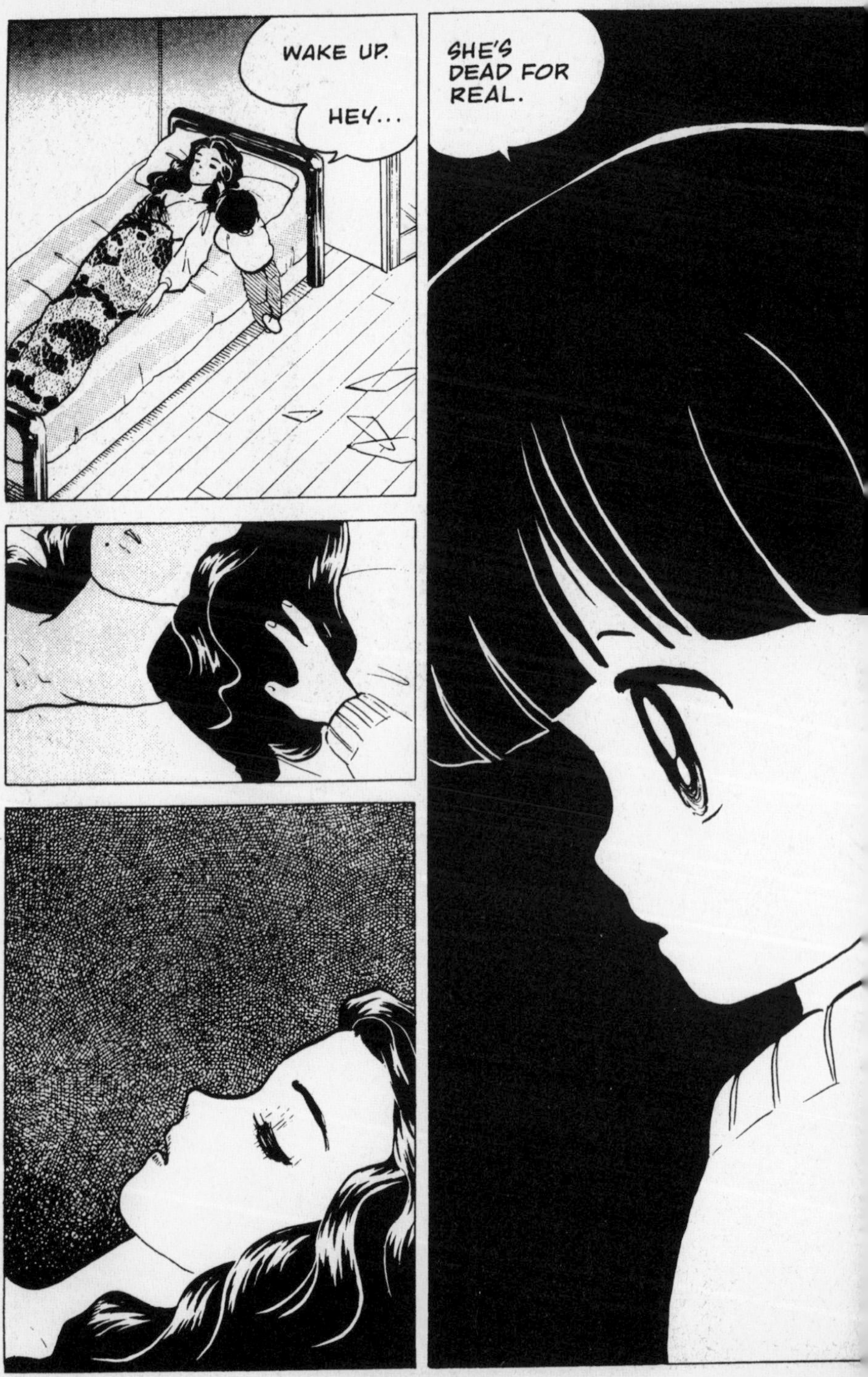
WAKE UP.
HEY...
SHE'S DEAD FOR REAL.

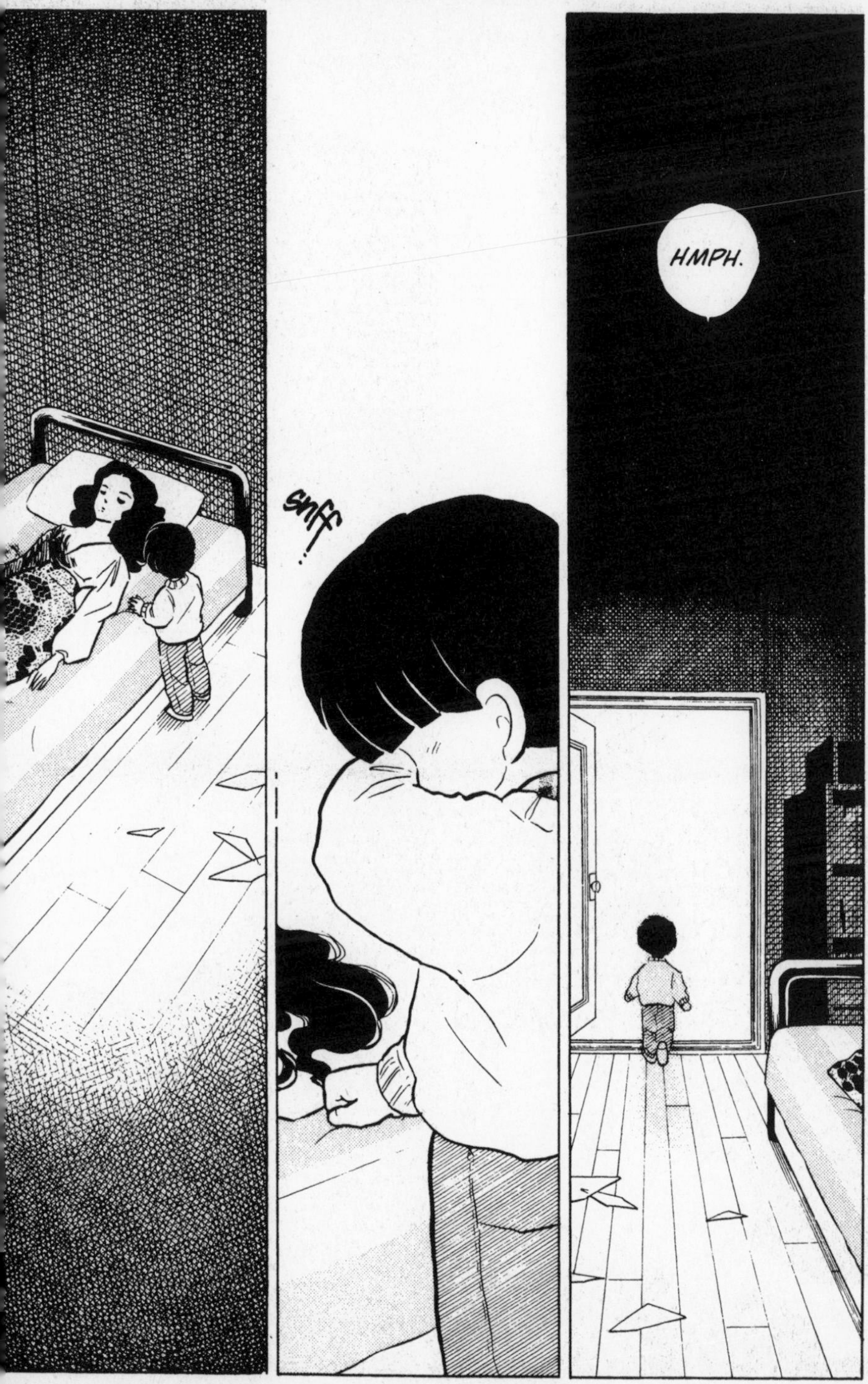
snff
HMPH.

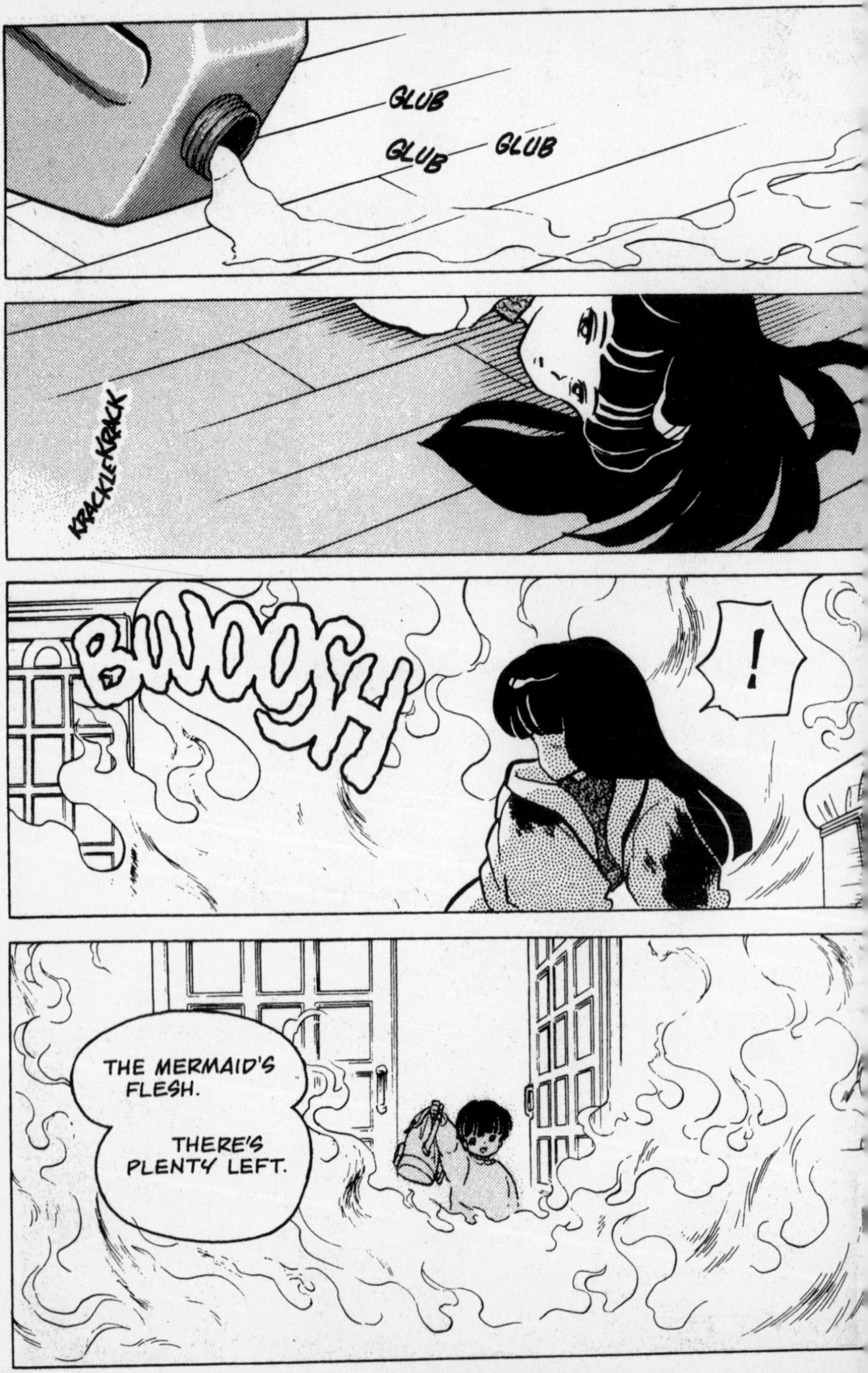
GLUB
GLUB
GLUB
KRACKLEKRACK
BWOOSH
!
THE MERMAID'S FLESH.
THERE'S PLENTY LEFT.

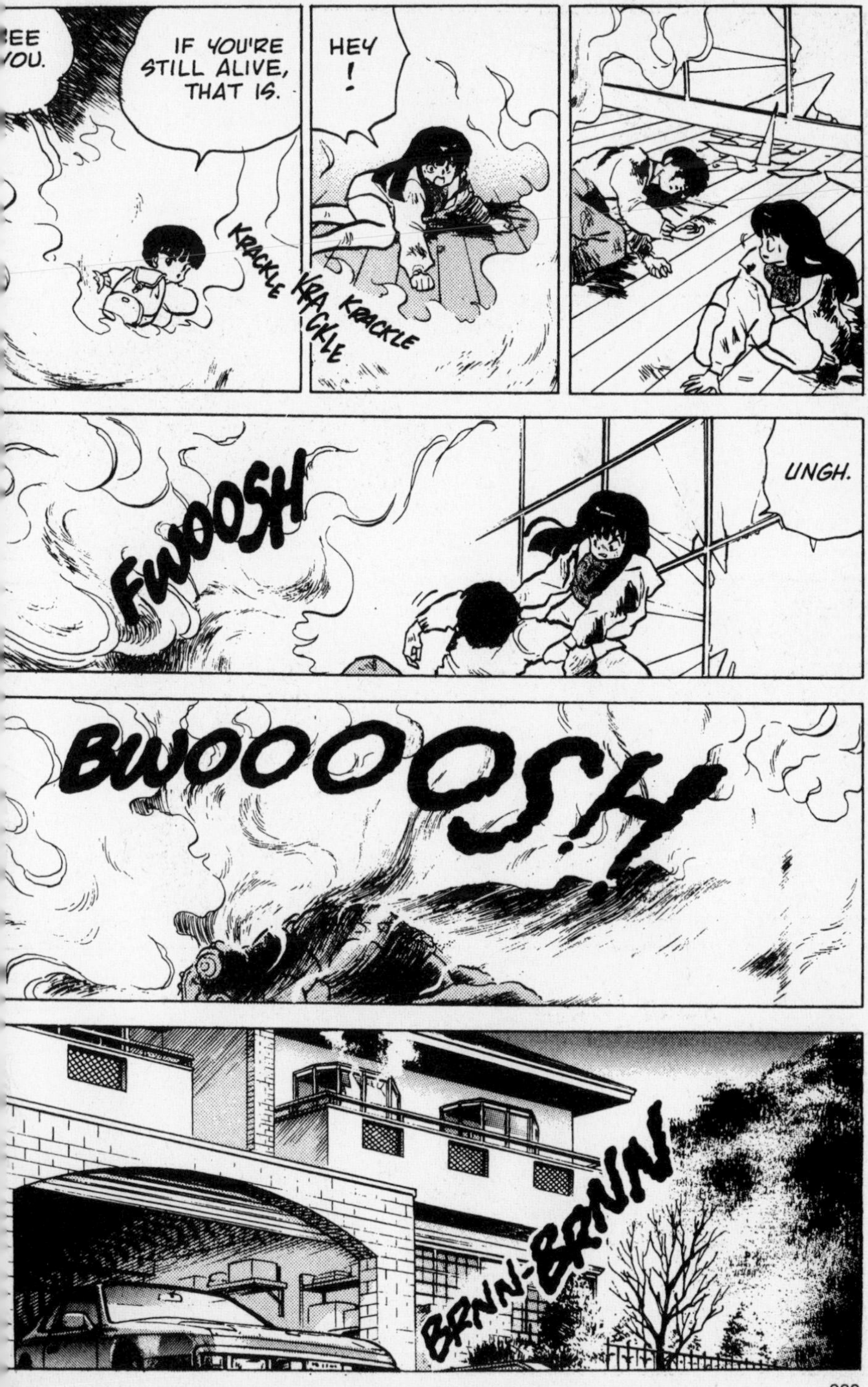
EE
YOU.
IF YOU'RE STILL ALIVE, THAT IS.
KRACKLE
KRACKLE
HEY !
KRACKLE
FWOOSH
UNGH.
BWOOOOSH
BRNN-BRNN

WHOOOO

KLANG
KLANG
KLANG

KLANG
KLANG KLANG
KLANG

230

B-DMP

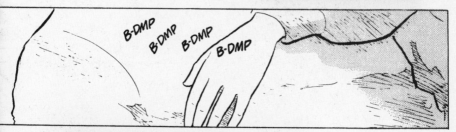

B-DMP B-DMP B-DMP B-DMP

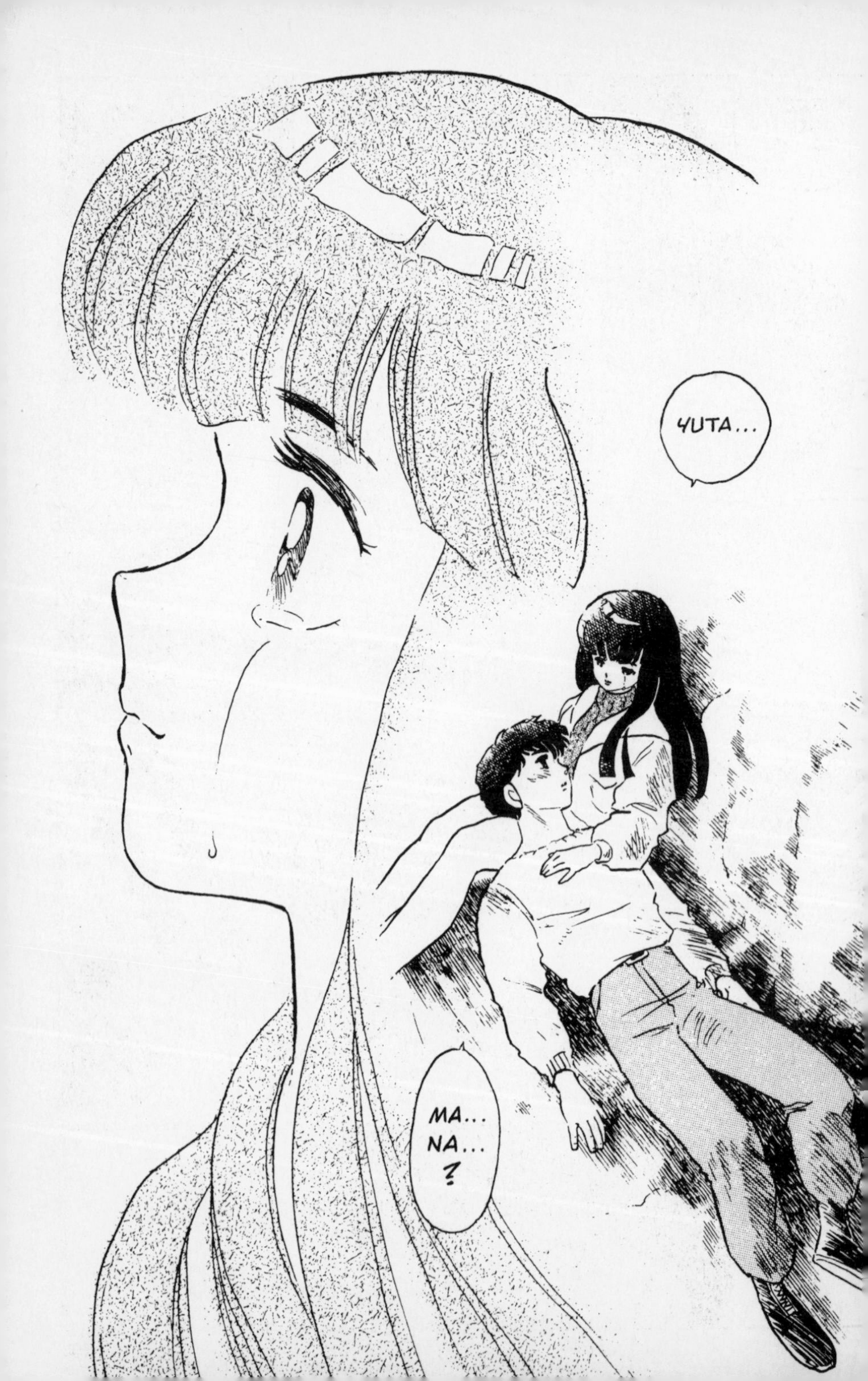
YUTA...
MA... NA... ?

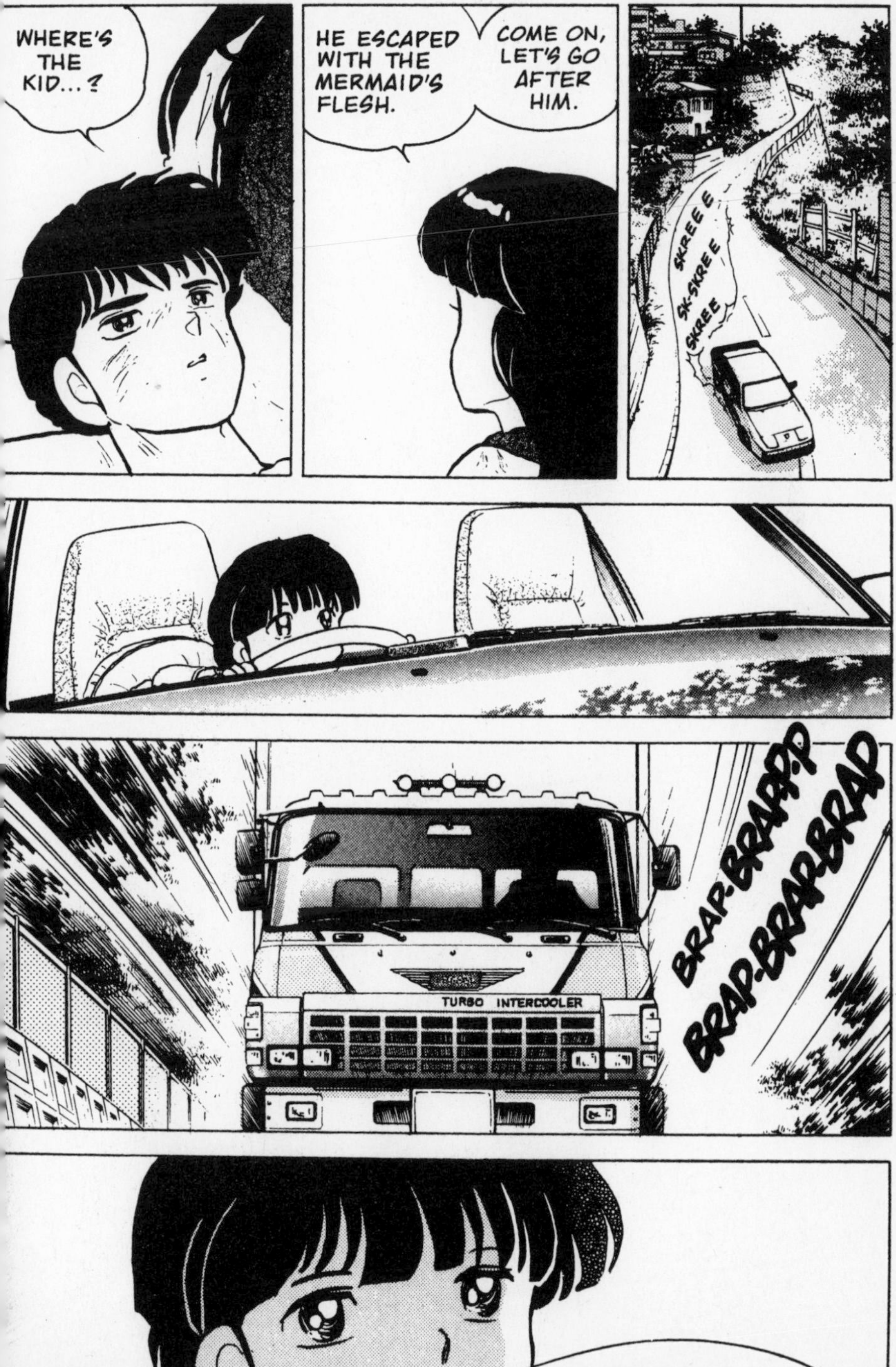
WHERE'S THE KID...?
HE ESCAPED WITH THE MERMAID'S FLESH.
COME ON, LET'S GO AFTER HIM.
SKREEE
SK-SKREEE
SKREEE
TURBO INTERCOOLER
BRAP-BRAPP-P
BRAP-BRAP-BRAP

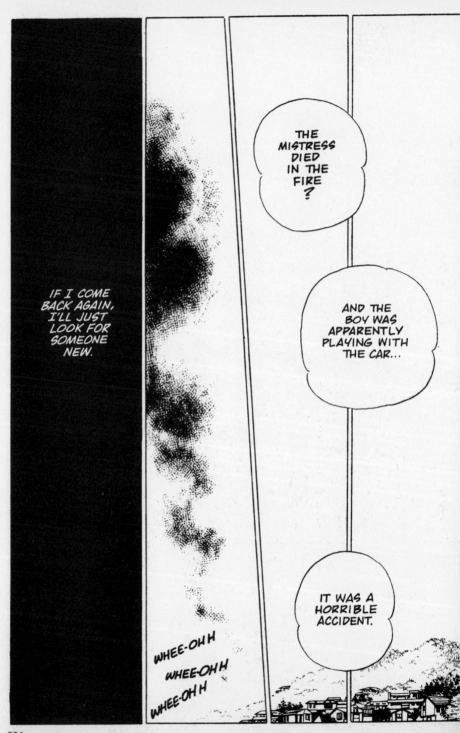

IF I COME BACK AGAIN, I'LL JUST LOOK FOR SOMEONE NEW.

THE MISTRESS DIED IN THE FIRE?

AND THE BOY WAS APPARENTLY PLAYING WITH THE CAR...

IT WAS A HORRIBLE ACCIDENT.

WHEE-OHH
WHEE-OHH
WHEE-OHH

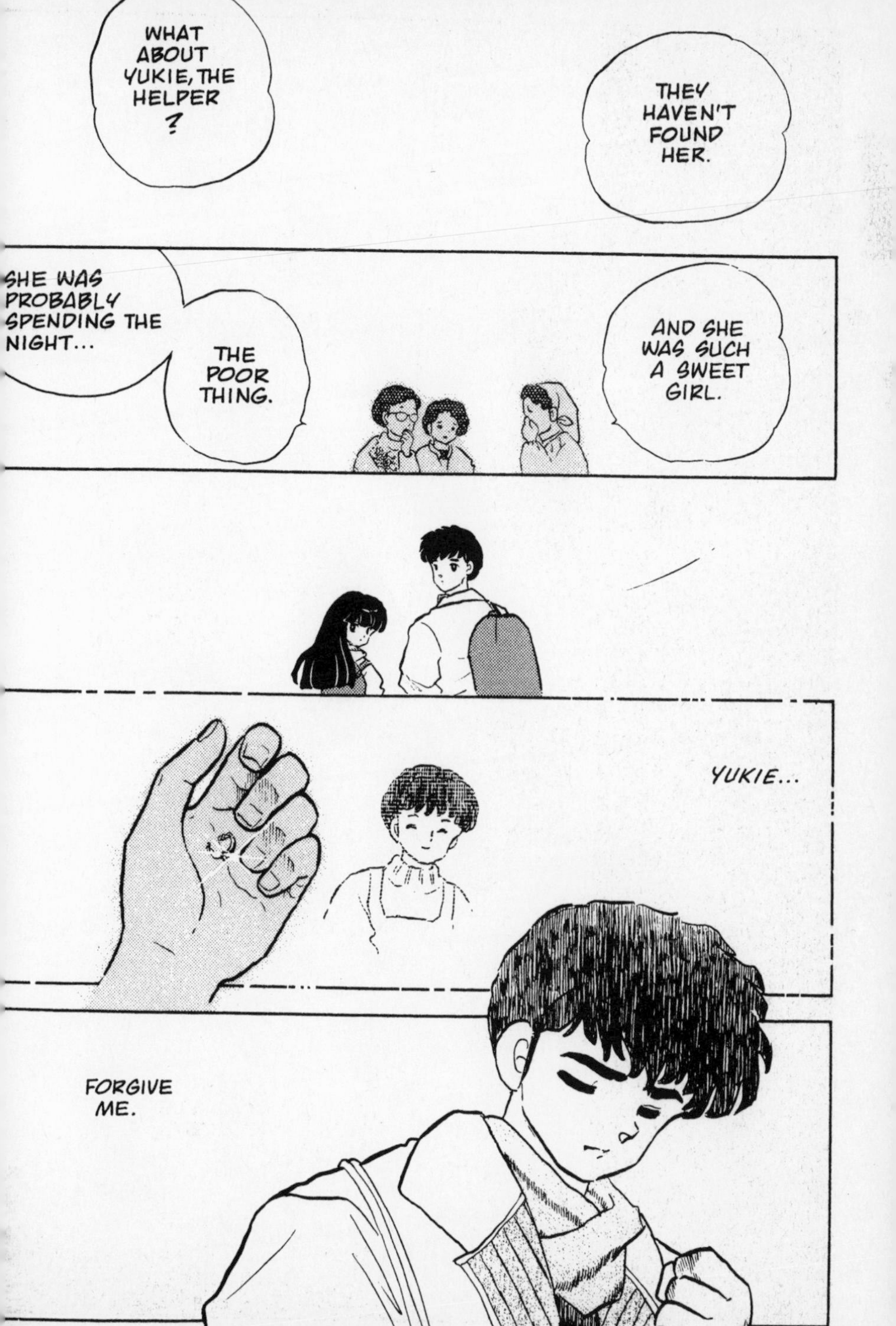
WHAT ABOUT YUKIE, THE HELPER?
THEY HAVEN'T FOUND HER.
SHE WAS PROBABLY SPENDING THE NIGHT...
THE POOR THING.
AND SHE WAS SUCH A SWEET GIRL.
YUKIE...
FORGIVE ME.

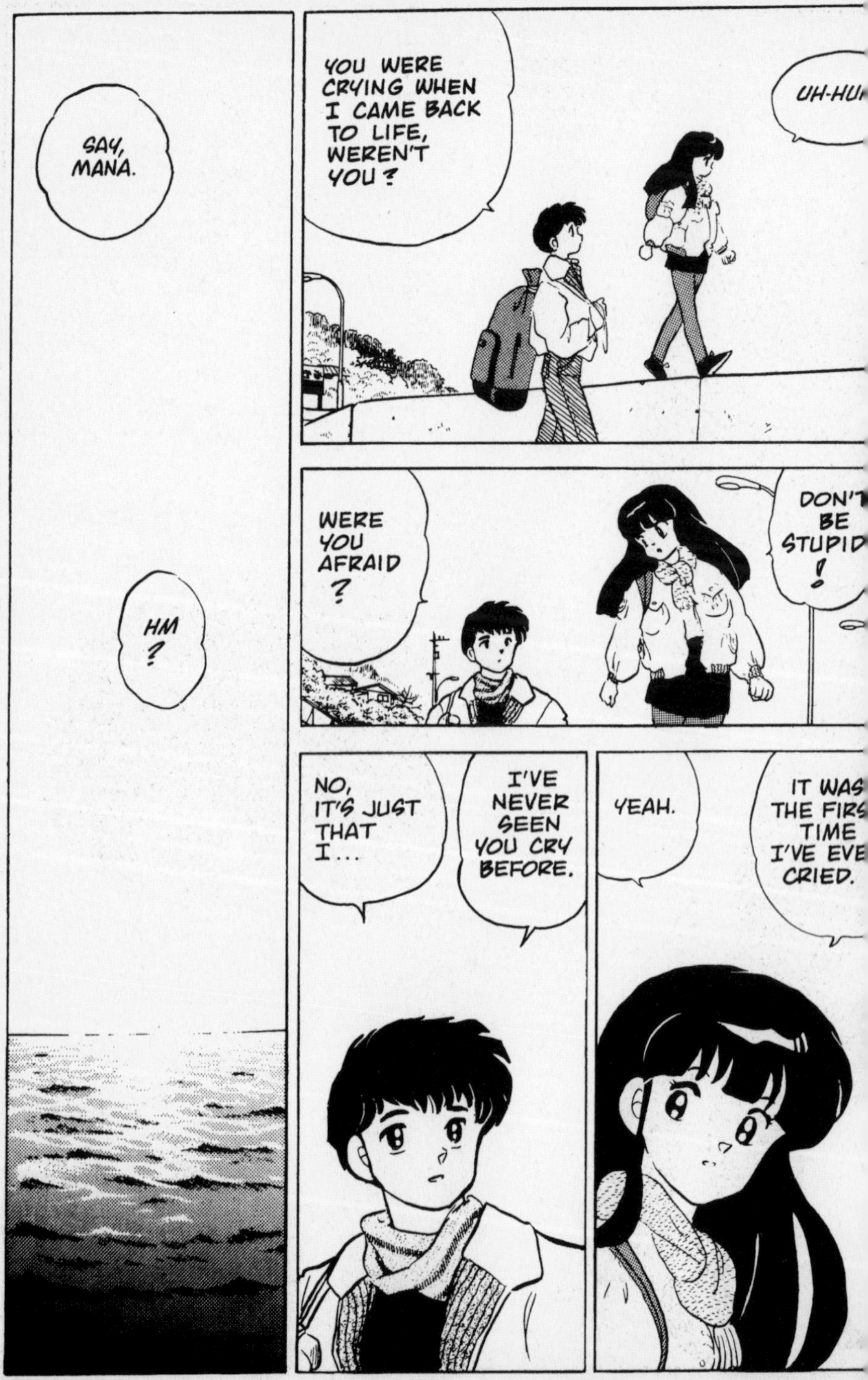
SAY, MANA.
HM ?
YOU WERE CRYING WHEN I CAME BACK TO LIFE, WEREN'T YOU ?
UH-HU
WERE YOU AFRAID ?
DON'T BE STUPID !
NO, IT'S JUST THAT I...
I'VE NEVER SEEN YOU CRY BEFORE.
YEAH.
IT WAS THE FIRS TIME I'VE EVE CRIED.

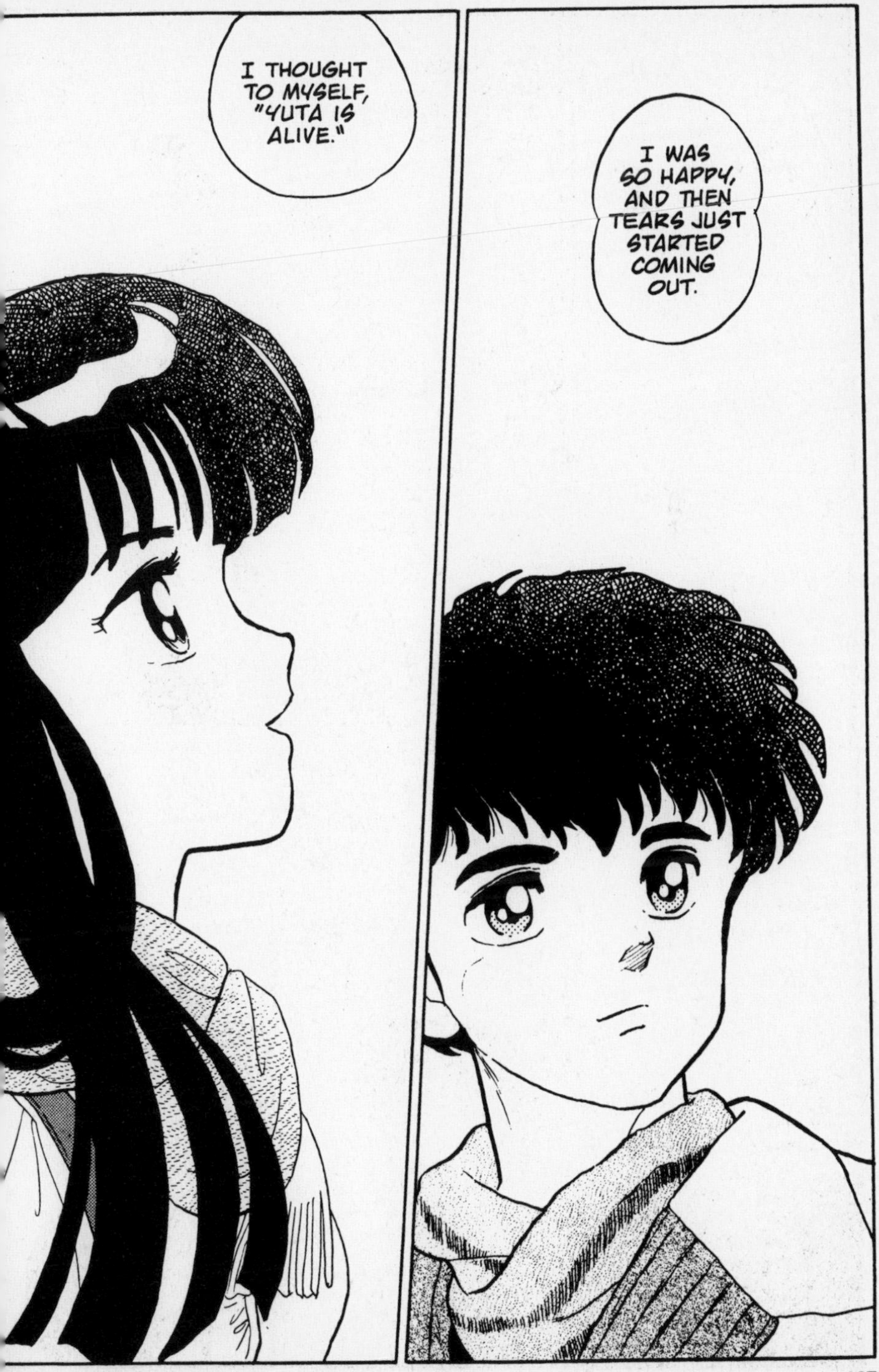
I THOUGHT TO MYSELF, "YUTA IS ALIVE."
I WAS SO HAPPY, AND THEN TEARS JUST STARTED COMING OUT.

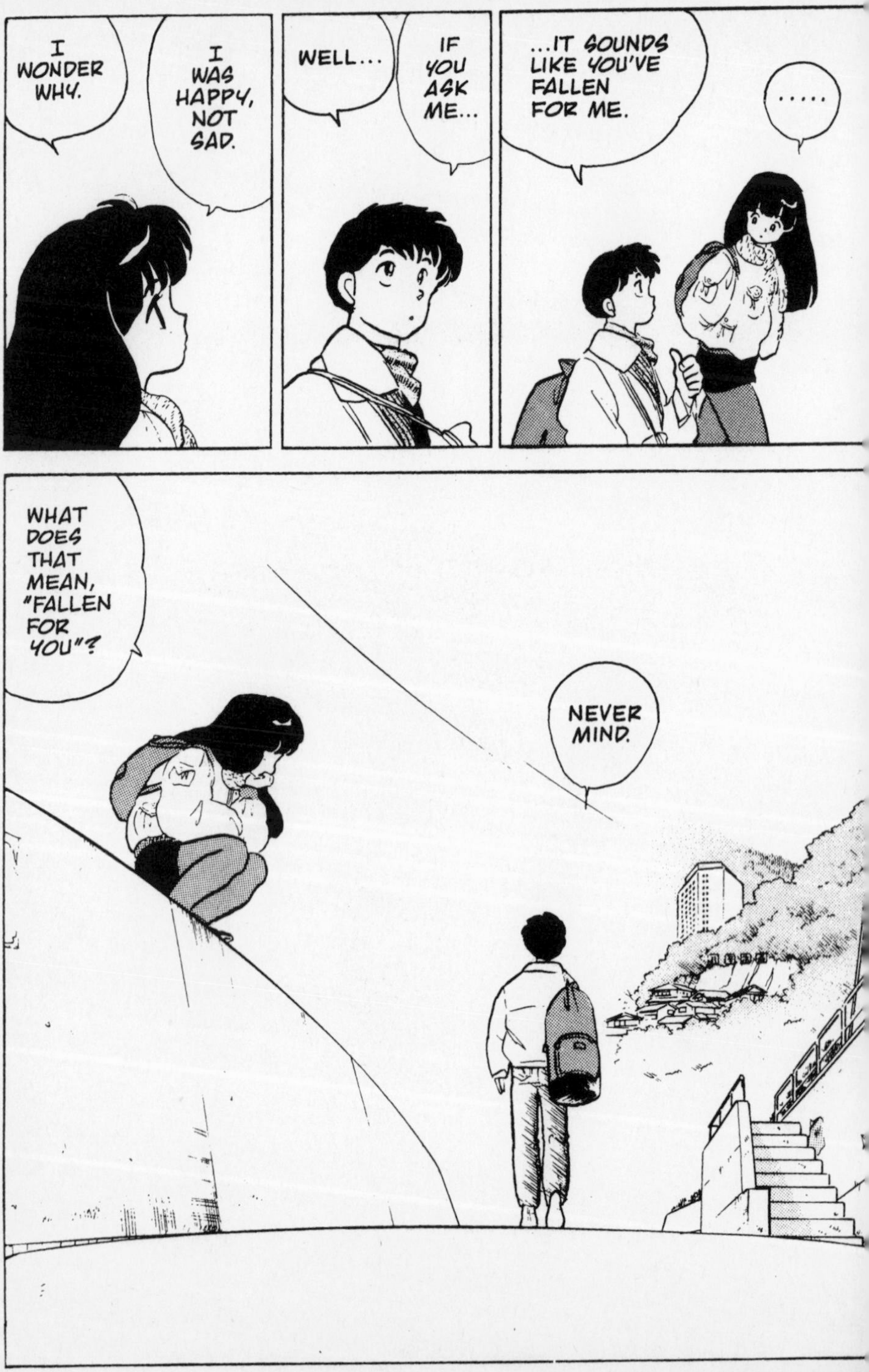
I WONDER WHY.
I WAS HAPPY, NOT SAD.
WELL...
IF YOU ASK ME...
...IT SOUNDS LIKE YOU'VE FALLEN FOR ME.
.....
WHAT DOES THAT MEAN, "FALLEN FOR YOU"?
NEVER MIND.

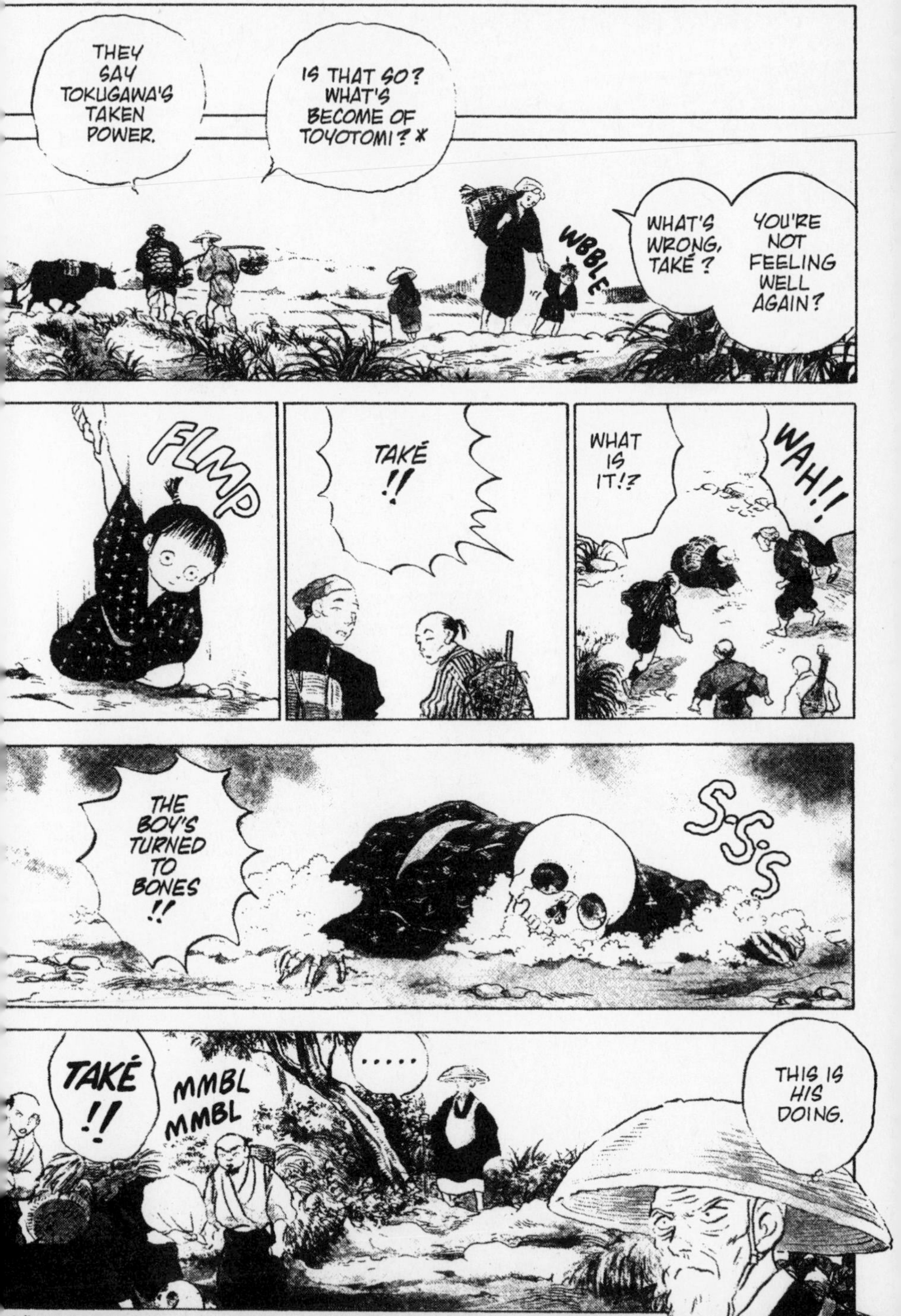
THEY SAY TOKUGAWA'S TAKEN POWER.
IS THAT SO? WHAT'S BECOME OF TOYOTOMI? *
WBBLE
WHAT'S WRONG, TAKÉ? YOU'RE NOT FEELING WELL AGAIN?
FLMP
TAKÉ !!
WHAT IS IT!?
WAH!!
THE BOY'S TURNED TO BONES !!
S-S-S
TAKÉ !!
MMBL MMBL
.....
THIS IS HIS DOING.

*"THE TOKUGAWA CLAN WRESTED CONTROL OF JAPAN FROM THE

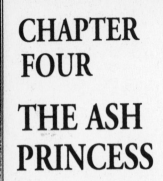

CHAPTER FOUR

THE ASH PRINCESS

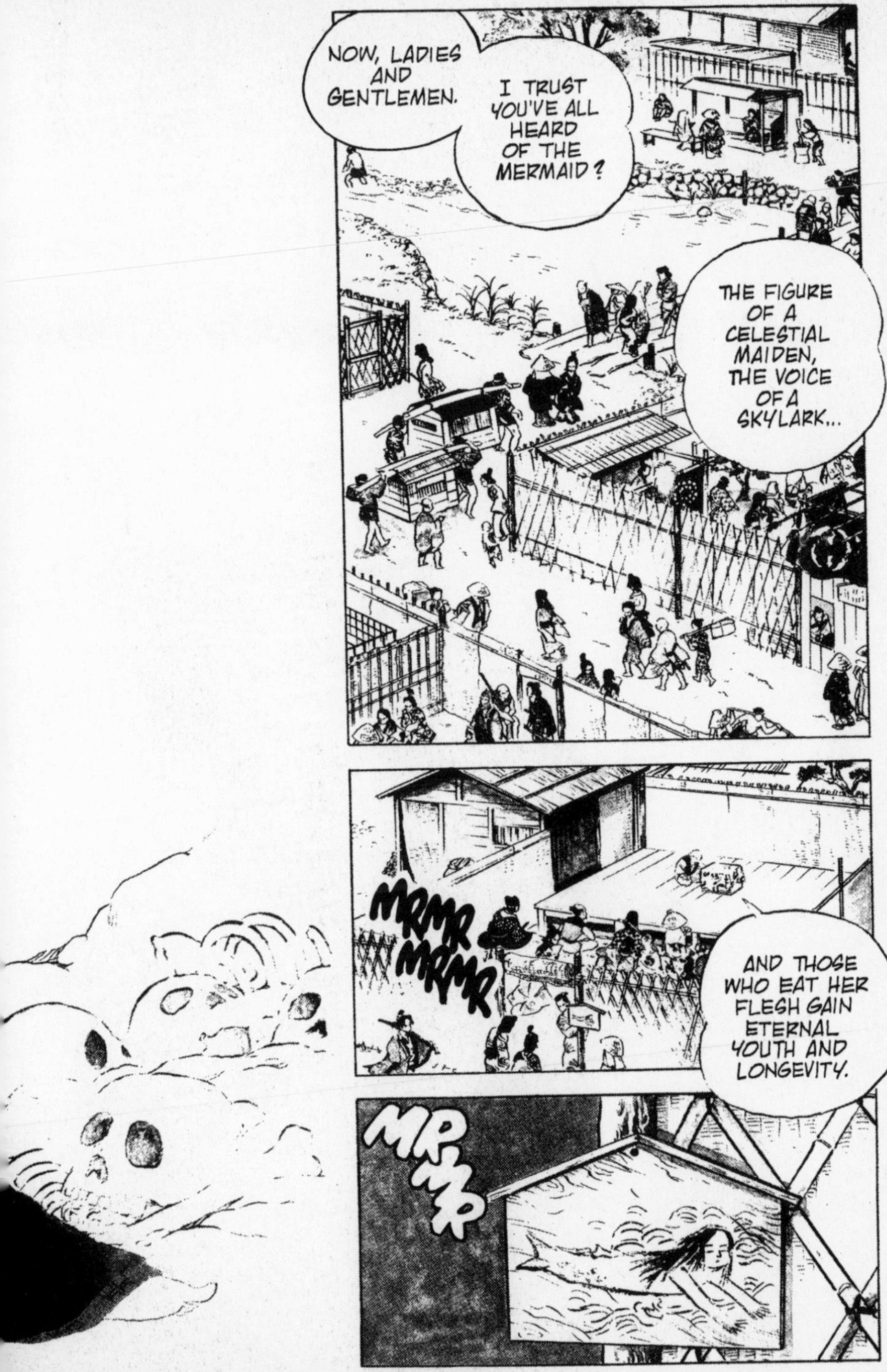
NOW, LADIES AND GENTLEMEN.
I TRUST YOU'VE ALL HEARD OF THE MERMAID?
THE FIGURE OF A CELESTIAL MAIDEN, THE VOICE OF A SKYLARK...
MRMR MRMR
AND THOSE WHO EAT HER FLESH GAIN ETERNAL YOUTH AND LONGEVITY.
MRMR

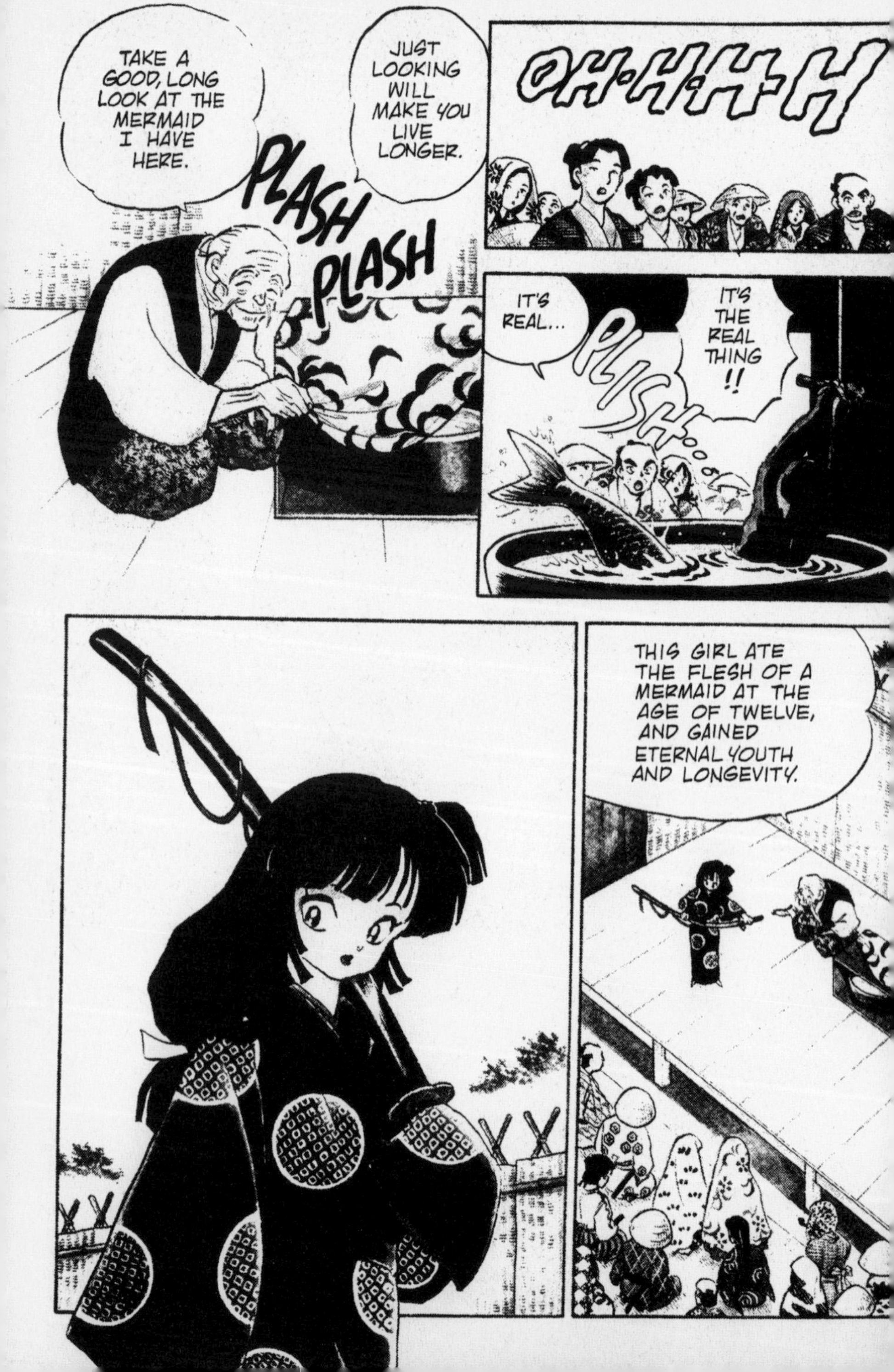
TAKE A GOOD, LONG LOOK AT THE MERMAID I HAVE HERE.
PLASH
PLASH
JUST LOOKING WILL MAKE YOU LIVE LONGER.
OH-H-H-H-H
IT'S REAL...
PLISH...
IT'S THE REAL THING!!
THIS GIRL ATE THE FLESH OF A MERMAID AT THE AGE OF TWELVE, AND GAINED ETERNAL YOUTH AND LONGEVITY.

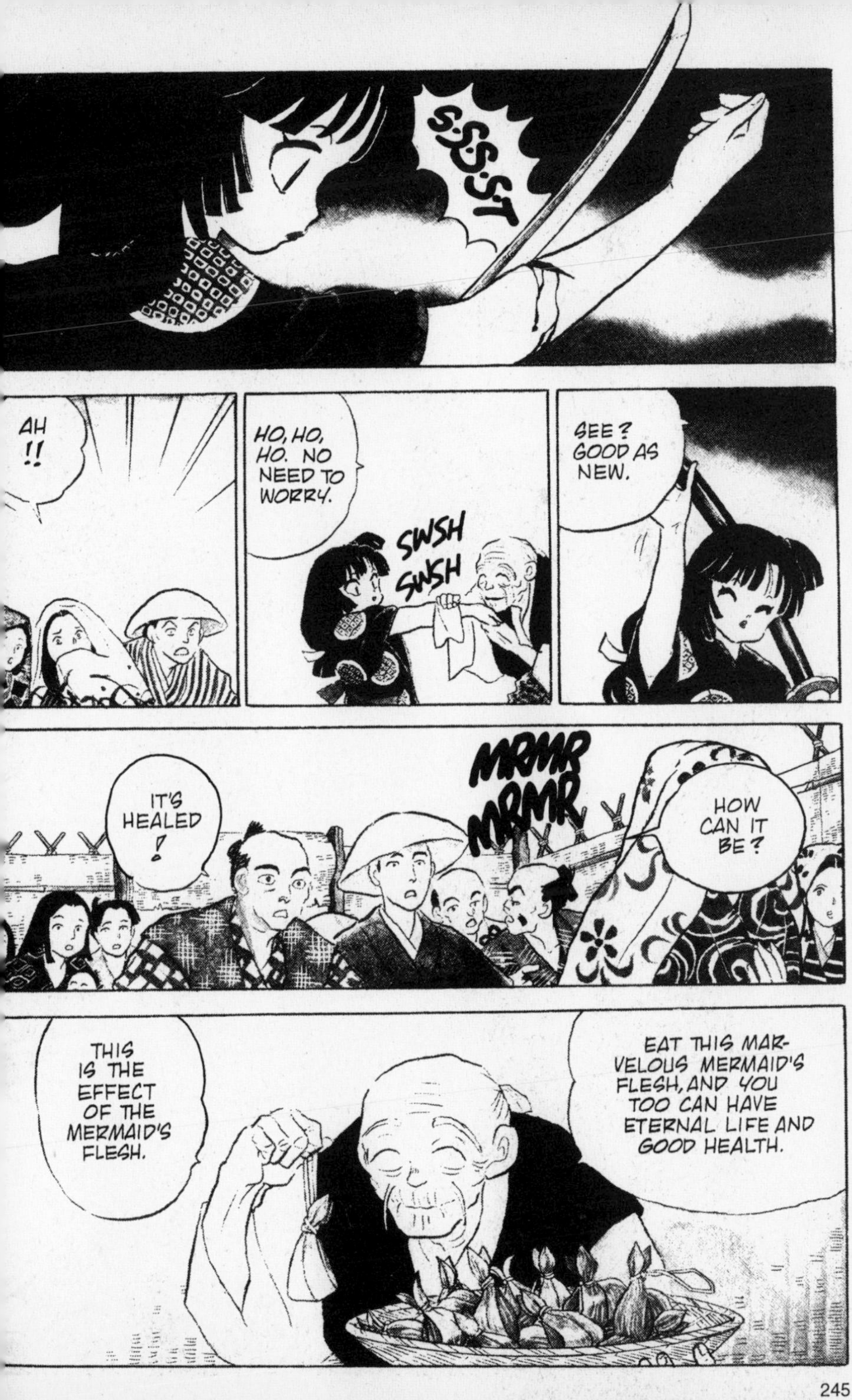
S-S-S-ST
AH !!
HO, HO, HO. NO NEED TO WORRY.
SWSH SWSH
SEE? GOOD AS NEW.
IT'S HEALED!
MRMR MRMR
HOW CAN IT BE?
THIS IS THE EFFECT OF THE MERMAID'S FLESH.
EAT THIS MARVELOUS MERMAID'S FLESH, AND YOU TOO CAN HAVE ETERNAL LIFE AND GOOD HEALTH.

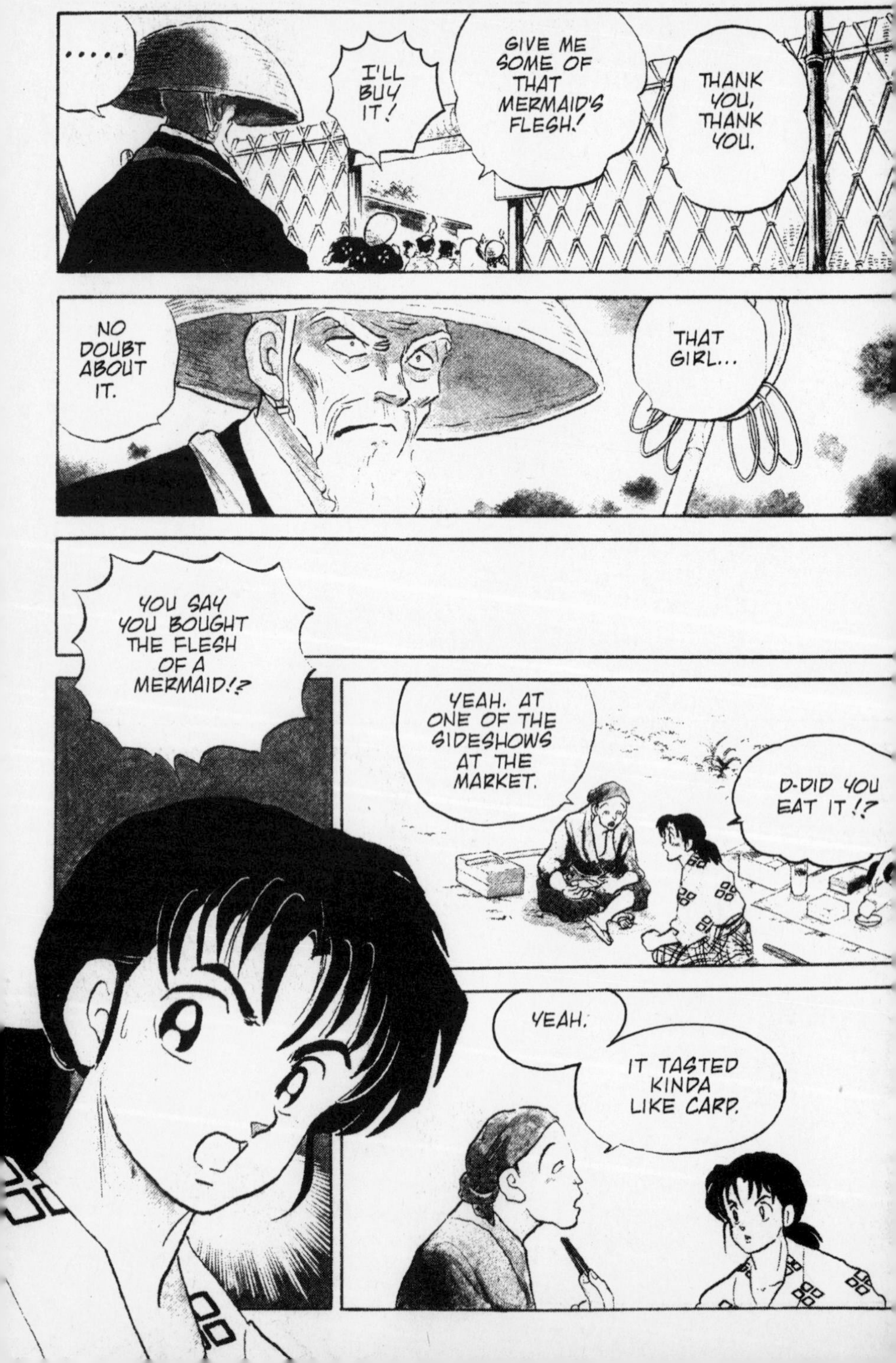
.....
I'LL BUY IT!
GIVE ME SOME OF THAT MERMAID'S FLESH!
THANK YOU, THANK YOU.
NO DOUBT ABOUT IT.
THAT GIRL...
YOU SAY YOU BOUGHT THE FLESH OF A MERMAID!?
YEAH. AT ONE OF THE SIDESHOWS AT THE MARKET.
D-DID YOU EAT IT!?
YEAH.
IT TASTED KINDA LIKE CARP.

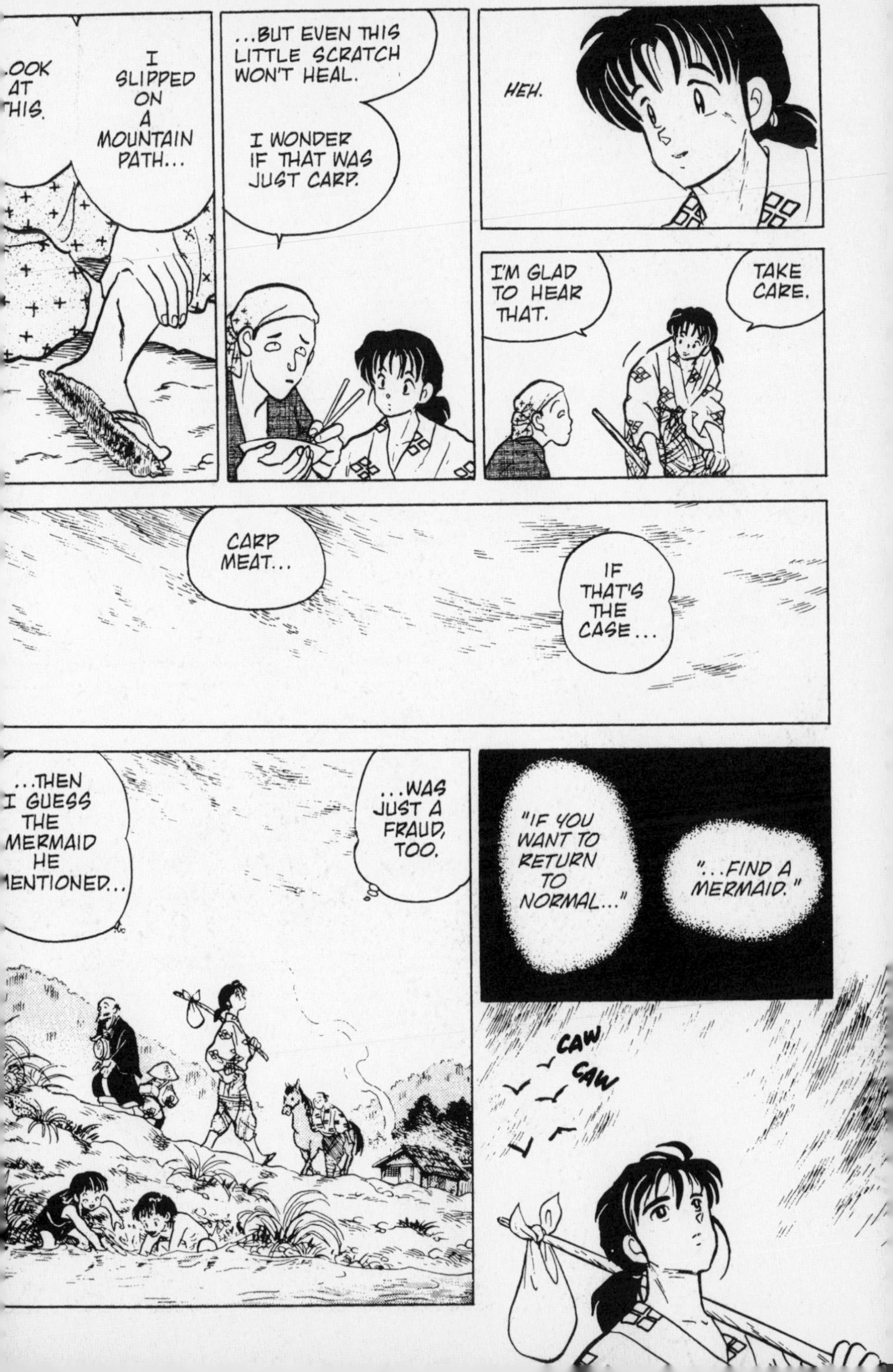
LOOK AT THIS.
I SLIPPED ON A MOUNTAIN PATH...
...BUT EVEN THIS LITTLE SCRATCH WON'T HEAL.
I WONDER IF THAT WAS JUST CARP.
HEH.
I'M GLAD TO HEAR THAT.
TAKE CARE.
CARP MEAT...
IF THAT'S THE CASE...
...THEN I GUESS THE MERMAID HE MENTIONED...
...WAS JUST A FRAUD, TOO.
"IF YOU WANT TO RETURN TO NORMAL..."
"...FIND A MERMAID."
CAW
CAW

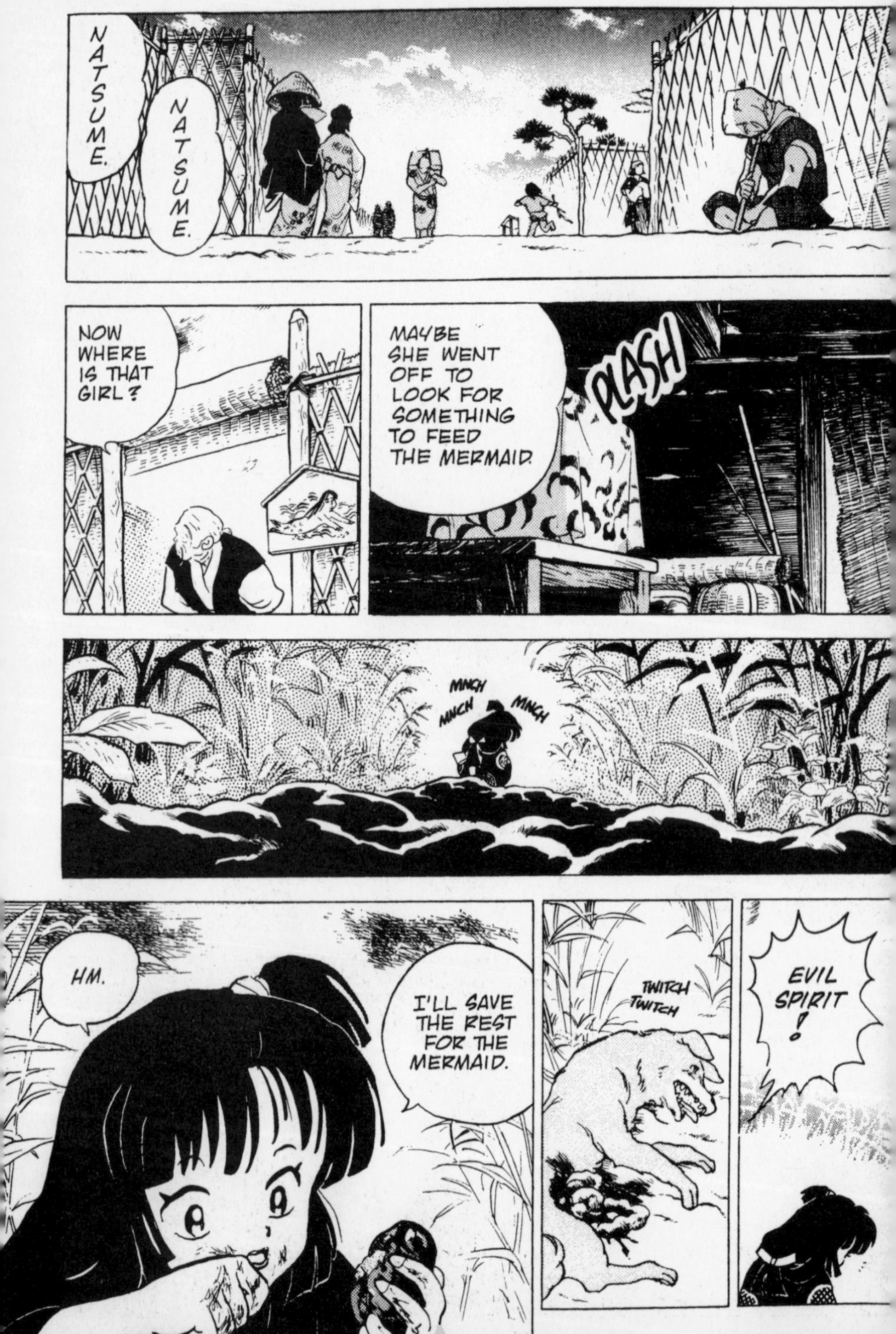
NATSUME.
NATSUME.
NOW WHERE IS THAT GIRL?
MAYBE SHE WENT OFF TO LOOK FOR SOMETHING TO FEED THE MERMAID.
PLASH
MNCH MNCH MNCH
HM.
I'LL SAVE THE REST FOR THE MERMAID.
TWITCH TWITCH
EVIL SPIRIT!

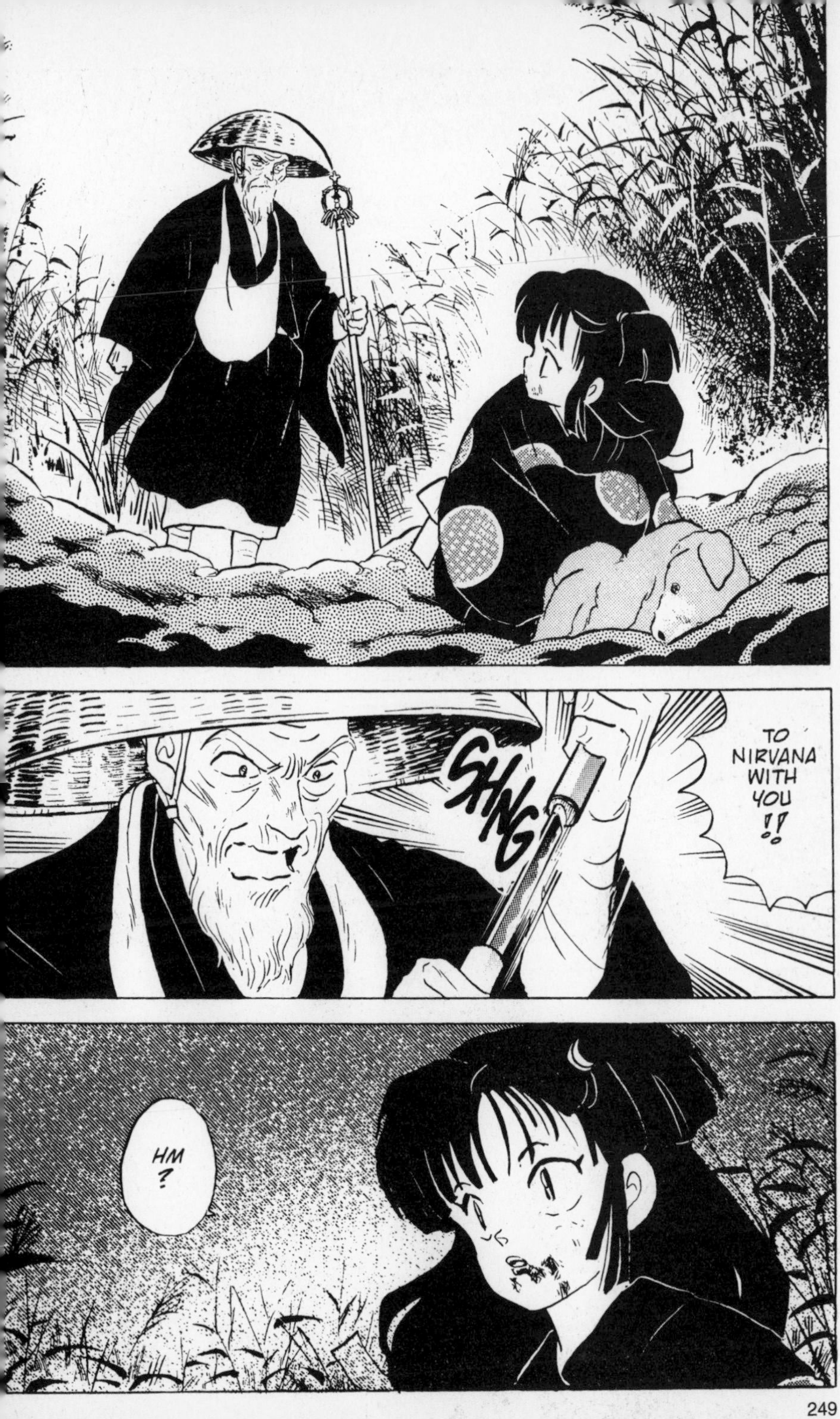
SHING
TO NIRVANA WITH YOU!!
HM?

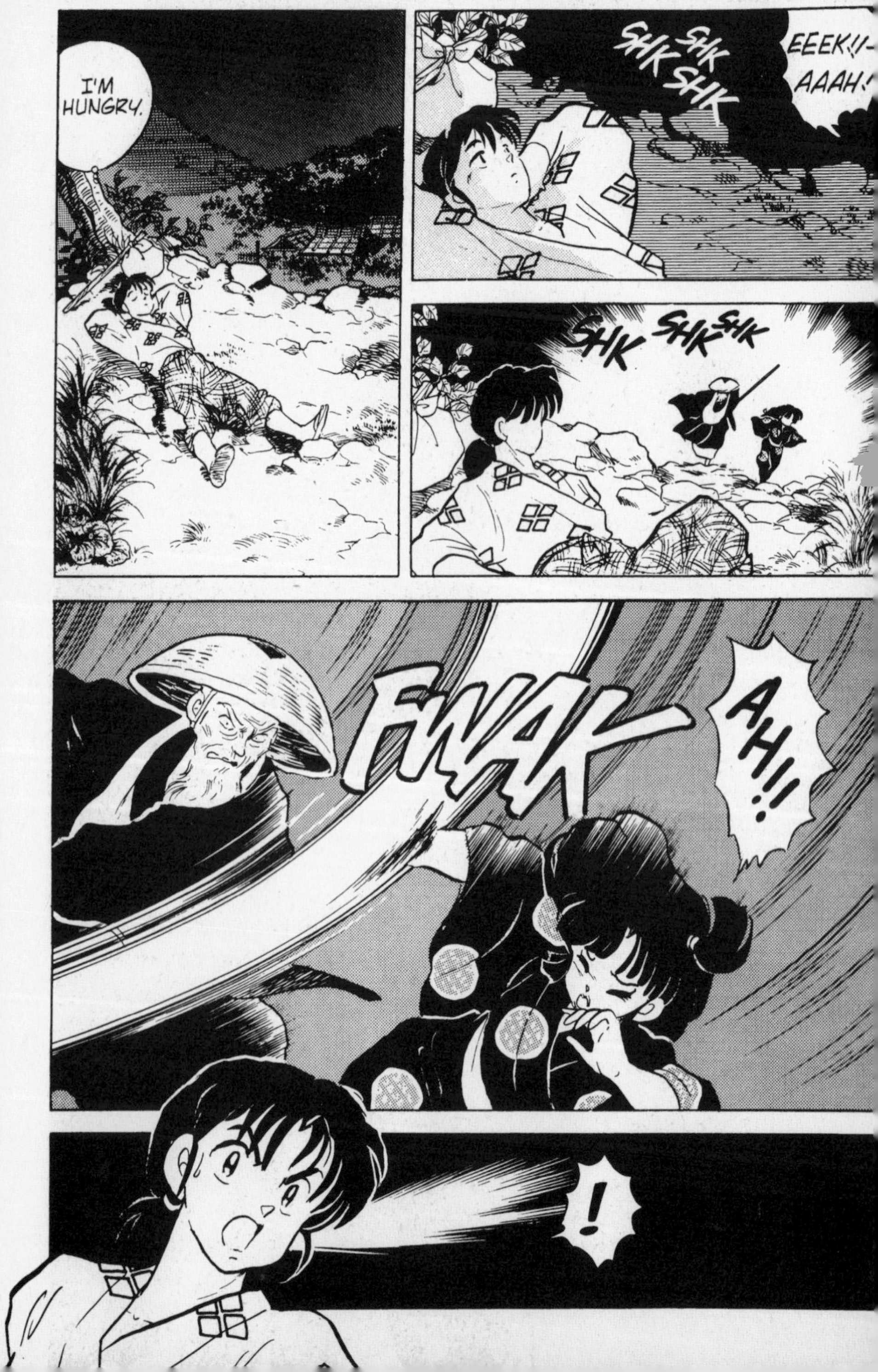
I'M HUNGRY.
SHK SHK SHK SHK
EEEK!!-AAAH!
SHK SHK SHK
FWAK
AH!!
!

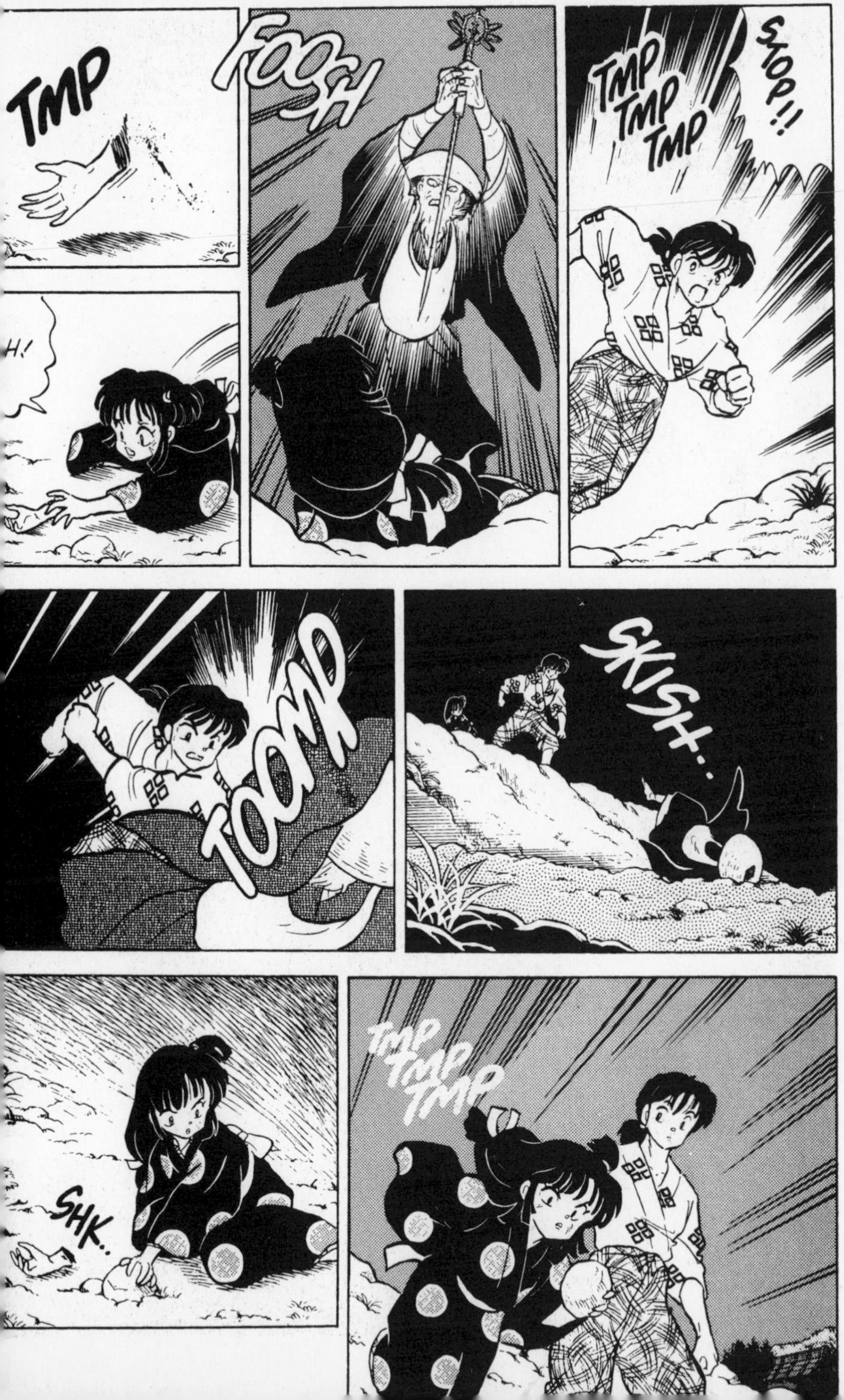

TMP
H!
FOOSH
TMP TMP TMP
STOP!!
TOOMP
SKISH...
SHK...
TMP TMP TMP

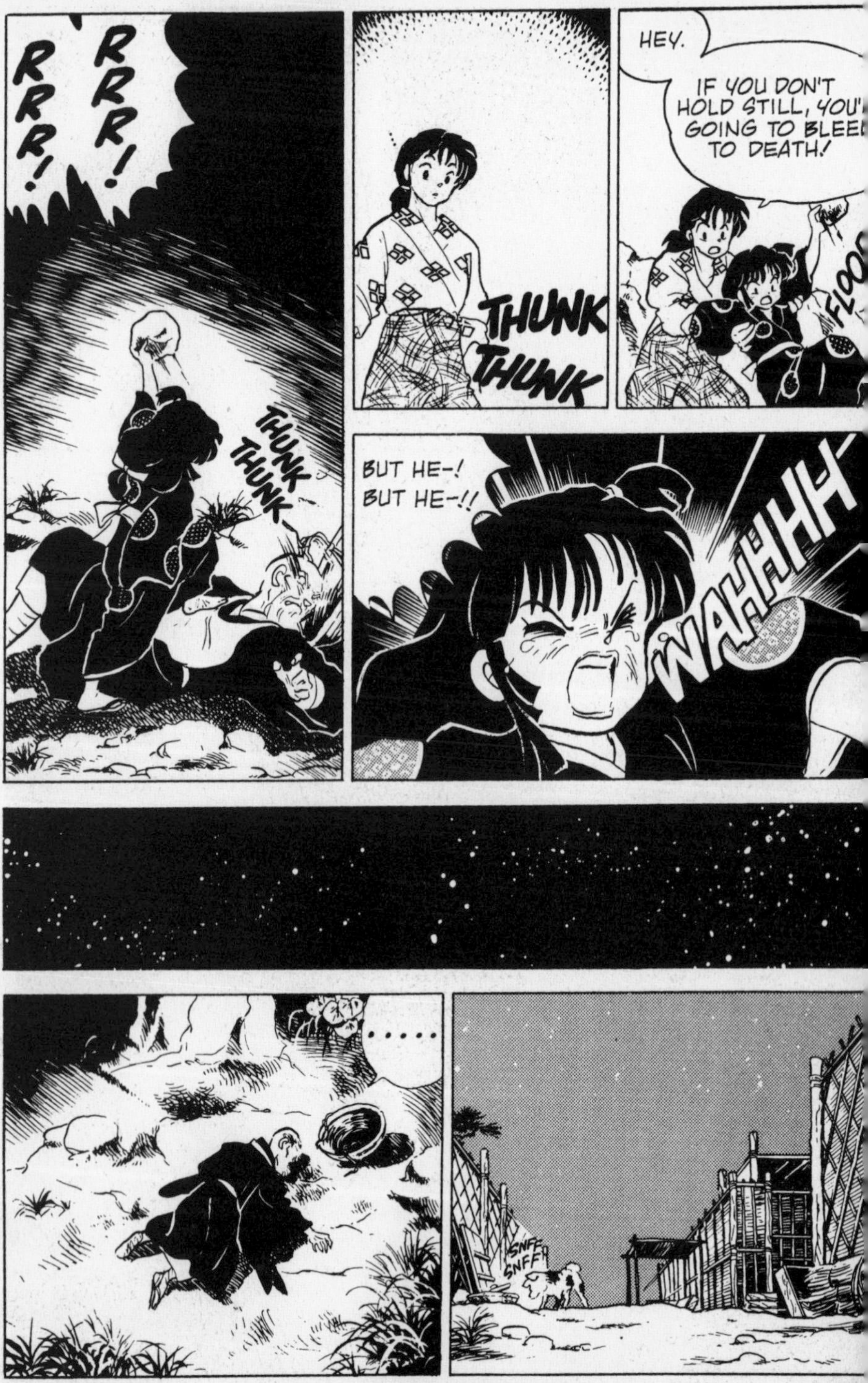
RRR!
RRR!
THUNK THUNK
THUNK THUNK
...
HEY.
IF YOU DON'T HOLD STILL, YOU' GOING TO BLEE TO DEATH!
FLOO
BUT HE-! BUT HE-!!
WAHHHH
......
SNFF SNFF

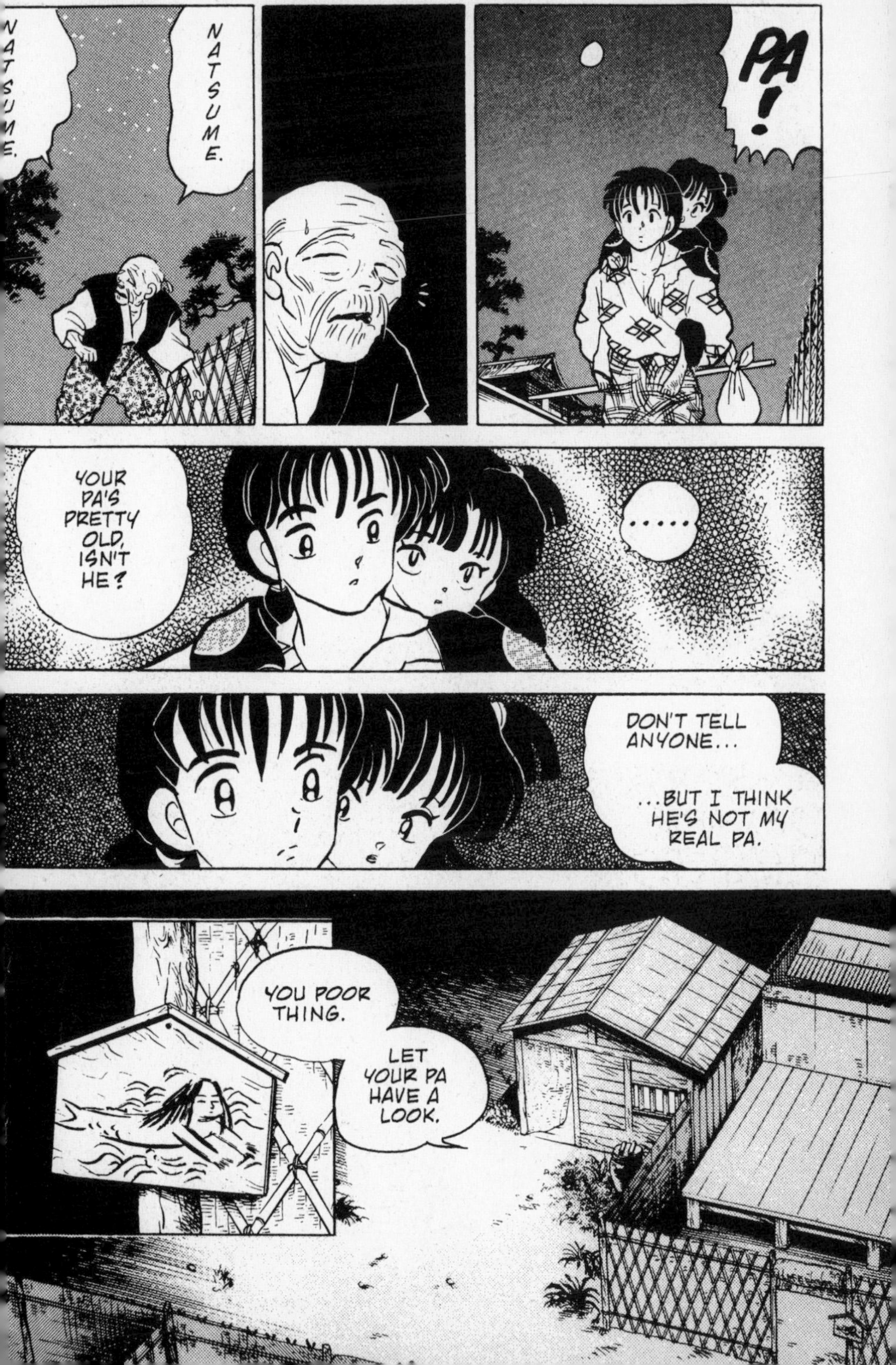
NATSUME.
NATSUME.
PA!
YOUR PA'S PRETTY OLD, ISN'T HE?
......
DON'T TELL ANYONE...
...BUT I THINK HE'S NOT MY REAL PA.
YOU POOR THING.
LET YOUR PA HAVE A LOOK.

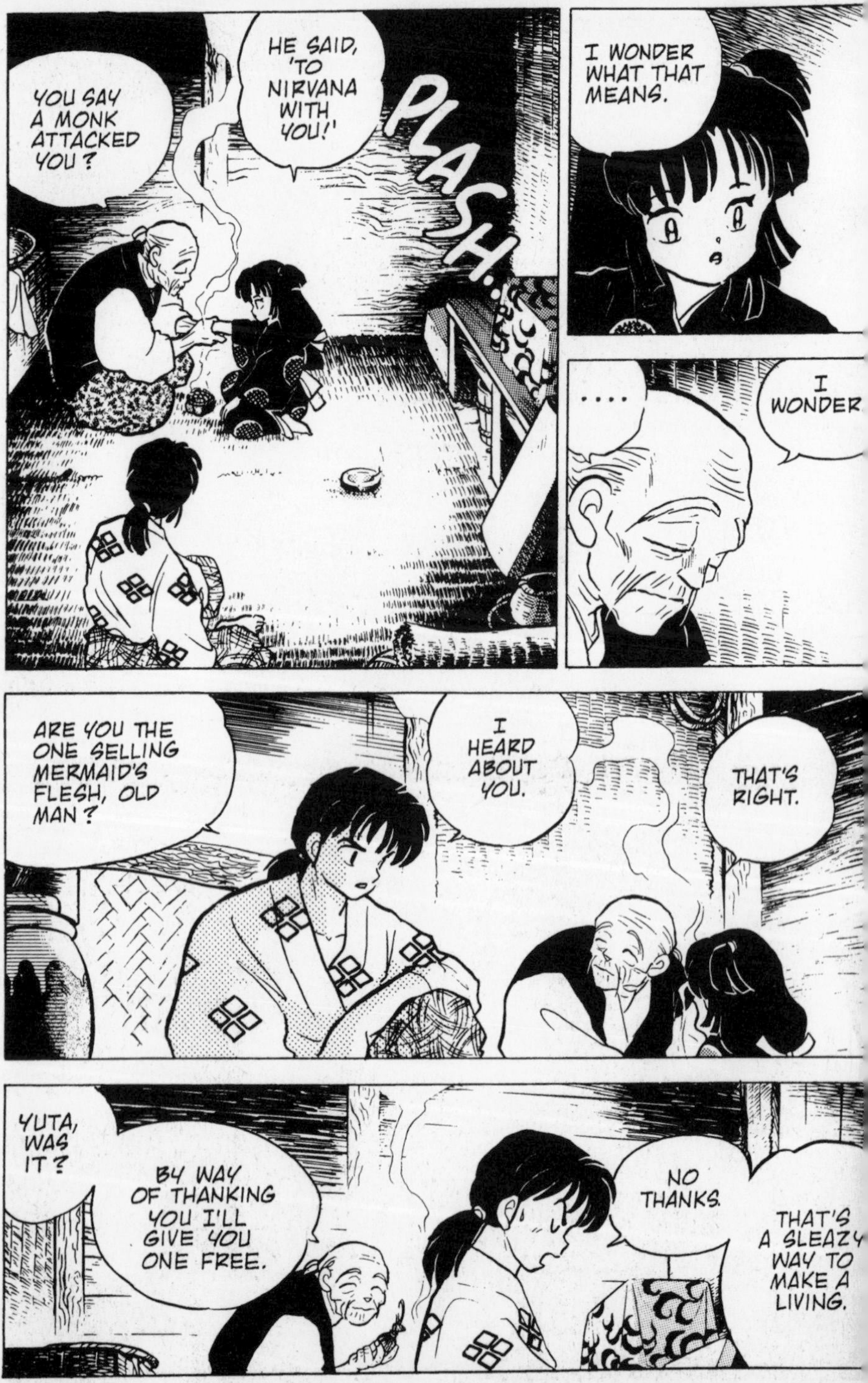

YOU SAY A MONK ATTACKED YOU?
HE SAID, 'TO NIRVANA WITH YOU!'
PLASH...
I WONDER WHAT THAT MEANS.
....
I WONDER.
ARE YOU THE ONE SELLING MERMAID'S FLESH, OLD MAN?
I HEARD ABOUT YOU.
THAT'S RIGHT.
YUTA, WAS IT?
BY WAY OF THANKING YOU I'LL GIVE YOU ONE FREE.
NO THANKS.
THAT'S A SLEAZY WAY TO MAKE A LIVING.

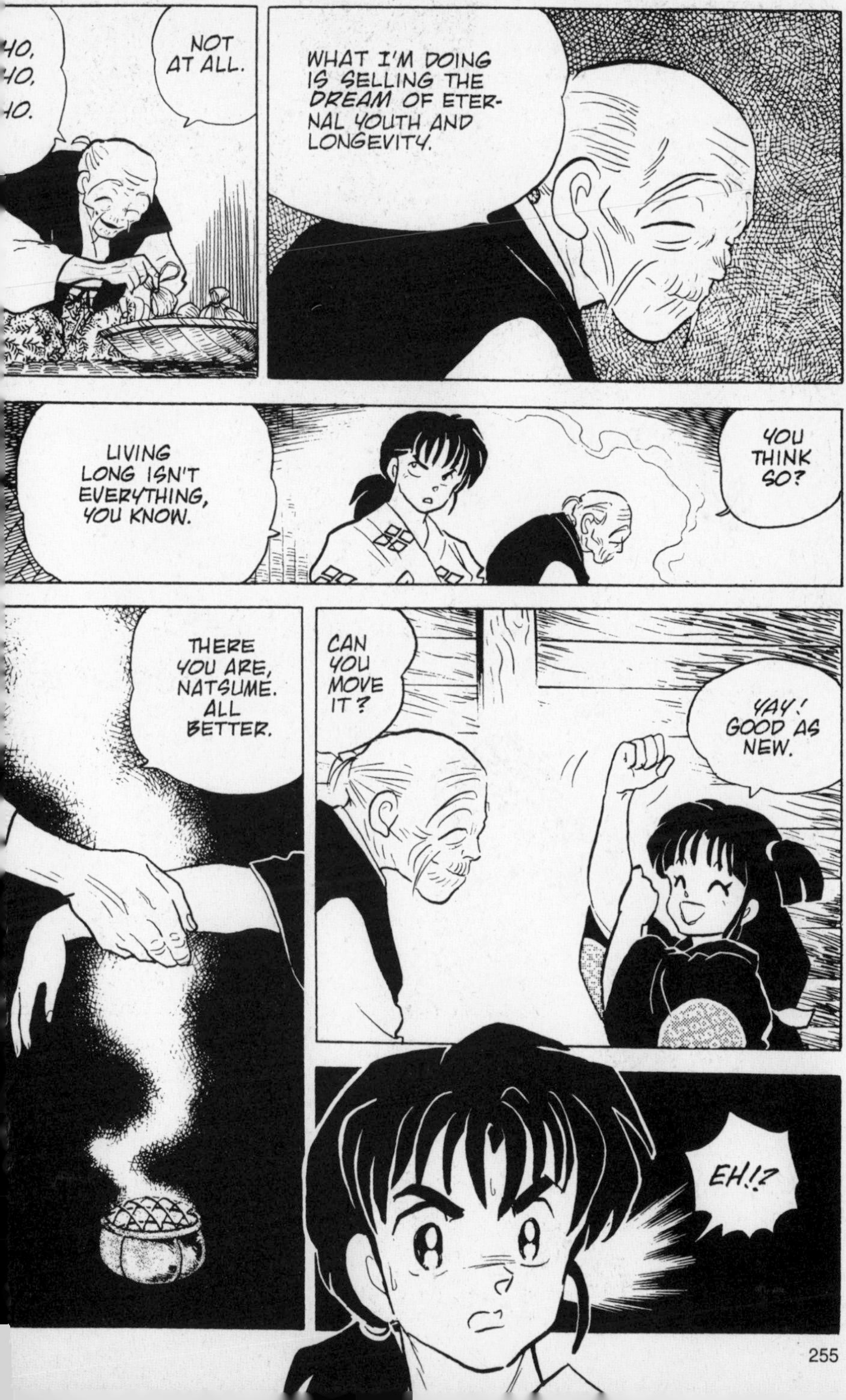
HO, HO, HO.
NOT AT ALL.
WHAT I'M DOING IS SELLING THE DREAM OF ETERNAL YOUTH AND LONGEVITY.
LIVING LONG ISN'T EVERYTHING, YOU KNOW.
YOU THINK SO?
THERE YOU ARE, NATSUME. ALL BETTER.
CAN YOU MOVE IT?
YAY! GOOD AS NEW.
EH!?

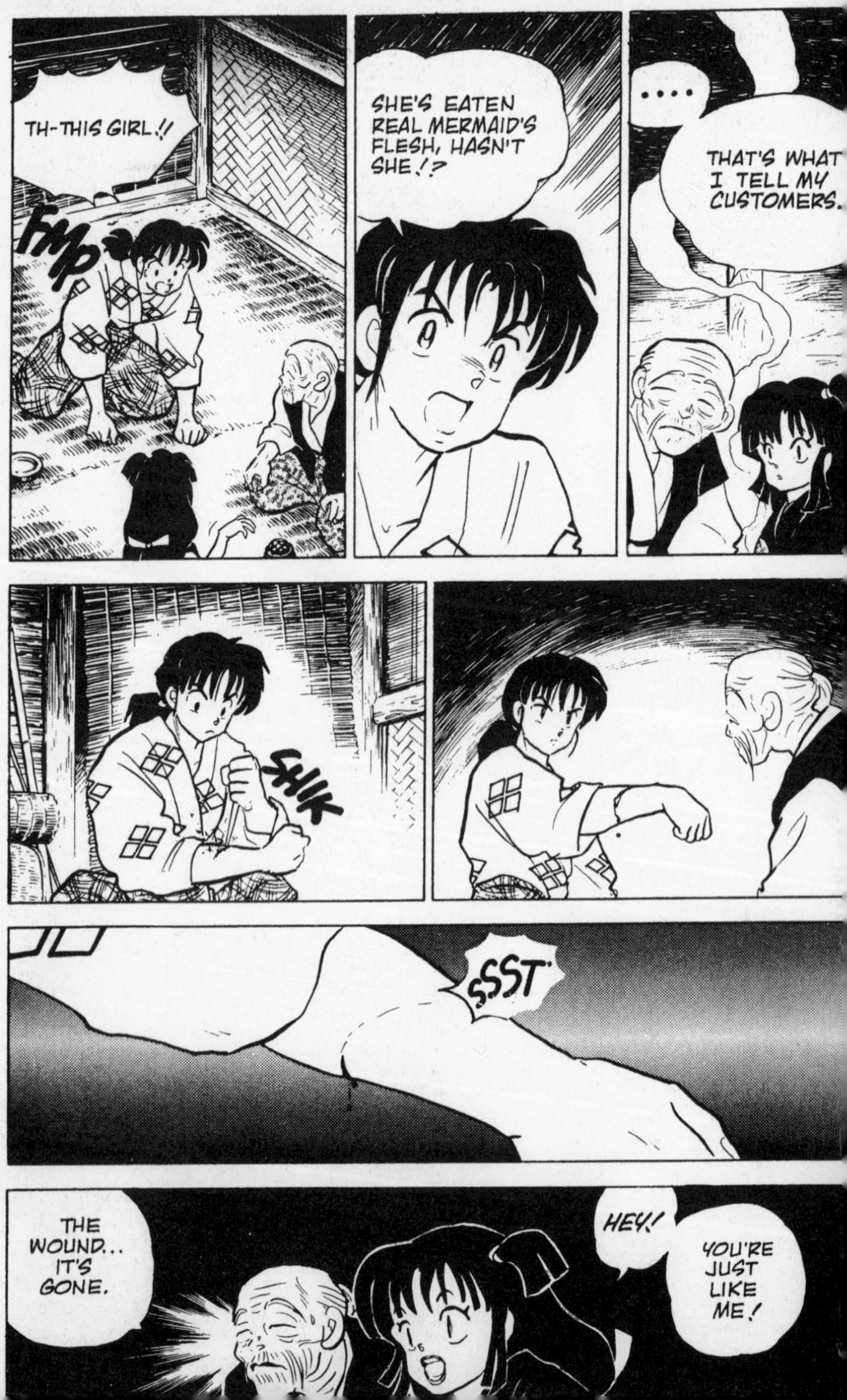
TH-THIS GIRL!!
FMP
SHE'S EATEN REAL MERMAID'S FLESH, HASN'T SHE!?
....
THAT'S WHAT I TELL MY CUSTOMERS.
SHIK
SSST
THE WOUND... IT'S GONE.
HEY!
YOU'RE JUST LIKE ME!

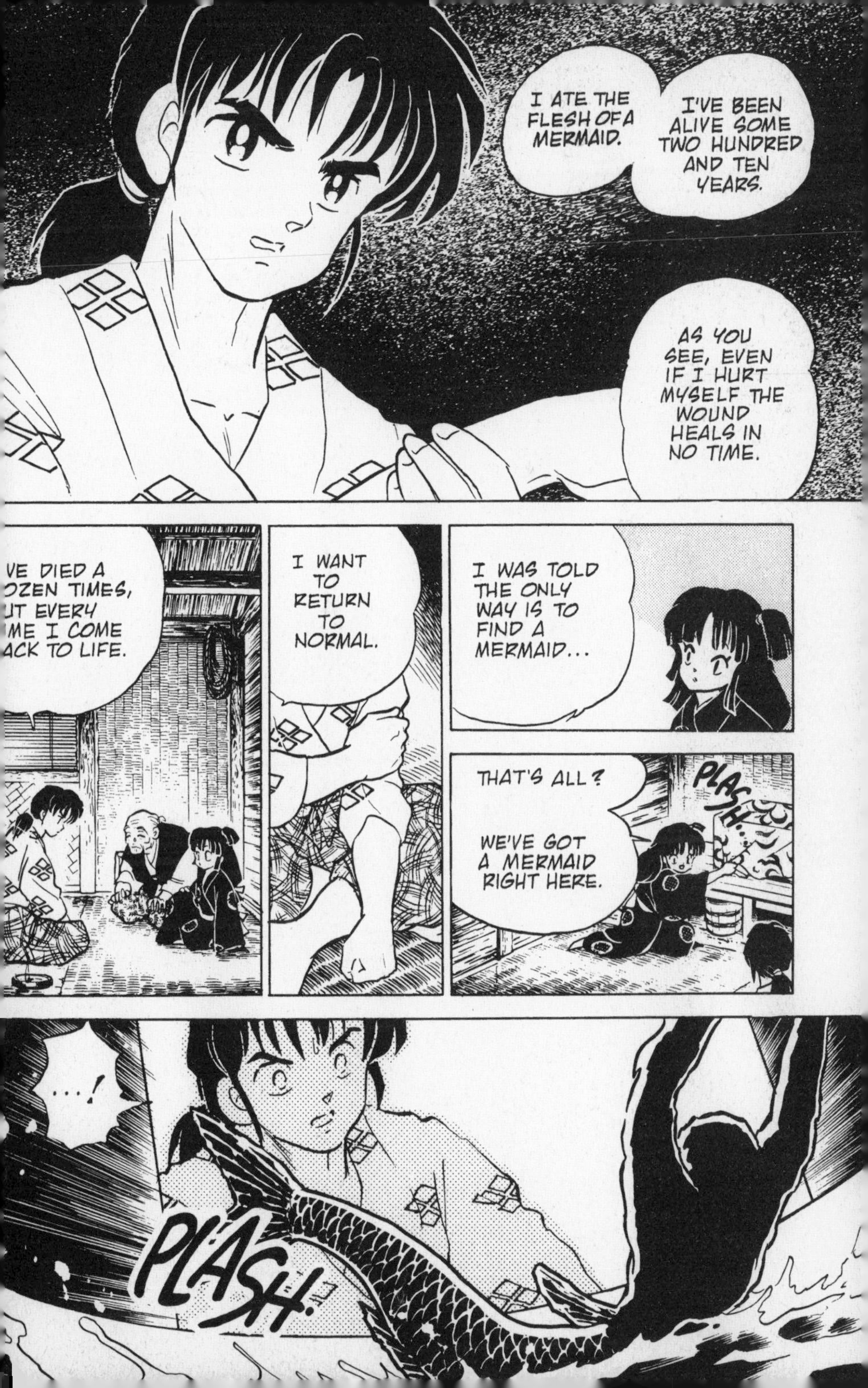
I ATE THE FLESH OF A MERMAID.
I'VE BEEN ALIVE SOME TWO HUNDRED AND TEN YEARS.
AS YOU SEE, EVEN IF I HURT MYSELF THE WOUND HEALS IN NO TIME.
VE DIED A OZEN TIMES, UT EVERY ME I COME ACK TO LIFE.
I WANT TO RETURN TO NORMAL.
I WAS TOLD THE ONLY WAY IS TO FIND A MERMAID...
THAT'S ALL?
WE'VE GOT A MERMAID RIGHT HERE.
PLASH...
...!
PLASH!

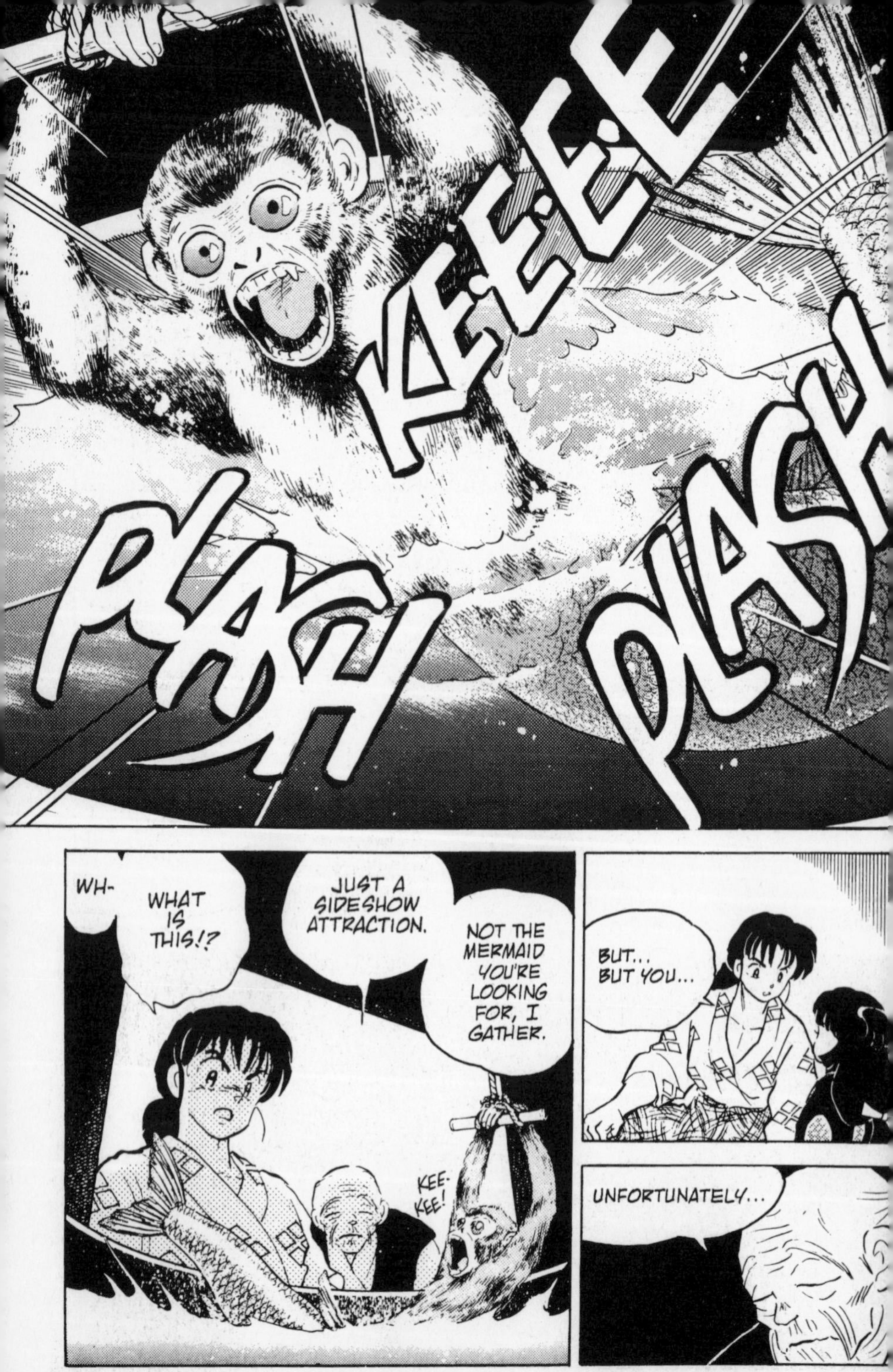
KEEEE
PLASH
PLASH
WH-
WHAT IS THIS!?
JUST A SIDESHOW ATTRACTION.
NOT THE MERMAID YOU'RE LOOKING FOR, I GATHER.
KEE-KEE!
BUT... BUT YOU...
UNFORTUNATELY...

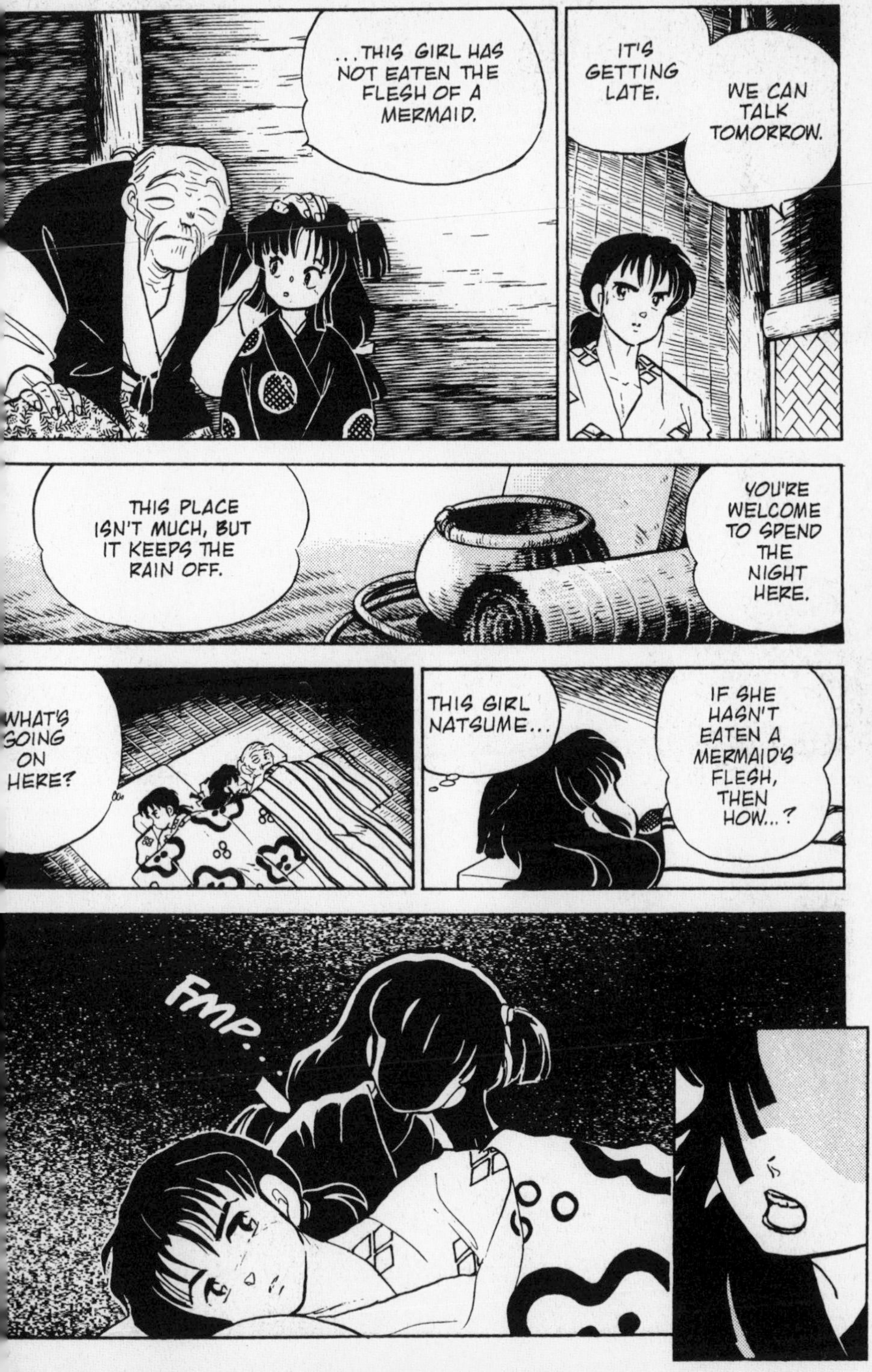
...THIS GIRL HAS NOT EATEN THE FLESH OF A MERMAID.
IT'S GETTING LATE.
WE CAN TALK TOMORROW.
THIS PLACE ISN'T MUCH, BUT IT KEEPS THE RAIN OFF.
YOU'RE WELCOME TO SPEND THE NIGHT HERE.
WHAT'S GOING ON HERE?
THIS GIRL NATSUME...
IF SHE HASN'T EATEN A MERMAID'S FLESH, THEN HOW...?
FMP...

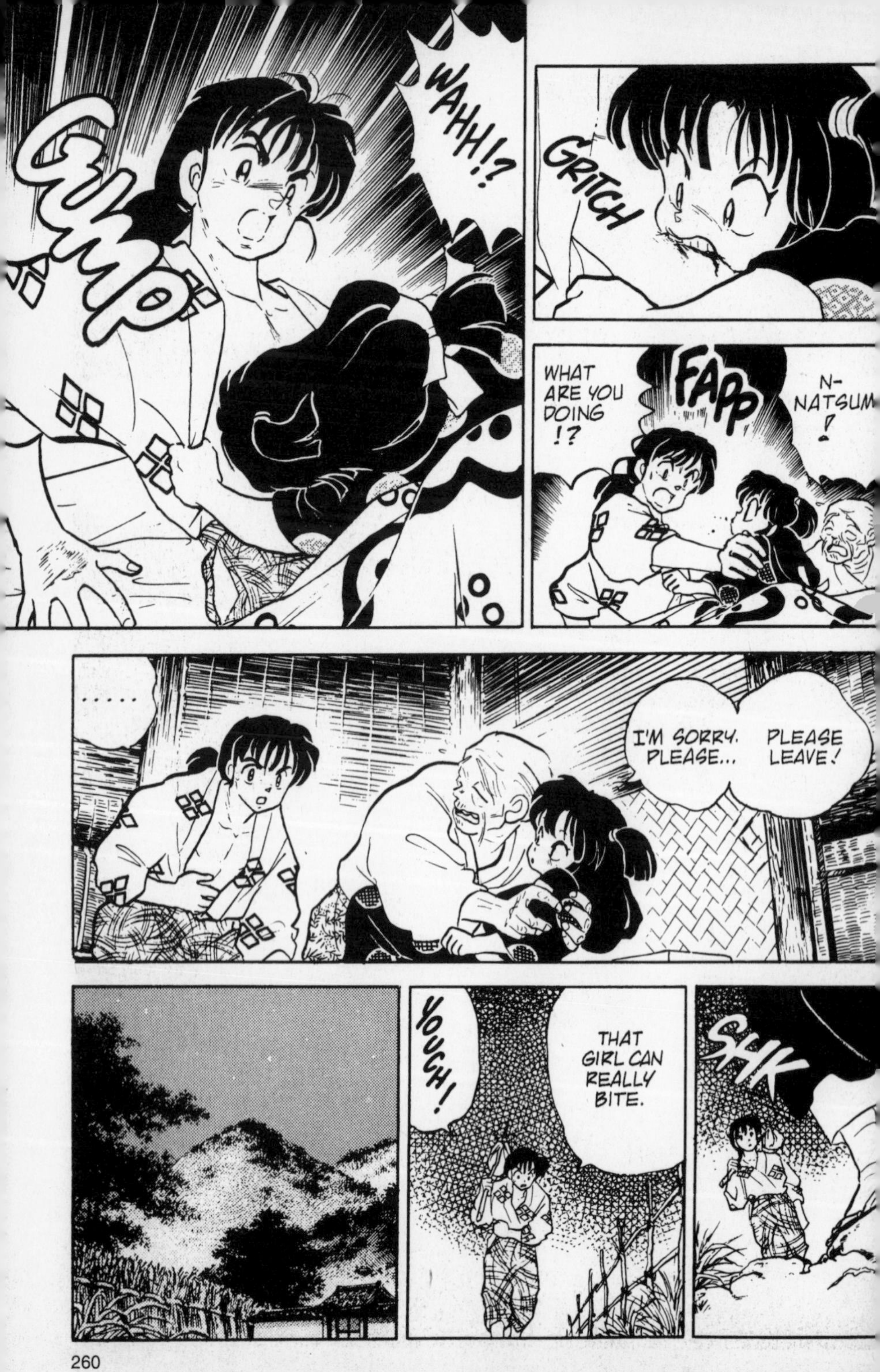
GUMP
WAHH!?
GRITCH
WHAT ARE YOU DOING !?
FAPP
N-NATSUM !
......
I'M SORRY. PLEASE...
PLEASE LEAVE!
YOUCH!
THAT GIRL CAN REALLY BITE.
SHK

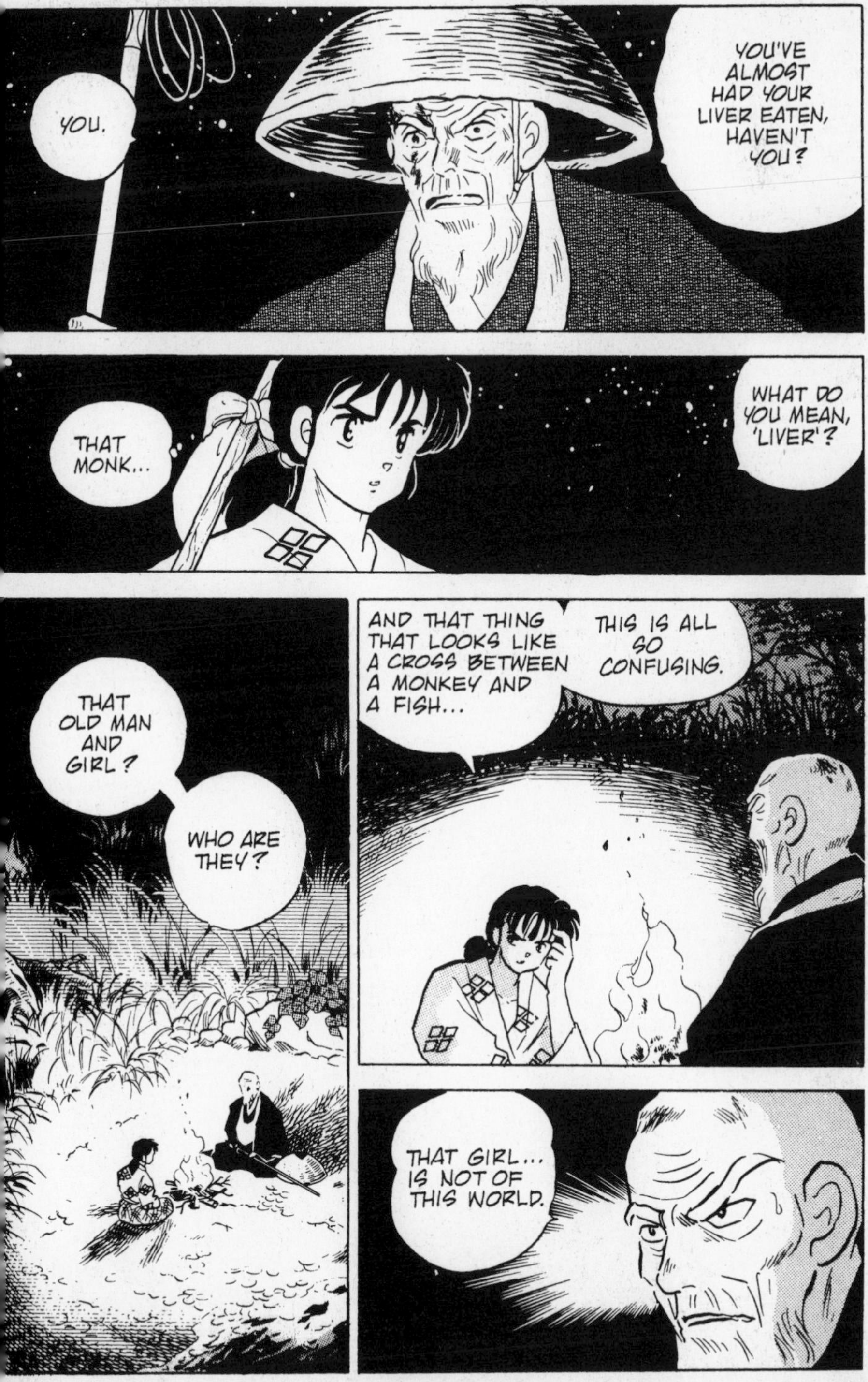
YOU.
YOU'VE ALMOST HAD YOUR LIVER EATEN, HAVEN'T YOU?
THAT MONK...
WHAT DO YOU MEAN, 'LIVER'?
THAT OLD MAN AND GIRL?
WHO ARE THEY?
AND THAT THING THAT LOOKS LIKE A CROSS BETWEEN A MONKEY AND A FISH...
THIS IS ALL SO CONFUSING.
THAT GIRL... IS NOT OF THIS WORLD.

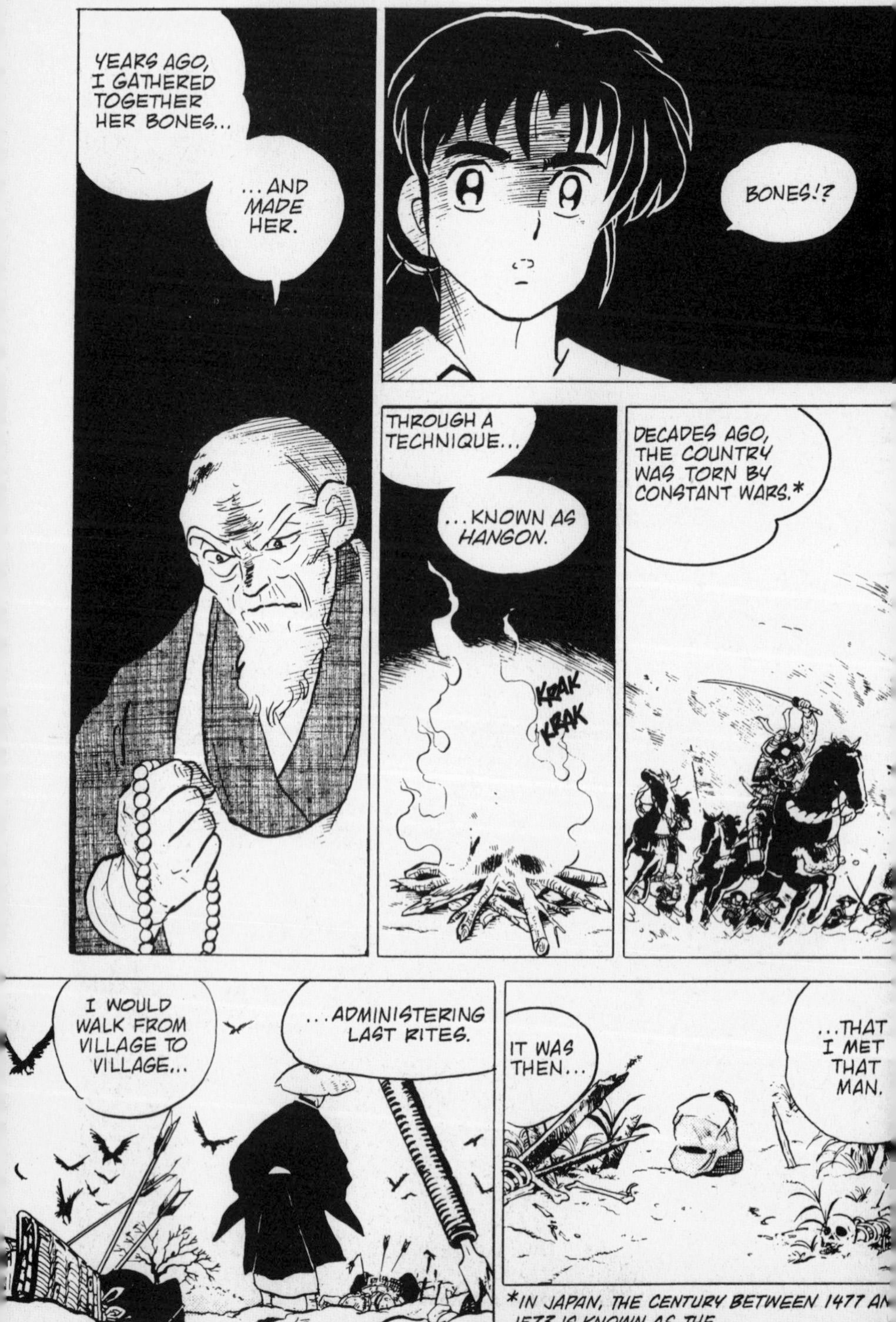
YEARS AGO, I GATHERED TOGETHER HER BONES...
...AND MADE HER.
BONES!?
THROUGH A TECHNIQUE...
...KNOWN AS HANGON.
KRAK KRAK
DECADES AGO, THE COUNTRY WAS TORN BY CONSTANT WARS.*
I WOULD WALK FROM VILLAGE TO VILLAGE...
...ADMINISTERING LAST RITES.
IT WAS THEN...
...THAT I MET THAT MAN.

*IN JAPAN, THE CENTURY BETWEEN 1477 AN[D] 1573 IS KNOWN AS THE 'WARRING STATES PERIOD.'

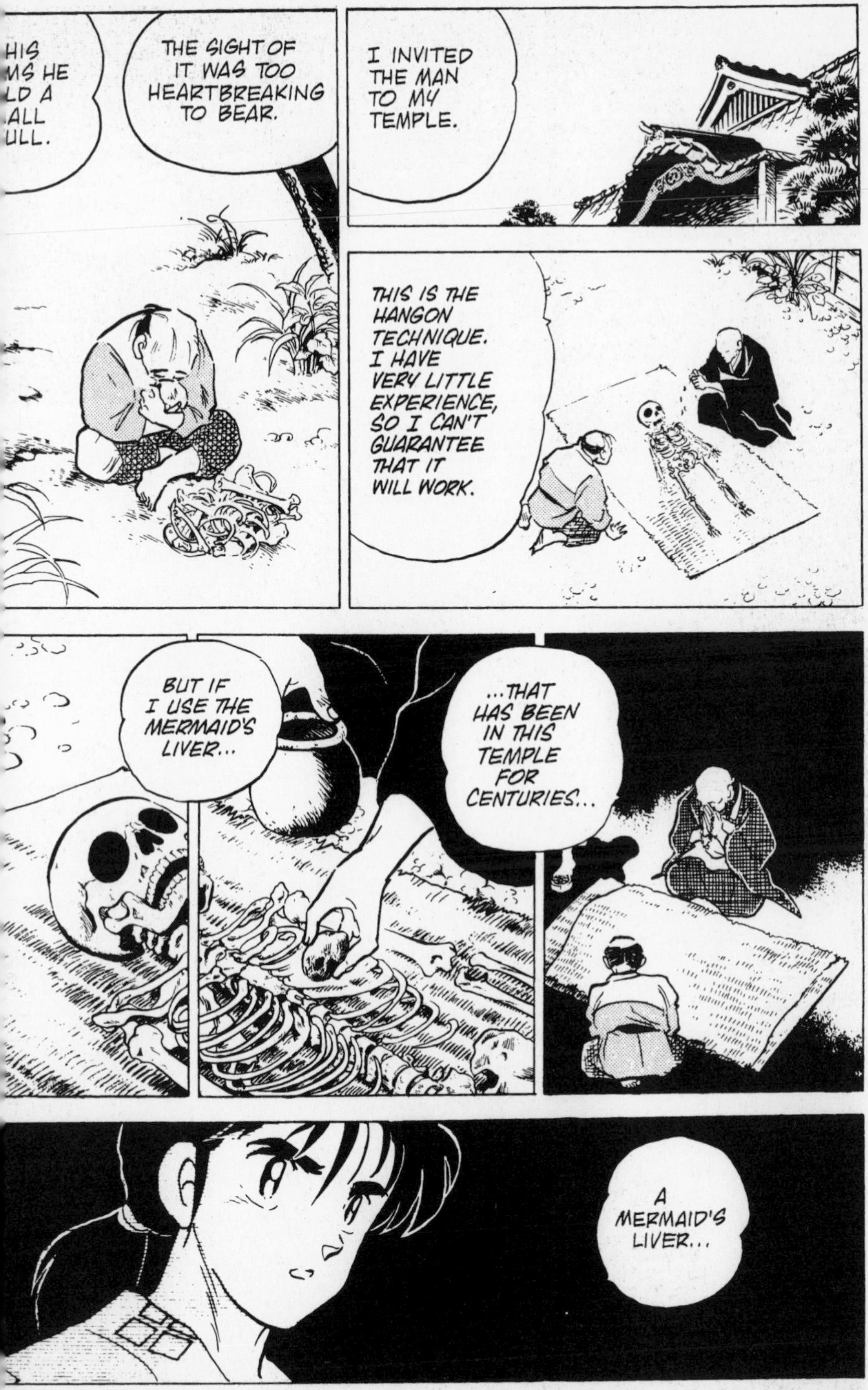
HIS
MS HE
LD A
ALL
ULL.
THE SIGHT OF IT WAS TOO HEARTBREAKING TO BEAR.
I INVITED THE MAN TO MY TEMPLE.
THIS IS THE HANGON TECHNIQUE. I HAVE VERY LITTLE EXPERIENCE, SO I CAN'T GUARANTEE THAT IT WILL WORK.
BUT IF I USE THE MERMAID'S LIVER...
...THAT HAS BEEN IN THIS TEMPLE FOR CENTURIES...
A MERMAID'S LIVER...

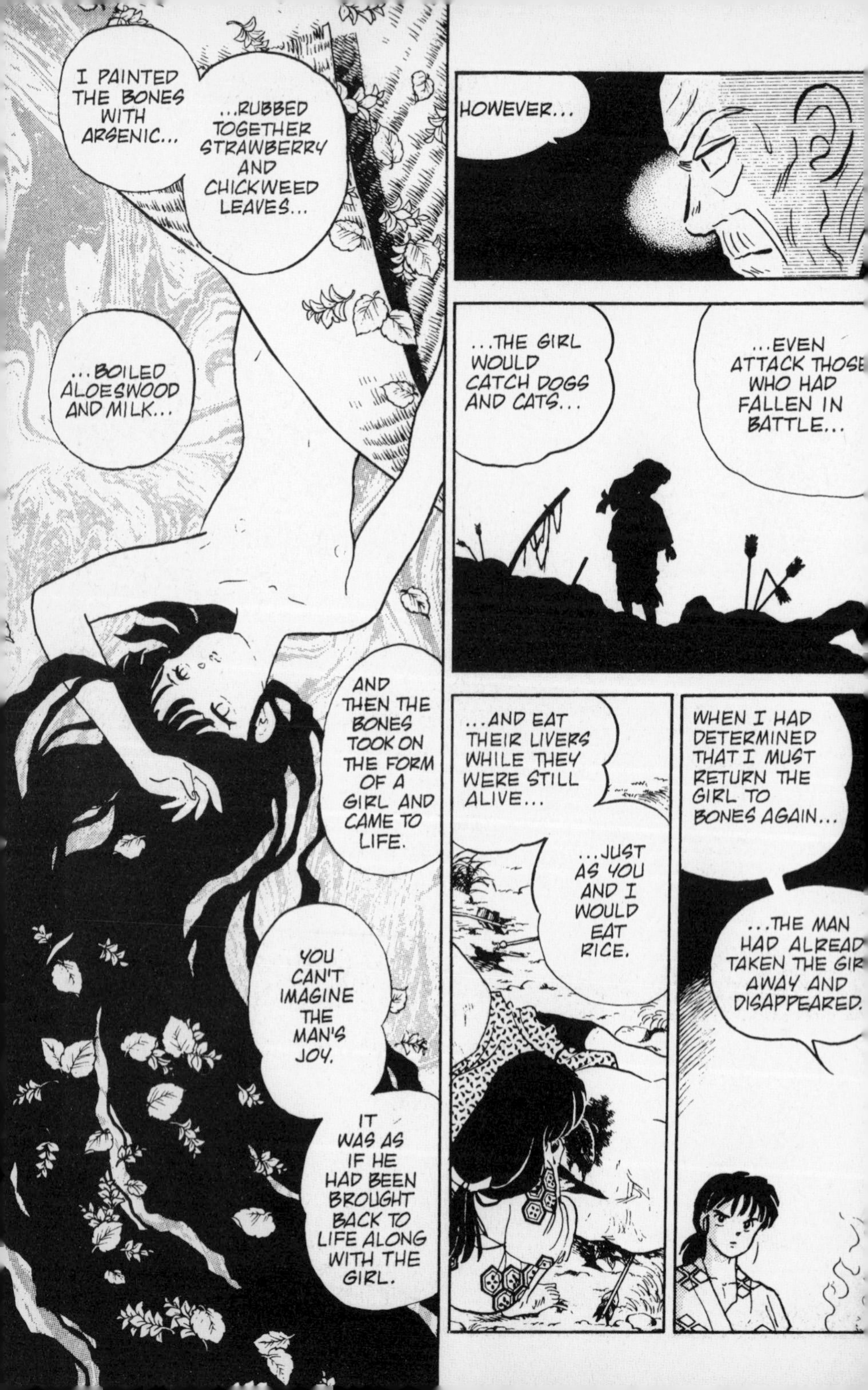
I PAINTED THE BONES WITH ARSENIC...
...RUBBED TOGETHER STRAWBERRY AND CHICKWEED LEAVES...
...BOILED ALOESWOOD AND MILK...
AND THEN THE BONES TOOK ON THE FORM OF A GIRL AND CAME TO LIFE.
YOU CAN'T IMAGINE THE MAN'S JOY.
IT WAS AS IF HE HAD BEEN BROUGHT BACK TO LIFE ALONG WITH THE GIRL.
HOWEVER...
...THE GIRL WOULD CATCH DOGS AND CATS...
...EVEN ATTACK THOSE WHO HAD FALLEN IN BATTLE...
...AND EAT THEIR LIVERS WHILE THEY WERE STILL ALIVE...
...JUST AS YOU AND I WOULD EAT RICE.
WHEN I HAD DETERMINED THAT I MUST RETURN THE GIRL TO BONES AGAIN...
...THE MAN HAD ALREAD TAKEN THE GIR AWAY AND DISAPPEARED.

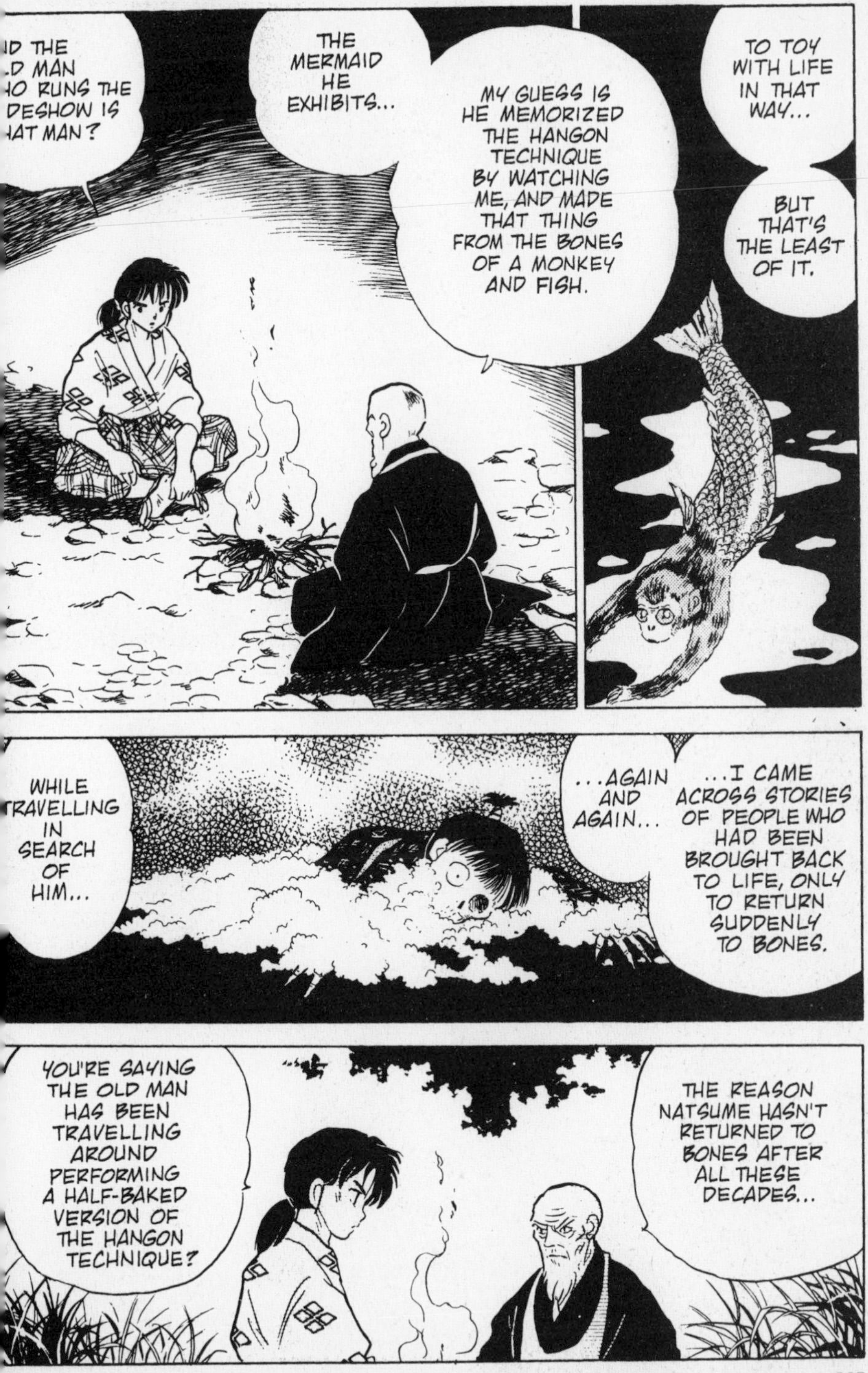

ID THE LD MAN HO RUNS THE DESHOW IS HAT MAN?
THE MERMAID HE EXHIBITS...
MY GUESS IS HE MEMORIZED THE HANGON TECHNIQUE BY WATCHING ME, AND MADE THAT THING FROM THE BONES OF A MONKEY AND FISH.
TO TOY WITH LIFE IN THAT WAY...
BUT THAT'S THE LEAST OF IT.
WHILE TRAVELLING IN SEARCH OF HIM...
...AGAIN AND AGAIN...
...I CAME ACROSS STORIES OF PEOPLE WHO HAD BEEN BROUGHT BACK TO LIFE, ONLY TO RETURN SUDDENLY TO BONES.
YOU'RE SAYING THE OLD MAN HAS BEEN TRAVELLING AROUND PERFORMING A HALF-BAKED VERSION OF THE HANGON TECHNIQUE?
THE REASON NATSUME HASN'T RETURNED TO BONES AFTER ALL THESE DECADES...

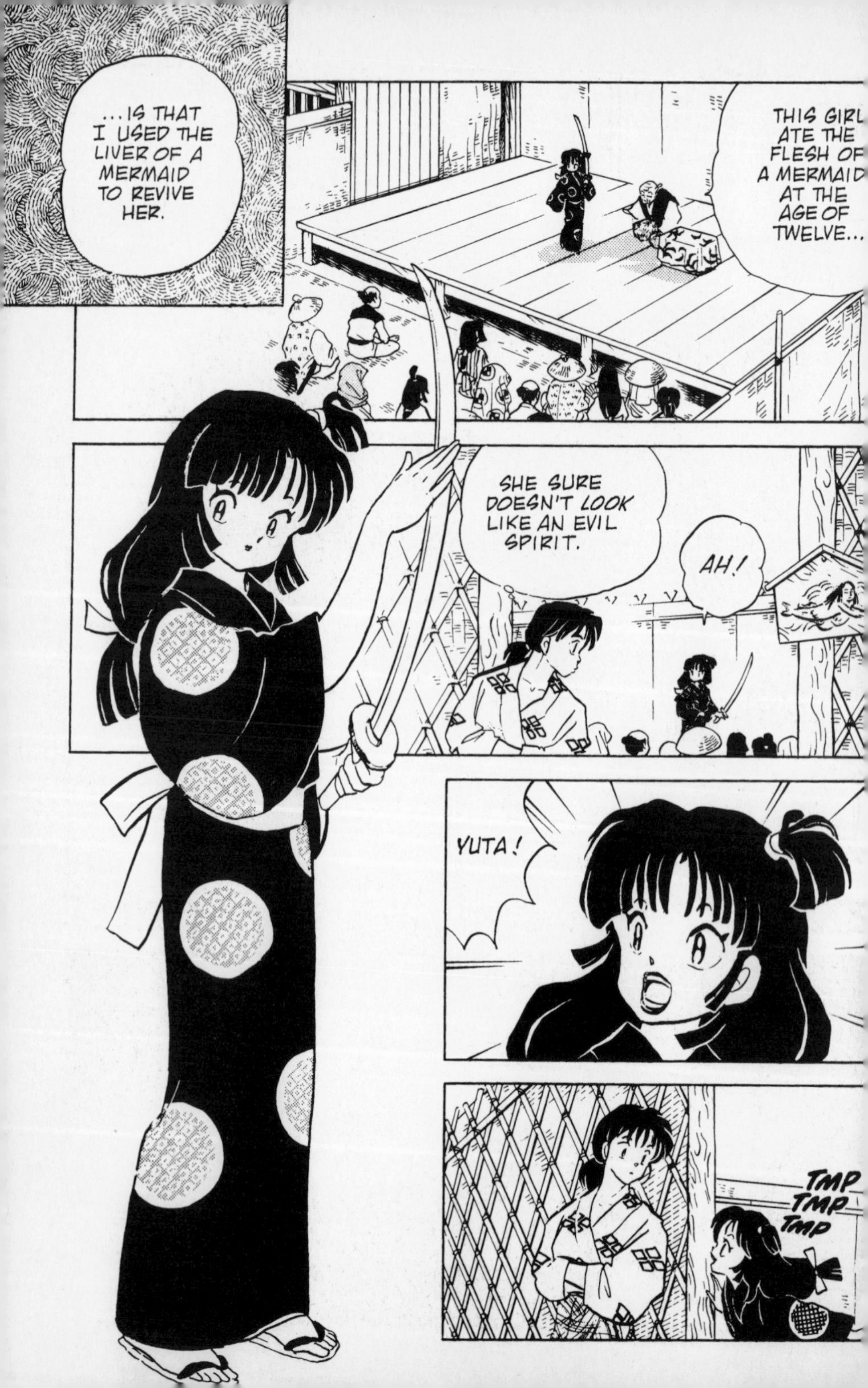

...IS THAT I USED THE LIVER OF A MERMAID TO REVIVE HER.
THIS GIRL ATE THE FLESH OF A MERMAID AT THE AGE OF TWELVE...
SHE SURE DOESN'T LOOK LIKE AN EVIL SPIRIT.
AH!
YUTA!
TMP TMP TMP

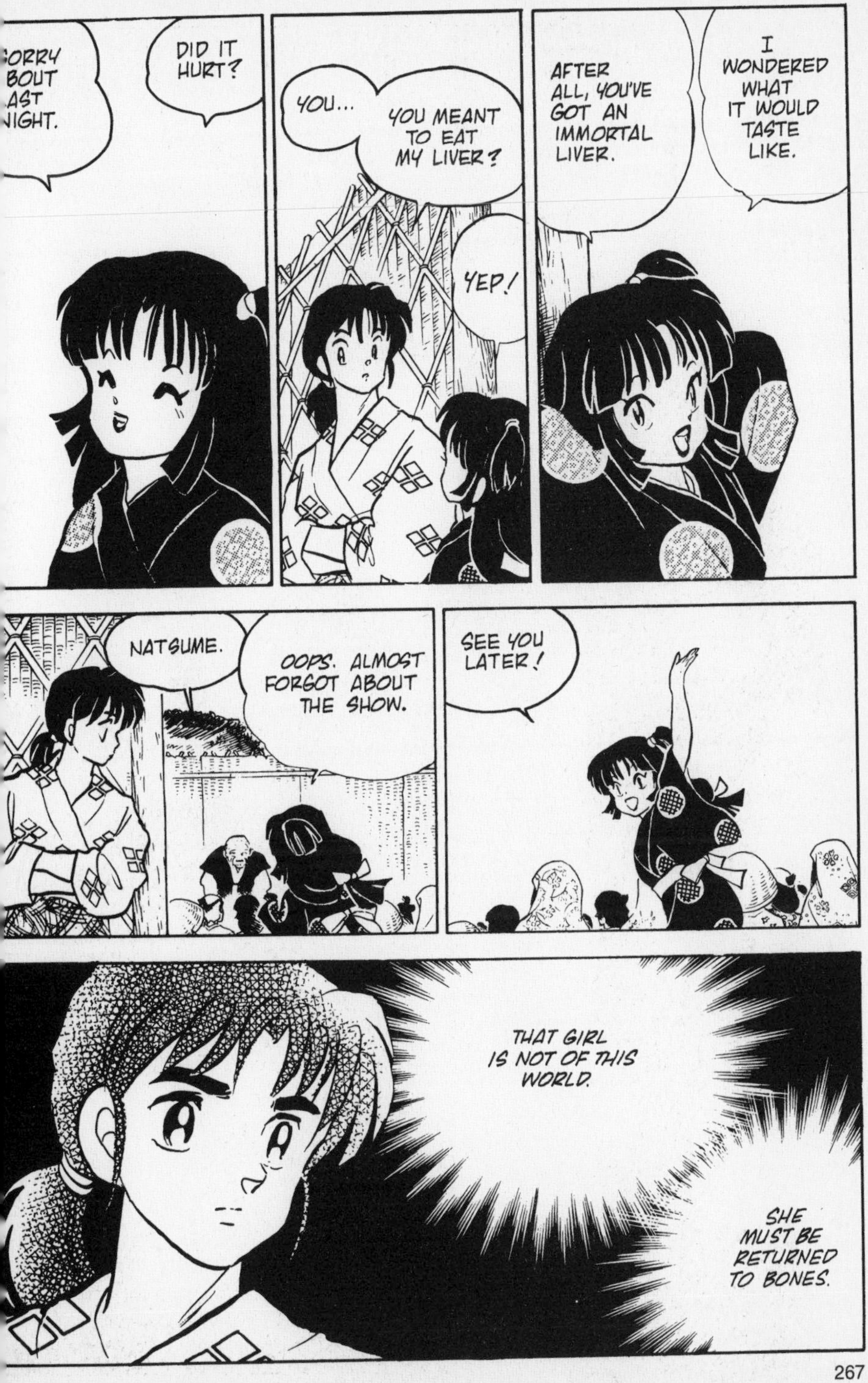

ORRY
BOUT
AST
IGHT.
DID IT HURT?
YOU...
YOU MEANT TO EAT MY LIVER?
YEP!
AFTER ALL, YOU'VE GOT AN IMMORTAL LIVER.
I WONDERED WHAT IT WOULD TASTE LIKE.
NATSUME.
OOPS. ALMOST FORGOT ABOUT THE SHOW.
SEE YOU LATER!
THAT GIRL IS NOT OF THIS WORLD.
SHE MUST BE RETURNED TO BONES.

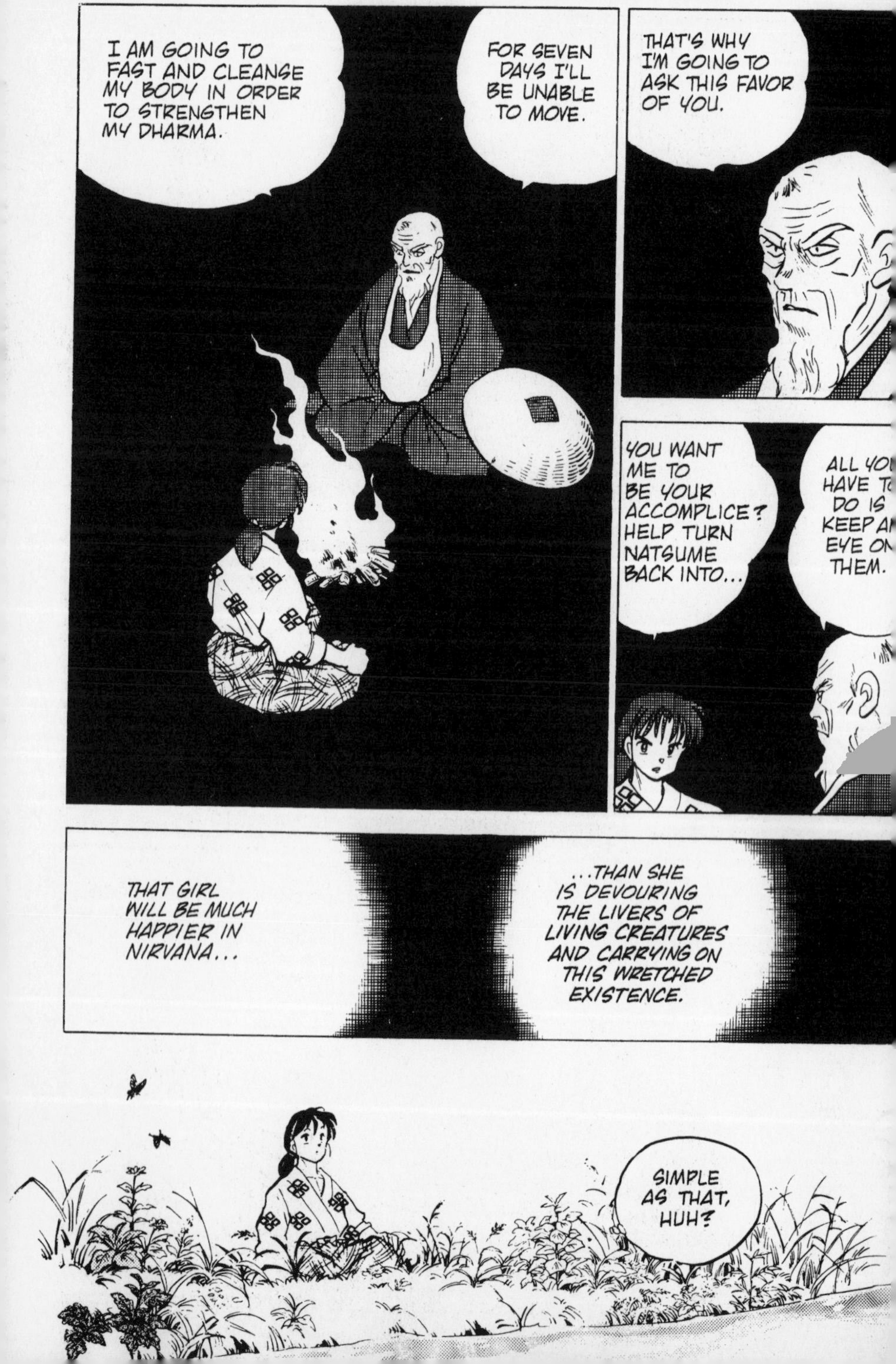
I AM GOING TO FAST AND CLEANSE MY BODY IN ORDER TO STRENGTHEN MY DHARMA.
FOR SEVEN DAYS I'LL BE UNABLE TO MOVE.
THAT'S WHY I'M GOING TO ASK THIS FAVOR OF YOU.
YOU WANT ME TO BE YOUR ACCOMPLICE? HELP TURN NATSUME BACK INTO...
ALL YO HAVE T DO IS KEEP A EYE ON THEM.
THAT GIRL WILL BE MUCH HAPPIER IN NIRVANA...
...THAN SHE IS DEVOURING THE LIVERS OF LIVING CREATURES AND CARRYING ON THIS WRETCHED EXISTENCE.
SIMPLE AS THAT, HUH?

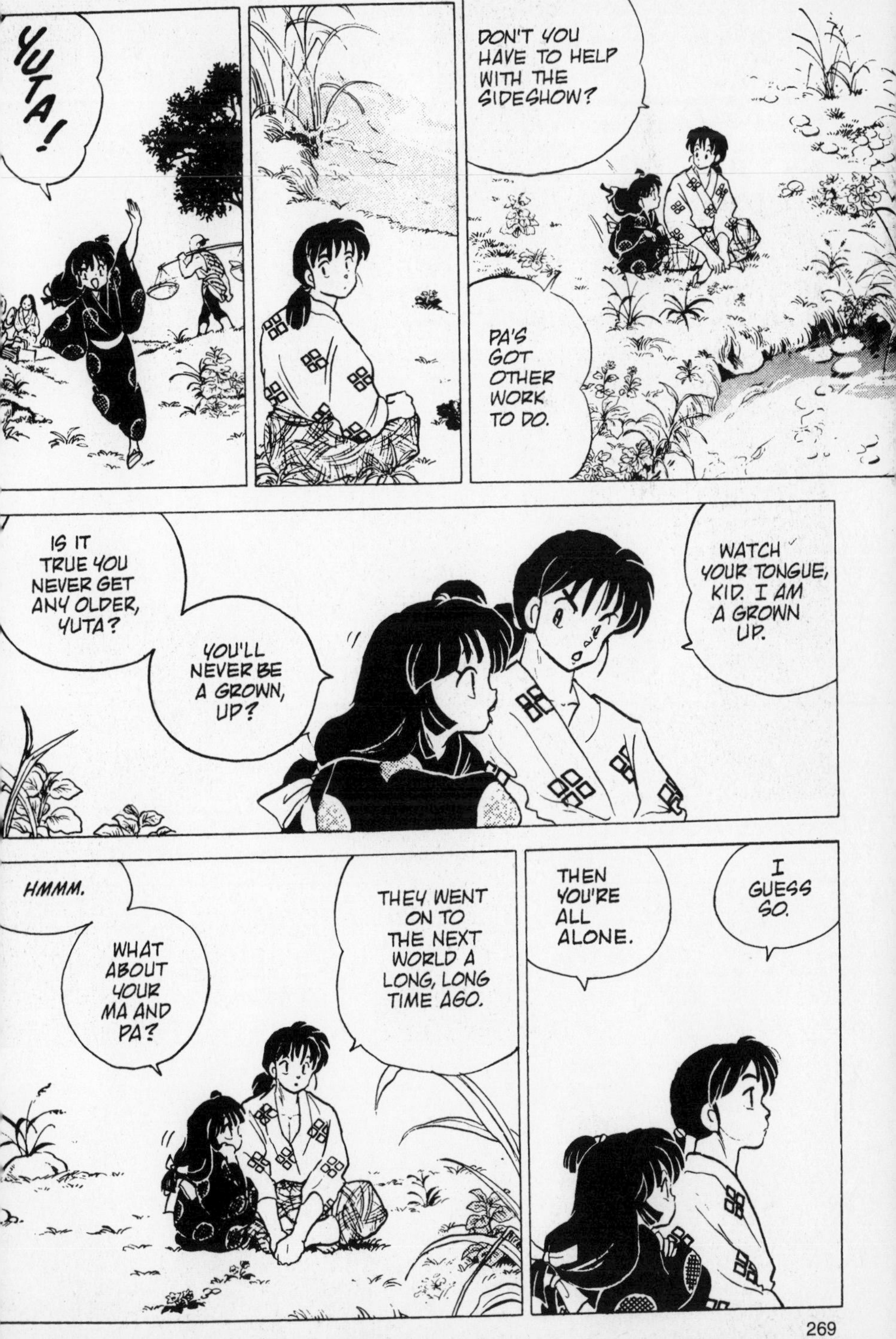
YUTA!
DON'T YOU HAVE TO HELP WITH THE SIDESHOW?
PA'S GOT OTHER WORK TO DO.
IS IT TRUE YOU NEVER GET ANY OLDER, YUTA?
YOU'LL NEVER BE A GROWN UP?
WATCH YOUR TONGUE, KID. I AM A GROWN UP.
HMMM.
WHAT ABOUT YOUR MA AND PA?
THEY WENT ON TO THE NEXT WORLD A LONG, LONG TIME AGO.
THEN YOU'RE ALL ALONE.
I GUESS SO.

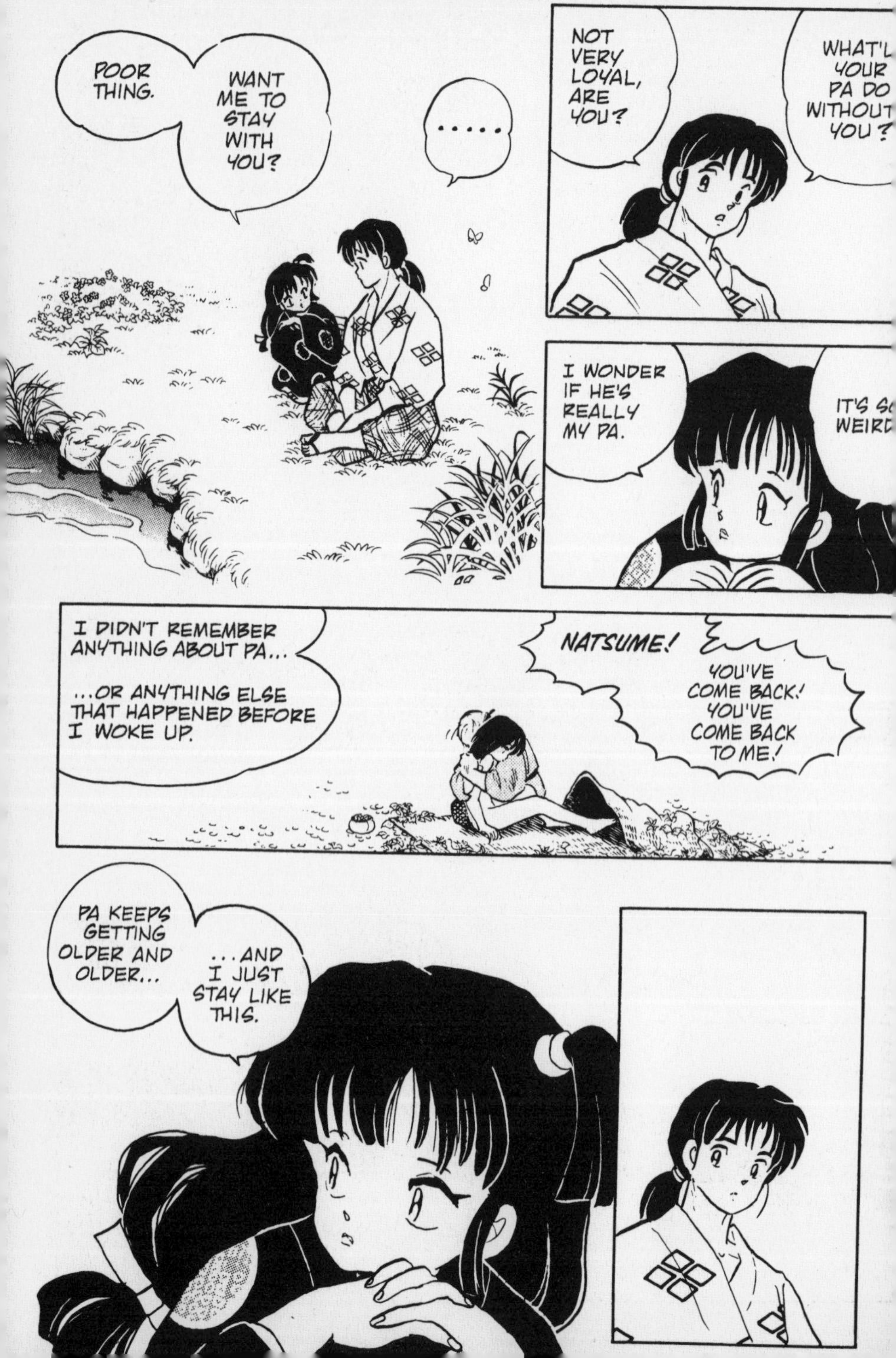
POOR THING.
WANT ME TO STAY WITH YOU?
.....
NOT VERY LOYAL, ARE YOU?
WHAT'L YOUR PA DO WITHOUT YOU?
I WONDER IF HE'S REALLY MY PA.
IT'S S WEIRD
I DIDN'T REMEMBER ANYTHING ABOUT PA...
...OR ANYTHING ELSE THAT HAPPENED BEFORE I WOKE UP.
NATSUME!
YOU'VE COME BACK! YOU'VE COME BACK TO ME!
PA KEEPS GETTING OLDER AND OLDER...
...AND I JUST STAY LIKE THIS.

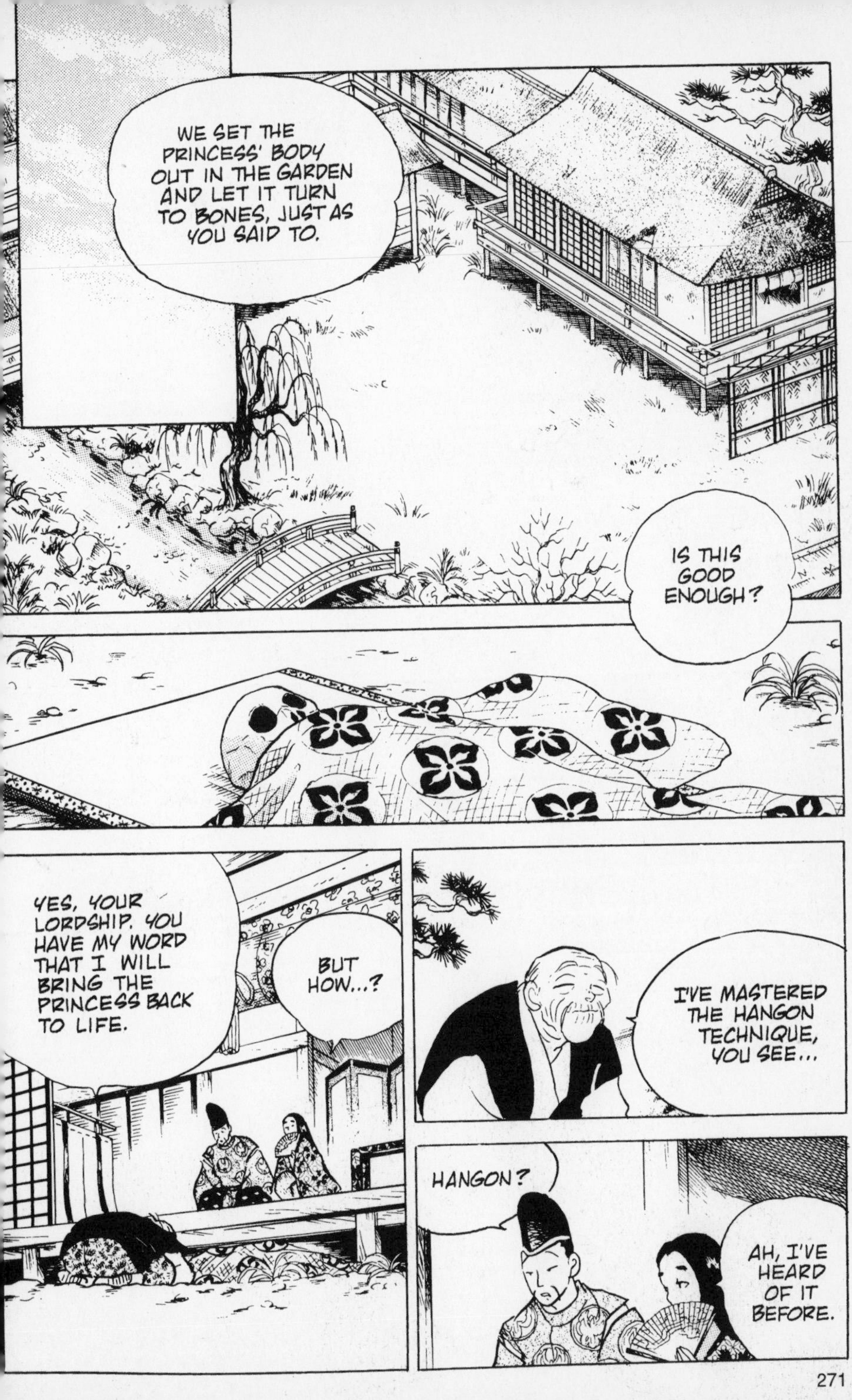
WE SET THE PRINCESS' BODY OUT IN THE GARDEN AND LET IT TURN TO BONES, JUST AS YOU SAID TO.
IS THIS GOOD ENOUGH?
YES, YOUR LORDSHIP. YOU HAVE MY WORD THAT I WILL BRING THE PRINCESS BACK TO LIFE.
BUT HOW...?
I'VE MASTERED THE HANGON TECHNIQUE, YOU SEE...
HANGON?
AH, I'VE HEARD OF IT BEFORE.

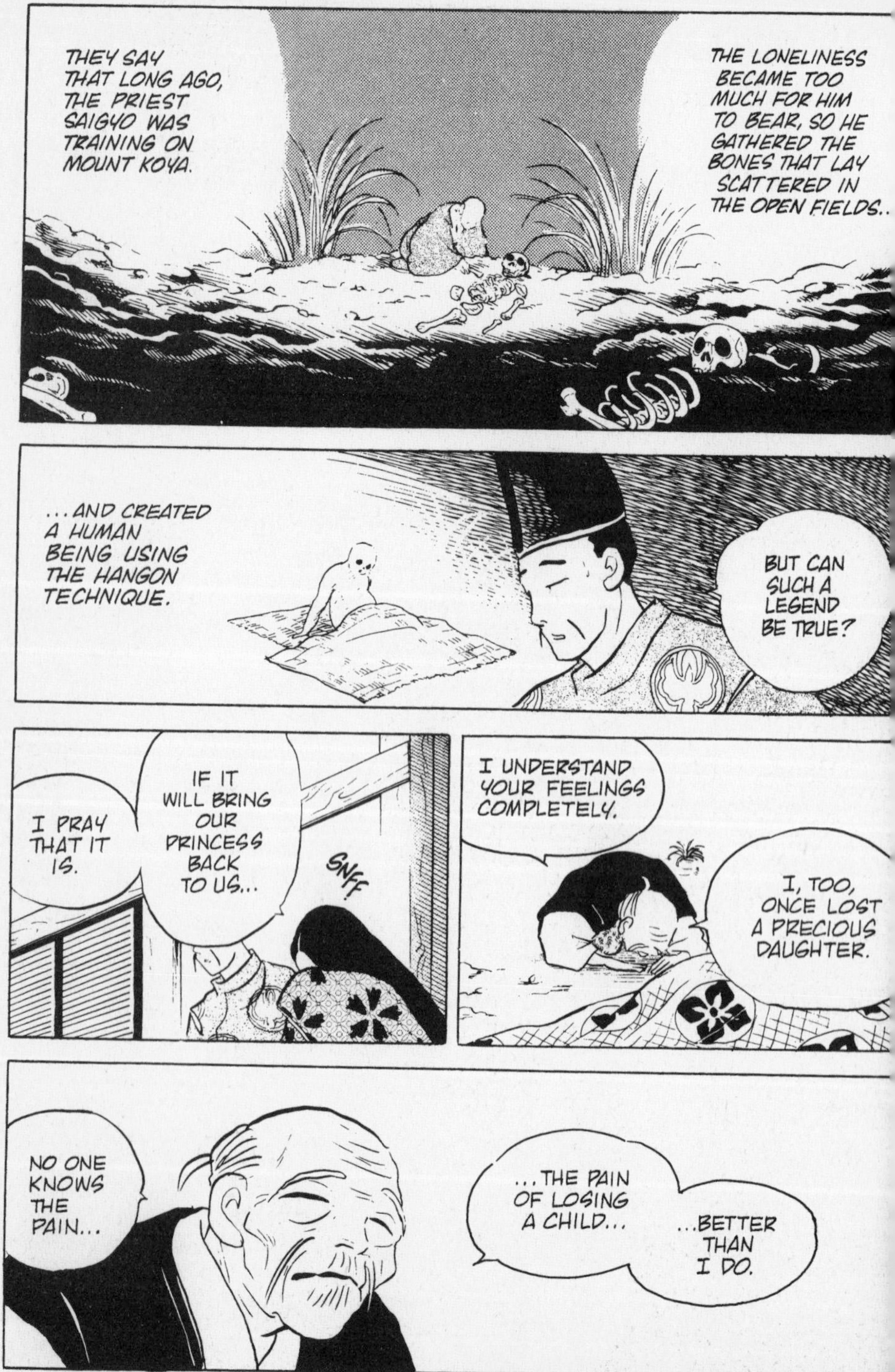
THEY SAY THAT LONG AGO, THE PRIEST SAIGYO WAS TRAINING ON MOUNT KOYA.
THE LONELINESS BECAME TOO MUCH FOR HIM TO BEAR, SO HE GATHERED THE BONES THAT LAY SCATTERED IN THE OPEN FIELDS...
...AND CREATED A HUMAN BEING USING THE HANGON TECHNIQUE.
BUT CAN SUCH A LEGEND BE TRUE?
I PRAY THAT IT IS.
IF IT WILL BRING OUR PRINCESS BACK TO US...
SNFF
I UNDERSTAND YOUR FEELINGS COMPLETELY.
I, TOO, ONCE LOST A PRECIOUS DAUGHTER.
NO ONE KNOWS THE PAIN...
...THE PAIN OF LOSING A CHILD...
...BETTER THAN I DO.

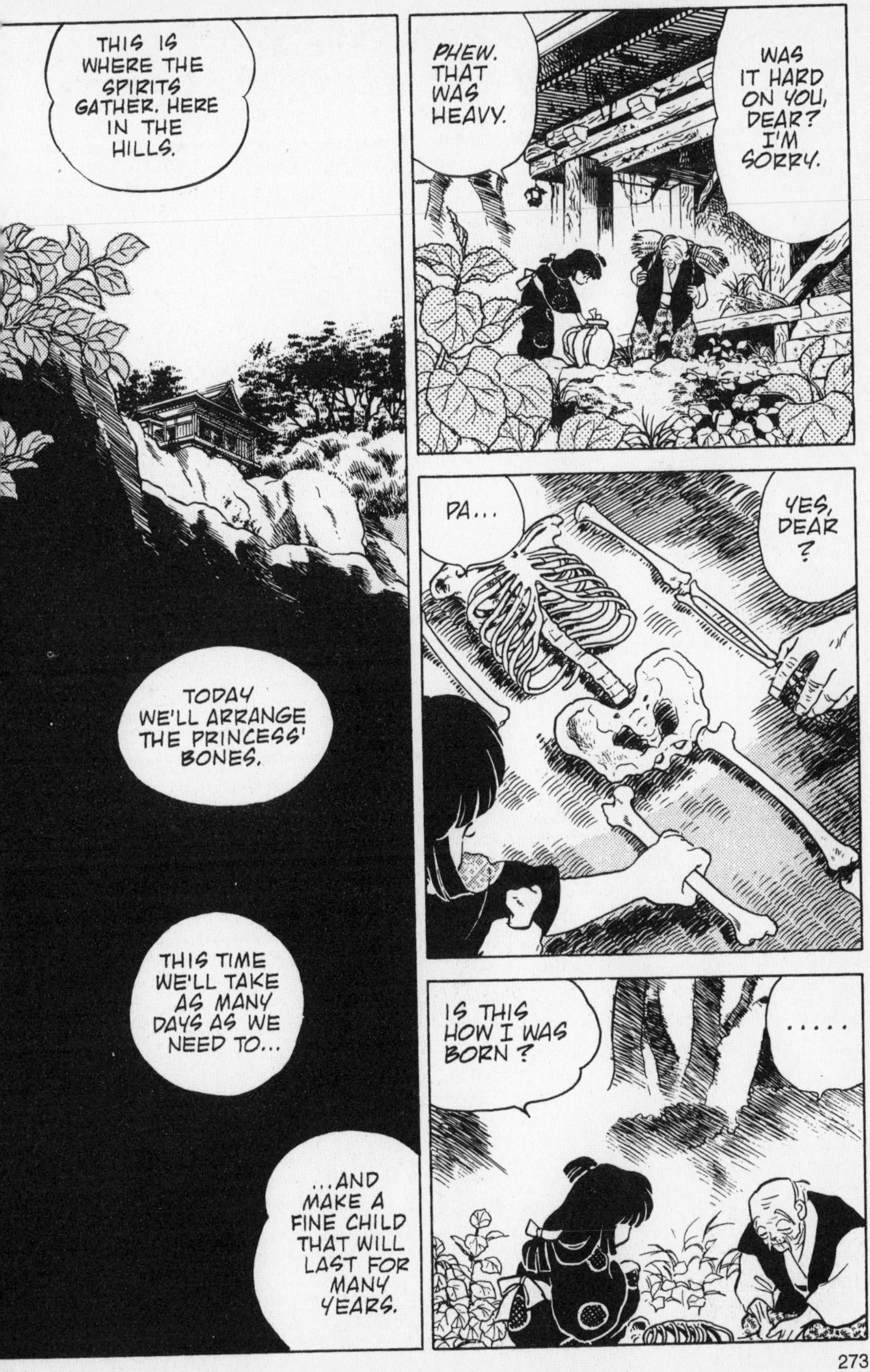
THIS IS WHERE THE SPIRITS GATHER. HERE IN THE HILLS.
TODAY WE'LL ARRANGE THE PRINCESS' BONES.
THIS TIME WE'LL TAKE AS MANY DAYS AS WE NEED TO...
...AND MAKE A FINE CHILD THAT WILL LAST FOR MANY YEARS.
PHEW. THAT WAS HEAVY.
WAS IT HARD ON YOU, DEAR? I'M SORRY.
PA...
YES, DEAR?
IS THIS HOW I WAS BORN?
......

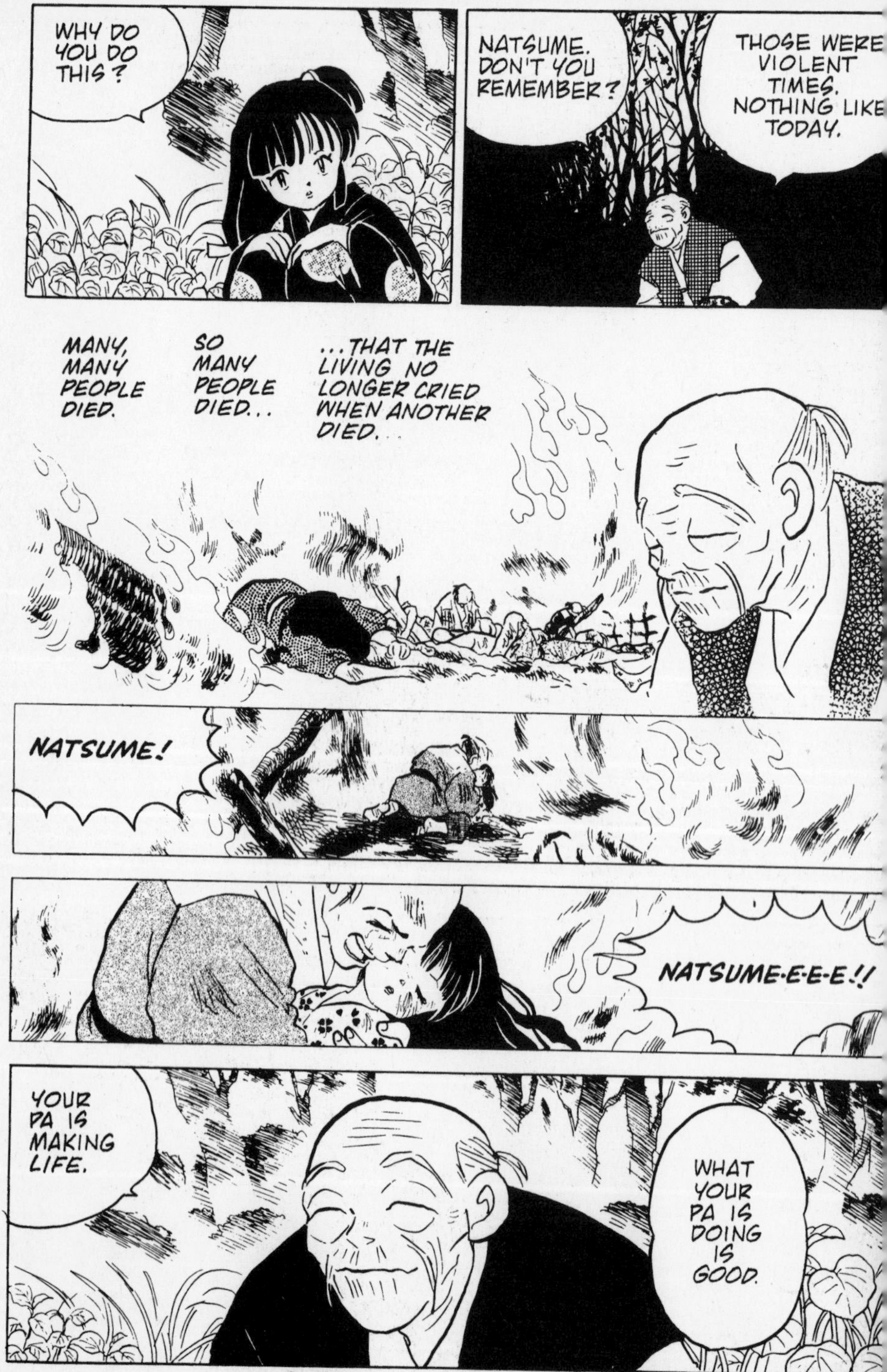
WHY DO YOU DO THIS?
NATSUME. DON'T YOU REMEMBER?
THOSE WERE VIOLENT TIMES. NOTHING LIKE TODAY.
MANY, MANY PEOPLE DIED.
SO MANY PEOPLE DIED...
...THAT THE LIVING NO LONGER CRIED WHEN ANOTHER DIED...
NATSUME!
NATSUME-E-E-E!!
YOUR PA IS MAKING LIFE.
WHAT YOUR PA IS DOING IS GOOD.

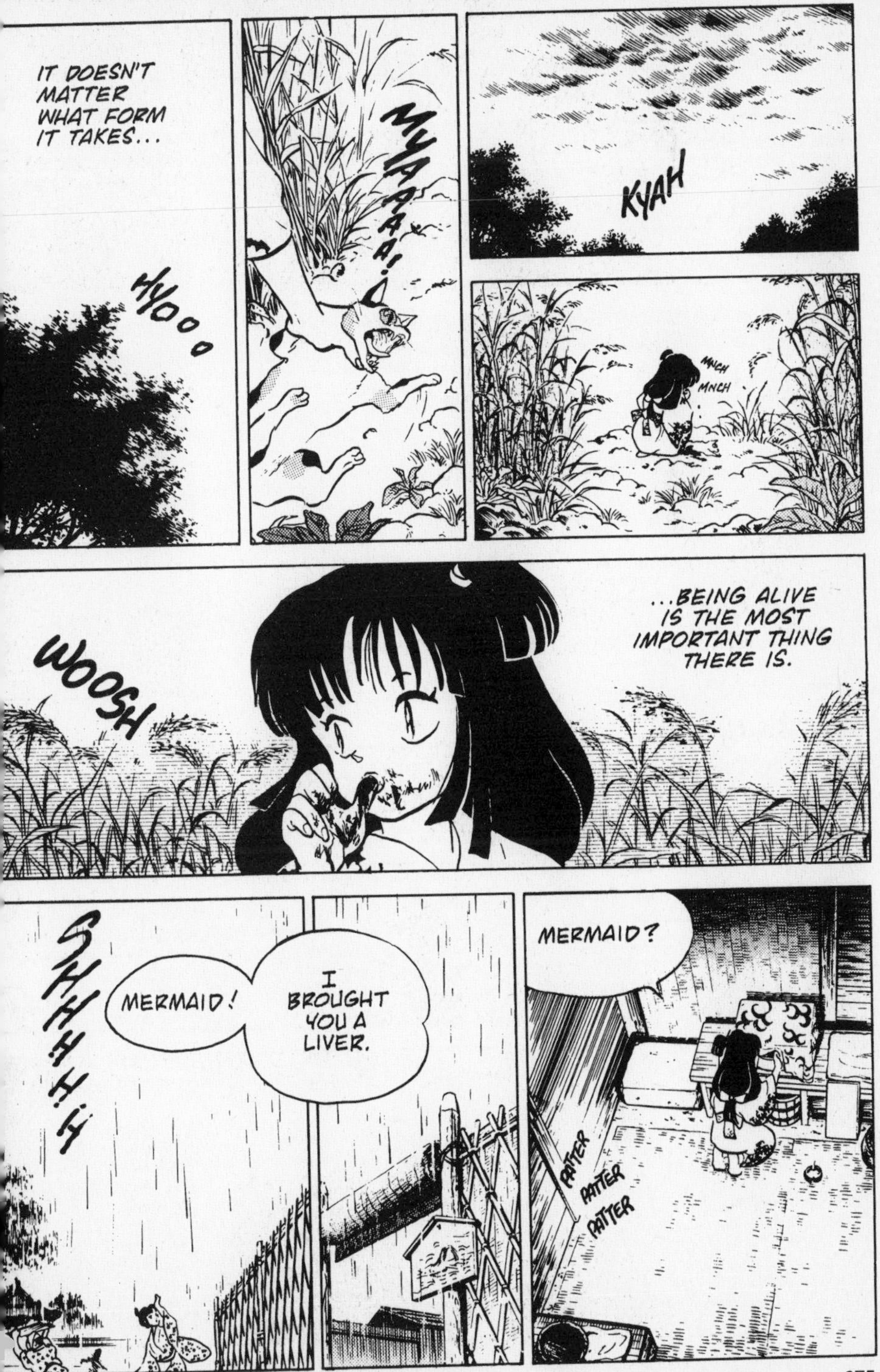
IT DOESN'T MATTER WHAT FORM IT TAKES...
HYOOO
MYAAAAA!
KYAH
MNCH
MNCH
WOOSH
...BEING ALIVE IS THE MOST IMPORTANT THING THERE IS.
SHHHHHH
MERMAID!
I BROUGHT YOU A LIVER.
MERMAID?
PATTER
PATTER
PATTER

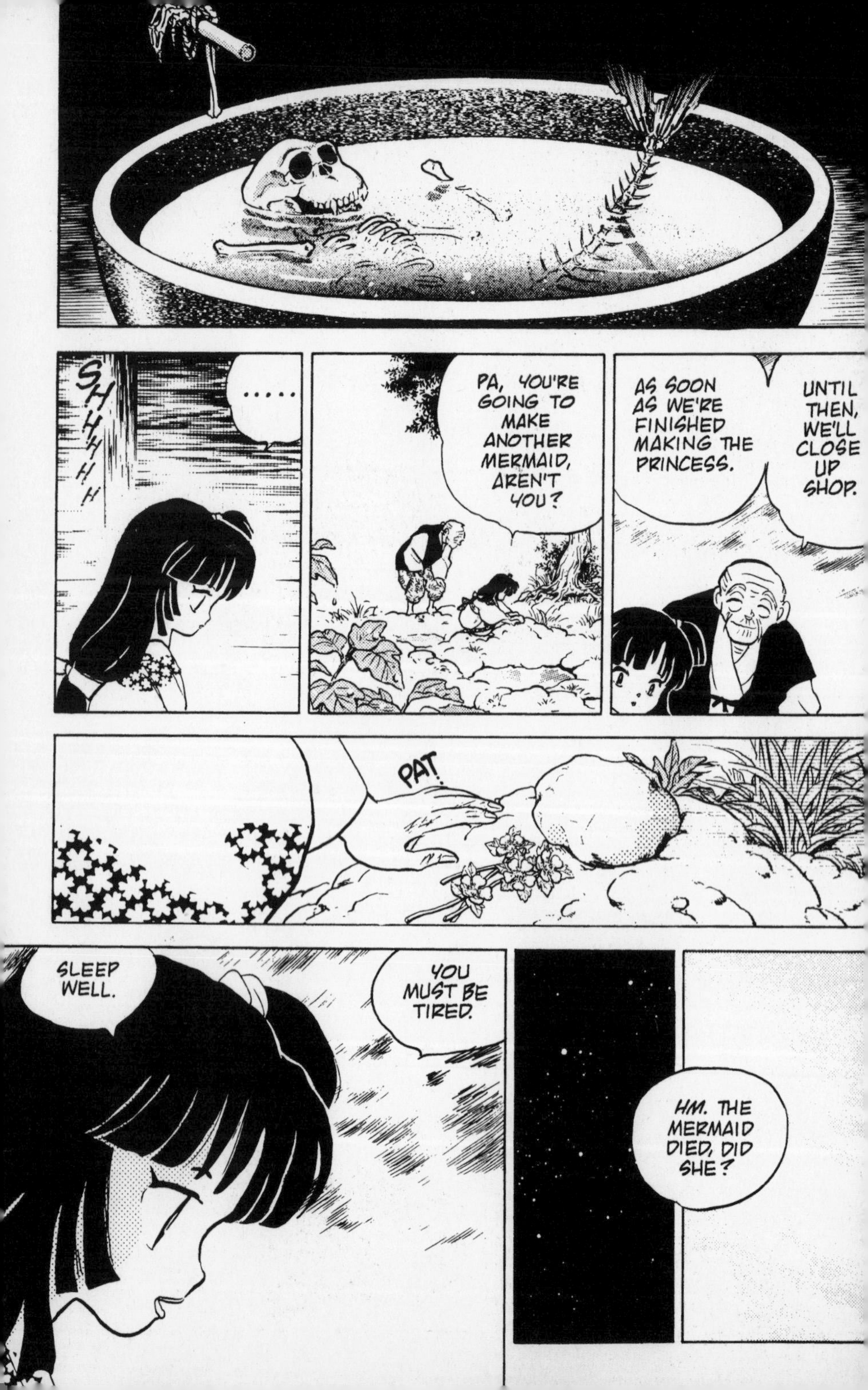
SHHHHHH
.....
PA, YOU'RE GOING TO MAKE ANOTHER MERMAID, AREN'T YOU?
AS SOON AS WE'RE FINISHED MAKING THE PRINCESS.
UNTIL THEN, WE'LL CLOSE UP SHOP.
PAT
SLEEP WELL.
YOU MUST BE TIRED.
HM. THE MERMAID DIED, DID SHE?

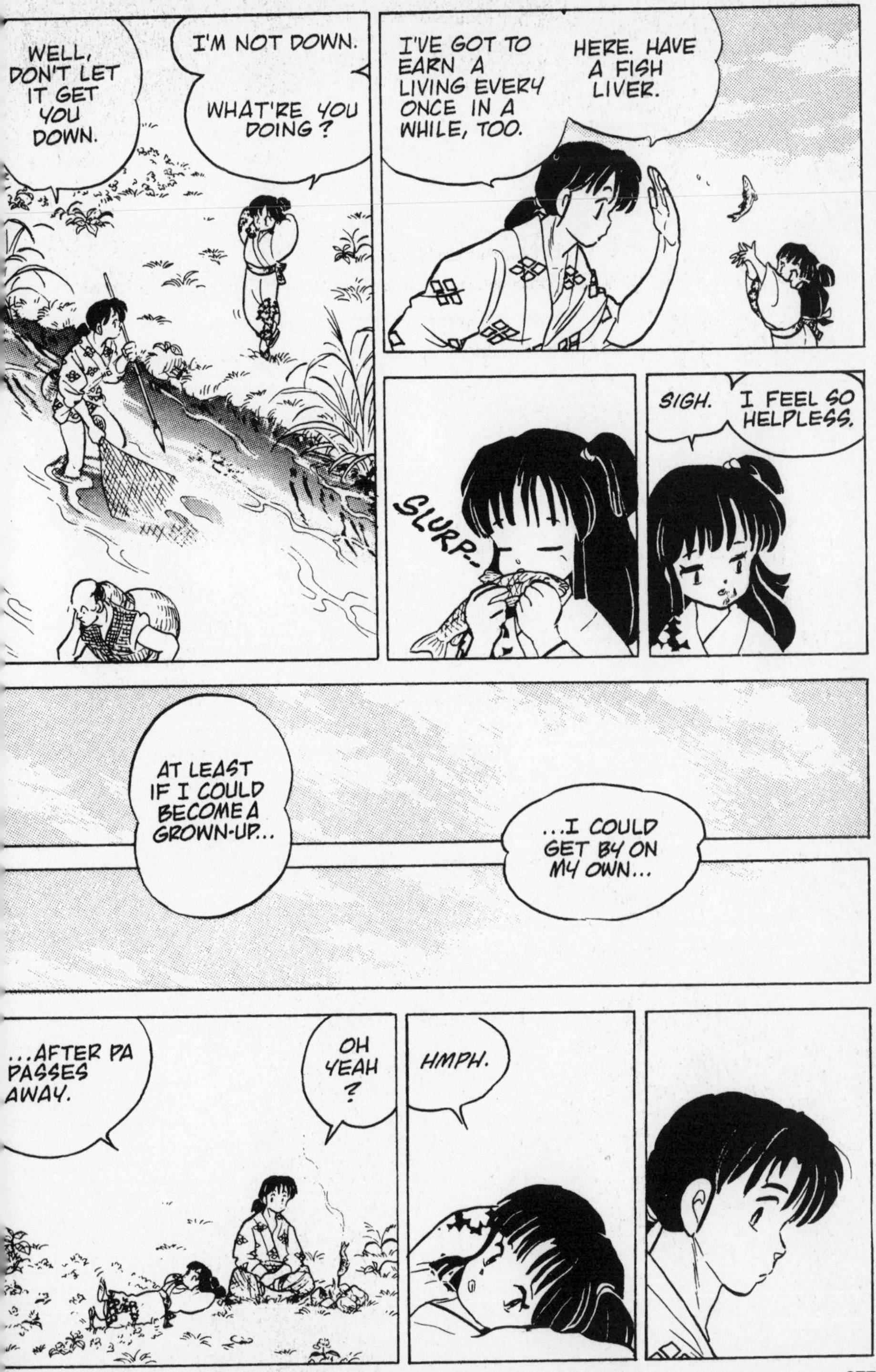

WELL, DON'T LET IT GET YOU DOWN.
I'M NOT DOWN.
WHAT'RE YOU DOING?
I'VE GOT TO EARN A LIVING EVERY ONCE IN A WHILE, TOO.
HERE. HAVE A FISH LIVER.
SLURP...
SIGH.
I FEEL SO HELPLESS.
AT LEAST IF I COULD BECOME A GROWN-UP...
...I COULD GET BY ON MY OWN...
...AFTER PA PASSES AWAY.
OH YEAH?
HMPH.

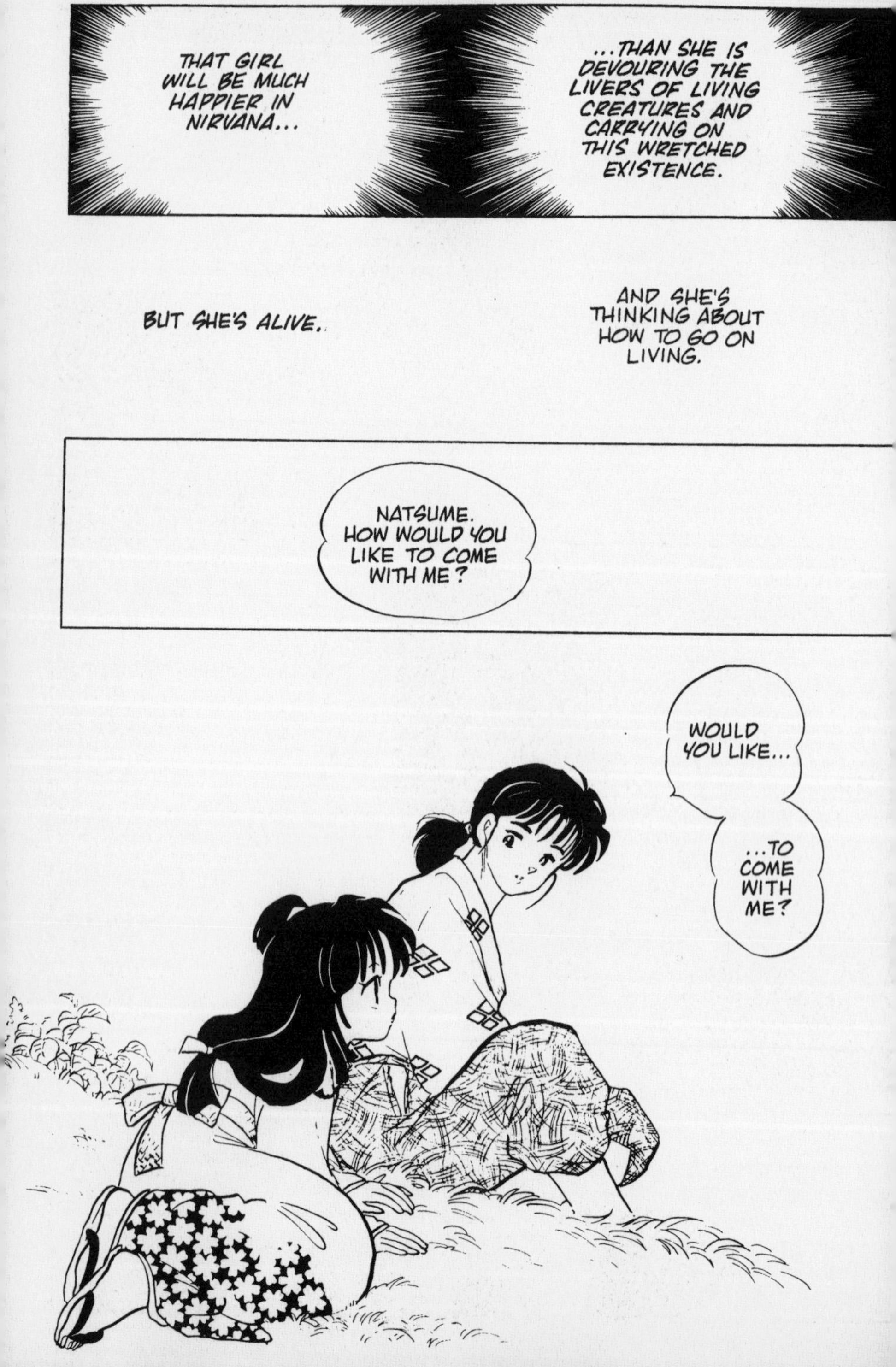
THAT GIRL WILL BE MUCH HAPPIER IN NIRVANA...
...THAN SHE IS DEVOURING THE LIVERS OF LIVING CREATURES AND CARRYING ON THIS WRETCHED EXISTENCE.
BUT SHE'S ALIVE..
AND SHE'S THINKING ABOUT HOW TO GO ON LIVING.
NATSUME. HOW WOULD YOU LIKE TO COME WITH ME?
WOULD YOU LIKE...
...TO COME WITH ME?

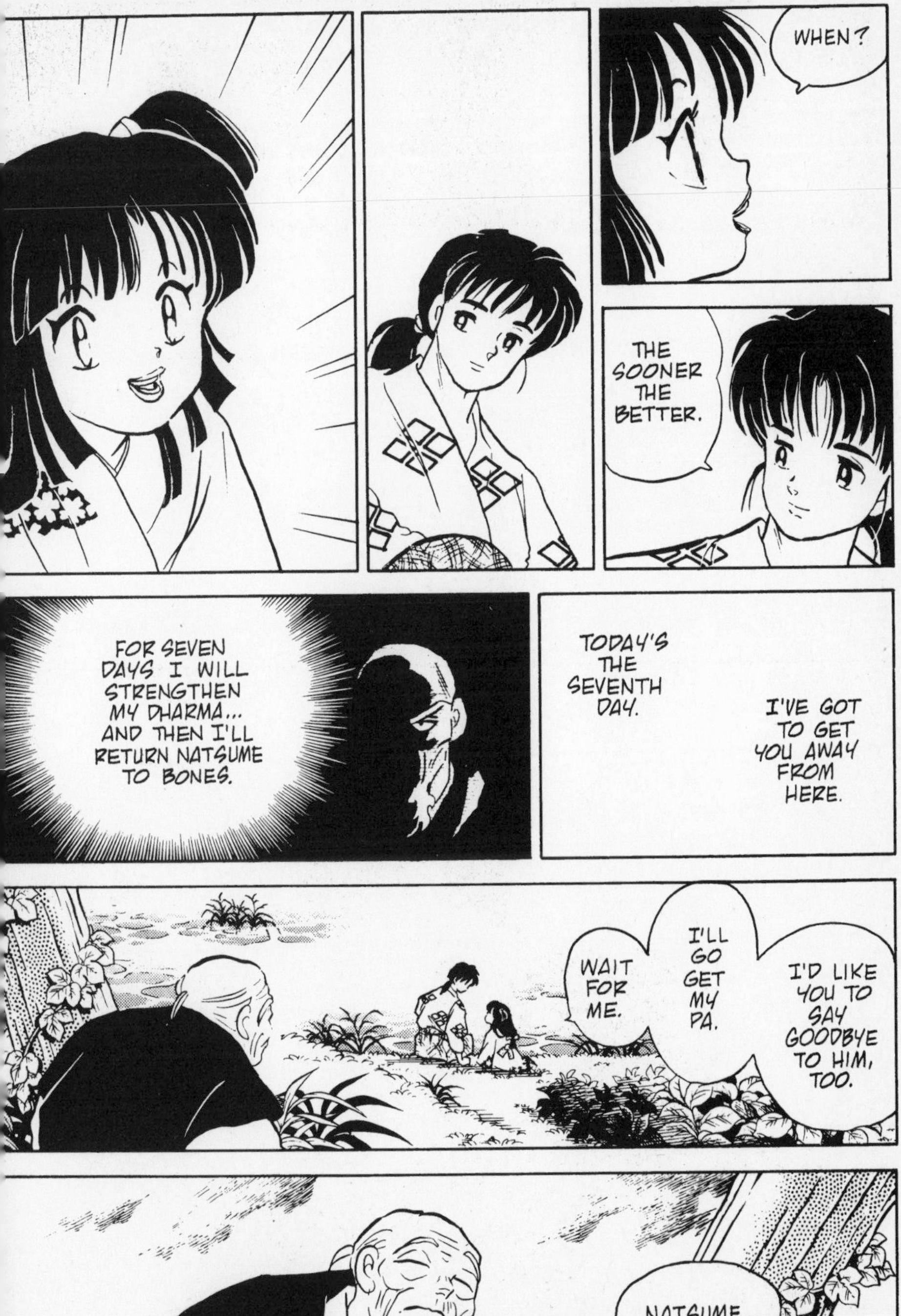

WHEN?
THE SOONER THE BETTER.
FOR SEVEN DAYS I WILL STRENGTHEN MY DHARMA... AND THEN I'LL RETURN NATSUME TO BONES.
TODAY'S THE SEVENTH DAY.
I'VE GOT TO GET YOU AWAY FROM HERE.
WAIT FOR ME.
I'LL GO GET MY PA.
I'D LIKE YOU TO SAY GOODBYE TO HIM, TOO.
NATSUME...

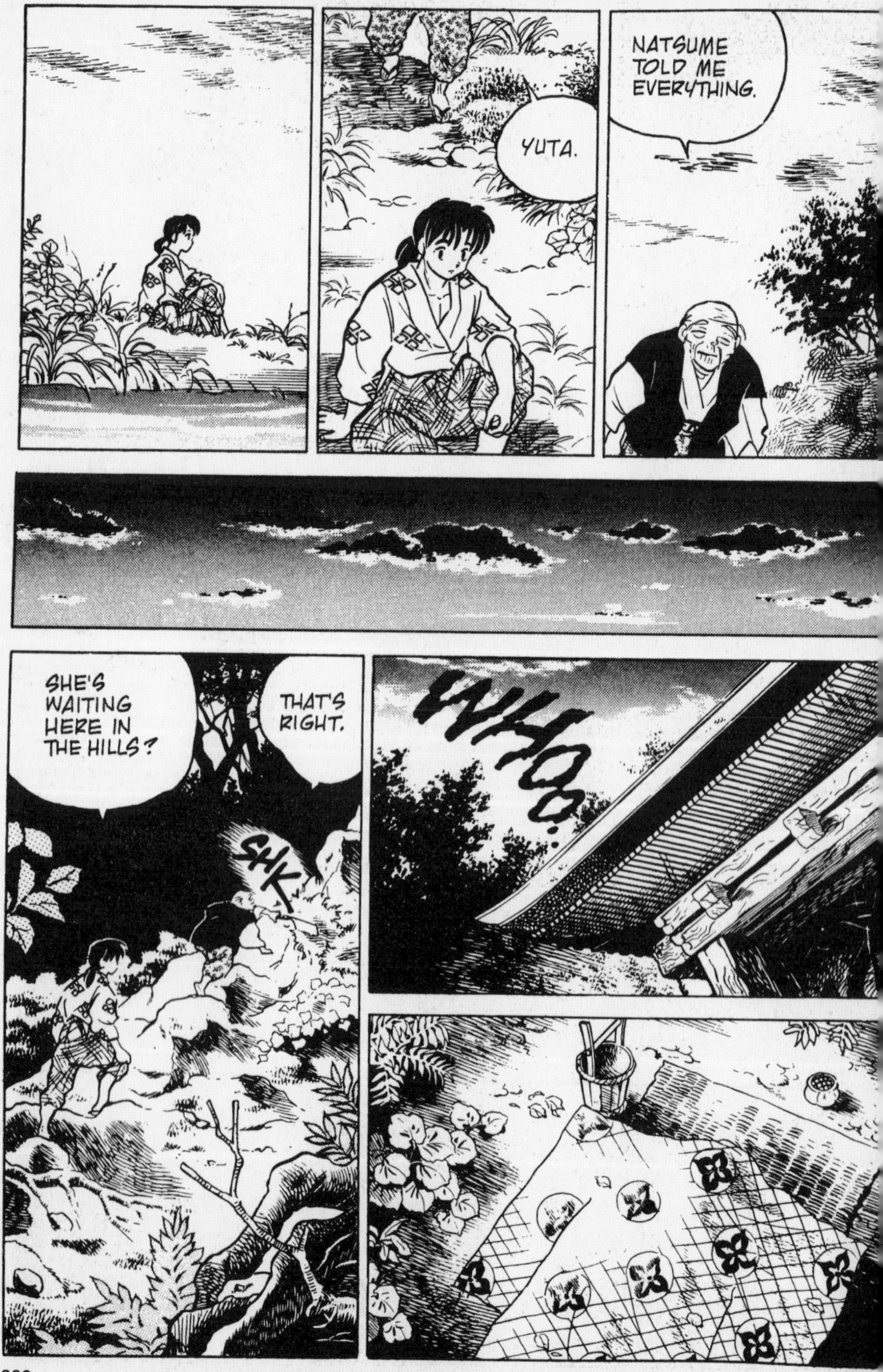
YUTA.
NATSUME TOLD ME EVERYTHING.
SHE'S WAITING HERE IN THE HILLS?
THAT'S RIGHT.
SHK
WHOO...

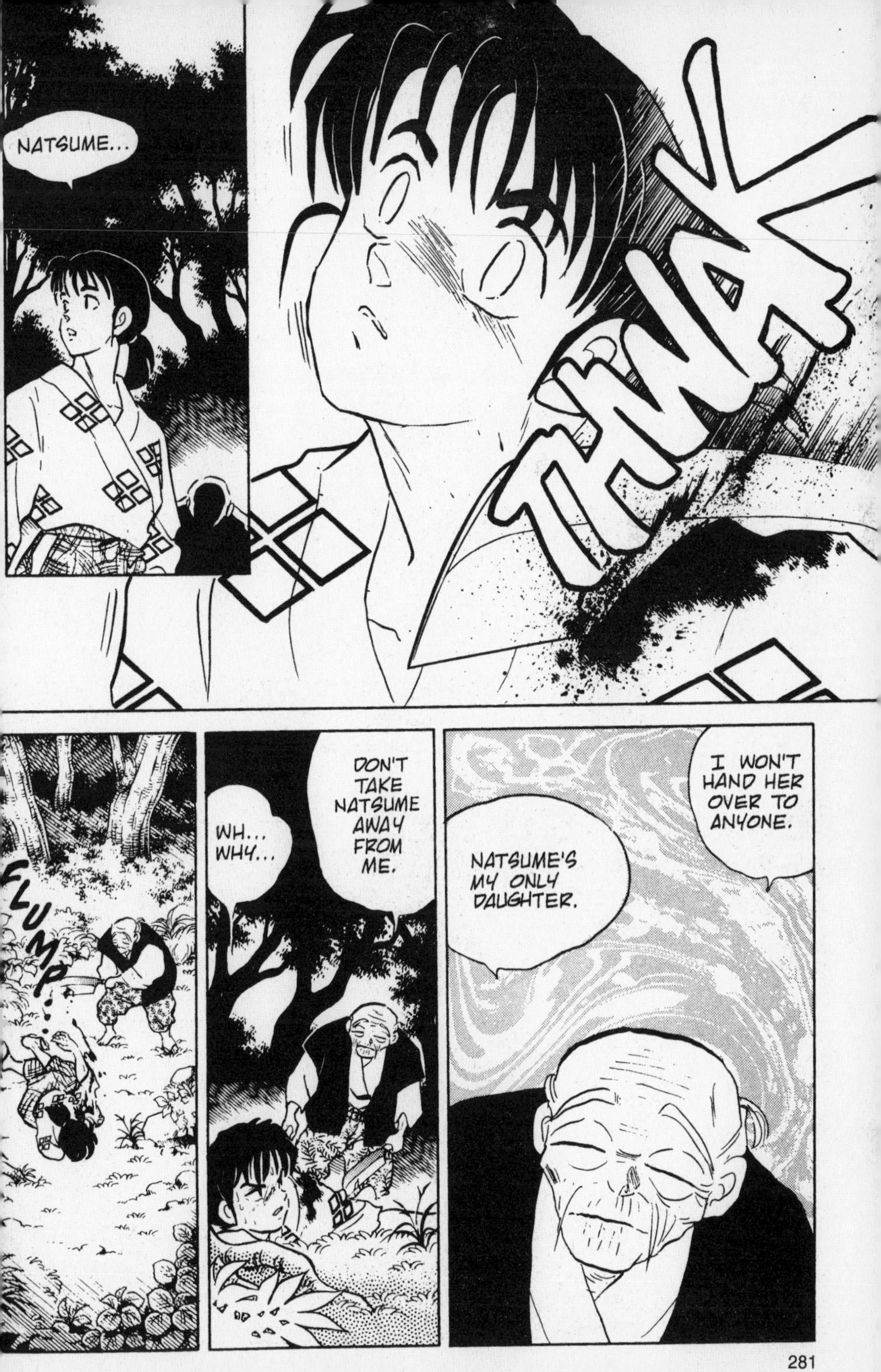
NATSUME...
THWAK
FLUMP
WH... WHY...
DON'T TAKE NATSUME AWAY FROM ME.
NATSUME'S MY ONLY DAUGHTER.
I WON'T HAND HER OVER TO ANYONE.

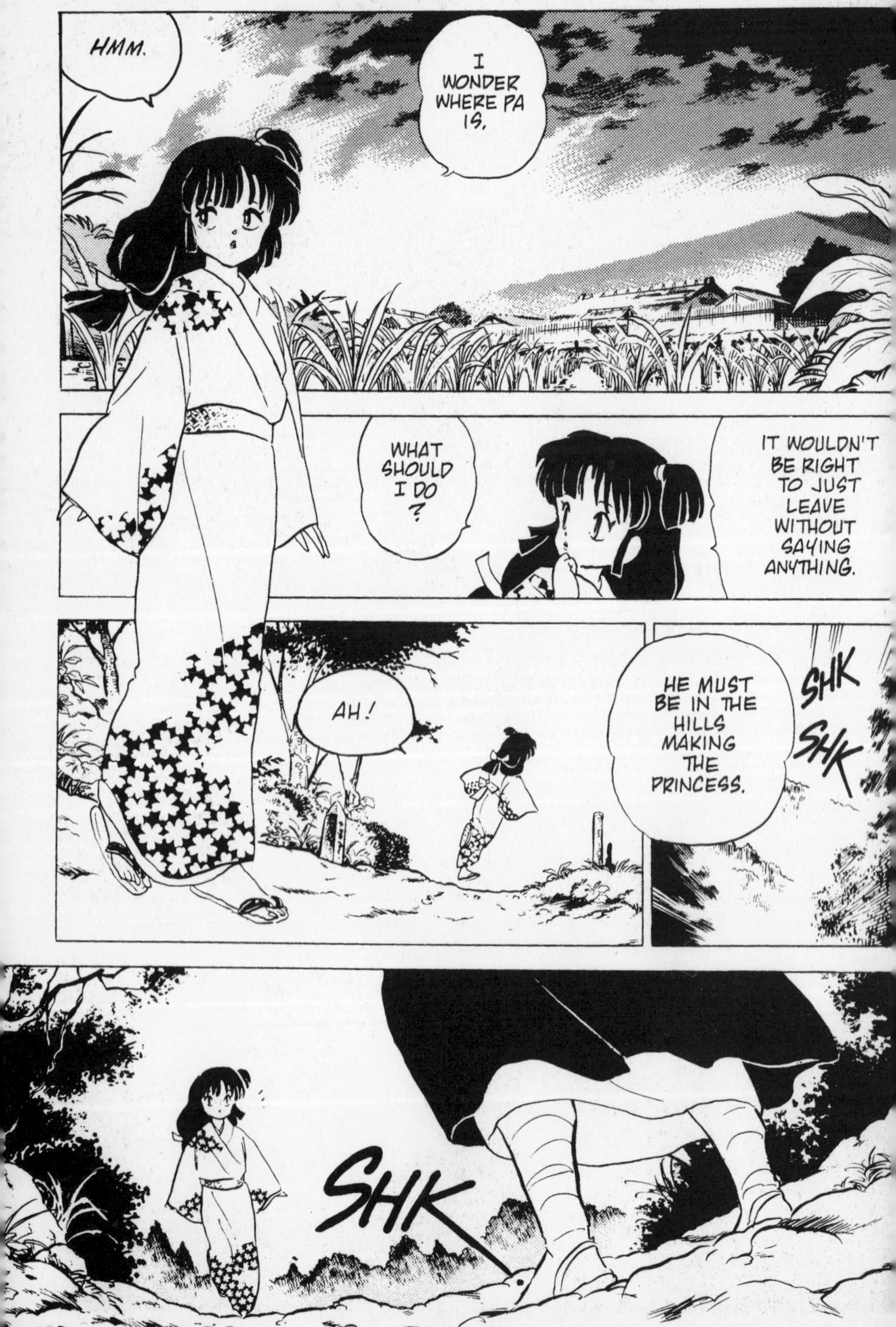
HMM.
I WONDER WHERE PA IS.
WHAT SHOULD I DO?
IT WOULDN'T BE RIGHT TO JUST LEAVE WITHOUT SAYING ANYTHING.
AH!
HE MUST BE IN THE HILLS MAKING THE PRINCESS.
SHK
SHK
SHK

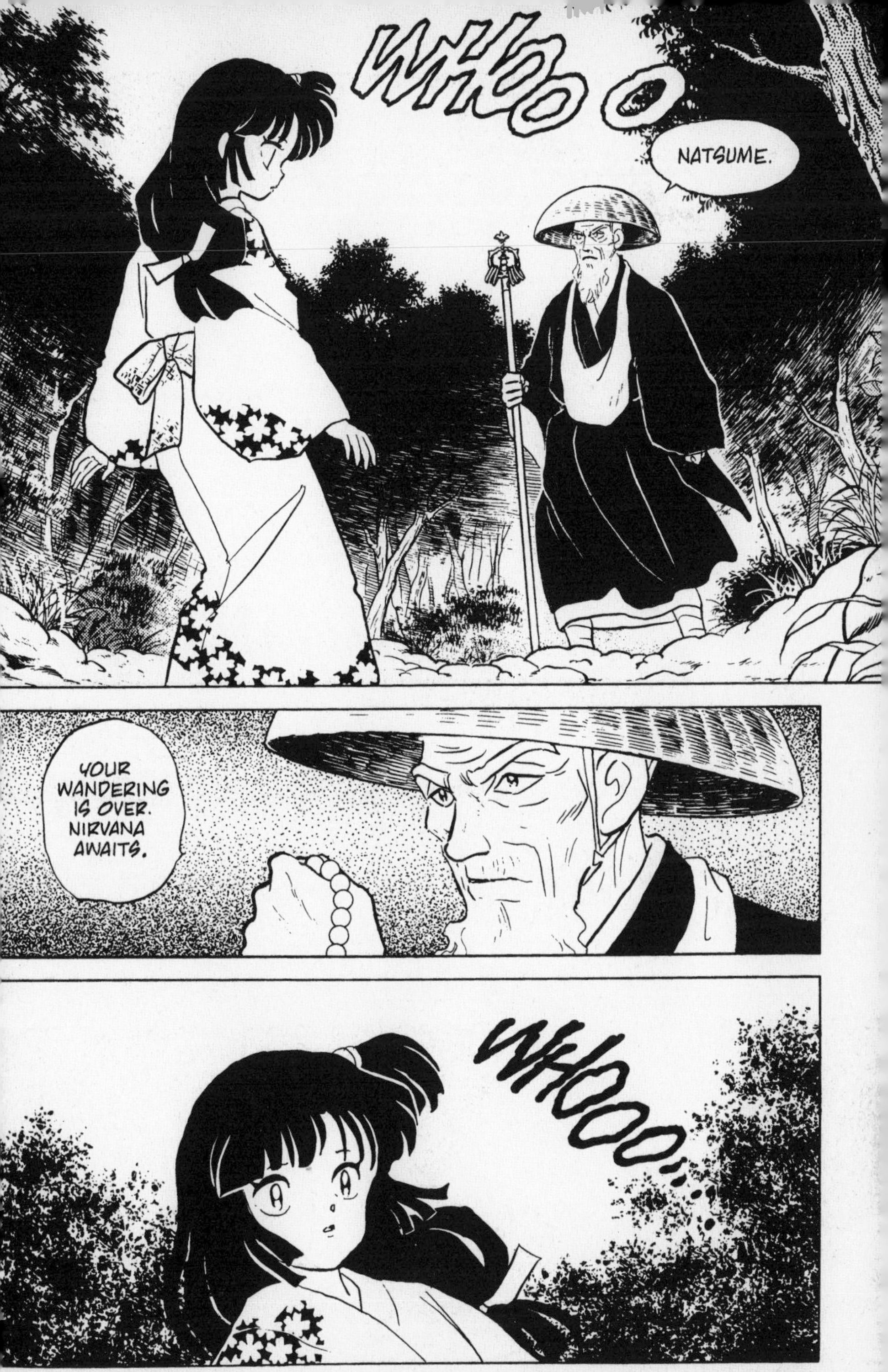
WHOOO
NATSUME.
YOUR WANDERING IS OVER. NIRVANA AWAITS.
WHOOO...

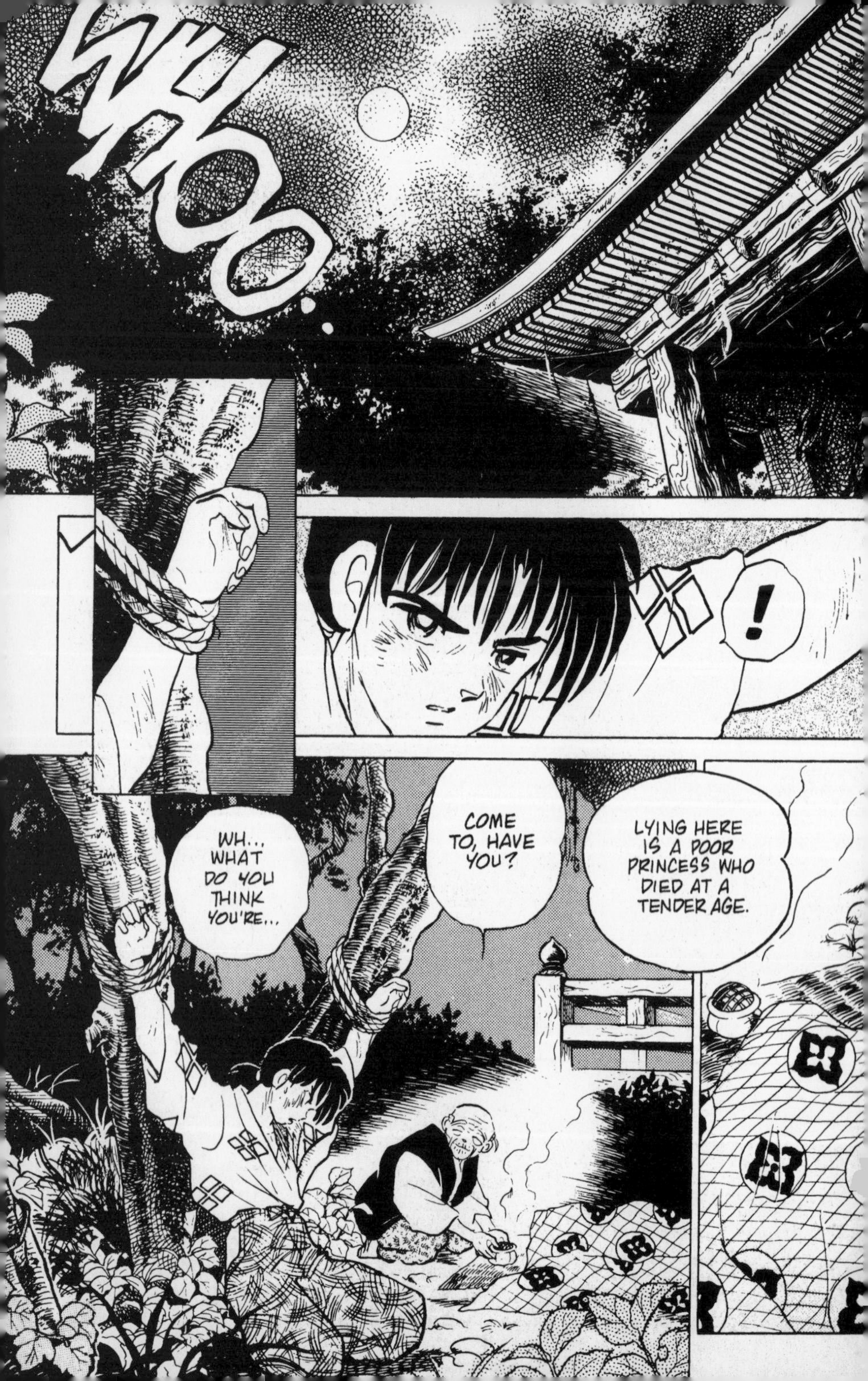
WHOOO...
!
WH... WHAT DO YOU THINK YOU'RE...
COME TO, HAVE YOU?
LYING HERE IS A POOR PRINCESS WHO DIED AT A TENDER AGE.

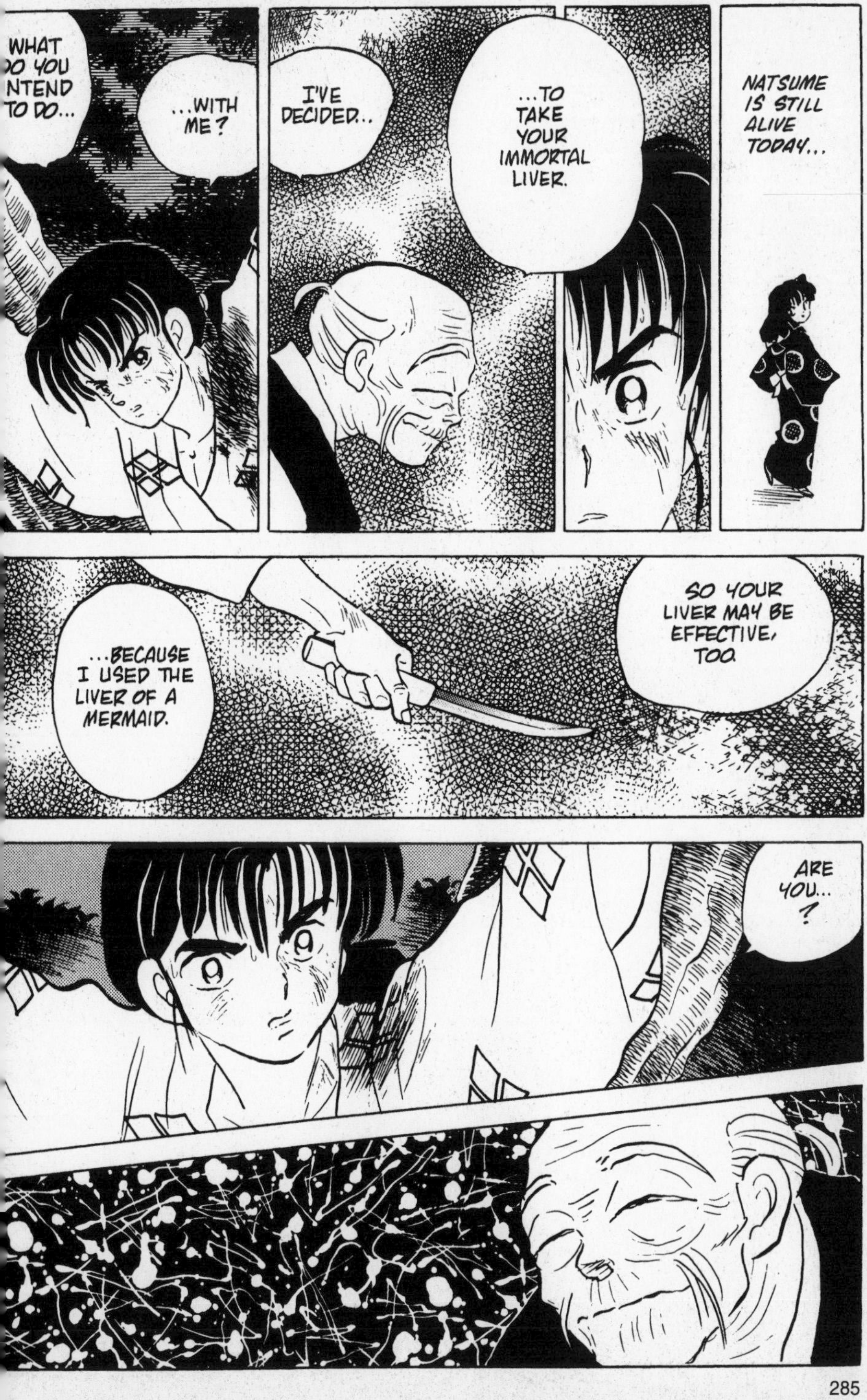

WHAT DO YOU INTEND TO DO...
...WITH ME?
I'VE DECIDED...
...TO TAKE YOUR IMMORTAL LIVER.
NATSUME IS STILL ALIVE TODAY...
...BECAUSE I USED THE LIVER OF A MERMAID.
SO YOUR LIVER MAY BE EFFECTIVE, TOO.
ARE YOU...?

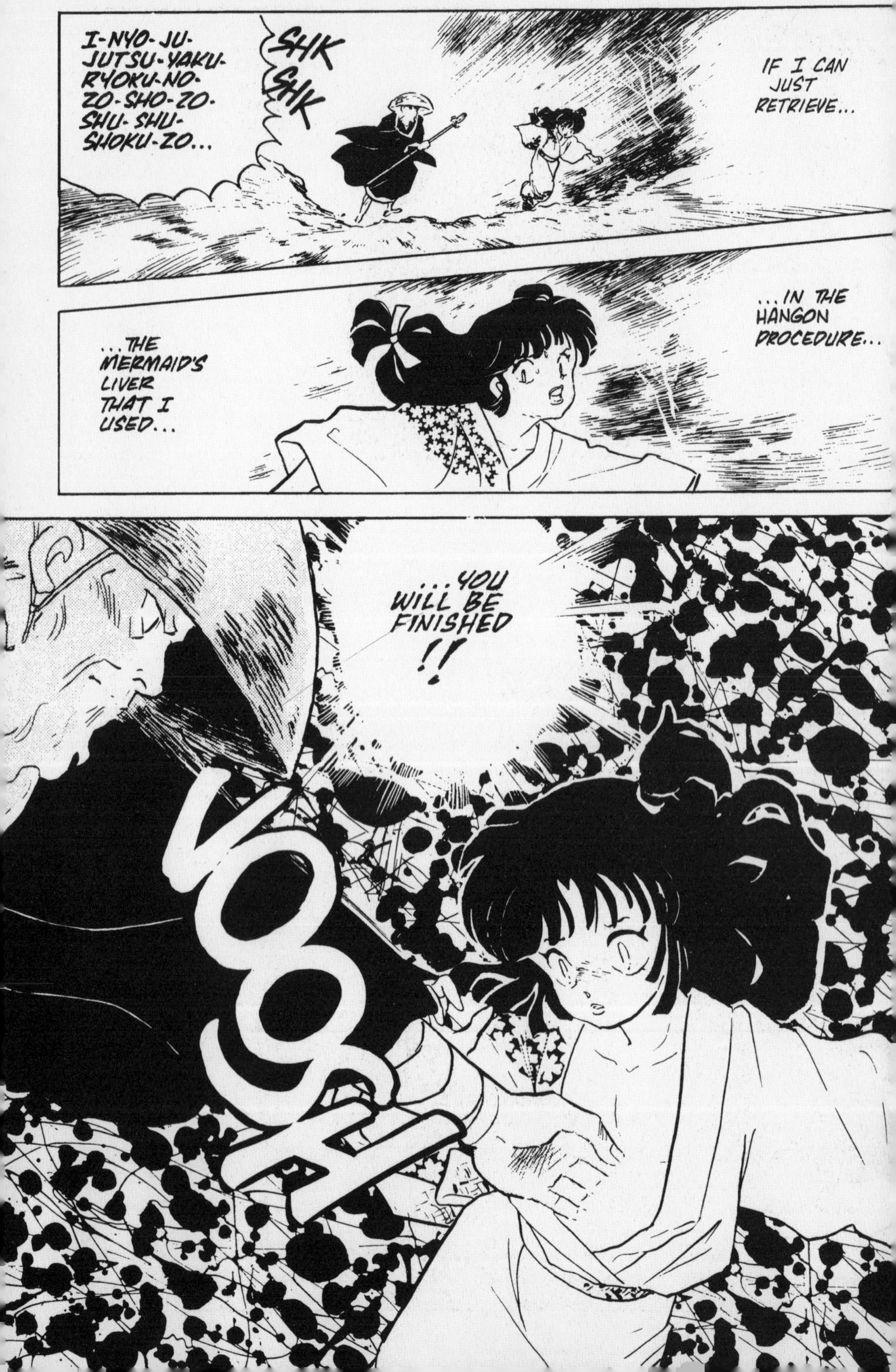
I-NYO-JU-JUTSU-YAKU-RYOKU-NO-ZO-SHO-ZO-SHU-SHU-SHOKU-ZO...
SHK SHK
IF I CAN JUST RETRIEVE...
...THE MERMAID'S LIVER THAT I USED...
...IN THE HANGON PROCEDURE...
...YOU WILL BE FINISHED!!
VOOSH

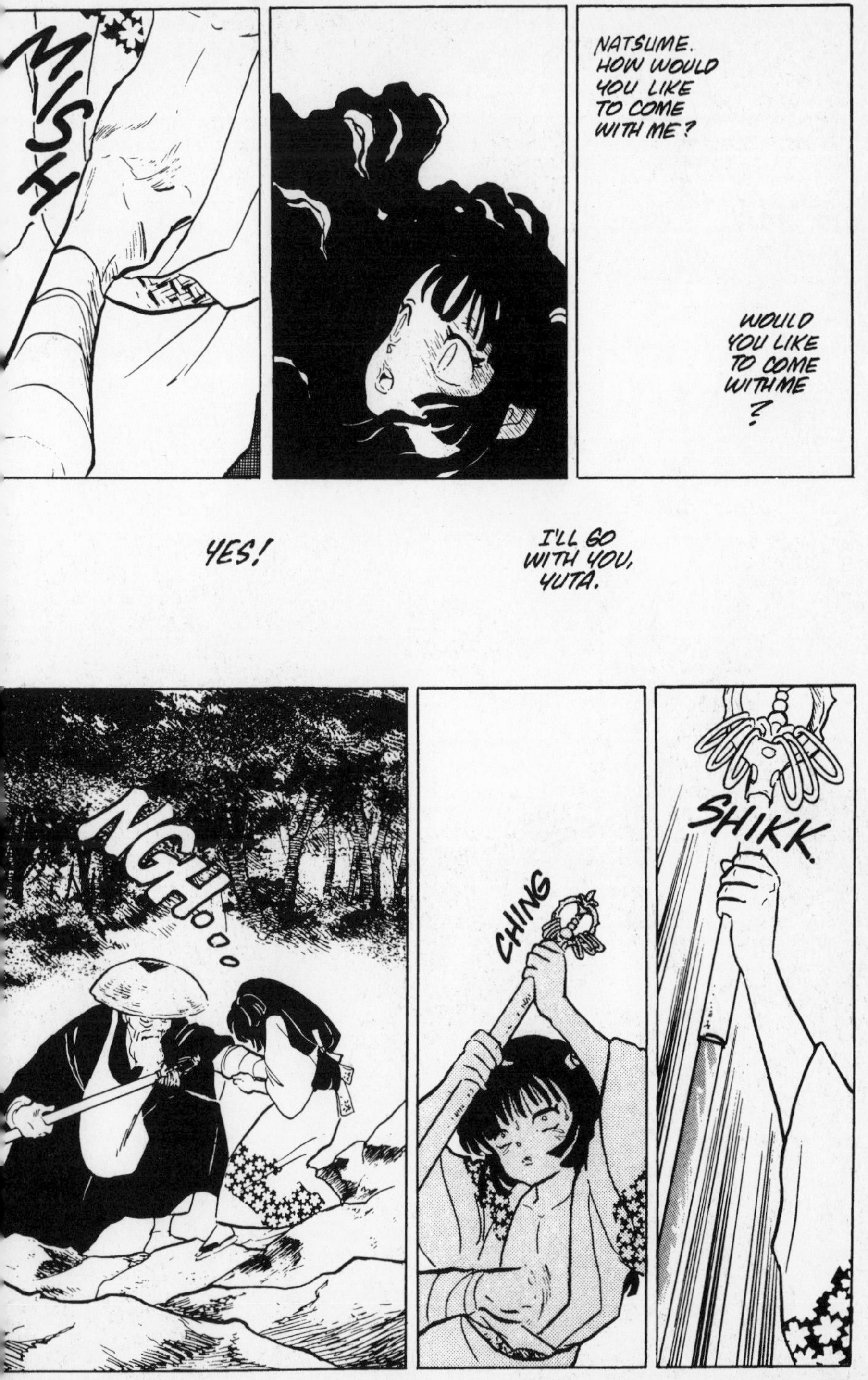

MISH
NATSUME. HOW WOULD YOU LIKE TO COME WITH ME?
WOULD YOU LIKE TO COME WITH ME ?
YES!
I'LL GO WITH YOU, YUTA.
NGH
CHING
SHIKK.

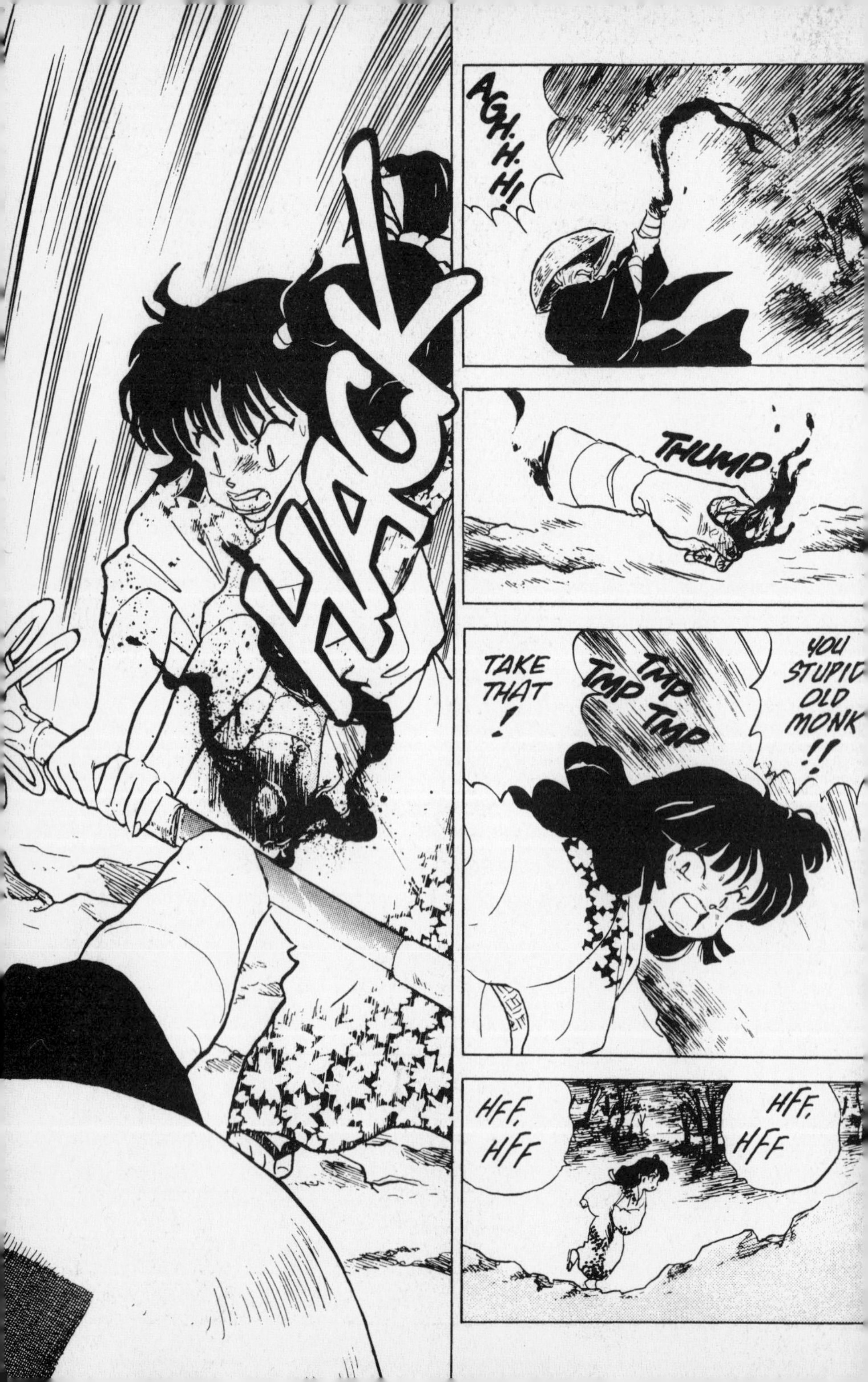
SHACK
AGH.H.H!
THUMP
TAKE THAT!
TMP TMP TMP TMP
YOU STUPID OLD MONK!!
HFF, HFF
HFF, HFF

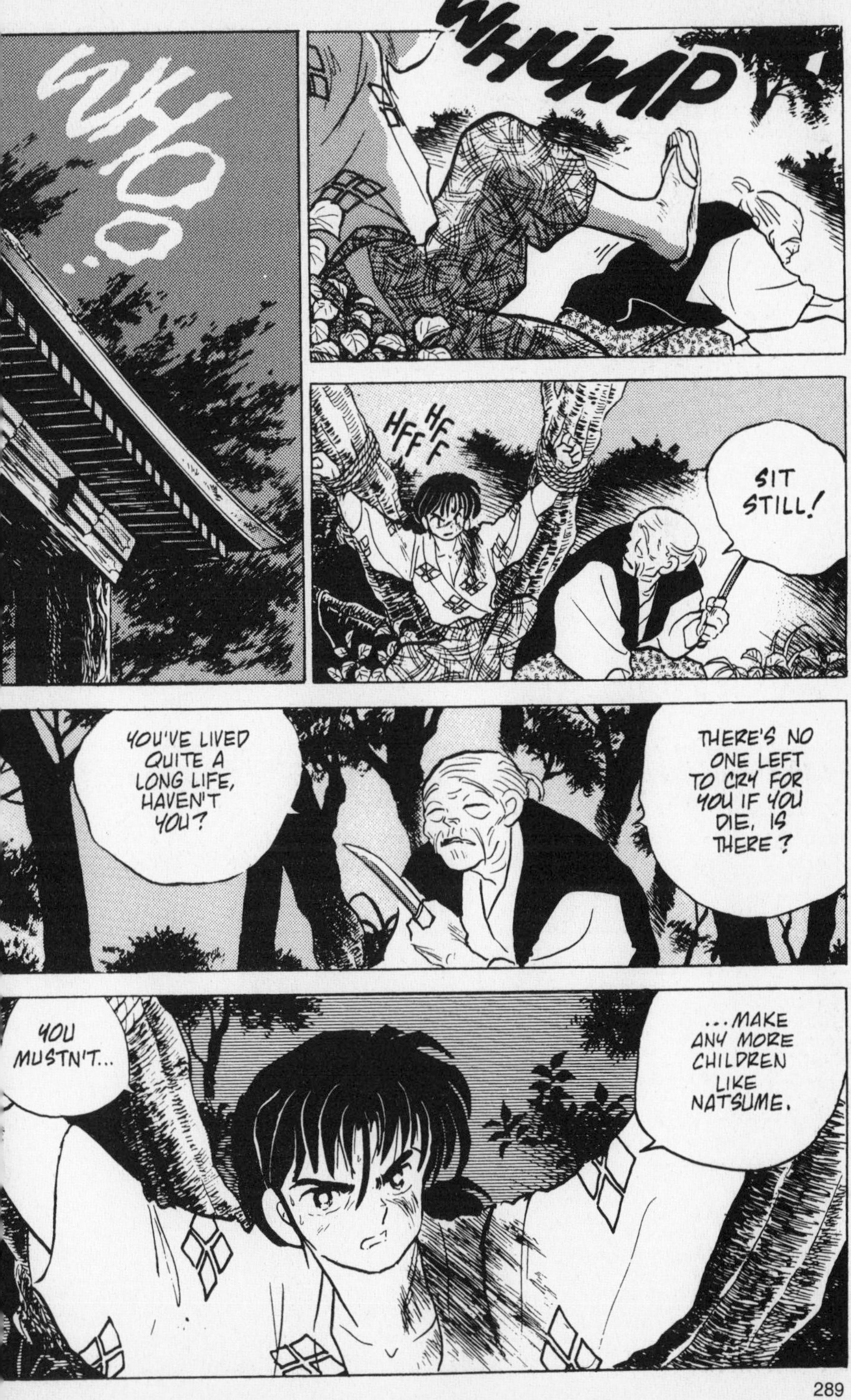
WHOO...
WHUMP
HFFF HFF
SIT STILL!
YOU'VE LIVED QUITE A LONG LIFE, HAVEN'T YOU?
THERE'S NO ONE LEFT TO CRY FOR YOU IF YOU DIE, IS THERE?
YOU MUSTN'T...
...MAKE ANY MORE CHILDREN LIKE NATSUME.

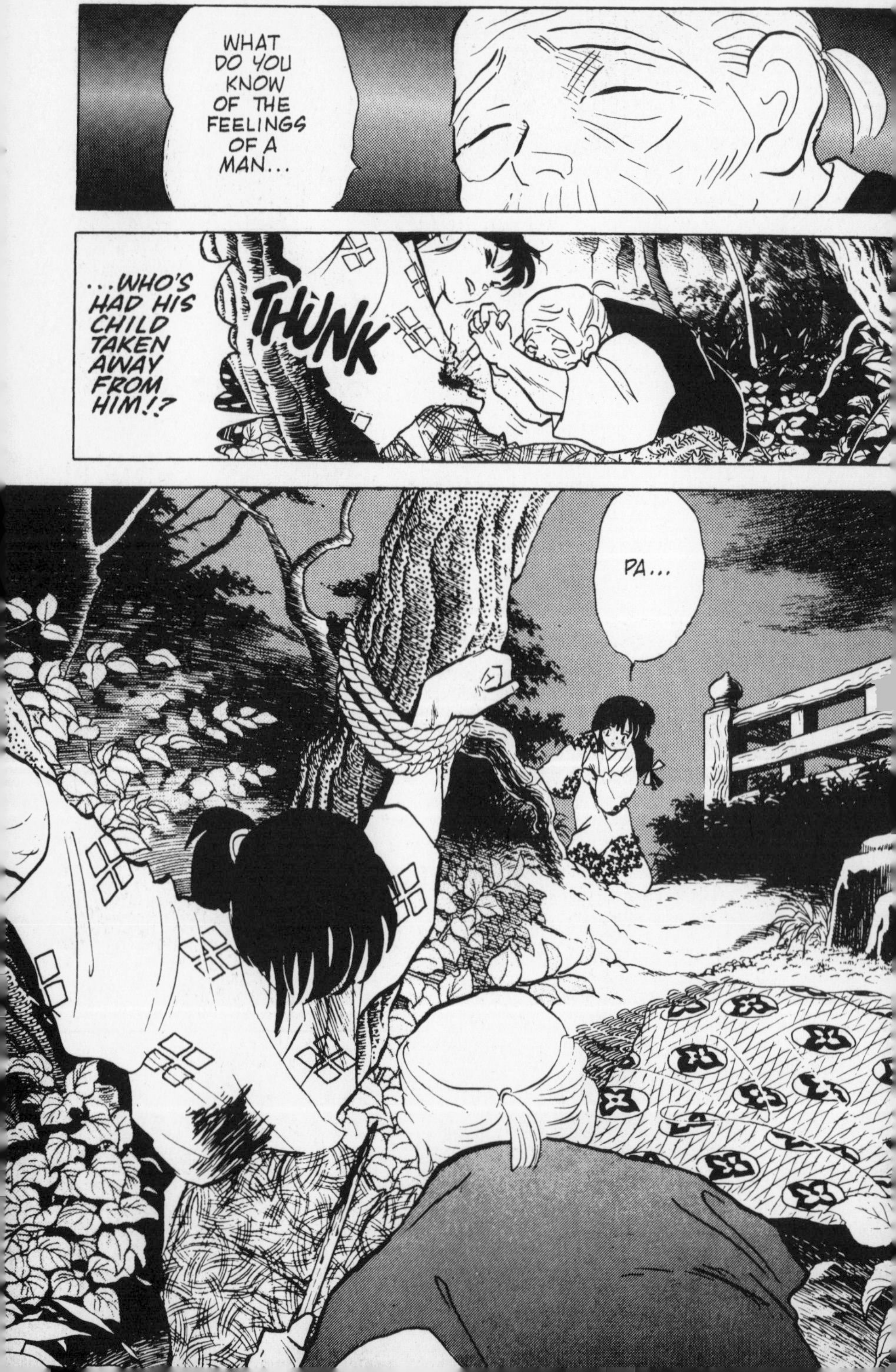
WHAT DO YOU KNOW OF THE FEELINGS OF A MAN...
...WHO'S HAD HIS CHILD TAKEN AWAY FROM HIM!?
THUNK
PA...

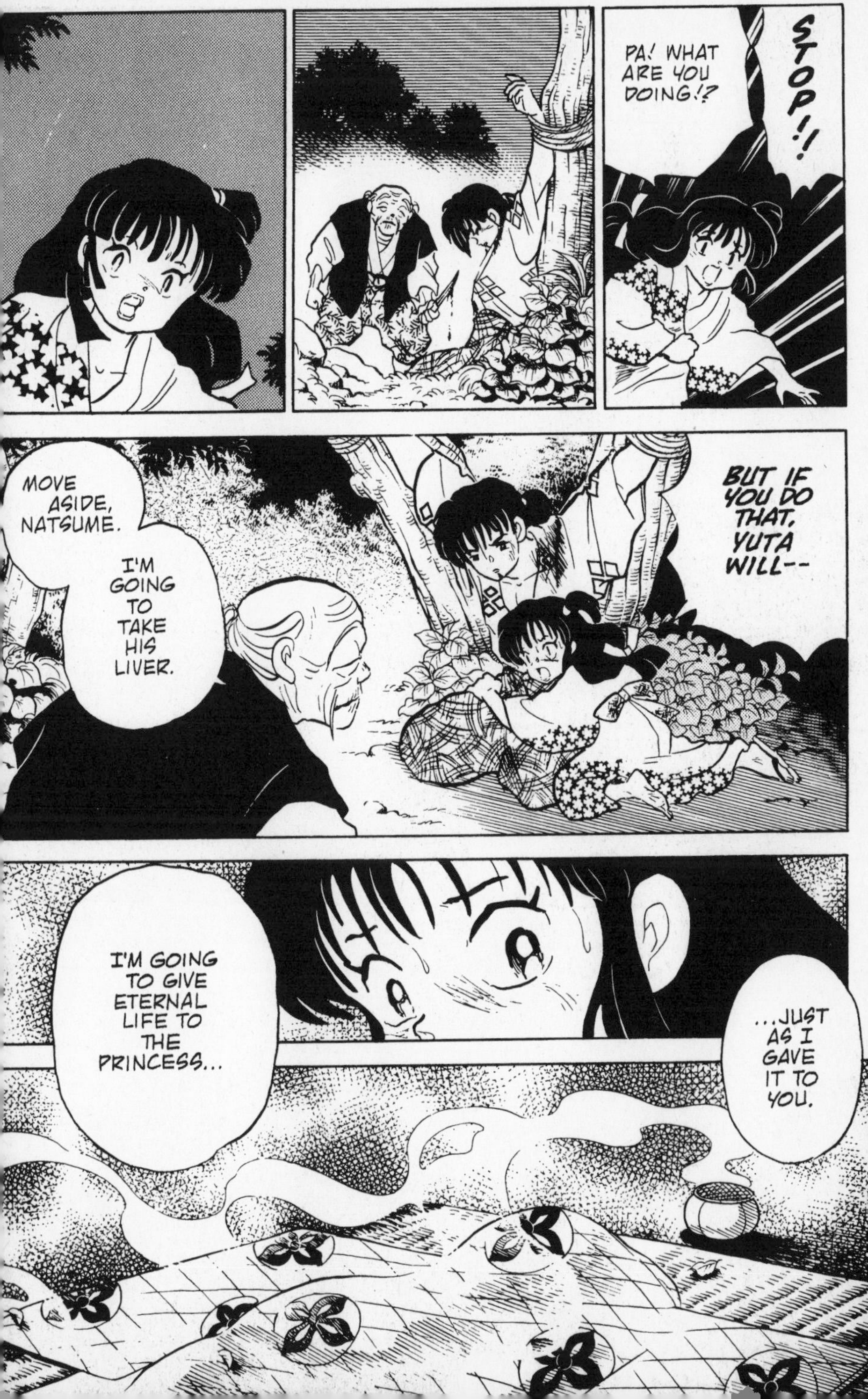
PA! WHAT ARE YOU DOING!?
STOP!!
MOVE ASIDE, NATSUME.
I'M GOING TO TAKE HIS LIVER.
BUT IF YOU DO THAT, YUTA WILL--
I'M GOING TO GIVE ETERNAL LIFE TO THE PRINCESS...
...JUST AS I GAVE IT TO YOU.

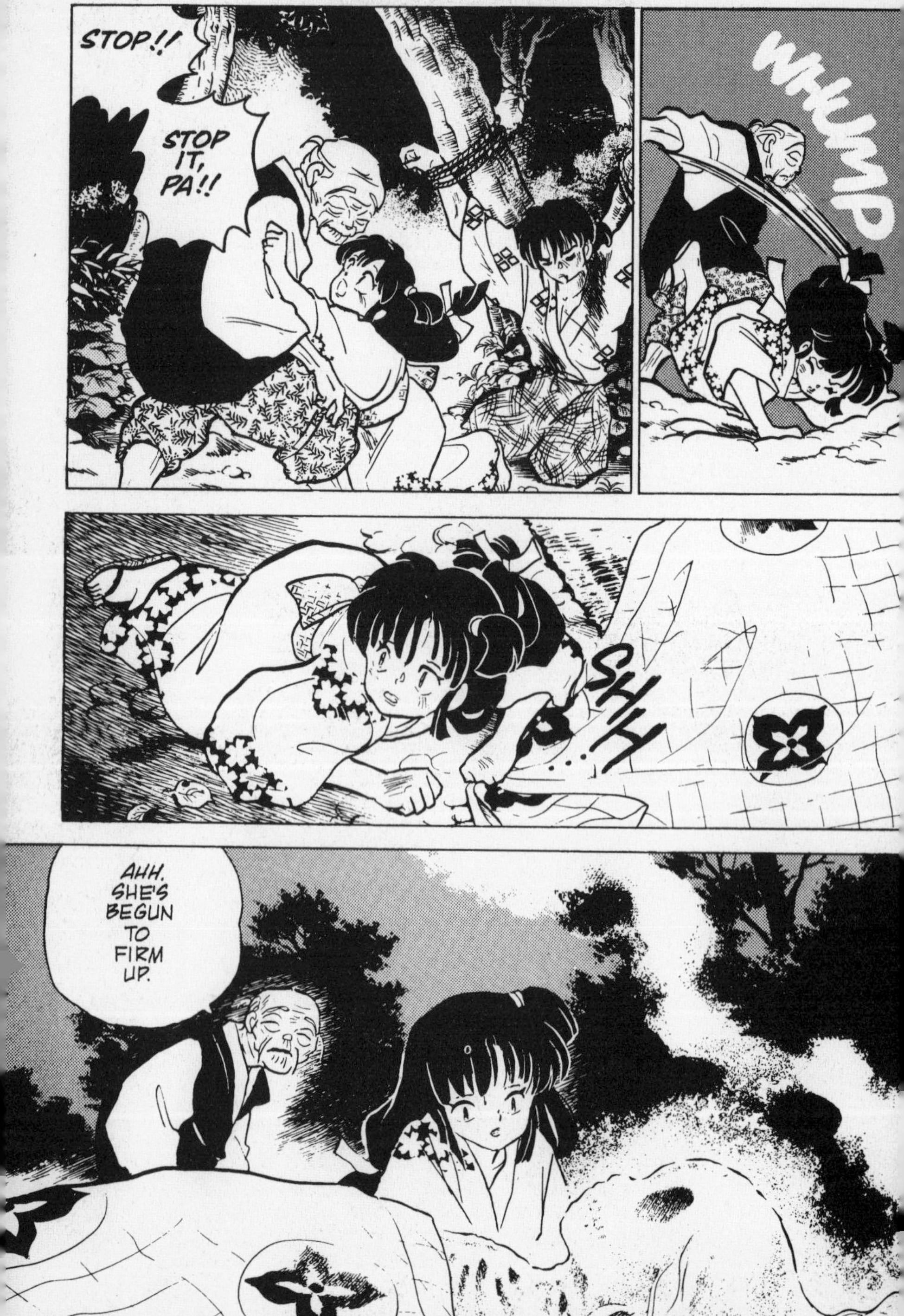
STOP!!
STOP IT, PA!!
WHUMP
SHH...!
AHH. SHE'S BEGUN TO FIRM UP.

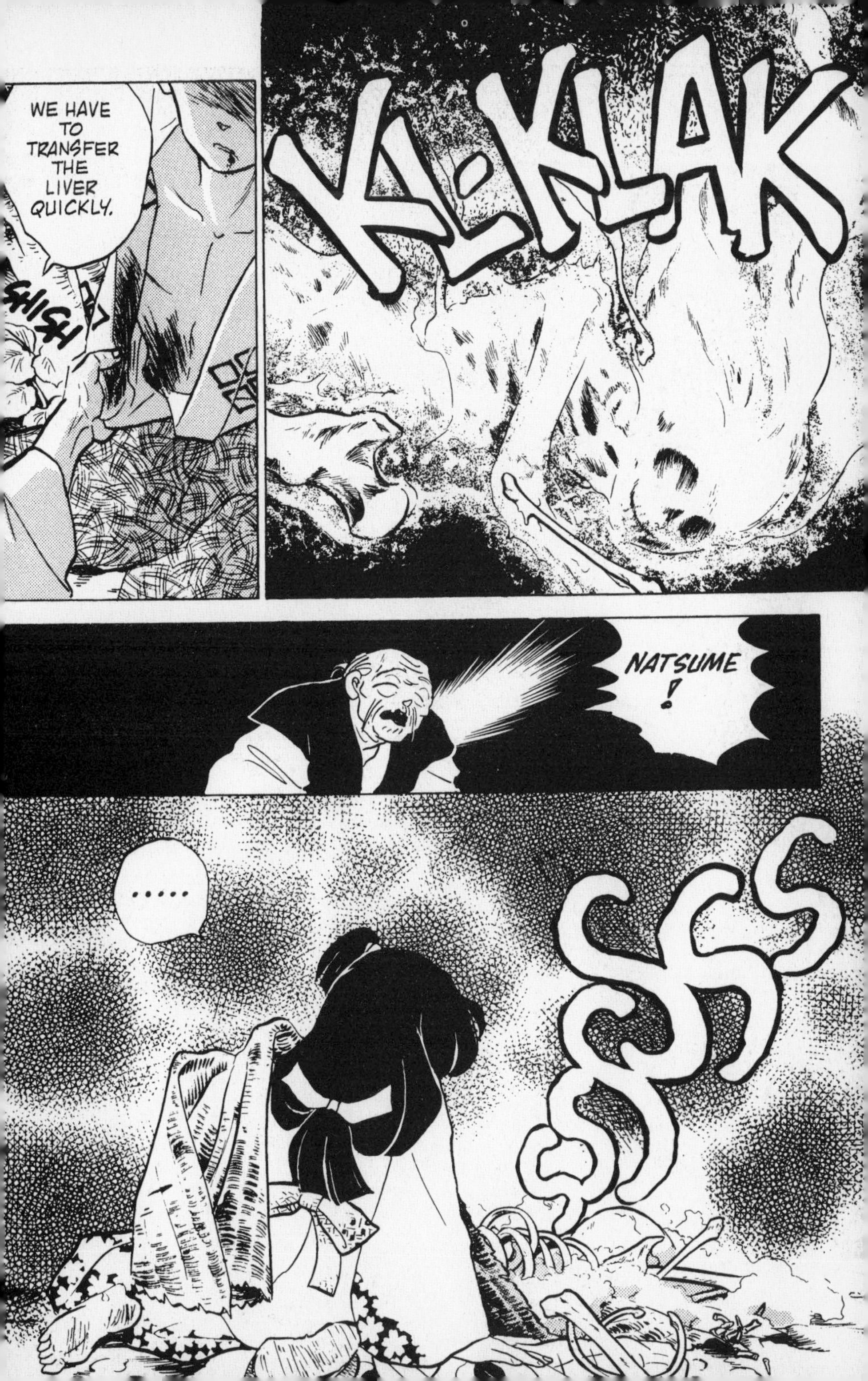
WE HAVE TO TRANSFER THE LIVER QUICKLY.
SHIGH
KL-KLAK
NATSUME!
.....
SSS

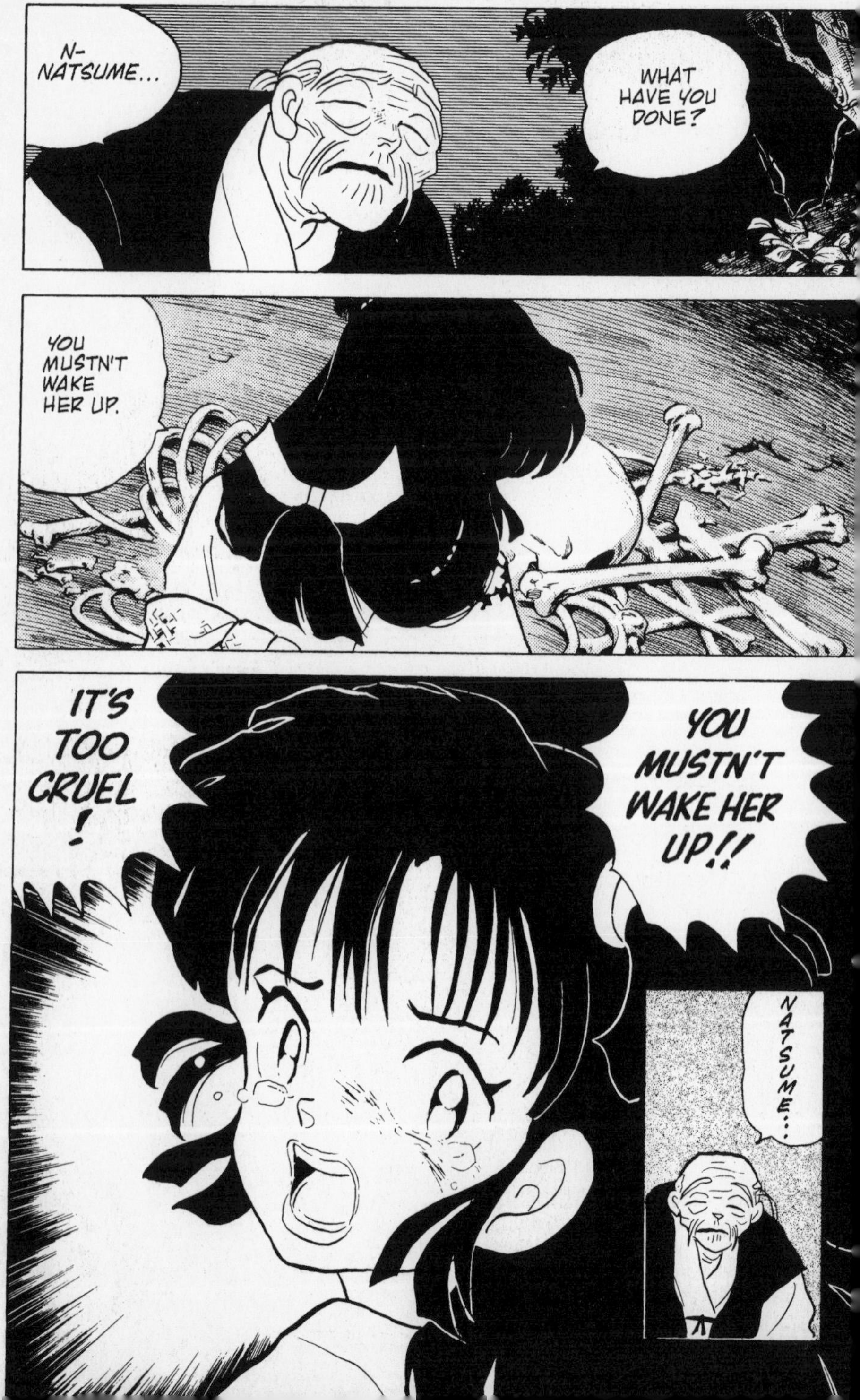
N-NATSUME...
WHAT HAVE YOU DONE?
YOU MUSTN'T WAKE HER UP.
IT'S TOO CRUEL!
YOU MUSTN'T WAKE HER UP!!
NATSUME...

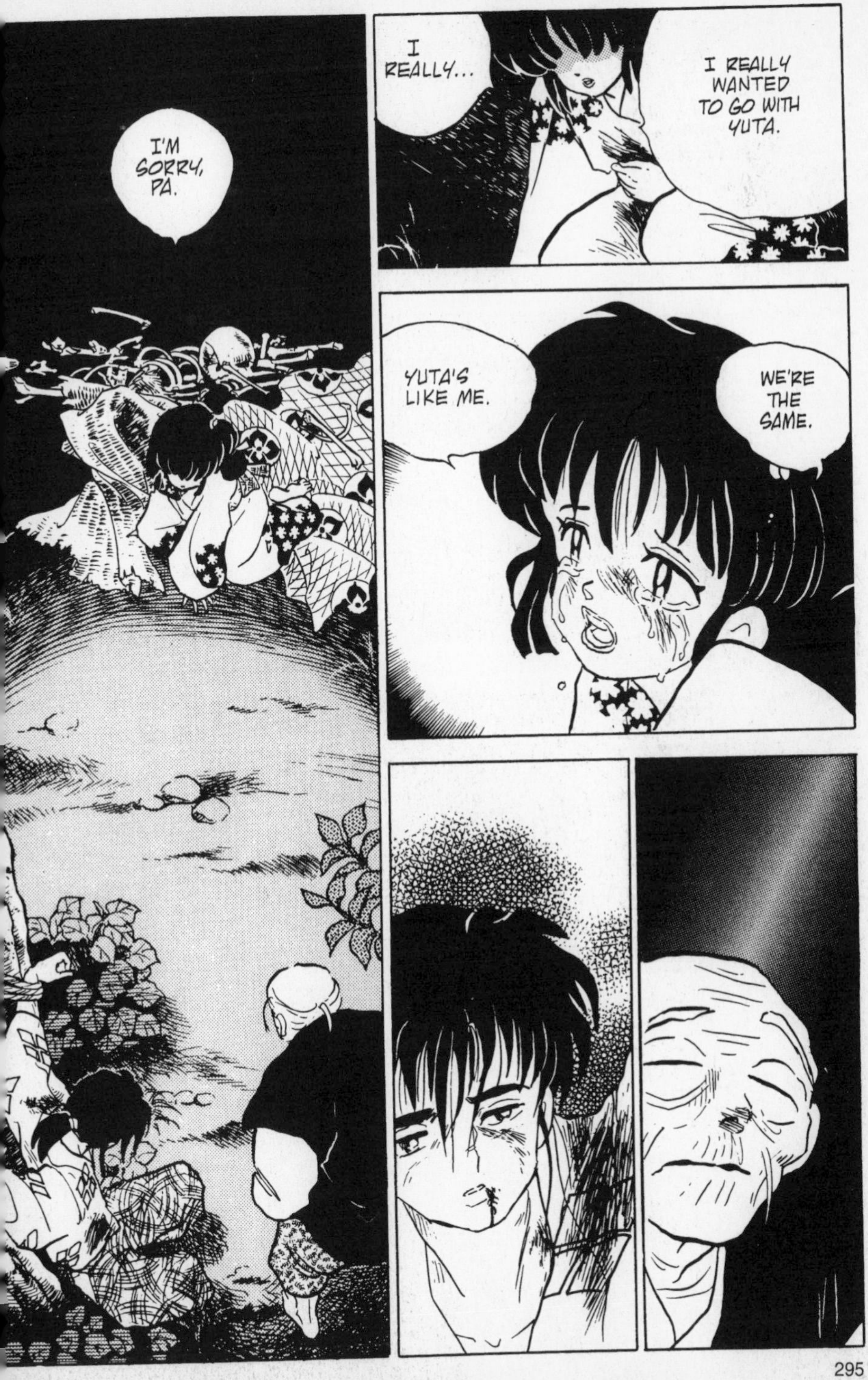
I'M SORRY, PA.
I REALLY...
I REALLY WANTED TO GO WITH YUTA.
YUTA'S LIKE ME.
WE'RE THE SAME.

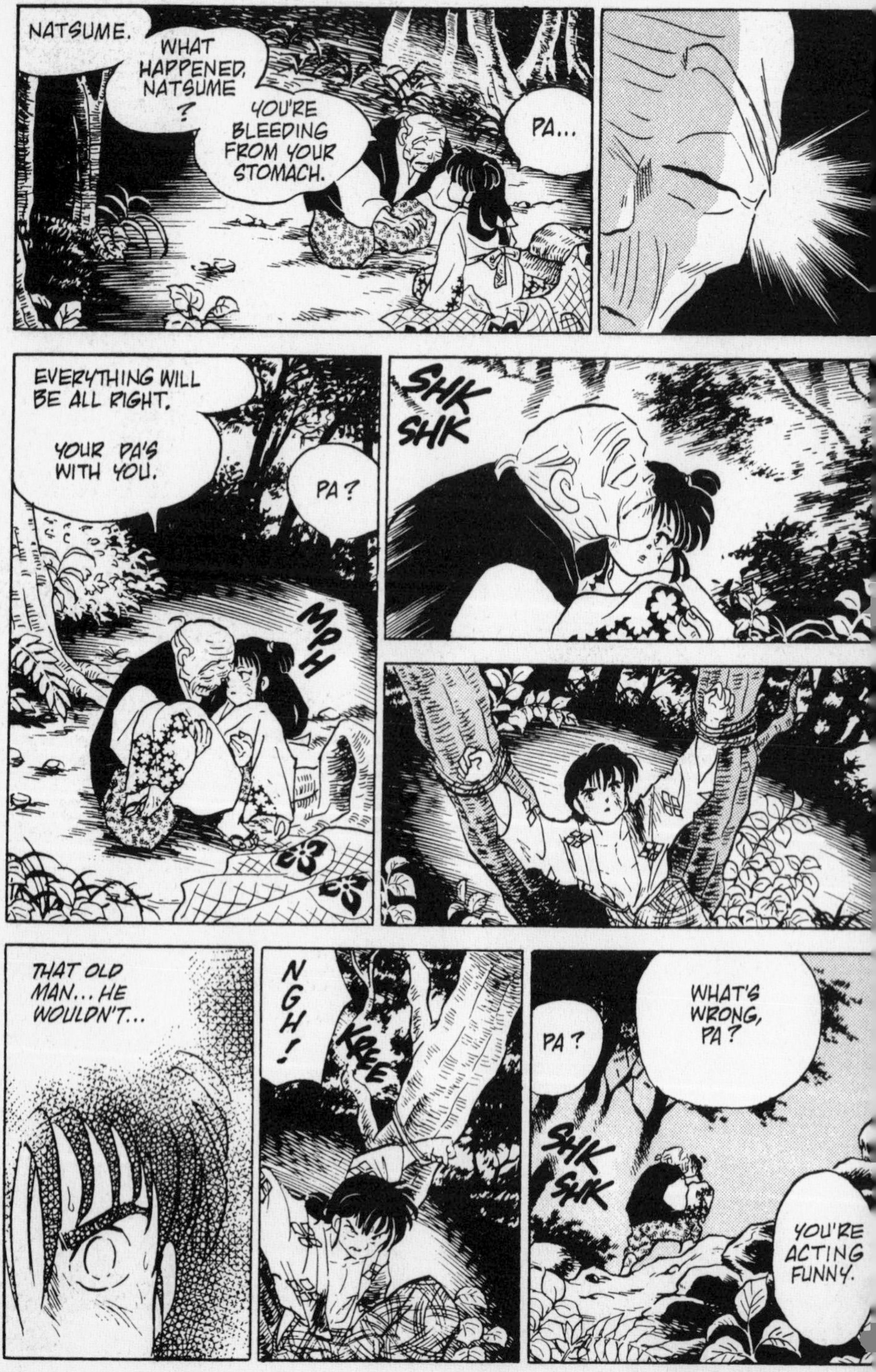
NATSUME.
WHAT HAPPENED, NATSUME?
YOU'RE BLEEDING FROM YOUR STOMACH.
PA...
EVERYTHING WILL BE ALL RIGHT.
YOUR PA'S WITH YOU.
PA?
MPH
SHK SHK
THAT OLD MAN... HE WOULDN'T...
NGH!
KREE
PA?
WHAT'S WRONG, PA?
SHK SHK
YOU'RE ACTING FUNNY.

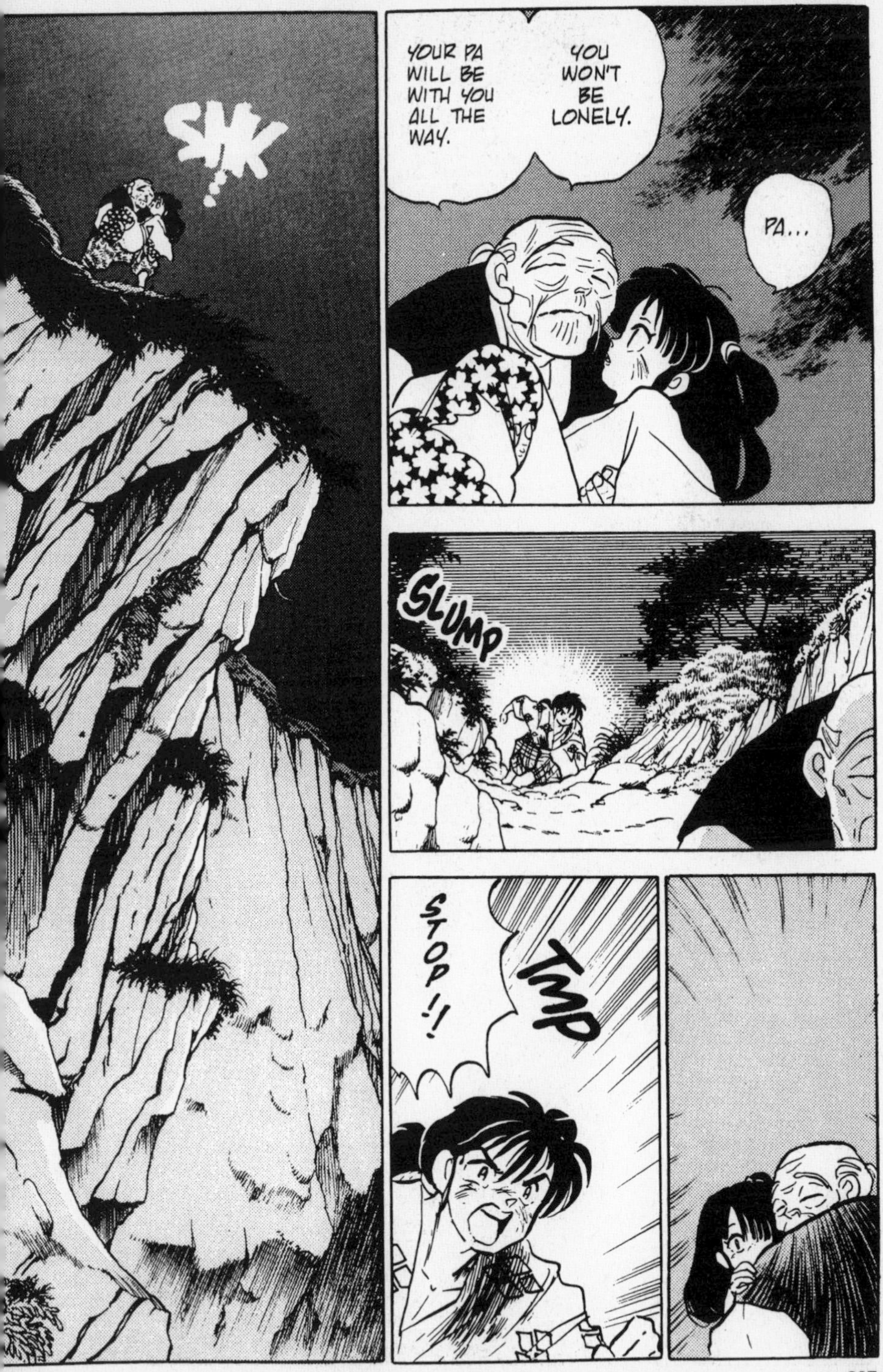
SHK
YOUR PA WILL BE WITH YOU ALL THE WAY.
YOU WON'T BE LONELY.
PA...
SLUMP
STOP!!
TMP

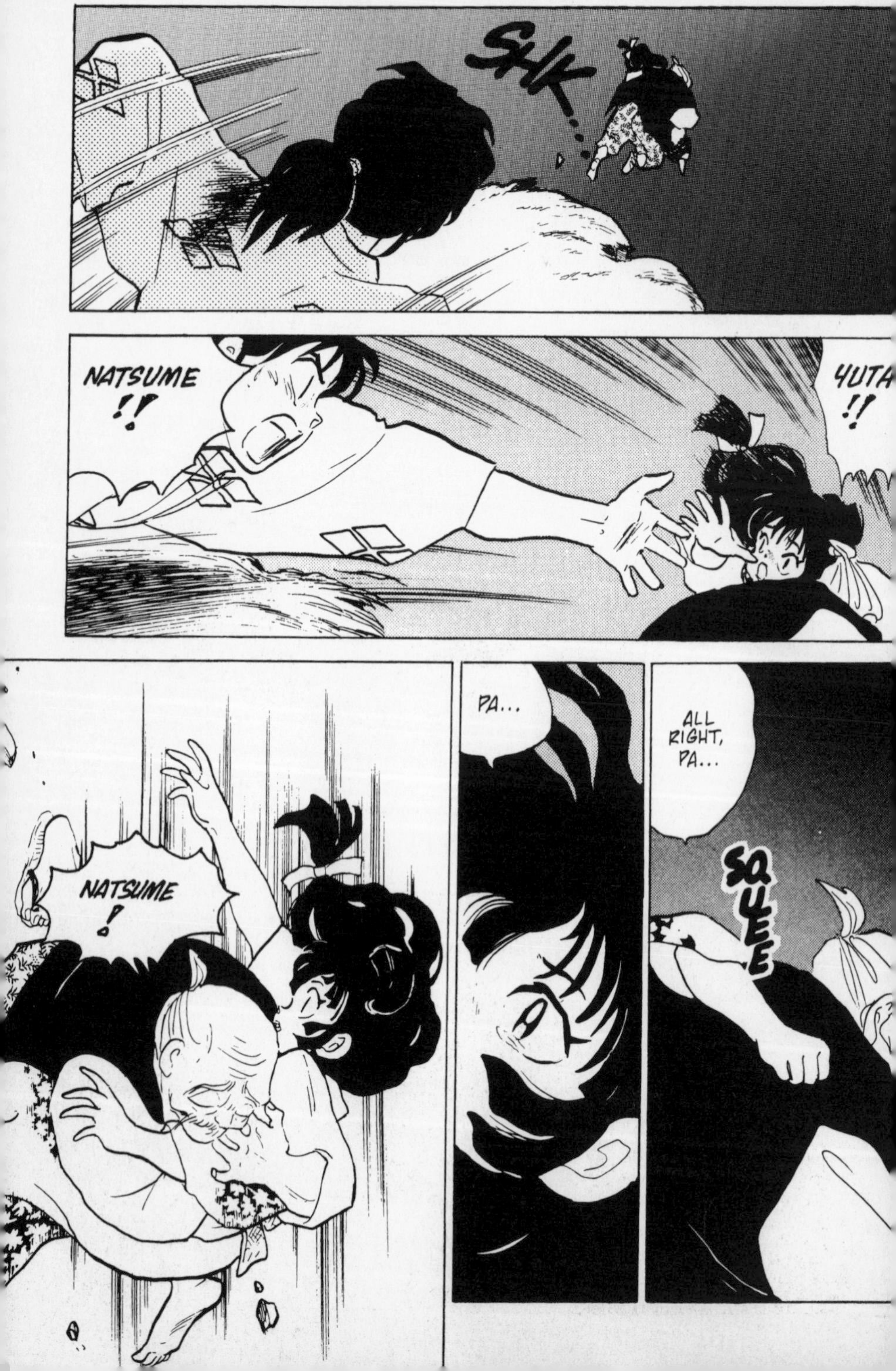
SHK...
NATSUME!!
YUTA!!
NATSUME!
PA...
ALL RIGHT, PA...
SQUEE

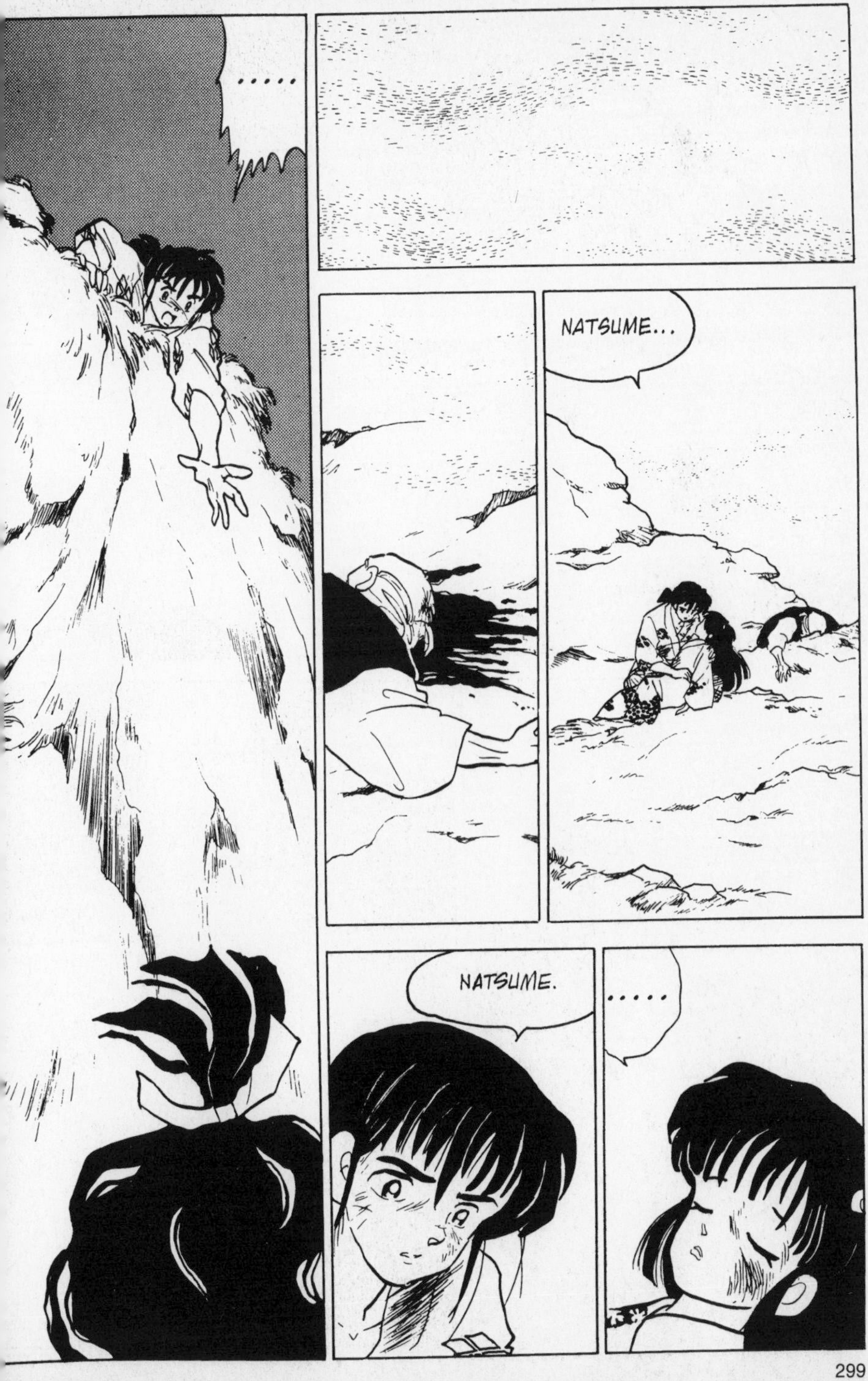
.....
NATSUME...
NATSUME.
.....

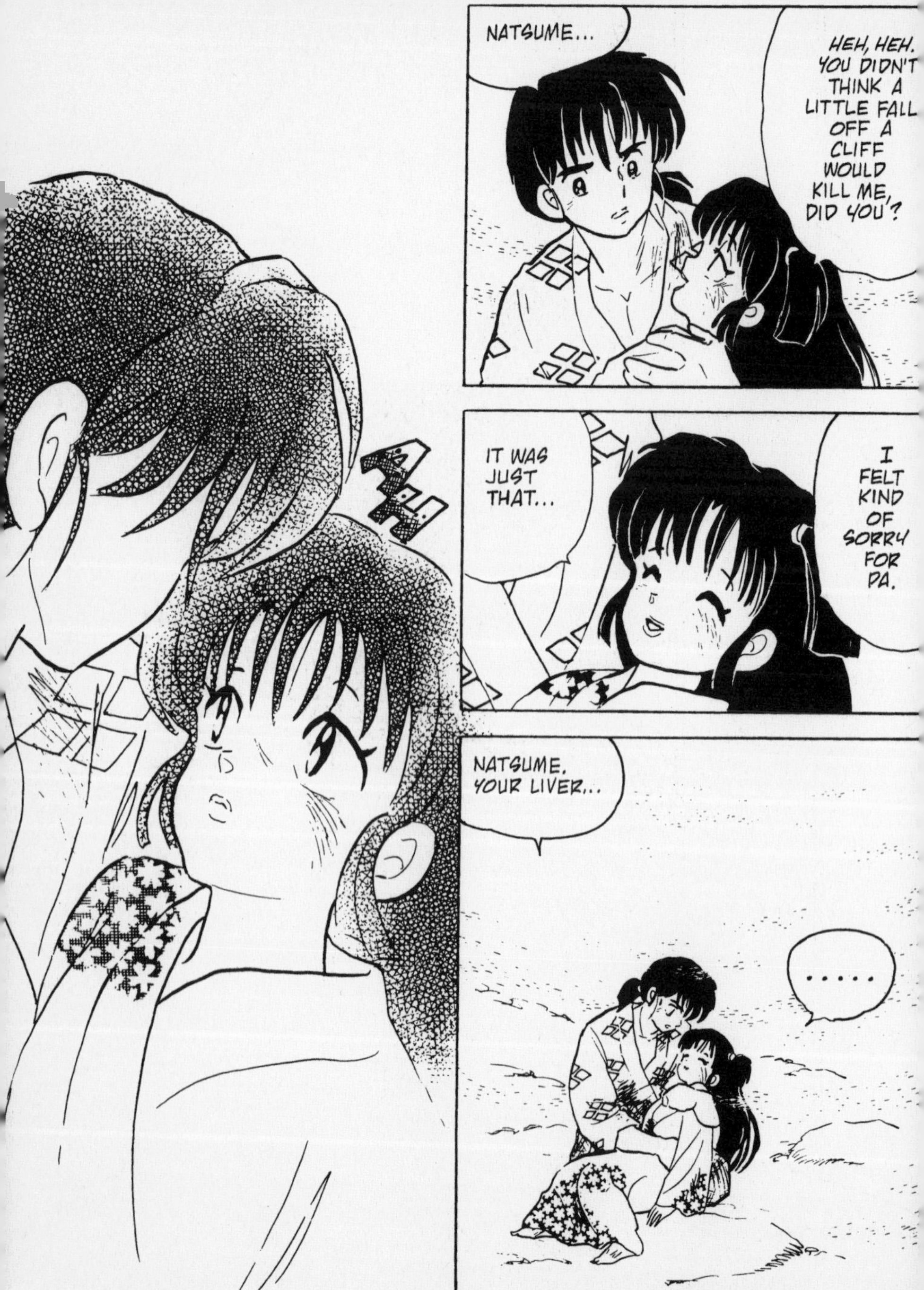
NATSUME...
HEH, HEH. YOU DIDN'T THINK A LITTLE FALL OFF A CLIFF WOULD KILL ME, DID YOU?
IT WAS JUST THAT...
I FELT KIND OF SORRY FOR PA.
NATSUME. YOUR LIVER...
.....

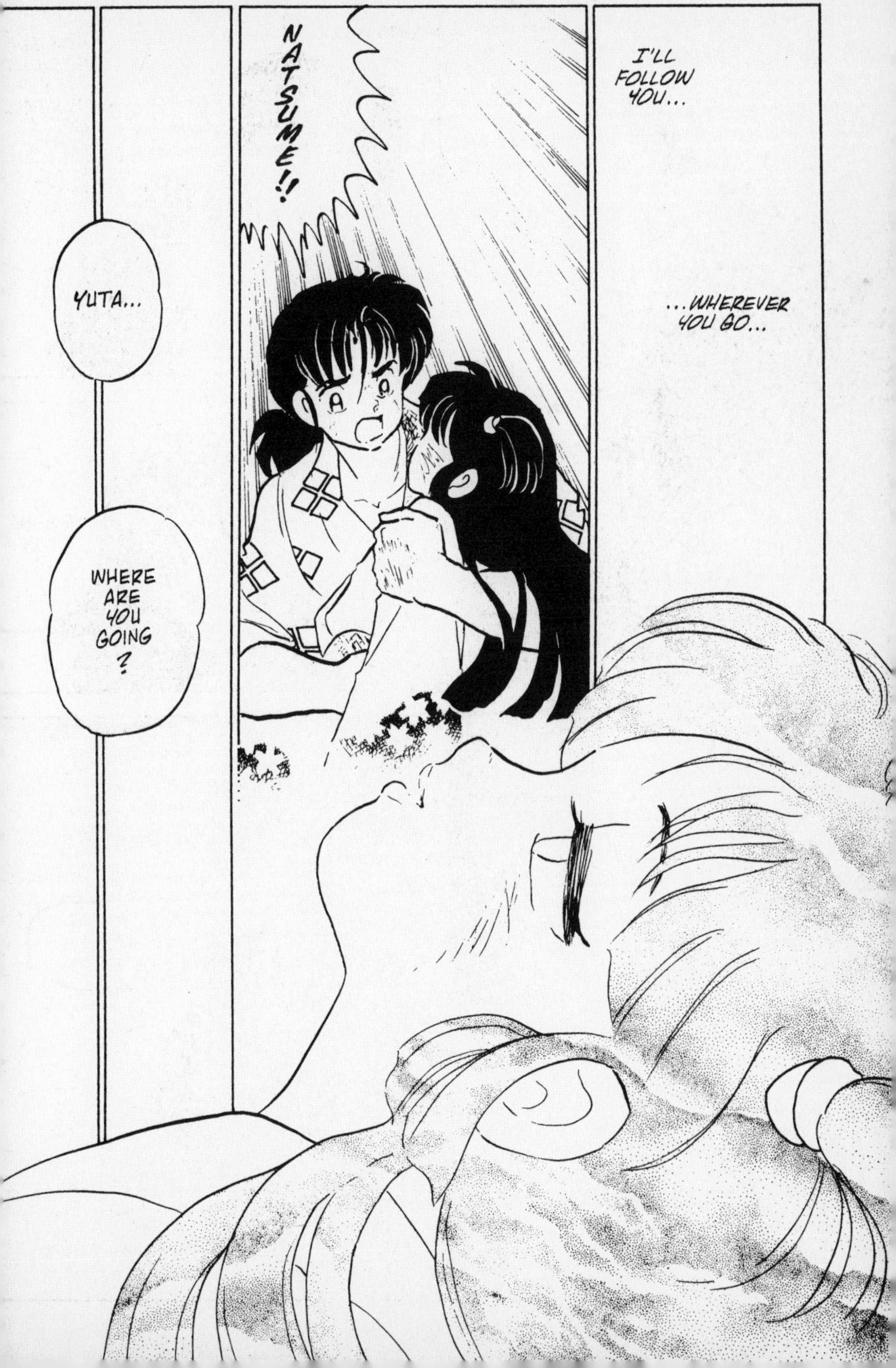
YUTA...
WHERE ARE YOU GOING?
NATSUME!!
I'LL FOLLOW YOU...
...WHEREVER YOU GO...

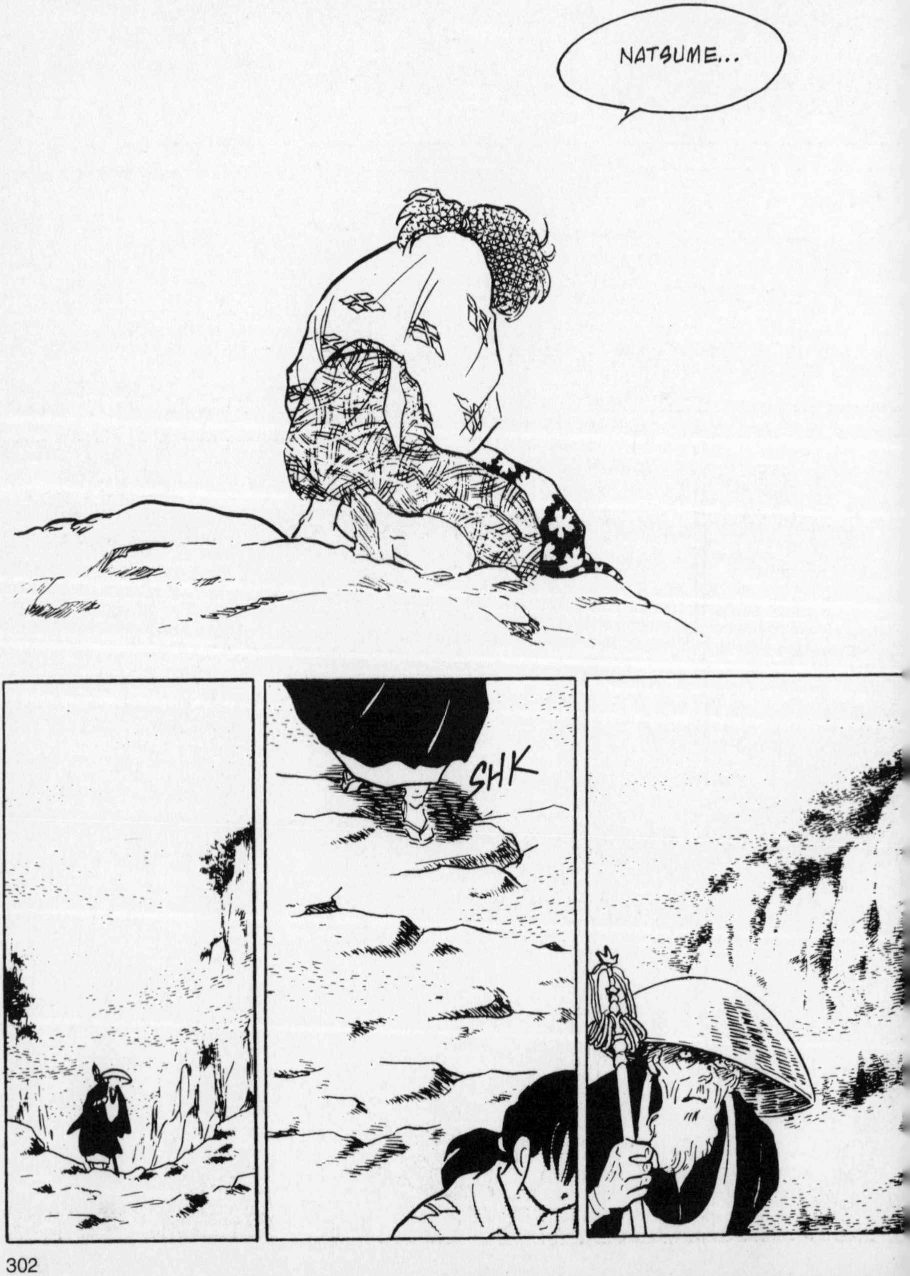
NATSUME...
SHK

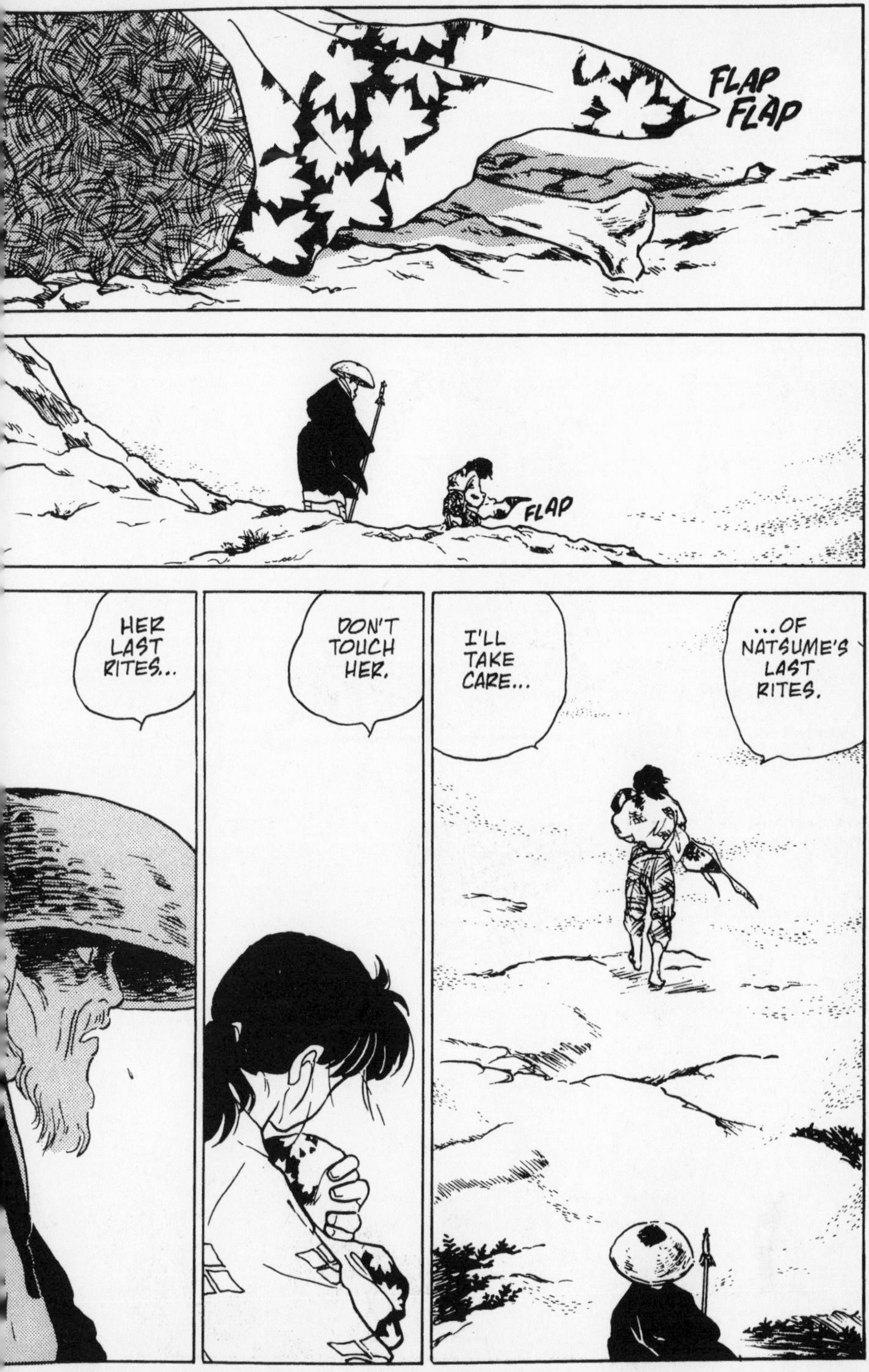
FLAP
FLAP
FLAP
HER LAST RITES...
DON'T TOUCH HER.
I'LL TAKE CARE...
...OF NATSUME'S LAST RITES.

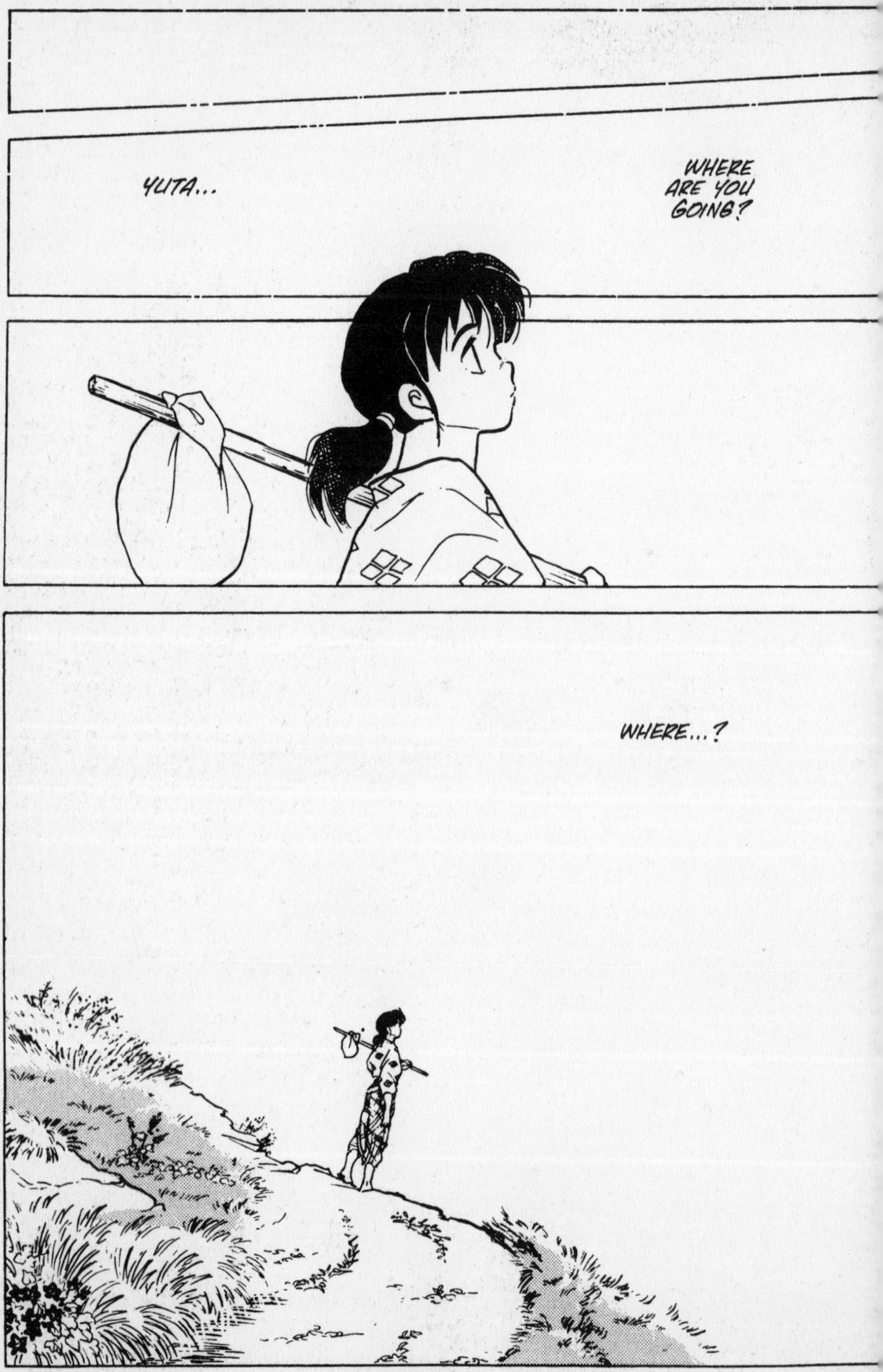
YUTA...
WHERE ARE YOU GOING?
WHERE...?

End